THE
INTERNATIONAL ENCYCLOPÆDIC DICTIONARY

of

NUMISMATICS

R. SCOTT CARLTON

Published by

700 E. State Street • Iola, WI 54990-0001
Telephone: 715/445-2214

Please call or write for our free catalog.
Our toll-free number to place an order or obtain a free catalog is 800-258-0929
or please use our regular business telephone 715-445-2214
for editorial comment and further information.

Library of Congress Catalog Number: 95-82430
ISBN: 0-87341-443-8
Printed in the United States of America

Gratefully Dedicated
to my Friends and Colleagues
at the
American Numismatic Association
for the
generous technical assistance
and constant encouragement
they have given me.

Appreciation is also expressed to
Albert Frey, Richard Doty,
Walter Breen, Ewald Junge,
and the other numismatic research scholars,
past and present,
whose efforts paved the way
for this present work.

.... R. Scott Carlton

Table of Contents

Encyclopædic Dictionary

The purpose of the Encyclopædic Dictionary is to provide definitions and relevant information on a wide range of numismatic topics and to give accurate and concise English translations of foreign numismatic terminology. The translations and many of the encyclopædic articles were supplied by some of the world's top numismatic and linguistic experts. The articles cover the entire gamut of numismatics from ancient times to the present. Topics range from cowry shells and ancient Greek staters to modern anti-counterfeiting devices and digital currency. Also included are biographies of key people who grace our coins and paper money.

Roman Alphabet

The Roman Alphabet section includes words in English, most European languages, Tagalog, and Turkish, plus romanized transliterations of non-Roman languages (Chinese, Hebrew, Greek, etc.). When transliterations are used, either the official versions have been chosen (such as the Pinyin system of Chinese) or the spellings most likely to be seen in English documents are included.

Alphabetization

This dictionary is arranged in strict English alphabetical order, meaning that diacritical marks, punctuation, spaces between words in multi-word entries, and capitalization are ignored. The alphabetizing does not take into account unusual letter combinations or configurations found in many other languages. For example, *ch* is one single letter of the Spanish alphabet (*a, b, c, ch, d, e,* etc.); *chelín* would follow *colección* in a normal Spanish dictionary, but in the present work *colección* precedes *chelín*. Also, the Turkish alphabet has both a dotted "I" (*İ* and *i*) and an undotted "I" (*I* and *ı*). Because there is no equivalent in English, these differences are ignored here. Foreign letters which do not resemble English letters are alphabetized as logically as possible, such as the German *ß* which is positioned as "ss."

Capitalization

In the Roman, Greek, and Cyrillic sections, entry words are only capitalized if they are *always* capitalized in normal use, such as proper names, accepted names of certain coins and types (e.g., Seated Liberty Quarter), all German nouns, etc.

Definitions

Many of the entries have non-numismatic as well as numismatic meanings, but the only definitions listed here are those with numismatic application. Every effort has been made to provide accurate and up-to-date definitions. Some archaic words and non-current definitions are included (and listed as such) because they are still found in English texts.

Abbreviations

The following abbreviations are used throughout this encyclopædic dictionary:

Ar.	Arabic	*Ger.*	German	*Pol.*	Polish
Bul.	Bulgarian	*Grk.*	Greek	*Port.*	Portuguese
Bur.	Burmese	*Heb.*	Hebrew	*Rom.*	Romanian
Cher.	Cherokee	*Hin.*	Hindi	*Russ.*	Russian
Chin.	Chinese[1]	*Hun.*	Hungarian	*Serb.*	Serbian
Cr.	Croatian	*Ice.*	Icelandic	*Srb.-Cr.*	Serbo-Croatian
Cz.	Czech	*Indo.*	Indonesian	*Slov.*	Slovak
Cz.-Sl.	Czech-Slovak	*Ire.*	Irish	*Span.*	Spanish
Dan.	Danish	*Ital.*	Italian	*Swed.*	Swedish
Dut.	Dutch	*Jpn.*	Japanese	*Tag.*	Tagalog
Eng.	English	*Kor.*	Korean	*Turk.*	Turkish
Finn.	Finnish	*Lat.*	Latin	*Viet.*	Vietnamese
Fr.	French	*Nor.*	Norwegian	*Wel.*	Welsh

Mid.	Middle	*c.*	noun, common	*m.-c.*	masculine-common[2]
abbr.	abbreviation	*f.*	noun, feminine		
q.v.	*quod vide* (cross-reference notation)	*f.adj.*	feminine adjective	*n.*	noun, neuter
		f.-c.	feminine-common[2]	*n.adj.*	neuter adjective
		m.	noun, masculine	*pl.*	plural
adj.	adjective	*m.adj.*	masculine adjective	*r.*	reale[3]
adv.	adverb			*v.*	verb

[1]Chinese transliterations appear either in the nineteenth-century Wade-Giles (*w.g.*) version which spells the name of the Chinese capital as *Peking,* or in the more recent Pinyin (*p.y.*) style in which that city is written *Beijing.* Similarly, words printed in Chinese characters can either be the traditional Complex Character (*c.c.*) still used in Hong Kong and Taiwan, or in the updated Simplified Character (*s.c.*) developed in the P.R.C.

[2]Some parts of the Dutch-speaking world still retain the masculine and feminine genders of nouns, while other areas have adopted the concept of common gender. Dutch nouns that fall into these categories are designated *m.-c.* and *f.-c.* in this dictionary.

[3]Reale is a form of neuter which corresponds somewhat to the common gender. It is found only in the Swedish language.

A a

a. [*abbr.*] about; almost.

aanpassingsteken (*n.*) [*Dut.*] adjustment mark.

aanwinst (*f.-c.*) [*Dut.*] acquisition.

Abbey crown Gold coin of 20 shillings first issued in 1526 by King James V of Scotland. These pieces are so named because they were struck at Holyrood Abbey instead of in Edinburgh, where other coins of this monarch were produced. Some were counterstamped with a cinquefoil, the family symbol of James, Earl of Arran, who supplied the gold and for whom the coins were probably intended.

[Peter Seaby & P. Frank Purvey, *Coins of Scotland, Ireland & the Islands*, p. 41.]

Abbey-piece Reference both to coins and tokens issued by some of the primary monastic establishments in Europe during the Middle Ages. Although some were legitimate coins in the strictest sense, many were tokens in the category of *Tesserae Sacrae*, meaning that they could only be used as money by the pilgrims and monks who journeyed from one religious house to another. In this sense, they bear a similarity to the haj money[q.v.] used by Muslim pilgrims today.

abbreviazione (*f.*) [*Ital.*] abbreviation.

ABC peso Popular name for the silver Cuban pesos of 1934-39. The name is a reference to the right-wing political group headed by Joaquín Martínez Sáenz, the Treasury minister responsible for the coins' existence. The pieces were not popular because they were only issued for whatever seigniorage[q.v.] they could generate to help bail the government out of its financial crisis. Many Cubans referred to them as "paper money printed on silver."

[Manuel Moreno Fraginals and José A. Pulido Ledesma, *Cuba: A Country and Its Currency*, National Bank of Cuba, p. 148.]

abgeändertes Datum (*n.*) [*Ger.*] altered date.

abjad see *gematria*.

Abkürzung (*f.*) [*Ger.*] abbreviation.

Abnutzung (*f.*) [*Ger.*] wear.

abreviatura (*f.*) [*Span., Port.*] abbreviation.

Abschnitt (*n.*) [*Ger.*] exergue.

Abstempelung (*f.*) [*Ger.*] cancellation.

abtat see *gematria*.

Abwertung (*f.*) [*Ger.*] devaluation.

acciaio (*m.*) [*Ital.*] steel.

accolated busts of William and Mary

accolated [also known as *conjoined* or *jugate*]. Design showing two or more heads or busts which face in the same direction and overlap.

This technique is first known to have appeared on Egyptian gold coins in the third century B.C. Ptolemy III and wife Berenice were portrayed in an accolated fashion to indicate that they were co-rulers, yet with one having more status than the other. Because of the infrequency of having two people rule the same country simultaneously, accolated portraiture did not become a widely-needed technique throughout ancient and medieval times, although it was used occasionally. In more recent times, the late seventeenth century English coins depicting William and Mary

display conjoined busts. In the event that the co-rulers had equal status, as in the case of Isabella and Ferdinand of Spain, the monarchs were portrayed facing each other and were not overlapped (see *vis-à-vis*), or their individual effigies appeared on the opposite sides of the same coin.

Although joint rule is no more common in the twentieth century than it was in previous times, the methods of deciding who will appear on coins and notes has changed immensely. Coins are no longer the exclusive domain of kings and queens. When two or three commoners are portrayed on the same coin in accolated fashion, all of them are presumed to have equal status, and the positioning of the individuals relative to each other usually has no particular significance.

Yet even in the twentieth century, the matter of positioning is very important when royalty is involved. If a reigning monarch is portrayed with someone else, then the ancient custom of placing the monarch's effigy in the forefront and of relegating the other person's portrait toward the back comes into play. For example, if Queen Elizabeth II and Prince Philip are depicted together, Elizabeth will traditionally appear in the front.

[Richard G. Doty, *Macmillan Encyclopedic Dictionary of Numismatics*, pp. 182-183.]

accolé [*Fr.*] accolated[q.v.], conjoined, jugate.

accollato [*Ital.*] accolated, conjoined, jugate.

accompte est requis, un [*Fr.*] deposit required.

account, money of see *money of account*.

accumulation Unsorted and usually unclassified and unattributed mixture of coins, tokens, or notes. The term is often used to describe coins offered in bulk which are not first sorted as to dates, mintmarks, or whatever, and are sold on an as-is basis.

aceitam-se cartões de crédito [*Port.*] credit cards accepted.

acél [*Hun.*] steel.

acélba vésés [*Hun.*] steel engraving.

acero (*m.*) [*Span.*] steel.

acharaktiristikos αχαρακτηριστικός [*Grk.*] unattributed (not fully identified or classified).

acheter (*v.*) [*Fr.*] to buy.

acheteur (*m.*) [*Fr.*] buyer.

à cheval [*Fr.*] on horseback. The term refers either to an "action" scene (e.g., the Austrian coin in the illustration) or a stationary position (the Canadian coin).

à cheval (action and stationary)

achiziție (*f.*) [*Rom.*] acquisition.

acht [*Ger., Dut.*] eight.

achtzig [*Ger.*] eighty.

acier (*m.*) [*Fr.*] steel.

acmonital An alloy of .815 iron and .185 chromium used by Italy in some of its coinage since 1939 and more recently by the Vatican. Its appearance is shiny grey-white, somewhat similar to freshly-struck nickel. This alloy is extremely hard and does not strike well during coinage. However, because it is actually stainless steel, it wears very well.

Acmonital is one of the two alloys, the other being bronzital[q.v.], which has been utilized by Italy and Vatican City in their bimetal 500 lira coins.

[Contributed by Halbert Carmichael.]

aço (*m.*) [*Port.*] steel.

acolado [*Span., Port.*] accolated[q.v.], conjoined, jugate.

acolat; acostat [*Rom.*] accolated, jugate, conjoined.

à condition [*Fr.*] on approval.

acont (*n.*) [*Rom.*] deposit.

acquisto (*m.*) [*Ital.*] acquisition.

acțiune (*f.*) [*Rom.*] (commercial) bond.

active Metallic object not covered by a thin layer of tarnish that protects the metal from additional oxidation, or a tarnished metallic object whose tarnish does not offer any protection. Most coins made of iron or steel fall into this category. Metal with a protective layer of tarnish is called *passive*.

acuñación (*f.*) [*Span.*] coinage.

acuñación a martillo [*Span.*] hammered coinage.

acuñación a molino [*Span.*] milled coinage.

adelaar (*m.-c.*) [*Dut.*] eagle.

adherent Any chemical substance that bonds to the metal of a coin through oxidation, causing visible tarnish or corrosion. The presence of adherents will cause a slight increase in the weight of the coin, if only by an infinitesimally small amount. Often the adherent will combine itself with some of the molecules of the coin's metal. If the adherent is removed, some of the molecules of metal will be removed with it, resulting in the coin's losing its original luster. If a large amount of metal has merged with the adherent, pitting or other forms of defacing will occur.

[Alan Korwin, "Shedding Light on Coin Cleaning," *The Numismatist*, June 1985, pp. 1089-1101; John C. Loperfido, "Airborne Particulates: The Silent Nemesis," *The Numismatist*, April 1983, pp. 706-709.]

adjustment 1. Filing metal from an overweight planchet or coin to bring it down to its correct weight. See *adjustment mark*.

2. Aligning a die in the coinage press to attain correct striking. Coins produced during the adjustment process exhibit a variety of abnormalities and are referred to as *adjustment trial pieces* or *set-up trial pieces*. Such coins usually display extremely weak designs due to inadequate pressure in the strike.

adjustment mark Evidence of filing done to an overweight silver or gold planchet to reduce it to its specified weight.

Modern machinery for making planchets is accurate enough that virtually all of today's blanks are of the correct size and weight. Those which are not are melted down and reprocessed. This was not always the case in the seventeenth and eighteenth centuries, particularly in smaller minting facilities, including the Philadelphia Mint in the United States. The equipment used to stamp round discs from strips of metal was not as sophisticated as the actual coinage presses, and many irregular blanks resulted. At some mints, underweight planchets were melted down, but overweight blanks were retained and adjusted. One or both of the flat sides of the planchet were filed down until the desired weight was achieved, and the blank was then struck in the normal way by the coinage dies. Although pressure from the coinage machinery obliterated most of the marks, some marks usually remained. The most obvious are frequently seen toward the center of the coin and on the areas of highest relief, because on those areas the planchet receives the least pressure from the die. Adjustment marks do not appear as sharp scratches but rather as soft parallel striations. Collectors do not regard coins with adjustment marks as mint errors, since the adjustments were done intentionally.

The term *adjustment mark* could conceivably be used to define filing done at the mint by mint employees to reduce an overweight finished coin instead of the planchet. However, the term is never used to describe fraudulent clipping or shaving of precious metal from the edge of a hammered coin during the Middle Ages. The clipped piece was kept and the coin was then spent as though it were intact. Unlike clipping, true adjustments were made to bring a coin down to its correct weight, not to reduce it below that level.

adjustment trial piece (known also as a *set-up trial piece* or simply as an *adjustment trial*.) See *adjustment*.

Adler (*m.*) [*Ger.*] eagle.

Ad Norman Conventionis [*Lat.*] To the standard of the convention. See *convention standard* and *Maria Theresa Thaler*.

adó [*Hun.*] tax.

adquisición (*f.*) [*Span.*] acquisition.

advers [*Nor.*] obverse.

adviesprijs (*m.-c.*) [*Dut.*] suggested bid.

AE. [*abbr.*] copper, bronze, or brass (from Latin *aes*).

ægte [*Dan.*] authentic, genuine.

ændre (*v.*) [*Dan.*] to alter.

aetos αετός (*m.*) [*Grk.*] eagle.

afkorting (*f.-c.*) [*Dut.*] abbreviation.

África del Sur [*Span.*]; **África do Sul** [*Port.*] South Africa. [Note: the accent mark over the "A" is usually omitted.]

Africa Star British military decoration given in World War II on behalf of King George VI to heroes of the North African campaign.

See page 311 for a color illustration.

Afrique du Sud [*Fr.*] South Africa.

Afryka Południowa [*Pol.*] South Africa.

afsnede (*f.-c.*) [*Dut.*] exergue.

aftokratoras αυτοκράτορας (*m.*) [*Grk.*] emperor.

ağırlık [*Turk.*] weight.

agnostos άγνωστος [*Grk.*] unknown.

agol עָגֹל [*Heb.*] round.

agorastis αγοραστής [*Grk.*] buyer.

agorazo αγοράζω (*v.*) [*Grk.*] to buy.

águia (*f.*) [*Port.*] eagle.

águila (*f.*) [*Span.*] eagle.

agujereado [*Span.*] holed.

agujero (*m.*) [*Span.*] hole.

agujeta (*f.*) [*Span.*] a crease (used specifically in reference to a banknote).

A.G.W. [*abbr.*] actual gold weight.

aigle (*f.*) [*Fr.*] eagle.

aihio [*Finn.*] planchet.

aito [*Finn.*] authentic, genuine.

ajánlani (*v.*) [*Hun.*] to offer.

ajánlat [*Hun.*] an offer.

ajánlott ár [*Hun.*] suggested bid.

akirosis kopis ακύρωση κοπής (*f.*) [*Grk.*] cut cancellation.

akkvisisjon (*m.*) [*Nor.*] acquisition.

akron άκρον (*n.*) [*Grk.*] edge.

äkta [*Swed.*] genuine.

akukloforita ακυκλοφόρητα [*Grk.*] uncirculated.

a la dobla [*Span.*] literally, *by doubles.*

On May 11, 1535, a decree was signed in Madrid authorizing the establishment of a mint in New Spain. This mint, constructed in what is now Mexico City, became the first minting facility in the New World. The same decree created a monetary system called *a la dobla*, because the system was based on the Castilian *real* with multiples of 2, 4, and 8 reales, as well as the fractional coins of 1/2 and 1/4 real. All of these coins were to be minted in silver.

The same *a la dobla* system was utilized about 150 years later when the Royal Decree of February 23, 1675, allowed for the minting of gold coins. The unitary coin upon which this system was based was the *escudo.* Denominations of 1/2, 2, 4, and 8 escudos were also struck.

The monetary system based on increments of two rather than of ten (i.e., the decimal system) was used throughout Spanish America for around 300 years. Mexico, for example, did not produce coins based on the decimal system until 1863.

[Miguel L. Muñoz, "Digits to Decimals," *The Numismatist*, May 1989, pp. 718-723, et al.]

aláírás [*Hun.*] signature.

alamă (*f.*) [*Rom.*] brass (the alloy).

Alankomaat [*Finn.*] Holland; The Netherlands.

alaosa [*Finn.*] bottom.

alaşım [*Turk.*] alloy (of metals).

alăturat [*Rom.*] accolated[*q.v.*], conjoined, jugate.

alb [*Rom.*] white.

aleación (*f.*) [*Span.*] alloy (of metals).

Alemanha [*Port.*] Germany.

Alemanha Ocidental [*Port.*] West Germany.

Alemanha Oriental [*Port.*] East Germany.

Alemania [*Span.*] Germany.

Alemania Occidental [*Span.*] West Germany (B.R.D.). [Official name in Spanish: *República Federal de Alemania.*]

Alemania Oriental [*Span.*] East Germany (D.D.R.). [Official name in Spanish: *República Democrática de Alemania.*]

Alexander eagle Variety of double eagle design (i.e., eagle with two necks and two heads, the heads facing in opposite directions) in which the eagle exhibits an unusually wide wing spread. This configuration appeared on the Russian silver coinage of 1826-31, as well as on gold coins of that general period. It is sometimes erroneously called the *Masonic* eagle.

[R. W. Julian, "The Russian Silver Coinage of 1796-1917," *The Numismatist*, December 1989, pp. 1957-58.]

aliaj (*n.*) [*Rom.*] alloy (of metals).

alıcı [*Turk.*] buyer.

alkuperäinen [*Finn.*] original.

allekirjoitus [*Finn.*] signature.

Allemagne [*Fr.*] Germany.

Allemagne de l'Est [*Fr.*] East Germany (D.D.R.).

Allemagne de l'Ouest [*Fr.*] West Germany (B.R.D.).

alliage (*m.*) [*Fr.*] alloy (of metals).

alloy 1. (*noun*) Any mixture of two or more metals. Mixing even a small amount of a common metal with a precious metal can give the precious metal considerable added strength and durability and make it much more suitable for coinage purposes. This is especially true with gold, which is an extremely soft metal in its pure form. Using alloys in coins can also serve to "stretch" a precious metal which might be in short supply.

Although most alloys used for coinage purposes are man-made, the very first coins, the Lydian stater[*q.v.*] of circa 620-600 B.C., were made from a natural alloy of approximately three parts gold to one part silver known as electrum.

When naming the alloy, the predominant or most important metal is mentioned first, such as *copper-nickel* or *nickel alloy*.

2. (*noun*) The less valuable metal added to a precious metal; e.g., copper is the alloy added to gold.

3. (*verb*) To mix two or more metals.

Almanya [*Turk.*] Germany.

almindelig [*Dan.*] common.

alminnelig [*Nor.*] common.

alphabets, numeric equivalents see *gematria*.

alt [*Ger.*] old; [*Turk.*] bottom.

általános [*Hun.*] common.

altera (*v.*) [*Rom.*] to alter.

alterar (*v.*) [*Span., Port.*] to alter.

alterare (*v.*) [*Ital.*] to alter; (*f.*) [*Rom.*] alteration.

alterazione (*f.*) [*Ital.*] alteration.

altered date The date of a common coin which has been changed to appear to be the date of a more valuable coin. This fraudulent practice is usually achieved by using various jeweler's and engraver's tools and techniques.

A coin with an altered date almost always shows scratches or some other evidence of re-tooling. When a U.S. 1944-D cent is altered to appear as a much rarer 1914-D cent (a coin frequently altered), three tell-tale signs remain. First, some microscopic scratches will surround the first digit "4" which has been altered to look like a "1". Second, there will be an

unnaturally wide gap between the "9" and the altered "1". Third, the three U.S. mints added the initials of Victor David Brenner, the coin's designer, to the underneath portion of Lincoln's shoulder in 1918. Altered 1944 cents show the initials, genuine 1914 cents do not. Even if the initials have been removed as part of the alteration, some re-tooling marks usually remain.

Not every altered coin exhibits as much evidence of altering as does the 1914-D cent, although some sort of evidence is usually present. The altered 1913 Liberty Head Nickel in the illustration (altered from a 1910 nickel) is reasonably well done, but the final digit shows telltale signs of alteration under magnification. Some alterations are made with such skill that they can only be detected by an expert using sophisticated magnifying equipment.

1913 nickels: genuine (above); altered from 1910 (below)

Some alterations involve portions of the coin other than the date. Mint marks are frequently changed or removed. Other extraneous marks can be altered to increase the value of a coin, such as adding a dot to a 1936 Canadian cent, ten cent piece, or quarter.

altın [*Turk.*] gold.

alto (*m.*) [*Ital.*] top.

aluminum [*U.S.A.*]; **aluminium** [*Can., U.K., Austl., N.Z., S.A., et al.*] Metal used for coinage. [element: group IIIa of periodic table; atomic

weight 26.98; atomic number 13; specific gravity 2.7; symbol Al.]

Aluminum is the lightest of all elements regularly used for coinage. It is usually alloyed with small but undisclosed amounts of other metals such as copper or magnesium. It was first used for coinage purposes by British West Africa in 1907. Its use in coinage only became widespread after World War II. Aluminum produces a bright and shiny coin when first struck, but it rapidly degrades to an unattractive light grey.

During the nineteenth century, aluminum was regarded as somewhat of a precious metal, largely because a good method for extracting it from bauxite was not developed until 1886. Only a few pattern coins were struck from this metal prior to that time. Even after it became inexpensive and widely available, it never found great popularity as a coinage metal, partly because it does not wear well and mostly because the general public does not perceive that coins made from this light-weight metal feel "genuine". Nevertheless, some minor coins are produced from it.

[Contributed by Halbert Carmichael.]

aluminum bronze [*U.S.A.*]; **aluminium bronze** [*Can., U.K., Austl., N.Z., S.A., et al.*] Coinage alloy of .920 copper with the remainder aluminum, although the French add a little nickel and the Italians some titanium. It has been a favorite for minor coins in much of the world since the 1920s. Examples include the Danzig 5 and 10 pfennig coins of 1932 and the French 50 centimes of 1931-44.

amarelo [*Port.*] yellow.

amarillo [*Span.*] yellow.

Amazonian Proof Set Unique six-piece pattern proof set of gold coins struck in 1872 by the U.S. Mint. The Amazonian Set consists of patterns in the denominations of $1, $2.50, $3, $5, $10, and $20, the same values as the gold coins which circulated in the United States during that era. The set was designed by mint engraver William Barber. All six coins share common designs: the obverse shows a flowing hair rendition of the head of Liberty, and and the reverse features an eagle and shield.

This proof set was once owned by King Farouk of Egypt and later by Dr. John E. Wilkinson of Springfield, Tennessee. It was purchased by Greg Holloway of Continental Investment Group, Inc., in 1987 for nearly one million dollars.

["Firm boasts ownership of two rare coin sets," *Numismatic News*, January 23, 1990, p. 28.]

American Numismatic Association The American Numismatic Association was founded in 1891 by Dr. George F. Heath to bring collectors together so they could expand their numismatic knowledge. Today the A.N.A. continues to serve the numismatic community as the world's largest nonprofit educational organization. The Association was chartered by Congress in 1912 for collectors of coins, paper money, tokens, and medals.

The A.N.A. annually organizes two major conventions in various parts of the nation, sanctions money shows in the U.S. and throughout the world, conducts coin grading seminars, offers week-long summer study seminars, and provides numismatic education through correspondence courses.

Members of the A.N.A. receive copies of the 160-page monthly journal, *The Numismatist*, started by Dr. Heath in 1888. It is filled with informative articles and columns, consumer news and tips, member benefit offerings, and world mintage updates.

The A.N.A.'s Resource Center allows members access to the world's largest circulating library of numismatic material— 30,000 titles of books, periodicals, auction catalogs, videotapes, and slide programs— for only the cost of postage and insurance.

The A.N.A. Authentication Bureau utilizes the best numismatic experts to determine the authenticity of numismatic material submitted by Association members. The World Money Museum in Colorado Springs houses more than 400,000 items, including some of the world's great numismatic rarities.

For membership information, contact the American Numismatic Association, 818 North Cascade Avenue, Colorado Springs, Colorado 80903-3279.

American Numismatic Association World Money Museum The three most significant numismatic museums in the United States are the Smithsonian Institution in Washington, D.C., the American Numismatic Society Museum in New York City, and the American Numismatic Association Museum in Colorado Springs, Colorado.

The museum's collection was initiated in 1928 by Moritz Wormser. Because the A.N.A. had no facility of its own at that time, the cabinet was housed in the Smithsonian Institution and was known as the Moritz Wormser Memorial Loan Collection. Emphasis was placed on post-World War I foreign coins.

Two dealers, James MacAllister and F. C. C. Boyd, donated a 1933 U.S. $10 gold piece in 1938. For fifty years this was the collection's most valuable piece.

The most momentous event in the museum's history came in 1967 when the A.N.A. moved into its permanent headquarters. Exhibits which had been on loan at the Smithsonian and at the Joslyn Museum in Omaha, Nebraska, became the nucleus of its new permanent display. The collection has been expanded to include virtually all areas of domestic and international numismatics.

Since moving into its permanent facility, the A.N.A. Museum has built an outstanding collection of U.S. paper money, now regarded as the finest in the world. Its Oriental currency collection is also regarded as extremely significant.

Aubrey and Adeline Bebee donated a 1913 Liberty Nickel in March 1989. This coin became the single most valuable item in the museum's approximately 400,000-piece collection. In 1991 the Bebees also donated an 1804 U.S. silver dollar.

One of the unique aspects of this museum is its Hall of Nations, which provides the visually impaired the opportunity to touch and feel coins by means of large, mint-production medals. Few museums permit the touching of anything; the A.N.A. Museum encourages it.

[David L. Ganz, "Building a World-Class Museum," *The Numismatist*, September 1989, pp. 1448-1452.]

American Numismatic Society For more than 130 years, the American Numismatic Society has been an international center for the preservation and study of coins, medals, and paper money, representing 2500 years of material culture. Scholars and collectors use the museum, which houses nearly one million objects, and the library, noted as the world's most comprehensive repository of numismatic literature.

The Society's magnificent library houses more than 100,000 volumes plus a unique photofile of more than 500,000 illustrations of published coins. A growing number of outreach programs includes a major exhibit, "The World of Coins," that traces the history of money as a medium of exchange from ancient to modern times. Traveling exhibits circulate to schools, libraries, and coin conventions.

The Society is the most active and respected non-profit numismatic publisher in the world. It is privately funded and is supported by individual and institutional membership fees and contributions, sale of publications, and foundation, corporate, and government grants.

For membership information, contact the American Numismatic Society, Broadway at 155th Street, New York, New York 10032.

Amerika Birleşik Devletleri [*Turk.*] United States of America (U.S.A.).

Amerikai Egyesült Államok [*Hun.*] United States of America.

Amerikan Yhdysvallat [*Finn.*] United States of America.

Amerikas Förenta Stater [*Swed.*] United States of America.

amiti אֲמִתִּי [*Heb.*] genuine.

amoedar por fundição (*v.*) [*Port.*] to cast.

Amors Centenary of Education Medalets Series of thirty-six small medals issued from 1976-84 to commemorate one hundred years (1880-1980) of public education in New South Wales (Australia). The various medalets were struck by the schools involved.

[R. J. Byatt and W. J. Mira, "Amors Centenary of Education Medalets for New South Wales," *Journal of the Numismatic Association of Australia*, July 1985, pp. 31-37.]

amtlich [*Ger.*] official.

amulet An object worn as a charm. Amulets have been worn since ancient times to guard against illness and witchcraft. They can be religious symbols or references to the monarchy, especially if the ruler has been given the status of deity. They often have astrological significance.

Chinese amulet

The illustrated item is from China and was cast in the style of cash[q.v.] coins. The inscription reads, "Under heaven, great peace."

amusement token Token used to operate juke boxes, pinball machines, slot (gambling) machines, trade stimulators, video arcade devices, etc.

Gambling tokens the size and weight of U.S. silver dollars were introduced by gambling casinos in Nevada in the 1960s to take the place of real silver dollars which were quickly leaving circulation due to the rising price of silver. See *casino token*.

Tokens made by amusement companies for use in their pinball machines and video arcade games are intended to discourage thievery. In some arcades, the customer must purchase tokens at a central location, as real coins will not fit into the machines. In this way, prospective thieves know that if they break into the amusement machines, they will only steal tokens which cannot be spent anywhere except at that arcade.

[Contributed by Robert Doyle. Stephen P. Alpert and Kenneth E. Smith, *Video Arcade, Pinball, Slot Machine, and Other Amusement Tokens of North America*, 1st edition, Redondo Beach, CA (1984).]

an (*m.*) [*Rom., Fr.*] year.

anagnorismeno αναγνωρισμένο [*Grk.*] conjoined, accolated, jugate.

anakseochreon kerma αναξιόχρεον κέρμα (*n.*) [*Grk.*] hammered coin.

anaparagogi αναπαραγωγή (*f.*) [*Grk.*] a copy; reproduction.

anbieten (*v.*) [*Ger.*] to offer.

anbud (*n.*) [*Swed.*] offer; bid.

anbudslapp (*r.*) [*Swed.*] bid sheet.

ancient coin In general, any coin struck prior to A.D. 476 (the fall of the western portion of the Roman Empire). The term is most often used in reference to Greek, Roman, and Judaic coins; it is used less often to refer to ancient coins of the Orient.

ändrat datum (*n.*) [*Swed.*] altered date.

anepisimon ανεπίσημον [*Grk.*] unofficial.

Angebot (*n.*) [*Ger.*] an offer.

Angel Gold bullion coin of the Isle of Man, so-named because its reverse depicts the archangel Michael slaying a dragon.

The Angel was first issued in 1984 to compete with the Krugerrand[q.v.], a coin highly in demand in the 1970s but which lost much of its popularity during the 1980s due to the apartheid policies of the South African government. Many nations, including the United States, banned the importation of all South African goods, including the Krugerrand. Yet the Krugerrand remained the first choice of many investors because it contains exactly one ounce of pure gold, the perfect unit for tracking the value of gold holdings.

The Angel was born to help fill the void left from the boycott of the Krugerrand. To make it as readily-accepted as possible, the Isle of Man produced these coins with the same specifications as the Krugerrand— the identical size, weight, purity, and gold content. The issue price was also the same as the prevailing price of the Krugerrand.

To make the coins even more marketable, an extremely beautiful reverse design was used, thus enhancing the coins' desirability in jewelry. The obverse portrays the traditional bust of Queen Elizabeth II.

Isle of Man Angel

Angleterre [*Fr.*] England.

Anglia [*Pol., Rom.*] England.

ấn hành đặc biệt [*Viet.*] commemorative.

ank अंक [*Hin.*] an issue, issuance.

anløbe [*Dan.*] tarnish.

anma (*adj.*) [*Turk.*] commemorative.

année (*f.*) [*Fr.*] year.

anno (*m.*) [*Lat., Ital.*] year.

annulation par découpage [*Fr.*] cut cancellation.

ano (*m.*) [*Port.*] year.

año (*m.*) [*Span.*] year.

anomaly Something that logically should not be the way it is. An anomaly differs from an error in that an error is an accident caused by carelessness or by an equipment malfunction, whereas an anomaly is intentional.

Anomalies are not absolute. What may seem an anomaly to one collector may be perceived as totally normal and logical to someone else. For example, the 1982 Polish coins showing Pope John Paul II[*q.v.*] holding a crucifix seemed like an anomaly to many people, because no communist country had ever before included a religious symbol on its coins. Yet other people were not surprised that Poland would honor its most famous son.

anote အနုတ် [*Bur.*] coin.

Ansell ribbon Variety of 1859 British sovereign showing an extra raised line on the lower portion of the ribbon in Queen Victoria's hair.

antallasso ανταλλάσσω (*v.*) [*Grk.*] to trade.

anthonize (*verb*) Word coined in the 1980s referring to a government's attempt to force its people to do something they don't want to do. The word is derived from the Susan B. Anthony Dollar, which was introduced in 1979 as the first possible step in eliminating the one dollar note. Despite extensive promotion by the U.S. Treasury Department, the Anthony Dollar failed. It was much smaller than previous dollar coins and so closely resembled the quarter dollar in size and color that many people confused the two coins, passing off dollars as though they were quarters. The American people also thought the government was trying to anthonize them by eliminating the dollar bill, a very popular fixture in domestic American commerce.

Anthony Dollar Short-lived U.S. dollar coin (1979-81) honoring Susan B. Anthony, American suffragette who fought to achieve women's right to vote and crusaded against slavery and for the prohibition of alcoholic beverages.

The dollars were designed by the U.S. Mint's chief engraver, Frank Gasparro. The coins were widely criticized for being ugly, hardly a valid criticism considering that Ms. Anthony herself was not an attractive woman. The reverse was retained from the Eisenhower Dollar of 1971-78, a coin also created by Gasparro. This design features the Apollo 11 insignia from the first moon landing.

With a diameter of 26.5 mm, the Anthony Dollar was far smaller in size than any previous U.S. silver (or silver-substitute) coin. The government's ultimate intent was to replace the popular one dollar bill with a coin in order to save millions of dollars annually in production costs. Unfortunately, the new coin was too similar in size and color to the Washington

Quarter. Many people got the two coins confused and gave out dollar coins as though they were quarters. This made the new coins instantly unpopular, and most Americans refused to accept them.

After only three years of production, the coins were discontinued. The approximately half-billion surviving pieces were stored until someone in the Treasury could figure out what to do with them. A partial solution presented itself in the 1990s with the proliferation of gambling casinos in the United States. It is cheaper for small casinos to buy slot machines which accept Anthony Dollars than to have great quantities of one dollar gambling tokens made. Hence, the Anthony Dollars found a new use.

Anthony, Susan Brownell Women's rights advocate and crusader for women's suffrage, temperance (the prohibition of alcoholic beverages), and the abolition of slavery. Born February 15, 1820, in Adams, Massachusetts; died March 13, 1906, in Rochester, New York.

Susan B. Anthony believed passionately in the democratic values upon which the United States was founded, but she never had the right to exercise the most basic of them all— the right to vote. She devoted her life fighting for the birthright of women and the privileges that are often taken for granted today: the right to vote, co-educational schools, the right to own property, and the opening of all professions on the basis of qualification and not gender.

Anthony helped establish the American Equal Rights Association in 1866 and the National Woman Suffrage Association in 1869. On November 28, 1872, she was arrested for voting illegally and was fined $100, a fine she never paid.

In 1906 at age 86, Susan B. Anthony died, with only four states having given women the right to vote. Finally in 1920, the centennial of her birth, the U.S. Congress passed the 19th Amendment to the Constitution which gave women in all states the right to vote.

In the 1970s Susan B. Anthony's name was used as a rallying symbol by various American gay and lesbian organizations in their quest for equal rights, because Anthony herself was a lesbian.

Anthony was elected to the Hall of Fame for Great Americans located at the Bronx Community College of City University of New York in 1950.

Anthony's numismatic genealogy goes back to the sixteenth century. Her ancestor, William Anthony, was the Chief Engraver of the English Royal Mint and Master of the Scales during the reigns of Edward, Mary, and Elizabeth I. His crest and coat of arms are listed in the royal enumeration.

Although Spain's Queen Isabella was featured on the 1893 U.S. commemorative quarter dollar, Susan B. Anthony was the first American woman to appear on a coin and the first woman of any nationality to have her effigy featured on a U.S. regular issue, the Anthony Dollar[q.v.] (1979-81).

[Contributed by Pamela Makricosta. Florence Horn Bryan, *Susan B. Anthony: Champion of Women's Rights*; Phyllis J. Read & Bernard L. Witlieb, *The Book of Women's Firsts*; Matthew G. Grant, *Susan B. Anthony: Crusader for Women's Rights*.]

antichità (*f.*) [*Ital.*] antiquity.

antichitate (*f.*) [*Rom.*] antiquity.

anticipo (*m.*) [*Ital.*] deposit.

anti-alteration device Any design or inscription on a coin or note intended to prevent the alteration of the denomination or of any other key information.

anti-alteration device: *un mil pesos*

The note in the illustration is a thousand peso note of Mexico. The denomination (stated as *un mil pesos*) was intentionally written using

an incorrect Spanish form. It should have been written simply as *mil pesos* with the word *un* ("one") omitted. Had it been written correctly, an unscrupulous person could easily have doctored the note by placing the word *diez* ("ten") in the space in front of *mil* to make the note appear to be worth ten thousand pesos. Few Mexicans would have been fooled by this deception, but many foreign tourists would have been cheated, creating a public relations problem for the Mexican government.

anti-counterfeiting device Anything included in the design or method of production of a coin or note which makes counterfeiting of that item more difficult or makes a forgery easier to detect. Security edges on coins could be considered as an anti-counterfeiting device, although they were originally intended to prevent clipping.

In today's world, most anti-counterfeiting devices are found in paper money. Silk threads embedded in the paper and watermarks are two traditional examples, but modern technology now allows for microprinting and color-shifting ink, as well as a whole host of possibilities for the future.

anticuado [*Span.*] obsolete.

antifalsificación (*f.*) [*Span.*] anti-counterfeiting. *dispositivo de antifalsificación*: anti-counterfeiting device.

antiforfalskningskarakteristika (*n.*) [*Dan.*] anti-counterfeiting device.

antigüedad (*f.*) [*Span.*] antiquity.

antiguo [*Span.*] ancient.

antiikinaikainen [*Finn.*] ancient.

antik [*Ger., Swed.*] ancient.

antimony A metallic element (group Va of periodic table; atomic weight 121.75; atomic number 51; density 6.69; symbol Sb.)

This element is used almost exclusively as a constituent of alloys such as pewter and type metal. It has the unique ability to expand on solidifying, making it particularly useful in making precise castings. Its only known use as a major constituent in a coinage alloy is in the Kweichow 10 cents of the year 20 of the Republic (1931 on the Western calendar).

[Contributed by Halbert Carmichael.]

anti-vervalsingkenmerk (*n.*) [*Dut.*] anti-counterfeiting device.

antoninianus Roman silver coin valued at two *denarii*. It was introduced by Emperor Caracalla, a.k.a. Marcus Aurelius Antoninus, in A.D. 214. By 295, the coin had become so debased that it was finally abandoned.

anverso (*m.*) [*Span.*] obverse.

anvil die Coinage die which remains stationary during the coinage process. The planchet (coin blank) is placed on the anvil die and is then struck by the hammer die (the movable die).

Anzahlung (*f.*) [*Ger.*] deposit.

anzahlungspflichtig [*Ger.*] deposit required.

aparcheomeno απαρχαιομένο [*Grk.*] obsolete.

à pied

à pied [*Fr.*] literally, *on foot*. The portrayed person on a coin or medal is shown in a standing position.

apodido αποδίδω (*v.*) [*Grk.*] to attribute.

apodiksis prosforon απόδειξη προσφορών (*f.*) [*Grk.*] bid sheet.

Apollo 11 insignia An insignia showing an eagle standing on the moon with the earth visible in the sky.

Apollo 11 insignia

Apollo 11 was the designation of the space expedition leading to the first moon landing in July 1969. To honor this event, Apollo 11's insignia was placed on the reverse of the Eisenhower Dollar (1971-1978). The insignia was later retained on the Susan B. Anthony Dollars (1979-81). No dollar coins were struck with the date 1975, and the 1976 issues were semi-commemorative (i.e., circulating commemorative) coins bearing a special U.S. Bicentennial design. The Apollo 11 insignia was brought back in 1977.

aprecia (*v.*) [*Rom.*] to grade.

apsogos άψογος [*Grk.*] perfect, flawless.

aquila (*f.*) [*Ital.*] eagle.

aquisição (*f.*) [*Port.*] acquisition.

år (*n.*) [*Dan., Swed, Nor.*] year.

ár [*Hun.*] price.

AR. [*abbr.*] silver (from Latin *argentum*).

arad אֲרָד (*m.*) [*Heb.*] bronze (the alloy).

árajánlat (*v.*) [*Hun.*] to bid (at an auction).

árajánlatot tesz [*Hun.*] (auction) bid.

aramă (*f.*) [*Rom.*] copper.

arany [*Hun.*] gold.

archeon αρχαίον [*Grk.*] ancient.

archeotis αρχαιότης (*f.*) [*Grk.*] antiquity.

arckép [*Hun.*] portrait.

árfolyam [*Hun.*] exchange rate.

argent (*m.*) [*Fr.*] silver; money.

argent du roi [*Fr.*] literally *the king's silver*. Term used in medieval French to refer to silver which is 23/24 pure.

Argentinien [*Ger.*] Argentina.

argento (*m.*) [*Ital.*] silver.

argentum (*n.*) [*Lat.*] silver.

argint (*n.*) [*Rom.*] silver.

argiros αργυρός [*Grk.*] silver.

Arjantin [*Turk.*] Argentina.

árjegyzék [*Hun.*] price list.

arka yüzü [*Turk.*] reverse.

arranhão (*m.*); **arranhadura** (*f.*) [*Port.*] scratch.

arruga (*f.*) [*Span.*] a crease, fold (as in a banknote or bond).

årstal (*n.*) [*Dan.*] date.

arte (*m./f.*) [*Span.*]; (*f.*) [*Port.*] art.

artificial toning The process of darkening a coin or medal to give it a more pleasing appearance or to hide flaws. This is done to make the item appear to be more valuable than it really is.

Old uncirculated coins with natural toning are frequently very beautiful and command higher prices than identical coins with unpleasant toning or pieces that have been poorly cleaned. The purpose of artificial toning is to make unpleasant coins look better and to make them appear to have toned or tarnished in a natural way. Regretfully, most attempts fail and the coins then look worse than they did before they were artifically toned.

Coins and medals are sometimes darkened to hide scratches or other surface blemishes, to hide the slight signs of wear on About Uncirculated coins to give them the appearance of being truly Uncirculated, or to disguise the fact that the item has been mis-handled in some way. In some cases, coins with a high book value are virtually impossible to sell because of their unpleasant appearance. The pieces are artificially toned not so much to increase their price but to provide for their marketability.

Coins and medals may be artificially toned by storing them in certain types of paper envelopes, by blowing tobacco smoke on them, or by soaking them in many different kinds of liquid substances. Applying high temperatures will often speed up the process. Some coin dealers sell special chemicals intended to be artificial toners.

Artificial toning is rarely done with the idea of making a true permanent improvement on a coin. The process is almost always done as a method of deception and fraud.

Also see *natural toning*.

[Anthony Swiatek, "The Facts Behind Natural and Artificial Toning," *The Numismatist*, June 1985, pp. 1102-1107.]

Artis Nostræ Conditor [*Lat.*] Author (founder) of our art (skill).

as Bronze coin of the Roman Republic equal to 1/16 denarius. When it became an Imperial coin, it was valued at 1/4 sestertius.

The name comes from its original use in the third century B.C. as a unit of weight, the *as libra* (Roman pound).

The letters "SC" seen on asses stand for *Senatus Consulto* ("By Decree of the Senate"). The emperor controlled gold and silver, but the Senate issued coins of lesser metals.

Juana de Asbaje

Asbaje, Juana de [a.k.a. *Sor Juana Inés de la Cruz* (*Sister Johanna Inés of the Cross*)]. Mexican poet, musician, scientist, and historian. Born 1648 or 1651 at San Miguel de Nepantla (near Mexico City); died of the plague in 1695 in the Convent of San Jerónimo.

Sister Johanna is regarded as the foremost Latin American poet of the seventeenth century and was called the "Tenth Muse" by her contemporaries. Her poetry reflects her deep religious faith.

One of the great intellects of her time, she conducted scientific experiments involving physics and astronomy and shared her observations with such European intellectuals as Sir Isaac Newton. Although she lived in a convent, she built a personal library of more than 4000 volumes.

Many of today's observers regard her as the world's first feminist because of her lifelong struggle against the establishment that sought to suppress women's intellect.

Sister Johanna's portrait appears on the Mexican 1000 peso note introduced in 1985.

[*Smithsonian World: Voices of Latin America* (script of television program), 1987, WETA (Washington, DC) & Smithsonian Institution; Angel Valbuena Briones, *Historia de la literatura española*, Vol. V, pp. 126-139.]

asfan matb'ot אַסְפָן מַטְבְּעוֹת (*m.*) [*Heb.*] coin collector; numismatist.

asimon אֲסִימוֹן (*m.*) [*Heb.*] token.

assignat The assignat provides an answer to the question, "If the government needs money, why doesn't it just print more?" In the 1790s France

French *assignat* (actual size)

did, and the result was a disaster. The uniface *assignat* notes were issued by the people who had overthrown the French monarchy just a few years earlier. The notes were an attempt to establish some sort of circulating money. Assignats were never backed by gold or silver but were supposedly backed by land confiscated from the Catholic Church, an institution which had opposed the French Revolution. But the notes were printed as fast as the presses could churn them out and quickly lost whatever value they once had. By the time they were discontinued, millions had been produced.

Even modern coin collectors do not value the assignats very highly, largely because so many specimens survive today. The note in the illustration is genuine and is more than 200 years old, yet it has a collector's value of only a few dollars.

A.S.W. [*abbr.*] actual silver weight.

'atik עָתִיק [*Heb.*] ancient.

atribución (*f.*) [*Span.*] attribution (the complete identification of a coin, medal, or banknote).

atribuição (*f.*) [*Port.*] attribution.

atribuir (*v.*) [*Span., Port.*] to attribute.

árverés [*Hun.*] auction, auction sale.

árverési katalógus [*Hun.*] auction catalogue.

árverési lap [*Hun.*] bid sheet.

arvo [*Finn.*] value.

arvokas [*Finn.*] valuable.

arvonalennus [*Finn.*] devaluation.

arvopaperi [*Finn.*] bond.

asgarî teklif [*Turk.*] minimum bid.

askeri madalya; askeri nişan [*Turk.*] military decoration.

assegno (*m.*) [*Ital.*] check, cheque; scrip.

assinatura (*f.*) [*Port.*] signature.

asta (*f.*) [*Ital.*] auction.

astro άστρο (*n.*) [*Grk.*] star.

atelier monétaire (*m.*) [*Fr.*] mint.

átmérő [*Hun.*] diameter.

Atocha, Nuestra Señora de *Our Lady of Atocha.* Spanish sailing vessel which sank in 1622 while carrying an enormous amount of treasure.

The Atocha and its sister ship, the Santa Margarita, set sail for Spain from Havana, Cuba, on September 4, 1622. Two days later the ships were hit by a hurricane and sank. Only five crew members from the two vessels survived.

In 1968, Mel Fisher, a former chicken farmer and dive shop owner from California, began a quest to locate the sunken ship. He and his son Dirk found evidence of its location in 1973. Their progress was interrupted by a series of court battles due to a claim by the State of Florida for 25% of the salvage and a claim by the U.S. federal government for 100%. In 1982 the U.S. Supreme Court granted Mel Fisher full ownership of any treasure found.

Tragedy struck in 1975 when Dirk Fisher, his wife, and a crew member drowned when their search/dive vessel capsized. Mel and his youngest son Kane continued the search.

Over the next few years the Fishers had a series of successes, especially in 1980 when they found the wreckage of the Santa Margarita with its more than $20 million in gold coins and artifacts.

The bulk of the Atocha's treasure was located on July 20, 1985. Later that year, work began on salvaging the Atocha's precious cargo, estimated to be worth more than $400 million. The salvage process has taken more than ten years.

Among the 300,000 items was an emerald-encrusted cross intended as a gift for the pope in Rome. Today the cross is valued at more than $20 million. One of the earliest finds was a group of 76 solid gold bars plus numerous gold disks, together weighing a total of more than 200 pounds.

Much of the salvaged treasure was not listed in the ship's manifest (the official inventory), indicating that the sailors had been smuggling valuables, especially emeralds, for their own benefit. This was probably a common activity in the seventeenth century, given that the king of Spain imposed very high taxes on his subjects and often "borrowed" from them whatever he wanted. Hence, men returning from the New World usually declared the silver they were bringing back (as silver was too big and bulky to smuggle), but they hid emeralds in their pockets and brought them

into Spain without being detected. The emeralds they smuggled could well have been worth more than the shipload of silver they were declaring to the king.

The Atocha is regarded as one of the richest of any Spanish galleons that sailed in the early seventeenth century. The pieces found in search and recovery missions will be studied and prized by historians and archaeologists for many decades to come.

[N. Neil Harris, "Coins of the *Nuestra Señora de Atocha*," *The Numismatist*, October 1986, pp. 2017-40. This article includes extensive photos of the salvage operation and of many of the coins which were retrieved.]

atrament (*m.*) [*Pol.*] ink.

atrybucja (*f.*) [*Pol.*] attribution (the complete identification of a coin, medal, or banknote).

atrybuować (*v.*) [*Pol.*] to attribute.

åtsida (*r.*) [*Swed.*] obverse.

åtta [*Swed.*] eight.

åtte [*Nor.*] eight.

åtti [*Nor.*] eighty.

åttio [*Swed.*] eighty.

attribuer (*v.*) [*Fr.*] to attribute.

attribuera (*v.*) [*Swed.*] to attribute.

attribuire (*v.*) [*Ital.*] to attribute.

attribute (*verb*); **attribution** (*noun*). The determination and classification of a coin, token, medal, or note's issuing agency (country, private individual, or whatever), place of manufacture, denomination, date or period of issue, kind of metal or paper, type, and variety. In some cases, other characteristics, such as grade, error, or pedigree, are also included in the attribution.

Anything that contributes to the complete and accurate identification of a numismatic item is part of its attribution. Until this identification is complete, the piece is referred to as *unattributed*.

attribuzione (*f.*) [*Ital.*] attribution.

AU. [*abbr.*] 1. gold (from Latin *aurum*). 2. About Uncirculated.

au buste enfantin [*Fr.*] Bust of the king or queen as a child. Refers to effigies of monarchs (e.g., France's Louis XV or Spain's Isabella II) who succeeded to the throne at a very young age and who remained on the throne long enough to require the updating of their effigies.

au buste enfantin (Louis XV)

aukcja (*f.*) [*Pol.*] auction.

aukcja na oferty pocztowe [*Pol.*] mail bid sale.

auksjon (*m.*) [*Nor.*] auction; auction sale.

auksjonskatalog (*m.*) [*Nor.*] auction catalogue.

auktion (*r.*) [*Swed.*] auction.

Auktion per Postweg [*Ger.*] mail bid sale.

auktionsförsäljning (*r.*) [*Swed.*] auction sale.

auktionskatalog [*Swed., Dan.*] auction catalogue.

Auktionskatalog (*m.*) [*Ger.*] auction catalogue.

auktionsnummer (*n.*) [*Dan.*] (auction) lot.

auktionssalg (*n.*) [*Dan.*] auction sale.

Auktionsverkauf (*m.*) [*Ger.*] auction sale.

aur (*n.*) [*Rom.*] gold.

aureate nickel A trademark of the Sheritt Mint for its nickel coated with 88% copper and 12% tin. Examples include the Canadian Loon Dollar coins issued since 1987.

aureus [*Lat.*] Gold Roman coin introduced by Augustus in the first century B.C. It was valued at twenty-five denarii. The aureus was the principal gold coin of Rome until the *solidus* was introduced in A.D. 309 by Constantine the Great.

aurum (*n.*) [*Lat.*] gold. Abbreviated *AU.* or *AV.*

Ausgabe (*f.*) [*Ger.*] an issue, issuance.

ausgezeichnet [*Ger.*] excellent.

ausländisch [*Ger.*] foreign.

Auslandswährung (*f.*) [*Ger.*] foreign currency.

ausstellen (*v.*) [*Ger.*] to exhibit.

Ausstellung (*f.*) [*Ger.*] exhibition.

austral (*m.*) [*Span.*] Argentine unit of currency introduced in 1985 as part of an austerity program to try to reduce Argentina's horrendous inflation. The austral was initially intended to be exchanged for one thousand pesos (the previously used denomination) or $1.25 in U.S funds. It was ultimately abandoned.

Australian Numismatic Society The Society was established in Sydney in 1913 and is the oldest numismatic organization in the Southern Hemisphere. Headquarters are located in Sydney with a branch in Queensland, which has its headquarters in Brisbane.

The Society has four principal aims: (1.) to encourage the collection and study of coins, medals, banknotes, and other numismatic items; (2.) to spread the knowledge of numismatics, using meetings, seminars, forums, and publications; (3.) to assist the interchange of ideas between members; and (4.) to encourage numismatic research and the publication of the results of that research.

Membership is open to any reputable person on a worldwide basis. Information can be obtained by contacting the Australian Numismatic Society, P.O. Box R 4, Royal Exchange, Australia, 2000.

Ausztria [*Hun.*] Austria.

Autriche [*Fr.*] Austria.

au verso [*Fr.*] on the back.

AV. [*Lat. abbr.*] gold (from *aurum*).

avamulyan अवमूल्यन [*Hin.*] devaluation.

avats אָבָץ (*m.*) [*Heb.*] zinc.

avbildning (*r.*) [*Swed.*] effigy.

avdp. [*abbr.*] avoirdupois[*q.v.*].

avers (*m.*) [*Fr.*]; (*n.*) [*Rom.*]; (*c.*) [*Dan.*] obverse.

Avers (*m.*) [*Ger.*] obverse.

avgift (*r.*) [*Swed.*] fee.

avoirdupois [from Middle English meaning *goods sold by weight*.] Measurement of weight as per the English system (i.e., 16 ounces to the pound and 16 drams to the ounce). For precious metals, one avoirdupois ounce equals 437.5 grains, 28.35 grams, or 0.9115 troy ounce. Abbreviated *avdp.*

avskärning (*r.*) [*Swed.*] exergue.

awers (*m.*) [*Pol.*] obverse.

axia αξία (*f.*) [*Grk.*] value.

ayant un défaut de frappe [*Fr.*] mis-struck.

ayar işareti [*Turk.*] adjustment mark.

aykırı [*Turk.*] anomaly.

aykserg אֶקסֶרג [*Heb.*] exergue.

ay'rech na'kuv עֶרֶךְ נָקוּב (*m.*) [*Heb.*] face value.

az bulunur [*Turk.*] scarce.

azul [*Span., Port.*] blue.

B b

baar (*f.-c.*) [*Dut.*] ingot.

babérkoszorús [*Hun.*] laureate.

Baby Bond Five dollar bond issued by the State of Louisiana in the 1870s to help pay off Civil War debts. Its distinguishing feature (and the source of its name) is the lovely vignette of a young child.

Virtually every surviving specimen looks exactly like the one in the illustration, with four coupons still attached. Just prior to the next redemption date, August 1884, the bonds were invalidated.

bạc [*Viet.*] silver.

bạch kim [*Viet.*] platinum.

back Reverse or secondary side of a banknote, bond, or other certificate. The front or primary side is called the *face*.

bag mark Surface abrasion caused when coins hit each other during the minting and wrapping process. Bag marks are more apt to be seen on large heavy coins like silver dollars, but they are also found on coins of any size or denomination. However, coins made from hard copper-nickel alloys are less prone to show bag marks than silver or gold coins.

Bag marks are not the result of circulation and do not disqualify a coin from being graded uncirculated. They are, however, taken into account when determining a coin's mint state level. A Morgan Dollar exhibiting heavy bag marks will probably be graded MS-60 while an identical coin with few bag marks might receive the grade of MS-65, commanding a higher price.

bái jīn 白金 [*Chin.-py./sc.*] platinum.

baik [*Indo.*] fine (grade or condition).

bakır [*Turk.*] copper.

bakside [*Nor.*] reverse. *på baksiden*: on the back.

bal [*Hun.*] left (direction or position).

banca (*f.*) [*Ital.*] bank; [*Span.*] banking (activity).

State of Louisiana "Baby Bond"

bancă (*f.*) [*Rom.*] bank.

banco 1. (*m.*) [*Span., Port.*] bank, i.e., a financial institution.

2. [*Russ.*] Generic category of any silver coin valued at 25 kopecks or more in Czarist Russia. Silver coins of less than 25 kopecks were known as *subsidiary.*

[R. W. Julian, "The Russian Silver Coinage of 1796-1917," *The Numismatist*, December 1989, p. 1956.]

banconota (*f.*) [*Ital.*] banknote.

bani (*m.pl.*) [*Rom.*] money.

bani fără acoperire în aur sau argint [*Rom.*] fiat money.

banka [*Turk.*] bank (financial institution).

bankbiljet (*n.*) [*Dut.*] banknote.

bankjegy [*Hun.*] banknote.

banknot [*Turk.*]; (*m.*) [*Pol.*] banknote.

banknota банкнота (*f.*) [*Russ.*] banknote.

banknote Paper money issued by a bank authorized by the government. Quantities are limited by legislative decree, and the method by which the notes can be redeemed is determined.

Bank of Montréal token Name given to several series of high quality copper tokens issued by the Bank of Montréal from 1835 to 1844. These tokens, valued at a halfpenny or penny, were intended both to alleviate a shortage of copper coins and to discourage individuals from making their own cheap brass tokens which the bank refused to accept. Despite the bank's good intentions, the issuance of these pieces spawned many lightweight imitations, most notably those known as *Bouquet Sous.*

The original 1835 and 1836 Bank of Montréal tokens featured a bouquet (from which the name of its imitators was derived) and the 1837 tokens showed a man standing (the *Habitant* tokens), but many later pieces showed a picture of the bank building itself. The 1838 specimens show the bank from an angle and are called *Side View* tokens.

In 1842, Upper and Lower Canada were united as the Province of Canada, and it authorized the Bank of Montréal to mint more copper tokens. As can be seen in the illustration, the new design showed the bank building from the front, hence their name *Front View tokens.* The pieces were struck by Boulton and Watt, the same company that had produced, among other things, the huge 1797 1d and 2d British "cartwheels." In 1842 and 1844 a total of 240,000 Bank of Montréal penny tokens were released, as well as just under two million halfpennies.

[J. E. Charlton, *Standard Catalogue of Canadian Coins* (10th Ed.), pp. 14-15; J. A. Haxby and R. C. Willey, *Coins of Canada* (9th Ed.), pp. 153-66.]

Bank of Montréal "Front View" token

banque (*f.*) [*Fr.*] bank (financial institution).

barang kuno [*Indo.*] antiquity.

Barber coinage U.S. dimes (i.e., ten cent pieces; 1892-1916), quarters (1892-1916), and half dollars (1892-1915) designed by Charles E. Barber, the Chief Engraver of the Mint from 1880 to 1917. These pieces were made possible by the Act of September 26, 1890, which permitted the Treasury Department to replace any coin design that had been in use for at least 25 years. As the dimes, quarters, and halves had exhibited Christian Gobrecht's Liberty Seated design since the 1830s, the Department decided to re-design those coins. After an unsuccessful attempt to convince ten of the most prominent artists to submit designs and after an even more unsuccessful effort to find a suitable design through open competition, Mint Director Edward O. Leech assigned Barber to the task. All three coins were introduced in 1892.

The design shows the head of the allegorical Liberty. Ms. Liberty is wearing a Phyrgian cap, symbol of freedom arising from the French Revolution. Surrounding the cap is a laurel wreath. Although Liberty has always been

personified as a woman, this particular rendition is sometimes considered to be somewhat masculine in appearance.

The reverse of the quarter and half dollar portrays a slightly stylized eagle reminiscent of that on the U.S. National Seal. The dime was too small for such an intricate design, so a wreath was substituted.

[David W. Lange, "The Underrated Barber Half Dollar." *The Numismatist*, May 1988, pp. 864-866; Stephen Epstein, "An Awakening in Barber Coin Collecting," *The Numismatist*, November 1990, pp. 1764-66 et al.]

barber shop token Type of token formerly used in large barber shops to facilitate bookkeeping. Each barber would be assigned a number. Upon completing a haircut, he would give the customer a token showing the barber's number and the amount owed. The customer would give the token to the cashier and would then pay the amount shown on the token. By using this system, the barbers did not have to handle money and the cashier was able to keep an accurate account of how much money each barber earned on any given day.

[David Schenkman and Joseph Levine, "Unusual Barber Shop Tokens," *The Numismatist*, April 1981, pp. 902-3.]

barbuda (*f.*) [*Port.*] Billon coin of medieval Portugal first minted by Ferdinand I "the Handsome" (1345-1383, ruled 1367-1383). It had a value of 3 dinheiros but was also issued in units of one-half and one-quarter barbuda.

bar coding Inclusion of a bar code on the reverse of paper notes to enable them to be read by high-speed sorting equipment. Canada began this practice with its 1986 issues so that its notes could be electronically sorted by the Bank of Canada.

[J. A. Haxby and R. C. Willey, *Coins of Canada* (9th Ed.), p. 200.]

Bargeld (*n.*) [*Ger.*] cash (ready money).

barna [*Hun.*] brown.

baros βάρος (*n.*) [*Grk.*] weight.

barre (*r.*) [*Dan.*] ingot.

Barren (*m.*) [*Ger.*] ingot.

barzel בַּרְזֶל (*m.*) [*Heb.*] iron (the metal).

bas (*m.*) [*Fr.*] bottom.

base metal For coinage purposes, any metal other than gold, silver, platinum, or palladium. Billon is sometimes called *base silver* because its actual silver content is less than 50%.

basilias βασιλιάς (*m.*) [*Grk.*] king.

basilissa βασίλισσα (*f.*) [*Grk.*] queen.

baskı makinesi [*Turk.*] (coinage) press.

basso (*m.*) [*Ital.*] bottom.

bathmologo βαθμολογώ (*v.*) [*Grk.*] to grade.

bathmos βαθμός (*m.*) [*Grk.*] grade, condition.

bathu (*v.*) [*Wel.*] to coin, to mint.

Batı Almanya [*Turk.*] West Germany (B.R.D.).

bătut defectuos [*Rom.*] badly struck; mis-struck.

bawbee Billon coin of Scotland introduced by James V in 1538 and continued through the reign of Mary. It was valued at sixpence. A half-bawbee and quarter-bawbee were also struck. Charles I did not issue this coin. The bawbee was brought back in 1677 by Charles II as a copper coin and was finally discontinued in 1697 by William II.

bawbee (Charles II)

B.C. 1. [*abbr.*] Before Christ, as used in Western dating systems. In the Middle East, *B.C.E.* (Before Christian Era) and *C.E.* (Christian Era, the equivalent of A.D., *anno Domini*) are preferred.

2. [*Span. abbr.*] buena conservación. Grade of banknotes approximating Very Fine. The note may have as many as three folds but no tears. All legends must be legible.

B.C.E. [*abbr.*] Before Christian Era. This and *C.E.* (Christian Era) are the preferred terms in Jewish and Arab societies to designate B.C. and A.D. for Western dating systems.

bead A raised dot that appears on the surface of a coin or medal as part of its design.

Beaded refers to a row of dots that encircles or partially encircles the coin just within the

rim. Canadian cents of 1965 exhibit two varieties of beaded borders: large beads and small beads.

If one bead appears by itself somewhere on the face of the coin, either intentionally or as the result of an error, it is usually called a dot[q.v.] rather than a bead. Probably the best known examples are the 1936 Canadian cents, ten cent pieces, and quarter dollars.

beaded rim

beau [*Fr.*] fine (grade or condition).
bedrag (*n.*) [*Dut.*] amount.
befejezetlen [*Hun.*] incomplete.
beğenilme şartiyle [*Turk.*] on approval.
Belag (*m.*) [*Ger.*] tarnish; incrustation; covering or coating of a foreign substance on a coin.
Belagerungsmünze (*f.*) [*Ger.*] obsidional coin.
belägrings- (*adj.*) [*Swed.*] obsidional.
belägringsmynt (*n.*) [*Swed.*] obsidional coin.
belasting (*m.-c.*) [*Dut.*] tax.
Belçika [*Turk.*] Belgium.
belejringspenge (*pl.*) [*Dan.*] obsidional money.
belge [*Turk.*] certificate.
Belgia [*Pol.*] Belgium.
Bélgica [*Span., Port.*] Belgium.
Belgien [*Ger.*] Belgium.
Belgio [*Ital.*] Belgium.
Belgique [*Fr.*] Belgium.
bell metal An alloy of approximately 20% tin and 80% copper.
bello [*Ital.*] beautiful; good (as the condition or grade of a coin).
belo [*Port.*] fine (grade or condition).
beløp (*n.*) [*Nor.*] amount.
belső [*Hun.*] intrinsic.
Benjamin Franklin National Memorial Award
Gold medals 64mm in diameter which were first awarded during 1990, the 200th anniversary of Franklin's death. The awards are funded by a bequest from Henry Bower (1896-1988), a Philadelphia chemical manufacturer.

The awards, made annually, are in two categories. *The Bower Award for Achievement in Science* is an international award granted without respect to nationality for achievement in science and is accompanied by a cash prize always in excess of $250,000 (U.S.). *The Bower Award for Business Leadership* is an American national award in business but does not include an honorarium.

The first science award, made in November 1990 went to Dr. Paul C. Lauterber, a pioneer and developer of magnetic resonance imaging technology, of the University of Illinois. The first business leadership award was presented to James E. Burke, retired chairman of Johnson and Johnson.

The medals, struck by Medallic Art Company, feature a seated Franklin on the obverse. A printing press adorns the reverse of the business medal, and the electro-static machine graces the reverse of the science medal.

[Contributed by Phil W. Greenslet. Larry E. Tise, *The Benjamin Franklin National Memorial Awards*, The Franklin Institute, Philadelphia, 1990.]

bercak [*Indo.*] tarnish.
beş [*Turk.*] five.
beschadigd [*Dut.*] damaged.
beschädigt [*Ger.*] damaged.
beschermend bod (*n.*) [*Dut.*] protective reserve bid.
Beschriftung (*f.*) [*Ger.*] inscription, lettering.
beskadiget [*Dan.*] damaged.
beställningssedel (*r.*) [*Swed.*] order form.
bestämning (*r.*) [*Swed.*] attribution.
bestelformulier (*n.*) [*Dut.*] order form.
Bestellformular (*n.*) [*Ger.*] order form.
bestillingsformular (*c.*) [*Dan.*] order form.
betalingsmerke (*n.*) [*Nor.*] token.
betét [*Hun.*] deposit.
Betrag (*m.*) [*Ger.*] amount.
betul [*Indo.*] authentic.
bevakningspris [*Swed.*] protective reserve bid.
beválthatatlan papírpénz [*Hun.*] fiat money.
bevonat [*Hun.*] tarnish.

bezel Ring into which a coin is inserted so that it can be attached to a chain or bracelet and worn as jewelry without damaging the coin. The bezel is usually of the same metal as the coin, either gold or silver.

biały [*Pol.*] white.

bianco [*Ital.*] white.

biàn sè 变色 [*Chin.-py./sc.*] tarnish.

biǎn zhí 贬值 [*Chin.-py./sc.*] devaluation.

bid sheet Order form submitted by mail by someone wishing to place a bid at an auction or mail bid sale. Just as with live participation at an auction, the highest bidder is legally obligated to pay for those items successfully bid upon.

bieden (*v.*) [*Dut.*] to bid (at an auction or mail bid sale).

biedformulier (*n.*); **biedingsformulier** (*n.*) [*Dut.*] bid sheet.

bien conservada [*Span.*] fine (grade or condition).

Bietempfehlung (*f.*) [*Ger.*] suggested bid.

bieten (*v.*) [*Ger.*] to bid (at an auction or mail bid sale).

bihira [*Tag.*] rare, scarce.

bilde (*n.*) [*Nor.*] effigy.

Bildnis (*n.*) [*Ger.*] effigy; portrait.

bilingue [*Ital.*] bilingual.

bilingüe [*Span.*] bilingual.

bilingv [*Rom.*] bilingual.

biljet (*n.*) [*Dut.*] note (i.e., banknote).

billet de banque (*m.*) [*Fr.*] note; banknote.

billet de propagande [*Fr.*] propaganda note.

billete (*m.*) [*Span.*] note.

billete de banco (*m.*) [*Span.*] banknote.

billete de propaganda [*Span.*] propaganda note.

billete expósito (*m.*) [*Span.*] Paper notes issued in Cuba in the 1880s to alleviate the shortage of small coins on the sugar plantations. See *foundling note.*

billet privé (*m.*) [*Fr.*] scrip.

bill-hook money Chinese bronze knives used as currency from 1125-255 B.C. See *knife money.*

billon A collective term for various alloys containing less than 50% silver and usually with the balance mostly copper. Billon was used for coinage as early as the third century A.D. by the Romans. The English used it during the sixteenth century debasement, and it was often found in coins of the seventeenth and eighteenth centuries. A twentieth century utilization of billon are the one peso coins of Mexico struck from 1957-67.

Billon was often treated at the mint to enhance its silvery appearance by being coated with a silver wash or by having part of the copper on the coins' surfaces bleached away with a mild acid. The acid treatment was done to the planchets prior to the coins' striking. Unfortunately, the silver coating deteriorates badly as soon as the coins start circulating, giving the coins a very unpleasant appearance.

If the copper content is more than 75%, the alloy is called *black billon* because the coins turn very black within a short period of time.

[Contributed by Halbert Carmichael.]

modern billon coin (Mexico)

bilti m'zoheh בִּלְתִּי מְזוֹהֶה [*Heb.*] unattributed (not fully identified).

bilti-yadu'a בִּלְתִּי יָדוּעַ [*Heb.*] unknown.

bimetallic token Token made of two dissimilar metals, frequently an aluminum insert in a brass ring, which is then struck as a single token. These items are often collected as a category in itself. They are also collected along with other tokens in the same type, i.e., bimetallic coal company store scrip is collected along with other coal company store scrip, etc.

[Contributed by Robert Doyle.]

bimetallism Monetary policy based on the use of both gold and silver as legal tender. The two metals are valued against each other in a fixed ratio, perhaps as sixteen units of silver equaling one of gold. Because the ratio is

determined by law and not by economic principles, the ratio does not reflect the relative abundance of the metals and may be changed by law, as was the case in the United States in 1834 when the former ratio of 15 to 1 (silver to gold) was changed to 15.988 (usually expressed as 16) to 1. In all cases, the ratio is expressed in terms of weight, usually with a fixed number of ounces of silver equaling one ounce of gold.

This system has often led to monetary problems which have caused countries to adopt a system of monometallism with gold as its standard. For example, the discovery of large quantities of gold, which happened in California and Australia, causes the value of gold to fall against that of silver and destroys the validity of the ratio. Also, when political units wish to merge, bimetallism must be abandoned if one unit has been using it and the others have not. This was the case in 1871 in Prussia when the German states merged following their success in the Franco-Prussian War. The resulting German Empire went on the gold standard.

Bimetallism was also abandoned in the United States in 1873. In 1878 the Bland-Allison Act allowed for the minting of a limited number of silver dollars, thus creating a system called limping bimetallism[q.v.], a monetary system partially dependent on the use of silver but primarily dependent on gold. The U.S. did not dissolve the last of its connections to bimetallism until 1967. It was during the mid-1960s when the rising price of silver finally forced the U.S. government to discontinue the production of silver coins and the redemption of silver certificates. In 1970 the federal government sold the last of its silver supply.

Birleşik Kırallık [*Turk.*] United Kingdom .

bisect Coin or note cut in half to make small change. A coin split this way is often referred to as *sheared*. A bisected banknote is also called a *cut note*. See pages 310 and 318 for color illustrations.

bit Piece sheared from Spanish 4 or 8 *real* coins to provide small change. A bit was supposed to equal 1 *real* in value, so the large crown-size 8 *real* coins were cut into eight pieces. It is from this practice that the American expression "two bits" (slang term for a quarter dollar) was derived, because a bit had the nominal value of 12 1/2 cents.

See page 310 for color photos.

bizonytalan származású [*Hun.*] unattributed.

bjuda (*v.*) [*Swed.*] to bid (at an auction).

blå [*Nor., Swed., Dan.*] blue.

bläck (*n.*) [*Swed.*] ink.

black billon [also known as *black money*]. Billon[q.v.] containing more than 75% copper. Coins made from this alloy turn very black within a short period of time after they enter circulation.

Most of the coins made from black billon were struck in the seventeenth and eighteenth centuries. Some of these coins acquired nicknames containing the word black, such as the *black dogg*.

black money See *black billon*.

Blacksmith's halfcrown Very crude silver halfcrown probably struck in 1642 or 1643 in Kilkenny, Ireland. It was issued by the Confederate Catholics who supported Charles I during the Great Rebellion. The Blacksmith's halfcrown is a poorly-struck copy of a similar piece made at the Tower Mint in London and is one of the many emergency coins resulting from the Rebellion.

Also see *Inchiquin money, Dublin money,* and *Ormonde money*.

Blacksmith's halfcrown

błąd (*m.*) [*Pol.*] error.

blanc [*Fr.*] white.

blanco [*Span.*] white.

blank Disc of metal upon which a coinage design is stamped. After the coin is struck, the disc is usually called a *planchet* (although many experts regard the words *blank, planchet,* and *flan* as synonymous).

blanket (*c.*) [*Dan.*] planchet.

blankett (*m.*) [*Nor.*] planchet.

blankiet (*m.*) [*Pol.*] planchet.

blau [*Ger.*] blue.

blauw [*Dut.*] blue.

blekk (*n.*) [*Nor.*] ink.

blind assistance Prior to World War II, few countries made any effort to make their coins and notes recognizable by blind people. Since the war, many nations have added a variety of changes to make circulating currency more user-friendly for the visually impaired.

U.K. 50 pence— a "blind-friendly" coin

The easiest way to make paper money recognizable to the blind is to print different denominations on different size paper. Another method is to print the notes with a heavy intaglio process that makes the ink so thick that the key information can actually be felt by a blind person running his fingers over it. An example is shown on page 320 of the color plates. The Dutch note on the top appears exactly as sighted people see it with its multiple shades of green and its modernistic design. The line drawing beneath it shows the portions printed in "heavy" ink which can be "read" by the blind with their fingers.

Coins can be more understandable to the blind if they are made of unusual sizes and if the numbers are large, in high relief, and not obstructed by the background design. The British 50 new pence coin is a good example

with its seven sides and large clear digits. Canada, Italy, and a few other countries have placed an interrupted reeded edge on certain coins; i.e., the edge design alternates between short reeded sections and plain sections. Italy has also issued coins with part of the inscription in braille.

It is ironic that the United States, which has passed more laws to assist handicapped people than any other country on earth, does so little to make its money accessible to the blind. Since 1929 all small-size notes have been the same size and texture, regardless of denomination. This was not changed in 1996 when the U.S. introduced its new series of notes with multiple anti-counterfeiting devices. The new notes are exactly the same size as the old notes and are indistinguishable to the visually impaired. U.S. coins are also difficult for the blind, especially foreigners. The inscriptions tend to be small and the denominations are written in words instead of numerals.

blind token A token with no mention of its issuer or of the city where it was issued, thus being difficult to attribute.

Blue Book See *Handbook of United States Coins.*

b'ma'khazor בְּמַחֲזוֹר [*Heb.*] circulated.

"Bo" Hobo who created the most popular hobo nickels. See *Hughes, "Bo"* for additional information.

bod (*n.*) [*Dut.*] (auction) bid.

bom (*m.adj.*); **boa** (*f.adj.*) [*Port.*] good.

bon (*m.adj.*); **bonne** (*f.adj.*) [*Fr.*] good.

bon de commande [*Fr.*] order form.

Scottish bonnet piece

bonnet piece Scottish gold ducat struck in 1539. Its name is derived from the obverse design which shows the king, James V, wearing a

broad flat cap. This coin is also notable for having been the first coin of the Scottish series to bear a date.

bono (*m.*) [*Span.*] (commercial) bond.

bon propagandowy (*m.*) [*Pol.*] propaganda note.

bord (*m.*) [*Fr.*] edge (of a coin or medal).

borde (*m.*) [*Span.*] rim.

bordo (*m.*) [*Port.*] rim; edge.

Bordüre (*f.*) [*Ger.*] bead (raised dot on the surface of a coin).

botten (*r.*) [*Swed.*] bottom.

bovenkant (*m.-c.*) [*Dut.*] top.

box Coin used to smuggle drugs, jewels, or other small precious items. Two identical large coins are needed to make a box. Usually the obverse and edge of one coin are retained and the reverse is hollowed out. On the other coin, the reverse (without the rim) is kept and a hinge is attached so that it can open and close somewhat like a woman's compact. When closed, the box resembles a normal coin. The ones with the best workmanship close together so cleanly and tightly that they have virtually no telltale marks of tampering.

The U.S. Trade Dollar was a favorite "host" coin for making boxes, partly because it was of a good size and thickness, and partly because much of the smuggling went on in areas of the world where the trade dollar circulated.

bracteate A flat, thin silver pfennig produced in German regions from about 1100 to the mid-fourteenth century. It is struck from one die and has only one readable side. The die is cut in relief and the coin is stamped from the back. Its purpose was to give moneyers a larger area to produce an artistic image than a coin of this weight would normally permit. In essence, a bracteate resembles what a round piece of aluminum foil would look like if it were pressed in a small notary seal.

branco [*Port.*] white.

brand piece Coin used to test a small die showing the logo of a large Mexican ranch.

Every ranch in Mexico and the Southwestern United States had its own distinct logo, known as a brand. A large version was burnt into the sides of cattle to prove ownership. A smaller version of the same brand was stamped into farm implements, tools, and all other movable property to make the items easily identifiable if they were stolen, much the same as Americans engrave their social security numbers on the backs of televisions, VCRs, and other valuables. The coins used for testing new dies are known as *brand pieces* and were merely convenient metal disks upon which new small dies could be tested.

Unlike many nineteenth-century coins of England, the United States, and elsewhere, Mexican coins with private counterstamps were usually not intended as advertising pieces.

[Gregory G. Brunk, "Merchant Advertising Countermarks of 19th-Century America," *The Numismatist*, February 1989, pp. 222-230.]

brass 1. Alloys of copper with varying amounts of zinc, typically 25% to 33%, but always more than 5%. Coins made from brass are usually bright shiny yellow when new but corrode easily.

In ancient times, brass was a fairly popular alloy for coinage because of its attractiveness and durability. However, brass became unpopular as a coinage alloy in the Middle Ages because of its strong resemblance to gold. Counterfeit gold coins were often produced from this metal. As a consequence, the general public began to perceive of brass as a worthless metal, and few legitimate coins were made from it. Even today, brass is not widely used for coins. The Guatemala one cent coin of 1949-54 is one of the few exceptions.

Since 1962 the U.S. Lincoln Cents have been made from an alloy of 95% copper and 5% zinc known as *gilding metal*. (Not included, of course, are the clad[*q.v.*] cents with a center layer of aluminum.) Although this alloy is sometimes mistakenly referred to as brass, it is actually bronze in the strictest metallurgical sense because it lacks a sufficiently high percentage of zinc.

Also see *cartridge brass* and *bronze*.

[Contributed by Halbert Carmichael.]

2. Archaic slang expression for *money*.

braun [*Ger.*] brown.

brąz (*m.*) [*Pol.*] bronze (the alloy).

brązowy [*Pol.*] brown.

Brésil [*Fr.*] Brazil.

brett (*m.*) [*Nor.*] a crease, a fold.

brevbudsauktion (*c.*) [*Dan.*] mail bid sale.

brick tea Blocks of pressed tea leaves used as a medium of exchange in some parts of Burma, China, and Tibet from around A.D. 1000 until the middle of the nineteenth century. The bricks were notched in such a way that they could easily be broken into however many pieces of approximately equal size for making small change. The name of the issuer and the value were stamped on each section.

bris de coin [*Fr.*] die break.

Britain Crown Popular name of two types of English gold coins issued under the reign of James I. The first was of five shillings and was struck from 1604-12. The second was of five shillings sixpence, a result of the decision in 1612 to raise the gold content of all gold coins by ten percent. The enhanced crowns were issued from 1612-19.

broadstrike In normal coin production, a collar rises above the anvil die (the stationary die) to retain the blank and keep it perfectly round. If the collar fails to rise, there is nothing to stop the spreading of the metal. The resulting coin is therefore larger than intended. The spread can vary from just a small amount to a large increase. A U.S. or Canadian 5 cent coin can appear as large as a quarter. Broadstrikes can be on-center or off-center and tend to be quite round.

[Contributed by Coleman Ezkovich.]

brockage [from Old English *brekken* or *brokken* meaning "broken" or "not of perfect quality"]. A coin inadvertently struck with either two obverses or two reverses, one of which is normal but the other of which is reversed and incuse. The error side usually exhibits a weak strike.

In normal modern minting procedures, a coin blank is placed between two dies which are then brought together under pressure. When the pressure is released, the newly-minted coin is ejected from the machine and another blank is inserted. If the coin fails to eject, the next blank will then be pressed between one die and the non-ejected coin, thus producing a new coin with one correct side and one side with an identical yet reversed and intaglio impression. In most cases, the non-ejected coin adheres to the hammer die (the die which moves up and down), but it occasionally attaches itself to the anvil die (the stationary die).

Since the metal from which the non-ejected coin was made is softer than the hardened steel in the die, the impression left on the error side of the brockage is weaker than the strike on the normal side. Similarly, the side of the non-ejected coin that strikes the new blank becomes somewhat flattened. If it remains stuck to the die for several strikings, the metal in the coin can spread outward and the piece begins to resemble a bottle cap before it is finally ejected from the machine. This type of error is referred to as a *cupped coin*.

Some brockages are known to have been struck in ancient and medieval times. But most have occurred since the advent of modern minting machines, largely due to the very high speeds used by today's coinage presses.

[Richard G. Doty, *The Macmillan Encyclopedic Dictionary of Numismatics*, pp. 37-38; Ewald Junge, *World Coin Encyclopedia*, p. 52.]

Brockageprägung [*Ger.*] brockage.

brøkdel (*c.*) [*Dan.*]; (*m.*) [*Nor.*] (mathematical) fraction.

b'ro'kej בְּרוֹקֵיג' [*Heb.*] brockage.

bronce (*m.*) [*Span.*] bronze (the alloy).

bronce amarillo (*m.*) [*Span.*] brass.

brons (*n.*) [*Dut.*]; (*r.*) [*Swed.*] bronze.

bronse (*m.*) [*Nor.*] bronze.

bronz [*Hun., Turk.*]; (*n.*) [*Rom.*] bronze.

bronze Alloy containing at least 90% copper. Countless different compositions have been used for coinage purposes throughout history. Current practice (since around 1850) is to use 95% copper with the balance tin and zinc. The content of tin varies from 4% in French bronze and in coins of the Bundesrepublik Deutschland (West Germany) to mere traces in post World War II United States coinage. Both the U.S. and British mints vary the tin content as the availability of tin changes.

Also see *brass*.

[Contributed by Halbert Carmichael.]

Bronze Star The Bronze Star is awarded to any person who, while serving in any capacity with the U.S. Army, Navy, Marine Corps, or Coast Guard on or after December 7, 1941, distinguishes himself (or herself) by heroic or meritorious achievement or service in connection with military operations against an enemy of the United States. It was authorized on February 4, 1944.

[Contributed by Robert A. Carpenter. Evans Kerrigan, *American Medals and Decorations*, pp. 22-23; Capt. H. Taprell Dorling, *Ribbons and Medals*, pp. 210.]

bronzital Name created by the Italians for their particular composition of aluminum bronze: 91.6% copper, 8.0% aluminum, and 0.4% titanium. Examples include the Italian 20 lira coins starting 1957 and the center of the bimetal 500 lira introduced in 1982.

Bruchteil (*f.*) [*Ger.*] fraction.

brugt [*Dan.*] used.

bruin [*Dut.*] brown.

brukt [*Nor.*] used.

brun [*Fr., Swed., Dan., Nor.*] brown.

bud (*n.*) [*Nor., Dan.*] bid (at an auction or mail bid sale).

budliste (*c.*) [*Dan.*] bid sheet.

bud uden øvre grænse accepteres ikke [*Dan.*] no unlimited bids accepted.

buena conservación [*Span.*] Grade of paper money roughly equal to Very Fine. The note may have as many as three folds but no tears. All legends must be legible. Abbreviated "B.C."

bueno [*Span.*] good.

bueno por... [*Span.*] good for....

Buffalo Nickel The Buffalo-Indian Nickel was designed by James E. Fraser and was issued from 1913 to 1938. It replaced the Liberty Head Nickel (1883-1912; five questionable specimens dated 1913). Its composition is the same as that used from 1866 to the present: 75% copper and 25% nickel.

The Indian portrayed on the obverse is actually a composite of three Native Americans who posed for Fraser. The buffalo on the reverse was modeled after "Black Diamond," a popular attraction at the New York Zoological Gardens.

The earliest 1913 Buffalo Nickels show the buffalo standing on a raised mound. The design was esthetically attractive, but the mound tended to wear too fast and was not well suited for circulation. The reverse was changed later in 1913 by adding a distinct exergue.

Buffalo Nickel: obv., 1st rev. (1913), & 2nd rev. (1913-38)

The obverse did not wear well, either, especially around the date. It was modified in the mid-1920s to make the date stronger.

The two most interesting coins of the series are both errors and both came from the Denver Mint. In 1918 some specimens were released showing the distinct overdate 1918/17. Some of the dies became excessively worn in 1937, producing what appears to be a three-legged buffalo.

The Buffalo Nickel was the favorite "host coin" for carving the so-called *hobo nickels*[q.v.]. Many beautiful and fascinating pieces were created.

Buffalo Nickels were discontinued in 1938 in favor of the current Jefferson Nickels.

buiten koers stelling [*Dut.*] demonetization.

buitenlands [*Dut.*] foreign.

buitenlandse valuta (*f.-c.*) [*Dut.*] foreign currency.

bulletin de commande [*Fr.*] order form.

bullion 1. Uncoined precious metal forged in the form of bars, rounds, or ingots. The weight and purity are usually inscribed. Most contemporary bullion items are in whole numbers or fractions of ounces, even in the majority of the world's countries which use the metric system because it has become traditional to quote the value of precious metals in ounces.

2. Non-circulating coin issued as a convenient medium for trading and holding precious metals. Bullion coins usually contain

exactly one ounce or a half, quarter, or tenth of an ounce of gold, silver, or platinum. These coins are regarded as a highly reliable way of trading bullion.

"Britannia" gold £100 bullion coin

Another advantage of bullion coins is that they allow small investors to purchase quantities of any size, including amounts far smaller than could be obtained through any other means. Trading commissions are low, and portfolios can be easily diversified to include any mixture of gold, silver, and platinum.

Although Mexico and several other countries issued coins intended as bullion in the twentieth century, the best known piece is the South African Krugerrand[q.v.], first struck in 1967. When the world began boycotting South African products in the 1980s over that nation's apartheid policies and it was no longer legal in many places to import Krugerrands, many countries started issuing their own bullion coins. Some of the key producers are Canada, China, Australia, and the United States. Australia is best known for its platinum bullion coins.

Some bullion coins show only their weight and purity instead of a denomination. The Mexican *Onza* ("Ounce") is a familiar example. In other cases, bullion coins show denominations which have no relationship to the actual value of the coin's metal content. The U.S. $50 bullion coins contain many times that amount of gold.

To attract collectors, some countries issue bullion coins with special designs. When it initiated gold and silver bullion coinage in 1986, the United States purposely chose to bring back two of the most popular and beautiful designs ever seen on U.S. coins— Augustus St. Gaudens' Liberty from the $20 gold pieces of 1907-1933 on the gold bullion coins, and A. A. Weinman's Liberty Walking motif used on half dollars from 1916-1947. Many of the U.S. bullion coins are also available in proof.

The Chinese have graced their bullion coins with pandas and with designs representing the Chinese lunar calendar. The 1983 and 1995 issues, for example, reflect the Year of the Pig and 1984 and 1996 coins honor the Year of the Rat, thus proving that coins do not have to be beautiful to be numismatically interesting.

Gold bullion coins are usually struck in one of two finenesses, either .9999 pure (24 carat) or .9167 fine (22 carat; known as *standard*, i.e., one part alloy to eleven parts pure gold to create a metal hard enough for circulating coins, even though many coins of this composition do not circulate). The difference in fineness is obvious to the naked eye: .9999 is a bright golden color while .9167 has a bit of a coppery tone. Krugerrands and U.S. bullion coins contain standard gold while Canadian *Maple Leafs* are of pure gold.

bumazhnyye dengi бумажные деньги (*pl.*) [*Russ.*] paper money.

bund (*c.*) [*Dan.*] bottom.

Bundesrepublik Deutschland [*Ger.*] Federal Republic of Germany (better known to English speakers as *West Germany*).

"bun head" penny

Bun Head Redesign of the Young Head type of Queen Victoria found on British bronze coinage from 1860 to 1894. This youthful effigy was

retained for many years even as Victoria turned 60 years of age. The design was finally replaced in 1895 with the *Old Head* coinage.

bunn (*m.*) [*Nor.*] bottom.

burélage [*Fr.*] Fine pattern or network of lines or dots covering the surface of a banknote or postage stamp as a security device. When it appears in the background of a banknote, it is called *underprint*.

The term can also apply to a solid network of vertical and horizontal lines covering the field of a coin. On coins or medals, it is strictly an artistic device. The Brazilian 2000 réis piece in the illustration shows one of the rare times when this technique has been used on a coin.

burélage in background

buronzu ブロンズ [*Jpn.*] bronze (the alloy).

bursă neagră (*f.*) [*Rom.*] black market.

business strike An issuance of coins intended for regular circulation, in contrast to proof or proof-like strikes done to create presentation pieces. In today's world, business strikes are produced in great quantities on high-powered coinage presses. Partly because of the speed with which these coins are made and partly due to the current tendency to mint coins from very hard nickel alloys, many business strikes lack sharp detail.

bust and harp token Halfpenny tokens struck in 1825 in Dublin but which circulated in Lower Canada. The first die was dated 1825, but the second die was intentionally overdated to 1820, probably to circumvent a law passed in 1825 prohibiting certain imports. A set of non-overdated 1820 dies also exists.

Around 1837 many imitations were produced, mostly in brass (see illustration). Some were of good quality, others much cruder. The latter group are referred to as *blacksmith* style.

The bust and harp token is among the huge number of colonial tokens issued during this era.

[J. A. Haxby and R. C. Willey, *Coins of Canada* (9th Ed.), pp. 148-49.]

bust and harp token (imitation)

buste enfantin, au [*Fr.*] bust (of the king or queen) as a child. See *au buste enfantin* for illustration.

buying blind Purchasing a coin through an auction without having first personally seen it. Some auction houses (but not all) will allow blind purchases to be returned if found unsatisfactory. If the lot has been seen by the bidder prior to the bid's being placed, then the successful bidder is legally obligated to purchase the lot. Returns are not normally permitted.

büyük [*Turk.*] large.

Büyük Britanya [*Turk.*] Great Britain.

büyüteç [*Turk.*] magnifying glass.

B.V. [*abbr.*] bullion value.

by (*v.*) [*Nor.*] to bid (at an auction or mail bid sale).

byde (*v.*) [*Dan.*] to bid.

by doubles See *a la dobla.*

bytte (*v.*) [*Nor.*] to trade.

byzant Large gold coin valued at 15 pounds Sterling. Its name comes from Byzantium, the place where it was struck.

C c

cabinet friction Hairline scratches on the surface of an uncirculated coin or medal caused from rubbing in a wooden cabinet. Since many fine collections were stored in cabinets, particularly during the eighteenth and nineteenth centuries, it is not uncommon to see some signs of cabinet friction on large brilliant uncirculated coins struck prior to 1900. Cabinet friction can also occur if the coin or medal has been stored in certain types of envelopes or albums.

Cabinet friction must not be confused with surface abrasions caused from circulation.

cạhn [*Viet.*] edge; rim.

cal (*m.*) [*Pol.*] inch.

calderilla (*f.*) [*Span.: Cuba*] Archaic colloquial term for coins of small face value, i.e., small change.

califica (*v.*) [*Rom.*] to grade.

cambio (*m.*) [*Span.*] exchange rate; small change, pocket change [also called *menudo* (*m.*)].

cameo head on S. Rhodesia crown

cameo head Small round or oval portrait included as part of a larger design of a coin or medal. It is so named because it resembles the style of cameo jewelry. The technique is attractive but seldom used until Canada adopted it for bi-metallic coinage in the 1990s. On the Canadian coins, a gold effigy appears in cameo form against a background of silver.

The illustration shows a standard cameo featuring the portrait of Cecil Rhodes. This cameo appears on the reverse of the 1953 Southern Rhodesian crown issued to commemorate the centennial of his birth.

Cameræ Computor Regiorum [*Lat.*] Computor of the vault of Royal Kingdoms.

campaigner Any of the U.S. presidential campaign medals which first appeared during the second presidential race between Andrew Jackson and John Quincy Adams in 1832.

[Barbara J. Gregory, "Marking the Campaign Trail," *The Numismatist*, November 1988, pp. 1906-10.]

Canadá [*Span., Port.*] Canada.

Canadian Numismatic Association The Canadian Numismatic Association was founded in 1950, and has members drawn from every Province in Canada, State of the United States of America, and many other countries.

Its objectives are to encourage and promote the science of numismatics through the acquisition and study of coins, paper money, medals, tokens, and all other numismatic items, with special emphasis on material pertaining to Canada. The C.N.A. aims to cultivate fraternal relations among collectors and students, and to assist and foster the interest of the new collector.

Membership includes a subscription to *The Canadian Numismatic Journal*, a monthly magazine devoted to Canadian numismatics. The Association maintains an extensive library; the books may be borrowed by members.

A convention is held annually where official business is transacted. Exhibits of numismatic

specimens, along with a dealers' bourse, provide both pleasure and profit. Advice, information, and entertainment can be found through association with others having similar interest.

For membership information, contact the Canadian Numismatic Association, P.O. Box 226, Barrie, Ontario L4M 4T2.

cancelación por perforación [*Span.*] punch cancellation.

cancelación mediante corte [*Span.*] cut cancellation.

cancelled 1. A coinage die obliterated in some way to prevent its reuse.

2. A note rendered worthless as money by having been officially overprinted, perforated, slit, or in some other way invalidated. Notes with their legal status revoked are less desirable to collectors than valid specimens. See *cut cancellation*.

cantidad (*f.*) [*Span.*] amount; quantity.

canto (*m.*) [*Span.*] edge (of a coin or medal).

çap [*Turk.*] diameter.

caparra (*f.*) [*Ital.*] deposit (of funds).

capicua (*f.*) [*Port.*] palindrome ("radar" serial number on banknotes).

capicúa (*f.*) [*Span.*] palindrome.

cara (*f.*) [*Span.*] front; face; obverse as it corresponds to the English term *heads*. [Note: the slang term for *tails* is *cruz*, literally meaning *cross*.]

carat [abbreviated *ct.*] 1. An indication of the parts per 24 by weight of gold. For example, 24 carat gold is 100% pure gold, 22 ct. is 22/24, or .916 fine, etc.

2. A unit of weight for gemstones (without much numismatic application).

carita (*f.*) [*Span.*] little face. See *dos caritas*.

carré (*adj.*) [*Fr.*] square.

carta (*f.*) [*Ital.*] paper.

carta di credito [*Ital.*] credit card.

carta moneta (*f.*) [*Ital.*] paper money.

carta moneta inconvertibile [*Ital.*] fiat money.

cartão de crédito [*Port.*] credit card.

carte de credit [*Rom.*] credit card.

carte de crédit [*Fr.*] credit card.

cărţi de credit acceptate [*Rom.*] credit cards accepted.

Mexican *cartón*

cartón (*m.*) [*Span.*] Small rectangular Mexican note printed on cardboard (which is what the word means in Spanish). Most *cartones* were issued in small denominations from 1914 to 1917 by Emiliano Zapata during the Mexican Revolution.

cartridge brass An alloy of 67-70% copper, 28-33% zinc, with small amounts of lead and iron.

1797 British 2d "cartwheel"

cartwheel 1. Popular name of the 1797 British twopence, a large coin containing two full ounces of copper. This and the 1797 penny were designed to permit the intrinsic value of

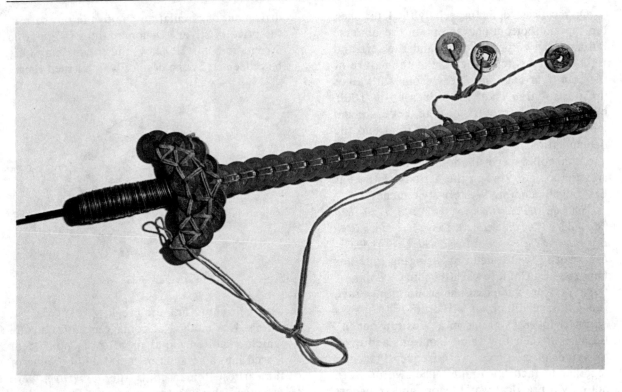

Chinese "cash" sword

their metal to approach their face value. They were manufactured at the factory in Birmingham owned by Matthew Boulton and James Watt, using technology that was state-of-the-art for its time. Although the coins were esthetically interesting, they were far too heavy and cumbersome to circulate and were soon discontinued.

2. Slang term for U.S. silver dollars (1794-1935), and particularly the Morgan Dollars of 1878-1921.

3. The expression *cartwheel effect* refers to visible flow lines which radiate from the center of a coin outward in every direction to the rim caused from pressure exerted on metal, especially silver, by a coinage press. The cartwheel effect is most noticeable on freshly-struck coins showing no signs of tarnish or wear. It is a phenomenon more likely to be seen on gem business strikes than on proof coins, even though silver proof specimens can exhibit flow lines.

casa da moeda (*f.*) [*Port.*] mint.

casa de moneda (*f.*) [*Span.*] mint. Also commonly called *ceca* (*f.*).

cash Popular type of base-metal coin used in China, Korea, Japan, and Annam (Vietnam). The cash coin is said to have been introduced in China at the beginning of the T'ang Dynasty in the seventh century A.D., but there is evidence that similar coins circulated for many centuries prior to that time.

Through the centuries, cash coins have been produced in enormous quantities, partly to satisfy the needs of a large population and partly because the coins were of such small value. It took one thousand to equal a *tael*, a Chinese unit of weight (37 grams of silver) slightly larger than the Western ounce (28.35 grams).

The coins were cast in the form of trees. When the metal cooled, the coins were broken off from the "branches" and their rough edges were smoothed.

On most cash coins, especially the later ones, the top and bottom characters on the obverse indicate the emperor's title, and the left and right characters tell something of the nature of the coin ("current coin," "heavy coin" for values up to 50, "large coin" for values up to 1000, etc.). The characters on the reverse can indicate such information as the mint and the denomination.

Cash coins were abandoned in the early twentieth century when the nations of the Far East began adopting Western-style money.

[William D. Craig, *Coins of the World: 1750-1850* (3rd Ed.), p. 76; Richard G. Doty, *The Macmillan Encyclopedic Dictionary of Numismatics*, pp. 47-48.]

cash sword Sword made by stringing together hundreds of Chinese cash[q.v.] coins. Coins of this type were valued at one thousand per *tael*, the Chinese ounce of silver (37 grams as opposed to 28.35 grams in a Western ounce). Because of their low value, hundreds and even thousands of cash coins were frequently strung together to facilitate trade. The swords were not only a practical way to store and transport these coins, but they were also interesting (and very masculine) works of art.

casi [*Span.*] almost.

casino token [Also called *gambling token*.]

1. In the great gambling casinos of Monte Carlo and elsewhere, tokens of various denominations are used at gambling tables instead of cash. At the end of play, the tokens are exchanged for cash (if, that is, the gambler still has any left!). These tokens are found in numerous shapes and sizes, and many are quite beautiful. The pieces from Monte Carlo are frequently inscribed with the name *Société des Bains de Mer de Monte Carlo*, the corporation which runs the casino.

[Thomas C. Day, "Casino Tokens of Monte Carlo," *The Numismatist*, June and July 1986, pp. 1124-1142 (June) and 1372-1379 (July).]

2. Silver dollar-size tokens that originally could be used interchangeably with real dollar coins in slot machines. Many of the gambling houses in Las Vegas and Reno, Nevada, started using these pieces in the mid 1960s to combat the shortage of silver dollars which had been driven out of circulation due to the increase in the price of silver. Denominations range from 5 cents to $500. By law, the tokens may only be redeemed by the casinos which issued them.

Las Vegas casino token

cassure de coin [*Fr.*] die break.

casting 1. A method of coinage manufacture in which a molten metal or alloy is poured or forced into a ceramic or metal mold. Some of the earliest Roman coins, the *aes grave*, were produced through this process. The method was used for 2000 years by the Chinese to make cash[q.v.] pieces, and has been utilized as recently as 1913 to make some of the revolutionary coins of Mexico by General Rafael Buelna. Coins made by this process are referred to as *cast coins*.

2. Popular way of counterfeiting coins from ancient times into the twentieth century. Cast copies of legitimate coins are easy to produce because molds are far easier to make than dies. Regrettably (for the counterfeiter), cast counterfeits are rarely of good quality and almost always exhibit certain flaws which are quite obvious to even the semi-knowledgeable observer. First, casting leaves a pitted or porous surface and the designs are not nearly as sharp and distinct as they would be on a genuine coin. Second, as molten metal becomes hard, it contracts. In other words, the counterfeit coin shrinks as it cools, leaving it smaller in diameter than a normal coin. This difference in size is readily noticeable in those types of coins produced during the past few centuries. Third, thick coins cast better than thin

ones, and many of the thin silver coins popular during the Middle Ages and early Modern Period were not really suitable for casting.

Casting counterfeit coins became more common in the twentieth century with the advent of the centrifugal casting method. This was a means of casting using centrifugal force to drive metal into the mold. It produces much more accurate, and therefore dangerous, copies.

The color illustrations on page 308 show a pair of 1816 British shillings. The specimen on the left is genuine, but the one on the right is a contemporary cast counterfeit of approximately the same grade. The counterfeit's faulty workmanship is obvious even in this photo.

[Contributed by Halbert Carmichael. Richard G. Doty, *The Macmillan Encyclopedic Dictionary of Numismatics*, pp. 48-50.]

catálogo (*m.*) [*Span., Port.*] catalog, catalogue.

catalogo d'asta [*Ital.*] auction catalogue.

catálogo de subasta [*Span.*] auction catalogue.

catalogue d'encan; **catalogue de vente aux enchères** [*Fr.*] auction catalogue.

Catherine Name of two Russian empresses.

1. Catherine I [née *Marta Skavronskaya.*] Born in 1682 or 1683 in Jakobstadt (now Jēkabplis, Latvia); died 1727.

Catherine I was born of peasant stock but was orphaned at an early age and raised by a pastor in Marienburg, Poland. In 1702 she was taken prisoner by the commander of the Russian troops who captured Marienburg. For years she lived among the soldiers until she came to the attention of Peter the Great who took her as his mistress and later as his second wife. (He divorced his first wife in 1699). Catherine became ruler of Russia in 1725 on the death of her husband, but she reigned only two years until her own death in 1727. She is remembered for her ability to control her husband, known for his violent temper.

Because Catherine I ruled for such a short time, the numismatic legacy she left is minimal. However, she is noted for being the first Russian ruler in many centuries *not* to issue silver wire money, simply because her husband had abandoned the practice in the 1710s in favor of machine-made coins.

2. Catherine II [née *Sophie Fredericke Auguste von Anhalt-Zerbst*; took the name *Ekaterina* (Catherine) *Alekseevna* when she converted to the Russian Orthodox faith in 1744; today known universally as *Catherine the Great*]. Princess Sophie was born on May 2, 1729, in Stettin (now Szczecin), Poland, the daughter of a Prussian prince. In 1745, at the age of 16, she married Grand Duke Peter of Holstein, heir to the Russian throne. Although this arranged marriage was unhappy for her, she was a brilliant woman who built up a circle of supporters. Peter became Czar Peter III upon the death of his mother, Empress Elizabeth, in 1761. But he proved to be such an incompetent and weak ruler that in 1762, just six months after he had been crowned, the Imperial Guards overthrew him and placed his wife Catherine on the throne in order to save Russia.

During Catherine's reign, artists, teachers, scientists, and actors came to Russia from all major European cities. She is noted for having built hospitals and schools, extending religious tolerance, introducing smallpox vaccination, modernizing the administration of government, promoting the education of women, adding to the Russian domain the areas of Crimea, most of Poland, and the land around the Black Sea. She even began the colonization of Alaska.

On the negative side, she refused to abolish serfdom (which she claimed to abhor), brutally suppressed peasant revolts, and only promoted the interests of the upper class.

Catherine the Great died on November 17, 1796, in St. Petersburg.

By virtue of having been empress for thirty-four years, Catherine II watched herself age on her coins. A collection of Catherine's coins shows her progression from a relatively young woman of thirty-three to a dowager in her golden years. Catherine's portrait issues are designated as Young Bust (1762-66), Mature Bust (1766-76), Older Bust (1777-82), and Aged Bust (1783-96).

[Contributed by Pamela Makricosta. Frank W. Weis, *Lifelines: Famous Contemporaries from 600 B.C. to 1975*, p. 246.]

cec (n.) [*Rom.*] check, cheque.

ceca (f.) [*Span.*] mint.

cédula (f.) [*Port.*] note, banknote.

ceitil (m.) [*Port.*] Small copper coin equal to 1/6 *real* issued by Portugal's John I in 1415. Its distinguishing feature is a three-towered castle.

The ceitil is noted for being the first European copper coin of modern times.

çek [*Turk.*] check, cheque.

cellophane Technically known as *cellulose acetate.* Cellophane is a clear packaging material used occasionally for storing coins. It is man-made from cellulose, either cotton or wood pulp. Although it does not seem to harm metals (including coins), it does become brittle with age.

cem [*Port.*] hundred.

cena (f.) [*Pol.*] price.

cena katalogowa [*Pol.*] catalogue value.

cena licytowana (f.) [*Pol.*] a bid (at an auction or mail bid sale).

cena szacunkowa (f.) [*Pol.*] suggested bid.

cennik (m.) [*Pol.*] price list.

cent 1. [*Fr.*] hundred.

2. Minor denomination valued at 1/100 of a dollar, rupee, or gulden. It has been used at various times by sixty-five nations, including Australia, Bahamas, Canada, New Zealand, and the United States.

The earliest date on a coin bearing that denomination is the 1791 Sierra Leone cent, but there is great speculation that the coins were actually struck some years later to celebrate the founding of the Sierra Leone Company.

The United States issued its first cent in 1793 and has produced coins of that value every year since then, except in 1815. The original issues were large cents and were struck through 1857. Starting in that year (or in 1856, if the popular Flying Eagle Cent pattern of that date is included), the small cent was introduced. Until 1864 it was a thick white coin with some nickel content. The switch over to bronze took place in 1864. The Lincoln Cent was introduced in 1909 and has had the greatest mintage of any type coin in history; since its inception, more than 250,000,000,000 have been struck.

Canada also started with the large cent (1858-1920) but eventually reduced the size of the coins. After its conversion to the small cent, Canada sold some large cent dies to China for recycling. (See *reused die.*)

centén [*Span.*] Spanish gold coin worth 25 pesetas.

centenaire (m.) [*Fr.*] centennial, centenary.

centenar (n.) [*Rom.*] centennial, centenary.

centenario (m.) [*Ital., Span.*] centennial, centenary.

centenário (m.) [*Port.*] centennial, centenary.

center dot Raised dot which appears in the center on the reverse side of some early U.S. coins.

centermark Round indentation that appears to be a punchmark found in the center of some ancient coins. It is possible that these marks resulted from some sort of lathe which was used to standardize the coin blanks. The striking of the coin failed to obliterate the mark.

centesimo (m.) [*Ital.*] hundredth (fraction).

centésimo (m.) [*Span., Port.*] hundredth (fraction).

centième (m.) [*Fr.*] hundredth (fraction).

centimetro (m.) [*Ital.*] centimeter, centimetre.

centímetro (m.) [*Span.*] centimeter, centimetre.

cento [*Ital.*] hundred.

Central America, S.S. Steamship that sank 160 miles off the coast of Cape Hatteras on September 12, 1857. Because it was carrying three tons of gold, much in the form of U.S. gold coins, the sinking of this ship triggered widespread international financial panic.

In July 1989, the Columbus-America Discovery Group, a multidisciplinary research project lead by Thomas G. Thompson, recovered about a third of the gold from the wreck of the *Central America.* Additional recovery was to follow. Most of the find consisted of mint-state 1857-S double eagles (U.S. $20 gold coins). One 1855-S specimen was of a previously unknown variety.

Many of the coins were recovered in oddly shaped encrusted configurations. The most interesting was a "coin tower", an encrusted stack of more than 300 mint-state U.S. $20 gold

pieces. To separate the coins without damaging them, the "tower" was soaked in what was described as a "buffered (pH 7.2) mixed sodium salts solution" which gently dissolved the iron oxide encrustation. Because the gold itself was not affected, the coins show no visible signs of cleaning.

In addition to the U.S. double eagles, some smaller U.S. gold coins and some European gold coins were recovered, as were a few silver coins. Nevertheless, most of the gold was in the form of $20 coins, presumably because one double eagle has the same weight as two $10 coins or four $5 coins but requires less space to store. The European coins were probably the property of individual passengers and were not part of the official cargo.

[Walter Breen, "The S.S. *Central America*: Tragedy and Treasure", *The Numismatist*, July 1990, pp. 1064-1072, et al.]

centrifugal casting See *casting*.

centymetr (*m.*) [*Pol.*] centimeter, centimetre.

cero [*Span.*] zero.

certificado (*m.*) [*Span., Port.*] certificate.

certificado de plata [*Span.*] silver certificate.

certificado provisional [*Span.*] provisional certificate; scrip.

cesarz (*m.*) [*Pol.*] emperor.

çeşit [*Turk.*] variety.

chad-panim חַד-פָּנִים [*Heb.*] uniface.

chalkos χαλκός (*m.*) [*Grk.*] 1. copper (the metal).
2. Bronze coin of ancient Greece valued at one-eighth obol.

chandra χάνδρα (*f.*) [*Grk.*] bead (raised dot on the surface of a coin or medal).

chân dung [*Viet.*] effigy.

change The coins carried in one's pocket or purse. This term usually refers to minor coins rather than crowns or silver dollars and has rarely ever been applied to gold.

Double-digit inflation has so lessened the value of coins that people seldom carry much small change with them these days. The decreased value and utility of pocket change has contributed to the demise of many once-popular coins, such as the British farthing and the New Zealand cent and two-cent piece,

although Canadians have taken the opposite route by doing away with their one- and two-dollar notes and replacing them with coins.

[Mark Goodman, "When a Penny Was Worth a Nickel," *The Numismatist*, May 1988, pp. 857-860.]

charactiristikon χαρακτηριστικόν (*n.*) [*Grk.*] attribution.

chartonomisma χαρτονόμισμα (*n.*) [*Grk.*] note, banknote; paper money; certificate.

Chaudoir, Baron Stanislaus de (1790-1858). Numismatic scholar whose works include *Aperçu Sur Les Monnaies Russes*, an important treatise on the history of Russian coins.

[R. W. Julian, "The Russian Silver Coinage of 1796-1979," *The Numismatist*, December 1989, pp. 1952-1959, et al.]

chek чек (*m.*) [*Russ.*] check, cheque.

chelín (*m.*) [*Span.*] (British) shilling.

cheque (*m.*) [*Span., Port.*] check, cheque.

chèque (*m.*) [*Fr.*] check, cheque.

cheshbon חֶשְׁבּוֹן (*m.*) [*Heb.*] account.

chidat ra'tso vashov חִידַת רָצוֹא וָשׁוֹב (*f.*) [*Heb.*] palindrome ("radar" serial number on banknotes).

chilia χίλια (*n.pl.*) [*Grk.*] thousand.

Chińska Republika Ludowa [*Pol.*] People's Republic of China (P.R.C.).

Chiny [*Pol.*] China.

chi-pe 지폐 [*Kor.*] banknote.

chistyy чистый [*Russ.*] fineness; fine (purity of metal).

chitanţă (*f.*) [*Rom.*] receipt.

chitos ogkos metallou χυτός ογκος μετάλλου [*Grk.*] ingot.

chong-dong 청동 [*Kor.*] bronze (the alloy).

chop mark [many spellings, including *schop mark*.] Small oriental character or special symbol counterstamped into the surface of a trade dollar or other large silver coin to show that the coin's weight and purity had been examined and approved. The practice of applying chops started in the mid-eighteenth century and was not discontinued until after World War I.

Each trader and banking firm in the Orient had a unique chop mark. Some trade coins show so many marks that their original designs are obliterated.

Unless the chop is one very rarely used, the presence of chop marks usually diminishes a coin's collector value. It must be pointed out, however, that some types of coins, particularly U.S. and British trade dollars, were specifically intended to circulate in the Far East. Thus, collectors should not be surprised to see chop marks on circulated specimens; the marks are simply a part of the coins' heritage.

British Trade Dollar with 8 chop marks

chotam חוֹתָם (*m.*) [*Heb.*] seal.
chrimata χρήματα (*n.pl.*) [*Grk.*] money; cash.
chrisos χρυσός (*m.*) [*Grk.*] gold.
Christogram Superimposition of the Greek letter χ (chi) over the letter P (rho), the first two letters in the Greek word for "Christ." The Christogram was a symbol used by early Christians as a way of identifying themselves to each other. It appeared on various coins from the late Roman period and even occasionally into the Middle Ages.

Christogram

Chrom (*n.*) [*Ger.*] chromium.
chromium A metal used for coinage. [element: group VIb of periodic table; atomic weight 51.996; atomic number 24; specific gravity 7.189; symbol Cr.]

An extremely hard, blue-white metal that is highly resistant to corrosion. It is present in all stainless steels and is used as such in Italian, Turkish, and Brazilian coins. It was also used as a plating on Canadian 5 cent pieces of 1944.
[Contributed by Halbert Carmichael.]
chroom (*n.*) [*Dut.*] chromium.
chū bǎ wù 出版物 [*Chin.-py./sc.*] an issue, issuance.
chu-jo-hwa-pae 주조화폐 [*Kor.*] coinage.
Churchill, Sir Winston [né *Winston Leonard Spencer Churchill.*] British prime minister (1940-45 & 1951-55). Born November 30, 1874, in Blenheim Palace, Oxfordshire, England; died January 24, 1965, in London.

Winston Churchill was the son of Lord Randolph Churchill, third son of the seventh Duke of Marlborough, and Jennie Jerome Churchill, daughter of Leonard W. Jerome, a New York financier. She was part Iroquois Indian and the great-granddaughter of Reuben Murray, a lieutenant in George Washington's Continental Army.

Churchill was noted as being a poor student, and yet he was famous for his fantastic memory. As a young man he served in the British Army in India, South Africa, and the Sudan. Throughout his life he was a prolific writer. His many works include the four-volume *A History of the English-speaking Peoples* (1956-58).

He was a multifaceted and talented man— a statesman, writer, painter, politician, journalist, and orator remembered as much for his failures as his successes. He was first elected to Parliament in 1900 as a Conservative, but he switched to the Liberal Party in 1904. In 1908 he became president of the Board of Trade in Herbert Henry Asquith's Liberal cabinet. As first lord of the admiralty (1911-15), one of Churchill's primary goals was the modernization of the navy. In 1924, he was appointed Chancellor of the Exchequer, and in 1925 presented his first budget which returned Britain to the gold standard.

Winston Churchill served as prime minister from 1940 to 1945. In response to Hitler's threat, the Grand Alliance was formed. In 1945

he met with Franklin D. Roosevelt and Joseph Stalin at the Yalta Conference.

Through his famous "Iron Curtain" speech in 1946, he called for a strong cooperation between Britain and the Unites States to stand as guardians of peace against Soviet expansionism. Churchill was also the leading advocate of a United States of Europe. He became prime minister again from 1951 to 1955. He received the Nobel Prize for Literature in 1953. In 1963 President John F. Kennedy declared him an honorary citizen of the United States.

Churchill crown

Although Churchill is universally regarded as one of the great figures of World War II, his personal life was less than exemplary. He was a heavy drinker who could be quite belligerent when he consumed too much alcohol. On one occasion, Lady Astor chided him for being drunk. He replied, "Madam, tomorrow I shall be sober, but you will still be ugly."

Churchill died on January 24, 1965, in London and received a state funeral reserved only for members of the royal family.

In the history of British coinage, only two commoners have ever appeared on British coins: Oliver Cromwell (on six types issued in 1656 and 1658, although these are said to be patterns even though some did circulate) and Winston Churchill, who appears on a commemorative 5 shilling crown issued in the year of his death. The coin is of copper-nickel and shows the Young Head of Queen Elizabeth II on the obverse. The Churchill side (technically the reverse) is in extremely low relief, in a sense symbolizing the dark days of World War II when Britain was under attack by Axis forces. Churchill's somber determination seems to be chiseled right into the heart of the coin.

[Contributed by Pamela Makricosta. Duncan M. White (editor), *Caesar to Churchill: The Years of Fulfillment*; Kenneth G. Richards, *People of Destiny: Sir Winston Churchill*, p. 16; James A. Moncure (editor), *Research Guide to European Historical Biography, 1450 to Present*, p. 428; Frank W. Weis, *Lifelines: Famous Contemporaries from 600 B.C. to 1975*.]

chûzôsho 鋳造所 [*Jpn.*] mint.

ciemny [*Pol.*] dark.

cien; ciento [*Span.*] hundred.

címlet [*Hun.*] denomination.

cimo (*m.*) [*Port.*] top.

Çin [*Turk.*] China.

Cina [*Ital.*] China.

cinc (*m.*) [*Span.*] zinc.

cinci [*Rom.*] five.

cincizeci [*Rom.*] fifty.

cinco [*Span., Port.*] five.

Çin Cumhuriyeti [*Turk.*] Republic of China.

Çin Halk Cumhuriyeti [*Turk.*] People's Republic of China (P.R.C.).

cincuenta [*Span.*] fifty.

çinko [*Turk.*] zinc.

cinq [*Fr.*] five.

cinquanta [*Ital.*] fifty.

cinquante [*Fr.*] fifty.

cinquefoil An ornament or design with five cusps, such as a rose with five petals. It is a common device on English coins of the late Middle Ages.

cinqüenta [*Port.*] fifty.

cinque [*Ital.*] five.

cinquième (*m.*) [*Fr.*] fifth (the fraction).

circolato [*Ital.*] circulated.

circolazione (*f.*) [*Ital.*] circulation.

circulação (*f.*) [*Port.*] circulation.

circulación (*f.*) [*Span.*] circulation.

circulado [*Span., Port.*] circulated.

circulante (*m.*); **circulación monetaria** (*f.*) [*Span.*] currency; circulating money.

circulat [*Rom.*] circulated.

46

circulatie (*m.-c.*) [*Dut.*] circulation.

circulaţie [*Rom.*] circulation.

circulating commemorative [a.k.a. *semi-commemorative.*] Commemorative coin issued for general circulation and intended to take the place of the prevailing regular-issue coins for one or two years. Some of the best-known examples are the 1976 U.S. Bicentennial coins (25 cents, 50 cents, and dollar) which replaced the regular coinage in 1975 and 1976, and the entire set of 1967 Canadian coins (cent, 5 cents, 10 cents, 25 cents, 50 cents, and dollar) struck to honor the hundredth anniversary of the formation of the Dominion of Canada. The Canadian designs replaced the regular issues for only the year 1967.

Probably the largest issuance of circulating commemoratives in recent history was the 1992 release of twelve quarter dollars in Canada, each honoring a different province or territory. *Canada 125*, as its 125th anniversary celebration was known, was a great boon to numismatics in that country because the promotion induced Canadian citizens to pay much more attention to their coins.

U.S. & Canadian circulating commemorative quarters

circulé [*Fr.*] circulated.

cirkulerad [*Swed.*] circulated.

cirkuleret [*Dan.*] circulated.

Civil War token [abbreviated *C.W.T.*] Any one of a large group of privately-struck tokens resembling the U.S. small cent, first issued in 1862 during the American Civil War (1861-65) to help alleviate an acute shortage of small change. Although these pieces became quite popular, an Act of Congress in 1864 forbade the issuance of additional tokens.

Civil War tokens may be divided into two broad categories: the patriotic type and store cards. The patriotic tokens have nationalistic slogans and devices on both sides. The store cards have a trademan's or merchant's advertisement on at least one side.

[Contributed by Robert Doyle. George and Melvin Fuld, *Patriotic Civil War Tokens*; same authors, *A Guide to Civil War Store Card Tokens*.]

Civil War token

çizik [*Turk.*] a scratch.

clad coinage [a.k.a. *sandwich coins*]. Coins made of three layers of metal bonded together. The outer layers are usually of the same alloy while the inner layer is different.

The United States introduced clad coinage in 1965 as a substitute for silver coins. Although a token coinage was needed because of the escalating price of silver, the replacements had to be the same size, shape, and weight as previous coins to be functional in vending machines. Clad coins proved satisfactory, even though the bonding occasionally comes loose and the coin splits apart. This is a very infrequent problem, however.

Most clad coins can be easily identified by the odd strip of color around the edge. On current U.S. dimes and quarters, the outer layers are of a copper-nickel alloy while the core is pure copper with its traditional reddish color.

The edge of a Kennedy Half Dollar does not clue the observer to the coin's clad characteristic, however, because all three layers are silver alloys, albeit that the outside layers contain considerably more silver than the inner core. There is no contrasting color of metal to appear around the rim.

Cladding is not to be confused with plating, in which only a thin layer of metal is applied to the base coin. In general terms, the clad outer layers comprise at least 10% of the total metal

of the coin, a much higher percentage than a plated surface would contain.

Spencer M. Clark

Clark, Spencer M. First-chief of the U.S. National Currency Bureau who placed his own portrait on a series of 5 cent fractional currency notes. The Treasury Department had ordered an issue honoring explorers Lewis and Clark, but Spencer Clark mistakenly thought that he himself was being honored so he placed his own portrait on the note. The U.S. Congress was furious and wanted him dismissed, but Secretary of the Treasury Salmon P. Chase intervened, thus temporarily saving Clark's job. Clark ultimately did lose his position because of his mistake.

This note is significant in American numismatic history because it was the inducement that caused Congress to pass a law forbidding the likeness of a living person to appear on any paper money or other obligation of the United States.

[David L. Ganz, "Researcher Reinterprets Living Portraits Law," *Coin World*, February 7, 1990, pp. 22-23, et al; John and Nancy Wilson, "United States Postage and Fractional Currency," *The Centinal*, Vol. 28, No. 3, Fall 1980, pp. 15-28.]

clasificación (*f.*) [*Span.*] classification.

clasificar (*v.*) [*Span.*] to classify; to grade.

classement (*m.*) [*Fr.*] classification.

classer (*v.*) [*Fr.*] to classify; to grade.

classificare (*v.*) [*Ital.*] to classify.

classificazione (*f.*) [*Ital.*] classification.

clean field 1. The area on a coin where a mintmark or other inscription or partial inscription has been inadvertently omitted. Some of the most common examples are the recent U.S. proof coins which lack the "S" mintmark. In this instance, a mint worker simply neglects to place the mintmark on the die, and the coin is struck without the necessary symbol.

In some cases, a clean field occurs when part of the die becomes accidentally filled with grease or some other foreign substance. Some 1989 U.S. quarters were reportedly struck with the mintmark obliterated in this manner. Almost immediately after the coins were reported, a few were found with scratches and other signs of altering in the area where the mintmark should have been, indicating that an unscrupulous person tried to remove the mintmark after the coin left the mint.

Even a legitimate filled die does not always leave a clean field. In 1922, no cents were struck at the Philadelphia Mint, which at that time did not use mintmarks; the only US cents issued that year were from the Denver Mint, which utilizes the "D" mintmark. Some of the cents were struck from a die containing a filled mintmark, thus giving the appearance of being 1922 "Plain" (*plain* being the term often used by U.S. collectors to refer to coins from the Philadelphia Mint). The mintmark was not completely filled, however, and genuine specimens will show a trace of the original mintmark.

["Altered Coin Mimics Error," *Coin World*, August 30, 1989, pp. 1 & 13.]

clean field design

2. A *clean field design* is a coin or medal motif which includes an effigy or symbolic

devise but no inscriptions or other lettering except perhaps for very faint marks such as designer's initials. The illustrated example is a 1973 10 franc coin of Belgium.

cleaning of coins The elimination of superficial dirt (indirect cleaning) or the removal of tarnish, rust, or other foreign substances caused by oxidation (direct cleaning) from a coin or medal.

Cleaning is done to enhance the coin's beauty and value. Most authorities agree that cleaning should only be done by an expert; otherwise, there is a great likelihood that permanent damage will occur and that the coin will look worse than it did before. But even when done by an expert, cleaning remains a controversial issue, because the coin is changed from its "natural" condition.

The methods of cleaning include dipping the piece into a chemical solution, physically scrubbing the piece with an abrasive, or using a can of compressed air to blow dust off of the coin. Many other ideas have been tried, including the use of sound waves.

When oxidation has taken place and is then removed through cleaning, some of the outermost molecules of metal will be lost, thereby altering the surface of the coin forever. The stripping away of these molecules destroys some degree of the original luster of the piece, and this luster can never be restored. If an abrasive is used, the coin or medal will usually show light scratch marks or very fine lines. Experienced numismatists can detect these and other signs of cleaning. As a general rule, a cleaned specimen is not worth as much as an uncleaned piece.

See *direct cleaning* and *indirect cleaning*.

[Alan Korwin, "Shedding Light on Coin Cleaning," *The Numismatist*, June 1985, pp. 1089-1101; Gerhard Welter, *Cleaning and Preservation of Coins and Medals* (New York: Sanford J. Durst Numismatic Publications, 1976-1980); John C. Loperfido, "Airborne Particulates: The Silent Nemesis," *The Numismatist*, April 1983, pp. 706-9; I. M. Allen and Anthony Wooten, "Cleaning Coins," *S.E.A.*, December 1960, p. 487.]

clipping Shaving off bits of gold or silver from the edge of a coin. Prior to the advent of milled coinage, the edges of coins were somewhat rough and irregular. It was common practice in the Middle Ages to clip bits of precious metal from the edge of a coin and then to spend the coin as if it were of full weight. Some coins were clipped so often that their weight and size became noticeably small. In some cases, all of the circulating coins in a kingdom had to be recalled and scrapped and new ones struck because such a large number of coins in circulation had been clipped.

The development of milled coins in the sixteenth century made clipping more difficult and noticeable. Coins were given round, uniform edges which could be reeded or lettered. This process also made counterfeiting more difficult.

cloning The use of dies to make punches from which additional dies can be made. The dies for the 1919 Australian pennies (Melbourne Mint) were produced in this manner.

[John Sharples, "Australian Coins 1919 to 1924," *Journal of the Numismatic Association of Australia*, July 1985, pp. 8-9.]

club See *coin club*.

c/m [*abbr.*] countermark, counterstamp.

C-note Slang expression, especially popular among criminals, for a U.S. or Canadian $100 note. It is derived from the Roman numeral "C" meaning "hundred".

coal company store scrip Metal tokens issued generally as an advance on wages for use only at the company store, deducted from wages on the next payday, thereby effectively keeping the miner constantly in debt to the coal mining company. It is said that some owners may have made more money at the company store than they did on the coal. Much of the coal scrip was manufactured as patented "systems," probably the largest of which were Ingle-Schierloh and Insurance Credit Systems (both of Dayton, Ohio) and *Orco* (Osborne Register, Cincinnati, Ohio).

See page 316 for a color photo.

[Contributed by Robert Doyle. Donald O. Edkins, *Edkins' Catalogue of Coal Company Store Scrip*.]

cob Crude Spanish-American coin struck from the sixteenth to the eighteenth centuries in

many parts of the New World. Most authorities believe that the word *cob* is derived from the Spanish term *cabo de barra* (loosely translated as "the end [or stump] of a bar"), but this may not be the case because the expression is used most often as an accounting term meaning "last payment" or "balance of account."

The planchets for cobs were cut from a quasi-round bar of silver, a procedure not unlike cutting slices off a salami. The resulting planchets were very irregular in shape, which explains why much of the coin design was lost in the minting process. Crude as the coins were, they served their purpose of allowing Spanish officials to mint great quantities of coins quickly.

cobre (*m.*) [*Span., Port.*] copper.

Codfish Note issued by Paul Revere during the American Revolution. The note is so named because its primary device is a codfish, a propaganda symbol which replaced the traditional crown of King George III of England that normally appeared on notes of this kind.

Also see *Sword in Hand.*

coin (*m.*) [*Fr.*] (coinage) die.

coin Metallic disk or small ingot, usually round, intended as a circulating medium of exchange worth a specified amount, and marked in some way so its source and monetary value can be identified. In today's world, coins are produced and dispensed by governments or other official agencies authorized to issue money

The Babylonians negotiated commercial transactions using gold and silver as means of exchange as far back as 2000 B.C., but the metals were not cast in a form to make for easy circulation. Every piece of precious metal had to be weighed and evaluated every time it was used in a transaction.

Around 620-600 B.C. the first coins (as we understand the term) were produced in Asia Minor. They were little more than thick lumpy blobs of electrum (an unrefined alloy of approximately three parts silver and one part gold as found in Nature), but they were marked with an indication of their weight and value. It is likely that these first coins were struck by merchants who needed a convenient way to assure a consistent weight and fineness of the pieces of metal they accepted in trade. Crude as these early coins were, they did serve their purpose, at least to a degree.

The first major improvement in coinage was to discontinue the use of electrum. Because it is an unrefined alloy, its ratio of gold to silver can vary considerably. To achieve a higher degree of consistency, moneyers realized they would have to separate the gold from the silver and produce coins primarily of gold, primarily of silver, or of a controlled mixture of the two. Although it became unpopular almost from the very beginning of coinage, natural electrum was used sporadically even into the Middle Ages.

Over the centuries, coin designs rose, fell, and then rose again in beauty and complexity. The first coins were quasi-uniface with a crude design on only one side and with nothing more than a simple punch mark on the other. Yet within a short time, coins of great artistic beauty were being struck in Greece and then in Rome. As the Roman Empire ultimately declined, so did the quality of its coins. By the Early Middle Ages, most of the coins being struck throughout the Western world were crude and ugly. But by the end of the Middle Ages, many lovely and artistic pieces were again being produced in Europe.

The integrity of the circulating coinage was sometimes compromised by rulers who debased coins as a way of inflicting a "hidden" tax on their subjects. Henry VIII of England was often guilty of this practice. He caused great harm to his nation's economy by reducing the purity of English gold and silver coins.

Prior to the sixteenth century, most coins were made by placing a round disk of metal between two dies and hitting it with a hammer (although a few coins were still being made by pouring molten metal into sand molds). Hammered coins, as they were known, could be very beautiful (as so many of the ancient coins can attest), but they tended to be somewhat crude and lacked well-formed edges. Because the edges were irregular, it was fairly simple to cut off thin slivers of gold or silver and then to

spend the coin as if it were of full weight. Some coins were clipped so many times that their value decreased considerably.

The sixteenth century saw a major change in the way coins were produced. For the first time, heavy machinery was used to mint coins. The first of these new mints were located in water-driven mills, thus giving the name milled coinage[q.v.] to pieces produced by this method. The technique was a quantum leap over hammering. Not only were milled coins more attractive and uniform, but continuous small cuts known as a milled edge, reeded edge, or crenelations could be placed around the coin, making it more difficult to clip small slivers of precious metal off the edge. (See *hammered coin* for comparative illustrations.)

Historically, coins of higher value have been made of precious metals, usually gold or silver, and minor coins were struck from copper alloys. In the second half of the twentieth century, gold has been relegated almost exclusively to non-circulating commemorative or bullion coins, and silver has been replaced with nickel or nickel alloys. Coins from this latter group are referred to as token coinage because they do not contain precious metals nor can they be exchanged for precious metals, placing them in the same category as fiat money[q.v.], paper currency not convertible to specie nor to gold or silver coins.

An argument can be made that the gold, silver, and platinum bullion pieces issued by Australia, Canada, the United States, Great Britain, and many other countries since the early 1980s are *not* coins in the truest sense, because they were never intended for circulation and their stated face values do not even approximate their intrinsic value. In other words, they are not really a form of money as much as they are a convenient way for individuals to hold precious metals. The only thing that separates them from privately-produced rounds and ingots is that the bullion "coins" are issued by governments instead of private corporations.

Coinage Act of 1873 U.S. coinage law act of February 12, 1873, which replaced the silver dollar with the slightly heavier Trade dollar to enable the dollar to compete better in the Orient against the Mexican 8 peso coin and against other silver crown-size coins. The framers of the Act did not intend for the new Trade dollars to have legal tender status within the boundaries of the United States, but such a provision was inadvertently included. The provision was soon removed.

The Act also eliminated the bronze 2 cent piece, the silver 3 cent piece, and the silver half dime, and slightly increased the weight of the dime, quarter, and half dollar. The weight adjustment was indicated by an arrow placed on each side of the date of the affected coins in 1873 and 1874.

Opponents of the Act referred to it as the *Crime of '73.*

[R. S. Yeoman, *A Guide Book of United States Coins* (44th Ed.), p. 9.]

coin club An organization where collectors meet to discuss their collections and to share their views on numismatics in general.

Coin clubs have been on the decline since the early 1970s when interest in numismatics began decreasing. The clubs that survived have often experienced poor attendance, apathy, and financial difficulties. Most significantly, few young people are participating, turning such organizations into senior citizens' groups.

Some of these problems are the result of a declining membership. A coin club increases its membership by promoting itself in whatever way it can, usually by starting with the local newspapers. The newspapers will almost always cover a club's events if the organization's officials merely make the request. Flyers placed on public bulletin boards, including on university campuses, and club newsletters sent to prospective members are also excellent promotional materials.

Boring meetings are another problem area for most numismatic associations. The single best way to alleviate boredom is to ask the club's own members to speak on whatever topic interests them the most. Although the more experienced members may be able to speak knowledgeably about technical topics, the

beginners and newer members should also be encouraged to speak. Their enthusiasm may more than compensate for their lack of experience, and their active participation may well generate the interest that will keep them involved in the hobby and in the organization throughout their lifetimes.

Young people will not participate unless they are shown how fascinating and intriguing the hobby really is. Adult volunteers from the club can speak at schools and can set up small exhibits. The club can easily devise youth activities, including junior competitive exhibits. In all respects, the young people must be made to feel welcome. Without an infusion of young people, the hobby will not survive.

The illustration shows a medal struck by the Ohio Valley Coin Association. The medal commemorates the organization's 20th anniversary in 1976 and features a U.S. Bicentennial theme.

[Michael Greenspan, "Rebuilding a Coin Club," *The Numismatist*, June 1988, pp. 1025-29.]

coin club medal

coin-medal Medal struck with the attributes of a coin (date, denomination, precious metal content, issuance by a government, etc.) but with no legal tender status. The piece cannot actually be spent nor can it be exchanged for spendable cash or specie.

Some Canadian proof coins fall into this category. Canadian Olympic commemorative coins were originally considered as non-circulating legal tender[q.v.] (N.C.L.T.) but were relegated to the coin-medal classification in 1990 when the Canadian government decided not to continue to redeem them.

coin struck [symbol: ↑↓] Alignment of the obverse and reverse dies on a coin, medal, or token such that the top of one side corresponds to the bottom of the other. To turn the piece over so that the reverse is right side up, the piece must be rotated on an axis running east and west. With few exceptions (such as some of the early Gobrecht silver dollars), virtually all U.S. coins have been struck with this alignment.

The other type of rotation is called *medal struck* and is designated ↑↑. Current British and British Commonwealth coins are medal struck.

coin tower An encrusted stack of more than 300 mint-state U.S. $20 gold pieces which were recovered from a shipwreck 1989. The coins had been stored in a wooden box which rotted away after the ship sank in 1857, thus allowing the coins to become encrusted in this very unusual configuration. See *S.S. Central America*.

[Walter Breen, "The S.S. *Central America*: Tragedy and Treasure", *The Numismatist*, July 1990, pp. 1064-1072, et al.]

coin weight A metal counterbalance used to check the weight of newly-struck coins. See *standard*.

coleção (*f.*) [*Port.*] collection.

colección (*f.*) [*Span.*] collection.

coleccionar (*v.*) [*Span., Port.*] to collect. [Note: the preferred spelling in Portuguese is *colecionar.*]

coleccionista (*m./f.*) [*Span.*] collector.

colecionador (*m.*) [*Port.*] collector.

colecionar (*v.*) [*Port.*] to collect.

collectionner (*v.*) [*Fr.*] to collect.

collectionneur (*m.*) [*Fr.*] collector.

collezionare (*v.*) [*Ital.*] to collect.

collezione (*f.*) [*Ital.*] collection.

collezionista (*m./f.*) [*Ital.*] collector.

colt Popular name for a series of ancient silver coins depicting Bellerophon's winged horse Pegasus. The pieces were were first struck around 570 B.C. in Corinth with a weight of 8.5-8.6 grams. The colt was also known as a *foal*. See *Pegasus* for additional information and illustration.

columnario [*Span.*] See *Pillar dollar*.

comemorativ (*adj.*) [*Rom.*] commemorative.

comemorativo (*m.; adj.*) [*Port.*] commemorative.

comerciar (*v.*) [*Span.*] to trade.

comes obryziacus [*from Lat.*] High-ranking official who guaranteed the quality of gold, no matter where coins from it would be struck. The abbreviation *COMOB* appears in the exergue of some late Roman coins (mostly after A.D. 395).

commémoratif (*adj.*) [*Fr.*] commemorative.

commemorative Temporary issue of a coin or note intended to honor a person or an event. Most commemoratives are produced for one or two years and rarely more than three.

Commemorative coins began in ancient Greece, but their impact was not really felt until the twentieth century when coins and notes of this type were marketed to generate profits. Commemorative coins are now issued to help finance the Olympics and many different charities and fund-raising activities, or the profits go into the country's general fund.

If a commemorative coin or note replaces a regular issue for a year or two, it is called a *circulating commemorative* or a *semi-commemorative*. Two well-known examples are the set of 1967 Canadian coins (cent through dollar) struck to honor Canada's hundredth anniversary, and the U.S. Bicentennial quarters, halves, and dollars of 1976, dated 1776-1976 but issued in 1975 and 1976.

Occasionally commemoratives have been placed in circulation as an addition to the regular issues, but this is rare in most countries. The 1965 British commemorative crowns honoring Winston Churchill were released by banks for circulation, but most were kept as souvenirs.

The 1932 U.S. Washington Quarter started as a circulating commemorative to honor the 200th anniversary of his birth. It was so popular that it was brought back in 1934 as a regular issue and is still minted today.

Commonwealth coinage Coins struck during the Republican Commonwealth of England, Scotland, and Ireland from 1649 to 1660. The coins were noted for having inscriptions in English instead of Latin, a language tied closely to the Vatican and regarded as anti-Protestant. Also, the royal portrait and royal arms were replaced with St. George's cross and the Irish harp.

Commonwealth coinage consisted of the gold unite, double-crown, and crown, as well as the silver crown, halfcrown, shilling, sixpence, halfgroat, penny, and halfpenny.

Pattern coins bearing the likeness of Oliver Cromwell were also struck, and some are known to have circulated. See *Cromwell, Oliver.*

Commonwealth gold "unite"

communion token Communion tokens (or *church tokens*) have been called the "leaden footprints of church history" by Mary McWhorter Tenny in her book on their origin, history, and use. It is probably that from very early times a token or something akin to it was used in all oath-bound societies.

The word *token* means a sign or proof mark or some sure promise to be kept. The earliest instance in history of such a sign is the rainbow token (*Genesis 9:13*). Of a similar sort was the bold token of the Passover. From the first time the word is used in the bible to the last, it is invariably a token of good, with one terrible exception: "He [Judas] that betrayed Him [Jesus] had given them a token (a kiss)." (*Mark 14:44.*)

The need of some safeguard for Christian privileges appeared early in the history of the church, and the subsequent adaptation of the token was used in different countries and in different times. The first mention of Protestant tokens is in the register of the Council of

Geneva, January 30, 1560. John Calvin, the noted theologian and reformer, petitioned the use of tokens to prevent the profanation of the Lord's Table. Each person should receive tokens for himself and those of his household who understood the meaning of communion. Strangers, on giving testimony of their faith, should also receive a token. Those who had no token should not be admitted to the table.

The request was not granted by the Council at that time for they saw "great difficulties" in such a practice. However, the token was in use in Geneva by 1605 and shortly thereafter in England, Scotland, Ireland, and Holland.

It was in Scotland that the communion token practice took its deepest roots, and the tokens are more closely identified with Presbyterianism than any other sect. The *tickets* of the Methodist class leaders were the same as tokens. The Methodists of Montrose used metal tokens; Episcopalians and Baptists used both metal tokens and cards.

The use of communion tokens in the Roman Catholic Church has been both affirmed and denied. There is no known specimen.

The communion token practice ultimately spread from Europe to all parts of the world, including the United States, Canada, Australia, New Zealand, Africa, Asia, New Hebrides, South America, and West Indies.

The sacrament was usually dispensed twice a year— spring, after the crops were planted, and fall, after the harvest. The "great occasions" lasted for several days and had to be held outside when people attended in large numbers. Before the celebration of the Lord's Supper, it was the general practice to hold a diet of examination on a day set from the pulpit, with the view of examining the candidates as to their Bible knowledge and their worthiness to partake of the sacrament. At the end of this service, the pastor or elder in charge would distribute the tokens, and only those who had a token could come to the table on Sunday. The taking up of the tokens was always carefully attended, for they were considered property of the church just the same as communion plates and baptismal vessels.

Communion tokens may be described as small disks of metal, commonly of lead or a mixture of lead and tin. However, many other metals were used, such as silver, bronze, copper, brass, porcelain, ivory, bakelite, and cardboard. They were of no prescribed shape or design. Most of the early specimens are square and small; later they were all shapes and sizes. They were struck from dies or cast from molds. Some were impressed on one side with a punch or indented with a chisel.

communion token

Beginning around 1800, inscriptions and designs began to appear which were delightful in variety and charm. Many Scottish and Canadian specimens bear the likeness of the sacred cup. In Edinburgh, Scotland, the Burgh arms appear on some of their tokens. Others have dates, ministers' initials, pictures of the church, scriptures, hearts, or the burning bush.

Ministers often made their own communion tokens with the occasional help of the village blacksmith. When new ones were needed, old tokens were melted to supply metal for the new issue. Some of the officials buried the discarded symbols lest they be profaned by being used for meaner purposes. By 1900 most churches had discontinued the use of tokens, some adopted the use of cards, and others practiced open communion.

It is impossible for a collector to obtain a complete collection of communion tokens. United States tokens are very rare and are either family keepsakes or repose in church vaults or in museums. Recently, churches have been striking replicas of early pieces or have issued new designs to commemorate anniversaries.

54

Reference books and articles written on communion tokens are not easily found, as most are out of print. However, if a collector is truly interested and is willing to spend time in research, this can be a rewarding hobby.

[Contributed by Autence A. Bason. Alexander Brook, *Communion Tokens of the Established Church of Scotland: Sixteenth, Seventeenth, and Eighteenth Centuries*; Rev. Robert Dick, *Scottish Communion Tokens, Other Than Those of the Established Church*; R. Kerr & J. R. Lockie, *Communion Tokens of the Church of Scotland: Nineteenth and Twentieth Centuries*; Rev. H. A. Whitelaw, *Communion Tokens with Descriptive Catalogue of Those of Dumfriesshire*; Mary McWhorter Tenny, *Communion Tokens, Their Origin, History, and Use*; Autence A. Bason, *Communion Tokens of the United States of America*.]

comoară (*f.*) [*Rom.*] treasure.

COMOB [*abbr. from Lat.*] see *comes obryziacus*.

concave coin Bowl-shaped coinage issued by Celts of the Danube region around the first century B.C. The coins were variously struck in gold and electrum[*q.v.*]. They show what are presumed to be religious designs on the deep concave side. Their name in German is *Regenbogenschüsselchen*.

[Ewald Junge, *World Coin Encyclopedia*, pp. 213-4.]

condecoração militar (*f.*) [*Port.*] military decoration.

condecoración militar (*f.*) [*Span.*] military decoration.

Conder token (one example)

Conder Tokens Large quantities of copper tokens struck from 1787 to 1802 to alleviate a shortage of coins of small denominations in England. The first were penny and two-penny tokens produced by the Anglesey Copper Mining Company. By 1802 private firms in nearly every city and town in the country had produced some form of farthing, halfpenny, or penny tokens, even though they had been declared illegal in 1797 when the regal coins of these denominations (the so-called *cartwheels*) were struck.

The Rev. James Conder began the task of classifying these tokens. He described them and assigned catalogue numbers. Due to his efforts, the whole series is now known as *Conder Tokens*.

condition Description of the amount of circulation a coin or note has experienced. It takes into account a coin or medal's surface wear or the degree to which a note has been folded or torn. Eye appeal also plays a role in determining condition.

In the past, the words *condition* and *grade* were used synonymously. However, since the advent of third-party grading services in the 1980s, the trend has been to use *condition* when describing a coin's state of preservation subjectively via words (*good, fine, uncirculated,* etc.), and to use *grade* when assigning a numerical value (such as MS-62, EF-40, G-4).

Although the term *proof condition* is often used, it is a misstatement that should be avoided. *Proof* is never a condition or grade but a type of strike, a method of manufacture.

The French term *fleur de coin* (F.D.C.) refers to uncirculated condition, even though it is often used to describe proof coins. It indicates coins or medals of very high quality, proof or otherwise.

condor 1. Gold coin of 25 sucres issued by Ecuador in 1928. It was struck in Birmingham, England, and shows the effigy of Simón Bolívar. It is named for the South American condor (*Vultur gryphus*), a large bird native to the region and an old symbol of Spanish-American independence from Spain.

2. Aluminum coin of Chile struck from 1956-59 and equal to ten pesos. The obverse features a South American condor in flight. The design was retained in 1962 after Chile's currency revaluation, but the name *condor* as a stated value was eliminated.

coniatura (*f.*) [*Ital.*] coinage.

conjoined (*adj.*) Also commonly known as *accolated* or *jugate*. Two or more heads or busts that face in the same direction and overlap. See *accolated* for additional information and illustration.

conjugado [*Port.*] accolated[*q.v.*], conjoined, jugate.

conmemorativo (*m.; adj.*) [*Span.*] commemorative.

con ó [*Viet.*] eagle.

conocidos (*m.pl. adj.*) [*Span.*] known. Usually used in the sense of a certain number of specimens known to exist, e.g., *cuatro conocidos* ("four known").

conscience money Money paid (usually anonymously) to relieve the conscience by restoring what has been wrongfully acquired.

cont (*n.*) [*Rom.*] account.

conta (*f.*) [*Port.*] account.

contante (*m.*) [*Ital.*] cash (ready money).

contant geld (*n.*) [*Dut.*] cash (ready money).

conto (*m.*) [*Ital.*] account.

contrafação (*f.*) [*Port.*] a counterfeit; a fake, forgery.

contrafazer (*v.*) [*Port.*] to counterfeit.

contraffare (*v.*) [*Ital.*] to counterfeit.

contraffazione (*f.*) [*Ital.*] a counterfeit.

contrahacer (*v.*) [*Span.*] to counterfeit; to falsify; to copy.

contrefaçon (*f.*) [*Fr.*] a counterfeit; a fake, forgery.

contrefacteur (*m.*) [*Fr.*] counterfeiter.

contrefaire (*v.*) [*Fr.*] to counterfeit.

conundrum Riddle or inexplicable situation that arises in numismatics.

Conventionsmünze (*f.*) [*Ger.*] Austrian silver coins minted on the 1753 Convention standard by which one Convention thaler equals 1/10 mark of fine silver by weight. The best known coin struck by this standard is the oft-restruck Maria Theresa Thaler[*q.v.*] bearing the date 1780.

[William D. Craig, *Coins of the World: 1750-1850* (3rd Ed.), pp. 28-29.]

Convention standard see *Conventionsmünze*.

Cook Islands' naked god See *Tangaroa* (the god's name) for illustration.

Copa Mundial de Fútbol [*Span.*] World Cup of Football (soccer).

copia (*f.*) [*Span., Ital.*] a copy; (*v.*) [*Rom.*] to copy.

copiar (*v.*) [*Port., Span.*] to copy.

copie prin electroplastie (*f.*) [*Rom.*] electrotype.

copper A popular metal used for coinage purposes. [element: group Ib of the periodic table; atomic weight 63.546; atomic number 29; specific gravity 8.96; symbol Cu.]

Copper is found in more coins than any other metal, since most coins made of precious metals (gold, silver, etc.) have used copper as an alloying agent. Since ancient times, copper has been utilized as the major constituent for minor coinage. Until around 1850 it was used as it came from smelter and was basically pure copper except for some small trace impurities. The coins made from this metal are properly called *copper* coins. Since the mid-nineteenth century, copper has been used as the major constituent of brass, bronze, bronzital, verenium, billon, and aluminum bronze[*qq.v.*].

A bright, shiny red when first struck, copper coins tone through a series of browns to dark chocolate. Exposure to sulfides can turn copper black. Green colors indicate carbonates and hydrated oxides caused by corrosion.

Examples of copper coins include the Roman dupondius, the British pennies since 1797, and the United States half cents and large cents of 1793-1857.

[Contributed by Halbert Carmichael.]

copper-nickel Also known as *cupro-nickel*. General name for several different alloys of copper and nickel. The most common is 75% copper and 25% nickel as found in the United States 5 cent pieces struck since 1866 and in the outside clad layers of the current U.S. dimes and quarter dollars. This alloy is used worldwide to produce white metal coins, often replacements for silver coinage. It can be shiny yet dark when new but wears to a dull grey. Judd used the term copper-nickel to refer to the 88% copper, 12% nickel alloy utilized in the United States Flying Eagle cents (1856-58) and the first Indian Head cents (1859-64). Some older authors have confused the issue further by referring to the 75% copper, 25% nickel alloy simply as nickel.

[Contributed by Halbert Carmichael.]

Coppernose See *Old Coppernose*.

cor (*f.*) [*Port.*] color, colour.

coroa (*f.*) [*Port.*] crown (royal headpiece; large silver coin).

coroană (*f.*) [*Rom.*] crown (royal headpiece; large silver coin).

corona (*f.*) [*Span., Ital., Port.*] 1. crown, i.e., the headpiece of a king or queen.

2. Popular name for the *escudo*[q.v.], a Spanish gold coin introduced in 1537.

3. British silver or cupro-nickel coin equal to five shillings referred to as a *crown*.

4. Generic term for any silver of silver-substitute coin approximately the same size as a U.S. or Canadian silver dollar or a British crown. See *crown*.

coronato di lauro [*Ital.*] laureate.

coroziune (*f.*) [*Rom.*] corrosion.

Corregidora see *Josefina*.

corte de anulação [*Port.*] cut cancellation.

cositor (*n.*) [*Rom.*] tin.

cospel (*m.*) [*Span.*] planchet.

cotisation (*f.*) [*Fr.*] fee.

couler (*v.*) [*Fr.*] to cast.

couleur (*f.*) [*Fr.*] color, colour.

counterfoil The part of a note which can be detached and kept as a record of issue. It may or may not have perforations where it is connected to the rest of the note. See illustration.

Costa Rican countermark (enlarged 3x to show detail)

countermark; counterstamp An official punchmark applied to a coin to change its value or to validate it for use in a country other than the one where it was made.

The coin in the illustration is a British sixpence countermarked in 1857 for use in Costa Rica. A large number of sixpences and shillings were punched in this way, and they are referred to as the *English series* of Costa Rican coins. The counterstamp shows a lion

note with perforated counterfoil

with the inscription *Habilitada por el gobierno* ("Qualified by the government").

The chop mark[q.v.] is one of the most commonly found countermarks. A chop mark was punched onto a silver trade coin to show that the coin had been checked and approved for correct weight and fineness by whatever Far East merchant or trading firm used that particular chop. Chop marks were used in many parts of the Orient from the mid-eighteenth century until just after World War I.

"Unofficial" countermarks are sometimes punched onto coins for satirical reasons or to make souvenirs.

1991 Ukrainian coupon

coupon (Ukraine) In order to protect their domestic market from the influx of Russian shoppers, the Ukraine S.S.R. Council of Ministers decided on October 28, 1990, that as of November 1 of that year, all goods could only be sold for coupons issued by the state (the initial issues of coupons also known as *consumer cards*) instead of Soviet rubles. The seller was obligated to cut off coupons from a sheet equivalent to the buying price. The coupons could be used only once. Workers received coupons from their employers.

Each month a new type of coupon was issued to discourage counterfeiting. The November 1990 issue was without district designations. From December 1990 to June 1991, the sheets had a 3-letter code, referring to the district where they could be used. Up to twenty-five different district codes can be found. No sheets were issued in July 1991, and from August to December 1991 the district indicators were removed.

In the first days of November 1990, there was a shortage of consumer sheets, so a black market sprang up. A 50-coupon sheet (valued at 50 rubles) cost one hundred rubles. Later, the situation reversed itself, and the black market price dropped far below face value. Consumer sheets were to be used in official shops, but there was still an open market where all deals were in rubles (but more expensive). In those places coupons were not necessary.

The system did not work well because many fake coupons appeared, and most service industries (transport, hair dressers, and the like) were still paid in rubles.

It is interesting to note that all of the above happened while the Soviet Union still existed. The U.S.S.R. was not officially dissolved until December 31, 1991. Because Ukraine was still a part of the Soviet Union and was not technically authorized to issue its own money, these consumer cards are regarded as coupons rather than banknotes.

On December 28, 1991, the Supreme Soviet of Ukraine issued a decree authorizing the use of *coupons of repeated using.* In anticipation of the split-up of the Soviet Union, Russia had started withdrawing rubles from Ukraine, leaving the latter short of ready money for the payment of salaries. Unlike consumer cards, which could only be used one time, coupons of repeated using were to start circulating as of January 10, 1992, and would function as ready cash. The intent was for one coupon (one Ukrainian *karbovanetz*) to equal one Russian ruble. Because the coupons are now circulating

money being issued by an independent nation with the right to issue its own currency, they can be regarded as banknotes.

Initially denominations ranging from one to one hundred coupons were placed in circulation. But the exchange rate did not hold, and the karbovanetz dropped in value against the ruble. Starting in 1993, denominations as high as one million coupons (karbovantzi) have been issued.

[Contributed by Flemming L. Hansen. Albert Pick, *Standard Catalog of World Paper Money* (7th Ed.), pp. 1186-87.]

courant [*Fr.*] common.

couronne (*f.*) [*Fr.*] crown (royal headpiece; large silver coin).

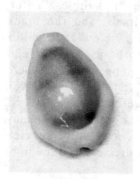

money cowry shell

cowry shell; cowrie shell Yellowish-green seashell (*Cypræa moneta*) used as a form of exchange. Although most come from the Maldive Islands, cowries have been found in nearly every part of the world. They were used in trade from ancient times until the mid-twentieth century. Their trade value has varied greatly, depending on the time and the place. For example, ten cowries equaled one cow in the Sudan in the sixteenth century, while 400,000 of them were worth one gold dinar in the Maldive Islands.

One of the reasons for the cowry shells' immense popularity is that no one ever found a way to counterfeit them, making them virtually unique in the annals of monetary history.

[Charles J. Opitz, *Odd and Curious Money: Descriptions and Values*, p. 23; Mort Reed, *Odd and Curious*, p. 39.]

Crane and Company Paper plant in Dalton, Massachusetts, which has supplied paper for the American Bank Note Company since 1842 and for the U.S. Bureau of Engraving and Printing since 1879. Countless millions of banknotes for a multitude of countries have been printed on this company's paper.

[Thomas S. LaMarre, "The Mills of Crane & Company," *The Numismatist*, April 1986, pp. 643-647.]

credit card Wallet-size plastic, cardboard, or metal plate which identifies the holder as having credit privileges with the company that has issued that plate. It is also referred to as a *charge card*. Because they are so often used as a substitute for cash money, the collection of these items is now regarded as an area of numismatics.

The predecessors of credit cards, known as *charge coins*, first appeared in the 1890s in the northeastern United States. The earliest were issued by department stores and only to the stores' more affluent customers. Later pieces were distributed by oil companies for use at service stations, and by hotels and other businesses. As a rule, these "coins" stated the customer's account number but not his or her name.

By the late 1920s, the first charge cards arrived on the scene. These were rectangular pieces of tin with the customer's name, address, and charge account number in raised letters. Attached to the reverse was a piece of cardboard that showed the name of the issuing company and allowed a space for the customer's signature. The card was kept in a small vinyl or leather sleeve.

During these first decades of credit card use, every company which wished to accept charge cards or coins issued its own and would not accept a card or coin given by a different company. Small stores obviously could not afford to issue their own and thus could not accept credit purchases from strangers. Furthermore, customers were not anxious to carry large numbers of credit cards in their purse or wallet. A better solution had to be found. In some cases, all of the department stores in a major city would issue one single tin

card, as described above. Round or square cuts would be made in specific places along the edges of the card. If a customer had an account at two stores but not at the others, her card would only fit into the charge card imprinting machines of those stores where she actually had her accounts.

In the early 1950s, Diners' Club® issued the first truly multi-purpose credit card. At first it was accepted at only a handful of New York hotels and restaurants, but its acceptability quickly spread. American Express®, which had specialized in selling travelers' checks, soon jumped on the bandwagon. Few of these cards from the 1950s were saved and are now highly prized by collectors. VISA® (né *BankAmericard*), MasterCard® (*Master Charge*), and Discover™ made their national and international appearances in the 1960s, 1970s, and 1980s. Some of these companies' earliest cards are also quite scarce.

Contemporary credit cards are almost always made of plastic, but they retain the raised letters so characteristic of the earlier tin plates. Virtually all current credit cards feature a magnetic strip containing encoded information which can be read by a computer. Computer chips with even more information can be included. Holograms are frequently added to make the plastic cards harder to counterfeit.

In the 1980s, this area of numismatics was expanded due to the emergence of debit cards, automatic teller machine cards, and various other similar items used to expedite financial transactions.

Collecting credit cards has one strange potential drawback: Who really owns these cards? Most credit cards clearly state that they remain the property of whatever company has issued them. They can be revoked and must be returned to the issuer upon demand. Even though collectors deal almost exclusively in expired cards and assume that their collections are their own, there is no guarantee that an issuer will never demand the return of an expired card (especially if it should someday become valuable).

The collecting of credit cards proves that numismatics will survive, even as we approach becoming a "cashless society."

[Walter R. Mack, "Collectors Are Indebted to Credit Cards," *The Numismatist*, January 1990, pp. 38-41 & 149-150.]

credit cards worden aangenomen [*Dut.*] credit cards accepted.

crédito (*m.*) [*Span., Port.*] credit.

crenation A cut or small slice on the edge of a coin. *Reeded edge* is the most common term used to describe an edge with continuous crenations.

Creole tempé [*Fr.*] Also known as *tempé, tampé, étampé,* or *stampée.* Base metal coin first struck in 1763 by the French for use in the French West Indies. See *stampée.*

creux [*Fr.*] sunken; *en creux* means *incuse.*

Crime of '73 Irreverent reference to the Coinage Act of 1873[qv.] of the United States.

Among its provisions, the Act replaced the standard silver dollar with the new Trade dollar. The 2 cent pieces, silver 3 cent pieces, and silver half dimes were eliminated, and the silver dimes, quarters, and half dollars were made slightly heavier.

[R. S. Yeoman, *A Guide Book of United States Coins* (44th Ed.), p. 9.]

crómio (*m.*) [*Port.*] chromium.

cromo (*m.*) [*Ital., Span.*] chromium.

Cromwell, Oliver [a.k.a. *Old Ironsides.*] Lord Protector of the Republican Commonwealth of England, Scotland, and Ireland (1653-58). Born April 25, 1599, in Huntington in Eastern England; died of malaria on September 3, 1658, in Whitehall.

In the English Civil Wars against King Charles I, Oliver Cromwell was one of the leading generals on the side of Parliament. He helped bring about the overthrow of the Stuart monarchy. A statesman of outstanding character and possessed of a deep Calvinist faith, he became Lord Protector of the Republican Commonwealth of England, Scotland, and Ireland in 1658. At the Battle of Marston Moor in 1644, he was given the nickname "Old Ironsides" because his ranks were so impenetrable. Regarded by some as a

dictator and an extreme Puritan, he was neither cruel nor intolerant but rather a patriotic ruler who restored order, stability, and religious tolerance to a country wracked by years of injustice and abuse by the kings and their supporters, the Royalists.

Cromwell died of malaria in 1658 on the anniversary of two of his greatest victories. Although he was buried secretly in Westminster Abbey on November 10, 1658, after the restoration of Charles II, his embalmed remains were exhumed and hung up at Tyburn where criminals were executed. His body was buried beneath the gallows, and his head was stuck on a pole on top of Westminster Hall where it remained until the end of Charles II's reign.

Oliver Cromwell is significant in numismatic history because he and Winston Churchill are the only two commoners ever to be portrayed on British coins. There is some dispute about this, however, because the coins bearing Cromwell's effigy are presumed to be patterns, even though it is certain that some of them did circulate, especially the 1656 halfcrowns and shillings.

Commonwealth coins known to be intended for circulation were not portrait pieces. These unites, double-crown, crowns, halfcrowns, shillings, sixpences, halfgroats, pennies, and halfpennies were variously issued from 1649 until the end of the Commonwealth in 1660. Coins portraying Cromwell included gold 50 shilling coins, broads (gold coins equal to 20 shillings), crowns, halfcrowns, shillings, sixpences, and farthings, and are all dated 1656 or 1658 (except the farthing which is undated).

What was lacking in Cromwell's Commonwealth was an authorized copper coinage. To alleviate the shortage of small change, many individuals struck their own farthing and halfpenny tokens (plus a few penny tokens) from around 1648 to the early 1670s. Most were round, but some interesting pieces were struck square, octagonal, or heart-shaped.

[Contributed by Ruth Ann Davis. Antonia Frasse, *Cromwell, The Lord Protector*; *Encyclopedia* *Britannica* (1981), Vol. 5, pp. 291-95; Stephen Mitchell & Brian Reeds (editors), *Coins of England and the United Kingdom* (Seaby, 1991), pp. 215-17.]

Crookston dollar

Crookston dollar [also spelled *Crookeston* dollar.] Popular name of the silver 30 shilling *ryal* issued from 1565 to 1567 by Mary Queen of Scots while she was married to Henry Darnley. Both of their names (*Maria & Henric*) appear on the obverse. The reverse is dominated by a tortoise climbing a crowned palm tree.

The coin reputedly got its name from the palm tree which is somewhat reminiscent of the old yew tree at Crookston Castle where Mary and Henry courted.

cross Ancient symbol found in many cultures. The tau (T-shaped) cross was a symbol of life to the ancient Egyptians; when combined with a circle, it represented eternity. To the ancient Greeks, the cross was a metaphor for the four indestructible elements of creation: air, earth, fire, and water.

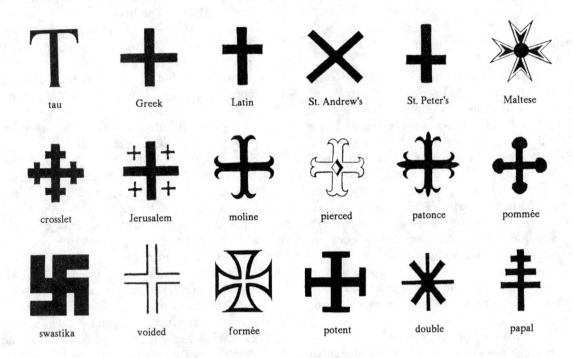

tau	Greek	Latin	St. Andrew's	St. Peter's	Maltese
crosslet	Jerusalem	moline	pierced	patonce	pommée
swastika	voided	formée	potent	double	papal

Styles of crosses used on coins and medals

In one form or another, the cross has appeared on coins virtually since their beginning. Some of the earliest Lydian staters show on their reverse a punch mark in the form of a mill-sail[q.v.], a stylized swastika.

Obviously the cross's greatest impact on numismatics has been as a symbol of Christianity. In this capacity, the cross has appeared in many forms and on a great many coins during the past fifteen hundred years.

The Christian cross was first seen on the coins on Constantine the Great around A.D. 312, and it remained a very popular device on Byzantine coins for many centuries. In the Middle Ages, so many coins showed a cross on the reverse, especially small silver coins like the penny, that the English expression "heads or tails" translates to "face or cross" in many European languages.

The cross has not lost its importance in modern times. The issuance of a set of commemorative coins in 1982 showing Pope John Paul II holding a crucifix would not have been such a shocking event had the issuer not been communist Poland, at that time an officially atheistic state. [See *John Paul II*.]

In addition to its symbolism, the cross has sometimes played a practical role in the development of coins. The designers of the "Long Cross" English pennies allowed the four arms of the cross to extend all the way to the rim in order to discourage clipping. If the edge were clipped, part of the cross would be clipped off with it, making the defacement more obvious.

The illustration shows some of the crosses apt to be seen on coins, especially those of the Middle Ages. These cross designs came from medieval heraldry, and each reflects some special symbolism.

crown 1. English coin of four shillings sixpence struck in 23 carat gold in 1526 and of five shillings in 22 carat gold from 1526-44. See *Crown of the Rose*.

2. Two types of English gold coins, one of five shillings (and later of five shillings sixpence) and the other of four shillings, both struck during the reign of James I. See *Britain Crown* and *Thistle Crown*.

3. Large British coin of five shillings issued occasionally from 1551 to 1937 in silver and from 1951 to 1965 in copper-nickel. The earliest silver crowns were issued by Edward VI in part to upgrade the state of Britain's money, something Henry VIII had allowed to deteriorate through his excessive debasement of silver coins. Nearly every monarch since Edward VI has issued crowns, but most of these coins struck in the twentieth century have been presentation pieces or commemoratives not intended for circulation. Even the vast majority of business-strike crowns issued in 1965 to honor Winston Churchill were kept as souvenirs and did not circulate.

4. Coins of traditional crown size issued by Britain since the switch to decimal coinage in 1971. The first, including the Silver Wedding Commemorative of 1972 and the Silver Jubilee Commemorative of 1977, were denominated at twenty-five new pence. (Note: The word "silver" refers to the Queen and Prince's 25th wedding anniversary and to the Queen's 25th anniversary on the throne; the coins were actually struck of copper-nickel.) In 1990 a crown commemorating the Queen Mother's 90th birthday was issued in the value of £5, establishing this as the new denomination for British crowns.

5. Generic name for any coin made from silver or from a silver substitute (such as nickel or copper-nickel) and having a diameter of approximately 35-50 mm. Often the crown is a coin equal in value to one unit of its nation's currency. An American or Canadian coin which would fit into a collection of crowns would most likely be a traditional silver dollar, although the recent Susan B. Anthony and Loon Dollars are too small in diameter to qualify.

In some languages, the translation of *crown* refers to a denomination or to a local coin of a specified value. As in the British example

above, prior to decimalization, a crown was a coin equal to five shillings.

[Stephen Mitchell & Brian Reeds (editors), *Coins of England and the United Kingdom* (Seaby, 1991), pp. 159-64, 340, et al.]

crown gold Gold of .916 fineness (22 carats), more commonly referred to in the twentieth century as *standard* gold.

Historically, this was regarded as inferior gold because coins struck prior to the reign of England's Henry VIII were of *fine* gold, i.e., 23 1/2 carats (.979 fine) or better. As part of his infamous coinage debasement, he reduced the gold content to 22 carats. The reduction was obvious to the naked eye, because crown gold has just a bit of a coppery tint and is less brilliant than purer gold.

In modern times crown or standard gold has been the preferred choice in coinage because pure gold (24 carats) is too soft to make coins intended for years of circulation. Gold coins of 22 carats are much harder and far more satisfactory for coinage purposes.

See *standard gold* and *fine.*.

Crown of the Double-Rose See *Crown of the Rose*.

Crown of the Rose English coin of four shillings sixpence struck in 23 carat gold in 1526 by Henry VIII to compete against the French *écu au soleil*. The coin was not a success and very few were struck, making this an extremely rare type coin.

A few months later it was replaced by the *Crown of the Double-Rose*, a five shilling coin struck in 22 carat gold. This was the first time British gold coins were minted with a fineness of less than 23 3/4 carats. These were far more accepted than the Crown of the Rose, so the mintage of them continued from 1526 until 1544. Because so many pieces were struck, today they are relatively inexpensive and easy to obtain.

[Stephen Mitchell & Brian Reeds (editors), *Coins of England and the United Kingdom* (Seaby, 1991), pp. 148-50.]

cruciform shield Shield design arranged in the form of a cross. The cross forms a divider to show four separate devices. This is a useful

configuration when, for example, the symbols of four political entities must be represented in the same shield.

cruz (*f.*) [*Span.*] cross; reverse, as it corresponds to the English term *tails*. [Note: the slang term for *heads* is *cara*, literally meaning *face*.]

csekk [*Hun.*] check, cheque.

csillag [*Hun.*] star.

cstp. [*abbr.*] counterstamp[*q.v.*].

ct. [*abbr.*] carat.

ctr. [*abbr.*] center, centre.

cu [*Rom.*] with.

cuadrado (*m.; adj.*) [*Span.*] square.

cuarenta [*Span.*] forty.

cuarto (*m.*) [*Span.*] a fourth, quarter.

cuatro [*Span.*] four.

cu defect [*Rom.*] defective.

cuenta (*f.*) [*Span.*] account (financial or transactional); *a cuenta*: on account.

cuirassed (abbreviated *cuir.*) Protected by armor on the breast and shoulder.

cuivre (*m.*) [*Fr.*] copper.

culoare (*f.*) [*Rom.*] color, colour.

cumpărător (*m.*) [*Rom.*] buyer.

cunhagem (*f.*) [*Port.*] coinage.

cunhagem com erro; cunhagem defeituosa [*Port.*] mis-strike.

cuño (*m.*) [*Span.*] (coinage) die.

cuò wü 错误 [*Chin.-py./sc.*] error.

cupellation Refining process used to separate gold and silver from lead and other impurities in their ores. The ore is placed into a cupel, a small shallow cup made of bone ash or some other porous material. When hit by a blast of very hot air, the tin, lead, copper, and any other unwanted metals become oxidized and partially sink into the porous cupel. The gold and silver remain on the surface of the cupel.

Cupellation can also be used to assay the fineness of those precious metals.

[James Mackay, *Key Definitions in Numismatics*, p. 25.]

cupon Spelling of *coupon* as seen on many transitional notes issued in the 1990s by Ukraine and other former Soviet states. See *coupon (Ukraine)*.

cupped coin A type of error that can occur when a freshly-minted coin gets stuck in a minting machine and fails to eject. The coin becomes cupped in shape because other coin blanks are fed into the machine and are pressed against the stuck coin. See *brockage*.

cupro-nickel See *copper-nickel*.

cupru (*n.*) [*Rom.*] copper.

currency Any form of circulating coins or paper money, and in particular, those with legal tender status. It is a commercial term referring to any circulating money produced by a government or any official agency authorized to issue money.

Although many people (including numismatists) use the word as if it were synonymous with paper money, this is not the case. *Currency* can include circulating coins. The term *paper currency* as a reference to paper money is acceptable.

As the term is generally used, currency does not include odd and curious forms of money, bars or ingots of precious metals, bullion coins, or non-redeemable coins (such as the Canadian Olympic commemoratives).

currency strikes A series of labor strikes in Cuba commencing on January 10, 1899, and extending well into 1907. Shortly after the Spanish American War of 1898, labor unrest broke out in Cuba due to massive confusion caused by changes in the types of money that were accepted as legal tender (basically the U.S. dollar) and the kinds of money actually in circulation (depreciated Spanish silver coins). In other words, the laborers were receiving less and less for their money than their wages would indicate. These *specie strikes* (in Spanish, *huelgas de la moneda*) first broke out among port workers in 1899 and concluded in 1907 when tobacco workers struck for nearly five months.

[Manuel Moreno Fraginals and José A. Pulido Ledesma, *Cuba: A Country and Its Currency*, National Bank of Cuba, p. 139.]

curs de schimb (*n.*) [*Rom.*] exchange rate.

cută (*f.*) [*Rom.*] a crease, fold.

cut cancellation Slits or wedges cut into a stamp or piece of paper money to cancel or invalidate it. The note in the illustration was cancelled with several V-shaped cuts. The

note showing cut cancellation

paper at those places has been rolled back to make the cuts more visible.

cut note Paper money officially cut into halves, quarters, or even smaller pieces with each division given its own value, often indicated by overprinting. It is usually an emergency measure to provide small change during a coin shortage. When a note is cut exactly in half, it can also be called a *bisect*. See page 318 for a color illustration.

C.W.T. (*abbr.*) Civil War token[q.v.].

cyna (*f.*) [*Pol.*] tin (the metal).

cynk (*m.*) [*Pol.*] zinc.

czarny [*Pol.*] black.

czarny rynek (*m.*) [*Pol.*] black market.

czek (*m.*) [*Pol.*] check, cheque.

czerwony [*Pol.*] red.

czterdzieści [*Pol.*] forty.

cztery [*Pol.*] four.

czysty [*Pol.*] fineness, fine (purity of metal).

D d

d. [*abbr.*] penny[*q.v.*] (or its plural form *pence*). Because the word *penny* is presumed to have been derived from *denarius*, an ancient Roman coin, the abbreviation of the traditional penny is "d." instead of "p." However, the "p." designation has been used since the switch-over to decimalization in 1970.

daftar harga [*Indo.*] price list.

dài yòng bì 代用币 [*Chin.-py./sc.*] token.

dalawa [*Tag.*] two.

dal-ro 달러 [*Kor.*] dollar ($).

dañado [*Span.*] damaged.

Danemark [*Fr.*] Denmark.

Dänemark [*Ger.*] Denmark.

danificado [*Port.*] damaged.

Danimarca [*Ital.*] Denmark.

Danmark [*Nor.*] Denmark.

danneggiato (*m.*) [*Ital.*] damaged.

d'argent [*Fr.*] of silver. A term which appears after the name of many French coins to distinguish its metal. For example, the *louis d'argent* is a silver coin while the *louis d'or* is of gold.

dàrlig preget [*Nor.*] badly struck.

dàrligt præget [*Dan.*] badly struck.

darn arian (*m.*) [*Wel.*] coin.

darn punt [*Wel.*] pound coin (£).

darphane [*Turk.*] mint.

darphane işareti [*Turk.*] mintmark.

data (*f.*) [*Port., Pol.*] date.

dată (*f.*) [*Rom.*] date.

data alterata (*f.*) [*Ital.*] altered date.

data falsificada (*f.*) [*Port.*] altered date.

dată shimbată (*f.*) [*Rom.*] altered date.

date changée (*f.*) [*Fr.*] altered date.

dato (*m.*) [*Nor.*] date.

datum (*n.*) [*Swed.*]; (*m.-c.*) [*Dut.*] date.

Datum (*n.*) [*Ger.*] date.

dátum [*Hun.*] date.

dátumváltozás [*Hun.*] altered date.

dead country A nation which formerly issued coins or notes but which no longer exists as an independent political entity. The term always refers to modern countries which have lost their political status, not ancient or medieval territories.

Republic of Biafra: banknote from a "dead" country

The nineteenth century saw some money-issuing countries come and go (Hawaii, the Republic of Texas, the Confederate States of America, et al), but the twentieth century has witnessed an enormous number of such national "deaths." On the one hand, the Soviet Union, Czechoslovakia, Yugoslavia, and a number of other countries have become dead in the numismatic sense by splitting apart. On the other hand, East Germany and West Germany merged.

The illustrated note represents a great human tragedy. The Republic of Biafra was an attempt in 1967 to create a secessionist state for the Ibo people of southeastern Nigeria. The secession triggered a civil war which lasted until January 1970 at which time the Biafrans signed a formal surrender. As many as a million people died of starvation as the result of that war. The banknotes and postage stamps of that nation are among the few surviving remnants of a people's attempt to create an independent nation for themselves.

deasupra [*Rom.*] top.

Canadian "death" dollar

death dollar Canadian silver dollar of 1958 honoring British Columbia. The principal device on the reverse is a totem pole. After the coin was released, some Native Canadians were supposedly alarmed that the top of the totem shows a raven, symbol of death. When the general public heard this story, the coin acquired its nickname *death dollar*.

Decadrachm Hoard See *Elmali Hoard*.

déchiré [*Fr.*] torn.

déchirure (*f.*) [*Fr.*] a tear (as in a banknote or bond).

dechomaste pistotikes kartes δεχόμαστε πιστωτικές κάρτες [*Grk.*] credit cards accepted.

decimo (*m.*) [*Ital.*] tenth (the fraction).

décimo (*m.*) [*Span., Port.*] tenth (the fraction).

decoraţie militară (*f.*) [*Rom.*] military decoration.

decoration Medallic badge, ribbon, or sash ornament awarded for valor or as a prize. Unlike other types of awards, decorations are intended to be worn, not just displayed.

Historians have traced decorations back to the ancient Greeks and Romans, although the decorations of those days were mostly in the form of buttons and wreaths. The ancient Olympic champions were awarded such wreaths rather than the gold, silver, and bronze medals given in the modern Games.

In the late Middle Ages, various types of decorations became popular. The recipient would wear his decorations to show that he was worthy of special recognition. This same attitude was prevalent in later centuries when awards for gallantry came into vogue.

During the past two hundred years, by far the greatest number of decorations awarded by governments have been bestowed to military personnel for valor in combat. The *Africa Star*, as seen in the illustration on the color plates, was given by Great Britain for participation in the North African campaigns of World War II. A well-known U.S. military decoration is the *Purple Heart*[q.v.], awarded to soldiers (or their families) who are killed or wounded in combat.

[Richard G. Doty, *The Macmillan Encyclopedic Dictionary of Numismatics*, p. 93.]

decorazione militare (*f.*) [*Ital.*] military decoration.

dedesubt [*Rom.*] bottom.

défaut (*m.*) [*Fr.*] defect.

défaut de frappe (*m.*) [*Fr.*] mis-strike.

defectivo; defeituoso [*Port.*] defective.

defecto de acuñación [*Span.*] mis-strike.

défectueux [*Fr.*] defective.

defectuoso [*Span.*] defective.

defeito (*m.*) [*Port.*] defect.

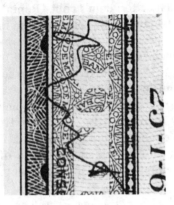

Mexican note with "de Gaulle" signature

defne yaprağı taçlı baş [*Turk.*] laureate.

defnostefis δαφνοστεφής [*Grk.*] laureate.

de Gaulle note Mexican one peso note with a signature on the lower left that bears a striking resemblance to the outline of Charles de Gaulle. When the signature of Luís G. Legorreta (the *consejero* or finance minister) is turned sideways, de Gaulle's profile is very distinct. See illustrations.

degem דֶּגֶם (*m.*) [*Heb.*] pattern.

değer düşürme [*Turk.*] devaluation.

değerli [*Turk.*] valuable.

değiştirme [*Turk.*] alteration.

Dei Gratia [*Lat.*] By the Grace of God. Abbreviated *D.G.* or *Dei Gra*. Motto seen on most coins of Great Britain and the British Commonwealth.

deka δέκα [*Grk.*] ten.

del (*r.*) [*Swed.*] fraction.

Dél-Afrika [*Hun.*] South Africa.

deltion paraggelion δελτίον παραγγελιών (*n.*) [*Grk.*] order form.

Demand Note On July 17, 1861, the United States Congress authorized the first issuance of Federal paper money as a way of helping to finance the Union Army (the North) in the U.S. Civil War. These notes were printed in denominations of $5, $10, and $20. Because their reverses were printed entirely in green ink, they quickly became known as *greenbacks*. They did not become legal tender until March of 1862; prior to that time, the bearer could demand payment in gold or silver whenever he chose. These notes saw limited circulation and were withdrawn in May 1862.

[Mary Jane Michael, "Greenbacks— The Controversial Currency," *The Numismatist*, April 1981, pp. 890-901.]

demi (*adj.*) [*Fr.*] half.

démonétisation (*f.*) [*Fr.*] demonetization.

Demonetisierung (*f.*) [*Ger.*] demonetization.

demonetyzacja (*f.*) [*Pol.*] demonetization.

demy Scottish gold coin introduced around 1390 as the *demy-lion* by Robert III. It was continued simply as the *demy* by his successors, James I and James II.

See *lozenge*.

denarius [pl.: *denarii*.] Primary silver coin of ancient Rome. It was introduced around 211 B.C., in part to raise money for Rome's involvement in the Second Punic War. Its original value was pegged at ten bronze asses, although it was later revalued to sixteen asses.

The coins became portrait pieces and were used by later rulers who issued them as propaganda tools. For example, Julius Caesar's portrait appeared on the denarii of his day, significant because this was the first time a living Roman had ever been featured on coins.

The denarius was discontinued in the mid-third century A.D., but many of the small silver coins introduced in Europe around the middle of the eighth century have their names derived from it: *denier, denaro, pfennig, penny*, etc. In

some cases, these derivations have stuck and are the current words in their languages which translate to *money*, such as *dinero* in Spanish and *dinheiro* in Portuguese.

denaro (*m.*) [*Ital.*] money. See *denarius*.

denga деньга [*Russ.*] Silver half kopeck coin of Russia first issued by Great Prince Dmitry Donskoy around 1375. Many feudal princes produced dengas, as did the consolidated monarchy in Moscow.

For about three centuries, dengas were a type of Russian wire money[*q.v.*]. But by the seventeenth century, the cost of producing them became prohibitive and they were finally replaced with copper dengas, the first of which were struck in 1700.

This coin became a permanent fixture in the Russian language, because the plural form (деньги, romanized as *dengi*) has become a general term meaning *money*.

[Randolph Zander, *Russian-English Numismatic Dictionary*, pp. 25-26.]

dengi деньги (*pl.*) [*Russ.*] money.

French *denier*

denier (*m.*) [*Fr.*] Small silver French coin first produced in the middle of the eighth century A.D. It became the prototype for the English and Scottish penny, Spanish dinero, Portuguese dinheiro, Italian denaro, and a host of similar coins struck throughout Europe. The names of all of the afore-mentioned coins were derived from the *denarius*, a popular silver coin of ancient Rome.

The denier was introduced by Pepin the Short (ca. 714-768, ruled 751-768) to facilitate trade. For several centuries France had no uniform regal coinage. The issuance of this coin not only helped commerce but was also politically expedient for Pepin. The coin it replaced was a small, thick, and somewhat crude silver coin also known as a denier, but it

bore little resemblance to Pepin's coin. Pepin's denier is an extremely important coin in numismatic history because it spawned so many similar coins throughout the continent. And in many kingdoms, this coin drove commerce, sometimes for centuries.

By the thirteenth century it had become debased and was beginning to lose its popularity. The denomination survived until the seventeenth century as a smaller coin of reduced silver content. The last pieces were struck in copper.

[Richard G. Doty, *The Macmillan Encyclopedic Dictionary of Numismatics*, pp. 97-98.]

denominação (*f.*) [*Port.*] denomination.

[#1] denticulated rim: 1700 Salzburg Thaler

denticulated rim [also known as *dentilated rim*.]

1. Rim of a coin created from a continuous circle of tooth-like indentations or ornaments. Denticles were sometimes applied in this way to compensate for a minting process which omitted the use of a collar. In other words, it

[#2] denticulated rim: 1948 Mexican 5 pesos

allowed the planchet space to spread out. The technique is mostly seen on European coins struck from the seventeenth to the nineteenth centuries.

2. Rounded, pointed, or squared design used as a rim decoration on modern coins. It may consist of serrations resembling the teeth on a saw or it may be something much more fancy and ornate.

depolanma esnasında aşınmış [*Turk.*] cabinet friction.

depósito (*m.*) [*Span., Port.*] deposit.

deposito obbligatorio (*m.*) [*Ital.*] deposit required.

deposit required Statement on an auction bid sheet indicating that a deposit must be submitted with the bid in order for the bid to be considered. The amount of the deposit will be a specified percentage of the total bid. If the bid is successful, the deposit is applied to the price of the item. If the bid is unsuccessful, the deposit is returned. The purpose of a required deposit is to help insure that the highest bidder will honor his bid as he is legally obligated to do.

depositum nødvendig [*Nor.*] deposit required.

depositum nødvendigt [*Dan.*] deposit required.

dépôt (*m.*) [*Fr.*] deposit (of funds).

dépôt est requis, un [*Fr.*] deposit required.

depozit obligatoriu [*Rom.*] deposit required.

derde [*Dut.*] third.

derecha (*f.*) [*Span.*] right (direction or position).

dertig [*Dut.*] thirty.

desconhecido [*Port.*] unknown.

desconocido [*Span.*] unknown.

desen [*Turk.*] pattern.

desenho (*m.*) [*Port.*] design.

desgaste por el uso (*m.*) [*Span.*] wear.

deslustre (*m.*) [*Span., Port.*] tarnish.

desmonetização (*f.*) [*Port.*] demonetization.

desmonetización (*f.*) [*Span.*] demonetization.

destrukt menniczy (*m.*) [*Pol.*] a mis-strike.

desuso (*m.*) [*Span.*] disuse; *en desuso*: obsolete.

desvalorização (*f.*) [*Port.*] devaluation.

deteriorat [*Rom.*] damaged.

deterioro por contacto (*m.*) [*Span.*] cabinet friction.

deuda pública (*f.*) [*Span.*] public debt.

Deutsche Demokratische Republik [*Ger.*] German Democratic Republic. More commonly known to English speakers as *East Germany.*

Deutschland [*Ger.*] Germany.

deux [*Fr.*] two.

de valor [*Span.*] valuable.

devaluatie (*f.-c.*) [*Dut.*] devaluation.

devaluering (*c.*) [*Dan.*]; (*m.*) [*Nor.*] devaluation.

devalvaatio [*Finn.*] devaluation.

devalvatsiya девальвация (*f.*) [*Russ.*] devaluation.

devalvering (*r.*) [*Swed.*] devaluation.

device Any design on a coin, medal, or token other than the date or other lettering. Portraits of specific people are usually not considered to be devices, but generic human forms (e.g., the Mountie on 1973 Canadian quarters and dollars) are included. Many devices have patriotic or nationalistic significance (eagles, rays, maple leaves, shields, swastikas, fasces, etc.) or show wildlife native to that region. Historical artifacts are also popular as devices, such as the Aztec Calendar Stone and Mayan Pyramid on Mexican coins and a group of formerly-used odd and curious items found on coins of Fiji.

Devil's Face Apparent likeness of the devil in the hair of Elizabeth II on the Series 1954 Canadian notes of all denominations ($1, $2, $5, $10, $20, $50, $100, and $1000).

The apparition was neither an error nor a prank but merely the faithful copying of the original photograph used as the model. George Gundersen, designer of the vignette, was "horrified" and "dumbfounded" at accusations that he had placed the face there on purpose; in point of fact, there is no evidence that he did. What appears to be the devil is nothing more than the way the queen's hair is highlighted.

Nevertheless, many Canadians refused to handle the notes and demanded that the vignette be changed. The Canadian government was hard pressed to do so quickly, because it had been recalling the old notes showing George VI. A fast recall would have left the nation without sufficient circulating paper currency.

normal Canadian note (left) and note with "Devil's Face"

The vignette was re-designed by darkening the hair highlights and removing part of the shading. The modifications were not extensive, but they sufficed to satisfy critics.

Despite whatever public outcry remained, most of the Devil's Face notes were not completely discontinued until 1959, and the "bedeviled" $1000 bill continued to circulate for several more years. The government apparently realized that changing the design on notes of such a high denomination was not a high priority, as they were seldom seen by anyone other than bankers.

[J. A. Haxby and R. C. Willey, *Coins of Canada* (9th Ed.), pp. 196-97; "Was it a demon, or did Elizabeth II have a bad hair day on Devil's Face notes?" *Coin World,* October 31, 1994, p. 10.]

devise (*f.*) [*Fr.*] motto.

Devise (*f.*) [*Ger.*] foreign exchange.

devise étrangère (*f.*) [*Fr.*] foreign currency.

deviză (*f.*) [*Rom.*] motto.

devlet kâr payı [*Turk.*] seigniorage.

dewaluacja (*f.*) [*Pol.*] devaluation.

dewizy (*f.pl.*) [*Pol.*] foreign currency.

deyutsmark [*Tag.*] mark (German unit of currency).

dez [*Port.*] ten.

D.G. [*Lat. abbr.*] *Dei Gratia* ("By the Grace of God"). Also abbreviated *Dei Gra.* Motto seen on many coins of Great Britain and the British Commonwealth.

diadochikos arithmos διαδοχικός αριθμός (*m.*) [*Grk.*] serial number.

diafilassomeni prosfora διαφυλασσόμενη προσφορά [*Grk.*] protective reserve bid.

diakanonismeno simio anagnorisis διακανονισμένο σημείο αναγνώρισης [*Grk.*] adjustment mark.

diakoptomeni sfragida nomismatos διακοπτόμενη φραγίδα νομίσματος [*Grk.*] die break.

diamètre (*m.*) [*Fr.*] diameter.

diâmetro (*m.*) [*Port.*] diameter.

diametros διάμετρος (*f.*) [*Grk.*] diameter.

diametru (*n.*) [*Rom.*] diameter.

die Iron or steel device used to transfer a design into a coin, medal, or token. Whether the pieces were minted by using a hammer, a screw press, or machinery, in each case a pair of dies is needed. One die remains stationary (the *anvil* die) and the blank is placed on it. The other is a movable die (the *hammer* die) which is pressed against the blank with enough pressure so that both dies will leave an impression.

die break A crack or break in a coinage die which leaves a line or mark on any coin struck from it. The mark on the coin appears in relief rather than incuse as a scratch would be.

dieci [*Ital.*] ten.

diepdruk (*n.*) [*Dut.*] intaglio.

Dieu [*Fr.*] God (in the Judaic-Christian sense).

diez [*Span.*] ten.

difetto (*m.*) [*Ital.*] defect.

difettoso [*Ital.*] defective.

digital currency Term coined in the 1990s by Bill Gates of Microsoft. It refers to the electronic transfer of funds using recently developed methods, such as via the so-called *smart cards*. See *money*.

digma δεῖγμα (*n.*) [*Grk.*] specimen.

di gran valore [*Ital.*] valuable.

dime 1. Official name of the U.S. 10 cent pieces issued since 1796. They were authorized through the Mint Act of April 2, 1792. The original spelling of this coin was *disme*, and a small group of pieces using this name were struck in 1792 at the fledgling Philadelphia Mint.

The word was presumably derived from the French word *dix*, meaning "ten."

2. Colloquial (but unofficial) term for the Canadian 10 cent piece.

dimoprasia δημοπρασία (*f.*) [*Grk.*] auction.

Dinamarca [*Span., Port.*] Denmark.

dinero (*m.*) [*Span.*] 1. Contemporary Spanish word meaning *money*.

2. Small Spanish silver coin of the same class as the French *denier* and the English *penny*. The name is derived from the *denarius*, a popular silver coin of ancient Rome. The dinero was introduced much later than the denier or the penny, probably because Spain was under Arab control from the eighth until the thirteenth century. In one form or another, it circulated from the late eleventh century until the sixteenth century but was usually struck from billon or copper rather than quality silver. It was minted as a silver coin during the reign of Ferdinand III (1230-52) who is sometimes credited for having introduced it, yet there is evidence that some sort of *dinero* coin circulated at least a hundred years earlier.

dinero contante y sonante (*m.*) [*Span.*] cash (ready money).

dinheiro (*m.*) [*Port.*] 1. Contemporary Portuguese word meaning *money*.

2. Small Portuguese coin similar to the Spanish *dinero* but always struck in base silver or copper instead of from quality silver. It

circulated from the twelfth to the fourteenth centuries. It is regarded as the first Portuguese coin.

dinheiro disponível (*m.*) [*Port.*] cash (ready money).

Dios [*Span.*] God (in the Judaic-Christian sense). The phrase *Por la gracia de Dios* ("By the Grace of God") is inscribed on some Spanish coins immediately after the king's name.

direct cleaning The removal from a coin or medal of tarnish, corrosion, rust, or other buildup caused by oxidation. When the foreign substance is removed, some of the coin's metal will also be eliminated due to the chemical reaction that has caused the oxidation in the first place. If indirect cleaning is used, only superficial dirt and grime are taken off, and the metal itself is not actually altered.

Also see *indirect cleaning*.

[Alan Korwin, "Shedding Light on Coin Cleaning," *The Numismatist*, June 1985, pp. 1091-93.]

direito [*Port.*] right (direction or position).

diritto (*m.*) [*Ital.*] front; obverse.

diritto di conio (*m.*) [*Ital.*] privilege of coinage; seigniorage. The preferred word in Italian is *signoraggio* (*m.*).

disegno (*m.*) [*Ital.*] design, pattern.

diseño (*m.*) [*Span.*] design, pattern.

disme Original name of the U.S. ten cent piece, authorized by the Mint Act of April 2, 1792. Some silver dismes and half-dismes were struck in 1792 at the Philadelphia Mint. The metal came from a silver service donated by George and Martha Washington. These coins are among the first U.S. Mint issues. When the first regular 10 cent coinage was begun in 1796, the denomination was changed to *dime*.

Disney Dollar Very popular scrip introduced by The Walt Disney Company in 1987. It is issued in denominations of $1, $5, and $10, and feature the portraits of Disney cartoon characters. The notes can be purchased at Disneyland, Walt Disney World, and the Disney retail stores. They are only good in trade at Disney-owned facilities.

The notes were originally intended as a one-time promotion, but they proved so successful

that Disney now releases new series on an annual basis. All of the Disney Dollars are printed by the American Bank Note Company or its affiliates.

[Paul Gilkes, "Disney Dollars," *Coin World*, August 14, 1995, p. 1 et al.]

dispositivo antifalsificazione (*m.*) [*Ital.*] anti-counterfeiting device.

dispositivo de antifalsificación (*m.*) [*Span.*] anti-counterfeiting device.

Distinguished Service Cross U.S. military decoration authorized on July 9, 1918, for any individuals serving in any capacity with the U.S. Army who have distinguished themselves by extraordinary heroism against an armed enemy, but not justifying the Medal of Honor.

This award can be granted posthumously and to officers and men of military forces allied to the United States. If a recipient is again cited for further acts of gallantry justifying the grant of the decoration, he is awarded a bronze oak cluster to be worn on the ribbon.

The first hundred of these decorations had the arms of the cross ornamented with oak leaves, but in subsequent issues the arms were of a simpler design. Beneath the eagle is a scroll bearing the words *For Valor*.

The Distinguished Service Cross has also been awarded to members of relief organizations serving with the army within the area of actual operations. The awarding of the Cross was retroactive to cover conspicuous service in wars or campaigns before the First World War. Additionally, in 1934 it was authorized to be presented to those persons who had received the Certificate of Merit.

[Contributed by Robert A. Carpenter. Evans Kerrigan, *American Medals and Decorations*, pp. 14-17; Capt. H. Taprell Dorling, *Ribbons and Medals*, pp. 205-6.]

disturbance Any unusual scratch, edge bump, hole, corrosion, odd tarnish spot, ink stain, or other irregularity that detracts from a coin or note's appearance. The term generally does not refer to surface wear, which is part of a coin's grade, unless the coin shows excessively heavy wear in just one spot.

An accurate description of a coin or note should include both the grade and any disturbances (e.g., "very fine condition but with a scratch on the obverse field").

divisa (*f.*) [*Span.*] motto; foreign currency.

dix [*Fr.*] ten.

dixième (*m.*) [*Fr.*] tenth (the fraction).

Dix note The State of Louisiana was originally a French-speaking area, and many people there still spoke French in the 1850s. When Louisiana banks issued $10 notes, the French word *dix* ("ten") was often included. According to legend, it was from these notes that the Confederacy became known as *Dixie*, a name still used today in reference to the southern United States.

dk. [*abbr.*] dark.

d'mut דְמוּת (*f.*) [*Heb.*] effigy.

dô 銅 [*Jpn.*] copper (the metal).

dobbelportrettert [*Nor.*] accolated[q.v.], conjoined, jugate.

doblez (*m.*) [*Span.*] a fold (as in a banknote or bond).

doblón (*m.*) [*Span.*; known in English as *doubloon*.] A Spanish or Spanish American gold coin ultimately valued at 8 escudos.

The coin, originally called a *pistole*, was first struck by Charles V of Spain in 1537 as a 22 carat (.9167 fine) replacement of the pure gold *excelente* introduced by Isabella and Ferdinand in 1497. The use of the name *doblón* was a carry-over from the "doubled" portraits of the king and queen which had appeared on the earlier *excelente* coins.

Later, the doblón became a larger coin valued at 8 escudos. Its denomination was derived from *escudo*, the Spanish word for *shield*. The primary device on the reverse of this coin is the Spanish coat of arms in the form of a shield, hence the name.

The doblón continued to be produced until around 1820, although coins of this metal and denomination were struck as late as the 1830s in Chile. A very similar coin (but denominated at 80 *reales*) was produced in Spain until 1849, the era of Isabella II's monetary reform which decimalized the system.

dobra (*f.*) [*Port.*] a crease, fold.

dobra gentil See *gentil*.

dobry [*Pol.*] fine, good (grade or condition).

dodeka δώδεκα [*Grk.*] twelve.

dog on a bridge Supposedly what the eye sees when the reverse of a U.S. Mercury Dime is rotated clockwise 90°. The ax blade of the fasces appears to be a dog about to cross a bridge.

Doğu Almanya [*Turk.*] East Germany (D.D.R.).

doi [*Rom.*] two.

dois (*m.adj.*) [*Port.*] two.

dökmek; döküm yapmak (*v.*) [*Turk.*] to cast.

dokuz [*Turk.*] nine.

dół (*m.*) [*Pol.*] bottom.

dô-la [*Viet.*] dollar ($).

dolar דוֹלָר (*m.*) [*Heb.*] dollar ($).

dólar (*m.*) [*Span., Port.*] dollar.

dollar Unit of currency created by the U.S. Coinage Act of April 2, 1792. The first coins of this denomination were struck two years later by the Philadelphia Mint. Silver crown-size dollar coins were issued intermittently in the United States from 1794 to 1935. They were again produced in 1971-78 but as copper-nickel clad coins (the Eisenhower Dollars) and then were issued as a smaller-size coin from 1979 to 1981 (Susan B. Anthony Dollars).

The dollar is significant because it was the first unit of currency intended to be broken into decimal units, i.e., one dollar equaling one hundred cents. In today's world, most countries use a decimal system similar to this; in 1792, the practice was unheard of.

The word dollar was derived from the German *Thaler*[*q.v.*] (a large silver coin first issued in Central Europe in the late fifteenth century) by way of the Dutch word *daaler*. The dollar's minor unit, the *cent*, simply means "hundred" in French.

Canada chose the dollar over the pound as its unit of currency in 1857, largely due to Canadian opposition to British control. Although no coins or notes by either the Province of Canada nor the Dominion of Canada were denominated in the d/s/£ system, Canada's earliest postage stamps (1851-59) were issued in values of 1/2d, 3d, 6d, 7 1/2d, 10d, and 12d. The first official coinage of 1858 consisted of 1 cent, 5 cent, 10 cent, and 20 cent pieces. Thus, in 1858 Canada became probably the only country in history to issue simultaneously coins in one currency and stamps in another.

Canada's first dollar coins were not issued until 1935, although three pattern specimens (two in silver, one in lead) were struck in 1911. The small-sized *Loon Dollar*[*q.v.*] was introduced in 1987 as part of the process to eliminate the $1 note.

Australia switched to the dollar in 1966 and New Zealand in 1967 as part of the decimalization reform which took place throughout Britain and the Commonwealth in the late 1960s and early '70s. Many smaller countries also made the changeover at the same time.

Coins or notes denominated in dollars have been issued at one time or another by Alderney, American Samoa, Anguilla, Antiqua & Barbuda, Australia, Bahamas, Barbados, Belize, Bermuda, British Virgin Islands, British West Indies, Brunei, Canada, Cayman Islands, China, Confederate States of America, Cook Islands, Danish West Indies, Dominica, East Caribbean States, Eritrea, Ethiopia, Fiji, Great Britain, Grenada, Guyana, Hawaii, Hong Kong, Jamaica, Japan, Kiribati, Liberia, Marshall Islands, Mauritius, Montserrat, Namibia, Nauru Island, New Zealand, Newfoundland, Niue, Palau Islands, Panama-Palo Seco, Pitcairn Islands, Puerto Rico, St. Kitts, St. Lucia, St. Vincent, Sierra Leone, Singapore, Solomon Islands, Straits Settlements, Texas, Tuvalu, Thailand, Trinidad & Tobago, the United States, and Zimbabwe.

Some of the above countries used the dollar in a very limited way. Great Britain, for example, limited its use to a group of emergency crowns and half-crowns in 1804 which were actually restruck silver Spanish-American 8 *real* coins. Some of the pieces were merely counterstamped while others were totally restruck. Its other use in British coinage is the trade dollar of 1895 to 1935, issued to facilitate British trade in the Orient. They do not portray the reigning monarch.

dos caritas ("two little faces") Mexican note

Some of the other countries listed above are tiny nations whose coinage either sees very limited use or it is non-circulating legal tender intended only to be marketed to collectors.

Panama does not print its own paper money. It uses the U.S. dollar but calls it a *balboa*.

[Walter Breen, *Complete Encyclopedia of U.S. and Colonial Coins*, pp. 423-84; Chester L. Krause and Clifford Mishler, *Standard Catalog of World Coins* (1995), p. 32.]

dollario δολλάριο (*n.*) [*Grk.*] dollar.

dong-jûn 동전 [*Kor.*] coin.

đồng tiền dập sai [*Viet.*] mis-struck.

đồng tiền giả [*Viet.*] token.

donker [*Dut.*] dark.

đơn vị tiền tệ [*Viet.*] monetary unit.

doorboord [*Dut.*] holed.

doppio (*m.; adj.*) [*Ital.*] duplicate.

d'or [*Fr.*] of gold, golden. This appears after the name of many French coins to distinguish its metal. For example, the *louis d'or* is a gold coin while the *louis d'argent* was struck from silver.

dört [*Turk.*] four.

doru ドル [*Jpn.*] dollar ($).

dos [*Span.*] two.

dos caritas [*Span.*] Literally, *two little faces*. This nickname was given to notes issued during the Mexican Revolution by the State of Chihuahua showing two unusually small portraits of the front side. The men pictured are Francisco I. Madero and Abrahám González. The notes were authorized by the military decree of Feb. 10, 1914, and were printed on many different types and qualities of paper.

[Carlos Gaytán, *Billetes de México*, pp. 33-34.]

dosh nivärana chinha दोष निवारण चिह्न [*Hin.*] adjustment mark.

doskonały [*Pol.*] perfect, flawless.

dot When George V died in January 1936, the Royal Mint in London began preparing new Edward VIII coinage dies for itself and for mints throughout the Commonwealth. But Edward's unexpected abdication in December 1936 disrupted the schedule, and the Royal Canadian Mint found itself unprepared to strike coins in 1937. Since the mint was not sure how long the delay in shipping new dies would be, a dot was added to the bottom of the reverse of its 1936 cent, ten cent, and quarter dollar dies to signify that any coins made from those dies were actually struck in 1937 on behalf of George VI.

According to mint records, 678,823 cents and 191,237 ten cent pieces were struck with the dot, yet only five of the cents and four of the ten cent coins are known to exist. The others were presumably melted. All nine known specimens are in uncirculated condition.

The quarter dollars are much more available to collectors. Their official mintage was 153,685. Some may have been melted, but enough survive— and in all grades— that they are within reach of the average collector. However, many of the extant specimens are not sharply struck because of ghosting[q.v.] problems caused by the old worn dies.

A variety of 1956 Canadian ten cent piece shows a dot under the date, but this was unintentional and resulted from a defective die. Some 1947 coins of various denominations show small irregular dots near the date, likely caused from flaking on a die which had been plated with chromium.

[J. A. Haxby and R. C. Willey, *Coins of Canada* (9th Ed.), pp. 24, 44, & 53; J. E. Charlton, *Standard Catalogue of Canadian Coins* (27th Ed.), pp. 27, 43, 45, & 49.]

Canadian 1936 "dot" 10 cents

douăzeci [*Rom.*] twenty.

double (*m.; adj.*) [*Fr.*] duplicate.

double denomination A coin of one denomination struck on an already-minted coin of a different denomination.

When coins are struck and ejected, they eventually end up in a bin for weighing. Occasionally, a struck coin remains in that bin. When another load of blanks for a different denomination is poured into the bin, the odd coin is struck by a different pair of dies. For example, a finished dime (U.S. 10 cent piece) could then be struck by dies meant for the cent. Both images are fairly clear, and each denomination can usually be determined.

A word of caution here— Since each blank slides down a chute of approximately the same diameter as the coin to be struck, the second strike must be of a coin which is physically larger than the first. It is impossible to strike a smaller coin over a larger one. Thus, since the U.S. dime has a slightly smaller diameter than the cent, a dime strike over a cent is impossible, but a cent over a dime is likely.

[Contributed by Coleman Ezkovich.]

doubled die A working die is made from a master. This master die usually strikes the surface of the die two or more times for enhanced sharpness. If there should be a slight rotation of the master on a second or subsequent impression, the lettering and/or the devices are doubled (or tripled). The coin struck from such a die will show double (or more) images. Some doubling is so faint that it can only be seen with a strong magnifying glass; in other cases, the doubling is so obvious that it can easily be seen with the naked eye. Some famous doubled die coins are the 1955 (see page 317 for color illustration) and 1972 Lincoln Cents, and the 1939 Jefferson Nickel.

This should not be confused with other types of doubling caused by the die bouncing on its strike. When only the date is doubled, in all probability the die is not doubled. Also, the doubling of mintmarks is not usually the result of a doubled die. A mintmark is normally added to the die after it is made. The mintmark may be punched several times and may be rotated or slightly shifted.

[Contributed by Coleman Ezkovich.]

double eagle 1. Portrayal of an eagle with two necks and two heads. This device was emblematic of Russia, the Austro-Hungarian Empire, and some German states and is featured on the reverses of many of their coins.

2. Official name of U.S. $20 gold piece issued from 1849 to 1933. It was introduced largely in response to the great quantities of gold discovered in California and elsewhere in the late 1840s and 1850s.

Only one specimen exists of the 1849 double eagle, and it is regarded as a pattern. It is now part of the numismatic collection of the Smithsonian Institution. Similarly, although nearly a half-million pieces were struck in 1933, they were never released. Two examples were retained for the Smithsonian and the others were supposedly destroyed. At least a few pieces did escape, however. They have been regarded as property stolen from the U.S. government and have been subject to confiscation.

James B. Longacre designed the Coronet type, used from 1849-1907. The St. Gaudens type (1907-1933) is regarded as one of America's most beautiful coins.

double rose The open double rose, such as that shown on the reverse of the first English sovereign (1489), symbolized the union of the White Rose of York and the Red Rose of Lancaster.

doubloon Anglicanized version of the Spanish word *doblón*[q.v.]. It is a Spanish or Spanish American gold coin valued at 8 escudos struck at various mints from the sixteenth to the nineteenth century. It is also the name Ephraim Brasher gave to his gold U.S. pattern coins of 1787.

doū zhǒng 多种 [*Chin.-py./sc.*] variety.

dove (Vatican 100 lire)

dove Christian symbol representing the Holy Ghost. In a more general sense, it also symbolizes spirituality or sublimation, i.e., the conversion of something inferior to something of a higher worth. It is also the universal symbol of peace.

The dove is found on various coins, particularly from the Middle Ages. Modern coins of the Vatican frequently display this symbol.

[J. E. Cirlot, *A Dictionary of Symbols* (2nd Ed.), Philosophical Library, New York, p. 85.]

downside Anything that detracts from the appearance of a coin or note without actually lowering its grade, such as unattractive tarnish.

drachm; drachma δραχμη [*Grk.*] 1. One of the basic denominations of ancient Greek coinage. It was a silver coin valued at six obols. Coins of multiples of the drachm were often struck, especially the tetradrachm (4 drachm coin). At various times and places, coins valued at 2, 4, 5, 6, 8, 10, and 12 drachmai were struck. See *Greek coinage (classical).*

Egyptian octadrachm (8 drachmai)

2. Series of thin silver Sassanian coins issued by the Persian dynasty of A.D. 226-641. Through the centuries the coins became progressively more abstract in design, especially after the fall of the dynasty when the area was under Arabian suzerainty. As can be seen in the illustration, some of the effigies were downright ghoulish, giving the coins the specter of death.

[Ewald Junge, *World Coin Encyclopedia*, p. 224.]

3. Unit of currency used by modern Greece since 1831.

Sassanian drachm

dreapta [*Rom.*] right (direction or position).

drei [*Ger.*] three.

dreißig [*Ger.*] thirty.

dreptunghiular [*Rom.*] rectangular.

drie [*Dut.*] three.

Drittel (*n.*) [*Ger.*] third (the fraction).

droite (*f.*) [*Fr.*] right (direction or position).

dronning (*c.*) [*Dan., Nor.*] queen.

drop-gate Iron grating on medieval buildings which was lowered to prevent entrance. It is found both as a mint mark and as a primary device on many British coins. See *portcullis* for additional information and illustration.

drottning (*f.*) [*Swed.*] queen.

drucken (*v.*) [*Ger.*] to print.

drukken (*v.*) [*Dut.*] to print.

drukować (*v.*) [*Pol.*] to print.

dua [*Indo.*] two.

duas (*f.adj.*) [*Port.*] two.

Dublin money Irish crowns and halfcrowns stamped from cut pieces of flattened silver plate in 1643. The crowns show a stamp with the letters "Vs" (five shillings) and the halfcrowns have "IIs VId" (two shillings sixpence). They were produced during the Great Rebellion.

Dublin crown

ducat Coin variously struck by Austria, Austrian States, Batavian Republic, Czech Republic, German States, Hungary, Indonesia, Kingdom of Holland, The Netherlands, Poland, Sweden, and the Swiss Cantons.

Its origin was that of a gold (or occasionally silver) coin, first struck in Venice in the late thirteenth century. The ducat was a very successful trade coin because of its fineness,

weight, and consistency. Although it was primarily an Italian coin, it was eventually adopted by other European countries. The coin in the illustration is a Netherlands 2 ducat gold piece of 1750.

1750 Netherlands 2 ducats

ducaton [also written *ducatoon*] Large silver coin of The Netherlands issued from the late sixteenth to the late eighteenth centuries. It was of high grade silver (.941 fine) and was intended to be equal in value to the gold ducat. Because of its design, it is often referred to as a *Silver Rider*[q.v.].

due [*Ital.*] two.

duì huàn lù 兑换率 [*Chin.-py./sc.*] exchange rate.

duizend [*Dut.*] thousand.

dunkel [*Ger.*] dark.

Dunmow token English trade token commemorating the Dunmow Flitch and issued to alleviate a coin shortage in the 1790s. They were struck by Peter Skidmore who probably made them not with the intent that they would actually circulate but to sell to collectors.

Two types exist, one showing the town arms with the inscription *MAY DUNMOW FLOURISH* and the other apparently displaying a headless pig and inscribed *PAYABLE AT DUNMOW ESSEX*.

The Dunmow Flitch is the odd story of a man named Fitzwalter who offered a flitch, an old term for a side of bacon, to any newly married couple who could swear under oath that after twelve months and one day of marriage, neither had transgressed against the other and neither had even for one moment regretted being married. After Fitzwalter's death, the custom was retained. According to

legend, for the next five centuries only six couples successfully claimed the flitch. It was from this tale that the expression "Bringing home the bacon" was coined.

[David Thompson, "Dunmow token reverses have nothing to do with Dunmow," *World Coin News*, November 7, 1994, p. 26.]

duplicaat (*n.*) [*Dut.*] a duplicate.

duplicado (*m.; adj.*) [*Span., Port.*] duplicate.

duplikat (*n.*) [*Nor.*]; (*m.*) [*Pol.*] a duplicate.

Duplikat (*n.*) [*Ger.*] a duplicate.

dupliziert (*adj.*) [*Ger.*] duplicate.

Durchmesser (*m.*) [*Ger.*] diameter, diametre.

durch Schnitt entwertet [*Ger.*] cut cancellation.

duro (*m.*) [*Span.*] crown (numismatic term for a large silver coin).

duży [*Pol.*] large.

dwa [*Pol.*] two.

dwadzieścia [*Pol.*] twenty.

dwt. (abbr.) pennyweight[*q.v.*]. The abbreviation *pwt.* is also used.

dyo δύο [*Grk.*] two.

dziesięć [*Pol.*] ten.

dziura (*f.*) [*Pol.*] hole.

E e

eagle 1. Symbol of high spiritual principle found on the coins of many nations. It is the bird association with courage, power, and war. Because the eagle lives in the full light of the sun, it is considered to be luminous in its essence and shares in the elements of air and fire. Its identification with the sun (which fertilizes female nature) makes it a symbol of masculinity.

In pre-Columbian America, eagles represented the struggle between the higher spirit and the lower world. The eagle with a serpent in its beak, as seen on Mexican coins, follows this line of symbolism. That eagle, which represents the higher order, conquers the snake, a symbol of evil. According to ancient Aztec legend, the Aztecs were foretold to build their capital where they saw the eagle and the serpent. As per the legend, they found such an eagle and built their capital where Mexico City now stands.

[J. E. Cirlot, *A Dictionary of Symbols* (2nd Ed.), pp. 91-92.]

Mexican eagle

2. Official name of the U.S. $10 gold piece authorized by the act of April 2, 1792. The first coins were struck in 1795 and produced intermittently until 1933.

The denomination is named for the national bird, the bald eagle (*haeliatus leucocephalus*). The renderings on the various reverse designs are either so stylized or unskilled that it is impossible to distinguish the bald eagle on the coins from the other eagle native to North America, the golden eagle.

The earliest issues (1795-1804) were of 22 carat gold (.9167 pure). Later issues were of .900 gold and .100 copper.

From 1795 to 1905, the obverse designs were of the Liberty Head types. The issues from 1838 to 1907 were known specifically as the *Coronet* type. In 1907 a stylized Indian Head design was introduced. Quarter eagles ($2.50, 1796-1929), half eagles ($5, 1795-1929), and double eagles ($20, 1849-1933) were also issued.

[Contributed by Halbert Carmichael.]

earliest known banknote A 10 kwan note of the Tang dynasty (A.D. 650-656) in China is considered to be the first banknote ever issued anywhere in the world. Although no specimens are known to exist today, an illustration of this note appears in *Ch'uan Pu T'ung Chih*, an early Chinese historical work. The note is presumed to be approximately 9" x 5 7/8" (22.8 cm x 14.9 cm) in size.

earliest known coin The earliest coins are believed to have originated in Lydia in western Asia Minor (now part of modern Turkey) around 620-600 B.C. These coins were made by stamping minute lumps of electrum, an unrefined mix of approximately three parts gold to one part silver as found in nature. The stamping consisted of a simple punch which went into the metal deeply enough to show that

the nugget was not merely a piece of plated base metal. The obverses featured a lioness, lion's head, or griffin. The reverse stamping showed little more than incuse squares or swastika-like designs.

See *electrum* and *Greek coinage (classical).*

eccellente [*Ital.*] excellent.

échanger (*v.*) [*Fr.*] to trade.

echt [*Ger., Dut.*] authentic, genuine.

echtheidskenmerk (*n.*) [*Dut.*] anti-counterfeiting device.

écu d'or of Philip VI

écu (*m.*) [*Fr.*] literally, *shield*.

1. French gold coin known as the *écu d'or* ("écu of gold"). It was introduced by Louis IX who ruled from 1226-70. The *écu d'or* was not on par with silver coins of its time and did not circulate.

Philip VI re-introduced the *écu d'or* during his reign (1328-50) as a highly regarded coin of pure gold. It remained the primary gold coin of France until Louis XIII replaced it with his *louis d'or* in 1640. As can be seen from the illustration, Philip's *écu d'or* is a magnificent coin showing the king sitting on the throne of France. The reverse shows a shield from which the coin got its name. The pieces issued by Philip's successors were slightly smaller and not of pure gold, but they were still considered quite reliable.

2. Large silver coin struck intermittently in France from 1641 until the overthrow of the monarchy in 1793. The *écu d'argent*, or "silver écu" as it is sometimes called, was introduced by Louis XIII as part of his monetary reform aimed at bringing integrity to the nation's coinage and at providing a rival for the popular Austrian *Thaler*.

As was the case with the *écu d'or*, the silver *écu*'s name was derived from the shield that appeared on the reverse of the first issues. The coin is noted for having been one of the earliest European coins regularly produced on a screw press.

See *Louis* for illustration of *écu d'argent*.

[Richard G. Doty, *The Macmillan Encyclopedic Dictionary of Numismatics*, pp. 116-18.]

3. Name chosen by the European Economic Community for its proposed common currency. The word *ecu* (usually written without the accent mark) is an acronym for "European Currency Unit."

edge The outside portion of a coin, medal, or token which lies at a 90° angle relative to the faces of the coin. In other words, it is the part of the coin that would touch paper if the coins were rolled.

Edges often are reeded, lettered, or show other devices as ways of preventing clipping or as anti-counterfeiting devices. In today's world of token coinage, fancy edges are mostly used as decorations.

See *lettered edge* and *security edge.*

Edward Name of eight British kings.

1. Edward I [a.k.a. *Longshanks*] (1239-1307, reigned 1272-1307); groat (silver fourpence) introduced during his reign. Edward II (1284-1327, reigned 1307-27); similar coinage to that of Edward I except that no groats were issued. Edward III (1312-77, reigned 1327-77); very extensive coinage; silver halfpennies and farthings were debased in 1335, yet an impressive gold coinage was introduced in 1344. Edward IV (1442-83, reigned 1461-70 and 1471-83); gold ryal and angel coins introduced. Edward V (1470-83; uncrowned king 1483); some dispute as to whether any coins were struck under this reign, if, in fact, there actually was a reign. Shortly after the death of his father, Edward IV, the 12-year-old Edward V and his brother were imprisoned in the Tower of London by their uncle, Richard, Duke of Gloucester, and were never seen again. Any coins attributed to his reign are in question. Edward VI (1537-53, reigned 1547-53); beginning of the coinage reforms

necessitated by the debasement of his father, Henry VIII[q.v.].

2. Edward VII [a.k.a. the *Peacemaker*.] King of Great Britain and Ireland and Emperor of India (1901-10). Born November 9, 1841, at Buckingham Palace in London; died there on May 6, 1910.

Although Edward VII waited until he was fifty-nine years old to become king, he had actually taken over many ceremonial duties from his mother, Queen Victoria, after his father, Prince Albert, died in 1861. Yet he had been totally excluded from the meaningful elements of his future position.. When he finally became king, he was far more interested in pleasure than in affairs of state. His marriage to Princess Alexandra of Denmark was harmonious, yet his extra-marital affairs with numerous women, both at home and abroad, often caused scandal and gossip.

Because he was king for only a short time, his coinage was limited. Among the most desirable coins bearing his likeness are some of the gold sovereigns minted in Canada and Australia, as well as the earliest Australian silver coins dated 1910, the year of his death.

3. Edward VIII [né *Edward Albert Christian George Andrew Patrick David*; known as the *Duke of Windsor* after his abdication.] Uncrowned king of Great Britain and Northern Ireland, and Emperor of India (January 20-December 11, 1936; born June 23, 1894, at Richmond Park in Surrey, England; died May 28, 1972, in Paris.

Edward VIII had hoped to make the monarchy reflect the social attitudes of the time. Although he had little interest in politics, he was concerned about the plight of the masses. During World War I, he served in Italy, France, and Egypt but could not serve on the front lines due to his status as Prince of Wales.

Ten months after his accession to the throne, he made it known that he wished to marry an American, Wallis Simpson, twice divorced. This marriage was so inconsistent with his position as Head of the Church of England that he was forced to choose. In announcing his abdication on December 11, 1936, he gave up the throne for, as in his own words, "the woman I love." From that time, he was known as "His Royal Highness, Prince Edward, Duke of Windsor."

Edward's unexpected abdication threw the mints of the British Commonwealth into turmoil. Dies which were being prepared with his effigy had to be scrapped and hastily replaced with those of his brother, now King George VI. Britain had been planning to introduce a new large brass 12-sided threepence intended to supplement and ultimately replace the smaller coins of low-grade silver which had circulated for many years. A few experimental brass threepences with Edward's likeness were struck and were to be sent to vending machine manufacturers. Several got into circulation and are now in the hands of collectors. Similarly, a small number of 1937 proof sets were struck with his effigy, but none was issued.

The most readily available coins of his reign are some colonial issues dated 1936. They were issued for British West Africa (copper-nickel penny, halfpenny, and tenth-penny), British East Africa (bronze 5 cents and 10 cents), Fiji (copper-nickel penny), and New Guinea (bronze penny). Most of these are inexpensive and easily obtained.

Edward VIII's portrait can be found on some paper money, such as the Canadian 1923 $2 notes. Because he was not yet king, his title is stated as Duke of Wales.

[Contributed by Ruth Ann Davis. *Encyclopedia Americana*, Vol. 9, pp. 745-46; Stephen Mitchell & Brian Reeds (editors), *Coins of England and the United Kingdom* (Seaby, 1991), pp. 323-25 et al.]

één [*Dut.*] one.

efigie (*f.*) [*Span.*] effigy.

efígie (*f.*) [*Port.*] effigy.

efterligne (*v.*) [*Dan.*] to duplicate.

efterligning (*c.*) [*Dan.*] imitation.

egcharaksi εγχάραξη (*f.*) [*Grk.*] intaglio.

egenværdi [*Dan.*] intrinsic.

egenverdi [*Nor.*] intrinsic.

egglifo έγγλυφο (*n.*) [*Grk.*] incuse.

égratignure (*f.*) [*Fr.*] a scratch.

egy [*Hun.*] one.

Egyesült Királyság [*Hun.*] United Kingdom (U.K.).

egyirányba néző kettős portré [*Hun.*] conjoined, accolated, jugate.

egyoldalú (pénz, érem) [*Hun.*] uniface.

egzerga (*f.*) [*Pol.*] exergue.

ehdotettu tarjous [*Finn.*] suggested bid.

Eichmarkierung (*f.*) [*Ger.*] adjustment mark.

eingekapselte Briefmarke (*f.*); **eingekapselte Marke** (*f.*) [*Ger.*] encased postage stamp.

eingraviert [*Ger.*] engraved.

eins [*Ger.*] one.

einstufen (*v.*) [*Ger.*] to grade.

einzigartig [*Ger.*] unique.

Éire [*Ire.*] Ireland.

Éirí Amac Na Casca 1916 [*Ire.*] Irish Easter Rising 1916. Edge inscription on Republic of Ireland 10 shilling commemorative coins of 1966 honoring Patrick Pearce.

Eisen (*n.*) [*Ger.*] iron (the metal).

ej cirkulerad [*Swed.*] uncirculated.

ejemplar (*m.*) [*Span.*] specimen.

ejemplar firmado (*m.*) [*Span.*] signed example. Reference to paper notes which include the signatures of the appropriate authorities.

ej utgiven [*Swed.*] not issued.

ekato εκατό [*Grk.*] hundred.

ekatommirio εκατομμύριο (*n.*) [*Grk.*] million.

ekatontaeterida εκατονταετηρίδα (*f.*) [*Grk.*] centennial, centenary.

ekdosi έκδοση (*f.*) [*Grk.*] an issue, issuance.

ek-myon-tan-wi 액면단위 [*Kor.*] denomination.

eksemplar (*n.*) [*Nor.*] specimen.

eksergi [*Finn.*] exergue.

eksponować (*v.*) [*Pol.*] to exhibit.

ekspozycja (*f.*) [*Pol.*] exhibition.

ekte [*Nor.*] authentic, genuine.

elachisti prosfora ελάχιστη προσφορά (*f.*) [*Grk.*] minimum bid.

eladni (*v.*) [*Hun.*] to sell.

eladó [*Hun.*] seller.

elcserélni (*v.*) [*Hun.*] to trade.

elde etme [*Turk.*] acquisition.

eldgammel [*Nor.*] ancient.

electro (*m.*) [*Span., Port.*] electrum.

electrotype A non-fraudulent copy or an illegal counterfeit copy of a coin or medal made by use of an electroplating process in which metal is electroplated onto a cast mold of the original coin or medal.

In the nineteenth and early twentieth centuries, reproductions of scarce pieces were made for educational or research purposes. Electrotypes were the highest quality copies which could be made with the technology of its day.

This same technique was also one method of producing counterfeit coins. A counterfeit piece manufactured by this method can most easily be detected by examining the edge. Because the plated objects are usually uniface, the obverse and the reverse of the coin are separate pieces which must be joined together to form one counterfeit coin (or, for that matter, a non-fraudulent copy). A seam will appear around the edge where the two pieces have been attached.

[Richard G. Doty, *The Macmillan Encyclopedic Dictionary of Numismatics*, pp. 119-20.]

electrum A mixture usually comprising approximately three parts gold to one part silver which is found in that state in Nature. It was from this natural alloy that the first coins (as we know the term) were minted. Most authorities believe that this earliest coinage originated around 620-600 B.C. in Lydia in western Asia Minor.

The use of natural electrum became unpopular for coinage because the ratio of gold to silver could vary considerably. Mixtures could be found with too much silver and not enough gold. In order to achieve consistency, the two precious metals were separated and coins were then minted with exclusively gold alloys, exclusively silver alloys, or controlled mixtures of the two. Nevertheless, natural electrum was still used sporadically even into the Middle Ages.

elektron [*Finn., Hun.*]; (*r.*) [*Swed.*]; ήλεκτρον (*n.*) [*Grk.*] electrum.

elektrotyyppi [*Finn.*] electrotype.

elektrum [*Turk.*]; (*n.*) [*Nor., Dan.*]; (*m.*) [*Pol.*] electrum.

Elektrum (*n.*) [*Ger.*] electrum.

elenco dei proprietari precendenti [*Ital.*] pedigree.

elettro (*m.*) [*Ital.*] electrum.

elhomályosodás [*Hun.*] tarnish.

Elizabeth I (nicknamed *Gloriana, Good Queen Bess*, and *The Virgin Queen.*) Queen of England and Ireland from 1558 to 1603. Born September 7, 1533, in Greenwich (near London). Died March 23 or 24, 1603, in Richmond (also near London).

Elizabeth was the daughter of King Henry VIII and Anne Boleyn. In 1536 Henry became disenchanted with Anne Boleyn and had her beheaded. Elizabeth, whom Henry now declared to be illegitimate, spent most of her early life at Hatfield House in Hertfordshire where she was virtually a prisoner. While she received an excellent classical education, she also had the chance to observe the endless parade of political and religious intrigue taking place around her. These experiences helped sharpen the skills she would someday need to survive the volatile political environment of her time.

In 1544 Elizabeth was reinstated to her proper place in line for the throne by an act of Parliament. While her half-sister Mary was queen, Elizabeth spent some time imprisoned in the tower of London for suspected treason. When Mary died in 1558, Elizabeth ascended to the throne at the age of twenty-five. One of her first acts as queen was to re-establish the Anglican Church which had been abolished by Mary in favor of Roman Catholicism. Since the majority of her subjects were Protestants, this act gained her immediate popularity which she retained throughout her reign.

Sixteenth-century England was nearly bankrupt and defenseless due to an unpopular war which was fought jointly with Spain against France. Using her extraordinary statesmanship, she brought to England a much-needed and relatively prosperous peace.

In 1587, Elizabeth followed the advice of one of her advisers, Sir Francis Walsingham, to execute her cousin, Mary Queen of Scots, because this Mary was another Roman Catholic whose supporters were trying to overthrow Elizabeth. The execution outraged Spanish King Philip II (himself a Roman Catholic), and

in 1588 he sent the Spanish Armada to attack England. Thanks in part to a great storm which sank many of the Spanish ships, Elizabeth's navy defeated the Armada, establishing England as a legitimate European power and Protestantism as a force in international politics.

Elizabeth, who never married and left no heirs, was the last of the Tudor rulers of England. It is from her famed virginity that the U.S. states of Virginia and West Virginia were presumably named.

Elizabeth's forty-five years of rule provided a wide range of coin denominations. Gold coins were struck both in *crown* gold (22 cts., .916 fineness) and *fine* gold (23 1/2 cts. to 23 3/4 cts., approximately .980 fineness). Base-silver shillings issued under Edward VI were called in and counterstamped for recirculation at reduced values. A silver coin with the rather curious denomination of three farthings was introduced as a way of making change if a purchase for one farthing were paid with a penny. A silver farthing would have been an impossibly small coin to strike.

Most of Elizabeth's reign saw the continuation of Edward VI's coinage reforms intended to undo the damage caused by Henry VIII's flagrant debasement. As part of her program, a new mintage facility was constructed, its completion coming in December 1560. It was known as the *Upper Mint* and later as the *Irish Mint* because it was ultimately used to strike coins for Ireland. Yet two years before her death in 1601, gold and silver coins were reduced in weight and purity.

One of Elizabeth's greatest contributions to numismatics was the introduction during her reign of the screw-type coinage press, partially powered by a horse-drawn mill. These *milled coins* were infinitely better in quality than the previous *hammered coins*, yet they did not achieve immediate popularity because the process was slow and inefficient. The inventor, Eloye Mestrelle, produced some coins with this method from 1561 until he was dismissed in 1572, six years before he was hanged for counterfeiting. The two coining techniques

The many faces of Queen Elizabeth II

were used more or less concurrently in Britain until 1662 when an improved version of the mechanical press permanently ended production of hammered coins. [See *hammered coin* for comparative illustrations of the two types of Elizabethan shillings.]

[Sir Authur Bryant, *The Elizabethan Deliverance*; Mary M. Luke, *Gloriana: The Years of Elizabeth I*; Stephen Mitchell & Brian Reeds (editors), *Coins of England and the United Kingdom* (Seaby, 1991), 168-76, 218; Clifton Potter, "Images of Majesty," *The Numismatist*, June 1991, pp. 858-62, et al.]

Elizabeth II (full name Elizabeth Alexandra Mary, of the house of Windsor.) Queen of Great Britain and Northern Ireland since 1952. Born in London in 1926 of (the future) King George VI and Queen Mother Elizabeth.

Unlike her namesake Elizabeth I, Queen Elizabeth II has never had to behead anyone to keep her throne. Her biggest threat is her own family. While Elizabeth II has always maintained the decorum of her position and is loved by the majority of her subjects, her children have scandalized their positions to the point of having weakened the very structure of the British monarchy. Only time will tell whether the throne will survive.

No matter what the future may bring, Elizabeth II has established an indelible place in numismatic history by having appeared on more different coins than anyone else in the history of the world. She is the only human being to have her effigy placed on more than a thousand type coins. These coins range from the common circulating coins of Britain, Canada, Australia, and New Zealand to the 1976 and 1988 Canadian Olympic commemoratives. They also include such diverse items as the *Angel* gold bullion pieces of the Isle of Man to the non-circulating legal tender[q.v.] coin sets of Gibraltar and even to the Cook Islands crowns which show on their reverse the blatant frontal nudity of the fertility god Tangaroa. A similar incarnation

has appeared on Commonwealth banknotes. In total, Elizabeth's portrait has appeared on the coins or notes of the United Kingdom, Canada, New Zealand, Australia, the Bahamas, Bermuda, Seychelles, South Africa, Gilbraltar, Southern Rhodesia, Rhodesia and Nyasaland, Cook Islands, Guernsey, Jersey, Nigeria, Fiji, British West Africa, the Gambia, Hong Kong, British Caribbean Territories, British Hondorus, Ceylon, Cyprus, Mauritius, Jamaica, Malaya and British Borneo, Isle of Man, East Africa, and Cayman Islands.

Elizabeth II has had the good grace to allow her coins to age as she herself has aged (unlike her great-great-grandmother Victoria whose 18-year-old effigy still appeared on some coins even when Victoria was in her sixties). As can be seen from the illustrations, coins and notes show Elizabeth's progression from a young woman to a mature dowager.

elle dövülerek yapılmış para [*Turk.*] hammered coin.

elli [*Turk.*] fifty.

Elmali Hoard Approximately 2000 ancient Greek and Lycian silver coins were supposedly excavated around April 1984 from a site near Elmali in the southern Anatolia region of Turkey and then illegally smuggled out of that country. Some of the coins were struck as early as the fifth century B.C. Included in the lot were 14 decadrachms, large rare coins from ancient Athens.

This collection is also known as the *Decadrachm Hoard.*

["Turkey Files Lawsuit to Regain Coin Hoard", *Coin World*, January 17, 1990, p. 1 et al; Ozgen Acar and Melik Kaylan, "Hoard of the Century," *Coin World*, July 6, 1988, p. 1 et al.]

elnök [*Hun.*] president.

előfizetés [*Hun.*] prepayment.

előlap; előoldal [*Hun.*] front; obverse.

elongated coin Oval-shaped souvenir made from a coin squeezed through a machine which also imprints a design on one side. The other side usually shows a flattened and stretched-out image of the original coin. This is also sometimes known as a *stretched coin* or *pinched penny.*

In the strictest sense, elongating U.S. coins is a violation of federal law which prohibits the defacing of money, but prosecutions for this type of activity are virtually nonexistent.

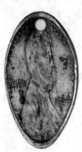

elongated cent

Elveţia [*Rom.*] Switzerland.

emas [*Indo.*] gold.

emergency currency Unofficial coins or paper money issued to fill a void when officially-issued money is not available.

The need for emergency money most frequently arises during times of war or economic depression. In wartime, military leaders sometimes have been forced to produce what is known as *campaign money* as a means of paying their troops. Coin shortages caused by war led to the production of *siege tokens*, unauthorized coins struck by the officials of cities and towns under attack to enable commerce to continue.

The third type of emergency money necessitated by war was *insurrectionists' coinage*, also known as *revolutionary money*[q.v.]. These pieces were issued by opposition military leaders during revolutions both for the purpose of paying followers and for the propaganda value inherent in issuing one's own coins. Pancho Villa's *Death Wish* peso from the Mexican Revolution is one of the most popular and best known of these pieces.

Economic crises have led to the creation of a wide variety of emergency coins and notes, ranging from the *Hard Times tokens*[q.v.] of nineteenth century United States to the German and Austrian *Notgeld* and French *Chamber of Commerce tokens* of the post-World War I era.

The American tokens were privately issued to combat the critical shortage of minor coins. The Notgeld coins and notes were both the result of and the contributor to the worst inflationary period that the world has ever seen. Virtually anyone with access to a printing press printed his own money.

[Ewald Junge, *World Coin Encyclopedia*, p. 99.]

emettere (*v.*) [*Ital.*] to issue.

émettre (*v.*) [*Fr.*] to issue.

emisión (*f.*) [*Span.*] issue, issuance.

emisja (*f.*) [*Pol.*] issue, issuance.

emissão (*f.*) [*Port.*] issue, issuance.

emission An issue of a coin or banknote; e.g., "The 1948 emission of Canadian silver dollars was much smaller than that of the previous year."

émission (*f.*) [*Fr.*] issue, issuance.

emissione (*f.*) [*Ital.*] issue, issuance.

emitir (*v.*) [*Span., Port.*] to issue.

emitować (*v.*) [*Pol.*] to issue.

emitteren [*Dut.*] to issue.

emlék- (*adj.*) [*Hun.*] commemorative.

emlékpénz [*Hun.*] commemorative coin.

e-money The electronic transfer of funds by way of *smart cards* and other technological innovations. Purchases, even small ones, are made without the use of coins or notes. In theory, this type of money is harder to steal and easier for police to trace. Ultimately, it is expected to become a form of international currency, in that a smart card keyed to the currency of one country can be used in any other participating country with the current exchange rate calculated automatically.

emperador (*m.*) [*Span.*] emperor.

empereur (*m.*) [*Fr.*] emperor.

Emperor of Canadian Coins Popular name of the 1911 specimen Canadian silver dollar. Only three are known to exist, one of which was struck in lead. The silver pieces were patterns, and the lead specimen is correctly referred to as a trial striking of a pattern. One silver specimen is in private hands; the other two pieces reside in museums.

No regular-issue silver dollars were struck in Canada until 1935, but then they became a regular fixture in Canadian coinage.

1911 Canadian Dollar: The "Emperor"

Similarly, the *King of Canadian Coins* is the 1921 half dollar, although these are regular-issue coins that just happen to be excessively rare.

emsalsiz [*Turk.*] unique.

en [*Nor., Swed.*] one.

ena ένα [*Grk.*] one.

encased cent in Good Luck charm

encased coin Usually a U.S. cent pressed into a prepared hole in an aluminum holder or encasement. The latter may be a simple ring or have the outline of a horseshoe (for good luck) or an old-fashioned "pottie", the type most sought after by collectors. Encased coins may be of the advertising type or the souvenir type, depending on the legends in the aluminum area. The scarcer pieces are those containing coins other than a U.S. cent.

See *greeting token*.

[Contributed by Robert Doyle.]

encased postage stamp One of two major catagories of postage stamps which have

circulated as money. Since the 1860s, sixteen countries have used stamps encapsulated in windowed tokens as a way to combat shortages of minor coins.

Encased postage stamps were born during the U.S. Civil War (1861-65). Economic panic forced hard money, even minor coins, out of circulation. To alleviate this shortage, the federal government authorized that stamps could be used in lieu of coins. Loose stamps were impractical for circulation because they easily became lost or torn. In 1862, John Gault, an inventor and entrepreneur from Boston, Massachusetts, devised an encasement that made the circulation of stamps more practical. The invention essentially consisted of placing a stamp between a brass disk and a mica window. The cost of the encasement was to be absorbed by local merchants who could place their advertising message on the back side of the token. His invention proved to be a marketing failure, however, because the government soon started issuing fractional currency[q.v.] notes and private merchants introduced a series of small unofficial coins known as Civil War tokens[q.v.]. The encased postage stamps were discontinued because they proved to be less economical and therefore less desirable than these other items.

U.S. encased postage stamp

Post-World War I Germany and Austria saw a revival of encased postage stamps. The economic chaos of that period resulted in the issuance of great quantities of emergency money known in German as *Notgeld*[q.v.]. Tens of thousands of different paper notes, metallic coins, and pieces of money fabricated from silk, coal, linen, leather, and a host of other substances were produced to deal with the uncontrollable inflation. Encased postage stamps were included in this avalanche of paper and non-paper currencies.

The second category of postage stamps which have circulated as money simply consists of stamps or paper notes resembling stamps which have been used "naked" without encapsulation or have simply been affixed to a piece of cardboard and have circulated in that fashion.

See *postage stamp money*.

[Albert Pick, *Briefmarkengeld*, 1970; Richard G. Doty, *The Macmillan Encyclopedic Dictionary of Numismatics*, pp. 122-123.]

enchère (*f.*) [*Fr.*] (auction) bid.

encre (*f.*) [*Fr.*] ink.

en creux [*Fr.*] incuse.

en desuso [*Span.*] obsolete; in disuse.

endiksi nomismatokopiou ἔνδειξη νομισματοκοπείου [*Grk.*] mintmark.

endommagé [*Fr.*] damaged.

en el reverso [*Span.*] on the back; on the reverse.

en espera de aprobación [*Span.*] on approval.

enestående [*Dan.*] unique.

engelsk pund (*c.*) [*Dan.*] pound (unit of weight).

Englanti [*Finn.*] England.

ensidig [*Nor., Swed., Dan.*] uniface.

entalhe (*m.*) [*Port.*] intaglio.

Entwurf (*m.*) [*Ger.*] design.

epäsäännöllinen [*Finn.*] irregular.

epätäydellinen [*Finn.*] incomplete.

epävirallinen [*Finn.*] unofficial.

epigrafi ἐπιγραφή (*f.*) [*Grk.*] inscription; legend.

epi pistosi ἐπί πιστώσει [*Grk.*] on approval.

epitagi ἐπιταγή (*f.*) [*Grk.*] check, cheque.

épreuve numismatique (*f.*) [*Fr.*] proof (*re*: coins or medals).

eredeti [*Hun.*] original.

érem [*Hun.*] medal.

Erhaltungsgrad (*m.*) [*Ger.*] grade, condition.

erhvervelse (*c.*) [*Dan.*] acquisition.

erinomainen [*Finn.*] excellent.

érme [*Hun.*] coin.

eroare (*f.*) [*Rom.*] error.

erro (*m.*) [*Port.*] error.

érték [*Hun.*] value.

értékes [*Hun.*] valuable.

Erwerbung (*f.*) [*Ger.*] acquisition.

esaminare qualitativamente (*v.*) [*Ital.*] to grade.

escaso [*Span.*] scarce. In the strictest sense, this term generally indicates that from 200 to 1000 specimens are assumed to exist. The expression *muy escaso* ("very scarce") designates the existence of approximately 20 to 200 known specimens.

escasso [*Port.*] scarce, rare.

Escocia [*Span.*] Scotland.

Escócia [*Port.*] Scotland.

escudo (*m.*) 1. [*Span., Port.*] shield.

2. Spanish gold coin first issued in 1537 by Carlos V (Charles V) and continued until 1833. The authorization for this coin was part of the monetary reforms initiated in 1535. The escudo, also known as the *corona* (Spanish word for "crown"), was intended to compete with the Italian and French gold trade coins of the time. It was made of .9167 fine gold (22 carats) and was pegged at the value of 350 maravedís[*q.v.*] (referring to money of account, not the small copper coin).

[Manuel Moreno Fraginals and José A. Pulido Ledesma, *Cuba: A Country and Its Currency*, National Bank of Cuba, p. 28.]

escuro [*Port.*] dark.

esemplare (*m.*) [*Ital.*] specimen.

esergo (*m.*) [*Ital.*] exergue.

esfalmeni charaksi εσφαλμένη χάραξη [*Grk.*] badly struck.

eski [*Turk.*] old; ancient.

eskilik [*Turk.*] antiquity.

esoteriki aksia εσωτερική αξία (*f.*) [*Grk.*] intrinsic value.

Espagne [*Fr.*] Spain.

España [*Span.*] Spain.

Espanha [*Port.*] Spain.

Espanja [*Finn.*] Spain.

espèces (*f.pl.*) [*Fr.*] cash (ready money).

espécime (*m.*) [*Port.*] specimen.

esplêndido [*Port.*] excellent (grade or condition).

esporre (*v.*) [*Ital.*] to exhibit.

esposizione (*f.*) [*Ital.*] exhibition.

esquerdo [*Port.*] left (direction or position).

essai Also spelled *essay*.

1. Design of an issued coin struck on a planchet of a different thickness or different metal.

2. As it applies to any type of paper money, certificate, bond, check, etc., an *essai* is a design which differs totally or in part from the accepted, issued design. An essai can be complete or incomplete and can be in black and white or in color. These designs, sometimes called *trials*, are usually impressed on India paper or card and are often submitted for approval in a series of developmental

essai of 1899 U.S. silver certificate

stages so that changes can be made without reworking the entire die. Even when the basic design is accepted, some minute changes may still be made, such as the strengthening of lines to intensify shadows and bring out highlights.

[Contributed by Gene Hessler. Dr. Howard S. Friedman, "Essays, Proofs and Specimens," *The Essay-Proof Journal*, Vol. 31, No. 1, 1974, p. 17; Gene Hessler, *U.S. Essay, Proof, and Specimen Notes*, BNR Press, p. 32.]

Estados Unidos de América (*abbr.:* EE.UU.; E.U.A.) [*Span.*] United States of America (U.S.A.).

estampador ng moneda [*Tag.*] (coinage) die.

estampilla encapsulada (*f.*) [*Span.*] encased postage stamp.

estanho (*m.*) [*Port.*] tin.

estaño (*m.*) [*Span.*] tin.

estragado [*Port.*] damaged.

estrangeiro [*Port.*] foreign.

estrela (*f.*) [*Port.*] star.

estrella (*f.*) [*Span.*] star.

Észak-Írország [*Hun.*] Northern Ireland.

étain (*m.*) [*Fr.*] tin.

étampé [*Fr.*] Also known as *tampé, tempé, Creole tempé,* or *stampée.* Base metal coin first struck in 1763 by the French for use in the French West Indies. See *stampée.*

état de conservation [*Fr.*] grade, condition.

États-Unis d'Amérique [*Fr.*] United States of America (U.S.A.).

Etelä-Afrikka [*Finn.*] South Africa.

étoile (*f.*) [*Fr.*] star.

etos έτος [*Grk.*] year.

étranger [*Fr.*] foreign.

etusivu [*Finn.*] obverse; front.

europino Monetary denomination chosen in the early 1950s by a group of Europeans interested in establishing a European federation. A large number of unofficial silver coins, including 300 proofs, was struck in Hamburg, Germany, in 1952. These pieces, denominated at 5 europinos, show the inscription *Europa Fœderata.*

[Leon Lindheim, "Coins" Column, *The Plain Dealer* (Cleveland, Ohio), April 2, 1985, p. 38P.]

év [*Hun.*] year.

évaluer l'état de conservation (*v.*) [*Fr.*] to grade.

Ex Candoris Decus [*Lat.*] An ornament of dazzling whiteness (brightness).

excelente de la granada

excelente de la granada Spanish gold coin, also known simply as an *excelente,* which was first issued by Isabella and Ferdinand in 1497 as part of the monetary reforms dictated by the Pragmatic Sanction of Medina del Campo. Spain continued to strike the coin until 1537. This piece was so named because its reverse exhibits a pomegranate (*granada* in Spanish) symbolizing the city of Granada where a battle had been fought and won by Spanish Christian forces just five years earlier. The Spanish victory brought to an end many centuries of Moorish domination in Southern Spain.

Presumably, these were the first European coins ever minted from gold mined in the New World. The 1497 excelentes contained 3.54 grams of .989 fine gold. Its fixed value was 375 maravedís, although in this case the term maravedí referred to money of account, not to the popular small copper coin of the time.

Although the coin quickly became popular, its name did not. Within seven years everyone began calling it a *ducado* ("ducat" in English), due to its similarity to the popular Venetian gold coin of the same name.

As can be seen in the illustration, the coin has additional numismatic significance because of the unusual *vis-à-vis* (face-to-face) portraits. This configuration was necessary to indicate that Isabella and Ferdinand each was monarch over his or her own territory and that neither was superior to the other in rank.

[Manuel Moreno Fraginals and José A. Pulido Ledesma, *Cuba: A Country and Its Currency,* National Bank of Cuba, pp. 27-28.]

exemplaar (n.) [*Dut.*] specimen.

exemplaire (m.) [*Fr.*] a specimen, copy.

exergă (f.) [*Rom.*] exergue.

exergo (m.) [*Span., Port.*] exergue.

exergue A distinct area on some coins, tokens, and medals which lies below the central portion of the design and is usually set off by a straight line. It can contain such information as the date, mint mark, denomination, and designer's initials.

Exergual inscriptions can be found on Greek and Roman coins and are usually encountered on the reverse. They are seldom on the side of the head (obverse). Although an exergue is featured on several Greek coins, most often is does not bear inscriptions. An example of a Greek coin with exergual legends is the Katane tetradrachm by Herakleidas whose signature is perfectly placed in the exergue below a breathtaking quadriga.

Exergual inscriptions and legends are encountered on early Roman coinage, including the pre-denarius period; they become a feature of Roman Republic coinage most often with the name of the moneyers placed in this area.

In coins of the higher Roman Empire, the exergual inscription marks either Consular dates or Senatorial authority ("SC"), or more importantly, it directly applies to the subject typified on the reverse. In the mintages of the lower Roman Empire, letters or sometimes symbols (or a combination of both) generally serve to indicate the cities in which they were struck.

Mintmarks placed in the exergue became the norm around A.D. 250. The study of these marks has produced fascinating theories as well as very amply documented essays and endless controversies. When a coin bears a mintmark, the numismatic attribution is quite easy, and most collectors will thank Philip I who inaugurated the system of *officina* marks (workshop marks). The innovation was welcomed by contemporaries, too, and lasted until the fifth century. The name of the mint is reasonably spelled out on the coinage of the third and fourth centuries; thus we can read exergues such as LON (for Londinium), ANT (for Antiochia), T (for Ticinum), and many more. From the late 360s to the end of the Roman Empire the gold coinage invariably bears the words COM or COMOB in the exergue. COM was an abbreviation for *comitatus* (the place where the emperor resided, thus enabling him to exercise direct control on the mintage of the most precious of metals). OB stands for *obryza* or *obryziacum aurum* (refined gold). After A.D. 395 the formula COMOB is regularly featured on Roman gold reference to a high ranking official (the *comes obryziacus*) who guaranteed the quality of the gold, wherever it was struck.

Following a similar pattern, the exergual inscriptions on late Roman silver begin with the abbreviated name of the mint followed by the letters PS (*pusulatum*, pure silver)— the purity and quality of the metal being a fundamental factor for the acceptance of the currency. Throughout the Roman Empire skepticism on the purity and quality of gold and silver had grown through the centuries. In fact, in previous centuries the central authority, when faced with financial problems, meddled with the gold and silver content/alloy of aureii and denarii, which we see as an early example of coin debasement.

[Contributed by Giorgio Migliavacca. Harold Mattingly, *Roman Coins from the Earliest Times to the Fall of the Western Empire*; Andrew Burnett, *Coinage in the Roman World*; Giorgio Migliavacca, "Mint Marks need further research," *Moneta International*; William Seth Stevenson, *A Dictionary of Roman Coins*; R. David Sear, *Greek Coins and Their Values*.]

exergues on Roman follis (A.D. 305-6) & Italian L.100 (1974)

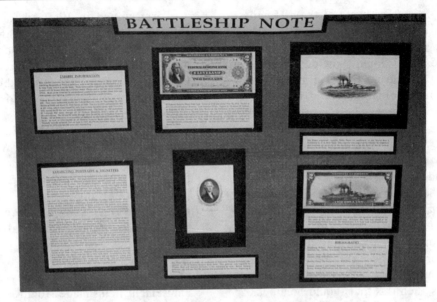

Exhibit of U.S. paper money created by John and Nancy Wilson

exhibiting The displaying of a coin, medal, token, or note collection for purposes of winning awards or of educating the public about numismatics.

Most exhibiting is competitive and takes place at local, regional, or national coin shows. The following information is based on the 1996 revised exhibiting rules and procedures established by the American Numismatic Association. Although A.N.A. exhibiting and judging criteria are not used universally, they are representative of the types of rules found everywhere.

Judging criteria do not place a premium on the collector value of the material being displayed. Rather, the rules emphasize information and creativity. The six principal areas of judging are,

—*Information* (35 points): Numismatic information must be accurate, thorough, relevant, timely, neat, concise, and interesting. It must be sufficiently complete to paint a clear and focused picture of what the exhibited material is all about. The information should help educate the viewer by supplying knowledge which is not generally known to most collectors, even to specialists in that type of material.

Numismatic exhibits should be treated the same as scholarly research papers. Factual information comes from some book, journal, or newspaper, and the names of all sources should be listed somewhere in the exhibit.

—*Presentation* (30 points): Originality, beauty, neatness, balance, and all other aesthetic elements fall under the heading of presentation. The best exhibits present good scholarship in an attractive and pleasing way.

The title should be the most noticeable single element in the exhibit. Not only must the title make a bold and clear statement but it must also be readily visible.

The informational sheets require absolute neatness as well as accuracy and easy visibility. Electric typewriters and word processors provide the highest quality work.

—*Completeness* (5 points): Completeness is the relationship between the title and material being displayed. Because the title is the single most important element in the exhibit, it should be very explicit and must not generalize. An exhibit is complete if and only if it contains all of the numismatic items indicated by its title.

—*Degree of difficulty* (10 points): This was added in 1996 to discourage exhibitors from limiting their displays to just one or two very

scarce pieces. It is an estimate of the difficulty that the exhibitor had in assembling the materials or in acquiring the information in the display. The exhibit should show dedication to collecting, in that the numismatic material or the related information was difficult to assemble or to present. This might include multiple rare pieces, new research, or a collection that took years to assemble.

—*Condition* (10 points): Exhibit rules instruct the judges only to award the maximum ten points if the displayed material is the best that is reasonably available to the collector. Exhibitors can greatly aid the judges by supplying information regarding any unusual grading matters. If the exhibited specimens really do compare well against all other existing pieces, then this fact should be noted.

—*Rarity* (10 points): The rarity of a numismatic item is judged by the number of like specimens believed to exist. The rules specify that the selling price should not be regarded as a measure for determining rarity.

And finally,

—*Best of Show* (separate judging): The criteria for determining Best of Show involve answers to the following questions: How consistently has the exhibit followed its announced title or theme? Does the display give a striking or exceptional effect, or is it merely average in its overall appearance? Does the exhibit add anything to numismatic knowledge not generally known to the average collector of this type of material? To what extent has careful research been accomplished as evidenced by the numismatic knowledge imparted to the viewer? Has credit been given to sources of numismatic written material? Would a non-collector understand the exhibit? To win Best of Show, an exhibit must provide affirmative responses to these questions.

[Information supplied by Joseph E. Boling and Robert L. Kriz. R. Scott Carlton, "The Art and Science of Numismatic Exhibiting," *The Numismatist*, April 1990, pp. 550-554, et al.]

exibição (*f.*) [*Port.*] exhibition.

exonumia [from Greek words *exo*, away from or out of, and *nomisma*, coin or custom.]

Term coined in 1960 by Russell Rulau to refer to most numismatic items other than coins, notes, or any other pieces issued by a government and intended as circulating money. Legitimate coins and notes which have been doctored in some way (e.g., love tokens) can fall into this group.

Although experts disagree as to exactly what should or should not be included in this category, the term is usually used to encompass tokens of all sorts, private scrip, advertising pieces resembling coins or notes, wooden nickels and flats, sales tax receipts, and other similar items. More peripherally are included medals, checks, encased coins, encased postage stamps and other philatelic items used as a temporary substitute for money, and jewelry or amusement items made from real coins.

Again, this list is not absolute. There currently exists no universally accepted definition of this word, except that everyone agrees that the term does not include coins and notes. Its meaning will continue to be modified until numismatists finally settle on one inclusive list of exactly which numismatic items the term encompasses.

See page 316 for color illustrations.

[Contributed by Robert Doyle.]

exonumist A numismatist who studies and collects exonumia.

exposition (*f.*) [*Fr.*] exhibition.

exposición (*f.*) [*Span.*] exhibition.

extranjero [*Span.*] foreign.

eye appeal Subjective characteristics of a coin which should not be taken into account when the coin is graded. Objective matters such as degree of wear and whether the coin has been cleaned determine the coin's grade. Nevertheless, a coin with attractive toning may well command a higher price than a similar coin of identical grade but with heavy unattractive tarnish.

The issue of eye appeal is the primary reason why many people refuse to buy coins sight-unseen, even when they have been graded by reputable grading services.

eyrekh nakuv עֵרֶךְ נָקוּב (*m.*) [*Heb.*] face value.

ezer [*Hun.*] thousand.

F f

face Front or primary side of a banknote or other certificate. The term *obverse* applies to coins and medals but should not be used in reference to paper money. The reverse side of a note is called the *back*.

face comerţ (*v.*) [*Rom.*] to trade.

Faciam Eos In Gentem Vnam [*Lat.*] I will make them one people (*Ezekiel 37:22*). Reference to the joining of England and Scotland in 1604 by James I (a.k.a. James VI of Scotland). This inscription appears on the gold unite[*q.v.*] issued to celebrate this event.

faire une mise; faire une offre (*v.*) [*Fr.*] to bid (at an auction or mail bid sale).

falsario (*m.*) [*Ital.*] counterfeiter.

fälschen (*v.*) [*Ger.*] to counterfeit.

Fälscher (*m.*) [*Ger.*] counterfeiter.

Fälschung (*f.*) [*Ger.*] a counterfeit; a fake, forgery.

Fälschungsschutz (*m.*) [*Ger.*] anti-counterfeiting device.

falsificação (*f.*) [*Port.*] a counterfeit; a fake, forgery.

falsificación (*f.*) [*Span.*] a counterfeit; a fake, forgery.

falsificador (*m.*) [*Span., Port.*] counterfeiter.

falsificare (*v.*) [*Ital.*] to counterfeit.

falskner (*c.*) [*Dan.*] counterfeiter.

falso (*m.; adj.*) [*Span., Ital.*] fake, forgery.

falsyfikat (*m.*) [*Pol.*] a fake.

fałszerstwo (*n.*) [*Pol.*] a counterfeit, fake, forgery.

fałszerz (*m.*) [*Pol.*] counterfeiter.

fałszować (*v.*) [*Pol.*] to counterfeit.

Falte (*f.*) [*Ger.*] fold, crease.

falten (*v.*) [*Ger.*] to crease.

Family ruble Large silver pieces struck at the Warsaw Mint in Poland in 1835 and 1836 under the auspices of the Russian government as part of the Russo-Polish series. The effigy of Czar Nicholas I appears on the obverse with the denomination given both in Russian (1 1/2 rubles) and in Polish (10 zlotych). However, it is the reverse design which is of the greatest interest to collectors. The czar's wife, Empress Alexandra, is shown in the center surrounded by their seven children. The bust at the top is that of Czarevich Alexander who later became Czar Alexander II. The designer was Heinrich Gube who patterned these pieces after a similarly-designed thaler issued by Bavaria in 1828.

Family Ruble

In the strictest sense, these items were not coins but a semi-official striking tolerated by Nicholas I, who presumably gave out most of

the original strikings to high-ranking collectors. The 1835 issues are considered patterns and are very rare, but there were dozens of 1836 pieces struck using three different dies. Most of the 1836 specimens in collections today were actually struck after 1875 to satisfy collector demand. Restrikes can be distinguished from originals by some reverse die deterioration on the lower right rim.

[R.W. Julian, "Russia takes over Poland and coinage," *World Coin News*, November 7, 1994, pp. 18-20.]

fǎn miàn 反面 [*Chin.-py./sc.*] reverse.

Farbe (*f.*) [*Ger.*] color, colour.

farge (*m.*) [*Nor.*] color, colour.

fare un'offerta (*v.*) [*Ital.*] to bid (at an auction).

färg (*r.*) [*Swed.*] color, colour.

Elizabeth II farthing

farthing   A small British coin valued at one fourth of a penny. Its name is derived from the *fourthling*, meaning "one fourth". The last of the modern farthings of Britain were dated 1956; they were demonetized in 1960.

The farthing was the heir apparent of the many tokens issued privately during the Middle Ages which were intended to help satisfy the need for small-denomination coins. This shortage was brought on by the sudden economic changes resulting from the devastating effects of the bubonic plague in the fourteenth century. For several centuries thereafter, tokens were issued in a variety of shapes, sizes, metals, and specific values, although all from this group were intended to be fractional units of the penny. Most of these tokens came from merchants, but others were issued by monasteries to aid those people taking pilgrimages to the shrine of St. Thomas à Becket at Canterbury.

Perhaps it can be said that the farthing did not achieve legitimacy until May 19, 1613, when King James I authorized John Lord Harrington to issue copper farthings for use in England, Wales, and Ireland. Prior to this time, most of the farthing tokens had been of tin or lead and were unauthorized issues. The various authorized copper farthings did not gain much popularity, largely because many of them were underweight and easily counterfeited. This weight deficiency could possibly be attributed to the method by which some of these pieces were manufactured. Instead of being individually minted, the Harrington farthings were mass-produced on copper strips.

The late seventeenth century saw a revival of the use of tin in farthings. The pieces authorized in 1684 by Charles II were basically of tin but contained a small square copper plug in the center. The copper gave the coins nominal value and theoretically made the coins harder to counterfeit, although this proved not to be the case. The ultimate demise of the tin farthing came in 1693 when William and Mary forsook tin and issued their farthings in copper.

The evolution of the farthing continued until 1821 at which time George IV issued a farthing for domestic use. The reverse shows the familiar helmeted Britannia, a design that was retained until 1937 when the wren was substituted.

[Saul B. Needleman, "The Farthing as an Economic Necessity," *The Numismatist*, April 1987, pp. 764-770; Junge, p. 103 & 131; David Thompson, "Private sector struck 17th-century farthings," *World Coin News*, September 25, 1995, pp. 15-16.]

fasces   Bundle of rods, usually bound by a leather cord or strap, and topped with an ax blade. It was an ancient Roman symbol of strength and authority. Among the coins exhibiting the fasces are the U.S. Mercury (Winged Liberty) Dimes of 1916-1945 and some of the 2 lira Italian coins issued by Benito Mussolini in the 1920s. Historians have pointed out the irony of these two issues: Mussolini removed the olive branch from the fasces on his coins and lost the war; the U.S. kept the olive branch and won.

[David W. Lange, "Mercury Dimes— Challenging Yet Affordable," *The Numismatist*, Feb. 1989, p. 289.]

fast [*Ger.*] almost.

faţă (*f.*) [*Rom.*] front.

faux (*m.; adj.*) [*Fr.*] fake.

fazer uma oferta (*v.*) [*Port.*] to make an offer; to bid (at an auction or mail bid sale).

F.D.C. [*Fr. abbr.*] *fleur de coin.* 1. Uncirculated condition; mint state. 2. Very high quality, often used to describe gem proof coins or medals as well as superior business strikes.

feble (*m.*) [*Span.*] Debased coin which circulated in Bolivia during the middle of the nineteenth century.

fecha (*f.*) [*Span.*] date.

fecha alterada (*f.*); **fecha retocada** (*f.*) [*Span.*] altered date.

Fehler (*m.*) [*Ger.*] defect; error.

fehlgeprägt [*Ger.*] mis-struck.

Fehlprägung (*f.*) [*Ger.*] a mis-strike.

feil (*m.*) [*Nor.*] error.

feilpregening (*m.*) [*Nor.*] a mis-strike.

feilpreget [*Nor.*] mis-struck.

fejl (*c.*) [*Dan.*] error.

fejlpræget [*Dan.*] mis-struck.

fejlprægning (*c.*) [*Dan.*] a mis-strike.

fekete [*Hun.*] black.

fekete piac [*Hun.*] black market.

fel (*n.*) [*Swed.*] error.

fél (*adj.*) [*Hun.*] half.

felaktig [*Swed.*] defective.

fele valaminek [*Hun.*] half (the fraction).

felt One of the more unusual materials upon which Notgeld[q.v.] (emergency money) was printed during the inflationary period in Germany and Austria from 1919-1922. Although most Notgeld was produced in the form of paper notes of varying sizes and designs, some was printed on silk, cloth, leather, and linen, and a number of metal coins were struck.

Much of the Notgeld, particularly those pieces made from these unusual substances, was not really intended to circulate as money but was manufactured as souvenirs and novelties. Many of the items were very bright and attractive, portraying comical or satirical motifs.

[Charles J. Opitz, *Odd and Curious Money: Descriptions and Values*, p. 30.]

felírás; felirat [*Hun.*] inscription; legend.

felpräglad [*Swed.*] mis-struck.

felprägling (*r.*) [*Swed.*] a mis-strike.

felülbélyegzés [*Hun.*] overprint.

fem [*Nor., Swed., Dan.*] five.

fém [*Hun.*] metal.

fémlapka [*Hun.*] planchet.

fémszál [*Hun.*] metal thread (put into banknote paper as a form of anti-counterfeiting device).

femti [*Nor.*] fifty.

femtio [*Swed.*] fifty.

fenék [*Hun.*] bottom.

fénynyomás [*Hun.*] photogravure.

fer (*m.*) [*Fr.*] iron (metal).

Ferracute Machine Company American manufacturer of coinage presses. This company, based in Bridgeton, New Jersey, gained a major reputation in this field when it was chosen to supply mintage equipment for the Philadelphia Mint in the late nineteenth century.

In 1896, Ferracute was asked to build three mints in China, two for the production of brass *tsen* ("cash") coins and one solely for the minting of silver coins. The Chinese recognized the need to modernize their method of coinage production, as they were still making coins by pouring molten metal into molds just as their ancestors had done generations before. Even more importantly, the Chinese wished to create a monetary system which was more in line with those of the Western world. They felt that Ferracute could help them in both regards.

Because of delays, thievery, and constant disputes with local government agents, the Chinese project turned out to be a much greater headache than the Ferracute executives ever imagined. The coinage equipment was so terribly rusted when it arrived at its various destinations that the top government officials thought that Ferracute was trying to unload old second-hand machinery on them. The dies, which were equally rusted, left unsightly blisters on the surfaces of the coins. Yet the top officials were delighted with the coins, noting that the blemishes would make the coins much more difficult to counterfeit.

As difficult as the China adventure was, it enhanced Ferracute's reputation so much that governments throughout the world asked the company to supply them with minting presses. Other governments even requested that Ferracute build entire minting facilities. In its day, Ferracute was truly regarded as one of the premier manufacturers of coinage machinery.

[Arthur J. Cox and Thomas Malim, *Ferracute: The History of an American Enterprise*, Bridgeton, New Jersey: Cowan Printing, Inc., 1985; Arthur J. Cox and Thomas Malim, "Ferracute Goes to China," *The Numismatist*, October 1988, pp. 1748-1756.]

ferro (*m.*) [*Ital., Port.*] iron (metal).

ferrugem (*f.*) [*Port.*] rust.

Feuchtwanger's metal See *German silver.*

feuille se soumission des offres [*Fr.*] bid sheet.

Feversham British frigate which sank off the coast of Nova Scotia on Oct. 7, 1711. Although salvage attempts were made as early as 1712, success was not achieved until 1982.

The 636 coins recovered from the wreckage have given numismatic scholars a great deal of new information regarding currency usage and distribution in Colonial America. Prior to the discovery of this hoard, numismatists had been unaware of the extent to which the Massachusetts silver pieces, including the Pine Tree shillings, had circulated. A number of the coins were also found to be sheared, i.e., cut into two or more equal pieces for use as small change.

The *Feversham* is the first known ship to have carried plugged[q.v.] coins. There were underweight Spanish-American 4- and 8-real pieces that were plugged with additonal silver to bring their weight up to par.

[Joseph R. Lasser, "The Remarkable *Feversham* Hoard," *The Numismatist*, February 1989, pp. 234-37 & 291-94.]

fiat money 1. Paper money which is good in trade only because its issuing agency (a government, bank, or whatever) has decreed that the money has value and people generally accept it as such. In recent years most fiat money has not been backed by gold, silver, or anything else of intrinsic value. Its acceptability is largely dependent upon people's confidence in the agency that issued it, such as the governments of the world's nations.

2. General term referring to any paper money which cannot be automatically exchanged for gold or silver.

ficha (*f.*) [*Span.*] token.

fiduciaire [*Fr.*] fiduciary; *monnaie fiduciaire* (*f.*): fiat money.

fijn [*Dut.*] fineness; fine (purity of metal).

filament de soie [*Fr.*] silk thread.

filigrana (*f.*) [*Span., Ital., Port.*] watermark.

filigrane (*m.*) [*Fr.*] watermark.

filo di seta [*Ital.*] silk thread.

fin 1. [*Swed., Dan.*] fine (grade or condition).

2. [*Fr., Rom.*] fine (purity of metal), fineness.

3. [*Nor.*] level of preservation approximating the British/North American grade of *good.*

finance minister In many countries, the title of the person who is in charge of the public treasury and whose signature often appears on paper money.

finansminister (*c.*) [*Dan.*]; (*m./f.*) [*Swed.*]; (*m.*) [*Nor.*] finance minister.

Finanzminister (*m.*) [*Ger.*] finance minister.

fine 1. Medium grade of a circulated coin, generally defined as ranging from a moderate to a considerable amount of even wear. The entire design should be bold. All lettering must be clearly visible even though it will have some weaknesses.

Because grading systems vary greatly from country to country, the term *fine* as a grade or condition is generic and lacks an absolute universal meaning.

2. Pure or virtually pure precious metal. In the Middle Ages, *fine gold* referred to a gold alloy of approximately 23 1/2 carats (97.9% pure) or better. Some sources claim that fine gold had to be 23 3/4 carat, but medieval coins seldom achieved that level of purity largely due to the inability of moneyers to purify metal to such a degree. Even if they had been able to do so, pure gold is relatively soft and not well suited for circulating coins.

Lowering the fineness of precious metal in a coin is known as *debasement* and was a common way of assessing a "hidden tax" during

the Middle Ages. Usually this idea backfired, because the general public would no longer accept the coins at their stated values.

When England's King Henry VIII wanted to debase his coins, he switched from *fine gold* to 22 carat gold known in those days as *crown gold* and currently called *standard gold.* Crown or standard gold has a slightly coppery tint and is not as brilliant as fine gold.

In today's world, the terms *fine gold* and *fine silver* simply refer to the quantity of pure gold or silver contained in a given coin and have no bearing on the coin's alloy. The terms are most commonly seen in descriptions of modern bullion coins, such as those produced by South Africa, Canada, and other nations.

The American Eagle bullion coin causes some confusion because it shows an inscription stating that the coin contains one ounce of fine gold. The coin's alloy is actually *standard* gold (22 carat, 91.67% pure), but the coin contains a full ounce of pure gold in addition to its copper and silver alloy. On the other hand, Canada's Maple Leaf contains one ounce of pure gold and virtually nothing of anything else; its alloy *is* fine gold (24 carat, 99.99% pure). Canada produces coins this way to enhance their marketability because the coins have a more attractive shine than the Eagles or the South African Krugerrands.

3. The percentage of precious metal in an alloy. See the following article on *fine; fineness* for additional information.

1953 Mexican 5 pesos showing weight and fineness

fine; fineness The percentage of precious metal in an alloy as written in the form of a decimal number. For example, .900 fine silver is 90.0% silver and 10.0% alloy. Commercially pure metals are often referred to as .999 fine even if they are actually more than 99.9% pure.

Many large silver coins, especially of the late nineteenth and early and mid-twentieth centuries, show their fineness inscribed directly on the coins along with the date, mintmark, country of issue, and other usual information. Among these are the U.S. Trade Dollars of 1873-85 and a wide range of Mexican silver coins extending throughout the twentieth century. On those Mexican pieces, the Spanish word *ley* indicates the fineness.

Canadian bullion coin: weight & fineness in English & French

The fineness determines the color of gold coins, most noticeably the recent bullion coins issued by South Africa, Canada, Mexico, the United States, Great Britain, and many other countries. South Africa's Krugerrand, America's Eagle, and the bullion coins of several other nations are 22 carat gold, meaning that they possess a fineness of .9167. Their color is darker and more coppery than the brilliantly gold-colored 24 carat (.9999 fine) bullion coins of Canada and many other countries. Irrespective of fineness, each of these coins contains the same quantity of gold (one ounce). Although the Canadian gold coins are more attractive, their pureness makes them metallically softer than the Krugerrands and thus less satisfactory for use in jewelry.

fine gold Gold alloy of approximately 23 1/2 carats (97.9% pure) or better. This was the purest gold that medieval moneyers could produce with the technology of their time. An

inferior alloy is *standard gold*, a.k.a. *crown gold* (22 carat, 91.67% pure).

Fingerabdruck (*m.*); **Fingerspuren** (*f.pl.*) [*Ger.*] fingerprint.

finhed (*c.*) [*Dan.*] fineness; fine (purity of metal).

finhet (*m.*) [*Nor.*] fineness; fine.

Finlandia [*Span., Ital., Pol., et al*] Finland.

Finlândia [*Port.*] Finland.

fino [*Ital.*] fineness; fine (purity of metal).

finom [*Hun.*] fineness; fine (purity of metal).

fio de seda [*Port.*] silk thread.

fir de mătase (*n.*) [*Rom.*] silk thread.

fire [*Nor., Dan.*] four.

firkantet (*adj.*) [*Dan.*] square.

firma (*f.*) [*Span., Ital.*] signature.

first-day-of-issue Idea borrowed from philately which failed to gain popularity in numismatics. It consists of obtaining a banknote or other collectible certificate on its first day of issue, and then of having a post office worker affix a postage stamp to the note and apply a postmark. This is supposed to prove that the note was obtained on the first day it was released (a fallacy in itself, because banknotes are sometimes given out by banks before their official release date).

On April 13, 1976, many thousands of U.S. $2 bills suffered the fate of being postmarked. They were issued on that day as part of America's Bicentennial celebration. The U.S. government encouraged all this hoopla because it hoped that the $2 note would finally become accepted by the American people, thus easing the pressure on the Bureau of Engraving and Printing to produce $1 bills. The results, however, were not encouraging. First, the $2 bill failed to circulate, largely because it is regarded as bringing bad luck. Secondly, the postmarked notes failed to generate any numismatic interest; today they seldom sell for much above their $2 face value.

fisă (*f.*) [*Rom.*] token.

Canadian "fish scale"

fish scale Colloquial term for Canadian 5 cent pieces issued in 1858 and again (with some gaps) from 1870 to 1921. In 1922 they were replaced with the now-familiar nickel 5 cent pieces.

[J. E. Charlton, *Standard Catalogue of Canadian Coins* (27th Ed.), pp. 31-34; Frank Van Valen, "Fishscales: My Favorite Canadian Import," *The Numismatist*, May 1987, pp. 991-994.]

fișic (*n.*) [*Rom.*] roll (of coins).

fissura de cunho [*Port.*] die break.

fisură în matriță (*f.*); **fisură în ștanță** (*f.*) [*Rom.*] die break.

first-day-of-issue postmarked U.S. $2 note

fiyat [*Turk.*] price.

fiyat arttırmak (*v.*) [*Turk.*] to bid (at an auction or mail bid sale).

fiyat listesi [*Turk.*] price list.

fjärdedel (*r.*) [*Swed.*] fourth (the fraction), quarter.

fjerdedel (*c.*) [*Dan.*]; (*m.*) [*Nor.*] a fourth, quarter.

fläck (*r.*) [*Swed.*] stain (on a banknote or bond).

flamante [*Span.*] crisp, i.e., a crisp uncirculated note containing no folds. Abbreviated "FL".

flan Disc of metal upon which a coinage design is stamped. See *planchet*.

1947 souvenir wooden "flat"

flat (*noun*) Wooden trade token made from a small thin sheet of wood. Collectors generally regard the 25 cent, 50 cent, and $1 tokens issued in early 1932 by the Tenino, Washington, Chamber of Commerce as the first flats, although some similar items were produced in the early 1920s in Germany (see *Notgeld* for additional information and page 319 of the color section for an illustration). The American flats were printed in response to a major shortage of circulating money caused by the Great Depression.

Many of the U.S. wooden nickels of the 1930s and 1940s were made in this manner. The example in the illustration is the 1947 Steubenville (Ohio) Sesquicentennial 5 cent flat manufactured by the John B. Rogers Producing Company of Fostoria, Ohio. The flats were popular souvenirs of that celebration and were issued in denominations of 5 cents, 10 cents, and 25 cents. The Rogers Company began issuing flats in 1938 and produced many thousands of 3-denomination sets.

The small wooden sheets from which flats were made is usually referred to as *slicewood*.

[William E. Pike, "Woodn't You Like to Collect Something Different?" *The Numismatist*, December 1989, pp. 1963-66.]

Fleck (*m.*) [*Ger.*] stain.

flekk (*m.*) [*Nor.*] stain; tarnish.

fleur de coin [*Fr.*] [abbreviated *F.D.C.*] literally, *flower of the die*. 1. uncirculated; mint condition. 2. Very high quality, often used to describe gem proof coins or medals as well as superior business strikes.

fleur-de-lis

fleur-de-lis [*Fr.*] literally, *flower lily*. A type of heraldic flower which does not exist in nature although it looks somewhat like an iris. It has been a symbol of royalty since ancient times. During the Middle Ages the *lis* was emblematic of illumination and of religious faith. It was popular among Christian monarchs because its central flower rises straight up from a horizontal connector creating something that resembles a cross.

The *fleur-de-lis* is usually associated with France because it appeared on many French regnal coins and because the term itself is in French. However, the first European appearance of the *lis* was on the florin issued by Florence in the mid-thirteenth century. During the duration of the Middle Ages, it was used as a decorative device on the coins of England and several other countries, and is still occasionally seen on coins today.

flip; **flipette**; **flippette** Vinyl pocket made for storing coins, medals, or tokens. The pocket area usually ranges from one to three square inches. Prior to 1970, most were manufactured from polyvinyl chloride[q.v.], also known as *P.V.C.*, a type of clear plastic which can harm coins. Since the 1970s, many flips have been made of an inert vinyl material which will not tarnish or corrode the coins stored within them, although some flips are still made of P.V.C. The ones without P.V.C. are usually marked as such.

Most experts agree that flips are not ideal for long-term storage. Although these items are not air-tight, they have either a flap for closing or a second pocket into which an information card can be placed.

flor de cuño [*Span.*] 1. proof (re: coins or medals). A more current word is *prueba*.

2. Archaic term for *uncirculated*.

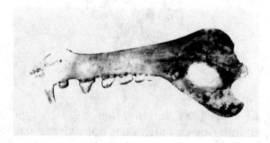

flying fox jaw (enlarged)

flying fox jaw Item used as money by the natives of New Guinea and Fiji. The jawbones were tar-blackened with all teeth intact. They were usually strung together so they could be worn or easily carried.

Flying foxes are not really foxes but small, fruit-eating bats. Their jaws had value in trade because the creatures are so hard to catch.

[Radford Stearns, "Tooth Money— A Great Way to Fill the Holes in Your Collection," *The Numismatist*, February 1987, pp. 269-74.]

"foal" silver stater

foal Name given to the Corinthian stater showing the winged horse Pegasus. This silver coin, more commonly known as a *colt*, was first issued around 570 B.C. and weighed approximately 8.6 grams. With some slight modifications, it was minted in Corinth and elsewhere for more than two hundred years.

foarte bun [*Rom.*] fine (grade or condition).

foglaló [*Hun.*] deposit.

foglaló kötelező [*Hun.*] deposit required.

foglio d'offerta [*Ital.*] bid sheet.

fokozat [*Hun.*] grade, condition.

folheto de propaganda [*Port.*] propaganda note.

Folkerepublikken Kina [*Nor., Dan.*] People's Republic of China (P.R.C.).

Folkrepubliken Kina [*Swed.*] People's Republic of China.

folosit [*Rom.*] used.

folt [*Hun.*] stain.

foncé [*Fr.*] dark.

fondo (*m.*) [*Span.*] bottom.

fondo a specchio (*m.*) [*Ital.*] proof (re: coins or medals).

font [*Hun.*] pound (16 ounces avdp. or 12 oz. troy of weight; pound Sterling - £).

food coupon see *food stamp*.

food stamp [technically known as *food coupon*.] Certificate distributed on behalf of the U.S. Department of Agriculture to low-income people who meet certain qualifications. It is used for the purchase of food items, excluding such things as prepared (already cooked) foods, tobacco products, and alcoholic beverages.

U.S. governmental studies of state poverty levels conducted in the early 1930s showed the highest rates in the Southern states. Food commodities distribution and a limited food stamp program functioned in those states from 1939 to 1943, initially to increase consumption of surplus farm products being stored at great expense by the U.S. government.

Surplus food distribution continued on a limited national basis through the early 1960s. The United States government reinstated the food stamp program in 1961 to supplement the resources of low-income people to provide food products for a more adequate diet. During this period households paid from one-quarter to one-half of the allowed amount of food stamps (for example, to pay $9 for $28 worth of food stamps).

It was discovered that these programs were not working properly due to state mismanagement and misuse of funds and products. A national consciousness aroused concern about rapid growth of poverty, hunger, and malnutrition. The Food Stamp Act of 1964 drastically reformed the program with strict federal rules of eligibility and distribution. Funding was apportioned from federal taxes, regulated by the Food and Nutrition Service of the U.S. Department Agriculture (U.S.D.A.), supervised by the states, and administered by each county. The program focus shifted at this time from disposal of surplus farm products (now becoming low in supply) to the nutritional needs of the poor.

A more comprehensive reform occurred with the Food Stamp Act of 1977, making the program more accessible to the needy. Other objectives were to be more cost effective through improved program and to reduce fraud. The purchase requirement was eliminated in 1979.

Food stamps are issued on a monthly basis. Recipients use them as cash to buy food from stores authorized by the U.S.D.A. to accept them. Eligibility is based on set federal rules of residency, household size, income (earned and unearned), assets (or resources), and shelter expenditures.

In the early 1990s, the U.S. government began working with the states to find ways of reducing program costs and fraud. Several states were authorized to experiment with the Electronic Benefits Transfer (E.B.T.) program in which recipients are given a card containing a computer chip programmed each month with their benefit amount. Stores are equipped with a chip card reader. Each purchase is deducted from the total benefit amount. Use of the E.B.T. card eliminates the need to print, transport, and store food stamp coupons, saving the government millions of dollars and greatly decreasing fraud.

[Contributed by Faith H. Barnett. *State of Ohio Food Stamp Certification Handbook*; *Encyclopedia of Social Work* (1973), Vols. 1 & 2.]

forældet [*Dan.*] obsolete.

föråldrad [*Swed.*] obsolete.

forandret årstal (*n.*) [*Dan.*] altered date.

forandret dato (*m.*) [*Nor.*] altered date.

forandring (*c.*) [*Dan.*]; (*m.*) [*Nor.*] alteration.

förändring (*r.*) [*Swed.*] alteration.

forato [*Ital.*] holed.

forbundet [*Nor.*] accolated, conjoined, jugate.

foreldet [*Nor.*] obsolete.

Forenede Stater [*Dan.*] United States of America (U.S.A.).

Forente Stater [*Nor.*] United States of America.

foreslået bud (*n.*) [*Dan.*] suggested bid.

förfalska (*v.*) [*Swed.*] to counterfeit.

förfalskare (*m./f.*) [*Swed.*] counterfeiter.

forfalsker (*m.*) [*Nor.*] counterfeiter.

forfalskning (*c.*) [*Dan.*]; (*m.*) [*Nor.*] a counterfeit, fake, forgery.

förfalskning (*r.*) [*Swed.*] a counterfeit, fake, forgery.

forgalom [*Hun.*] circulation.

forgalomba nem bocsátott [*Hun.*] uncirculated.

forgalomban lévő [*Hun.*] circulated.

forgalomból kivont [*Hun.*] demonetization; obsolete.

forhåndsbetaling (*m.*) [*Nor.*] prepayment.

forkortelse (*c.*) [*Dan.*]; (*m.*) [*Nor.*] abbreviation.

förkortning (*r.*) [*Swed.*] abbreviation.

formulario de pedido (*m.*) [*Span.*] order form.

formulário de pedido (*m.*) [*Port.*] order form.

formularz ofertowy (*m.*) [*Pol.*] bid sheet.

formularz zamówienia (*m.*) [*Pol.*] order form.

foros φόρος (*m.*) [*Grk.*] tax.

forside (*c.*) [*Dan.*]; (*m.*) [*Nor.*] front; obverse.

förskottsbetalning (*r.*) [*Swed.*] prepayment.

förstoringsglas (*n.*) [*Swed.*] magnifying glass.

forstørrelsesglas (*n.*) [*Nor., Dan.*] magnifying glass.

forte 1. [*Span., Port.*] strong, solid.

2. [*Port.*] Term used to differentiate coins of substantial silver content from coins made of baser metal in Portugal during the Middle Ages.

fortjeneste (*c.*) [*Dan.*] seigniorage.

Fortuna Variabilis / Omnia Cum Pondere Numero & Mensura [*Lat.*] Changing fortune / All things with weight, number and measurement.

Fortuna Volubilis Errat [*Lat.*] Fortune varies erratically. Inscription found on some German *Schauthalers* circa 1600.

[Arthur R. Doumaux, Jr., "The Hamburg Connection," *The Numismatist*, February 1989, p. 243.]

forudbetaling (*c.*) [*Dan.*] prepayment.

förvärv (*n.*) [*Swed.*] acquisition.

fotoincisione (*f.*) [*Ital.*] photogravure.

foundling note Type of paper note printed in the 1880s in Cuba to alleviate the shortage of small coins on the sugar plantations. These notes bore the same denominations as the copper coins of the time. They acquired the nickname *foundling notes* (in Spanish, *billetes expósitos*) because both their physical condition and their value deteriorated quickly shortly after their issuance. The privately-owned stores outside of the sugar plantations would only accept them in trade for much less than their face values. In 1886 an association of private shopkeepers decided not to accept in trade any paper money with a denomination of less than one peso and would only accept the larger notes at a greatly inflated rate. Foundling notes and other house coins continued to circulate in the plantations until the 1930s, when laws were passed to prohibit their use.

[Manuel Moreno Fraginals and José A. Pulido Ledesma, *Cuba: A Country and Its Currency*, National Bank of Cuba, pp. 69-77.]

fourthling Middle English word meaning a fourth of something. It was from this word that the modern word *farthing*[q.v.] was derived.

fout (*f.-c.*) [*Dut.*] defect; error.

foutief [*Dut.*] defective.

fraai [*Dut.*] fine (grade or condition).

fracción (*f.*) [*Span.*] fraction.

fractional currency 1. Any of the U.S. notes issued from 1862-1876 bearing a denomination of less than one dollar. These notes were popularly known as *shinplasters*.

During the early years of the U.S. Civil War (1861-65), in response to the political uncertainty of the time, the banking industry suspended the redemption of paper money for coin. The net effect of this action was to place a premium on coins vis-à-vis paper money, which resulted in a widespread hoarding of coins by the public.

All forms of coinage were involved in the hoarding, not just coins of silver and gold. This created a serious situation for merchants, who were unable to make change to carry on the normal course of their business.

Merchants and the general public did whatever they could to deal with the problem. They even tried barter. The most significant idea from the standpoint of the development of fractional currency, was the public's resort to postage stamps as change. These had the obvious advantage of existing in small enough denominations. They also had the equally obvious disadvantage of gummed backs, which became sticky and soiled after only a short period of circulation.

The solution, generally credited to General Francis E. Spinner, Treasurer of the United States during the Lincoln administration, was the issuance of a form of fractional notes similar in appearance to the postage stamps they were designed to replace in circulation.

In all there were five different issues, or major design types, printed from 1862 until 1876, when production of these notes ceased. The designs were changed with some frequency in response to an alarming rate of counterfeiting— in itself an interesting comparative commentary on times then and

now. Modern counterfeiters seldom bother with any denominations lower than a twenty dollar bill, whereas their Civil War counterparts busied themselves with denominations as low as three and five cents.

U.S. postage currency

During the 14 years these notes were in production, almost 369 million dollars worth were printed. According to the latest available figures from U.S. Treasury Department records, less than $500,000 are still unredeemed. How much of that total has been lost or destroyed forever is anybody's guess.

The first general emission (August 21, 1862 to May 27, 1863) was issued in denominations of 5, 10, 25, and 50 cents. These notes were called *Postage Currency*, so named because they actually picture 5 and 10 cent postage stamps. They were designed in such a manner so as to convince the public that these notes were legitimate substitutions for postage stamps, but far more suitable for circulation. Also, some of these notes resembled postage stamps in that they had perforated edges.

These first fractional notes were actually issued illegally under the Act of Congress of July 17, 1862. That Act only permitted the acceptance of postage stamps as currency but did not authorize the printing of notes, even if those notes pictured the images of postage stamps.

The second general issue (October 10, 1863 to February 23, 1867; denominations of 5, 10, 25, and 50 cents), third (December 5, 1864 to August 16, 1869; 3, 5, 10, 25, and 50 cents), fourth (July 14, 1869 to February 16, 1875; 10, 15, 25, and 50 cents), and fifth (February 26, 1874 to February 15, 1876; 10, 25, and 50 cents) were officially titled *Fractional Currency* rather than *Postage Currency*. The change in name was part of the Congressional Act of March 3, 1863, which not only authorized the emission of the second and subsequent issues of these notes, but also legalized the Postage Currency (first issue) notes.

The notes of the second issue are distinguished by the inclusion of a bronze-colored oval frame overstamped around the portrait of Washington and the overprinting of the denomination in bronze on the reverse. Many different kinds of paper were used in an attempt to find a paper which would deter counterfeiting. Some notes were produced on a fiber paper similar to the fiber papers used in modern U.S. currency. No signatures nor the Treasury Seal were used on this issue. Serial numbers were not to appear on the notes of any of the five series. Again, the most significant change was the designation *Fractional Currency* on the face of the notes in lieu of the previous *Postage Currency*.

This issue established several precedents which have continued to the paper money used by the United States today. It started the use of a special paper exclusively for use on United States Government Obligations. It was the first time an identifying fiber was incorporated in the paper. It established the use of engraving as the preferred method of printing currency.

Unlike the second issue, which only showed the portrait of George Washington, the notes of the third issue presented a variety of people.

One of those men, Spencer M. Clark, Superintendent of the National Currency Bureau, mistakenly believed that he had been given orders to place his own portrait on the 5 cent note and actually did so. His action led to a Congressional uproar and the passing of a still-existing rule forbidding the use of the image of a "living American" on the notes, coinage, or obligations of the United States Government. [See *Clark, Spencer M.*]

The third issue eliminated the oval overprints but kept the overstamped denominations on the reverse as an anti-counterfeiting device. Again, the Treasury Seal was not included.

The fourth issue, just like the previous two, was initiated because of extensive counterfeiting. This issue also had many experiments with paper to find a deterrent to counterfeiting. Watermarks were tried and discontinued because of the short life of the note due to the weakened paper. A strip of blue fibers imbedded between two layers of paper was also tried. The bronze surcharge (denominational overprint) was left off on this issue. The Treasury Seal appeared on this series for the first time and was maintained on the fifth issue.

The production of the fifth issue exhausted the appropriations for printing Fractional Currency and no new funds were provided. The paper in this issue was all fiber, watermarked paper. The Treasury Seal appeared on all of the notes along with signatures.

The retirement of Fractional Currency started in 1876, with the Act of Congress of April 17, 1876, calling for the emission of fractional silver coins to redeem fractional currency.

[Contributed by John and Nancy Wilson. Taken from their article "United State Postage and Fractional Currency," *The Centinel*, Vol. 28, No. 3, Fall 1980, pp. 15-28.]

2. Notes of Canada issued in the single denomination of 25 cents. The first emission of these notes came in 1870 as a response to the large quantities of U.S. silver coins entering circulation in Canada. The U.S. coins proved troublesome because the American dollar was only worth 80% as much as a Canadian dollar at that time, and Canadian merchants took a loss whenever they accepted those coins in trade. Unfortunately, the American coins were needed, inferior as they were, as there were not nearly enough Canadian coins in existence to satisfy the demand.

Canadian 25 cent fractional currency note

To give the Canadian government a bit more time to mint an adequate supply of silver coins, the fractional notes were issued as a temporary solution. Much to the surprise of the government, the notes proved to be so popular that additional printings were necessitated in 1900 and again in 1923, thus providing three separate series of fractional currency notes.

As in the case of the U.S. fractional currency notes described above, the Canadian fractional notes were also colloquially known as *shinplasters*.

[J. A. Haxby and R. C. Willey, *Coins of Canada* (9th Ed.), pp. 181-3.]

fractionary coinage 1. Coins whose denomination is less than one of the prevailing unit of currency. For example, since the dollar is the unit of currency in the United States and Canada, any coin with a value of less than one dollar (e.g., ten cents) is fractionary.

2. Coins of low denomination, particularly from countries such as Japan and Italy whose units of currency are so small as to preclude issuing coins of fractional values.

fracţiune (*f.*) [*Rom.*] fraction.

fragko φράγκο (*n.*) [*Grk.*] franc (French unit of currency).

frakcja (*f.*) [*Pol.*] fraction.

framsida (*r.*) [*Swed.*] front.

França [*Port.*] France.

Francia [*Ital., Span.*] France.

Franciaország [*Hun.*] France.

Francja [*Pol.*] France.

franco (*m.*) [*Port., Ital, Span.*] franc (French unit of currency).

Generalísimo Francisco Franco

Franco, Francisco [né *Francisco Paulino Hermenegildo Teodulo Franco Bahamonde*; a.k.a. *El Caudillo* ("The Commander").] Spanish Chief of State (1947-75). Born December 4, 1892, in El Ferrol, Galicia (Spain); died of acute heart disease on November 20, 1975, in Madrid.

General Franco was leader of the Nationalist forces that overthrew the Spanish Democratic Republic in the Spanish Civil War (1936-39). He entered the army in 1907 at the age of fifteen. Because of his military capabilities, his rise through the military ranks was meteoric. In 1926, he became Europe's youngest Brigadier-General.

During World War II, Franco was sympathetic to the Axis but refused to officially enter the war, calling Spain's position "non-belligerent." But as the Allied armies started to advance, he drew back closer to a position of "neutrality." In 1947, after re-organizing the government and proclaiming Spain a monarchy, he made himself Chief of State, a position he kept until his death.

In July 1969 Franco chose Prince Juan Carlos de Borbón as his eventual successor. At Franco's death, Juan Carlos was sworn in as King Juan Carlos I on November 22, 1975.

[Contributed by Ruth Ann Davis.]

frangi [*Finn.*] franc.

frank [*Hun., Turk.*]; (*m.*) [*Pol.*] franc.

Benjamin Franklin

Franklin, Benjamin American author, printer, inventor, diplomat, and scientist, and one of the leaders of the American Revolution. Born January 17, 1706, in Boston, Massachusetts; died April 17, 1790, at his home in Philadelphia, Pennsylvania.

Although his talents encompassed many areas of human endeavor, Franklin is best remembered for his wisdom and diplomacy in effecting an alliance between France and the American colonies and later in bringing about a peace treaty forcing Great Britain to recognize American independence. An elder statesman of the American Revolution, he was the oldest man to sign the Declaration of Independence and the United States Constitution.

Born into a family of seventeen children, Franklin attended school just long enough to learn to read and write. Yet despite his limited education, he became the publisher of the

Pennsylvania Gazette and the highly respected *Poor Richard's Almanac.*

In 1727 he formed the Junto, or Leather Apron Club, a social and philosophical club for young craftsmen. Four years later, the Junto Club's library became the basis for the Library Company of Philadelphia, regarded as the first circulating library in America.

Franklin obtained a lucrative printing contract to print Pennsylvania's paper money after he published a pamphlet in 1729 called *A Modest Inquiry into the Nature and Necessity of Paper Currency* that called for the issuance of more paper money.

His long illustrious career in public office began at the age of thirty when he was chosen as Clerk of the Pennsylvania Legislature. He accepted a second office in 1737 when he became Philadelphia's Deputy Postmaster in order to improve the city's distribution of mail.

His life was not without controversy. His first son was born out of wedlock. The two disliked each other so much that the son took the side of the British during the American Revolution. Franklin's behavior in France when he was trying to obtain support for the American cause was far from exemplary, as he had quite a reputation for being a heavy drinker and womanizer. Even his experiments with lightning and electricity proved controversial, because many preachers in American and Europe believed that being hit by lightning was God's punishment for sinners, and that Franklin had no business interfering with the will of God.

Nevertheless, Benjamin Franklin will always be remembered as one of America's greatest patriots. Thomas Jefferson summed it up by calling him "the greatest man and ornament of the age and country in which he lived."

Franklin's likeness is found on the half dollars of 1948 to 1963 (see *Franklin Half Dollar*) and the U.S. $100 bill, as well as on the $1000 U.S. Saving Bond. An unusually large portrait of Franklin generated a considerable amount of controversy in 1996 when it appeared on the new $100 bill, the first in a series of re-designed U.S. notes. His face is also the first to be seen in a watermark on modern U.S. paper currency.

Franklin has been featured on many commemorative medals, some of which are described in this dictionary (see *Franklin Bicentennial Medallion, Franklin Medal of the United States Congress,* et al).

[Contributed by Ruth Ann Davis. David C. Whitney (editor), *Founders of Freedom in America.*]

Franklin Bicentennial Medallion Approved by an Act of Congress (U.S.) in 1904, this 102mm bronze medallion was struck to commemorate the 200th anniversary of the birth of Benjamin Franklin on January 17, 1906.

One medallion was issued in gold and presented to the Republic of France. One hundred fifty were produced in bronze. These were manufactured by Tiffany of New York and are edgemarked *Tiffany Co.* However, there is evidence that additional medallions were struck, presumably by the U.S. Mint.

The obverse has Franklin facing left with 1706/1790 to his right. The inscriptions read *BENJAMIN FRANKLIN: PRINTER — PHILOSOPHER / SCIENTIST — STATESMAN / DIPLOMATIST.*

The medallion is the work of Augustus and Louis St. Gaudens and is monogrammed *LSTGA* on the reverse. It was mostly the work of Louis, as Augustus was quite ill at the time.

The medallions were to be distributed at the discretion of the president of the United States, with 50 copies assigned to be distributed by the American Philosophical Society.

In 1964, a die trial of this medallion was brought to light. This medallion is similar to the regular design, with the following exceptions: Franklin's bust is un-clothed and his head is adorned with a laurel wreath. A larger version of this medallion, which is 102mm, is alluded to in Fuld (FR.M.UN.6).

[Contributed by Phil W. Greenslet. George and Melvin Fuld, "Medallic Memorials to Franklin," *The Numismatist,* December 1956; George J. Fuld, "New Franklin Medal by St. Gaudens," *TAMS Journal,* Token and Medal Society, March-April 1966; Burton M. Saxton, "The Franklin Bicentennial Medallion," *The Numismatist,* December, 1956.]

Franklin Half Dollar U.S. 50 cent coin issued from 1948 to 1963 to honor Benjamin Franklin, American statesman, scientist, printer, writer, and philosopher.

The coin was designed by John R. Sinnock, who had created the Roosevelt Dime two years earlier. The simplicity of the Franklin Half Dollar lies in stark contrast to the very ornate Walking Liberty Half Dollar[q.v.] it replaced.

The reverse of the Franklin Half features the Liberty Bell, a symbol of American Independence. This bell is in higher relief than the design used by Sinnock in 1926 for the Sesquicentennial commemorative half dollar. In fact, the Franklin Half's striking is so strong that the words "Pass and Stow, Philada., MDCCLIII" can be seen immediately above the upper terminus of the crack on the bell. This is the name of the firm that recast the bell after it cracked while being tested for tone, and the year (1753) it was recast. The Philadelphia Assembly had ordered the inscription as a courtesy to Pass and Stow.

An odd feature of the reverse of the Franklin Half Dollar is the unusually small eagle seen at the right of the Liberty Bell. It was included in the design solely to satisfy an 1873 U.S. federal mandate that all silver coins with a face value greater than ten cents must show an eagle on the reverse.

A few 1955 specimens show a small obverse die break in the area of Franklin's mouth, giving Franklin what appears to be a severe overbite. These coins have been nicknamed the *Bugs Bunny* halves.

[Clifford Mishler, *Coins: Questions and Answers*, pp. 76-79.]

Franklin Medal of The Franklin Institute Gold medal which has been awarded annually to those workers in physical science or technology, without regard to country, whose efforts have done most to advance a knowledge of physical science or its application. The first recipient was Thomas Alva Edison in 1914.

The 51 mm medal was designed by R. Tait McKenzie, the Canadian-born, self-taught sculptor, who doubled as the director of physical education at the University of Pennsylvania, the school Franklin helped found. The medals are produced by the Medallic Art Company.

[Contributed by Phil W. Greenslet. George and Melvin Fuld, "Medallic Memorials to Franklin," *The Numismatist*, December 1956; Phil W. Greenslet, "Drs. McKenzie and Franklin," *The Numismatist*, April 1990, pp. 538-41; Helen and Clarence Jourdan, "Benjamin Franklin's Unfinished Business," The Franklin Institute, 1956.]

Franklin Medal of the United States Congress Medal authorized by an Act of Congress to be awarded to learned scientific, educational, and welfare societies of which Benjamin Franklin was a member, founder, or sponsor.

The 76mm medals were designed by Laura Gardin Frazer and struck by the U.S. Mint in 1956. The original medals were struck in silver. Among the recipients were the American Philosophical Society, the Medical Society of London, Académie Nationale de Médecine (Paris), the University of Pennsylvania, and the cities of Boston and Philadelphia.

An additional 50 were struck in bronze for presentation by the 250th Anniversary Committee of The Franklin Institute.

[Contributed by Phil W. Greenslet. Helen and Clarence Jourdan, "Benjamin Franklin's Unfinished Business," The Franklin Institute, 1956; George and Melvin Fuld, "Medallic Memorials to Franklin," *The Numismatist*, December 1956.]

Franklin National Memorial Award, Benjamin See *Benjamin Franklin National Memorial Award*.

Frankreich [*Ger.*] France.

Frankrig [*Dan.*] France.

Frankrijk [*Dut.*] France.

Frankrike [*Nor., Swed.*] France.

frånsida (r.) [*Swed.*] reverse.

Franţa [*Rom.*] France.

fraternal order The source of many non-military decorations. Fraternal orders are defined as voluntary, nonprofit associations established for the mutual aid and sociability of their members. They appeared in England as early as the sixteenth century and were called *friendly societies*. Various parts of

Order of DeMolay

Europe had benevolent secret societies modeled on the order established by the Freemasons. In present-day Canada and the United States, fraternal orders are fellowship organizations where members can develop friendships and conduct social activities.

Badges and various other types of numismatic collectibles are often presented as part of the initiation ritual. The illustrated item is the Order of DeMolay from the 1930s.

frazione (*f.*) [*Ital.*] fraction.

Freiheit (*f.*) [*Ger.*] liberty.

fremd [*Ger.*] foreign.

Fremdwährung (*f.*) [*Ger.*] foreign currency.

fremragende [*Dan.*] excellent.

French bronze The standard bronze alloy of the nineteenth century. It consists of 95% copper, 4% tin, and 1% zinc. Its name supposedly originated from diluting the bell metal of confiscated French church bells with additional copper. Examples include the German 2 pfennig coins, issued since 1950.

frente (*m.*) [*Span.*] front.

fresco [*Span.*] crisp (*re*: the condition of banknotes).

fricção de arrumação (*f.*) [*Port.*] cabinet friction.

fukan shihei 不換紙幣 [*Jpn.*] fiat money.

fundir (*v.*) [*Span., Port.*] to cast.

fundo (*m.*) [*Port.*] bottom.

fünf [*Ger.*] five.

Fünftel (*n.*) [*Ger.*] fifth.

fünfzig [*Ger.*] fifty.

funt (*m.*) [*Pol.*] pound (unit of weight).

funt szterling (*m.*) [*Pol.*] pound Sterling (£).

fuoricorso [*Ital.*] (*m.*) demonetization; (*adj.*) obsolete.

furo (*m.*) [*Port.*] hole.

F.V. [*abbr.*] face value.

G g

gaikoku tsûka 外国通貨 [*Jpn.*] foreign currency.

gakumenkakaku 額面価格 [*Jpn.*] face value.

galben [*Rom.*] yellow.

Gales [*Span.*] Wales.

Galles [*Ital.*] Wales.

galvanismeno γαλβανισμένα [*Grk.*] electrotype.

galvanoplastica (*f.*) [*Ital.*] electrotype.

galvanoplastie (*f.*) [*Fr.*] electrotype.

Galvanotypie (*f.*) [*Ger.*] electrotype.

gambling token See *casino token* and *poker chip.*

gammal [*Swed.*] old.

gammel [*Dan.*] old.

gangbar mynt (*m.*) [*Nor.*] currency.

garantibevis (*n.*) [*Nor.*] certificate.

gauche (*f.*) [*Fr.*] left (direction or position).

Gebot (*n.*) [*Ger.*] bid; bid sheet.

gebraucht [*Ger.*] used.

gebruikt [*Dut.*] used.

Gebühr (*f.*) [*Ger.*] fee.

gebyr (*n.*) [*Nor., Dan.*] fee.

geçici özel para [*Turk.*] scrip.

geçici para [*Turk.*] emergency currency.

gecirculeerd [*Dut.*] circulated.

Gedenk- [*Ger.*] commemorative.

Gedenkmünze (*f.*) [*Ger.*] commemorative coin.

geel [*Dut.*] yellow.

geelkoper (*n.*) [*Dut.*] brass (the alloy).

geen ongelimiteerde biedingen geaccepteerd [*Dut.*] no unlimited bids accepted.

gegraveerd [*Dut.*] engraved.

gehämmerte Münze (*f.*) [*Ger.*] hammered coin.

gelaagde munten; gelaagd muntmetaal [*Dut.*] clad coinage.

gelauwerd [*Dut.*] laureate.

gelb [*Ger.*] yellow.

geld (*n.*) [*Dut.*] money.

Geld (*n.*) [*Ger.*] money.

Geldanweisung (*f.*) [*Ger.*] money order.

Geldeinheit (*f.*) [*Ger.*] monetary unit.

Geldschein (*m.*) [*Ger.*] note, banknote.

Geldscheine (*m.pl.*) [*Ger.*] paper money.

geldstuk (*n.*) [*Dut.*] coin.

gelegeerde munten [*Dut.*] clad coinage.

gelocht [*Ger.*] holed.

gematria [from Hebrew גִּימַטְרִיָּה, originally Greek γεωμετρια.] The system of using letters of the alphabet as numerals. This was done extensively on Greek, Jewish, and Moslem coinage, and occasionally on Latin coins and medals (although only a few of the Latin letters have numeric values). In Greek, Hebrew, and Arabic/Farsi, all letters have a numeric equivalent and hence every word has a numeric value. Sometimes letters are used as numerals without any reference to any words they may form, as in the dates on ancient Greek coins and modern Israeli coins. Other times the words are important and the numeric values become a type of shorthand. Medals and coins have been issued by Moslems which use 66 as the number for God (الله), 92 for Mohammed (محمد), and 786 for the *Basmala*— *In the name of God, the Compassionate, the Merciful* (بسم الله الرحمن الرحيم). Israeli commemoratives for the state's 18th (חַי *khay* "life") and 28th (כֹּח *ko'akh* "strength") anniversaries base their designs on words with the anniversary's numeric value.

Historically, gematria started with the Greeks. They introduced the concept to the Jews after Alexander's conquest of Judea (323 B.C.E.). The Jews, in turn, used gematria in Moslem countries, using the Arabic letter equivalents of their own Hebrew, known in Arabic as *abjad* (ابجد). Tipu Sultan introduced

	ones		tens		hundreds		1000
	1 2 3 4 5 6 7 8 9		1 2 3 4 5 6 7 8 9		1 2 3 4 5 6 7 8 9		
Greek	A B Γ Δ E S Z H Θ		I K Λ M N Ξ O Π ϟ		P Σ T Y Φ X Ψ Ω ϡ		
Hebrew	א ב ג ד ה ו ז ח ט		י כ ל מ נ ס ע פ צ		ק ר ש ת		
Abjad	ا ب ج د ه و ز ح ط		ي ك ل م ن س ع ف ص		ق ر ش ت ث خ ذ ض ظ		غ
Abtat	ا ب ت ث ج ح خ د ذ		ر ز س ش ص ض ط ظ ع		غ ف ق ك ل م ن ه و		ي
Latin	I	V	X	L	C	D	M

forms of gematria

a method of gematria which used Arabic's natural alphabetic sequence around 1790 C.E., which is known as *abtat* (ابتت).

The various forms of gematria appear on the illustrated chart.

[Simcha Kuritzky, "Give Credit Where Credit Is Due," *N.I. Bulletin*, Oct. 1990, pp. 240-241; Raymond J. Hébert, "Abjad and the Basmala—786," *N.I. Bulletin*, July 1986, pp. 162-165; *Encyclopedia Judaica*, Vol. 7, p. 370; Richard Plant, *Arabic Coins and How to Read Them*, pp. 102-103; *Webster's New World Dictionary*, 2nd Collegiate ed., p. 1691.]

gentil [*Port.*] Gold coin of Ferdinand I "The Handsome" (1345-1383, ruled 1367-1383) of Portugal. The distinguishing feature is a portrayal of the king seated under a canopy. The reverse shows a display of five shields. This piece was also sometimes known as a *dobra gentil.*

George Name of six British kings, some of whom are extremely important in numismatics.

1. George I was born in Osnabrück, Hannover (now Lower Saxony in Germany), on May 28, 1660, to Ernest Augustus, elector of Hannover, and Sophia, granddaughter of King James I of England. He died in Osnabrück on June 11, 1727.

He succeeded Queen Anne in 1714 through provisions of the Act of Settlement. He never learned to speak English, a fact which hardly enamored him to his British subjects. His inability to communicate in the local tongue (not to mention his lukewarm attitude about being king) caused him to turn much of the rule over to his chief minister. This initiated the role of Prime Minister as a leading political figure, an arrangement which, of course, persists today.

The initials S.S.C. and W.C.C. are found under his bust or on the reverse of some silver coins struck from 1723 through 1726. These refer to the South Sea Company and the Welsh Copper Company who supplied the bullion. Similarly, roses and plumes intertwined on the reverse refer to bullion provided by the Company for Smelting Pit Coale and Sea Coale.

Copper farthings and halfpennies issued from 1717 to 1724 are known as *dump* issues. They are much thicker than most coins of those denominations.

2. George II was also born in Hannover, largely because his parents spent so much time there instead of attending to their duties in London. He was born on November 10, 1683, at Herrenhausen Palace and died on October 25, 1760, in Kensington Palace, London. His titles were king of Great Britain and Ireland and elector of Hannover.

George II shared his father's lack of enthusiasm for England and spent much of his life in Hannover. During his frequent absenses he usually left his wife, Caroline of Ansbach, to act as regent. She was a very capable woman who persuaded her husband to make several decisions which helped strengthen Britain's economy.

In 1742 he attended one of the earliest performances of George Frideric Handel's *The Messiah*. George II was so moved by the music that he stood up during the playing of the *Hallelujah Chorus*, a tradition still observed today.

In many respects George II left a very small numismatic legacy. Silver coins were struck only sporadically during his rule, and no copper coins were produced after 1754. Probably the most interesting pieces issued during his reign were some gold coins of five guineas, one guinea, and one-half guinea, plus a group of silver crowns, halfcrowns, shillings and sixpences made from bullion seized by Commodore George Anson during his circumnavigation of the world. The admiral captured the specie from the Spanish ship *Nuestra Señora de Copadonga* and from a custom house in Payta, Peru. On coins struck from this seized metal, the word *LIMA* appears under the kings effigy. See *Lima Coinage*.

3. George III (nicknamed, among other things, *Mad King George*) is by far the most interesting of the six British kings to share this name. Born in London on June 4, 1738, he was the eldest son of Frederick Louis, Prince of Wales, and was the grandson of George II. To his credit, George III was a truly English king who wanted to be an effective ruler. Unfortunately he lacked the statesmanship to achieve his lofty goals, and he failed to show good judgment when it came to delegating authority. He made the mistake of choosing Frederick North, 2d earl of Guilford, as his prime minister. Lord North's handling of royal policy did much to spark the American Revolution, a political disaster that nearly forced George III to abdicate.

George III's official titles were king of Great Britain and Ireland and elector of Hannover, basically the same titles shared by his two predecesors. But he was ultimately given a third title, that of king of Hannover, which he kept from 1815 until his death at Windsor Palace on January 29, 1820. The decision to chose him as king of Hannover by the Congress of Vienna seems very bizarre considering that he had become blind in 1809 and had long suffered from severe dementia, probably the result of a metabolic disorder called porphyria which he had inherited. By 1811 he had succumbed so totally to this disease that his son, the future George IV, had to act as regent for the remainder of George III's reign. It seems strange to imagine that someone so demented would be declared king of Hannover.

George III is a type collector's dream. During his 60-year reign, many beautiful and unusual coins were struck, as well as a wide range of tokens (including some satirical pieces), overstruck foreign coins, banknotes, and the like. Several unlikely denominations were issued, such as emergency bank tokens of three shillings and of eighteen pence (both struck from 1811-1816) and the Bank of England dollars re-struck in 1804 from Spanish American 8 real coins.

A noteworthy experiment was the attempt in 1797 to strike pennies and twopences containing their true value of copper. The results were rather ludicrous because the coins were far too big to be practical. The twopence piece in particular was given the name *cartwheel* for its large size and weight [see *cartwheel* for illustration]. In 1806 and 1807 pennies were again struck, albeit in a smaller size, but copper twopences were never again issued. Only one single specimen is known to exist of the 1808 penny.

George III's greatest numismatic achievement took place in 1816 when he was too demented to appreciate it. In that year steam-powered minting machinery was purchased to replace forever the old hand-operated presses. This dramatically increased the production capability of the mint and also enabled the facility to create coins of great artistry.

The most enduring art to come from this transformation was Benedetto Pistrucci's magnificent reverse design known as *St. George Slaying the Dragon*. This classic work, first seen on the crowns of 1818, has reappeared throughout the 19th and 20th centuries.

Not all of George III's coins are attractive. See *wart on nose*, the term for an 1806 farthing with an unusual die break.

4. George IV, the eldest son of George III, was born in London on August 12, 1762, and died June 26, 1830, in Windsor Palace. Although he officially became king on the death of his father in 1820, he had been the acting regent since 1811 due to George III's incapacity.

George IV was not popular with his subjects, largely due to the debts he accrued from his extravagances and because of his personal peccadillos. Somewhat reminiscent of Henry VIII, George IV went through two clumsy marriages complicated by religious conflicts (although George IV was hardly in the position to have his wives beheaded, since they were far more popular than he). On his death he was succeeded to the throne by his brother, William IV.

George IV left a very meager numismatic legacy. Although the new mintage facility built at Tower Hill in 1816 produced coins of high technical quality, the coinage issues were rather straightforward with no particular innovations other than the issuance of a £2 gold piece in 1823 and the reinstatement of copper farthings in 1821.

King George V

5. George V (born June 3, 1865, in London; died January 20, 1936, at Sandringham House, Norfold) was the first British monarch to realize the need to become accessible to his subjects, starting a trend which has shown mixed results in the late twentieth century.

Although he was born into the house of Saxe-Coburg-Gotha, he renounced his German titles at the beginning of World War I and changed the royal name to the house of Windsor. As a sailor who had entered the Royal Navy in 1877 and had risen to the rank of vice admiral in 1903, George V took an active interest in the "War to end all wars" and achieved great popularity with his subjects.

Unlike his Georgian predecessors, this king not only inherited the title of king of Great Britain and Ireland but also that of emperor of India. He lost his reign of Ireland in the rebellion of 1922 but retained Northern Ireland as part of his domain.

His numismatic legacy in Britain is fairly minimal, yet he was the first King George to see his effigy on a significant number of Commonwealth coins. The three extant 1911 Canadian pattern silver dollars bearing his portrait (two in silver, one in copper) are called the *Emperor* of Canadian coinage, while the scarce 1921 Canadian half dollars are referred to as the *King* of that country's coins. One of the most significant issues in New Zealand history is the Waitangi Crown of 1935, celebrating the cooperation of European and Aboriginal cultures on the reverse while portraying George V's effigy on the obverse. He appeared on the coins of India and many other Commonwealth Countries during his reign. [Also see *pig rupee* and *ghosting*.]

6. George VI was not groomed to be king. As second in line to the throne, everyone always assumed that his older brother Edward would be king. But, then, "everyone" did not assume that Edward would renounce his throne after only nine months to marry an American divorcée. Prepared or not, George VI became king of Great Britain and Northern Ireland and emperor of India in 1936.

George VI was born in Sandringham, Norfolk, on December 14, 1895. He married Lady Elizabeth Bowes-Lyon who would later be known to her many loving subjects as Queen

Mother Elizabeth. Just as his father had done, George VI faced a major war and dealt with it admirably. He was a symbol of strength during World War II and helped his people overcome the Nazi aggression. George VI died on February 6, 1952, and was succeeded by his daughter, Elizabeth II.

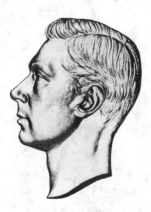

King George VI

Under George VI Britain changed its threepence coin from a small, round silver piece to a larger, thicker, twelve-sided nickel-brass coin. Patterns with the effigy of Edward VIII had been produced to send to vending machine companies so they could make necessary adjustments to their equipment, but the first regular issue coins of this type showed George VI.

Much of his numismatic legacy can be seen in Canada, where two separate events caused a disruption in the production of normal coinage. First, of course, no one was prepared for the abdication of Edward VIII. Coinage matrices and punches with his effigy had to be junked, and mint officials did not expect dies portraying George VI to be ready on time. Thus, some Canadian cents, ten cent pieces, and quarter dollars were struck with old dies of George V but with a dot placed under the date or under the wreath to show that the coins were produced during the reign of George VI. This was a wasted effort, because the 1937 dies showed up soon enough for a significant quantity of coins to be issued. The cents and

ten cent pieces are exceedingly scarce; only the quarter dollars are relatively common and within the budget of the average collector. But even some of those were struck on over-used dies and show signs of *ghosting*[q.v.].

The second disruption came in 1948 when India achieved its independence. Coins of the British world could no longer state that George VI was king "and emperor of India" (*ET IND. IMP.* as abbreviated in Latin). Again, there was the possibility of a delay in getting revised obverse matrices and punches to Canada. Because of a pressing coin shortage, the Canadian Mint used 1947 dies but added a small maple leaf next to the date to indicate that the coins were actually struck in 1948. When the corrected dies arrived, normal 1948 coinage was issued, although the ten cent pieces and dollars of that date are somewhat scarce.

[Stephen Mitchell & Brian Reeds (editors), *Coins of England and the United Kingdom* (Seaby, 1991), pp. 247-333; *Funk & Wagnalls New Encyclopedia* (1984), Vol. 11, pp. 290-2; J. A. Haxby and R. C. Willey, *Coins of Canada* (9th Ed.), pp. 24-53.]

gerçek [*Turk.*] authentic.

gerepareerd [*Dut.*] repaired.

Germania [*Ital., Rom.*] Germany.

Germania de Est [*Rom.*] East Germany (D.D.R.).

Germania de Vest [*Rom.*] West Germany (B.R.D.).

German silver Despite its name, this coinage alloy contains no actual silver. It is an alloy of copper, nickel, and zinc. Typically the makeup is 55-65% copper, 18% nickel, and the balance zinc. German silver can have a bright yellow appearance when new, but wears rapidly to a dull white with a possible yellowish cast. German silver was used in some United States patterns as early as 1854. It is also found in the 1952 5 and 10 centavo pieces of El Salvador.

One particular composition of German silver is called *Feuchtwanger's metal*, so-named for Dr. Lewis Feuchtwanger, the metallugist who created it and who tried to convince the U.S. Congress to issue coins made from it as a replacement for copper coins.

[Contributed by Halbert Carmichael.]

ghetto money: 50 pfennig and 1 mark notes

gettone (*m.*) [*Ital.*] token.

gewicht (*n.*) [*Dut.*] weight.

Gewicht (*n.*) [*Ger.*] weight.

gewijzidge datum (*m.-c.*) [*Dut.*] altered date.

gewöhnlich [*Ger.*] common.

gewoon [*Dut.*] common.

ghetto money (a.k.a. *ghetto crown* from the German *Gettokronen*). Special coins and paper money produced by the Germans during World War II for use by Jews who were imprisoned in detention camps and ghettos. These pieces were actually receipts given in exchange for German or Polish money, as the ghetto money was the only form of currency that the Jews were permitted to use while in these camps.

Ghetto money was officially issued for the ghettos in Lodz, Poland, and Theresienstadt, Czechoslovakia; and detention camps in Cremona, Italy, and Westerbork, The Netherlands. The most significant of these issues were the notes printed for the Theresienstadt ghetto, a place near the small town of Terezin which was used to house "privileged" Jews such as German World War I heroes. The Theresienstadt notes, available in seven denominations (1, 2, 5, 10, 20, 50, and 100 kronen), show a vignette of Moses holding the Ten Commandments (i.e., the decalog) and are often called *Moses Crowns*[*q.v.*]. [See page 312 for color illustration].

It is believed that the ghetto notes were invented for propaganda purposes to show that the Jews had a semblance of a normal life and autonomy. However, in reality there was nothing to buy with the notes. The Jews in the ghetto were forced into crowded conditions with little food, and many died of starvation and disease. Many Jews were also deported to death camps. Of the 140,000 Jews interred in Theresienstadt, fewer than 20,000 survived the war.

Both the coins (aluminum and magnesium 5, 10, and 20 marks dated 1943) and the notes (50 pfennig, 1, 2, 5, 10, 20, and 50 marks dated

May 15, 1940) were issued for use in the Lodz (Litzmanstadt) Ghetto in Poland. The large 20 mark coin is sometimes called a *ghetto crown*.

Ghetto 10 mark coin

For many years it was believed that in Poland, some illegal ghetto currency was printed by Jewish postal authorities confined in the ghetto. These unofficial pieces were particularly symbolic and historically significant in that they show a group of Stars of David, a barbed wire fence, and a flame containing the SS insignia. However, this background information has not been confirmed and the notes are now regarded as being of questionable origin.

[Contributed by Simcha Kuritzky. Zvi Stahl, *Jewish Ghettos' and Concentration Camps' Money (1933-1945)*; Steven A. Feller and Barbara Feller, "Ghetto Money of the Nazi Holocaust," *The Numismatist*, April 1981, pp. 875-881; Arlie Slabaugh, *Prisoner of War Monies and Medals* (Chicago: Hewitt Brothers, 1966); Evzen Sknouril, "Theresienstadt's Bleak Bank Note Story," *The Shekel*, September-October 1982; Alan York, "The Paper Money Used in the Theresienstadt Ghetto: The Inside Story," *The Shekel*, March-April 1983, pp. 27-33.]

ghost coin An authorized coin which is never issued. The *dominicano* of the Dominican Republic is one example. It was to have been introduced in 1889 but was never struck, presumably for economic reasons.

ghosting Ghost-like image of the obverse effigy which inadvertently appears on the reverse side. This is not a minting error in the usual sense but is instead a bad strike resulting from poorly designed dies. Ghosting can occur when both the obverse and reverse dies have too much relief in the same spots opposite each other, especially if the planchet is rather large and thin. There is not enough pressure from a single strike of the coinage press to force the metal into all areas of both dies. Since the obverse effigy is often broader, deeper, and more extensive than the reverse design, the metal is sucked into the obverse die and away from the reverse die. Ghosting can most readily be seen on British pennies of Edward VII and George V.

Worn dies can cause ghosting problems of a different nature. The unexpected abdication of Edward VIII in December 1936 prevented the Royal Mint from preparing new dies in time for 1937 production of Commonwealth coins. The Ottawa Mint tried to recycle 1936 dies of its cents, 10 cents, and quarter dollars by placing a dot at the bottom on the reverse to indicate that the coins were actually struck in 1937. But the old quarter dollar dies were so worn that the ghosting effect caused most of the specimens to be weakly struck and with the first three letters of the word CANADA bearly readable. The same problem is found on many Canadian large cents of the early twentieth century, especially those of Edward VII and George V. (See *reused die* for an illustration.)

As a rule, proof specimens do not exhibit ghosting because the coins are struck at least twice, giving the metal the chance to flow into every possible crevice.

[J. A. Haxby and R. C. Willey, *Coins of Canada* (9th Ed.), p. 53.]

ghosting on British penny

giá ghi trên bản mục lục [*Viet.*] catalogue value.

giallo [*Ital.*] yellow.

Giampaoli, Pietro Chief Engraver of the Rome Mint (1937-63). Born February 14, 1898, in Buia (Udine), Italy.

Giampaoli was called into the army at eighteen years of age to participate in the First World War. While trying to conquer Mount Grappa during the Austrian offensive, he was taken prisoner and subsequently interned in Hungary. While in a Hungarian concentration camp, he met Russian prisoners who were specialists in engraving. From them he had the occasion and the opportunity to learn this art. He subsequently became involved with other artistic specialties of the various laboratories in the concentration camp. After he was sent home at the end of the war, he attended schools where he specialized in engraving and sculpture.

Working as an engraver for the Johnson Company in Milan, he took part in various national contests. In 1924 he won first prize for relief sculpture and four years later, first prize for engraving. In 1937 he acquired the position of Chief Engraver of the Rome Mint.

Shortly after the end of World War II, he was called to Baden-Baden as technical consultant to the French Ateliers in the Occupation Zone. In 1949 Giampaoli participated in the First International Exhibition of the post-war medallions in Paris where the critics singled out the medallions and praised the technique and sensitivity of the modeling. Later that year, he was given the job of making the models and engraving Vatican coins for the Holy See of 1950.

The year 1951 saw Giampaoli take part in the International Exhibition of the Medallions of Madrid, winning first prize. His expertise was again put to the task in 1953 when he was called upon to create a magnificent group of medals and plaquettes for the coronation of Britain's Queen Elizabeth II. Three years later the Ministry of Finance for Turkey gave him the job of preparing the models and making the engraving of the cons for the State of Turkey by the Istanbul Mint.

Giampaoli was honored in 1959 by the Governor of the National Bank of Tunisia who requested that he make four new gold coins to commemorate Tunisian independence. From 1960 until his retirement on March 1, 1963, he executed for the Vatican the official medallions commemorating key events of Pope John XXIII and Pope Paul VI.

During his long career, Pietro Giampaoli was a major contributor to the field of medallic art.

[Contributed by Emil Voigt, largely based on personal correspondences between Mr. Voigt and Mr. Giampaoli.]

Giappone [*Ital.*] Japan.

giá tiền [*Viet.*] price.

giá trị [*Viet.*] value.

giá trị pháp dịng [*Viet.*] face value.

giấy bạc [*Viet.*] paper money; banknote.

gießen (*v.*) [*Ger.*] to cast.

gieten (*v.*) [*Dut.*] to cast.

gin 銀 [*Jpn.*] silver.

ginkôken 銀行券 [*Jpn.*] banknote.

ginto [*Tag.*] gold.

giro (*m.*) [*Span.*] money order.

gizô bôshikaku 偽造防止策 [*Jpn.*] anti-counterfeiting device.

gizzi penny [with many other spellings, including *kissi* penny.] Twisted iron rod flattened on both ends. It was used as a unit of

African gizzi penny

exchange in Sierra Leone, Liberia, and French Guinea. This item was often referred to as the "coin with a soul," because if it were broken, a witch doctor had to repair it and "restore" the soul.

The value of the gizzi penny was pegged according to the number it took to buy a wife, usually 240. More were needed if the pennies were not in good condition.

gjuta (v.) [*Swed.*] to cast.

glanslöshet (r.) [*Swed.*] tarnish.

gnision γνήσιον [*Grk.*] genuine, authentic.

god [*Dan., Swed.*] good.

George V "Godless" obverse

Godless coinage Coins, particularly of Britain or the Commonwealth, which fail to show the inscription *Dei Gratia* ("By the Grace of God") or its abbreviation D.G. Its omission has always caused a public outcry which has prompted the restoration of the motto, usually the following year.

Among the coins in this category are the 1849 British florins of Queen Victoria and the 1911 Canadian coinage (all denominations) of King George V.

goed [*Dut.*] good.

gôkin 合金 [*Jpn.*] alloy (of metals).

gokuin 極印 [*Jpn.*] (coinage) die.

gold A precious metal used extensively for coinage. [element: group 1b of the periodic table; atomic weight 196.967; atomic number 79; specific gravity 19.32 (at 68° F (20° C); symbol Au.]

Gold has been used since ancient times in coinage and is regarded as the "king" of coinage metals. The very first coins (as numismatists define the term) were made in Asia Minor circa 620-600 B.C. of a natural mixture of approximately three parts gold and one part silver known as *electrum*[q.v.], although this ratio could vary greatly. In the succeeding century, the two metals were separated using the best technology of the time, and coins were made primarily of one metal or the other. The refining process was done primarily to guarantee consistency and to assure that the coinage alloy of gold coins actually contained enough gold. This process has continued to the present day. The technology has progressed to the degree that Canada, the United States, and many other countries are issuing bullion coins made of gold so pure that it is in excess of .999 fine.

Gold was not only regarded as a precious metal by the ancients but was also a favorite metal for producing beautiful artifacts. Because these people held gold in such high esteem, it logically followed that the coins made from this metal would be as artistically superb as the ancient moneyers could produce. The lovely Arsinoe octadrachm of the Ptolemaic Kingdom is one such example. The whole realm of Greek stater[q.v.] coins and Roman aureus[q.v.] pieces falls into the category of magnificence.

Gold coinage as an art form reached its pinacle during the late Middle Ages. Hundreds of incredibly impressive coins were struck throughout Europe and beyond. In particular, the German states and Italian states produced a dazzling array of gold coins and medals which display a superlative level of workmanship. England, Spain, and many other countries also issued gold pieces of great artistry.

The nineteenth and twentieth centuries have witnessed a resurgence in gold coin splendor. The St. Gaudens double eagle ($20 gold piece), especially the 1907 specimens with Roman numerals and high relief, are surely the finest coins ever produced by the United States Mints. The Isle of Man bullion coin known as the *Angel*[q.v.] is an example of a late-twentieth century piece exhibiting magnificent designs and craftsmanship. The most beautiful gold

coin in history may well be the 1839 English £5 gold masterpiece called *Una and the Lion*[q.v.], so named because of its depiction on the reverse of the young Queen Victoria in the role of William Spencer's character Una from *The Fairie Queene*. This issue has been called the high point of the English engraver's art. The coin illustrated here is another beautiful Victorian £5 coin, the 1887 specimen featuring Pistrucci's famous *St. George Slaying the Dragon* on the reverse.

British gold: 1887 £5 of Queen Victoria

Although many gold coins are beautiful, the history of gold is not. Throughout recorded history, countless atrocities have been committed by unscrupulous people in their quest for gold. The Spanish and other Europeans exploited the inhabitants of the New World in order to acquire gold and other precious commodities. South Africa, the creator of the famous *Krugerrand*[q.v.], was accused for many years of using its huge gold production to help perpetuate its widely criticized racial policies.

In gold's defense, the lust for gold has sometimes brought positive changes. The discovery of gold in California in 1849 began a gold rush of epic proportions which significantly contributed to the development of the American West. Of course, it also hastened the demise of the way of life of the American Indians.

Whether gold is a hero or a scoundrel, it has played a truly major role in the history of numismatics. Because it is so precious, it allows coins of sizable value to be struck. It is an attractive metal which retains its beauty largely due to its molecular inertness; i.e., in its pure state, its atoms do not normally attach to the atoms of other elements as do silver and copper atoms, so pure gold does not tarnish or corrode. Because gold is so soft, it is usually alloyed with copper to make it harder for coinage purposes: the more copper, the darker and more orange-colored its appearance. Its composition is measured in either carats or fineness.

From the days of the Great Depression in the early 1930s until 1973, the U.S. government tried to regulate the price of gold and to keep it at $35 an ounce. Americans citizens were not permitted to own gold, except in jewelry and collectable coins minted prior to 1934. Raising the price to $42.22 in 1973 did not help, because gold was trading on the free market in Europe for as much as five times that amount. The ban on private ownership of gold by U.S. citizens was lifted at the beginning of 1975, and the price of gold rose as high as $850 an ounce in early 1980.

Golden Cycle The period between 1492 and 1525 when the conquest and settlement of Santo Domingo took place. Europeans made repeated voyages to the Caribbean during those years in search of gold and spices which were sent back to Europe to bolster the economies of the home countries.

[Manuel Moreno Fraginals and José A. Pulido Ledesma, *Cuba: A Country and Its Currency*, National Bank of Cuba, p. 12]

Goldsilberlegierung (*f.*) [*Ger.*] gold-silver alloy. This term is used to refer to *electrum*[q.v.], a naturally-found alloy of approximately three parts gold and one part silver from which the earliest coins were minted just prior to 600 B.C. The preferable word in German is *Elektrum* (*n.*).

goloid An alloy containing small quantities of gold in copper. It was promoted as a method for making small denomination coins with intrinsic value.

go-momme gin

go-momme gin Rectangular silver Japanese coins issued from 1765 to 1772. They are also known as *Meiwa go-momme gin* because they were issued during the Meiwa era. The coins were valued at 1/12 ryo or 5 momme (18.75 gr. of silver). The mintmaster's name is shown on the reverse.

[William D. Craig, *Coins of the World: 1750-1850* (3rd Ed.), p. 344.]

50 cent *good for*

good fors (*noun*) Small trade tokens issued by merchants as advertising promotions. Their name comes from the inscription "good for (a certain amount) in merchandise" or "good for (one beer or some other item)."

In the nineteenth and twentieth centuries, thousands of *good fors* were issued in many parts of the world. This type of token is called a *bon* in French and a *gut für* in German. They come in an endless variety of shapes and styles, but most are made of aluminum or other base metal.

See *trade token* for additional information, and page 316 for color illustrations.

góra (*f.*) [*Pol.*] top.

Görögország [*Hun.*] Greece.

"Gothic" crown

Gothic Ornate design used on British silver crowns (1847 and 1853) and florins (1851-1887). The obverse shows the crowned head of the young Queen Victoria. The inscriptions are in gothic lettering and the dates are stated in gothic-style roman numerals.

gotówka (*f.*) [*Pol.*] cash (ready money).

goud (*n.*) [*Dut.*] gold.

goú wáng 国王 [*Chin.-py./sc.*] king.

grabado [*Span.*] engraved.

grabado en acero (*m.*) [*Span.*] steel engraving.

Grã-Bretanha [*Port.*] Great Britain.

grad (*r.*) [*Swed.*] grade, condition.

grade Determination of a coin or medal's surface wear, or the degree to which a note has been folded or torn. The grade reflects the amount of circulation a piece has seen. It also takes into account the quality of strike,

whether the piece has been cleaned, number of bag marks, etc.

Starting in the 1980s, the word *grade* has no longer been synonymous with *condition*. Since the advent of third-party grading services, the word *grade* usually refers to an objective measure of a coin's state of preservation determined on a scale ranging from 1 to 70. The grade is thus given as MS-65, EF-45, F-12, or whatever. Coins struck in proof are graded as PR-60 to PR-70, or as PR-59 or less if they are impaired.

The word *condition* is currently utilized more as a subjective measure, using the terms *good, very good, fine, very fine, extremely fine* (or *extra fine*), *about uncirculated*, and *uncirculated*, with or without such qualifying adjectives as *brilliant*, but almost always without the numbering system.

gradera (*v.*) [*Swed.*] to grade.

grado de conservación; graduación (*f.*) [*Span.*] grade, condition.

graduar (*v.*) [*Span.*] to grade.

gráfila (*f.*) [*Span.*] bead (raised dot on the surface of a coin or medal).

graffio (*m.*) [*Ital.*] a scratch.

graining [*Eng.: U.K., Austl., N.Z., S.A., et al*] Continuous indentations around the edge of a coin to prevent metal from being clipped off fraudulently. Also known as *serrated edge*, *crenations*, *reeded edge*, and *milled edge*, the latter two terms being particularly common in the U.S. and Canada (although *milled edge* is now considered somewhat archaic).

grammatio γραμμάτιο (*m.*) [*Grk.*] note, banknote.

Gran Bretaña [*Span.*] Great Britain.

Gran Bretagna [*Ital.*] Great Britain.

grand [*Fr.*] big, large.

grande [*Ital., Span., Port.*] big, large.

Grande Bretagne [*Fr.*] Great Britain.

gratsoynia γρατσουνιά (*f.*) [*Grk.*] a scratch.

grau (*m.*) [*Port.*] grade, condition.

gravada [*Port.*] engraved.

grave [*Port.*] Billon coin issued during the reign of Ferdinand I "The Handsome" (1345-1383, ruled 1367-1383) of Portugal. Its distinguishing feature is a crowned "F" on the reverse.

graverad [*Swed.*] engraved.

graveret [*Dan.*] engraved.

gravert [*Nor.*] engraved.

graviert [*Ger.*] engraved.

gravură în oţel (*f.*) [*Rom.*] steel engraving.

gravure en creux [*Fr.*] intaglio.

gravure sur acier [*Fr.*] steel engraving.

Amelia Earhart medal, reverse

Great Moments in Manned Flight Set of six medals presented in the early 1970s to Trans World Airline's frequent-flyer passengers. Each medal shows one or more aviation innovators on the obverse and their means of air transportation on the reverse. The people portrayed are Amelia Earhart, aviatrix who pioneered trans-Atlantic flight in 1932; Leonardo da Vinci, who conceptualized manned flight in 1490; Stephan and Joseph Montgolfier, whose hot-air balloon provided the first ascent of man in 1783; Wilbur and Orville Wright, responsible for the first heavier-than-air flight in 1903; Charles Lindbergh, who made the first one-man trans-Atlantic flight; and astronauts Aldrin, Armstrong, and Collins who made the first moon landing.

The medals are 38 mm in diameter and have an antique silver anodized finish. The set was created as a marketing promotion for TWA and is housed in a stand-up holder intended to be displayed on a desk and seen by the recipient's colleagues. Despite their commercial purpose, the medals are attractive and historically interesting.

[Clifford Mishler, "New decade offers untold collecting opportunities," *Numismatic News*, January 16, 1990, p. 52.]

Great Seal of the United States Official seal of the United States as adopted in 1782.

Unlike the seal of any other nation, the Great Seal of the United States has two sides. The obverse depicts an American eagle, symbolizing national sovereignty. On its breast is the national shield with its traditional thirteen bars. In its right talon, the eagle grasps an olive branch of thirteen leaves and thirteen olives representing peace. The left talon clutches 13 arrows signifying the fight for liberty and independence. The eagle's beak holds a scroll with the Latin inscription *E Pluribus Unum*, the official U.S. motto meaning "From Many, One." Above the eagle is a cluster of thirteen stars surrounded by a cloud of glory. In each case, the number thirteen refers to the thirteen original colonies which banded together to form one government.

The reverse is dominated by an Egyptian-style pyramid, symbolic of permanence and strength. Yet this pyramid is unfinished, representing the young country and its promise to build and grow. The "Eye of Providence", based on an ancient Egyptian symbol of understanding and truth, sits atop the pyramid. At the bottom of the pyramid is engraved the date 1776, the year in which the Declaration of Independence was signed. This is regarded as the founding date of the U.S.A. Surrounding the pyramid are two additional Latin inscriptions: *Annuit cœptis* ("God has smiled on our undertakings") and *Novus ordo seclorum* ("New Order of the Ages").

Although the Great Seal was commissioned shortly after the signing of the Declaration of Independence on July 4, 1776, the final design was not adopted by the U.S. Congress until June 20, 1782.

Both sides of the Great Seal are depicted on the reverse of the US one dollar notes which have been issued since the mid-1930s. The *Heraldic Eagle*, found on the reverse of many early U.S. gold and silver coins, is a variation of the front of the Great Seal. Another variation is the Presidential Coat of Arms as seen on the reverse of the Kennedy Half Dollars.

Grecia [*Span., Ital., Rom.*] Greece.

Grécia [*Port.*] Greece.

Grecja [*Pol.*] Greece.

Greek coinage (classical) Reference to all coins struck in the Mediterranean and Black Sea regions from the first coinage (ca. 620-600 B.C.) through the first century B.C., except for those issued from Rome or its provinces starting in the third century B.C.

The great artistry that characterized the production of ancient Greek coins has been a virtually endless source of inspiration for ancient and modern medalists and coin designers as well as sculptors and painters. It is no surprise then, that as early as the sixteenth century A.D., coin collectors became fascinated with the gold, silver, and bronze numismatic output of the Greek world.

But early modern collectors as well as today's numismatists are not the only individuals to become enamored with Greek coinage. It is said that the Roman Emperor Augustus was a great admirer of Greek numismatic art. He was particularly impressed by the portraits of ancient rulers and shared his delight by donating old coins to guests and friends.

The first coins were minted in western Asia Minor (Turkey) shortly before 600 B.C. Before that time, money existed in various primitive forms. At this early stage, a wide range of objects or commodities were used by various civilizations as money. Xenophanes of Colophon is recorded as saying that coinage was invented by the Lydians. Shortly thereafter, the Greek historian Herodotus also tells us that the first people to have struck coins in silver and gold were the Lydians. Later sources give us confusing accounts, but modern research tends to confirm that Herodotus was right. However, a negligible discrepancy can be noted in his account, for the early coinage is neither made of silver nor gold but of an alloy of both metals called *electrum*[q.v.] ("pale gold"). This alloy occurs naturally in alluvial deposits such as the ones identified near Mount Tmolus and Mount Sipylus in Lydia; later the alloy was produced artificially at various mints by mixing the two

metals and eventually adding some copper to improve the hardness of the metal.

These early "pale gold" coins were made by stamping minute lumps of electrum. The stamping consisted of a simple punch which went deep enough into the metal to prove that the nugget was not made from a base metal core plated with a precious metal. The obverse depicted a lioness, or a lion's head or that of a griffin. The reverse was also punched, usually resulting in an incuse sinking with one or more squares.

After this first phase, gold and silver pieces were minted by the legendary King Crœsus of Lydia (ca. 560-547 B.C.). These coins encountered great favor, and the second half of the sixth century B.C. brought improved technology and saw a number of cities of western Asia Minor setting up their own mints.

The Greek world— from the Black Sea and throughout the Mediterranean— soon became acquainted with this new currency. The invention of coins as a form of currency was quickly adopted by many city-states and islands. Territories under Persian rule, namely Cyprus and Cyrenaica, did not fail to grasp the importance of the novelty.

Minting began in mainland Greece around 550 B.C. when Aegina, an island in the Saronic Golf between the Peloponnese and Attica, struck its first silver coinage. At this point in time, different standards of weight, different alloys, and lack of small denominations generated enormous confusion. The silver coinage of Aegina, however, grew in prominence in the Greek world for its consistency in weight standards and alloy. So much so, the Aeginetan standard became one of the two prevailing standards, the other being the Euboic-Attic.

Very much aware of the political and civic prestige to be gained by minting their own coins, the dictators of the city-states of mainland Greece began striking their own coins. Athens, Abdera, and Corinth began minting their own coins within the period 550-525 B.C. Huge quantities of silver were mined at Laurium in Attica, which gave further impetus to the Athenian coinage and in time established Athens as a political and economic superpower.

Once it became clear that the more widespread and consistent the coinage of a given city, the more political and economic clout it had, cities began engaging in outdoing each other in the distinction of their coinage and its artistic beauty. Sacred, mythical figures and deities were portrayed on coins; religious emblems, badges or symbols of cities, and even local products adorned the silver output of the many mints.

By the third quarter of the sixth century, the cities of Carystus, Eretria, and Chalcis (all situated on the large island of Euboea) began to produce silver coins struck only on one side, but in due course both obverse and reverse were utilized.

Athens moved from its early series displaying heraldic emblems to a new and more popular type depicting a helmeted head of Athena on the obverse and an owl together with the abbreviated name of the city on the reverse. This new silver coinage was adopted as early as 500-510 B.C. and became known as *Owls*. Its basic denomination was the tetradrachm (four drachmæ) with a weight of about 17 grams. The Athenians did not adopt the weight standard of hostile Aegina; instead they produced their coins on the "Attic-Euboic" standard which had as its basic unit the drachm weighing about 4.25 grams. The Aeginatan standard was based on a 6 gram drachm. The *owls* had a wide circulation and an extremely long life.

As early as 570 B.C., Corinth inaugurated a series of silver coins depicting the winged horse Pegasus. These coins were nicknamed *colts* or *foals* and are characterized by a light unit consisting of a drachm of three grams. The Corinthian stater of three drachmæ had a weight of about 8.6 grams (half the weight of the Athenian owl). Concerned about the identification of their coinage, the Corinthians inscribed their "colts" with the city's initial— the archaic letter *koppa*. The reverse moved from an archaic "Union Jack" type to a more

defined "swastika" pattern; later (ca. 500 B.C.) the pattern was replaced by a head of Athena within an incuse square. Corinth owed its prominence and wealth to its strategic location, positioned as it was at the isthmus between the Ionian and the Aegean Seas.

Northern Greece had rich silver mines which contributed to the opulent Macedonian coinage. Beginning about 520 B.C. Macedonian output distinguished itself for large denomination pieces such as the octadrachm (eight drachm coin). The high weight was not the only appeal Macedonian coins had; their popularity was further enhanced by very artistic designs and compositions depicting a lion attacking a variety of animals (stags, boars, bulls, etc.).

Bœtia and most cities gravitating around Thebes began minting silver towards the end of the sixth century B.C. A number of islands off the coast of Thrace also began their coinage in about 525 B.C.

The southern region of the Italian peninsula and Sicily had been under Greek influence since the eighth and seventh centuries B.C. This crucial area of geo-political influence was later labeled by the Romans as *Magna Græcia* ("Great Greece"). Although numismatists have put forward several contrasting theories as to when coinage started in southern Italy, some of the most authoritative experts tend to agree that Sybaris was the leader when— shortly after 550 B.C.— it began producing coins depicting a bull as the river-god Crathis and inscribed with the abbreviated name of the city. Sybaris had gained widespread reputation for its wealth and, its *spread flan* coinage was a further ostentation of grandeur. The Sybarite dominance stretched from the Adriatic to the Etruscan coast, thus granting virtual monopoly over trade between north and south. The rapid and affluent hegemony came to an end in 510 B.C. when Sybaris received a fatal blow from its neighbor, Croton. Shortly thereafter the victors began minting their own coins depicting a tripod.

The coinage of Sybaris (as well as that of Metapontum and Croton before and after the Sybarite debacle) was produced with a very sophisticated technology that required extreme accuracy. These incuse[q.v.] coins show the same design on both sides, but on the obverse it is in relief while on the reverse it is "struck in" with an intaglio technique. The flan was stunningly thin and the technique required an almost perfect alignment of the two dies— a very difficult feat.

By this time, Syracuse in southern Sicily was considered by many to be the most important city in the entire Greek world. For a while Syracuse had been importing currency from its trading partners, but by the end of the sixth century B.C. it began a long-lived and glorious coinage.

[Contributed by Giorgio Migliavacca.]

greenback 1. Popular name for the Demand Notes[q.v.] issued by the U.S. in 1861 and 1862. They acquired their name due to their reverses' being printed entirely in green ink.

[Mary Jane Michael, "Greenbacks— The Controversial Currency," *The Numismatist*, April 1981, pp. 890-901.]

2. Slang expression for any U.S. note whose reverse is printed exclusively in green ink, including all of the paper money currently being issued.

Israeli greeting token

greeting token Commemorative token or medal sent to subscribers of the Israel Government Coins and Medals Corporation as a New Year's greeting.

The first was issued in 1964 (5724) and consisted of a genuine Israeli one agora coin set in a brass frame (see illustration). The inscription on the brass frame (obverse)

translates as *Good Year 7524*. The reverse inscription reads *The Israel Company for Medals and Coins* (the organization's name prior to 1970). The company's official seal appears at the bottom.

In 1965 (5725) the commemorative gift was a bookmark into which a small medal was inserted. The following year and thereafter, the greeting tokens have been in the form of a medal. The obverse design is changed each year to give the medal a realistic character.

Similar greeting tokens have also been issued by the American-Israel Numismatic Association. The name and emblem of the A.I.N.A. appear in place of those of the Israel Corporation.

[Contributed by Rabbi John Spitzer.]

greșeală (*f.*) [*Rom.*] error.
Griechenland [*Ger.*] Greece.
Griekenland [*Dut.*] Greece.

Scottish groat of James III (1460-88)

groat 1. British silver coin of four pence issued variously from 1279 to 1855. Later pieces were also issued: 1888 for colonial use only, and fourpence coins struck for Maundy[*q.v.*] sets being issued up to the present day.

2. Scottish silver coins valued at fourpence when they were first released in 1357; later valued at 6d, 12d, 14d, and 18d.
groen [*Dut.*] green.
grøn [*Dan.*] green.
groot [*Dut.*] large.
Groot-Brittannië [*Dut.*] Great Britain.
groot zilverstuk (*n.*) [*Dut.*] crown (large silver coin).
groß [*Ger.*] large, big; great.
Großbritannien [*Ger.*] Great Britain.
grön [*Swed.*] green.
grønn [*Nor.*] green.

gros [*Fr.*] big, large.
grün [*Ger.*] green.
gǔ bì de 古币的 [*Chin.-py./sc.*] numismatic.
gǔ bì shōu cáng jiā 古币收藏家 [*Chin.-py./sc.*] numismatist.
gǔ dài 古代 [*Chin.-py./sc.*] ancient.
Guide Book of United States Coins, A Retail price guide of U.S. coins which has been issued annually since 1946. More commonly known as the *Red Book*.

The Red Book was born as a companion publication to the *Handbook of United States Coins*[*q.v.*] (known as the *Blue Book*), which was introduced in 1942 as a wholesale price guide of U.S. coins. Both books were authored by R S. Yeoman and published by Whitman Publishing Company of Racine, Wisconsin.

Yeoman would have introduced the Red Book earlier had not World War II interfered. The first edition was printed in late 1946 but with the cover date of 1947. Current editions are released on July 1 of every year with the following year's cover date.

The books contain a great deal of information in addition to prices. They encompass all areas of U.S. coins from the Colonial period to the present day, including commemoratives, territorial gold, and Confederate issues. Prices are calculated by surveying a large group of numismatic experts, primarily dealers.

The Red Books are so popular that they themselves are collected by numismatists and book specialists. Many are becoming quite valuable, especially the first, third, and fifth editions.

Richard S. Yeoman died in 1988, but the books are being continued under a different authorship.

[Ginger Rapsus, "The Red Book Story," *The Numismatist*, September 1988, pp. 1561-65.]

guilloche (*m.*) [*Fr.*] Circular or symmetrical machine-generated pattern found on many banknotes, bonds, and various other types of certificates. Although these designs can be extremely attractive, especially when done in multiple colors, they are used on paper money primarily because *guilloche* designs are hard to

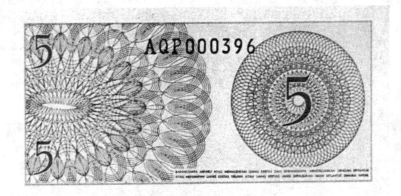

note with multiple *guilloche* designs

counterfeit. The patterns tend to be intricate with very fine lines.

The technique was created by Asa Spencer, an American inventor who built a geometrical lathe capable of engraving such a design onto a steel engraving plate. The patterns soon became popular and are now used worldwide.

guinea British gold coin valued at 20 shillings when it was first struck by Charles II in 1663. It became a 30 shilling coin in 1694 and then dropped to the unlikely value of 21 shillings 6 pence from 1698-1717 when England scrapped most of its coins and struck new ones as a way of ridding itself of badly debased silver coins. The value of the guinea value finally settled at 21 shillings in 1717 and has remained so until the present day, even though coins of this value were discontinued in 1813.

From 1814 until the coinage decimalization of 1970, the guinea was strictly a money of account. Prices of luxury items were usually quoted in guineas (at 21 shillings) rather than pounds (worth only 20 shillings) so that the seller could legitimately draw a five percent advantage.

guk-in 국인 [*Kor.*] (coinage) die.

guld (*n.*) [*Dan., Swed.*] gold.

gull (*n.*) [*Nor.*] gold.

gümüş [*Turk.*] silver.

Güney Afrika [*Turk.*] South Africa.

gun money; gunmoney Coins struck by James II in 1689 and 1690 when he was in exile in Ireland. He was attempting to regain his English throne but lacked the necessary funds to wage war. As a way of raising money, he issued brass coins made from old cannons, bells, and other scrap metal. James claimed the coins were "official," and he promised to redeem them in sterling silver after he regained his throne (which he never did). The coins were originally called *brass money* but eventually became known as *gun money*.

Irish gun money: 1690 crown (year only)

A unique feature of gun money is that many of the coins were dated not only with the year but also the month. The shilling in the illustration is an example. On the reverse under the crown can be seen the abbreviation "Apr" which indicates that the coin was issued in April 1690. To complicate matters, during this era the new year officially began on March 25, not January 1. Thus, January 1689 *followed* December 1689, and the coins dated

March 1689 and March 1690 were actually struck in the same month of the same year.

[Peter Seaby & P. Frank Purvey, *Coins of Scotland, Ireland & the Islands* (Seaby), p. 154-58.]

Irish gun money: shilling of April 1690

gut [*Ger.*] good (grade or condition).

gù yǒu de 固有的 [*Chin.-py./sc.*] intrinsic.

gwiazda (*f.*) [*Pol.*] star.

gyöngy [*Hun.*] bead (raised dot on the surface of a coin or medal).

gyűjtemény [*Hun.*] collection.

gyűjteni (*v.*) [*Hun.*] to collect.

gyűjtő [*Hun.*] collector.

gyűjtő (pénz, érem, stb.) [*Hun.*] coin collector; numismatist.

gyűrődés [*Hun.*] a crease, a fold (as in a banknote or bond).

H h

habitant token [also known as *Papineau* token.] One of the many types of penny and halfpenny copper tokens issued by the Bank of Montréal and its affiliated banks in the 1830s and '40s. The tokens were struck by Boulton and Watt. The Bank of Montréal issued 240,000 penny and 480,000 halfpenny tokens; the Québec Bank, the City Bank, and the Banque de Peuple each issued half as many.

Although dated 1837, the habitant tokens were released early the following year. They were strongly identified with Louis Joseph Papineau, leader of the Lower Canadian rebels who staged an unsuccessful revolt against the British in 1837. Contrary to popular belief, it is not he who is portrayed on the tokens, even though the course heavy clothing worn by people known as habitants was the "uniform" of his soldiers.

Also see *Bank of Montréal token*.

[E. B. Banning, *Exploring Canadian Colonial Tokens*; Richard G. Doty, "Boulton, Watt and the Canadian Adventure," *Canada's Money* (John M. Kleeberg, ed.), p. 43; J. A. Haxby and R. C. Willey, *Coins of Canada* (9th Ed.), p. 160.]

habitant token

Haganah defense token Small, thin brass 1/2 mil token issued by the Jewish Agency (forerunner of the Israeli government) in Palestine in 1938. The tokens were issued to facilitate a voluntary tax on most commodities which was used to buy weapons to defend Jews against the on-going Arab riots (1936-39). These tokens are 18 mm in diameter and are uniface in the sense that the reverse is retrograde. They have a shield with the inscription כֹּפֶר הַיִּשּׁוּב (*Redemption of the Community*) above, the date split by the shield (תרצט—5699 or late 1938), and מִיל 1/2 בַּר-תָּו (*Tax Tag Son 1/2 mil*) below. The term כֹּפֶר (*redemption*) is also used by the Bible (*Exodus: 30:16*) in reference to the temple tax[*q.v.*]. An estimated 510,000 tokens were issued by the Pliz Metal Works in Holon, and they circulated widely among the Jewish Palestinians.

[Contributed by Simcha Kuritzky. David T. Alexander, "Brass Tokens Recall Israel Birth Pangs," *The Shekel*, July-Aug., 1986, pp. 28-31.]

Haganah defense token

haika 廃貨 [*Jpn.*] demonetization.

hairline Minute scratches on a coin or medal usually caused either by rubbing against a cabinet or album (also known as *cabinet friction*) or from improper cleaning.

haj pilgrim note As a part of their religious faith, Muslims are supposed to make a journey at least once during their lifetime to the Islam capital of Mecca in Saudi Arabia. This pilgrimage is call *haj*. To assist its people on this journey, the Pakistani government has issued special multi-lingual 10 and 100 rupee banknotes. The notes are inscribed *FOR HAJ*

Pakistani *haj* note

PILGRIMS FROM PAKISTAN — FOR USE IN SAUDI ARABIA ONLY. [An additional illustration is shown on page 318 in color.]

[Clovis Von T. Crummett, "World Paper Money—Footnotes to History," *The Numismatist*, July 1986, pp. 1362-1371.]

hajtás [*Hun.*] a crease, fold (in a banknote or bond).

hakiki [*Turk.*] genuine.

hakkedilmiş [*Turk.*] engraved; incuse.

hakkô 発行 [*Jpn.*] an issue, issuance.

hål (*n.*) [*Swed.*] hole.

halagang nakatakda [*Tag.*] face value.

halb (*adj.*) [*Ger.*] half.

Halbtaler (*m.*) [*Ger.*] crown (numismatic term for a large silver coin).

Hälfte (*f.*) [*Ger.*] half (the fraction).

halkaisija [*Finn.*] diameter.

hallitsija [*Finn.*] sovereign.

halv (*adj.*) [*Nor., Swed.*] half.

halvdel (*c.*) [*Dan.*] half (the fraction).

halvfjerds [*Dan.*] seventy.

halvpart (*m.*) [*Nor.*] half (the fraction).

halvtreds [*Dan.*] fifty.

Hamilton, Alexander [called the *Prime Minister*, so completely did he dominate the government.] American statesman. Born (out of wedlock) on January 11(?), 1755, in Charlestown on the island of Nevis, British West Indies; died from being mortally wounded in a duel with Aaron Burr on July 12, 1804.

At an early age, Hamilton distinguished himself in a number of military missions and soon became aide-de-camp to General George Washington. Later as a politician, Hamilton was a tireless, hard-boiled realist who believed that money was the key driving force and that government would not last unless the wealthy class could make money by it. This put him in constant conflict with Thomas Jefferson, who wanted the United States to remain a country of farmers and craftsmen instead of bankers and industrial workers. When Hamilton and Jefferson clashed over policy issues at cabinet meetings, Hamilton, who by this point was secretary of the treasury, generally prevailed because he enjoyed Washington's support.

In the presidential election of 1800, Jefferson and Aaron Burr, both political enemies of Hamilton, were tied in votes. The House of Representatives was called upon to break the deadlock. Hamilton, wishing to show his stature as a statesman, urged his supporters to vote for Jefferson, his old enemy, instead of Burr, a man he considered to have dangerous ambitions. His support of Jefferson caused him to lose much prestige with his own Federalist Party and practically ended his career.

In 1804 Hamilton again used his influence to prevent Burr's election, this time for the New York governorship. Burr, in turn, demanded retribution by challenging Hamilton to a duel. Hamilton was opposed to dueling because his son had been fatally shot in a duel in 1801. But as a public figure, Hamilton could not avoid the issue. The duel was fought on July 11, 1804, in Weehawken, New Jersey, the same place where Hamilton's son had died three years earlier. Hamilton did not take aim but shot harmlessly in the air. Burr shot Hamilton, mortally wounding him. Hamilton died the following day in New York City.

Hamilton's face is well known to Americans because it appears on the $10 bill as well as on $500 U.S. Savings Bonds. Numismatically, Burr's face is virtually unknown because the duel discredited him as a politician.

[Contributed by Ruth Ann Davis. Roger Butterfield, *The American Past*.]

Alexander Hamilton

hamisítás elleni eszköz [*Hun.*] anti-counterfeiting device.

hamisító [*Hun.*] counterfeiter.

hamisítvány [*Hun.*] a counterfeit, forgery.

hamkha'ah הַמְחָאָה (*f.*) [*Heb.*] check, cheque.

hammarpräglat mynt (*n.*) [*Swed.*] hammered coin.

hammer die Coinage die which moves up and down during the coinage process and physically strikes the planchet (coin blank) using great pressure. The die which remains stationary during this process is known as the anvil die.

hammered coin A coin struck by hand and without the benefit of mechanical machinery. The method generally consisted of placing a planchet between two dies and striking the back of the top die with a hammer. The blow would press the images from the dies into the planchet, thereby producing a recognizable coin. Although the coins minted by this method appear extremely crude by today's standards, many of the ancient pieces are surprisingly beautiful and are now considered great works of art. Perhaps more importantly, these coins served their purpose well and even provide modern researchers with considerable insights about the ancient peoples who produced them.

Chinese money trees and a few other metallic currencies have been produced by casting. Yet during the past twenty-six centuries, the vast majority of hand-made coins have come from one variation or another of the hammering technique. From the very first coinage of the seventh century B.C. until around A.D. 1600, nearly all coins were made by this method.

The technology for producing milled coinage[*q.v.*] (coins made by machinery) was developed in the sixteenth century and eventually became popular, even though initially the process was slow and cumbersome. In some countries, there was political opposition to the switch to milled coinage, in part because the process's inventor, Eloye Mestrelle, was executed in England for counterfeiting.

Some hammered coins continued to be struck even until the end of the nineteenth century, usually as a way of satisfying a need for coins when coining machinery was not available. Spanish cobs[*q.v.*] made from the sixteenth to the eighteenth centuries are a good example, since hammering gold and silver from the New World into crude coins was the most expedient way of converting the raw metal into a more transportable form. Even more recent than the cob is the Nepal mohar which was sometimes handstruck as late as 1882. This coin is considerably less crude than many of its hammered predecessors.

Elizabeth I: hammered shilling (above); milled shilling (below)

Both methods of coinage were used during the reign of England's Elizabeth I. The two types of shillings are illustrated for comparison. As the photos show, hammered coins can be most easily distinguished from milled coins by their shapes and edges. Rarely are hammered coins perfectly round and virtually never do they have what could be called finished rims. The hammering process did not provide for any type of raised rim which reduces the wear on the coin's surface and makes the coins easier to stack. Hence, the edge tends to be somewhat thin and irregular. Other differences between the two systems can also be noted, depending upon where and when the coins were made. For example, some hammered coins are usually thick in the center because the planchets used to make them were globular instead of flat.

Hammerprägung (f.) [Ger.] hammered coin.

hammerpreget mynt (m.) [Nor.] hammered coin.

Handbook of United States Coins Commonly known as the *Blue Book*. It is a wholesale price guide of U.S. coins which has been issued annually since 1942. The Blue Book was created by Richard S. Yeoman and is published by Whitman Publishing Company of Racine, Wisconsin. Prices are determined by surveying a large group of expert professional numismatists.

In 1946 the success of the Blue Book spawned the *Guide Book of United States Coins*[q.v.] (more commonly known as the *Red Book*), a retail price guide of U.S. coins. It, too, was authored by Yeoman and is published by Whitman.

[Ginger Rapsus, "The Red Book Story," *The Numismatist*, September 1988, pp. 1561-65.]

Handheller

Handheller [Ger.] Small thin silver coin originating at Schwäbisch-Hall (Würtemberg) during the Middle Ages. It was intended to replace the *denier*-style coins which had become debased.

Unfortunately, the heller also became debased, ultimately degenerating to a copper coin which survived in Germany until the mid-nineteenth century.

handlować (v.) [Pol.] to trade.

handmatig geslagen munt (m.-c.) [Dut.] hammered coin.

handpenning (r.) [Swed.] deposit.

handpenning erfordras [Swed.] deposit required.

hankinta [Finn.] acquisition.

han'pakah הַנְפָּקָה [Heb.] an issue, issuance.

hansatsu [Jpn.] Notes issued by Japanese clans from around 1680 until the early reign of Meiji (literally, *Enlightened Government*), the name taken by Prince Mutsuhito when he became emperor of Japan in 1867 (his reign continued until 1912). The demise of the hansatsu came as part of a national revolution known as the Meiji restoration, a movement intended to give Japan a stronger government and to obtain Western technology in order for Japan to avoid foreign domination.

The term is a generic title for all non-central Japanese government paper issues of

the pre-modern period (which is virtually all of the pre-modern era notes, as there were only three short series of government issues before Meiji). Approximately 1700 different types are known to have been issued, some of which are inexpensive and readily available to today's collectors.

See *hatamoto satsu*.

[Contributed by Joseph E. Boling.]

Hanukka: 1985 1 new shekel, above; 1989 10 agorot, below.

Hanukka money [from Yiddish חַנוּכָּה גֶעלט , *Khanukah gelt*]. Money, usually small change, given as presents to children on the Jewish holiday of Hanukka. Hanukka celebrates the rededication of the Second Temple by Yehudah HaMakabi on Kislev 25 (late December) 165 B.C.E. Judea was then under Selukid rule, and Antiochus IV had declared himself divine, outlawed Jewish practices, and insisted that his subjects worship him. He desecrated the Temple in Jerusalem by placing an idol of Zeus there. The Jews, under Yehudah HaMakabi, revolted and eventually won autonomy.

Hanukka is celebrated for eight days with the lighting of special lamps and eating fried foods (the oil is in memory of the sacramental oil used in the Temple). Among Eastern European Jews, it became customary also to give gifts of candy or money to children, and to play a gambling game using a spinning top (called *dreydle* or *s'vivon*). The money given was usually local currency, but some institutions have issued tokens and some companies make candy or chocolate money for the purpose.

1983 Hanukka coin with lamp from Theresienstadt ghetto

The State of Israel issued a series of copper-nickel one lira (pound) coins for use as Hanukka *gelt* from 1958 to 1963. These were discontinued when circulating one lira coins were issued. However, Hanukka coins were reintroduced in 1972, as silver 5 lirot. The metals and denominations changed owing to inflation, but Hanukka coins have been issued every year since then. From 1982 to 1990, Hanukka coins were issued as an uncirculated one shekel[q.v.] and proof two shekalim in silver. Circulating Hanukka coins were introduced in 1984. These coins are identical to their trade counterparts except for a small lamp and the word *HANUKKA* in Hebrew and English. Only the highest denominations were used from 1984-86, but all denominations have been used since then.

[Contributed by Simcha Kuritzky. Sylvia Haffner Magnus (ed.), *Israel's Money and Medals*, Section H.]

hap-gum 합금 [*Kor.*] alloy (of metals).

harapan [*Tag.*] obverse.

hardhead [also known as a *lion*.] Very debased Scottish billon coin valued at 1 1/2 pence. It was issued by Mary Queen of Scots from 1555 to 1560. At the end of its production, it contained only about four percent pure silver. It proved unpopular and was abandoned.

hardness Degree of purity of the precious metal from which a coin is made. For example, a gold coin that is .980 fine is "harder" than a coin of similar size and weight but containing only .950 fineness. In this sense, the "hardness" is financial, not physical.

Hard Times token

Hard Times token (a.k.a. *Jackson cent*). Any one of a group of tokens, usually copper and about the size of a U.S. large cent, which were privately issued from about 1833 to 1844. Their issuance spanned the Andrew Jackson and Martin Van Buren presidential administrations (1829-1841) which included the financial Panic of 1837 and the depression which followed. Many such tokens poke fun at Jackson, a man of little formal education, or refer to the controversy of the time concerning the Bank of the United States. Others are advertising tokens (known as *store cards*) and some are quite similar to the U.S. large cents.

[Contributed by Robert Doyle. Russell Rulau, *Hard Times Tokens 1832-1844* (3rd ed.)]

harga [*Indo.*] price; value.

Irish 1/2d with harp

harp Symbol of Ireland which has appeared on most Irish coins since the reign of Henry VIII. In mythology, the harp was a bridge between heaven and earth.

The first Irish coins to show this symbol were the "harp" groats and half-groats of 1534-40. The Republic of Ireland has maintained the tradition. Most of its modern issues have shown a harp on one side and some form of wildlife on the other.

harvinainen [*Finn.*] rare.
hasta pública (*f.*) [*Port.*] auction.
hata [*Turk.*] error.

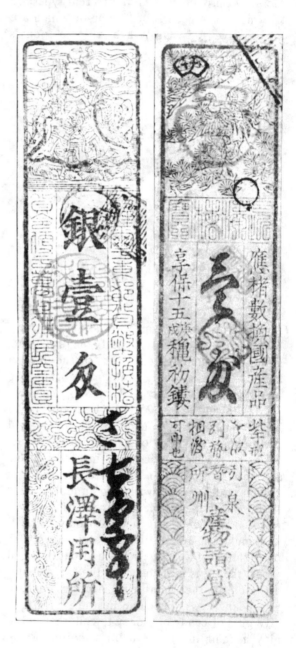

hatamoto satsu

hatamoto satsu 旗本札 [*Jpn.*] Notes issued by Japanese *hatamoto* families. The hatamoto are also called bannermen; they were *samurai* who

were direct retainers of the *shogun* without fief. Hatamoto satsu is similar in nature to the *hansatsu*[q.v.], notes issued by Japanese clans (rather than families) from around 1680 until the late 1860s.

The illustrated piece is a typical example of this type of note. It is from Mikawa Province, issued by the Nagasawa hatamoto. It is denominated 1 momme of silver and is dated Kyoho 15 (1730). It was actually issued in the 1860s. The dates Kyoho 14 and 15 were widely used on notes of clans and other issuers because of a Shogunate ban on new issues in Kyoho 15; notes dated earlier could pretend to be legitimate.

[Contributed by Joseph E. Boling.]

hätäraha [*Finn.*] emergency currency.

hatıra (*adj.*) [*Turk.*] commemorative.

hátlap; hátoldal [*Hun.*] reverse.

hátoldalon [*Hun.*] on the back.

hatsa'at m'khir minimum הַצָּעַת מְחִיר מִינִימוּם (*f.*) [*Heb.*] minimum bid.

haut (*m.*) [*Fr.*] top.

hazine [*Turk.*] treasure.

HDA. [*Span. abbr.*] hacienda (large farm or estate). This abbreviation appears on some Mexican hacienda tokens as a part of the farm's name.

heikko [*Finn.*] good.

heimisch [*Ger.*] domestic.

hé jīn 合金 [*Chin.-py./sc.*] alloy (of metals).

helft (*f.-c.*) [*Dut.*] half (the fraction).

Heliogravüre (*f.*) [*Ger.*] intaglio.

Hellas Ελλάς [*Grk.*] Greece.

Hellenic Numismatic Society The Hellenic Numismatic Society was founded in 1970 to serve the interests of Greek and foreign numismatists concerned with every aspect of Greek numismatics from earliest times to the present day.

The journal of the Society, *Numismatika Khronika* ("NomKhron") which has appeared since 1972, contains articles by Greek and foreign numismatists, covering a whole range of the history of coins in the Greek world. It is now bilingual with all articles printed in their original language with full translation in Greek or English as required.

For membership information, contact the Hellenic Numismatic Society, 45 Didotou Street, 10680 Athens, Greece.

Heller see *Handheller*.

helmi [*Finn.*] bead (raised dot on the surface of a coin or medal).

Henry Name of eight kings of England.

1. Henry I (1068-1135), third Norman king of England (1100-35). Only silver pennies were coined for general circulation during his reign. Halfpences were authorized, but very few specimens have survived. Henry II (1133-89, reigned 1154-89); best known for his *Tealby* coinage (cross and crosslets) and his *Short Cross* coinage which began during his reign (1180) and continued with his name on the coins throughout the reigns of his sons Richard and John and his grandson Henry III. Henry III (1207-72, reigned 1216-72); introduced *Long Cross* coinage in 1247 as a way of discouraging clipping of silver coins. Henry IV (1367-1413, reigned 1399-1413); under his reign the standard weights of the coinage were reduced, partly for lack of bullion and partly as a way of raising revenue. Henry V (1387-1422, reigned 1413-22); increased use of privy marks which distinguished the various issues. Henry VI (1421-71), last of the house of Lancaster (reigned 1422-61 and 1470-71); few gold coins struck due to a dwindling supply of that metal. Henry VII (a.k.a. *Henry Tudor*, 1457-1509, reigned 1485-1509); best known for having introduced the gold pound which quickly became known as a sovereign because of its design showing the enthroned king.

2. Henry VIII (1491-1547, reigned 1509-47). Henry VIII's importance to numismatics cannot be understated. Although his policies created great harm to the coinage of his reign, a collector could devote a lifetime to the study of Henry VIII's coins and the effects they had on his successors.

Henry VIII was one of the strongest English rulers. As absolute political head of state and supreme head of the Church, he was the spiritual and temporal ruler of England.

His first act upon succeeding to the throne was to marry his brother's wife, Catherine of

Aragón. Catherine bore him five children but only one survived— Mary, who later became queen.

But Henry wanted a son so he ordered his Prime Minister, Thomas Cardinal Wolsey, to ask Pope Clement VII to annul his marriage to Catherine so that he could marry Anne Boleyn, a maid of honor at court. Pope Clement refused. Henry promptly dismissed Wolsey.

At Henry's insistence, Parliament passed two acts declaring that the pope and the Roman Catholic Church had no authority in England and established Henry as supreme head of the Church of England. The marriage of Catherine and Henry was annulled and Henry promptly married Anne Boleyn (who bore him the daughter who was to become Queen Elizabeth I). In 1536 the king had Anne beheaded on a charge of infidelity.

The remainder of Henry's reign was marked by successive marriages to Jane Seymour (who bore him his only legitimate son, Edward, who later became King Edward VI), Anne of Cleves, Catherine Howard, and Catherine Paar. Catherine Howard, his fifth wife, was also convicted of misconduct and beheaded.

From a numismatic perspective, the complications of Henry's personal life and loves impacted on England's coinage in a number of ways. First, his split with the Roman Catholic Church led to the abolishing of the Church's coining privileges in England and ultimately to the closing of the ecclesiastical mints at York and Durham.

Secondly, there was a question as to which of his children were legitimate heirs to the throne, a debate which arose because the two churches involved did not recognize the same marriages. Three of his children, Edward, Mary, and Elizabeth, ultimately ruled England. They were left with the job of fixing the monetary problems left by their father.

This leads to the third point, that Henry VIII liked to spend money. In order to pay for his extravagances, he often debased the coins. He ultimately reduced the silver content of his coins to billon (an alloy of less than 50% pure silver) but with an unexpected consequence.

After billon coins were struck, they were washed with an acid solution which extracted the copper atoms from the surface, leaving the coins with a bright silvery appearance intended to fool the unenlightened. But as soon as the coins were circulated, the highest points started turning a coppery brown. The highest point on Henry's coins was his nose. He became known as "Old Coppernose," and the expression "brown-nosing" was created.

His gold coins were also debased by changing from *fine* gold (23 3/4 carats, the purest gold that could be obtained with the technology of the day) down to 23 carat gold, and finally to what became known as *crown* gold, that of 22 carats (91.67% pure). Crown gold (known in today's world as *standard* gold) is slightly more coppery in color than fine gold, so the debasement was obvious to the naked eye.

During Henry's reign, a large number of types and denominations were issued, many of them short-lived. Some (e.g., the Crown of the Rose[q.v.]) were struck to compete with coins on the Continent. Others reflected the debasement.

By the time he died, Henry VIII had allowed his coinage system to degenerate so much that few people still had confidence in it. His coinage policies had a detrimental effect on trade. The damage was not undone until around the end of the sixteen century when Elizabeth I took drastic steps to restore the integrity of England's coinage.

[Contributed by Ruth Ann Davis. *World Book Encyclopedia*, Vol. 9, p. 179; Stephen Mitchell & Brian Reeds (editors), *Coins of England and the United Kingdom* (Seaby, 1991), pp. 148-58 et al; *Compton's Encyclopedia*, Vol. 12, pp. 137-38.]

herausgeben (*v.*) [*Ger.*] to issue (coins, notes, etc.).

herdenkings- (*adj.*) [*Dut.*] commemorative.

herkomst (*m.-c.*) [*Dut.*] pedigree.

hersker (*m.*) [*Nor.*] sovereign (i.e., a king or queen). The English word *sovereign* is used to refer to the gold coin of that designation.

hét [*Hun.*] seven.

hetven [*Hun.*] seventy.

hiányos; hibás [*Hun.*] defective.
hiba [*Hun.*] defect; error.
hibás veret [*Hun.*] mis-strike.
Hibernia [*Lat.*] Ireland.

Father Hidalgo on 1953 Mexican 5 pesos

Hidalgo y Costilla, Fr. Miguel (known as *El Zorro*, "The Fox," by his classmates). Leader of the Mexican liberation movement. Born 1753 on the Hacienda San Diego Corralejo in the Bajio district near Guanajuato, Mexico; died by execution on May 8, 1811.

Father Hidalgo is remembered as the foremost liberator who fought to enable Mexico to gain its independence from Spain. He was ordained a priest in 1778. As a liberal, revolutionary thinker who was unconventional in performing his priestly duties, he had a hand in convincing the Catholic Church to relax somewhat its stern dogma which had created difficulties for him with the Church's hierarchy.

In championing the cause of the Mestizos and the Indians, Hidalgo joined a secret society dedicated to freeing Mexico from Spanish oppression. He wanted to reform the government, remove the Spanish-born agents from control, and free the working classes from the tyranny of slavery.

He rallied an army of Mestizos and Indians, but they were sadly lacking in discipline and their weapons consisted mostly of machetes. The rebels, with Hidalgo as their leader, routed the mining town of Celaya and then followed that with a bloody attack on Guanajuato. After successful attacks on several other cities, his forces seemed invincible until they themselves were routed by a small band of Spanish soldiers near Guadalajara on January 11, 1811. Hidalgo fled north but was ultimately captured when he became trapped in a narrow ravine on March 21. After his capture, the Catholic Church and its Inquisition condemned him for heresy and sacrilege.

Father Hidalgo was executed by a firing squad on May 8, 1811, in the courtyard of a Jesuit College. In deference to his former priesthood, he was granted two requests: to be shot in the chest instead of in the back, and to face the firing squad unbound and without a blindfold. Before his execution, he embarrassed his captors by giving them candy.

Mexico honors Hidalgo by celebrating its Independence Day on September 16, the date in 1810 when he proclaimed his revolt. His effigy appears on a wide range of gold and silver coins, including the magnificent *Año de Hidalgo* 5 peso silver crown issued in 1953 to commemorate the 200th anniversary of his birth.

See *Josefa*.

[Contributed by Ruth Ann Davis. Clarke Newlon, *The Men Who Made Mexico*.]

hieno [*Finn.*] fineness, fine (purity of metal).
hierro (*m.*) [*Span.*] iron (the metal).
hilo de seda [*Span.*] silk thread.
hindi ipinalabas [*Tag.*] not issued.
hinnasto [*Finn.*] price list.
hinta [*Finn.*] price.
hintaluettelo [*Finn.*] price list.
Hiszpania [*Pol.*] Spain.
hitel [*Hun.*] credit.
hiteles [*Hun.*] authentic.
hitelkártya [*Hun.*] credit card.
hitelkártya-elfogadás [*Hun.*] credit cards accepted.
hitkhak'khut bateyva הִתְחַכְּכוּת בַּתֵּיבָה (*f.*) [*Heb.*] cabinet friction.
hivatalos [*Hun.*] official.
hobo nickel Standard U.S. Buffalo Nickel that has had the likeness of either the Indian or the Buffalo modified so that it represents a different design. On various pieces, the buffalo has been turned into donkeys, men with packs on their backs, and elephants, among other

things. The Indian has been redesigned to represent clowns, other Indians, friends, loved ones, or self. Hobo nickels are unique pieces of metal that combine the fields of numismatics, art, and history.

The Buffalo Nickel[q.v.], the hobo artist's base, is one of the most loved of all the coins of the United States. The obverse shows an Indian and the reverse a bison— true examples of Americana. The years of its reign, 1913 to 1938, take us through some of the most memorable years in the history of the United States— the First World War, Prohibition, the Roaring '20s, and the Great Depression.

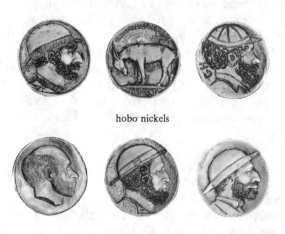

hobo nickels

Each of the *original* hobo nickels, sculpt before 1952, is unique. They were all hand-carved by yesterday's homeless and were traded for meals, a place to sleep, a ride, or other favors. The nickels were carved of loved ones as mementos of better times, or to honor those lost to time.

George Washington "Bo" Hughes was the foremost creator of Hobo Nickels. See *Hughes, "Bo"* for additional information.

[Contributed by Gail Kraljevich. Delma K. Romines, *Hobo Nickels*.]

höger [*Swed.*] right (direction or position).

hogge money [also known as *hog money* or *hoggies*.] Earliest coinage struck for the English colonies in North America. The colony in question was Hogge Islands, later renamed Sommer Islands and now known as the Bermuda Islands.

As legend has it, the Spanish explorer Juan Bermúdez stopped there in 1515 on his way to the West Indies and left behind some hogs. When Sir George Sommers and his crew were shipwrecked there in 1609, they found the islands overrun with hogs, providing a needed food supply.

The silver-washed copper coins produced for the islands around 1616 feature a wild hog. The coins were struck in values of twopence, threepence, sixpence, and one shilling.

Hogmouth Descriptive term for the effigy of Leopold I of the Holy Roman Empire who suffered a grotesque deformity of his lower lip. This deformity is seen on all denominations of the coins of his reign (1658-1705). He insisted that he be portrayed exactly as he really looked, so this bizarre effigy was used with his approval.

"Hogmouth" crown of Leopold II

hoja de licitación (*f.*); **hoja de oferta** (*f.*) [*Span.*] bid sheet.

højre [*Dan.*] right.

Holanda [*Span., Port., et al*] Holland, Netherlands.

holyland token A piece issued sometime after 1926 which portrays a 1 mil coin of the British Mandate of Palestine dated 1927 (though the Arabic date might be ١٩٦٧—1967 and a legend surrounding which states ' HISTORICAL ' HOLYLAND ' COIN ' (1927) in English on one side and in Arabic on the other. It is not known who issued them or for what purpose. Only about 150 are known. They are much

larger than the 1 mil coin (28.5 mm vs. 21 mm for the 1 mil) and are in bronze. Multiple varieties suggest more than one set of dies may have been used. There are too few pieces for commercial souvenirs (unless the issuer was threatened with prosecution for counterfeiting), and too many for a pattern issue.

[Contributed by Simcha Kuritzky. Sylvia Haffner Magnus, "Palestine Numismatics: Part III," *The Shekel*, May-June, 1986, pp. 17-18.]

holyland token

Homma Medal Commemorative medals designed and issued by Lieutenant General Masaharu Homma (1888-1946) of the Japanese Army. General Homma presented these medals to his officers in 1942 following the Japanese conquest of the Philippines. The pieces were overstruck on silver Philippine one peso coins. Although the exact mintage is unknown, it is estimated that several hundred were produced.

Following World War II, Homma was convicted of war crimes and executed.

[James W. Young, "The Homma Medal," *The Numismatist*, January 1986, pp. 21-29.]

honderd [*Dut.*] hundred.

honderdjarig [*Dut.*] centennial, centenary.

hopea [*Finn.*] silver.

horned eagle Variety of 1787 Massachusetts cent with a peculiar die break on the reverse side that makes the eagle appear to have a horn.

hornyolt érem [*Hun.*] milled coin.

hors circulation [*Fr.*] uncirculated.

horse blanket Nickname for any large-size U.S. note issued prior to 1929. Also known as *saddle blanket*.

host coin A coin which is counterstamped for purposes of being revaluated or reissued. In some cases an attempt is made to totally obliterate the host coin's original design.

Hôtel de la Monnaie (*m.*) [*Fr.*] mint.

hotsa'ah mitokef הוֹצָאָה מְחוֹקֶף (*f.*) [*Heb.*] demonetization.

hòu bì de 货币的 [*Chin.-py./sc.*] monetary.

house coin Token distributed to a company's employees for use at the company store or other company-owned facility. In some cases, these pieces are issued to help alleviate a general coin shortage, yet most often their purpose is to assure that the employees' wages go back into the company's coffers.

huáng dì 皇帝 [*Chin.-py./sc.*] emperor.

huáng hòu 皇后 [*Chin.-py./sc.*] queen.

huáng tóng 黄铜 [*Chin.-py./sc.*] brass (the alloy).

hueco [*Span.*] incuse.

huecograbado (*m.*) [*Span.*] intaglio.

huelgas de la moneda [*Span.*] Labor strikes in Cuba between 1899 and 1907 caused by massive confusion over changes made in the types of money that began circulating. [See *currency strikes*.]

Hughes, "Bo" [né *George Washington Hughes*.] Hobo. Born ca. 1900; presumably died in the early 1980s.

Although most of the identities of hobo nickel[q.v.] artists are unknown; George Washington "Bo" Hughes is the exception. His nickels are of superior quality and workmanship, and his styles are unique.

"Bo" was the youngest of ten or eleven children, the son of a freed slave. He was born around the turn of the century and went "on the bum" about 1915. He was a true hobo from the time he left home right up to the early 1980s when he disappeared, hopping train after train, going from one adventure to another. He learned the art of nickel carving from his friend, mentor, and fellow hobo, Bertram "Bert" Wiegand, and sold his first nickels around the time of the First World War. Today his nickels are highly prized and sought after by collectors.

[Contributed by Gail Kraljevich. Delma K. Romines, *Hobo Nickels*.]

huippu [*Finn.*] top.

huit [*Fr.*] eight.

hükümdar [*Turk.*] sovereign.

hundert [*Ger.*] hundred.

Hundertjahrfeier (*f.*) [*Ger.*] centennial, centenary.

Hundertstel (*n.*) [*Ger.*] hundredth (the fraction).

hundra [*Swed.*] hundred.

hundraårsjubileum (*n.*) [*Swed.*] centennial, centenary.

hundradel (*n.*) [*Swed.*] hundredth (the fraction).

hundre [*Nor.*] hundred.

hundredårsdag (*c.*) [*Dan.*] centennial, centenary.

hundrede [*Dan.*] hundred.

hundrededel (*c.*) [*Dan.*]; (*m.*) [*Nor.*] hundredth (the fraction).

huò bì xué 货币学 [*Chin.-py./sc.*] numismatics.

huonosti lyöty [*Finn.*] badly struck.

hŭ pò jīn 琥珀金 [*Chin.-py./sc.*] electrum.

húsz [*Hun.*] twenty.

huutokauppa [*Finn.*] auction, auction sale.

huutokauppakohde [*Finn.*] (auction) lot.

huutokauppaluettelo [*Finn.*] auction catalogue.

hüvelyk [*Hun.*] inch.

huy-chương [*Viet.*] medal.

hwang-dong 황동 [*Kor.*] brass (the alloy).

hwang-gum 황금 [*Kor.*] gold.

hyômen 表面 [*Jpn.*] obverse.

hypo-cycloid Geometric figure resembling a diamond but with concave sides.

hyväksyttäväksi [*Finn.*] on approval.

I i

I/ Symbol of the Peruvian monetary unit known as the *inti*. It was introduced in 1985 and equals 1,000 soles.

Icelandic Numismatic Society The Icelandic Numismatic Society was founded in 1969 and currently has about 250 members, some of which live outside of Iceland.

The goal of the Society is to promote, stimulate, and advance the study and knowledge of numismatics.

Membership is available to anyone interested in numismatics. Information may be obtained by contacting the Icelandic Numismatic Society, P.O. Box 5024, Reykjavik, Iceland.

idatosimo υδατόσημο (*n.*) [*Grk.*] watermark.

idegen valuta [*Hun.*] foreign currency.

identifikasjonsmerke (*n.*) [*Nor.*] attribution.

idioma (*m.*) [*Span.*] language.

idiotiko prosorino nomisma ιδιωτικό προσωρινό νόμισμα [*Grk.*] scrip.

Ierland [*Dut.*] Ireland.

igemonas ηγεμόνας [*Grk.*] sovereign.

ijzer (*n.*) [*Dut.*] iron (the metal).

iki [*Turk.*] two.

iki yönden de aynı okuma [*Turk.*] palindrome ("radar" serial number on banknotes).

ikke identificeret [*Dan.*] unattributed.

ikke katalogført [*Nor.*] unpublished.

ikke udgivet [*Dan.*] not issued.

ikke utgitt [*Nor.*] not issued.

ikke været i cirkulation [*Dan.*] uncirculated.

ikosi είκοσι [*Grk.*] twenty.

imerominia ημερομηνία (*f.*) [*Grk.*] date.

imperador (*m.*) [*Port.*] emperor.

imperatore (*m.*) [*Ital.*] emperor.

imposto (*m.*) [*Port.*] tax.

impresión calcográfica (*f.*); **impresión intaglio** (*f.*) [*Span.*] intaglio.

impresso de oferta [*Port.*] bid sheet.

imprimer (*v.*) [*Fr.*] to print.

imprimir (*v.*) [*Span., Port.*] to print.

impuesto (*m.*) [*Span.*] tax.

imputation (*f.*) [*Fr.*] attribution (the complete identification of a coin, medal, or banknote).

inatribuído [*Port.*] unattributed.

Inchiquin money Irish crowns, halfcrowns, shillings, ninepence, sixpence, and groats stamped from cut pieces of flattened silver plate in 1642. They were produced during the Great Rebellion and were named for Lord Inchiquin who was appointed to command the Protestant forces in Munster.

The coins are very crude. The stamps merely show the coins' weights in pennyweights and grains.

Also see *Blacksmith's halfcrown, Dublin money, and Ormonde money.*

incisione su acciaio [*Ital.*] steel engraving.

inclusione (*f.*) [*Ital.*] brockage.

inconnu [*Fr.*] unknown.

incrinatura del punzone [*Ital.*] die break.

incus [*Ger.*] incuse.

incusa (*f.*) [*Span.*] brockage.

incuso [*Ital., Span., Port.*] incuse.

incusum (*n.*) [*Dut.*] incuse; brockage.

incuus [*Dut.*] incuse.

Indian Head Cent Popular U.S. small cent struck from 1859 to 1909. Although the coin supposedly shows an Indian princess, the model was actually designer James Longacre's daughter.

The first pieces (1859-64) used the same thick white blanks of 88% copper and 12% nickel as had the Flying Eagle Cents of 1856-58. The reverse of the 1860 coins was revised with modifications in the wreath and the addition of a shield.

The copper-nickel coins proved unpopular and were replaced with bronze planchets in 1864. The bronze Indian Cent was struck until 1909 when the coin was replaced with the Lincoln Cent. Some 1908 and 1909 Indian Cents were minted in San Francisco, the first time non-silver and non-gold coins had ever been made at a U.S. branch mint.

Indian Institute of Research in Numismatic Studies The Institute was founded in 1980 and its campus at Anjaneri was inaugurated in 1984.

The main objectives of the Institute include promoting study and research in Indian numismatics; providing specialized training, creating research facilities, and helping scholars in their research; collecting photographs, materials, and information relating to numismatics and sigillography; creating a museum to preserve a visual display of the numismatic heritage of India; publishing literature such as journals, books, bulletins, etc.; and organizing meetings, lectures, and symposiums.

There is no membership to the Institute. The research facilities are open to all. Anyone can visit and utilize the facilities. Accommodations and dining are available in the Scholars' Residence, which has well-furnished rooms and is located on the campus itself.

indirect cleaning The removal of incidental dirt or grime from the surface of a coin or medal. This does not include the removal of tarnish or other forms of oxidation in which the foreign substance being eliminated has actually combined with some of the molecules of metal from the specimen. Theoretically, the weight of an uncirculated coin which has received indirect cleaning should be exactly the same as the weight of that same coin when it was first minted. If tarnish has been removed, then some molecules of the original metal have been removed along with it, thereby causing the cleaned uncirculated coin to weigh slightly less than it did when it was manufactured, even if only by an infinitesimally small amount.

Also see *direct cleaning*.

[Alan Korwin, "Shedding Light on Coin Cleaning," *The Numismatist*, June 1985, pp. 1090-91.]

îndoitură (*f.*) [*Rom.*] a fold, crease.

indragning (*r.*) [*Swed.*] demonetization.

indskåret [*Dan.*] intaglio.

indslået [*Dan.*] incuse.

Inghilterra [*Ital.*] England.

İngiliz lirası [*Turk.*] pound Sterling (£).

İngiltere [*Turk.*] England.

Inglaterra [*Span., Port.*] England.

inkus prägling (*r.*) [*Swed.*] incuse strike.

inländisch [*Ger.*] domestic.

inndraging (*m.*) [*Nor.*] demonetization.

inneboende [*Swed.*] intrinsic.

innskrift (*m.*) [*Nor.*] legend.

inofficiell [*Swed.*] unofficial.

in omloop geweest [*Dut.*] circulated.

Inschrift (*f.*) [*Ger.*] legend.

inscrição (*f.*) [*Port.*] inscription; legend.

inscripción (*f.*) [*Span.*] inscription; legend.

inskrift (*r.*) [*Swed.*] legend.

inskriptio [*Finn.*] inscription.

instructional money: Union College currency

inskrypcja (*f.*) [*Pol.*] inscription.

instructional money A variation of play money used by students in classrooms to enable them to better understand problems in finance and economics. This educational tool became popular among colleges and universities specializing in business during the first half of the twentieth century. The more recent trend is to use this fictitious money in elementary schools to teach young children the basics of money management.

See illustration on previous page.

[Barbara J. Gregory, "Ute City Residents Pay the Price," *The Numismatist*, May 1988, pp. 843-846.]

intaglio [*Ital.*] literally, *indentation*.

1. A method of printing postage stamps, paper money, or other printed material in which a mirror image of the design is etched onto a plate, the plate is inked, and the excess ink on the plate's surface is removed leaving only the ink in the etchings. When paper is pressed against the plate, the ink within the etchings transfers to the paper, thus producing a normal image of the design.

When the etching is done manually with engraver's tools, the method known as *line engraving* is generally chosen. The portraiture or lettering is broken down into many small lines of varying lengths, thicknesses, and curvatures.

Photographs can be reproduced using a mechanical method known as *photogravure*. A screen is placed over the photo which breaks the picture into small black dots. The larger and denser the dots, the darker that particular area of the photo will be. Magazine and newspaper pictures are usually done with this method.

As a way of assisting the blind, an exaggerated intaglio process can be used for printing paper money which produces inking so thick that the printing can be felt by a blind person. The color illustration and accompanying diagram on page 320 show what sighted people see when looking at a recent Dutch note as compared to what blind people "see" when they run their finger over that same note.

2. An incuse design on a coin or medal in which the lettering and effigy appear to be cut into the metal rather than being raised up from its surface (known as *relief*).

International Numismatic Commission The International Numismatic Commission was founded in 1934 "to facilitate cooperation among scholars and between institutions in the field of numismatics and related disciplines."

The Commission now has 132 members from 35 countries. These include museums, university institutes, numismatic societies, and mints. Its activities are coordinated by a council of nine members elected by representatives of constituent institutions at the International Numismatic Congress.

Membership is open to institutions and organizations only. Interested representatives should contact the Secretary of the Council, Dr. A. M. Burnett, Department of Coins and Medals, The British Museum, London, WCIB 3DG.

internazionale [*Ital.*] international.

inti Monetary unit of Peru. Introduced in 1985 as a way of fighting inflation, the inti equals 1,000 soles. Its symbol is I/.

intrínseco [*Span., Port.*] intrinsic.

intrinsèque [*Fr.*] intrinsic.

intrinsic The market value of the metal from which a coin, medal, or military decoration is made, or the value of the precious metal for which a note or bond can be exchanged.

intrinsisch [*Ger.*] intrinsic.

învechit [*Rom.*] obsolete.

invento contra falsificação [*Port.*] anti-counterfeiting device.

investment club Any group of individuals who pool their financial resources to invest in rare coins, stamps, or other collectibles.

According to the laws of most Western countries, a "legal entity" is created whenever two or more people form a business relationship. Thus, any group wishing to form such a club should start by consulting a legal professional to learn what that group's rights and obligations are.

When an investment club is formed, certain decisions should be agreed upon in writing:

who collects the money, who spends it, who decides which items will be purchased, where the purchases will be stored, how the profits (or losses) will be divided, etc. Provision must also be made for the loss of interest or death of a member.

[David L. Ganz, Jerrietta R. Hollinger, and Steven I. Welinsky, "Forming an Investment Club", *The Numismatist*, July 1990, pp. 1075-1076, et al.]

invio a scelta [*Ital.*] on approval.

inwaarts [*Dut.*] incuse.

ipotimisi υποτίμηση (*f.*) [*Grk.*] devaluation.

ipourgos ikonomikon υπουργός οικονομικών (*m.*) [*Grk.*] finance minister.

Irish Mint See *Upper Mint.*

Irland [*Nor., Swed.*] Ireland.

Irlanda [*Span., Port., Ital.*] Ireland.

İrlanda [*Turk.*] Ireland.

Irlanda del Nord [*Ital.*] Northern Ireland.

Irlanda del Norte [*Span.*] Northern Ireland.

Irlande [*Fr.*] Ireland.

Irlande du Nord [*Fr.*] Northern Ireland.

Irlandia [*Pol.*] Ireland.

Irlandia Północna [*Pol.*] Northern Ireland.

Ireland, Numismatic Society of see *Numismatic Society of Ireland.*

Irlanti [*Finn.*] Ireland.

iron Metal rarely used for coinage. [element: group VIII of the periodic table; atomic weight 55.847; atomic number 26; specific gravity 7.874; symbol Fe.]

A dark grey, easily corroded metal used exclusively for emergency coinage of minor denominations or alloyed to make certain types of stainless steel coins. Commercial iron always contains some carbon and depending on the carbon content can be referred to as steel, as in the US "steel" cent of 1943 issued to combat a wartime shortage of copper. Other examples are the Norwegian 1, 2, and 5 øre coins of 1917-1921, as well as some post-World War I Notgeld[q.v.] coins from Germany and Austria. See page 319 for color illustrations.

[Contributed by Halbert Carmichael.]

Iron Cross Prussian decoration first established in 1813 during the Napoleonic Wars as an award for battlefield bravery. It was reinstituted in three classes for bravery and leadership in 1870 during the Franco-Prussian War. Its final appearance as a Prussian decoration came in 1914 when Kaiser Wilhelm II awarded four classes of it. The Iron Cross pictured in color on page 311 is a 2nd Class Medal made of silver and iron. In 1939 the Iron Cross was given as a German national decoration.

Írország [*Hun.*] Ireland.

irregolare [*Ital.*] irregular.

irregular Something unusual or unintentional on a coin or note which is generally regarded as an error.

isa [*Tag.*] one.

isandaan [*Tag.*] hundred.

işaret [*Turk.*] motto.

iscrizione (*f.*) [*Ital.*] inscription.

isipoumeni prosfora εισηγούμενη προσφορά (*f.*) [*Grk.*] suggested bid.

İskoçya [*Turk.*] Scotland.

Ísland [*Ice.*] Iceland.

ısmarlama formu [*Turk.*] order form.

ismeretlen [*Hun.*] unknown.

Iso-Britannia [*Finn.*] Great Britain.

Isolierreibung (*f.*) [*Ger.*] cabinet friction.

İspanya [*Turk.*] Spain.

İsrail [*Turk.*] Israel.

İsveç [*Turk.*] Sweden.

İsviçre [*Turk.*] Switzerland.

Italia [*Ital., Span., Nor., et al*] Italy.

Italie [*Fr.*] Italy.

Italië [*Dut.*] Italy.

italma A coinage alloy consisting of 96.2% aluminum, 3.5% magnesium, 0.3% manganese. It has been used by Italy for its smallest coins since World War II. It is usually listed in catalogs as aluminum (aluminium), whose characteristics it generally shows.

İtalya [*Turk.*] Italy.

Itä-Saksa [*Finn.*] East Germany (D.D.R.).

itseis- [*Finn.*] intrinsic.

itur dafna עָטוּר דַּפְנָה (*m.*) [*Heb.*] laureate.

iturevet [*Dan.*] torn.

itur tsva'i עָטוּר צְבָאִי (*m.*) [*Heb.*] military decoration.

Iugoslavia [*Rom.*] Yugoslavia, Jugoslavia.

Iugoslávia [*Port.*] Yugoslavia, Jugoslavia.

izquierda (*f.*) [*Span.*] left (direction or position).

Izrael [*Hun., Pol.*] Israel.

J j

jaar (*n.*) [*Dut.*] year.

Jackson, Andrew [nicknamed *Old Hickory* by his troops because of his toughness.] U.S. Army general; later president of the United States (1829-37). Born March 15, 1767, in Waxhaws County, South Carolina; died of tuberculosis on June 8, 1845, at the Hermitage (his plantation home).

As seventh president of the United States, Jackson was the first to be called the "People's President." As founder of the Democratic Party, he was the first poor boy with little education to be elected to this high office.

His spectacular service in the War of 1812 was the turning point in his life. His victories over the Creek Indians at the Battle of Horseshoe Bend, Alabama, won him great acclaim. He was commissioned Major-General of the regular Army. His next assignment was to defend New Orleans where he decisively routed the British troops. In 1817, he captured Pensacola in Florida and stemmed the attacks of the Seminole Indians. For this, he was made first Governor of Florida.

Tiring of politics, Jackson wished to retire to private life, but his friends felt he was the only man who could break the power of the East in the national government. He was inaugurated president March 4, 1829.

In his second term of office, Jackson dissolved the Bank of the United States which he detested. He ordered government funds removed from it and deposited into state banks. Wild speculation occurred as they began to issue large quantities of paper money. Financial panic struck in 1837. The ensuing economic depression caused him (as well as many other Americans) to lose most of his money. His health grew progressively worse

and he died at his Hermitage Home on June 8, 1845.

Numismatically, his greatest claim to fame is his likeness on the current U.S. $20 bill, although he also appeared on earlier U.S. notes. In years past when $20 had more buying power, the $20 note with his portrait was widely counterfeited.

Andrew Jackson

Jackson also has an indelible spot in numismatic history because of the so-called Hard Times tokens[q.v.] issued from the late 1830s into the 1840s as a result of the economic depression of 1837. Historically, people tend to hoard good money, even copper coins, during bad times. The tokens were issued by many individuals in part to fill the need for small change and in part to express views on political and social issues. Since a great many people blamed Jackson and his successor, Martin van Buren, for the economic chaos, Jackson and Van Buren were frequently satirized on the tokens. Some of the most popular tokens show Jackson caricatured as a mule because of his stubbornness. The degree to which Jackson

was responsible for the Depression 1837 is up for debate, but there is no doubt that the Hard Times tokens are significant in numismatic Americana.

Also see *Hard Times token, Van Buren token, scrip,* and *store card.*

[Contributed by Ruth Ann Davis. Charles van Doren (editor), *Webster's American Biographies*; *Compton's Encyclopedia and Fact Index*, Vol. 13.]

Jahr (*n.*) [*Ger.*] year.

jäljennös [*Finn.*] reproduction.

jäljentää (*v.*) [*Finn.*] to copy; to duplicate.

jäljitelmä [*Finn.*] imitation.

jälki leimasimien lyömisestä yhteen [*Finn.*] brockage.

jälki metallin poistamisesta [*Finn.*] adjustment mark.

Janus

Janus Roman deity who is portrayed with two faces looking in opposite directions. He is a symbol of wholeness and the desire to master all things.

Janus appears on many Roman bronze and silver coins. The ancient Romans associated him with destiny, time, and war. He also symbolized simultaneous knowledge of history and of the future.

[J. E. Cirlot, *A Dictionary of Symbols* (2nd Ed.), 1983, Philosophical Library, New York, pp. 161-62.]

jarang [*Indo.*] rare, scarce.

järn (*n.*) [*Swed.*] iron (the metal).

jaune [*Fr.*] yellow.

jeden [*Pol.*] one.

jedna czwarta (*f.*) [*Pol.*] fourth (the fraction).

jedna dziesiąta (*f.*) [*Pol.*] tenth.

jedna piąta (*f.*) [*Pol.*] fifth.

jedna setna (*f.*) [*Pol.*] hundredth.

jedna trzecia (*f.*) [*Pol.*] third.

jednostka monetarna (*f.*) [*Pol.*] monetary unit.

jednostronny [*Pol.*] uniface.

jedwabna nitka (*f.*) [*Pol.*] silk thread.

Jefferson Nickel U.S. 5 cent piece issued since 1938. It honors Thomas Jefferson, third president of the United States and the writer of the Declaration of Independence.

The design of the Jefferson Nickel was the first ever chosen through open competition in the United States. Its creator was Felix Schlag, a sculptor who was awarded $1000 for beating the entries of 390 other artists.

The obverse shows Jefferson in pigtail and high collar as he likely appeared when he was a member of the Second Continental Congress. The reverse features a front view of Monticello, the Virginia home he designed and built.

From 1938 to 1942 and again from 1946 to the present, the metallic composition of the Jefferson Nickel has been .750 copper and .250 nickel, the same alloy used in the outer layers of U.S. dimes and quarters since 1965, and half dollars and dollars since 1971.

However, during World War II, nickel was eliminated from the five cent pieces because it was a critical metal for the war effort. In mid-1942 the U.S. mints changed the metallic composition of the Jefferson Nickel to one of 56% copper, 35% silver, and 9% manganese. These coins are now referred to as *wartime nickels* or simply *warnicks.* To indicate which coins had been changed, a large mintmark was placed over Monticello's dome on the reverse. The Denver and San Francisco Mints had always used mintmarks, but this was the first time the Philadelphia Mint ever designated its issuances with a "P" mintmark. In 1946 the old copper-nickel alloy was reinstated and is still being used today. (See page 312 for color illustrations of U.S. and Canadian wartime coins.)

[Kenneth W. Leish, *The American Heritage: Pictorial History of the Presidents of the United States*; David C. Whitney, *Founders of Freedom.*]

Jefferson, Thomas Third president of the United States (1801-1809) and the writer of the Declaration of Independence. Born April 13, 1743, at Shadwell, Albemarle County, Virginia; died July 4, 1826, at Monticello (his Virginia home).

The range of Jefferson's multiple interests and talents was incredible. Above all else a statesman and politician, he was also an outstanding writer, lawyer, architect, farmer, musician, classicist, linguist, naturalist, botanist, surveyor, geographer, ethnologist, and philosopher.

The Declaration of Independence, which he drafted for the Second Continental Congress in June 1776, reflects his political philosophies, especially where he declares that the tyrannical acts of the British government gave the American colonists the right to "dissolve the political bands" which tied them to England.

After the Revolutionary War was won, he held many positions in the fledgling American government. He was secretary of state (1790-94) in President Washington's first administration, vice president (1797-1801) under John Adams, and finally president for two terms (1801-1805 and 1805-1809). During his first run for the presidency, he tied in the voting with Aaron Burr. The House of Representatives had to break the deadlock and chose Jefferson, largely due to the support of Alexander Hamilton. This was one of the principal reasons for the feud between Hamilton and Burr which ultimately led to their duel in 1804 in which Burr fatally shot Hamilton.

On the whole, America's founding fathers were not the best of friends. Jefferson in particular seems to have had a great many enemies, including John Adams, the man under whom Jefferson had served as vice president. When Adams was on his deathbed, he is reported to have said that his greatest regret was that he had not out-lived his old nemesis, Thomas Jefferson. Adams could not know that Jefferson had died several hours earlier. In a strange quirk of fate, John Adams and Thomas Jefferson, America's second and third presidents, both died on July 4, 1826, fifty years to the day after the signing of the Declaration of Independence. To add to the irony, James Monroe, America's fifth president, died exactly five years to the day later (July 4, 1831).

Jefferson has been portrayed on the U.S. 5 cent piece since 1938. The Jefferson Nickel is special because it was the first U.S. coin design to be chosen in open competition. The reverse features Monticello, Jefferson's Virginia home which he himself designed. His likeness is also on the $2 bill, but that denomination is so unpopular in the United States that few people ever see it. Although his face has also appeared on a variety of U.S. Savings Bonds, early banknotes, and the like, one of the more unusual items bearing his likeness is the so-called Jefferson Head cent of 1795. Today's experts believe it was a sample struck by a private manufacturer, John Harper, who was trying to get a contract from the government to produce America's coins.

[Contributed by Ruth Ann Davis. David C. Whitney (editor), *Founders of Freedom in America*.]

jelkép [*Hun.*] symbol.

jelmondat [*Hun.*] motto.

jern (*n.*) [*Nor., Dan.*] iron (the metal).

jeton (*m.*) [*Fr.*] token.

język (*m.*) [*Pol.*] language.

jià gé 价格 [*Chin.-py./sc.*] price.

jià mù biǎo 价目表 [*Chin.-py./sc.*] price list.

jiǎng zhāng 奖章 [*Chin.-py./sc.*] medal.

jīn 金 [*Chin.-py./sc.*] gold.

jó [*Hun.*] good.

Joachimsthaler see *Thaler*.

jobb [*Hun.*] right (direction or position).

John XXIII [né *Angelo Giuseppi Roncalli*; nicknamed *John-outside-the-walls* by the citizens of Rome.] Pope of the Roman Catholic Church (1958-63). Born November 25, 1881, in Sotto il Monte, near Bergamo, Italy; died in the Vatican on June 30, 1963.

Pope John XXIII was above all a pastor. He wanted Catholics to look on other Christians as members of the same family, the children of a common father. His motto as a bishop,

Obedientia et Pax ("Obedience and Peace"), characterized the kindness and peace that was a part of his nature. In the non-Catholic world, John XXIII is best remembered for having helped rescue many Jews, especially children, from Nazi-controlled Hungary during World War II.

Because John XXIII was only pope for five and a half years, he did not leave as much of a numismatic legacy as most other popes of the twentieth century. The numismatic highlight of his papacy is a series of impressive coins (1, 2, 5, 10, 20, 50, 100, and 500 lire) commemorating the 1962 Ecumenical Council which he convened to promote unity among Christians.

[Contributed by Ruth Ann Davis. Eric John (editor), *The Popes: A Concise Biographical History.*]

John Paul I [né *Albino Luciani.*] 263rd Pope of the Roman Catholic Church. Born 1912 in Forno di Canale, Italy; died at the Vatican in Rome on September 28, 1978.

Pope John Paul I, the first pope to choose a double name, died just 34 days after becoming pontiff. By dying so unexpectedly in 1978, he left a rather odd numismatic legacy. It is customary for the Vatican to issue *sede vacante* ("vacant see") coins to note the death of a pope. Because of the time it takes to prepare dies, the coins, showing the year of the interregnum, are issued after the fact and are a form of commemoration. But John Paul's death provided two interregnal periods within the same calendar year. Hence, two sets of 1978 *sede vacante* coins were struck, but the second set also shows the month (September). This is one of the few times a month-year date has appeared on a modern coin.

John Paul II [né *Karol Wojtyla.*] Pope of the Roman Catholic Church (1978-). Born May 18, 1920, in Wadowice, Poland.

Pope John Paul II is the first non-Italian pope since 1523. His election to the papacy had great political significance because he came from Poland, a country still under communist control at the time of his ascension.

In March 1979, Ellen Jacobsen, president of a public relations firm in New York City, took it upon herself to convince the Polish government (and specifically the Polish National Bank) to issue a commemorative coin honoring Poland's first pope. The difficulty, of course, was that the communist government in Poland was officially atheistic. Through her persuasion and marketing expertise, Polish officials finally agreed to her suggestion, and the issuance of a set of commemorative coins was approved. The set, dated 1982, consists of five coins: silver 100 and 200 złoty pieces, plus gold coins of 1000, 2000, and 10,000 złotych. In addition, Poland released a number of circulation-quality 1000 złoty silver coins as a separate issue.

Polish coin of Pope John Paul II

This was the first time any communist government permitted the striking of coins with religious significance. In fact, the gold coins show the Pope holding a crucifix, the only time any communist country has struck coins bearing a religious symbol. This was an incredible tribute to the world's first Polish pope.

[Contributed by James Galownia. Ed Reiter, "Minting the Impossible: This American Lady Persuaded the Poles to Change Their Coinage," *Coinage* Magazine, October 1983, pp. 90-92.]

Josefina [née *Josefa Ortiz de Domínguez*; known by the popular title *La Corregidora.*] Key figure in Mexico's struggle for independence from Spain. Born 1770 in Vallodolid (now Morelia, capital of the State of Michoacán), Mexico; died 1829.

Josefina was a Creole of pure Spanish blood. She was born of well-to-do parents who gave her the standard education expected of young women of her class: music (piano), sewing, dancing, riding, etc. At the age of thirteen she

married Don Miguel Domínguez, the *Corregidor* (Chief Administrator), a position of great political importance in the province of Querétaro.

During the Mexican rebellion against both the Spanish rule and the Spanish Inquisition, Josefa and Don Miguel held many secret meetings in their home. Señora Domínguez planned lavish events at her home to conceal the plotting sessions that were being conducted in an adjoining room. She and her husband were actively engaged in the conspiracy headed by Father Miguel Hidalgo[q.v.] along with Captains Allende and Aldama.

On September 12, 1810, word reached Querétaro that traitors had revealed the plot to the authorities who immediately ordered the arrest of Miguel Hidalgo and his followers. At the risk of her life and that of her husband, *La Corregidora* (as she was affectionately called) sent word to Hidalgo that the plot had been discovered and that his arrest and probable execution were imminent.

When word reached Hidalgo, he made the immediate decision to start the rebellion. At first his forces were unstoppable and a cruel and bloody onslaught ensued in which the revolutionists emerged victorious. However, on March 21, 1811, Hidalgo's and his troops were ambushed in a narrow ravine heading to Guadalupe. Two months later Hidaglo was executed by a firing squad.

Without the determination and courage of La Corregidora, the fight for independence might have been delayed for many years. She is honored among her countrymen as the heroine of the rebellion and the precursor of Mexican independence.

Her likeness has appeared on Mexican 5 and 20 pesos notes, as well as several types of 5 centavo coins from 1942 to 1976. The coins are called *josefinas* in her honor. Unlike the other types which were all minted in brass or bronze, the 1950 5 centavo coin was struck in copper-nickel and is referred to as *josefa blanca* ("white josefa").

On all these coins and notes, Josefa is portrayed artistically as a strong woman of plain features, not unlike Susan B. Anthony on the U.S. dollar coins. Josefa's strong and chiseled face is itself a symbol of Mexico's struggle for independence.

[Contributed by Ruth Ann Davis. Clarke Newlon, *The Men Who Made Mexico*.]

jóváhagyással [*Hun.*] on approval.

Juana de Asbaje See *Asbaje, Juana de.*

Jubilee Head Effigy of Queen Victoria[q.v.] introduced in 1887 to honor the fiftieth anniversary of her reign as Queen of the United Kingdom of Great Britain and Ireland. The design was used from 1887 until the early 1890s (the exact cut-off date varies among the different denominations) when the *Old Head* design was introduced.

Victoria "Jubilee Head"

Judea capta coins Group of coins issued by the Roman Empire to commemorate the conquest of Judea (67-70 C.E.). The Romans traditionally issued coins to announce the conquest of new provinces, but the Judean pieces were unusual in that they were issued for 26 years, under Vespasian, Titus, and Domitian. The coins generally portray a Roman soldier by a palm tree, standing over a weeping woman. The palm tree is symbolic of Judea. The image of a ruined Jerusalem as a weeping widow appears in Isaiah, Jeremiah, Lamentations, and other Biblical works (though they refer to the destruction of Jerusalem by the Babylonians 650 years before the Roman War).

The image captured on these coins was so powerful that the State of Israel issued a medal, almost 19 centuries later, with a Judea Capta

coin on the obverse with the legend *JUDAEA CAPTIVE 70 C.E.* The reverse portrays the same palm tree with a young man planting a new tree and a joyous woman playing with her infant child, with the legend *ISRAEL LIBERATED 1948.*

[Contributed by Simcha Kuritzky. D. Bernard Hoenig, "The Weeping Woman of Judea," *The Shekel*, September-October 1983, pp. 19-23.]

Judea capta coin

Judenpfennig [*Ger.*] literally, *Jews' pennies.* Small copper tokens issued by merchants in the city of Frankfurt and the Rhineland to relieve a coin shortage during and after the Napoleonic War (1807-22). These tokens have various designs, including shields, stars, lions, and chickens, and carry various denominations such as *halbag*, *atribuo*, *theler*, *heller*, and *pfennig.* They are called Jewish pennies

because most, if not all, of the issuing merchants were Jews. The Jewish community of Frankfurt was quite significant numismatically. The Rothschilds were from Frankfurt, and their financial empire had its beginnings in selling coins to nobility. Frankfurt was the numismatic capital of Europe until the Nazis came to power.

[Contributed by Simcha Kuritzky. Chester L. Krause and Clifford Mishler, *Standard Catalog of World Coins* (1985); Chet Needelman, "The House of Rothschild," *Coin Illustrated*, July, 1978, pp. 40-42; *Encyclopedia Judaica*, Vol. 10, p. 406.]

2 *Judenpfennig* coins

jugate Also known as *accolated* or *conjoined.* Design which shows two or more heads or busts that face in the same direction and overlap. See *accolated* for additional information and illustrations.

jûgun kisho 征軍徽章 [*Jpn.*] military campaign medal.

julkaisematon [*Finn.*] unpublished.

jumătate (*f.; adj.*) [*Rom.*] half.

junking Rummaging through a dealer's "junk" box with the hopes of finding something rare or unusual.

[Frank Van Valen, "Still Junking After All These Years," *The Numismatist*, July 1986, pp. 1346-48.]

junsui 純粋 [*Jpn.*] fineness; fine (purity of metal).

jurmana जुर्माना [*Hin.*] fineness; fine (purity of metal).

Justierspur (*f.*) [*Ger.*] adjustment mark.

K k

kabinettslitasje (*m.*) [*Nor.*] cabinet friction.

kağıt para [*Turk.*] note, banknote; paper money.

kahei 貨幣 [*Jpn.*] coin.

kahei no chûzô 貨幣の鋳造 [*Jpn.*] coinage.

Kaiser (*m.*) [*Ger.*] emperor.

kaiverrettu [*Finn.*] engraved.

kakaunti [*Tag.*] rare, scarce.

kaksi [*Finn.*] two.

kaksikielinen [*Finn.*] bilingual.

kaksikymmentä [*Finn.*] twenty.

kaksois- (*adj.*) [*Finn.*] duplicate.

kalın para [*Turk.*] piéfort, piedfort.

kalıp [*Turk.*] (coinage) die.

kalıp çatlağı; kalıp kırığı [*Turk.*] die break.

kaloupono καλουπώνω (*v.*) [*Grk.*] to cast.

kalp [*Turk.*] a counterfeit.

kalpazanlığı önleme cihazı [*Turk.*] anti-counterfeiting device.

kambiyo kuru [*Turk.*] exchange rate.

Kanada [*Ger., Finn., Swed., Hun., Turk., et al*] Canada.

kane 金 [*Jpn.*] money.

kangaroo piece Group of Australian pattern coins struck in Port Philip in 1853. They were issued in values of 1/4, 1/2, 1, and 2 ounces of gold. Kangaroo pieces denominated at 1/2 and 1 sovereign were also made. Gilt copper re-strikes exist of the four coins valued in ounces. All of the kangaroo pieces are extremely scarce today.

The coins are named after the kangaroo which appears as the principal obverse device. This is the first time a kangaroo appeared on a coin, but Australia used it often as a principal motif on its coins in the twentieth century.

kansainvälinen [*Finn.*] international.

kansio [*Finn.*] album.

kant (*c.*) [*Dan.*]; (*r.*) [*Swed.*]; (*m.-c.*) [*Dut.*]; (*m.*) [*Nor.*] edge; rim.

kaparo [*Turk.*] deposit (of funds).

kara [*Tag.*] obverse; "heads" side of coin.

kararma [*Turk.*] tarnish.

karcolás [*Hun.*] a scratch.

karta kredytowa (*f.*) [*Pol.*] credit card.

kartal [*Turk.*] eagle.

käsinlyöty [*Finn.*] hammered coin.

käsiraha [*Finn.*] (monetary) deposit.

kasowanie (*n.*) [*Pol.*] cancellation.

kasowanie przez dziurkowanie (*n.*) [*Pol.*] punch cancellation.

kasowanie przez nacięcie (*n.*) [*Pol.*] cut cancellation.

kaspi כַּסְפִּי [*Heb.*] monetary.

kasu Copper coin introduced in the mid-1700s by the Indian state of Mysore. Its name is the Hindi equivalent of the Chinese word *cash*[*q.v.*].

[James Mackay, *Key Definitions in Numismatics*, p. 70.]

katalog [*Turk.*]; (*n.*) [*Dan., Swed.*]; (*m.*) [*Pol., Nor.*] catalogue, catalog.

Katalog (*m.*) [*Ger.*] catalogue.

katalog aukcyjny (*m.*) [*Pol.*] auction catalogue.

katalogos κατάλογος (*m.*) [*Grk.*] catalogue.

katalogos plistiriasmou κατάλογος πλειστηριασμού (*m.*) [*Grk.*] auction catalogue.

katalogus (*m.-c.*) [*Dut.*] catalogue.

katalógus [*Hun.*] catalogue.

Katalogwert (*m.*) [*Ger.*] catalogue value.

katastasi κατάσταση (*f.*) [*Grk.*] grade, condition (of a coin or note).

käteinen raha [*Finn.*] cash (ready money).

katharos καθαρός [*Grk.*] fineness; fine (purity of metal).

katonai kitüntetés [*Hun.*] military decoration.

katseh קָצֶה (*m.*) [*Heb.*] edge (of a coin or medal).

katteeton raha [*Finn.*] fiat money.

kaucja (*f.*) [*Pol.*] deposit (of funds).

kaufen (v.) [*Ger.*] to buy.

Käufer (m.) [*Ger.*] buyer.

käytöstä poistettu [*Finn.*] obsolete.

käyttämätön [*Finn.*] uncirculated.

kazıntı [*Turk.*] a scratch.

kebalikan [*Indo.*] reverse.

kehäkirjoitus [*Finn.*] legend.

Kelet-Németország [*Hun.*] East Germany (D.D.R.).

kẽn [*Viet.*] nickel (the metal).

kenar [*Turk.*] edge; rim.

kendetegn (n.) [*Dan.*] attribution.

Kennedy Half Dollar U.S. 50 cent piece struck since 1964 to honor President John F. Kennedy, assassinated on November 22, 1963. It replaced the Franklin Half Dollar (1948-63). The coins were designed by Gilroy Roberts, Chief Engraver of the Mint.

Some controversy erupted when the coins were released in 1964. Gilroy Roberts had placed his initials on the truncation of Kennedy's neck. But to the naked eye, they resemble the Soviet hammer and sickle. Because this coinage issue came so soon after Kennedy's involvement in the Cuban Missile Crisis, the American public had to be reassured that there was no communist conspiracy and that the designer's initials were exactly what they were supposed to be.

The first issues of 1964 were of 90% silver, the same used in all U.S. silver coins (10 cents and larger) since 1837. However, the very next year saw the changeover to clad coinage. The half dollars were not immediately switched to the same clad compositions as the 1965 dimes and quarters (outer layers of 75% copper, 25% nickel; inner core of pure copper) but to outer layers of 80% silver and 20% copper bonded to a core of 20.9% silver and 79.1% copper. In 1971 the composition was changed to that of the dimes and quarters, and has remained so to this day.

The most desired coins of the series are the 1970-D pieces which were only released via official U.S. mint sets; no halves of this date and mint were struck for general circulation.

The 1976 halves were part of the U.S. Bicentennial series, which included special reverses for the quarter, half dollar, and dollar coins. The obverse carried the dual date 1776-1976, and the presidential coat of arms on the reverse was replaced with Independence Hall (located in Philadelphia).

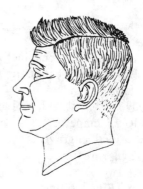

John F. Kennedy

Kennedy, John Fitzgerald President of the United States (1961-63). Born May 29, 1917, in Brookline, Massachusetts; shot to death on November 22, 1963, in Dallas, Texas.

Born into a political family of Irish descent and Roman Catholic faith, J.F.K. was quiet and shy. It was expected that he would become a writer or teacher. However, when his brother Joe was killed in 1944 while serving in World War II, John turned to politics. John had also fought in that war, distinguishing himself as the captain of the U.S. Navy torpedo boat PT-109. He rescued several of his crewmen when the boat was rammed by a Japanese destroyer off the Solomon Islands.

Elected to the United States Senate in 1952, he was appointed to the powerful Foreign Relations Committee. He supported a program of aid to underdeveloped countries and worked for legislation to end corruption in the labor unions. In 1958 he won re-election to the Senate.

Upon being inaugurated president on January 20, 1961, J.F.K. initiated a program known as the "New Frontier" and established the Peace Corps.

The highlight of his brief presidency was his handling of the Cuban Missile Crisis in 1962

in which he succeeded in lessening Cold War tensions with the Soviet Union and avoided a possible atomic war.

Kennedy was assassinated by Lee Harvey Oswald in 1963. He will always be remembered for his famous words to the American people during his inaugural address in 1961: "Ask not what your country can do for you—Ask what you can do for your country."

Within a year of his death, his effigy was placed on the Kennedy Half Dollar.

[Contributed by Ruth Ann Davis.]

kennzeichnen (v.) [Ger.] to attribute.

Kennzeichnung (f.) [Ger.] attribution.

kenourgio καινούργιο [Grk.] new; crisp (in reference to paper money).

képmás [Hun.] effigy.

keräilijä [Finn.] collector.

kerätä (v.) [Finn.] to collect.

kerek [Hun.] round.

kereskedni (v.) [Hun.] to trade.

kesatuan moneter [Indo.] monetary unit.

kesef כֶּסֶף (m.) [Heb.] money; silver.

kesef kheyrum כֶּסֶף חֵרוּם (m.) [Heb.] emergency currency.

kesef mukhraz כֶּסֶף מוּכְרָז (m.) [Heb.] fiat money.

készpénz [Hun.] cash (ready money).

ketem כֶּתֶם (m.) [Heb.] stain; tarnish.

keter כֶּתֶר (m.) [Heb.] crown (royal headpiece; large silver coin).

kétnyelvű [Hun.] bilingual.

kétszeres; kettős (adj.) [Hun.] duplicate.

key 1. Symbol of the Cuban Mint.

2. The scarcest, most expensive, or hardest to obtain coins in a series are called *keys* or *key dates*. Coins which command a premium but are not among the scarcest in their series are referred to as *semi-keys*.

kézi veréssel készült pénz [Hun.] hammered coin.

khad-panim חַד-פָּנִים [Heb.] uniface.

kheshbon חֶשְׁבּוֹן (m.) [Heb.] account (financial or transactional).

khidat ratso vashov חִידַת רָצוֹא וָשׁוֹב (f.) [Heb.] palindrome ("radar" serial number on banknotes).

không lưu hành [Viet.] uncirculated.

khotam חוֹתָם (m.) [Heb.] seal (in the numismatic sense).

kiadás; kibocsátás [Hun.] an issue, issuance.

kiadatlan [Hun.] unpublished.

kiadni; kibocsátani (v.) [Hun.] to issue.

kiállítani (v.) [Hun.] to exhibit.

kiállítás [Hun.] exhibition.

kibdilon κίβδηλον (n.) [Grk.] a fake, forgery.

kibocsátásra nem került [Hun.] not issued.

kicsi [Hun.] small.

kiegyenlítési jegy [Hun.] adjustment mark.

kieli [Finn.] language.

kierrossa ollut [Finn.] circulated.

kierto [Finn.] circulation.

kiiltolyönti [Finn.] proof (re: coins or medals).

Kiina [Finn.] China.

Kiinan kansantasavalta [Finn.] People's Republic of China (P.R.C.).

Kiinan tasavalta [Finn.] Republic of China (Taiwan).

kilenc [Hun.] nine.

kilencven [Hun.] ninety.

kim-loại [Viet.] metal.

ki-myom-ui 기념의 (adj.) [Kor.] commemorative.

kin 金 [Jpn.] gold.

Kina [Nor., Dan., Swed.] China.

Kína [Hun.] China.

Kínai Köztársaság [Hun.] Republic of China.

Kínai Népköztársaság [Hun.] People's Republic of China (P.R.C.).

kincs [Hun.] treasure.

King of Canadian Coins Popular name for the 1921 half dollar of which only about 100 are known to exist. Although 206,398 were minted, nearly all (plus about 300,000 of other dates) were melted in 1929. The mint then used that metal to strike halves with the 1929 date. This strange occurrence happened because the mint had produced far more half dollars than were needed in the late 1910s and early 1920s, about a half million of which were never distributed. When a demand for halves arose in the late 1920s, the mint feared that the public would question the authenticity of shiny new coins with ten-year-old dates. Hence, the stockpile was melted and recycled, causing the 1921 coins to become extremely scarce.

Similarly, the *Emperor of Canadian Coins* is the 1911 dollar, two of which exist in silver and one in copper. Unlike the King, the Emperor was strictly a pattern, not a regular issue.

[J. A. Haxby and R. C. Willey, *Coins of Canada* (9th Ed.), p. 60; *Coin World*, "Carroll Reports Find of Canadian Rarity," November 30, 1977, p. 1.]

King of Siam Proof Set In 1834 the U.S. State Department requested that the Philadelphia Mint prepare a special eleven-piece proof set of U.S. coins to be given to the King Ph'ra Nang Klao of Siam as a diplomatic gift. The set was housed in a plush hand-tooled leather presentation case. A similar set was prepared for Sayid Sayid bin Sultan, Imām of Muscat.

The regular designs of the coins in circulation in 1834 were used and all but two of the coins showed that date. The two exceptions were the silver dollar and gold eagle ($10 gold piece). When mint officials checked the records and found that no coins of those denominations had been struck since 1804, dies bearing that date were prepared. Perhaps the officials did not realize that the dollar coins manufactured in 1804 were actually struck from the previous year's dies and were in fact dated 1803. Hence, the eight 1804 silver dollars produced in 1834 and 1835 for presentation sets were a whole new issuance and not simply a restrike. The King of Siam specimen is one of the finest known. [Note: Seven specimens of the 1804 dollar are known as *restrikes*, but they were produced by mint employees from 1858 to 1860 to satisfy a demand from collectors. The eight made in 1834-35 are called *originals*.]

Although 1804-dated gold eagles had been struck in that year, four restrikes were minted in 1834 for various presentation sets. The four restrikes, all in proof, are of a separate variety and can be distinguished from the specimens actually minted in 1804.

The other coins in the set include a half cent, large cent, dime, quarter dollar, half dollar, no motto Classic Head quarter eagle (gold $2.50), and no motto Classic Head half eagle (gold $5). The set as it now exists has two pieces missing. One of them is almost assuredly a half dime. Instead of a coin, the other missing piece may well be a gold medal for President Andrew Jackson's second inauguration. This is highly likely, as there were no other type coins issued by the United States in 1834.

After its presentation to the King of Siam, the set disappeared from numismatic annals. It resurfaced briefly at the 1962 American Numismatic Association convention, then again disappeared.

The set first appeared on auction in October 1987. But with a reserve bid of two million dollars, it failed to attract an opening bid. Then in 1989 the set appeared on auction again. This time it was purchased by Martin Paul of The Rarities Group and Greg Holloway of Continental Investments for a sum reported to be substantially in excess of two million dollars.

See page 309 for color illustration.

["King of Siam proof set sells," *Numismatic News*, p. 1 et al; Walter Breen, *Complete Encyclopedia of U.S. and Colonial Coins*, p. 431.]

kinkyû shihei 緊急紙幣 [*Jpn.*] emergency currency.

kinzoku 金属 [*Jpn.*] metal.

kraliçe [*Turk.*] queen.

király [*Hun.*] king.

királynő [*Hun.*] queen.

kirjoitus [*Finn.*] inscription.

kissi penny see *gizzi penny*.

kitűnő [*Hun.*] excellent.

kjøpe (*v.*) [*Nor.*] to buy.

kjøper (*m.*) [*Nor.*] buyer.

klassificering (*r.*) [*Swed.*] classification.

klassifikasjon (*m.*) [*Nor.*] classification; grade, condition.

klasyfikować (*v.*) [*Pol.*] to classify; to grade.

klein [*Ger.*] small.

kleur (*f.-c.*) [*Dut.*] color, colour.

Knick (*m.*) [*Ger.*] a fold, crease.

knife money Bronze knives used as currency in China from 1125-255 B.C. They have also been called *razor, sword,* or *bill-hook* money. The Chinese name for these items is *tao*.

According to theory, money (as we know the term) developed in three stages: pure

Chinese knife money

barter, an exchange of items resembling barter items, and coins. Knife money would fit into the second stage, as they resemble real knives which had exchange value.

[Charles J. Opitz, *Odd and Curious Money: Descriptions and Values*, p. 41; Richard G. Doty, *The Macmillan Encyclopedic Dictionary of Numismatics*, pp. 185-86.]

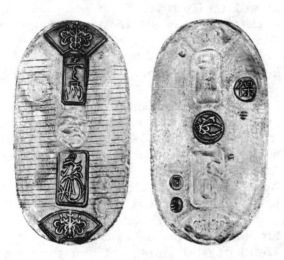

Japanese *koban*

koban Large oval-shaped Japanese coin of the Tokugawa Shogunate (1599-1868). These pieces were minted from an alloy of gold and silver but always with a predominance of gold. The types were changed periodically and every new type had a slightly different fineness. They were held in high esteem as trading coins.

The designs are actually a series of punches, each providing a needed piece of information. Because the pieces were trade coins circulating in the Far East, many exhibit chop marks.

The koban in the illustration is one of the last of its size (32 x 61 mm) to be issued. It was produced from 1837 to 1858, and its metallic content is .568 gold and .432 silver. A few slightly smaller specimens were made in 1859, but in 1860 the coins were reduced in size to 21 x 36 mm. In 1868 the koban was abandoned when the shogunate was deposed.

køber (*c.*) [*Dan.*] buyer.

kobber (*n.*) [*Nor., Dan.*] copper.

ko-dae-ui 고대의 [*Kor.*] ancient.

kohtalainen [*Finn.*] fine (grade or condition).

koin コイン [*Jpn.*] coin.

kokhav כּוֹכָב (*m.*) [*Heb.*] star.

kokoelma [*Finn.*] collection.

kolekcja (*f.*) [*Pol.*] collection.

kolekcjoner (*m.*) [*Pol.*] collector.

kollektsioner коллекционер (*m.*) [*Russ.*] collector.

kollektsionirovat коллекционировать (*v.*) [*Russ.*] to collect.

kollektsiya коллекция (*f.*) [*Russ.*] collection.

kolmasosa [*Finn.*] third (the fraction).

kolme [*Finn.*] three.

kolor (*m.*) [*Pol.*] color, colour.

kondekorsayon militar [*Tag.*] military decoration.

koneella lyöty raha [*Finn.*] milled coin.

konge (*c.*) [*Dan.*]; (*m.*) [*Nor.*] king.

König (*m.*) [*Ger.*] king.

Königin (*f.*) [*Ger.*] queen.

koning (*m.-c.*) [*Dut.*] king.

koningin (*f.-c.*) [*Dut.*] queen.

konserveringsgrad (*c.*) [*Dan.*] grade, condition.

konst (*r.*) [*Swed.*] art.

kontant [*Dan., Nor.*] cash (ready money).

kontanter (*r.pl.*) [*Swed.*] cash (ready money).

konto (*n.*) [*Pol., Swed.*]; (*c.*) [*Dan.*]; (*m.*) [*Nor.*] account (financial or transactional).

Konto (*n.*) [*Ger.*] account.

köpare (*m./f.*) [*Swed.*] buyer.

kopás [*Hun.*] wear.

kopeck; kopek копейка (*f.*) [*Russ.*] Minor denomination of Russia and the Soviet Union. The coin was introduced in 1534-5 as part of the monetary reform of Elena Glinskaya. Its name comes from the design on the earliest pieces which portray the czar carrying a spear ("копье" in Russian).

Over the years the kopeck evolved from being a silver wire coin (see *wire money*) to a copper coin and finally to an aluminum coin issued by the Soviets.

This coin is historically significant because it was equal in value to one-hundredth of a ruble, making it the world's first true decimal coin.

[Randolph Zander, *Russian-English Numismatic Dictionary*, p. 36; James Mackay, *Key Definitions in Numismatics*, p. 71.]

koper [*Dut.*] (*m.-c.*) buyer; (*n.*) copper (the metal).

kopie (*f.-c.*) [*Dut.*] copy; reproduction.

Kopie (*f.*) [*Ger.*] copy; reproduction.

koppar (*r.*) [*Swed.*] copper (metal).

korjattu [*Finn.*] repaired.

Korn Jude medals [from German for *grain Jew*]. A series of medals issued in Germany in 1694-96 and again in 1770-73. These medals blame high grain prices on Jewish grain merchants rather than on the grasshoppers and bad weather which destroyed much of the harvests in those years. They show on the obverse a well-fed man carrying a sack of grain with a small devil or goat perched on it and the legend *DU KORN JUDE* ("You Grain Jew"). The reverses show a grain sifter with a quote from Proverbs against grain speculation (*Proverbs 21:26*). Some varieties show the figure hanging from a tree, and others show the figure walking into the open jaws of an alligator.

[Contributed by Simcha Kuritzky. Daniel M. Friedenberg, "Anti-Semitic Medals of Late Medieval Europe," *The Shekel*, July-August 1984, pp. 4-14.]

korona [*Hun.*]; (*f.*) [*Pol.*] crown (royal headpiece; large silver coin).

korozja (*f.*) [*Pol.*] corrosion.

korrosjon (*m.*) [*Nor.*] corrosion.

korrózió [*Hun.*] corrosion.

kosengaku 古銭学 [*Jpn.*] numismatics.

kosengaku no 古銭学の [*Jpn.*] numismatic.

koteloitu postimerkki [*Finn.*] encased postage stamp.

koter קֹטֶר (*m.*) [*Heb.*] diameter.

kotka [*Finn.*] eagle.

kötü vurulmuş [*Turk.*] badly struck.

köztársaság [*Hun.*] republic.

kral [*Turk.*] king.

kras (*m.-c.*) [*Dut.*] a scratch.

kratiko kerdos apo ekdosi nomismaton κρατικό κέρδος απο έκδοση νομισμάτων [*Grk.*] seigniorage.

Kratzer (*m.*) [*Ger.*] a scratch.

krawędź (*f.*) [*Pol.*] rim.

krążek monetarny (*m.*) [*Pol.*] planchet, coin blank.

krediet (*n.*) [*Dut.*] credit.

kredietkaarten aanvaard [*Dut.*] credit cards accepted.

kredi kartı [*Turk.*] credit card.

kredi kartı kabul edilir [*Turk.*] credit cards accepted.

kredit (*c.*) [*Dan.*]; (*r.*) [*Swed.*] credit.

Kredit (*m.*) [*Ger.*] credit.

Kreditkarte (*f.*) [*Ger.*] credit card.

Kreditkarten akzeptiert [*Ger.*] credit cards accepted.

kreditkort (*n.*) [*Dan., Swed.*] credit card.

kreditkort gäller [*Swed.*] credit cards accepted.

kreditt (*m.*) [*Nor.*] credit.

kredittkort (*n.*) [*Nor.*] credit card.

kredittkort akseptert [*Nor.*] credit cards accepted.

Kreikka [*Finn.*] Greece.

król (*m.*) [*Pol.*] king.

królowa (*f.*) [*Pol.*] queen.

krom (*n.*) [*Nor., Dan., Swed.*] chromium.

króm [*Hun.*] chromium.

kromi [*Finn.*] chromium.

kron [*Turk.*] crown (a large silver coin).

krona (*r.*) [*Swed.*] crown (royal headpiece; large silver coin).

krone (*c.*) [*Dan.*]; (*m.*) [*Nor.*] crown (royal headpiece; large silver coin). In Danish and Norwegian, a large silver coin is often referred to by the English word *crown* if it is foreign and *krone* if it was struck in Denmark or Norway.

Krone (*f.*) [*Ger.*] crown (royal headpiece; large silver coin).

kroon (*m.-c.*) [*Dut.*] crown (royal headpiece). The generic Dutch term for a large silver coin is *groot zilverstuk* (*n.*).

Kruger, Paul né *Stephanus Johannes Paulus Kruger.* South African statesman and military leader who led the Boers in their fight against the British. Born October 10, 1825, in Colesberg, Cape Colony; died July 14, 1904, in Clarens, Switzerland.

Kruger began his military career as a fighter against the Zulus and other African tribes who attacked Boer settlers (including his family) after England recognized the independence of Transvaal State in 1852. His reputation as a military man helped him get elected to the position of commandant general of the Transvaal forces in 1864. Kruger was dismissed from this rank by the British a year after they annexed the Transvaal in 1877 because of his refusal to accept the annexation. He became a military leader in the Boer Rebellion in 1880 and helped negotiate a peace agreement with Britain the following year. Kruger became president of the Transvaal in 1883 and kept that position until the Boers ultimately accepted British domination in 1902. At the beginning of the Boer War in 1899, Kruger travelled to Europe in an attempt to gain the support of key European powers, but he was unable to prevent a British takeover of the Transvaal. He remained in Europe until his death in 1904.

Kruger's effigy appears on the South African gold Krugerrand, a bullion coin named after him. This coin has been issued since 1967 and contains one ounce of pure gold. South Africa has also issued the half-, quarter- and tenth-Krugerrand.

Krugerrand Gold bullion[q.v.] coin struck in South Africa since 1967 and named for Paul Kruger, leader of the Boers in their fight against Great Britain. The Krugerrand was issued as a convenient medium for trading and holding gold. It contains one ounce of pure gold at a fineness of .9167 (known as *standard,* i.e., one part alloy to eleven parts pure gold to create a metal hard enough for circulating coins). Some proof and proof-like specimens have been struck for collectors. Fractional Krugerrands are now available in one-half, one-fourth, and one-tenth ounce coins.

Because South Africa is a major gold-producing country, it was logical for the South Africans to want to find a better way to market their product. The Krugerrand was the ideal solution until the 1980s when most of the countries of the world, led by the United States, imposed a boycott against all South African products because of that nation's apartheid policies. Although it was still legal for Americans and others to own Krugerrands, it was illegal to import them. In the 1990s after apartheid was disassembled, the worldwide boycott was dropped and Krugerrands became legal virtually everywhere.

However, in the 1980s and early 1990s, Australia, Canada, the United States, China, Great Britain, and many other countries filled the void by introducing their own gold bullion coins (as well as those of silver and platinum), thus severely cutting into South Africa's market.

kruunu [*Finn.*] crown (royal headpiece; large silver coin).

kseno nomisma ξένο νόμισμα (*n.*) [*Grk.*] foreign currency.

kuitti [*Finn.*] receipt.

kukloforimeno κυκλοφορημένο [*Grk.*] circulated.

ku-la-wun-hwa 크라운화 [*Kor.*] crown (numismatic term for a large silver coin).

külçe [*Turk.*] ingot.

kullanılmış [*Turk.*] circulated.

kulta [*Finn.*] gold.

kuluma [*Finn.*] wear.

kun faste bud akseptert [*Nor.*] no unlimited bids accepted.

kung (*m.*) [*Swed.*] king.

kuningan [*Indo.*] brass (the alloy).
kuningas [*Finn.*] king.
kuningatar [*Finn.*] queen.
kunst (*f.-c.*) [*Dut.*]; (*c.*) [*Dan.*]; (*m.*) [*Nor.*] art.
Kunst (*f.*) [*Ger.*] art.
kuntoluokka [*Finn.*] a grade (condition).
kupari [*Finn.*] copper.
Kupfer (*n.*) [*Ger.*] copper.
kurs (*m.*) [*Nor.*] exchange rate.
kurs wymiany (*m.*) [*Pol.*] exchange rate.
kuşatılmış bölge parası [*Turk.*] obsidional.
kusursuz [*Turk.*] perfect, flawless.
kuvio [*Finn.*] pattern.
kuvio tai kirjoitus syvennöksenä [*Finn.*] incuse.
kuwarta [*Tag.*] money.
kuwartang papel [*Tag.*] banknote; paper money.

Kuzey İrlanda [*Turk.*] Northern Ireland.
kvadratisk (*adj.*) [*Nor., Dan.*] square.
kvadratiskt (*adj.*) [*Swed.*] square.
kvalitet (*c.*) [*Dan.*]; (*m.*) [*Nor.*] grade, condition.
kvalitetsbedømme (*v.*) [*Dan.*] to grade.
kvittering (*c.*) [*Dan.*]; (*m.*) [*Nor.*] receipt.
kvitto (*n.*) [*Swed.*] receipt.
kwadratowy (*adj.*) [*Pol.*] square.
kwalificeren (*v.*) [*Dut.*] to grade.
kwaliteitsaanduiding (*f.-c.*) [*Dut.*] condition, grade.
kwota (*f.*) [*Pol.*] amount.
kyay ၍: [*Bur.*] copper.
kykloforia κυκλοφορία (*f.*) [*Grk.*] circulation (of a coin or note).
kymmenen [*Finn.*] ten.
kymmenesosa [*Finn.*] tenth (the fraction).
kyôbai 競売 [*Jpn.*] auction; auction sale.

L l

l. [*abbr.*] left (direction or position).

laagste bod (*n.*) [*Dut.*] minimum bid.

labarum A square flag, also known as a *vexillum* or *imperial standard*, which bears the coat of arms or other official emblem of the last Roman emperors. They often included the Christogram, an ancient symbol of Christianity formed by overlapping the Greek letters χ and Ρ (chi and rho), the first two letters of the word *Christus* (the Greek word for Christ).

The labarum with the Christogram first appeared on the bronze coins of Constantine I the Great (Flavius Valerius Constantinus, joint emperor A.D. 306-323; sole emperor 323-327) and later on the coins of Magnentius and Decentius who attempted a revolt against Constantine II (reigned 337-340).

[Michael Grant, *The Roman Emperors*, 227-240; Christopher T. Connell, "Christian Icons on Byzantine Coins," *The Numismatist*, October 1989, pp. 1610-14.]

labas; limbag [*Tag.*] an issue, issuance.

Labbé, Philippe (1607-67). French scholar who wrote the first numismatic bibliography, a work titled *Bibliotheca Nummaria*, in 1664.

lachnos λαχνός (*m.*) [*Grk.*] lot (at an auction or mail bid sale).

Lafayette Dollar U.S. commemorative silver dollar struck on December 14, 1899 (the one hundredth anniversary of the death of George Washington), but with the date 1900. One of the first U.S. commemorative coins and the very first of this denomination, the Lafayette piece was authorized by the Act of March 3, 1899, and was struck to raise money for the completion of a statue of Marie Joseph Paul Yves Roch Gilbert du Motier, Marquis de Lafayette (1757-1834), the French military leader and statesman who aided the American colonists in their revolution against the British and who later participated in the French Revolution. Because American schoolchildren had contributed approximately $50,000 to the Lafayette Monument Fund, the dedication on the reverse of the coin reads, "Erected by the youth of the United States in honor of Gen. Lafayette/Paris 1900."

Charles E. Barber engraved the dies. The obverse portrays the accolated busts of Lafayette and Washington. Barber borrowed the design of Washington from a now-famous bust sculpted by Jean Antoine Houdon in 1785. The depiction of Lafayette came from an 1824 French medal created by Caunois. The reverse shows Lafayette on horseback.

Although named for Lafayette, this piece is not only the first coin to portray a U.S. President but is also the first to feature *any* American citizen (except for a few women who served as artists' models). For that reason it will always have a special place in numismatics.

[Thomas LaMarre, "The Lafayette Dollar: The Commemorative That Broke All the Rules," *The Numismatist*, July 1986, pp. 1359-61.; Arlie R. Slabaugh, *United States Commemorative Coinage*, pp. 17-22.]

lagad [*Swed.*] repaired.

lagerkransad [*Swed.*] laureate.

lagkagelegering (*c.*) [*Dan.*] Literally, *layer cake alloy*. The term refers to *clad* or *"sandwich"* coinage.

LaGrange, Jean (1831-1908) Chief Engraver of the Paris Mint from 1880 to 1896. In addition to preparing French coins, he also created coins for Guatemala, Tunis, and Ethiopia.

laiton (*m.*) [*Fr.*] brass (the alloy).

lamination A thin layer of metal which peels off the surface of a coin due to flaws in the

alloy from which the planchet[q.v.] was made. Except for clad coins or coins with plated surfaces, coin planchets are normally disks of a single solid metal. The disks can lose their solidity if foreign substances get mixed into the alloy or if the various metals in the alloy fail to blend properly. Layers of metal form which can break away from each other. These breaks may be as small as the head of a pin or may be large enough to cover a major portion of the coin's surface. Some coins have even been known to split in half.

Coins made of nickel alloys are most likely to have laminations. The extreme hardness of these alloys is both their biggest quality and their greatest fault. Although the coins are so hard that they can endure being in circulation for a long time, the alloys are hard to mix, causing quality control to suffer.

lanço (*m.*) [*Port.*] (auction) bid.

Landesmünze (*f.*) [*Ger.*] literally, *boundary coin.* Copper or billon coin intended to circulate only within some specific German province rather than to be valid for use throughout an entire kingdom. This concept first appeared in the mid-1600s and continued until the advent of the German Empire in 1871.

langued Heraldic term indicating an exposed tongue.

Länsi-Saksa [*Finn.*] West Germany (B.R.D.).

lantay [*Tag.*] fineness; fine (purity of metal).

lantti [*Finn.*] coin (colloquial term).

laos [*Tag.*] obsolete.

läpimitta [*Finn.*] diameter.

larawan [*Tag.*] portrait.

large cent 1. Numismatic name for the copper one cent pieces coined in the United States from 1793 to 1857. The cents struck since that time are of a reduced size and are called small cents.

It is widely held that the large cents and their companion half cents were the first coins struck for general circulation by the fledgling Philadelphia Mint, although a few experts feel that the various dismes, half dismes, silver center cents, and Birch cents of 1792 were intended as the first regular issues. All of the large cents and half cents were produced by the Philadelphia Mint, even though the U.S. government established other minting facilities prior to the discontinuance of these two series in 1857. No copper or nickel coins of any type were struck outside of Philadelphia until the San Francisco Mint issued Indian Head Cents in 1908.

Half cents and large cents, as well as silver and gold coins, were authorized through the Mint Act of April 2, 1792. A key aspect of this Act was the creation of a decimal system of coinage, something virtually unheard of in 1792 but used by nearly every country on earth today. One hundred cents were to equal one dollar. In fact, the word "cent" itself comes from the identical French word meaning "hundred."

Although the half cent and large cent were regarded as token coinage, an effort was made to give these coins enough copper to allow their intrinsic values to approach their face values. The coins were large and cumbersome which contributed to their demise in 1857. Even the reduction of the cent's weight from 13.48 grams to 10.89 grams in 1795 did not make the coins appreciably more convenient. As a point of comparison, today's U.S. bronze cents have a weight of 3.11 grams, but it should also be noted that the cent of today has considerably less purchasing power than the cent of two hundred years ago.

All of the half cents and large cents portray an allegory of Liberty, a popular motif found on most U.S. coin designs of the eighteenth and nineteenth centuries. The reverse design of the very first large cents showed the denomination encircled by a 13-link chain, one link for each of the 13 original American colonies. On all of the half cents and on all subsequent large cents, the chain was replaced with a wreath. Some of the earliest U.S. coins, especially the coppers, exhibit weak designs and poor workmanship, deficiencies which were substantially corrected by the time the Philadelphia Mint had been in existence for ten years.

The half cents and large cents ultimately fell victim to inflation, as their continued issuance became impractical due to the rising

price of copper. In 1857 the half cent was discontinued forever and the large cent was replaced with the smaller and more convenient Flying Eagle Cent.

[William H. Sheldon, *Penny Whimsy*; R. S. Yeoman, *A Guide Book of United States Coins* (44th Ed.), pp. 8-10 & 69-89; Richard G. Doty, *The Macmillan Encyclopedic Dictionary of Numismatics*, pp. 191-92.]

1911 "Godless" Canadian large cent

2. Bronze one cent coins minted in Canada from 1858-1859 and (with interruptions) from 1876-1920. There were no corresponding half cents issued.

Canada began issuing large cents just one year after the United States discontinued its series. Canada's decision to mint the larger coins resulted from the confusion it faced in the 1850s in its attempt to create its own monetary system. Unlike the United States, which had achieved its independence from Britain by 1792 and could make whatever monetary decisions it chose, Canada was still an English province and had to follow the dictates of London. Furthermore, in creating its own coinage Canada had to deal with the practical problem of reaching a compromise between the English coins which were supposed to be circulating in Canada and the decimal coins of the United States and elsewhere which were often found in circulation.

The initial large cents of the Province of Canada had a weight of 4.536 grams. Enough were struck in 1858 and 1859 to satisfy demand for nearly twenty years. When the next batch was minted by the Dominion of Canada in 1876, the weight of the coins was increased, not decreased. The new weight of 5.67 grams corresponded to that of the English halfpennies which were quite popular among Canadians.

As is the case with current Canadian coins, the reigning British monarch appeared on all of the large cents. Victoria's effigy graced the cents of 1858-1901, Edward VII's from 1902-1910, and George V's from 1911-1920. In 1920 the series was replaced with the small cents of 3.24 grams.

The 1911 pieces, the first of George V, were the most controversial of the series due to the omission of the Latin words *Dei Gratia* ("By the Grace of God") from the obverse inscription. Because of complaints from the public, this "Godless" inscription was modified the following year and the missing words (in abbreviated form) were restored.

In the early 1920s, Canada disposed of some of its old large cent dies by selling them to China for "recycling." See *reused die* for illustration.

[J. A. Haxby and R. C. Willey, *Coins of Canada* (9th Ed.), pp. 19-23.]

largest medal A 14-karat gold medal weighing 365 pounds and measuring one meter (39.37 inches) in diameter is presumed to be the largest medal ever produced anywhere. This medallic monster, containing exactly 3,123 troy ounces of gold, was minted by the Leach & Garner Company of Attleboro, Massachusetts, for the Vancouver World's Fair in 1986.

The size of this medal was chosen so as to guarantee that the gold content would be worth more than one million dollars, both in Canadian and U.S. funds. The price of gold needed only to exceed $320 (U.S.) per ounce to assure that the medal would indeed be worth that amount.

[Robert Obojski, "World's Fair Medal Weighs 365 Pounds," *Coin World*, October 15, 1986, p. 82.]

laskea liikkeeseen (*v.*) [*Finn.*] to issue.

laskos [*Finn.*] a fold.

latão (*m.*) [*Port.*] brass (the alloy).

Late Oincta Profundit [*Lat.*] That which is joined together, stretches far and wide.

lathos λάθος (*n.*) [*Grk.*] error.

Latin Union; Latin Monetary Union Economic entity formed in 1865 by France, Italy, Belgium, and Switzerland to form a bimetallic monetary standard and to determine the amount of silver which could be coined annually by each of the member countries. In order to create a common

European currency, each nation's unit of money was to be standardized so that the common unit would be a silver coin (franc, lira, or whatever) of 5.000 grams, .835 silver, .1342 ounce A.S.W. The common currency was intended to expedite trade and minimize confusion.

Many other countries, including some outside of Europe, ultimately joined. The Union never enjoyed the success it desired, partly because of fluctuations in the relative value of gold and silver but mostly because Great Britain refused to join. The British gold sovereign was a perpetual mismatch against the other currencies, just as the pound Sterling sank the European Economic Community's attempt to establish a common *écu*[q.v.] in the 1990s when the British refused to participate.

Whatever was left of the the Latin Union dissolved after World War I when most European countries discontinued their gold coinage. In today's world, the French, Italian, Belgian, and Swiss units of currency (as well as the currencies of the other various members of the Union) have no particular relationship to each other.

[Ewald Junge, *World Coin Encyclopedia*, pp. 149-50; *Standard American Encyclopedia*, Vol. 10., p. 96.]

latón (*m.*) [*Span.*] brass (the alloy).

laur. [*abbr.*] laureate.

lauré; lauréate [*Fr.*] laureate.

laureate head

laureate Head crowned with a laurel wreath. The laurel is an ancient symbol of honor and victory and also serves to identify the hero with the motives and goals of his accomplishments. This motif has been placed on many coins throughout history.

[J. E. Cirlot, *A Dictionary of Symbols* (2nd Ed.), 1983, Philosophical Library, New York, p. 181.]

laureato [*Ital.*] laureate.

English laurel of James I

laurel English gold coin of 20 shillings (one pound) issued by James I from 1619 to 1625. The roman numeral XX by the king's head indicates the denomination. The coin is so named because James is portrayed with a laureate head.

Laurier, Sir Wilfrid Canadian Prime Minister (1896-1911). Born November 20, 1841, in Saint-Lin (now Laurentides), Québec; died February 17, 1919, in Ottawa, Ontario.

Sir Wilfrid Laurier was the first French-Canadian Prime Minister of the Dominion of Canada. An advanced liberal with anticlerical and republican views, he dedicated his life to Canadian unity. Through his statesmanship and perseverance, he was able to bridge the gap between conservative churchmen and liberal politicians.

In 1874 he was elected to the Canadian House of Commons, and then in 1877 became minister of inland revenue. When he became Prime Minister in 1896, his primary objectives were to bring all Canadians together on issues of church and state and to improve relations with the United States and Great Britain (while keeping Canada independent of Britain).

Laurier's land and emigration policies were among the primary achievements of his administration. His government settled boundary disputes between British Columbia

"Lazy Deuce" U.S. National Bank Note   [Photo courtesy Stanley Morycz]

and Alaska, created the precursor of the Canadian National Railways, and expanded trade. He governed during a period of great prosperity for which he provided the slogan, "The Twentieth Century belongs to Canada."

To his faithful followers, he was a hero. His great personal charisma, character, dignity, and dedication won him the admiration of Canadians and non-Canadians alike.

Laurier is portrayed on the Canadian $1000 notes of 1935 and 1937, the $5 multicolored note of 1969-75, and the $5 note introduced in 1986 as part of the *bar code* issues.

[Contributed by Ruth Ann Davis.]

Lawful Money   Official exchange rate in the eighteenth century equating the Spanish milled dollar to six English shillings. Thus, 1 penny = 1/72 dollar = 1/9 bit.

Lazy Deuce   U.S. National Bank Note from the First Charter Period, Series of 1863-1875. The vignette on the front portrays an allegorical woman holding an American flag. The note receives its name from the large digit "2" which is stretched out and lying on its side.

[Fred Reinfeld, *The Story of Paper Money*, p. 88.]

lead   Metal rarely used for coinage purposes. [element: group IVa of periodic table; atomic weight 207.2; atomic number 82; specific gravity 11.35; symbol Pb.]

Lead is a heavy, soft, dark grey metal sometimes used in patterns and in some ancient Roman tokens but mostly found in nineteenth and twentieth century counterfeit coins. Among its few uses in standard coins were

those issued in India during the Andhra dynasty (also known as Satavahana) of ca. 230 B.C.-A.D. 230.

[Contributed by Halbert Carmichael.]

leather   1. Medium of exchange among many ancient peoples. There is evidence that before the advent of copper coins, the ancient Romans stamped leather skins and used them as a form of currency.

2. Substance from which some pieces of money were produced in Europe from the Middle Ages into the sixteenth century. In most cases, the pieces were produced as necessity money by cities under siege. For example, in 1124 the Doge of Venice issued leather coins made of horse hide for the beleaguered city of Tyrus.

Not all leather money has been obsidional. Because his treasury had been depleted due to war reparations, King John II of France was forced to issue small leather coins in 1360. The coins contained slim gold threads sewn into the leather or stamped upon it.

[Albert R. Frey, *A Dictionary of Numismatic Names* (1973 reprint), pp. 131-132.]

3. One of the more unusual materials upon which Notgeld[q.v.] (emergency money) was printed during the inflationary period in Germany and Austria from 1919-1922. Although the vast majority of Notgeld pieces were produced in the form of paper notes of varying designs and denominations, a few were printed on silk, felt, and linen, and some metal coins were struck.

The leather Notgeld "notes" were not really intended to circulate as money but were produced as souvenirs or novelties. Such was the case with much of the Notgeld, irrespective of the material from which it was made.

[Charles J. Opitz, *Odd and Curious Money: Descriptions and Values*, p. 42.]

leaved edge Type of security edge consisting of indefinitely repeated twin leaves instead of milled ridges or lettering. This device is most commonly found on Latin American silver crown-size coins.

leértékelés [*Hun.*] devaluation.

left side of coin When used as part of a description of a coin or note, the terms *left* and *right* refer to positioning from the viewer's perspective, not the coin's perspective.

lega (*f.*) [*Ital.*] alloy (of metals).

legalacsonyabb ár [*Hun.*] minimum bid.

legenda [*Finn.*]; (*f.*) [*Port., Pol.*] legend.

legal tender Any form of circulating coin or paper money which the law compels a creditor to accept in payment of a debt when offered by the debtor in the right amount. For example, because U.S. paper money has been decreed legal tender by the U.S. government, it can be used in payment for any debts owed in the United States. A person owed $1000 in the United States must accept payment in any form of U.S. currency and cannot demand to be paid in silver or gold coins or in some other form of payment.

[*Black's Law Dictionary*, 4th Ed., p. 1637.]

legal tender note Series of U.S. paper money initiated on March 10, 1862. Various issues extended into the 1920s. Legal tender notes exist in denominations of $5, $10, $20, $50, $100, $500, and $1000, and most are categorized as United States Notes. Legal tender notes are so named because of their stated obligation: *This note is a legal tender at its face value for all debts public and private, except duties on imports and interest on the public debt.* [The exact phrasing of this obligation varies somewhat from issue to issue.]

The notes were introduced during the U.S. Civil War (1861-65), a time when citizens were hoarding gold, silver, and even copper coins. Unsecured paper money (notes not backed by gold or silver) was distrusted by the general public and not always accepted in payment. Making these notes legal tender was the government's way of requiring people to accept them in trade.

[Fred Reinfeld, *The Story of Paper Money*, pp. 61-70.]

legend 1. The inscription surrounding the head or bust of a monarch on a coin or medal. It usually gives the sovereign's name and title but may also include territory ruled, sanction by God, and whatever other information is deemed necessary to support the monarch's legitimacy. The legend need not be in the national language and may include abbreviations.

The 1902 British crown in the illustration shows a lengthy and complicated legend: EDWARDVS VII (the king's name and numbering, "Edward VII"), DEI GRA*tia* ("By the Grace of God"), BRIT[T]*anniarum* OMN*ium* REX ("King of all the Britains"), FID*ei*

U.S. legal tender note showing obligation   [Photo courtesy Stanley Morycz]

DEF*ensor* ("Defender of the Faith"), IND*iae* IMP*erator* ("Emperor of India").

extensive legend on British crown

2. Any inscription approximating the above, especially a circular inscription running parallel to the rim. If the legend is a patriotic or religious slogan, it is called a motto.

Legende (*f.*) [*Ger.*] legend.

legering (*f.-c.*) [*Dut.*]; (*c.*) [*Dan.*]; (*r.*) [*Swed.*]; (*m.*) [*Nor.*] alloy (of metals).

leggenda (*f.*) [*Ital.*] legend.

Legierung (*f.*) [*Ger.*] alloy (of metals).

leike [*Finn.*] exergue.

leikkaamalla mitätöity [*Finn.*] cut cancellation.

leilão (*f.*) [*Port.*] auction.

leilão por correspondência [*Port.*] mail bid sale.

leimauspuristin [*Finn.*] (coinage) press.

Leitmotiv (*n.*) [*Ger.*] A brief musical theme associated with a specific character in Wagnerian operas. The term is sometimes used numismatically in reference to some particular device or design that recurs frequently on the coins or banknotes of a given country. Coats of arms and various national symbols (Mexican and American eagles, Canadian maple leaves, Australian kangaroos, etc.) fall into this category.

leke [*Turk.*] tarnish; stain.

lekopott [*Hun.*] cabinet friction.

lema (*f.*) [*Span., Port.*] motto.

lempira Unit of currency of Honduras established through that nation's monetary reform decreed on April 3, 1926. It is the denomination of a silver coin (12.500 grams, .900 silver, .3617 oz. A.S.W.) first minted in 1931. Its minor unit is the *centavo de lempira* equal to 1/100 of a lempira. The word comes from the name of a famous native chieftain (Lempira, 1497?-1536) who temporarily held off a Spanish advance into the interior of that country and who is now regarded as a national symbol of liberty and valor.

[Paul J. Holsen II, "Honduras Notes Interest Young Collector," *World Coins,* February 1970, pp. 206-10.; Frank Nuessel, "Currency Designations in Spanish-Speaking Nations," *The Numismatist,* November 1986, pp. 2260-65.]

lengua (*f.*) [*Span.*] language.

Lenin, Vladimir Ilich né *Vladimir Ilich Ulyanov.* Russian statesman who created the Bolshevik Party and the Soviet state. Born April 22, 1870 (as per current calendar; April 10, 1870, on the calendar in use at that time) in Simbirsk (now Ulyanovsk), Russia; died January 21, 1924, in Gorkiy (near Moscow) of a paralytic stroke.

After the overthrow and execution of Czar Nicholas II in 1917, the Bolsheviks, led by Lenin, ultimately took control of Russia and renamed it the Union of Soviet Socialist Republics. His basic goal was to build a workers' state from what had been a peasant society. Lenin's political theory was a modified version of Marxism, especially in that he opposed both the feudal system of the Russian czars and the capitalist system of the West. In his eyes, both systems took power and land away from the workers. Unfortunately, the new socialist system to which he gave birth did not furnish sound economic answers. The twentieth century saw the Soviet Union become an increasingly large and militarily powerful nation, but one with an ever-worsening economy until its ultimate dissolution in 1991.

Because regular-issue Soviet coins do not usually portray individuals, Lenin has not appeared on a great number of coins. He is seen on a few Soviet commemorative coins, as well as some non-circulating legal tender[*q.v.*] coins of such places as Equatorial Guinea.

[*Funk & Wagnalls New Encyclopedia* (1984), Vol. 16, pp. 54-56.]

lente de aumento [*Span.*] magnifying glass.

lente d'ingrandimento (*f.*) [*Ital.*] magnifying glass.

leopard 1. Gold coin valued at a half-florin struck by Edward III in 1344. The florin of this series was known as a double leopard and the quarter-florin was called a helm. All three pieces are extremely rare.

[Stephen Mitchell & Brian Reeds (editors), *Coins of England and the United Kingdom* (Seaby, 1991), p. 102.]

2. Animal which has appeared on numerous coins, even though the technical distinction between the leopard and the lion has sometimes been blurred. See *lion*.

leprosy Technically known as Hansen's Disease, leprosy is a severe affliction of the skin and peripheral nerves which often affect the eyes, larynx, and mucous membranes. It is the focus of many commemorative medals as well as outstanding service awards, especially the Damien-Dutton, given to individuals who have contributed to the eradication of this horrible disease. Those honored with the Damien-Dutton Award include Mother Teresa (1984) and John F. Kennedy (posthumously, 1965). Since 1976 the American Leprosy Missions, Inc., has awarded its bronze medal to supporters, key staff members, and others who have helped alleviate the problems of those suffering from this terrible affliction.

[Dennis F. Marr, "Crusaders Against a Misunderstood Disease," *The Numismatist,* April 1988, pp. 657-662.]

lepton [from Greek λεπτόν, based on λεπτός (*leptos*), *small* or *thin*.]

1. Generic term used by the ancient Greeks for the smallest coin of a series, regardless of the metal.

2. Small copper coins of local issue (as opposed to Imperial issues) in the eastern part of the Roman Empire.

3. In first-century Judea and Syria, a lepton was a small copper coin, two of which equalled a Roman quadrans, Greek chalko, or Hebrew pruta. This denomination is also known in English as a widow's mite, based on the King James translation of a passage in the Gospels, where an offering made by a poor widow is declared by Jesus to be worth more than gold given by the wealthy (*Mark 22: 41-44*).

4. In Modern Greece, a unit of account worth one-hundredth of a phoenix (1828-1831) or drachma (1831 to the present). It was issued as a small copper coin from 1828 to 1879 in Greece, 1900 and 1901 in Crete, and 1834 to 1862 in British-occupied Ionian Islands.

Due to inflation, all Greek lepta-denominated coins were phased out in the late 1980s.

[Contributed by Simcha Kuritzky. Albert R. Frey, *A Dictionary of Numismatic Names* (1973 reprint), pp. 133-134; *Encyclopedia Judaica*, Vol. 5, p. 697.]

LeSouef Collection Numismatic collection amassed by A. M. LeSouef, Deputy Master of the Melbourne Branch of the Royal Mint from 1919 to 1926. This fine group of Australian coins and medals forms a significant portion of the Museum of Victoria's numismatic holdings.

LeSouef was not a wealthy collector. He mostly acquired samplings of new coins as they were minted in Australia. Nevertheless, this accumulation is of great numismatic importance to that country.

[A. M. LeSouef, "Catalogue of Coins, Medals, and Checks in the A. M. LeSouef Collection," *Journal of the Numismatic Association of Australia*, July 1986, pp. 25-36.]

letét [*Hun.*] deposit.

lettered edges: in relief (above); incuse (below)

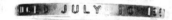

lettered edge Inscription placed around the edges of some coins as a way of making the coins harder to clip, file, or counterfeit. Lettered edges fall into the category of security edges.

Lettered edges have been a popular yet clumsy way of giving protection to the edges of coins since the seventeenth century. Prior to

the advent of milled coinage in the sixteenth century, this process was impossible because of the way coins were hammered by hand. Edges were ragged and coins were not perfectly round, permitting unscrupulous people to clip or file some of the precious metal from the edge without the adjustments being readily noticeable. The crude appearance of so many hammered coins also made the counterfeiting of them relatively easy. Because these illicit activities were widespread, measures had to be taken to protect the integrity of the coinage.

The invention of coinage machines gave moneyers more options. One such option was to place either incuse or relief lettering around the edge, thus making any illegal adjustments obvious. Also, lettered edges made the creation of passable counterfeits more difficult.

When a coin is minted by machine, the planchet is placed in a ring called a collar. This prevents the coin from "spreading out" when the planchet is struck by the obverse and reverse dies. To obtain a lettered edge in relief (raised letters), the coin can be struck in a segmented collar. In other words, the collar is in pieces, permitting the finished coin to be removed from the collar after the minting process is completed. The edge tends to show seam marks where the segmented pieces met.

The lettering can also be incuse (recessed rather than raised), but this requires a different process. Usually the planchet's edge is lettered prior to the minting process. If a collar is used, the lettering suffers. If no collar is used, the shape and quality of the coin suffer.

The late twentieth century has seen a revival of lettered edges, although not for the same reasons for which they were introduced in the seventeenth century. In the modern world, adding a lettered edge gives commemorative and other special coins a certain "flair" which makes them more marketable.

letters used as numerals see *gematria*.

lewa strona (*f.*) [*Pol.*] left (direction or position).

leyenda (*f.*) [*Span.*] legend.

libbra (*f.*) [*Ital.*] pound (unit of weight).

libertad (*f.*) [*Span.*] liberty.

Libertas Americana Medal U.S. commemorative medal struck in 1783 by the Paris Mint for distribution to various French leaders who were contributing to America's successful war of independence against the British. The words *Libertas Americana* are Latin for "American Liberty."

Benjamin Franklin, who authorized the production of these medals, also helped to design them. He suggested a depiction of the infant Hercules grappling with two serpents. The child symbolizes the young American nation, and the serpents represent the armies of British Generals Burgoyne and Cornwallis. France, depicted by the goddess Minerva, stands over the child and protects him from the English rampant lion. Completing the design are the dates October 17, 1777 (Burgoyne's surrender at Saratoga), and October 19, 1781 (Cornwallis' surrender at Yorktown), and the Latin inscription *Non Sine Diis Animosus Infans* ("The courageous child was not without divine assistance").

The opposite side portrays the allegorical Ms. Liberty with dishevelled hair and a look of determination on her face. Included is a Phrygian cap, an ancient symbol of freedom. At the bottom is the French abbreviation for the date July 4, 1776.

Franklin is said to have ordered 200 pieces in bronze, 50 in silver, and 2 in gold. The gold medals were given to French King Louis XVI and his wife Marie Antoinette. These pieces disappeared in the 1790s when the French monarchy was overthrown and have not been seen since. Some of the bronze and silver specimens have survived but are very rare and command high prices.

To commemorate America's Bicentennial in 1976, Pierre de Haye, director of the Paris Mint, suggested restriking these medals using the original dies that still existed in the Mint's archives. The suggestion was well received and new medals were produced. So that the new pieces could not be confused with the originals, certain design changes were made. In particular, the diameter was increased from

47 mm. to 77 mm. and the new pieces were made noticeably thicker.

Perhaps the greatest significance of the 1783 *Libertas Americana* Medal is the impact of its Liberty design on the early regular coinage of the United States. The very portrayal of Liberty on US coins, a tradition that continues even to the present time, may have been inspired by this beautiful medal.

[Louis C. Sass, "Medals of Friendship and Thanks", *The Numismatist*, July 1990, pp. 1080-1084; Martha L. Turner, "Commemorative Medals of the American Revolution and the War of 1812," *The Numismatist*, January 1975, pp. 5-18.]

liberté (*f.*) [*Fr.*] liberty.

Liberté, egalité, fraternité on 1918 10 centime coin

Liberté, egalité, fraternité [*Fr.*] Liberty, equality, fraternity. Rallying cry of the French revolutionists in 1789. This motto has appeared on many French coins and notes since the 1790s. It dominates the reverse on the World War I-era 10 centime coin in the illustration.

Liberty Allegorical woman who has appeared on many series of American coins. Ms. Liberty was portrayed on the first coins officially produced by the U.S. Mint: the 1792 silver center cent, silver half disme, silver disme, and pattern quarter dollar, as well as all of the regular-issue coinage from 1793 well into the nineteenth century. The Walking Liberty Half Dollar was minted as late as 1947. Two Liberty designs were brought back in 1986 when the United States began issuing gold and silver bullion coins.

Placing the personification of Liberty on United States coins was not the first choice of many members of the earliest U.S. Congress. The general consensus was to place George Washington's effigy on coins, although some congressmen objected that such a practice resembled the actions of a monarchy. Since Washington himself reportedly disapproved of using his own likeness on coins, the decision was made to portray a representation of Liberty.

[R. S. Yeoman, *A Guide Book of United States Coins* (44th Ed.), p. 63.]

1883 "No Cents" Liberty Nickel

Liberty Head Nickel Popular U.S. 5 cent piece designed by mint Chief Engraver Charles Barber and struck from 1883-1912.

The initial issue in 1883 showed the Roman numeral "V" on the reverse as a way of indicating the coin's denomination. However, the actual word "cents" was not to be found. Some unscrupulous people reeded the edge and gold plated many of these coins to pass them off as $5 gold pieces which became known as racketeer nickels. The mint soon realized its mistake and changed the reverse design to include the word "cents". Hence, two major varieties of the 1883 Liberty Head Nickel exist, designated as "without cents" and "with cents."

The nickels were officially issued through 1912, although five specimens of questionable origin dated 1913 are known to have been struck. They were probably fraudulently made by mint employees to satisfy collector demand. No matter what their origin, the 1913 Liberty Head Nickels remain among the most popular and desirable of all U.S. coins and are in great demand.

McDermott-Bebee 1913 Liberty Nickel

The 1913 nickel shown in the illustration is the famed McDermott-Bebee specimen, donated by Aubrey Bebee to the American Numismatic Association. The piece now resides in the A.N.A. Museum.

[Dustin Goglin, "Charles Barber's Liberty Head Nickel," *The Numismatist,* June 1994, pp. 846-49; Ted Schwarz, "Ups and Downs of the U.S. Nickel," *Coins,* July 1983, pp. 56-61; R. S. Yeoman, *A Guide Book of United States Coins* (44th Ed.), pp. 105-106.]

Liberty Seated coins see *Seated Liberty coins.*

Liberty Standing Quarter see *Standing Liberty Quarter.*

Liberty Walking Half Dollar see *Walking Liberty Half Dollar.*

libra (*f.*) [*Span., Port.*] pound (unit of weight).

libra esterlina (*f.*) [*Span., Port.*] pound Sterling (£).

libranza (*f.*) [*Span.*] money order.

libre [*Turk.*] pound (unit of weight).

licita (*v.*) [*Rom.*] to bid (at an auction or mail bid sale).

licitación (*f.*) [*Span.*] (auction) bid.

licitación mínima (*f.*) [*Span.*] minimum bid.

licitación sugerida (*f.*) [*Span.*] suggested bid.

licitar (*v.*) [*Span.*] to bid.

licitare (*f.*) [*Rom.*] (auction) bid.

licitaţie (*f.*) [*Rom.*] auction, auction sale.

licitaţie prin poştă (*f.*) [*Rom.*] mail bid sale.

licytować (*v.*) [*Pol.*] to bid.

liga (*f.*) [*Port.*] alloy (of metals).

Lighthouse, John C. Born in Rochester, New York, in 1844, John C. Lighthouse ("J. C." as he was known) was one of the foremost numismatic collectors of the nineteenth century. He was a discriminate collector and usually bought only the best. His collection included most of the great U.S. rarities of the eighteenth and nineteenth centuries as well as many of the most desirable ancient coins.

Lighthouse spent a good deal of his life in San Francisco. Although he usually kept his collection locked in the Safe Deposit Company's facilities in that city, he removed the collection from the vault in mid-April 1906 to show the pieces to his friend Farran Zerbe. In the early morning of April 18, 1906, San Francisco was severely ravaged by its

famous earthquake and subsequent fire. The Safe Deposit Company building and all of its contents were totally destroyed, but Lighthouse's collection mercifully was saved.

"J. C." died in Rochester in 1909, but his collection was kept intact in a bank vault until 1936. In that year, J. C. Morgenthau and Company auctioned off a portion of it, including 660 rare proof U.S. coins, in New York City.

[Charles J. Ricard, "John C. Lighthouse: Numismatic Giant," *The Numismatist,* January 1988, pp. 47-54.]

lignée (*f.*) [*Fr.*] pedigree (list of previous and present owners).

liikkeeseen laskematon [*Finn.*] not issued.

lille [*Dan.*] small, little.

lilies on the ends of the cross on Monaco *écu d'or*

lily Stylized flower seen on many coins and heraldic emblems. The term *fleur-de-lis*[*q.v.*] is more correct, because the flower as it appears in heraldry does not exist in nature, whereas a lily does. The English word *lily* is often seen in catalogues to describe this type of design, especially when the flower is attached to something else rather than being shown by itself. An example is the coin in the illustration, an *écu d'or*[*q.v.*] of Monaco ca. 1515. The lilies are connected to the four ends of the cross.

lima [*Indo., Tag.*] five.

Lima Coinage English silver and gold coins struck in 1745 and 1746 by George II using

specie (i.e., coinage and bullion) captured from the Spanish ship *Manila Galleon* (known in Spanish as *Nuestra Señora de Copadonga*) and from a custom house in Payta, Peru, by Commodore George Anson, commander of the English vessel *Centurian.* The bulk of the treasure was part of a $3 million bounty seized when Anson and his men surprised the *Manila Galleon* off Cape Espíritu Santo in the Philippines in June 1743. Because the English were at war with the Spanish over trading practices in the North American colonies, the *Centurian,* along with seven other ships under Anson's command, were sent to circumnavigate the world in order to destroy whatever Spanish ships and towns they might encounter and to bring back plunder. In Anson's favor was the British prize-money system which guaranteed every member of a victorious crew a predetermined portion of the booty, thus giving his men an incentive to push onward even when they faced overwhelming odds.

"Lima" crown of George II

Anson's voyage was more successful than anyone could have expected, and he returned to England a hero. To commemorate Anson's achievement as well as the successes of other privateers, George II had coins struck from the captured gold and silver. Under his bust appears the word *LIMA* which served both as an honor to Anson and his crew and as a slap in the face to the Spanish who had not forgotten nor forgiven the English for destroying their Armada a century and a half earlier.

The Lima coinage consists of silver sixpence pieces (1745 & 1746, "old bust" effigy of the king), shillings (1745 & 1746, "old bust"), halfcrowns (1745 & 1746, "old head"), and crowns (1746, "old bust"), and gold half-guineas (1745, "intermediate head"), guineas (1745, "intermediate head"), and five guineas (1746, "old bust").

[Stephen Mitchell & Brian Reeds (editors), *Coins of England and the United Kingdom* (Seaby, 1991), pp. 251-55; Thomas H. Sebring, "Commodore Anson and the Lima Coinage," *The Numismatist,* November 1985, pp. 2164-71.]

Lima Mint On August 21, 1565, King Philip II of Spain signed a decree establishing a mint in what is now Lima, Peru. This mint, one of the oldest in the New World (the very oldest having been established in Mexico), was desperately needed to alleviate a severe coin shortage in that territory, to standardize the local medium of exchange, and to assure that the precious metals mined there would be properly taxed.

The first coins were not struck at that mint until 1568, due largely to a delay in obtaining the proper equipment. Within a very few years, the mint was temporarily closed because of accusations of fraud. Although a new mint was built farther inland at Potosí in 1573, some limited coinage was struck in Lima for the next fifteen years. The mint was closed in 1588 and remained so until 1683, except for an unauthorized reopening in 1658. Its re-establishment in 1683 proved to be permanent, as it has been in operation ever since.

The most significant change in the mint's status transpired in 1824 and 1825 upon the establishment of the Republic of Peru (or, *República Peruana,* as its national name appears on coins). The Napoleonic Wars had weakened Spain's grip on its Latin American colonies, thereby enabling the revolutionists in these various territories to gain their independence. The mints were taken over by the new national governments: the Lima Mint became the property of the Peruvian government, the Potosí Mint went to the Bolivian government, etc.

Despite facing wars, inflation, earthquakes, and even a devastating fire which destroyed

the original building in 1620, the Lima Mint is alive and well and remains one of the most historically significant minting facilities in the world.

[Glenn S. Murray, "Exploring the Historic Lima Mint," *The Numismatist*, July 1988, pp. 1200-1212, including a detailed chronology of the mint's history.]

Lima Style Doubloon Privately-struck gold doubloons produced in America ca. 1786 and attributed to Ephraim Brasher. Its name comes from its design which resembles the 8 escudo gold pieces struck during the mid-18th century in Lima, Peru.

Only two specimens are known to exist, as opposed to the eight specimens of the so-called New York Doubloons which numismatists regularly refer to as Brasher Doubloons. Both types were probably intended for circulation in the American colonies, maybe to expedite large payments between merchants rather than for export to the West Indies. Brasher may have chosen the Lima Mint design, weight, and purity as his prototype because of the mint's reputable weight standard.

The earliest published reference appeared in 1894 in the Scott Stamp & Coin Company's auction catalog of the "Paris" Collection. The second specimen (the finer of the two) came to light in 1914 when Waldo Newcomer acquired it and submitted it to the American Numismatic Society for examination.

Even though the coins have the "E.B." touchmark and that the punch used to make it shows the same exact design and the same rust area as the punch used on the New York specimens, some scholars question whether these pieces were designed by Brasher, in part because of the poor quality of the reverse die. One possible explanation is that Brasher himself designed the obverse but then allowed an apprentice to prepare the reverse.

Many questions remain about these pieces. For example, we do not know why Brasher used two different letter punch sets for his name on his Lima and New York style doubloons, considering the high cost and personal nature of a silversmith's punch set during this period. We also don't know why he

placed *NEW YORK* on the Lima specimens and not on the New York pieces. And researchers have not yet proved conclusively that Brasher was in fact the designer of these pieces.

[Michael Hodder, "Ephraim Brasher's 1786 Lima Style Doubloon," *Money of Pre-Federal America*, pp. 127-157.]

limping bimetallism Monetary system with some limited dependence on the use of silver while primarily dependent on gold. This is in contrast to the normal definition of bimetallism[q.v.] which is a monetary system pegged on two metals, usually silver and gold, which have a fixed ratio of value relative to each other, and both of which have legal tender[q.v.] status.

The term came into vogue in 1878 when the United States through the Bland-Allison Act allowed a limited number of silver dollars to be coined, despite America's abandonment of bimetallism in 1873. Limping bimetallism in the U.S. ended in 1900 when America officially went on the gold standard (even though the silver dollar was still given special status) but revived to some degree in the 1930s as a result of new banking restrictions necessitated by the Great Depression.

[*Funk & Wagnalls New Encyclopedia* (1984), Vol. 4, pp. 76-77; R. S. Yeoman, *A Guide Book of United States Coins* (44th Ed.), p. 14.]

Lincoln, Abraham (nicknamed *Honest Abe* and *The Great Emancipator*). Sixteenth president of the United States. Born February 12, 1809, in Hardin County, Kentucky; shot by John Wilkes Booth on April 14, 1865, in Washington, D.C., and died the following morning.

Abraham Lincoln was president during the U.S. Civil War (1861-65), one of the most turbulent periods in American history. The war itself was fought primarily over the issue of slavery. In 1861 eleven of the southern states bonded together in an attempt to secede from the U.S.A. and to form a separate nation known as the Confederate States of America. It was the intent of the C.S.A. to permit the ownership of black slaves.

Lincoln's primary objective was to keep the Union intact. His second goal was to eliminate

slavery throughout the country. In this latter regard, he issued the *Emancipation Proclamation* on January 1, 1863, which officially abolished slavery, although the proclamation had no practical effect until 1865 when the Confederacy was defeated.

Lincoln is regarded as one of the greatest U.S. presidents because he had worthy goals and was capable of achieving them. He proved himself a compassionate leader by being merciful to the defeated Confederacy and by doing everything possible to bring those states back into the mainstream of American society quickly and painlessly. Although many members of his own party strongly objected to these tactics, history has shown that he made the right decision.

Lincoln was shot to death while watching a play in the Ford Theater in Washington, D.C. He had just begun his second 4-year term as president. His assassin was John Wilkes Booth, a Southern sympathizer.

Although Lincoln's portrait appears on the current $5 note of the United States as well as on a variety of commemorative coins and medals, his effigy on the Lincoln Cent, the type coin with the greatest mintage in history, is his greatest numismatic claim to fame.

Abraham Lincoln

Lincoln Cent Popular U.S. coin introduced in 1909 to commemorate the hundredth anniversary of the birth of Abraham Lincoln. It was the first regular-issue U.S. coin to portray a real person and replaced the Indian Cent[q.v.] which had circulated since 1859.

The coin was designed by Victor David Brenner whose initials "V.D.B." appear on the bottom of the reverse of the earliest strikes. Because the initials were deemed too noticeable, they were removed later in 1909 only to reappear in 1918 but placed discretely under Lincoln's shoulder on the obverse.

From 1909-1958 the main device on the reverse was two stalks of wheat, giving these coins the nickname "wheaties.". In 1959 the Lincoln Memorial was added to the reverse in honor of Lincoln's 150th birthday. Chief Engraver Frank Gasparro created the design.

Due to a shortage of copper during World War II, 1943 Lincoln Cents were struck from zinc-plated steel ("steelies"). The coins soon turned black and rusted, forcing the government to pull them out of circulation. Many of them were disposed of simply by dumping them into San Francisco harbor where they quickly rusted into an unidentifiable blob. A few 1943 bronze cents were struck in error, as were several 1944 steel cents.

Some 1944-1946 cents were made from melted-down rifle cartridge cases. Although their color varied somewhat from that of previous bronze cents, this alloy proved satisfactory. The old alloy was resumed in 1947.

When the price of copper began to skyrocket in the early 1970s, the U.S. Congress started looking for a cheaper alternative. Aluminum was the obvious choice, but an all-aluminum cent was rejected. Instead the decision was made to mint an inexpensive copper-plated zinc coin which would retain the quality and detail of previous Lincoln Cents.

The Lincoln Cent series includes several key double-die issues, most notably those of 1955 and 1995, plus some non-existent 1922 Philadelphia specimens which are really Denver issues with a defective die.

Since 1909 more than a quarter *trillion* Lincoln Cents have been struck, making it the most common type coin ever produced by any country in history and assuring it a permanent place in numismatic history.

Lincoln Memorial Monument completed in 1922 in Washington, D.C., and dedicated to the life and work of Abraham Lincoln. The building itself was designed by Henry Bacon, and the famous white marble statue of Lincoln which rests in the central chamber was sculpted by Daniel French. Above the statue is engraved the inscription, "In this temple, as in the hearts of the people for whom he saved the Union, the memory of Abraham Lincoln is enshrined forever."

The Lincoln Memorial appears on the reverse of the small-size U.S. five dollar notes first issued in 1929. It was also placed on the reverse of the Lincoln Cents in 1959 to commemorate the 150th anniversary of Lincoln's birth.

[David L. Ganz, "A Milestone for a Monumental Coin," *The Numismatist,* January 1994, pp. 42-46 et al; *Funk & Wagnalls New Encyclopedia* (1984), Vol. 16, pp. 140-41.]

linen One of the materials upon which Notgeld[q.v.] (emergency money) was printed during the inflationary period in Germany and Austria from 1919-1922. Although most Notgeld was printed on paper, some was produced on silk, leather, and felt, as well as in the form of metal coins.

Much of the Notgeld, particularly those pieces made from unusual substances, was not really intended to circulate as money but was manufactured as souvenirs and novelties. Many of the pieces were bright and attractive, portraying comical or satirical motifs. The color photo on page 319 shows one such example, a linen Notgeld "note" made in Bielefeld, Germany.

[Charles J. Opitz, *Odd and Curious Money: Descriptions and Values*, p. 47.]

lingot (*m.*) [*Fr.*] ingot.

lingote (*m.*) [*Span., Port.*] ingot.

lingotto (*m.*) [*Ital.*] ingot.

lingua (*f.*) [*Ital.*] language.

linked rings on Fugio Cent

linked rings One of the earliest symbols of unity among the original American colonies, the linked rings consist of a large circle made up of thirteen interlocking smaller rings with each ring showing the name (or abbreviation) of one of the colonies. The design was loosely modeled after a similar motif used on Greco-Roman commemorative reliefs from around 150 B.C. to A.D. 200. Because a circle has no end, ancient peoples regarded it as a symbol of eternity, continuity, and wholeness.

Unlike the eagle and the allegorical figure of Liberty, linked rings did not remain popular as a U.S. national symbol. They made their first documented numismatic appearance on fractional currency issued by the Continental Congress on Feb. 17, 1776. The rings also appeared on the Continental Dollar pattern coins which were the first crown-size silver coins ever proposed for the United States (even though many of the specimens were struck in pewter or brass) and on the 1787 Fugio Cents, the first coins issued by authority of the United States. Linked rings continued to appear on various tokens, notes, medals, and pattern coins until around 1815 when the design simply went out of vogue.

No regular-issue U.S. coins were ever struck using this exact motif, but the first large cents minted in 1793 did show a circle of thirteen interlocking links of a chain. The design proved so unpopular that it was replaced with a wreath after only 36,103 pieces were made.

[David P. McBride, "Linked Rings: Early American Unity Illustrated," *The Numismatist,* November 1979, pp. 2373-93; R. S. Yeoman, *A Guide Book of United States Coins* (44th Ed.), pp. 32, 61, & 75.]

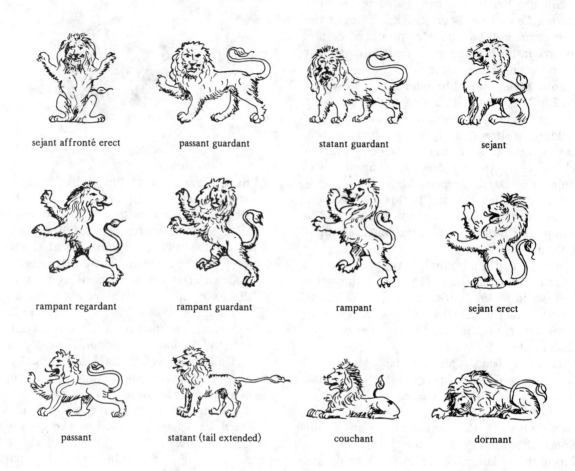

sejant affronté erect	passant guardant	statant guardant	sejant
rampant regardant	rampant guardant	rampant	sejant erect
passant	statant (tail extended)	couchant	dormant

Heraldic lions found on coins and medals

links [*Ger., Dut.*] left (direction or position).

lint mark Small irregular incuse line resembling a scratch on the surface of a coin caused by a piece of lint on the die or planchet during the minting process. It most often occurs on proof coins. Unlike scratches, lint marks have odd thread-like shapes, a uniform depth, and no raised ridges on their borders. Because they occur in the mint during the striking process, they generally have less negative impact on the value of a coin than do scratches.

[James L. Halperin, *N.C.I. Grading Guide*, p. 15.]

lion 1. Popular symbol of regal dignity, virility, and victory which has appeared frequently on coins since the beginning of coinage 2600 years ago. Because of the lion's status as "king" among animals, it gained wide acceptance as a symbol of the ruling king or lord.

In medieval heraldry, the lion was shown in many different poses and positions. These same symbolic lions were often portrayed on coins. The most popular styles are shown in the illustration.

For hundreds of years there has been some debate as to exactly how these animals should be defined. In Continental Europe, a large cat in a standing posture was considered a lion, while a cat in a walking stance was regarded as a leopard. In Britain, however, all of them

were seen as lions. Similarly, Continental heraldry dictated that two or more cat-like creatures on the same shield were to be called leopards, but Britain placed no such restriction.

The popularity of the lion on coins is indisputable. The lion appeared on some of the earliest electrum coins of ancient Greece. The first thaler[q.v.], known as the Joachimsthaler (1519), portrayed a rampant lion on the reverse. In modern times the lion appears on a wide variety of coins ranging from the symbolic crowned *passant guardant* lion on modern British ten pence pieces to the biologically correct lion of East Africa.

2. Denomination of coins used in various parts of Europe during the Middle Ages, usually so named because a lion appeared as the center figure of the coin's design. The list of "lions" includes the Scottish billon coin (a.k.a., the "hardhead") of Queen Mary struck in 1555-56, the Scottish gold 5-shilling piece first issued during the reign of Robert III around 1390, and the gold florin struck in Flanders by Louis de Mâle (1346-1384). Because of the nature of its design, this last piece is referred to as the *lion heaumé* ("helmeted lion").

The *lion d'or* ("golden lion"), a French gold piece struck in the fourteenth century during the reign of Philip VI, is unique in that the lion is not the primary focus of the coin's design. In this instance, a lion is shown lying at the foot of the throne.

[L.E. Clow, "Heraldic Lion Popular on Coins," *World Coins*, May 1973, pp. 678-680, et al. Included is a list of 46 names and descriptions of the lions found in heraldry.]

lion's head of Samos Samos is one of the Greek islands in the Ionian region lying just off of Asia Minor. It was an important trading center in the sixth century B.C. and was a member of the Athenian confederacy. It was also a noted naval power that had substantial dealings with Egypt.

The island's coinage is notable for two devices appearing on its specimens: the forepart of an ox, but most especially a lion's head. The lion's head was depicted on all tetradrachms and was frequently utilized on other denominations such as the stater, half-stater, twelfth-stater, forty-eighth stater, drachm, tetraobol, triobol, didrachm, diobol, trihemiobol, hemidrachm, obol, hemiobol, tridrachm, and trihemidrachm. Metals are principally silver with a few gold and bronze issues, plus electrum.

Six weight standards prevailed during the striking era of Samian coinage. The island's small silver deposits gave it little to draw from for coinage, and it must have acquired its metal from other sources via trading, appropriation, capture, etc.

The lion's head device may well be of oriental origin and could have come from bronze work or ivory carving of Syria and Phoenicia that had begun to influence Greek art. The lion may also have had religious significance.

The lion's head was first noted as early as 600-530 B.C. It was of crude character but susceptible of discernment. Refinements occurred in design over a period of some one hundred years, and by the end of this time the device looks much better. It was not to be conjoined with a reverse of a ship's prow on certain specimens. With the passage of another 25-50 years, it had become quite detailed and recognizable. The lion's head is of the Ionian style, but not in great congruence. It is basically consistent with the prevailing styles of Samian art. The lion's head was exported to the Magna Græcia area and appeared on emissions therefrom, notably those of Zankle and Rhegion.

Samian fortunes ebbed and flowed. The island reverted between independence and several captors, with a concomitant stemming of the flow of its coinage. A decline in the caliber of its specimens became notable, and in 129 B.C. it became a part of the Roman Empire in the Province of Asia.

[Contributed by William F. Mross. John Ward, *Greek Coins and Their Parent Cities*; John Penrose Barron, *The Silver Coins of Samos*; *Catalogue of Greek Coins— Ionia— in the British Museum.*]

lira (*f.*; pl.: *lire*; symbol: L) [*Ital.*] 1. Derived from the Latin *libra* ("pound"). The lira was

originally a unit of account equaling one pound of silver from which 240 Roman denari could be minted.

The first coin of this denomination was struck by Nicolò Tron, doge of Venice, in 1472. The piece weighed 6.5 grams and was 27 mm. in diameter, making it the largest silver coin circulating in Europe at that time. For political reasons the coin became unpopular because the doge (an elected position) had dared to put his own portrait on it, a "royal" practice opposed by the Venetians who were anti-monarchy.

At around the same time, Galeazzo Maria Sforza, duke of Milan, minted a 10-gram lira. The lira was occasionally revived in the sixteenth, seventeenth, and eighteenth centuries in Savoy and Genoa but didn't see any great acceptance until the early nineteenth century when Napoléon Bonaparte proclaimed the lira to be the Italian equivalent of the silver French franc, a valuation which continued until his Italian kingdom collapsed in 1814.

2. The lira is the present unit of currency of Italy, San Marino, and the Vatican, and has also been used in the Italian colonies of Eritrea and Somaliland. The modern lira was adopted by Italy in 1861 when the Kingdom of Italy was created with Victor Emmanuel, king of Sardinia, on the throne. It was to be part of Italy's contribution to the Latin Monetary Union[q.v.], established in 1865 to equalize the currencies of France, Italy, Belgium, and Switzerland in order to create a common European currency. Although the Union ultimately failed, Italy has retained the lira to the present day.

The lira's minor denomination is the centesimo (1 lira = 100 centesimi), but because the lira has dropped so dramatically in value against other currencies (e.g., it now takes hundreds of lire to equal one dollar or one pound Sterling), all modern Italian coins are denominated in lire, so the centesimo no longer has a functionable value.

3. Arabic, Hebrew, and Turkish translation of *pound* used by Israel (לִירָה singular and לִירוֹת *lirot* plural) from 1948 to 1980, by Lebanon and Syria (ليرة singular and ليران *lirat*

plural) from 1920 to the present, and by Turkey from 1873 to the present. On the Lebanese and Syrian pieces, the French *livre(s)* is used as the translation. Turkish notes before 1930 used the French and Arabic spellings, and after 1930 used *lirasi* as the plural. The Israeli lira was replaced with the shekel[q.v.] in 1980, with 10 lirot equal to one shekel.

[Contributed by Simcha Kuritzky. René Sédillot, *Historia de las principales monedas*, pp. 121-32; Richard G. Doty, *The Macmillan Encyclopedic Dictionary of Numismatics*, pp. 197-98; Chester L. Krause and Clifford Mishler, *Standard Catalog of World Coins* (1985), pp. 1139-47.]

modern Israeli lira

lira sterling לִירָה שְׁטֶרְלִינְג (*f.*) [*Heb.*] pound Sterling (£).

lisäpainama [*Finn.*] overprint.

lista de precios [*Span.*] price list.

lista de preços (*f.*) [*Port.*] price list.

liste de prix [*Fr.*] price list.

listel (*m.*) [*Fr.*] rim.

liste over tidligere eiere [*Nor.*] pedigree (list of previous and present owners).

listino prezzi [*Ital.*] price list.

liten [*Nor., Swed.*] small.

lithography Printing technique developed in 1798 by Aloys Senefelder (1771-1834), a German map inspector. This method was the forerunner of modern offset printing.

Lithography is based on the principle that water and grease repel each other. An image (actually a reversed, "mirrored" image) was drawn on a piece of flat, polished limestone with a greasy crayon. The entire piece of limestone would then be wetted. The water would not stick to the image but would be absorbed into the porous surface of the bare

limestone keeping it moist. A greasy ink would then be applied to the entire area but would only adhere to the greasy image. If a sheet of paper were pressed against this, the image (i.e., a "normal" image) would transfer to the paper.

The frequent use of the word "greasy" should not be misconstrued as meaning that the finished work was crude or sloppy. To the contrary, some very beautiful works of art exhibiting exquisite shading have been produced through this process. Yet the use of lithography as a means of printing paper money has usually proved unsatisfactory. The technique lacks the sharpness normally seen on banknotes, making lithographed notes easy to counterfeit. If the work is not done by an expert, the paper can wrinkle during the printing process, resulting in a flawed reproduction (as can be seen in the illustration).

As a means of manufacturing notes, lithography has often been the desired method in emergency situations. A number of lithographed notes appeared in Europe after both World Wars, particularly in those countries experiencing hyperinflation. The Confederacy (the southern states during the U.S. Civil War of 1861-1865) used lithography to print its notes because it had no alternatives. The notes were of poor quality but they served their purpose, as did the rather crude lithographed Mexican revolutionary notes printed in the 1910s.

When lithography is used to counterfeit engraved notes, the difference is obvious, not only because of the lack of sharp detail but also because of the way the finished work feels to the touch. The intaglio process (using etched or engraved plates) leaves the ink sitting on the paper rather than being completely absorbed into it. Some Dutch notes have been intentionally produced with such deep etchings that the inked inscriptions can be felt and "read" by the blind (see *blind assistance*; also see page 320 for color illustrations). Lithography produces no such feel. The finished note feels essentially the same as a blank sheet of paper.

Little Eagle [known in French as *l'Aiglon*]. See *Napoléon II*.

Little Princess Popular name of the U.S. 1841 quarter eagle (gold $2.50), struck only in proof. It is considered to be the most famous and desirable of all the Coronet Type quarter eagles, minted from 1840 to 1907. Twelve examples are known to exist, one of which is unverified.

liú tōng de 流通的 [*Chin.-py./sc.*] circulated.

Livingstone, **David** Scottish physician and missionary who is considered one of the most important modern explorers of Africa. Born March 19, 1813, in Blantyre, Scotland; died April 30(?), 1873, in Zambia.

After completing his medical studies in Glasgow in 1840, he was sent as a medical

lithographed Mexican Revolutionary note with printing flaws (white streaks) caused by wrinkled paper

missionary by the London Missionary Society to South Africa. He and his family traveled into regions of Africa never before explored by white Europeans. He was the first European to locate the Zambezi River, Lake Ngami, Victoria Falls, Lake Nyasa, the Lualaba River, and many other key geographic spots.

His greatest contribution to society was his condemnation of the last remnants of black slavery, still practiced by the Arabs and Portuguese. Because of his work, his portrait was placed on the £10 note issued by the Clydesdale Bank of Scotland. The back of the note features three African slaves as a reminder of Livingstone's tireless efforts to abolish slavery.

[Pat Carrigan, "Clydesdale Bank Plans New Note Trio," *World Coins,* April 1973, p. 532; *Funk & Wagnalls New Encyclopedia* (1984), Vol. 16, pp. 168-69.]

livră (*f.*) [*Rom.*] pound (unit of weight; pound Sterling - £).

livre (*f.*) [*Fr.*] 1. pound, i.e., weight of 16 ounces (avdp.) or 12 ounces troy. Derived from the Latin word *libra.*

2. pound Sterling (£).

3. Unit of currency used in France from medieval times until the advent of the decimal system in 1795. Its origins go back to the monetary system of Charlemagne, as do the British pound, Italian lira, and various other European currencies.

The livre was actually a money of account, as no coins were issued using that denomination. During the last centuries of its existence, it was valued at 20 sous or 240 deniers; 5 livres equaled one écu (silver crown). This valuation fluctuated when silver coins were debased.

loại tiền [*Viet.*] denomination.

løbenummer (*n.*) [*Dan.*] serial number.

lobolo ring Metallic ring used in Zulu marriage ceremonies which represented the price paid for the bride. The bridegroom would wedge a coin inside the ring and toss it at his bride's feet. Her father would keep the ring and use it at his next daughter's wedding.

[Mort Reed, *Odd and Curious,* p. 93.]

Loch (*n.*) [*Ger.*] hole.

Lochentwertung (*f.*) [*Ger.*] punch cancellation.

logam [*Indo.*] metal.

logam campuran [*Indo.*] alloy.

lo mitkablot hatsa'ot bilti mugbalot לֹא מִתְקַבְּלוֹת הַצָּעוֹת בִּלְתִּי מֻגְבָּלוֹת [*Heb.*] no unlimited bids accepted.

Scottish "Long Cross" penny of Alexander III

Long Cross coinage Series of English silver pennies (including a few specimens in gold) struck from 1247 to 1278 by Henry III and Edward I. A similar series was introduced in Scotland around 1250 by Alexander III. In each case the reverse shows a cross (specifically the *voided cross*) with both arms extending across the entire diameter of the coin all the way to the rim. The purpose of this design was to discourage clipping, the act of shaving off slivers of precious metal and then of spending the coin as though it were full weight.

By 1247 so many of the circulating coins were either worn down or badly clipped that Henry decided essentially to create a whole new coinage. The previous pennies struck during his reign were of the Short Cross variety, where the points of the cross only reach a circle inside the inscription. Extending the voided cross (with its characteristic double lines, causing these pieces sometimes to be referred to as *Double Cross* coinage) all the way to the edge served to make clipping more difficult. It also provided fairly accurate marks to show where to cut the coins into halves or quarters in order to make small change.

From 1247 to 1250 at least 80 moneyers working at 20 mints produced well over a million Long Cross pennies. Edward I, Henry's successor, continued the concept from 1272 to 1278 but finally abandoned it in 1279 in favor of a modified design featuring a *cross patté* in place of the voided cross. Another major change was the introduction of the groat (equal

to four pennies) plus the half-penny and farthing (quarter-penny) which made the practice of cutting pennies into fractions no longer necessary. Some scholars (e.g., Ewald Junge) refer to the 1279-1310 issuance as Long Cross; other sources (such as the Seaby U.K. Catalogue) claim that the Long Cross coinage ended in 1278.

[Ewald Junge, *World Coin Encyclopedia*, p. 156; Stephen Mitchell & Brian Reeds (editors), *Coins of England and the United Kingdom* (Seaby, 1991), pp. 91-99; Peter Seaby & P. Frank Purvey, *Coins of Scotland, Ireland & the Islands* (Seaby), pp. 8 & 110.]

Longacre, James Barton (1794-1869). Chief Engraver of the U.S. Mint from 1844-1869 whose designs include the Flying Eagle Cent, Indian Head Cent, two-cent piece, three-cent pieces (both silver and nickel), Shield Nickel, gold dollar, $3 gold piece, and Coronet double eagle ($20 gold piece), plus two U.S. Mint medals.

The Indian Cent was significant because it was the first U.S. coin to portray the representation of a Native American, even though the model was probably his own daughter Sarah who had posed for him on a number of occasions when he was designing other coins. His two-cent piece was important because it was the first U.S. coin to include the motto *In God We Trust*.

Longacre's career had its share of controversy, partly because of some strange mistakes which were made either by Longacre himself or by his employees, such as punching the date upside-down before repunching it right-side-up on one of the 1844 large cent working dies and of misspelling the word "LIBERTY" as "LLBERTY" on a master die for the 1850-1858 $20 gold pieces. Some of the mistakes may have been made by subordinates of chief coiner Franklin Peale who disliked Longacre and constantly complained about his work.

He was also criticized for not putting more imagination in his designs, yet it must be remembered that prior to the introduction of his Indian Head Cent, U.S. coins portrayed nothing but eagles and allegorical representations of Liberty. His conservative rendition of an American Indian was a radical concept for its day, and he probably made it as artistic as public opinion would bear. But whatever his designs might have lacked in artistic merit they made up for in patriotic symbolism, and this nationalistic influence is still seen on U.S. coins today.

Irrespective of any faults Longacre may have had, he was an outstanding artist whose worked graced U.S. coins for more than 60 years. He left a lasting impression on numismatics which cannot be denied.

[Tom DeLorey, "Longacre: Unsung Engraver of the U.S. Mint," *The Numismatist,* October 1985, pp. 1970-78; Lee F. McKenzie, "Longacre's Influence on Numismatic Art," *The Numismatist*, December 1991, pp. 1922-24 et al; *Coin World Almanac* (6th Ed.), pp. 202-3.]

Canadian Loon Dollar

Loon Dollar Small-size $1 coin (26.5 mm) introduced in Canada in 1987. Its name comes from the beautiful yet common native bird pictured on the reverse, the Canadian Loon.

The coin was intended for widespread circulation as a permanent replacement for the one dollar note. So that the general public would not confuse this coin with a 25 cent piece (the main reason for the failure of the Susan B. Anthony Dollar[q.v.] in the early 1980s in the U.S.), the pieces are struck from aureate nickel (pure nickel plated with bronze) giving the coins a yellow-gold color. To make them easily identifiable by visually handicapped people and by coin-operated machines, the coins are twelve-sided instead of round and have plain edges.

The Canadian Mint originally intended to use the traditional Voyageur design which had

appeared on most Canadian dollar circulation strikes since 1935. However, a set of dies mysteriously disappeared while en route to the mint facility in Winnipeg, Manitoba, forcing officials to choose a different design. The loon motif designed by artist Robert Carmichael was adopted.

[Hans Lee, "The Changing Face of Canada's Dollar," *The Numismatist*, July 1987, pp. 1441-1445; J. A. Haxby and R. C. Willey, *Coins of Canada* (9th Ed.), p. 78.]

lorbeerbekranzt [*Ger.*] laureate.

Los (*n.*) [*Ger.*] (auction) lot.

lost wax process (*cire perdue* in French). Method of casting used by artisans in many parts of the world for thousands of years to create medals and other metallic art objects.

The object is first modeled in wax. The wax model is then encased in moist clay or plaster, often mixed with silica, with a drainage hole in the bottom. The mold, known as the "investment," is allowed to dry slowly so it will retain as much of the original wax mold's design as possible. After the investment hardens, it is heated to make the wax melt and run out through the hole ("burnout"). Molten metal, usually bronze for medals or brass for other art objects, is poured into the hole and allowed to cool. When the metal hardens, the investment is broken and the object removed. Any lingering burrs are filed off.

Today, if the piece is a medal, the finishing stage is usually to colorize it ("patination"). This consists of treating it with any of a variety of chemicals, depending on the color desired (browns, blacks, or greens) to enhance details and give it an "old" look. The patinated bronze medal is coated with a thin layer of clear wax to preserve the color.

[Jean Schonwalter, "'Lost Wax' Cast Medals," *The Numismatist*, July 1994, pp. 1014-15; Mort Reed, *Odd and Curious*, pp. 58-59.]

lot One or more items sold as a single unit at an auction or mail bid sale.

lote (*m.*) [*Span., Port.*] (auction) lot.

lottery ticket Odd type of currency issued by the revolutionary French government in the late 1790s. In an attempt to give value and stability to the paper money, lottery tickets (*billets de loterie*) were circulated as currency. Not only were they to be accepted in trade, but the holder of the winning "note" would acquire 12 million francs. The tickets became worthless after the draw and were never popular as currency.

[Colin Narbeth, *Collecting Paper Money*, pp. 53-54.]

lotto (*m.*) [*Ital.*] (auction) lot.

Louis Popular name of French kings. Reigning dates are as king of France except where noted: Louis I (lived 778-840; reigned 814-840; also, Holy Roman emperor 814-840, king of Germany 814-840, and king of Aquitaine 781-840); Louis VI, a.k.a. *Louis the Fat* (1081-1137; reigned 1108-37); Louis VII, a.k.a. *Louis the Young* (1121?-1180; reigned 1137-80); Louis VIII (1187-1226; reigned 1223-26); Louis IX, a.k.a. *St. Louis* (1214-70; reigned 1226-70; canonized in 1297); Louis X, a.k.a. *Louis the Headstrong* (1289-1316; reigned 1314-16); Louis XI (1423-83; reigned 1461-83); Louis XII (1462-1515; reigned 1498-1515); Louis XIII (1601-43; reigned 1610-43); Louis XIV, a.k.a. *The Sun King* (1638-1715; reigned 1643-1715); Louis XV (1710-74; reigned 1715-74); Louis XVI (1754-93; reigned 1774-92); Louis XVII (1785-95; titular king of France 1793-95); and Louis XVIII (1755-1824; reigned 1814-15 and 1815-24).

The reigns of Louis XIII through Louis XVIII are extremely significant to numismatists. Louis XIII's greatest claim to fame was the *louis d'or*, considered by experts as the most significant French gold coin of the seventeenth and eighteenth centuries. Additionally, the *louis d'argent*, a popular silver crown, was also introduced during Louis XIII's reign. Both pieces resulted from Louis XIII's monetary reforms which included manufacturing coins by machine rather than by hammering them by hand. These milled coins[*q.v.*] were not only more attractive than their predecessors but were far more functional because they were harder to counterfeit and because any clipping of gold or silver from the edge of the coins would be more noticeable.

Louis XIV ruled for nearly 72 years, longer than the reign of any other European monarch.

His influence on France was immense. He imposed absolute rule and fought a series of wars in his attempt to dominate Europe. As he was a great supporter of arts and letters, culture flourished during his reign. Those many years that he spent on the throne assured that his effigy would appear on a great number of coins of various metals and denominations. Not surprisingly, many different types of the above-mentioned louis d'or and louis d'argent pieces were minted during his reign.

Louis XV continued the tradition of issuing the louis d'or and louis d'argent. Yet one of the most numismatically interesting aspects of his reign was the issuance of some small ugly billon coins known to the French as *sols marqués* (and to the English simply as *black doggs*). Because of their billon composition, they turned black almost as soon as they were placed in circulation. The coins were intended for use in the French West Indies, but they were accepted in trade even in the non-French areas.

Louis XVI was overthrown in 1789 and was guillotined with his family in the 1790s. In 1791 they escaped their imprisonment and attempted to flee to Austria. As legend has it, a peasant recognized Louis from his effigy on a coin, leading to the family's recapture and ultimate execution. Although the tale probably lacks historical validity, it serves to show the impact of the louis d'or and its sister silver coins on French society. What is historically certain is that the louis d'or was so important that it continued to be struck even after the overthrow and death of Louis XVI.

Louis XVII was the young son of Louis XVI and never actually took title to the French throne. He was regarded by royalists as the titular king from 1793-1795 until he, too, was executed. From a numismatic point of view, he remained a minor character.

Louis XVIII was the younger brother of Louis XVI. After the initial overthrow of Napoleon, he ascended to the throne as a constitutional monarch. He fled to Belgium when Napoleon returned to power in 1815 but regained his throne later that same year after Napoleon's final defeat at Waterloo. Monetarily, Louis XVIII's concession to the French Revolution was to retain the decimal system (100 centimes = 10 décimes = 1 franc) adopted in 1795 rather than to revert back to the old system using deniers, sols, liards, livres, etc.

louis d'argent (silver *écu*) of Louis XV

louis d'argent Popular name of the silver crown-size *écu* introduced in France in 1641 during the reign of Louis XIII. It remained the most popular silver coin of that country for more than 150 years and was even struck (along with its fractional parts) in the early 1790s after the overthrow of the monarchy.

The louis d'argent and its gold companion piece, the louis d'or, were part of Louis XIII's coinage reforms. Because they were milled coins (made by machine) rather than hammered (made by hand), they were more difficult to counterfeit or clip. The coins were regarded as reliable and were trusted by the French people.

As with the louis d'or, the louis d'argent was issued for such a long period of time that a

significant number of types and varieties were struck, thus making this a popular coin among numismatists.

louis d'or Very important French gold coin first issued by Louis XIII (for whom the coin was named) in 1640. This denomination (as well as its multiple and fractional forms) was retained for more than 150 years, even until 1793 after Louis XVI (the last king before the revolution) had been overthrown and executed.

louis d'or of Louis XIII

The louis d'or and its companion *louis d'argent* ("louis of silver," a.k.a. *écu*) were part of Louis XIII's monetary reform. Unlike previous French coins which had been hammered by hand, the louis d'or and louis d'argent pieces were made by machine. In Louis XIII's day the advent of milled coinage gave coins an increased consistency and credibility. The coins became difficult to counterfeit and any clipping of precious metal from the edge was more visible.

Adding to the credibility of the louis d'or was the concerted effort to keep it at a high intrinsic value. It was originally minted in 22-carat gold and at a weight of 6.69 grams with a conversion value of ten livres. The coin was never debased. In fact, its weight was increased to 8.16 grams in 1726 and its value was changed to 24 livres.

Because this coin circulated for a long period of time and because it was issued by four kings and a revolutionary council, a very large number of different types was struck. Many exhibit exquisite workmanship and are highly regarded by numismatists. The last issues were produced after the overthrow of the monarchy and are basically satirical (if not downright sarcastic) in nature. They showed a

very unflattering portrait of the king, who by 1793 had already been guillotined. Later in 1793, a small group of gold coins denominated simply as "24 livres" appeared. They displayed an angel instead of the king's effigy but were of the same weight and metallic content as the louis d'or. Shortly thereafter, a decimal system of coinage was adopted and the louis d'or was to appear no more.

[William D. Craig, *Coins of the World: 1750-1850* (3rd Ed.), pp. 99-103; Richard G. Doty, *The Macmillan Encyclopedic Dictionary of Numismatics*, pp. 199-200.]

lương [*Viet.*] ounce.

loupe (*f.*) [*Fr.*] magnifying glass.

love token A coin, medal, or other small metallic disk which has been made smooth on one or both sides and has then been engraved with initials or other configurations. A loop is usually attached so the piece can be worn as jewelry.

Most love tokens were made from gold and silver coins because they were the most readily available small disks of precious metal. If only one side were to be engraved, the less attractive side of the coin would be chosen, leaving the more beautiful side of the coin as the reverse of the token. The illustration shows such an example.

love token

The pieces are so named because they were often given as gifts to one's true love. Nonetheless, any token similar to these in design and style are categorized by this name, irrespective of the purpose for which it was intended.

Most love tokens were produced in the eighteenth and nineteenth centuries. Although a few came from throughout the Western World, their greatest popularity lay in English-

speaking countries, particularly the United States, Canada, and Australia.

The worksmanship on many love tokens is gorgeous and some beautiful collections have been amassed. Regretfully, this has never been one of the most popular areas of numismatics. Due to the lack of a huge demand, many interesting specimens can be acquired at a reasonably low price.

[Peter Lane, "The Love Tokens of Thomas Alsop," *Journal of the Numismatic Association of Australia*, July 1985, pp. 58-60; Lloyd L. Entenmann, "Love Token Pricing," *The Numismatist*, February 1988, pp. 271-3; Lloyd L. Entenmann., "A Token Love Affair," *The Numismatist*, February 1992, pp. 187-90.]

lozenge on Scottish gold demy of James I

lozenge Geometric shape of four equal sides with two acute and two obtuse angles, resembling the shape of a diamond on playing cards. In coin descriptions, squares rotated so that their angles point north, south, east, and west are often erroneously referred to as lozenges. A lion or other device is sometimes found within a lozenge, particularly on medieval coins such as the Scottish gold demy of James I in the illustration.

lt. [*abbr.*] light.

Lucite Dupont tradename for polymethyl methacrilate[*q.v.*].

Lucky Bucks Comic strips written in the format of play money during the 1930s. They appeared in Sunday newspapers and featured a wide range of cartoon characters such as Felix the Cat, Popeye and Olive Oyl, Barney Google, Dumb Dora, and Polly and Her Pals. No one knows exactly how many different Lucky Bucks were printed, but the number was probably well into the thousands.

Children growing up during the Great Depression had few toys, so these "bucks" were very popular. Millions were cut out of newspapers and used for play, but most were ultimately discarded. Few survive in collectible condition.

[Jim Ruehrmund, "Lucky Bucks," *The Numismatist*, November 1990, pp. 1814-15.]

luettelo [*Finn.*] catalog, catalogue.

luetteloarvo [*Finn.*] catalogue value.

lumber company store scrip Metal tokens issued by logging and lumber companies, naval store and turpentine operations, paper companies, and related forest product operations. Usually these pieces are an advance on wages, usable only at a certain store, and deducted from wages the next payday. For those logging operations out in the forest, a company commissary may have been

"Lucky Buck" featuring Popeye and Olive Oyl

on a railroad flat car, while less isolated operations may have utilized a local general store. Similar in usage to coal company store scrip[q.v.].

[Contributed by Robert Doyle. Terry Trantow, *Lumber Company Store Tokens*.]

luokitella (v.) [*Finn.*] to classify; to grade.

luokitus [*Finn.*] classification.

luotto [*Finn.*] credit.

luottokortit hyväksytään [*Finn.*] credit cards accepted.

luottokortti [*Finn.*] credit card.

lupa (f.) [*Span., Port., Pol.*] magnifying glass.

lupă (f.) [*Rom.*] magnifying glass.

luster; lustre Natural degree of shine on an uncirculated coin caused by the centrifugal flow of metal when the coin is struck. Normal circulation destroys a coin's luster quickly, as do most forms of oxidation. Because they are active metals[q.v.], copper and silver tend to lose their luster the fastest, yet coins of all metals are subject to this destruction. Once the luster is gone, it cannot be restored through chemical means.

To make them more marketable, uncirculated (or *presumed* uncirculated) coins which have lost their luster are sometimes artificially toned to hide the lack of natural sheen. This "doctoring" is usually obvious to experts.

lưu hành [*Viet.*] circulated.

lyöntivero [*Finn.*] seigniorage.

lyuk [*Hun.*] hole.

M m

ma'arekht haksafim מַעֲרֶכֶת הַכְּסָפִים (*f.*) [*Heb.*] monetary system.

määrittää (*v.*) [*Finn.*] to attribute.

määrittelemätön [*Finn.*] unattributed.

määritys [*Finn.*] attribution.

macchia (*f.*) [*Ital.*] stain (as on a banknote or bond).

Macdonald, Sir John Alexander First Prime Minister of Canada (1867-73 and 1878-91). Born January 11, 1815, in Glasgow, Scotland; died June 6, 1891, in Ottawa, Ontario.

Sir John Macdonald emigrated from Scotland to Kingston (in what is now Ontario) in 1820. He became Prime Minister of the Province of Canada in 1857. Largely through his efforts and the efforts of Sir George Étienne Cartier and George Brown, the British Parliament passed the British North America Act in 1867, creating the Dominion of Canada. Macdonald became its first Prime Minister.

Under his direction, the Dominion quickly expanded to include the provinces of Manitoba, British Columbia, and Prince Edward Island. But Macdonald was forced to resign during the Pacific Scandal of 1873 in which the government was accused of taking bribes regarding railway contracts. He returned as Prime Minister five years later and retained that position until his death in 1891.

He always remained loyal to the British Commonwealth and directed his efforts to maintaining independence from the United States. He remained loyal to his motto, "A British subject I was born; a British subject I will die."

Macdonald is featured on such paper money issues as the 1935 $500 note, the 1937 $100 note, and the $10 multicolored issue of 1969-75.

[Contributed by Ruth Ann Davis.]

machinaal geslagen munt (*m.-c.*) [*Dut.*] milled coin.

machine token A coin-like disc which can be inserted into an appropriate slot and thereby operate a mechanical or electro-mechanical device. Among the varieties are tokens for amusement and vending, brewery (amusement), car cleaning and parking, gas, laundry, locker, telephone, telescope, toilet, and weights and measures.

[Contributed by Robert Doyle. Ralph Hayes, *British Machine Tokens* (1st ed. & supplement).]

macuquina (*f.*) [*Span.*] Gold or silver coin minted by authority of Spain for use in Spanish America during the eighteenth century. These pieces had rough corners and lacked reeded edges. See *cob*.

maden değeri [*Turk.*] intrinsic.

madeni para [*Turk.*] coin.

madeni paradaki portre [*Turk.*] effigy.

madraygah מַדְרֵגָה (*f.*) [*Heb.*] grade; condition.

magán szükségpénz [*Hun.*] scrip.

magnamet A specially formulated copper nickel alloy proposed by a German supplier for the Anthony dollar. It was rejected. Some planchets of the material exist.

magnesium Metal with some limited coinage applications. [element: IIa of the periodic table; atomic weight 24.305; atomic number 12; specific gravity 1.738; symbol Mg.]

Frequently small quantities of magnesium are alloyed with aluminum (aluminium) for coinage purposes. Examples include the Cyprus 1 mil coin of 1963. It was reportedly used as the major constituent in some, but not all, Lodz ghetto tokens. Magnesium can easily be detected by its low specific gravity.

mail bid sale Type of auction sale where all bids are placed by mail; there is no live bidding

done on the auction floor. The company conducting the sale usually places a minimum bid on the more expensive items. Unlike at a regular auction, purchases found to be unsatisfactory may usually be returned for a full refund, unless some provision has been made for prospective bidders to examine the items prior to the sale.

makapal na moneda [*Tag.*] piéfort, piedfort.

Makel (*m.*) [*Ger.*] stain; blemish; fault.

makellos [*Ger.*] unblemished, faultless.

makhbeysh matb'ot מַכְבֵּשׁ מַטְבְּעוֹת (*m.*) [*Heb.*] (coinage) press.

makina ng moneda [*Tag.*] (coinage) press.

makinede basılmış para [*Turk.*] milled coin.

maksu [*Finn.*] fee.

maksumääräys [*Finn.*] money order.

mala acuñación (*f.*) [*Span.*] mis-strike.

mala conservación [*Span.*] Grade of coins or notes corresponding to Poor. A piece in this condition is not normally considered collectible. Abbreviated "M.C."

mal acuñado [*Span.*] badly struck; mis-struck.

Malaysia Numismatic Society The Society was formally registered on October 2, 1968. The organization's objectives are to promote the interest of members in the study of coins, medals, notes, and other matters of numismatic interest; to bring members into closer relations with one another by discussion and interchange of ideas on matters of numismatic interest; to issue to members the latest information about the numismatic world through new bulletins, books, etc. (the Society issues six news bulletins per year); to arrange the exchange or sale of material of numismatic interest among members; to arrange the exchange of numismatic material between the Society and other organizations having similar interests; to arrange the general collection and disposal of numismatic material for the benefit of any charity, funds, or other cause; and to display coins at public or private exhibitions and by other means to foster interest in the science of numismatics.

For membership information, contact the Malaysia Numismatic Society, P.O. Box 12367, 50776 Kuala Lumpur, Malaysia.

mal battuto [*Ital.*] badly struck; mis-struck.

mal cunhado [*Port.*] badly struck; mis-struck.

mal frappé [*Fr.*] badly struck; mis-struck.

maliye bakanı [*Turk.*] finance minister.

mallikappale [*Finn.*] specimen.

mal stampato [*Ital.*] badly struck.

mały [*Pol.*] small.

mancha (*f.*) [*Span., Port.*] stain (as on a banknote or bond).

mandat (*m.*) [*Fr.*] money order.

mandat poştal (*n.*) [*Rom.*] postal money order.

manganese Metal with some coinage applications. [element: group VIIb of the periodic table; atomic weight 54.938; atomic number 25; specific gravity 7.3; symbol Mn.]

Hard, silvery metal used exclusively as an alloying element. It is found in the U.S.S.R. 10 kopek to 1 ruble coins after 1961 and in a few 1923 British silver coins. The largest fraction of manganese used in any one coin was the 9% found in the so-called *wartime nickels*[q.v.] of the United States, 1942-45 (see page 312 for color illustration).

[Contributed by Halbert Carmichael.]

mangel (*m.*) [*Nor.*] defect.

mangelfull [*Nor.*] defective.

mangelhaft [*Ger.*] defective.

mångfald (*r.*) [*Swed.*] variety.

mangfoldighet (*m.*) [*Nor.*] variety.

maple leaf 1. All Canadian coins struck from 1911 to 1947 included the obverse inscription *ET IND. IMP.* (Latin abbreviation meaning "And Emperor of India") as part of the king's title. When India became an independent nation in 1947, new dies for 1948 had to be prepared with the reference to India omitted.

While awaiting its new matrices and punches from the Royal Mint in London, the Royal Canadian Mint tried to alleviate a coin shortage in Canada by continuing to use 1947 dies. A small maple leaf was placed next to the date on all denominations to signify that the coins had actually been struck in 1948. Later that year when the new dies were ready, the coins struck from them were correctly dated 1948.

This procedure created a number of rarities. With every denomination from cent to dollar,

1947 maple leaf 5 cents

the 1948-dated coins are scarcer than their 1947 maple leaf counterparts. The ten cent pieces, in particular, are much scarcer. However, all of the half dollars and dollars struck in that year, whether dated 1947 ML or 1948, are quite scarce. A few very rare die varieties of the 1947 ML versions also exist.

[J. A. Haxby and R. C. Willey, *Coins of Canada* (9th Ed.), pp. 25 & 62; J. E. Charlton, *Standard Catalogue of Canadian Coins* (27th Ed.), pp. 28 & 64.]

2. The *Maple Leaf* is the name of Canada's gold and silver bullion coins. [plural: *Maple Leafs.*]

marabotín (*m.*) [*Span.*] 1. Spanish name for the Muslim gold coin known as the *Murabit dinar*. This coin circulated extensively in Spain prior to the thirteenth century and was the predecessor of the Spanish gold *maravedí*[q.v.]

2. Popular but unofficial name in Spain for the above-mentioned gold maravedí.

maravedí (*m.*) [*Span.*] 1. Gold Spanish coin issued in the late twelfth and early thirteenth centuries by Alfonso VIII of Castile. It evolved from the Muslim coin known as the *Murabit dinar* or *marabotín* and was the first gold coin issued in Western Europe by a Christian monarch.

2. Silver Spanish coin produced only a short time by Alfonso X "the Wise" in the late thirteenth century. The silver piece, also known as the *Burgos maravedí*, had a value of one-sixth of a gold maravedí.

3. Small copper Spanish coin first struck in the late fifteenth century by Isabella and Ferdinand and issued intermittently until 1843. This piece, known locally as a *blanco novenes*, originally had a value of one-sixtieth of an original gold maravedí or one-tenth of a silver one.

During those centuries the copper maravedí depreciated so much in value that its issuance became impractical, at which point the maravedí continued to be a money of account (similar to the U.S. mill or the contemporary British guinea) but was no longer a circulating coin. The color illustration on page 310 shows a copper maravedí of 1622 but overstruck with the date 1641. Overstriking coins such as these was a way of devaluating them.

[Manuel Moreno Fraginals and José A. Pulido Ledesma, *Cuba: A Country and Its Currency*, National Bank of Cuba, p. 27; Richard G. Doty, *The Macmillan Encyclopedic Dictionary of Numismatics*, p. 203.]

marca de agua (*f.*) [*Span.*] watermark (when used in reference to a banknote; the more general term is *filigrana*).

marca de ajuste [*Span., Port.*] adjustment mark.

marca de autenticidad (*f.*) [*Span.*] authentication mark.

marca de ceca (*f.*) [*Span.*] mintmark.

marca de cunhagem [*Port.*] mintmark.

marché noir (*m.*) [*Fr.*] black market.

marco (*m.*) [*Span., Ital., Port., et al*] mark (German unit of currency).

mare [*Rom.*] large.

Marea Britanie [*Rom.*] Great Britain.

margine (*f.*) [*Rom.*] edge; rim.

Maria Theresa Archduchess of Austria and Queen of Hungary and Bohemia (1740-80). Born in Vienna on May 13, 1717; died November 29, 1780, also in Vienna.

Maria Theresa was the eldest daughter of Charles VI, Holy Roman Emperor. In 1736 she married Francis Stephen of Lorraine, later to become Holy Roman Emperor Francis I. They had sixteen children, including two who would become Holy Roman emperors (Joseph II and Leopold II). One of their daughters was Maria Antoinette, the ill-fated Queen of France who was ultimately beheaded along with her

husband, Louis XVI, during the French Revolution.

When Maria Theresa became empress upon the death of her father in 1740, she also became the first woman to rule the Hapsburg Dynasty in its 650-year history. At the time of her succession to the throne, Hapsburg finances were in shambles. The debts were enormous and most of the royal domains had been mortgaged. The army was at half strength and unpaid, and the ministers were aged and ineffectual. In 1745 she acquired the title Holy Roman emperor for her husband. Together they made sweeping internal reforms that gave strength to the central administration. They also made many improvements in the army. When Francis died in 1765, Maria Theresa made her eldest son Joseph co-regent, but she retained ultimate authority for herself because she disagreed with many of his ideas. He became sole emperor upon her death in 1780.

During her reign, many important educational reforms were put in place, including the adoption of better ways for preparing university students. She encouraged agriculture, industry, and trade. She brought the Catholic Church under state control and greatly diminished the power of the Inquisition which was ultimately abolished during her sons' reigns. Her own reign is remembered for its cultural, artistic, educational, musical, financial, and governmental advances.

Maria Theresa would be regarded as a relatively minor character in the numismatic scene were it not for one type coin which emblazoned her name in numismatics forever: the famed Maria Theresa Thaler[q.v.]. Because of this coin (and countless restrikes of it), her face became known to millions of people throughout the civilized (and not-so-civilized) world from 1773 until well into the twentieth century.

[Contributed by Pamela Makricosta. James A. Moncure (editor), *Research Guide to European Historical Biography, 1450 to Present*, p. 327; Karl A. Roider, Jr., *Maria Theresa*, p. 97.]

Maria Theresa Thaler [also known as *Mariatheresientaler* (in German).] Austrian silver crown first minted in 1773 at the Günzburg

Maria Theresa Thaler

Mint. It was struck on the 1753 Convention standard (one thaler = 1/10 mark of fine silver by weight). The name is derived from the obverse design which shows the veiled bust of Empress Maria Theresa of the Holy Roman Empire.

It became very popular as a trade coin, especially in the Levant, a region on the eastern shores of the Mediterranean stretching from Italy to Egypt. The coin quickly became so recognizable that no other design was accepted by merchants, even if the coins presented were of the same weight and standard. Thus, Maria Theresa's death in 1780 posed a huge problem because featuring her effigy on coins would no longer be appropriate.

The solution was to restrike these coins and to freeze the date at 1780, the last year coins of this type would logically have been struck. The idea worked better than anyone expected, because the demand for them persisted even into the 1960s, making them the most widely used trade coins in history.

At one time or another, Maria Theresa Thalers have been minted in Vienna, Milan, Venice, Rome, London, Paris, Bombay, Brussels, and Birmingham, as well as Günzburg. Although every effort was made to keep all of them true to the original design, slight differences can be found which enable experts to tell in most cases the exact mint where a given specimen was struck.

While eighteenth and nineteenth century merchants valued the Maria Theresa Thalers for their fineness and consistency, modern collectors prize them for their beauty and historical importance.

[William D. Craig, *Coins of the World: 1750-1850* (3rd Ed.), pp. 28-29; Ewald Junge, *World Coin Encyclopedia*, p. 161.]

marka (*f.*) [*Pol.*] mark (German unit of currency).

márka [*Hun.*] mark (German unit of currency).

Marke (*f.*) [*Ger.*] token.

markedsverdi [*Nor.*] intrinsic value.

markka [*Finn.*] mark (German unit of currency).

marko μάρκο (*n.*) [*Grk.*] mark (German unit of currency).

marque d'ajustage [*Fr.*] adjustment mark.

marque d'atelier (*f.*); **marque monétaire** (*f.*) [*Fr.*] mintmark.

marque noire (*f.*) [*Fr.*] Literally *black mark*. Colloquial term for a French billon (base metal) coin valued at 2 sols (24 deniers) which was first minted in 1738. In 1763 many of these pieces were counterstamped and reissued for use in the French West Indies. See *stampée*.

marques de frottement [*Fr.*] cabinet friction.

marrom [*Port. (Brazil)*] brown.

marrón [*Span.*] brown.

marrone [*Ital.*] brown.

maskinfremstilt mynt [*Nor.*] milled coin.

másolat [*Hun.*] a copy, reproduction; a duplicate.

másolni (*v.*) [*Hun.*] to copy; to duplicate.

Masonic eagle Erroneous name for the *Alexander eagle*, a variety of the double eagle design (i.e., an eagle with two necks and heads) in which the eagle's wings are spread unusually far apart. It appeared on Russian silver coins

of 1826-31 and on gold coins of that general period.

[R. W. Julian, "The Russian Silver Coinage of 1796-1917," *The Numismatist*, December 1989, pp. 1957-58.]

mässing (*r.*) [*Swed.*] brass (the alloy).

mat (*adj.*) [*Rom.*] tarnish.

matalliko krama μεταλλικό κράμα (*n.*) [*Grk.*] (metal) alloy.

mata wang [*Indo.*] currency.

mata wang asing [*Indo.*] foreign currency.

matba'at מַטְבַּעַת (*f.*) [*Heb.*] (coinage) die.

matbeya מַטְבֵּע (*m.*) [*Heb.*] coin; currency.

matbeya m'kursam מַטְבֵּע מְכוּרְסָם (*m.*) [*Heb.*] milled coin.

matbeya mutsav bapatish מַטְבֵּע מְעוּצָב בַּפַּטִישׁ (*m.*) [*Heb.*] hammered coin.

matbeya tlat shikhvati מַטְבֵּע תְּלַת שִׁכְבָתִי (*m.*) [*Heb.*] clad coinage.

matbeya zar מַטְבֵּע זָר [*Heb.*] foreign currency.

matbeyot kheyrum מַטְבְּעוֹת חֵרוּם [*Heb.*] obsidional.

matekhet מַתֶּכֶת (*f.*) [*Heb.*] metal.

matriţă (*f.*) [*Rom.*] (coinage) die.

matriz (*f.*) [*Span.*] (coinage) die.

mặt sau [*Viet.*] reverse.

maudrik [*Hin.*] monetary.

1962 Maundy coins

Maundy money Set of four small silver coins consisting of a penny, twopence, threepence, and fourpence. The sets are produced annually by Great Britain and are given by the reigning monarch (or his or her representative) to elderly poor people who are deemed worthy. The presentation is a ritual performed on Maundy Thursday (the Thursday before Easter) as part of a religious ceremony dating back to medieval times.

The word "Maundy" comes from *mandatum*, a Latin word referring to Christ's mandate as

He washed the feet of His disciples as an act of humility (*John 13:1-16*). Originally the Maundy ritual did not include money. Coins were not given until the reign of Edward II in the early fourteenth century. From then until 1670, the only coins presented were regular issue pieces, usually silver pennies.

The earliest known sets of these four denominations of silver coins are undated and were issued by Charles II in the 1660s. All four were likely intended for general circulation, and probably the tiny silver penny was the only one distributed in the royal Maundy ceremony. Most experts believe that the first true Maundy coins were the four-piece sets struck in 1670 and which bear that date. They, too, were issued by Charles II.

With the obvious exception of Edward VIII (who abdicated in 1936 only a few months before his expected coronation), every British monarch since Charles II has issued Maundy coins, although the sets were issued somewhat sporadically from 1670 to 1820. George III was the first to strike Maundy coins in proof. In 1822 George IV began minting Maundy coins annually, a custom which has continued unbroken to this day.

maverick token

maverick A token which does not have the information in its legends to be attributed to both a specific city and to that city's U.S. state, Canadian province, or whatever. Thus, a token which has the legend "Broadway, NYC" can be readily attributed to New York City (which obviously is in the state of New York), but one with "10 Main St., Springfield" cannot be attributed with certainty to any specific state unless some other information is available. Other mavericks might show only the region

while others might lack any mention of any city or region.

Tokens issued for use by businesses or activities operating region-wide or in several regions and which do not fit this city/region pattern may be listed as *non-local*. The collecting of tokens from a single state or province, usually of one's home state or state of origin, is extremely popular with U.S. and Canadian collectors. Hence, those tokens which cannot be identified by both city and state or those which are properly attributed non-local are not as desirable to collectors.

[Contributed by Robert Doyle.]

maykapangyarihan [*Tag.*] sovereign.

M.B.C. [*Span. abbr.*] muy buena conservación. Spanish term approximating Extremely Fine to About Uncirculated condition of paper money.

M.C. [*Span. abbr.*] mala conservación. Grade of Poor of a coin or banknote.

m/c [*abbr.*] multicolored, multicoloured.

med медь (*f.*) [*Russ.*] copper (the metal).

medaglia (*f.*) [*Ital.*] medal.

medaille (*f.-c.*) [*Dut.*] medal.

Medaille (*f.*) [*Ger.*] medal.

médaille (*f.*) [*Fr.*] medal.

médaille militaire (*f.*) [*Fr.*] military decoration.

medal Coin-like metallic object struck for purposes other than to circulate as money. Medals are created as awards or commemorations. They differ from decorations which are intended to be worn, while medals are not.

Although cast medallions were made in ancient times, the first modern medals were struck in Italy during the sixteenth century and were among the first items produced on the newly-invented screw press.

Historically the word *medal* has been reserved for a large piece (at least 35 mm in diameter), while *medalet* refers to a smaller piece of similar intent. But in recent years private mints have blurred these definitions by using them more or less as they please in their effort to market their product. Even such notable organizations as the Olympics have muddled the meaning of this word. For example, the "medals" awarded to first, second,

and third place winners at the 1994 Winter Games in Lillehammer, Norway, were actually made of crystal trimmed in gold, silver, or bronze.

In the late twentieth century, coin designs started becoming progressively more bland (in part to keep them simple so they could be easily produced on high-speed equipment), but medal designs have become more imaginative. Modern medals encompass a wide range of shapes, sizes, metals (or crystal!), thicknesses, and designs, and they are issued to commemorate or honor just about every conceivable person or event. Some fine examples are the Jewish-American Hall of Fame Medals which are trapezoidal in shape and very modernistic in design. [See *Wiesel, Elie* for an illustration.]

Medallic art is a very special area of numismatics, and it is gratifying to see how many excellent pieces are currently being produced.

medalha (*f.*) [*Port.*] medal.

medalie (*f.*) [*Rom.*] medal.

medalje (*c.*) [*Dan.*]; (*m.*) [*Nor.*] medal.

medaljepræg [*Dan.*] proof (*re:* coins or medals).

medalla (*f.*) [*Span.*] medal.

medal struck [symbol: ↑↑] Alignment of the obverse and reverse dies such that the top of both sides is on the same end of the coin or medal. To turn the piece over so that the reverse is right side up, the piece must be rotated on an axis running north and south. Current coins of Britain and the British Commonwealth are normally aligned this way, although earlier coins of Canada and elsewhere are found with the other type of alignment, known as *coin struck* and designated ↑↓. All current U.S. coinage are coin struck. Some countries, such as Mexico, use both methods.

medaru メダル [*Jpn.*] medal.

med hål [*Swed.*] holed.

medida de seguridad (*f.*) [*Span.*] anti-counterfeiting device.

medieval coin In general, any coin struck from A.D. 476 (the fall of the western portion of the Roman Empire) to around 1500.

medio (*adj.*) [*Span.*] half.

medium of exchange Anything which is accepted as a standard of value by all parties participating in a transaction. The valued item may have been chosen voluntarily by the participants or may have been forced upon them by legal decree (e.g., U.S. notes are "legal tender for all debts, public and private").

Although money is the most common medium of exchange in today's world, exchange has sometimes been transacted with such diverse items as coffee, live animals, shells, beads, tobacco, chocolate, and nails.

[A. George Mallis, "A Numismatic Primer— Part 1", *The Numismatist*, July 1988, pp. 1215-18.]

megenthitikos fakos μεγενθυτικός φακός (*m.*) [*Grk.*] magnifying glass.

megrendelőlap [*Hun.*] order form.

megrongált [*Hun.*] damaged.

megváltoztatni (*v.*) [*Hun.*] to alter.

Mehrschichtgepräge (*n.pl.*) [*Ger.*] clad coinage.

mei 銘 [*Jpn.*] inscription; legend.

meio (*adj.*) [*Port.*] half.

Golda Meir

Meir, Golda [née *Goldie Mabovitz* (or *Mabovich*).] Israeli prime minister (1969-74). Born May 3, 1898, in Kiev, Russia (now Ukraine); died December 8, 1978, in Jerusalem.

Golda Meir started her career as a schoolteacher in Milwaukee, Wisconsin. An

avowed Zionist, she and her husband moved to Palestine in 1921. She became active in Zionist affairs and in the labor movement. Throughout the 1930s and 1940s, she served in various Zionist organizations in Palestine, Europe, and the United States.

Her perilous secret meeting with King Abdullah of Jordan just before the Arab invasion in 1948 was a dramatic attempt for last minute conciliation. Appointed Minister of Labor in 1949, Golda initiated large-scale housing and road-building programs, and vigorously supported the policy of unrestricted immigration despite the great economic difficulties faced by the young Jewish State. As Foreign Minister (1956-65), she was often Israel's spokesperson at the United Nations. Among her main achievements in foreign relations was the extension of Israeli aid to the emerging African nations, and the establishment of friendly relations accomplished through personal visits to Liberia, Ghana, Nigeria, and the Ivory Coast.

After the death of Levi Eshkol in 1969, Golda Meir became the fourth Prime Minister of Israel. Originally thought to have been a stop-gap appointment, she went on to lead her party to victory in the next general elections. She held this critical position, continuing to carry on indirect negotiations with Egypt, through the outbreak of the Yom Kippur War in 1973. Despite her eminence, she was and continues to be called simply "Golda."

Golda Meir is portrayed on the 1984 10,000 shekel note of Israel and the 1985 10 shekel monetary reform note which replaced the larger note (three zeroes were dropped as part of the reform). As seen in the illustration, Golda's vignette also appears on an earlier £5 Israeli note.

Her effigy is featured on the 1995 bimetallic 10 shekel coin which was introduced to replace the 1985-series note, part of the worldwide trend to eliminate small-denomination paper money. And, of course, she is honored on many commemorative medals.

[Contributed by Mel Wacks on behalf of the Magnes Museum.]

meisti [*Finn.*] (coinage) die.
meistivirhe [*Finn.*] die break.
Méjico; México [*Span.*] Mexico.
Meksika [*Turk.*] Mexico.
Meksyk [*Pol.*] Mexico.
mektupla müzayede [*Turk.*] mail bid sale.
melago μεγάλο [*Grk.*] large.
melkein [*Finn.*] almost.
melko harvinainen [*Finn.*] scarce.

survivor of official melt: 1957-H B.W.A. 3d

melt, official The melting down of coins by the government or official agency that minted them.

Patterns and test pieces are sometimes melted to prevent them from getting into the hands of collectors, as was the case of the Martha Washington test pieces. In the mid-1960s the U.S. Mint needed to find an acceptable substitute for silver coins. Some pattern pieces made from clad planchets were minted showing Martha Washington's effigy. After the decision was made to switch the nation's silver coinage to a non-silver or low-silver clad coinage, the patterns were destroyed. Rumors persist that a few specimens escaped the melting pot, but this story has never been confirmed, largely because the pieces would be subject to confiscation if they were found to exist.

Occasionally coins are melted if they are struck prior to the decision being made not to release that denomination for whatever reason. An example is the 1954 British penny. A small quantity was produced but never released. All of the 1954 pennies were melted except for one surviving specimen.

Official melts can take place when the country or political unit no longer exists. An example is the illustrated coin, a 1957-H British West African threepence. British West Africa

had been an administrative grouping of four British Commonwealth countries, Nigeria, Gambia, Sierra Leone, and Gold Coast (now Ghana). Beginning in 1907 they were supplied with a common coinage and banknotes by the West African Currency Board, an arrangement which continued until 1958. But shortly after 800,080 threepences were minted in 1957, the B.W.A. administrative group was dissolved. The threepences, which had not yet been shipped, were no longer needed and 800,000 of them were melted. Probably fewer than fifty survive today. Because British West African threepences had not been issued since the days of King George VI, the official melt of the 1957-H issue resulted in the surviving pieces' becoming one of the scarcest British Commonwealth types of coins portraying Queen Elizabeth II.

Official melts should not be confused with the melting of precious-metal coins by private individuals to achieve financial gain. This was the case in 1979 when the price of silver rose so dramatically that the intrinsic value of most silver coins exceeded the coins' numismatic value. Within a short time, great hoards of silver coins were destroyed.

mélyített veret [*Hun.*] incuse.

mennica (*f.*) [*Pol.*] mint.

mennictwo (*n.*) [*Pol.*] coinage.

menorah

menorah Candelabrum symbolizing the universe, used in Jewish worship. The menorah appears on one of the ancient coins of Antigonus Mattathias. In modern times, it has been featured on some of the coins of Israel. The coin in the illustration is a half-lira coin struck from 1963-1908 (5723-5740 on the Jewish calendar).

měnová soustava (*f.*) [*Cz.*] coinage.

menudo (*m.*) [*Span.*] small change; the coins in one's pocket.

mercado negro (*m.*) [*Span., Port.*] black market.

mercato nero (*m.*) [*Ital.*] black market.

merchant advertising countermarks During the nineteenth century, many coins, particularly from the United States, England, and China, were counterstamped with the names of companies which used these coins as a source of advertising. The American and English coins were countermarked and then placed back into circulation where the advertising message would presumably be seen by anyone receiving these coins in change. The Chinese cash coins were counterstamped on their wide flat rims and were then imported into various countries where they could be used as gambling chips.

Edward Lloyd, publisher of *Lloyd's Weekly Newspaper* in London, stamped so many coins with his own advertising that his marketing efforts became regarded as a public nuisance. Because of him and because of others who were equally guilty of this practice, the English Parliament passed an act in 1853 prohibiting the defacement of current coin of the realm. Unfortunately, the English lawmakers failed to anticipate that the "counterstampers" could get around this law simply by countermarking foreign coins of similar weight and metallic composition to the English coins and by passing them into circulation. The influx of foreign coins may have proven to be a greater nuisance than the counterstamping had been.

Whereas counterstamped coins, done for advertising purposes or otherwise, were regarded as a major headache in England and other parts of Europe, some researchers surmise that such was not a serious problem in the United States or Canada. Presumably fewer than one percent of the circulating coins in these two countries were countermarked, and those few pieces were more or less ignored.

Mexican coins with private counterstamps were usually not consciously intended as advertising pieces. Rather, the host coins were merely convenient metal disks upon which

small dies could be tested. Every ranch had its own distinct logo, known as a brand. A large version was burnt into the sides of cattle to prove ownership. A smaller version of the same brand was stamped into all movable property to prevent its easy disposal if it were stolen, much the same as Americans engrave their social security numbers on the backs of televisions, VCRs, and other valuables. The coins used for testing new dies are known as *brand pieces*.

Most U.S. coins which exhibit advertising countermarks are large cents (issued 1793-1857), although some silver coins and a very few gold coins have also been found which show advertising messages.

[Gregory G. Brunk, "Merchant Advertising Countermarks of 19th-Century America," *The Numismatist*, February 1989, pp. 222-230.]

merchant token See *trade token*.

Mercury Dime Misnomer yet universally-used name for the 10 cent pieces struck in the United States from 1916 to 1945. See *Winged Liberty Dime*.

Messico [*Ital.*] Mexico.

messing (*n.*) [*Dut., Dan.*]; (*m.*) [*Nor.*] brass (the alloy).

Messing (*n.*) [*Ger.*] brass.

messinki [*Finn.*] brass.

met [*Dut.*] with.

metà (*f.*) [*Ital.*] half (the fraction).

metaal (*n.*) [*Dut.*] metal.

metade (*f.*) [*Port.*] half (the fraction).

metall (*n.*) [*Nor.*] metal.

Metall (*n.*) [*Ger.*] metal.

metalli [*Finn.*] metal.

metalliharkko [*Finn.*] ingot.

metallion μετάλλιον (*n.*) [*Grk.*] medal.

metalliraha [*Finn.*] coin.

metalliseos [*Finn.*] alloy (of metals).

metallo μέταλλο (*n.*) [*Grk.*] metal.

metapiimeni hmerominia μεταποιημένη ημερομηνία [*Grk.*] altered date.

met gat [*Dut.*] holed.

met lauwerkrans [*Dut.*] laureate.

mettere in mostra (*v.*) [*Ital.*] to exhibit.

metallo (*m.*) [*Ital.*] metal.

meydalya מֶדַלְיָה (*f.*) [*Heb.*] medal.

mezat [*Turk.*] auction.

mezat kataloğu [*Turk.*] auction catalogue.

mezzo (*adj.*) [*Ital.*] half.

miàn é 面额 [*Chin.-py./sc.*] denomination; face value.

mic [*Rom.*] small.

michanismos anagnorisis plastografias μηχανισμός αναγνώρισης πλαστογραφίας [*Grk.*] anti-counterfeiting device.

mie [*Rom.*] thousand.

miedź (*f.*) [*Pol.*] copper.

mi ekdothenta μή εκδοθέντα [*Grk.*] not issued.

mikhuts l'makhazor מחוץ למחזור [*Heb.*] obsolete.

mikro μικρό [*Grk.*] small.

mil [*Span., Port.*] thousand.

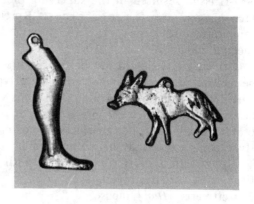

two *milagros*

milagro (*m.*) [*Span.*] literally, *miracle*. Small amulet worn in conjunction with prayer to ask God to protect someone or something. Usually made of low-grade silver, it is cast in the shape of whatever needs to be protected such as a leg or arm, one's livestock, or the whole person. Milagros are popular in many parts of Latin America.

milhão [*Port.*] million.

milímetro (*m.*) [*Span., Port.*] millimeter, millimetre.

milione [*Ital.*] million.

militær orden (*m.*) [*Nor.*] military decoration.

militaire onderscheiding (*f.-c.*) [*Dut.*] military decoration.

Militärorden (*m.*) [*Ger.*] military decoration.

military decoration Badge, ribbon, or other wearable award given for military valor or for

such reasons as being wounded in battle. This type of award can also be presented posthumously. See *decoration* for additional information and page 311 for color illustrations of the *Iron Cross*, *Purple Heart* and *India Star*.

military token Token used in payment in military PXs, canteens, service clubs, ship service stores, and disabled veterans' homes. They may be of metal, often brass or anodized (colored) aluminum, or of plastic.

Some nineteenth-century tokens were issued by sutlers, merchants named by the Secretary of War to sell personal-use items to military personnel during the U.S. Civil War (1861-1865). See *sutler token*.

[Contributed by Robert Doyle. David E. Schenkman, *Civil War Sutler Tokens and Cardboard Scrip*; James J. Curto, *Military Tokens of the United States, 1866-1969*.]

miljoen [*Dut.*] million.

miljoona [*Finn.*] million.

mille [*Fr., Ital.*] thousand.

milled coin 1. A coin made from the primitive coinage machinery of the mid-sixteenth century through the nineteenth century.

Prior to the advent of mechanical coinage equipment, coins were individually struck by being hammered between two dies. Although some of the pieces produced in this manner were beautiful and are regarded as works of art, the general lever of quality of hammered coins was quite poor. [See *hammered coin* for comparative illustrations.]

In the middle of the sixteenth century, the French began producing coins with the kind of water-driven machinery used in mills to grind wheat into flour, which is why these coins are referred to as *milled*. Although such coins were by no means up to twentieth-century standards, they were a vast improvement over hammered coins in terms of beauty and consistency.

2. Generic term for any machine-made coin.

millimetri [*Finn.*] millimeter, millimetre.

millimetro (*m.*) [*Ital.*] millimeter, millimetre.

millió [*Hun.*] million.

mill-sail pattern Swastika-like design found in the form of an incuse punch on the reverse of many early Greek stater coins. Early Athenian coins show a panther peering from one of the square's incuse compartments, and the first coins of Syracuse show the head of Artemis from one of them.

[David Van Meter, *Collecting Greek Coins*, pp. 19-20.]

mill-sail pattern

mince (*f.*) [*Cz.*] coin.

mince ražená za obléhání [*Cz.*] obsidional coin.

mindennapos [*Hun.*] common.

míng kè 铭刻 [*Chin.-py./sc.*] inscription.

minimibud (*n.*) [*Swed.*] minimum bid.

minimum bid The lowest acceptable bid as determined by the seller in an auction or mail bid sale.

minimum müzayede değeri [*Turk.*] protective reserve bid.

minimumsbud (*n.*) [*Dan.*] minimum bid.

minne- (*adj.*) [*Nor.*] commemorative.

minnes- (*adj.*) [*Swed.*] commemorative.

minstebud (*n.*) [*Nor.*] minimum bid.

minstepris (*m.*) [*Nor.*] minimum price; protective reserve bid.

mint Facility where coins are produced.

The concept of what constitutes a mint has changed radically from ancient times to the present. The earliest mints were probably little more than glorified blacksmith shops where metal was refined, formed into blanks, and hammered into coins. The process was slow and cumbersome, yet many of the coins produced in these places are magnificent works of art. Today's mints are huge modern factories with powerful high-speed equipment capable of turning out thousands of coins per minute.

Most large countries own their own minting facilities, but this has not always been the case.

In the Middle Ages, private moneyers produced many of the coins under contract with the crown. Sometimes the king would allow the moneyer to debase the coins by a specified percentage; the moneyer would keep that amount as his "commission."

The advent of milled coinage in the sixteenth century changed the design of mints forever. They began resembling flour mills more than blacksmith's shops because of the need to be located near a power source, in this case a river whose flowing water ran the mill's coinage presses. Other new mints used horse-driven machinery. Another innovation which changed the design of the mint was the invention of the screw press, although its earliest use was limited mostly to the striking of medals.

The great debate in the sixteenth century was whether to switch to the new milled system and to abandon hammered coins[q.v.]. Milled coins were clearly superior in quality to hammered coins, but the milling process was even slower and more cumbersome than the hammering technique. The technology was still in its infancy stage. To complicate matters, the moneyers who operated the hammering "mints" usually had some clout with the monarch. Additional political opposition to milled coins arose in the late 1500s when Eloye Mestrelle, the inventor of the process, was executed in England for counterfeiting.

In today's world, most smaller countries do not choose to operate their own mints. The Royal Mint in London produces coins for many of the Commonwealth countries. In 1967 it inadvertently matched an obverse die from Bahamas with a reverse die from New Zealand to create a mule[q.v.]. [See page 317 for color illustrations.] The United States mints are often called upon to produce coins for various nations. Panama, for example, not only gets its coins minted in the U.S., but they are exact matches in size and metallic content to the current circulating U.S. coins.

One of the most storied minting facilities in the world is the second U.S. Mint in San Francisco, now a museum. It was one of the few government buildings still standing after the 1906 earthquake and temporarily housed the offices of many governmental agencies until new facilities could be built. Today, tourists can strike their own commemorative medal as a souvenir of their visit.

visitor's medal from the San Francisco Mint

minta [*Hun.*] design; specimen.

mintmark; **mint mark** Letter or symbol placed on a coin to indicate which mint produced it. In today's world, mintmarks are usually the initials of the place where the mint is located ("S" for San Francisco, "C" for Canada, "KN" for the private firm of King's Norton Mint, etc.). Modern Spanish mints are indicated by the number of points on the star near the date. Some mintmarks have been in the form of monograms, such as the "M" with the small "o" above it representing Mexico City. A wide variety of symbols have at one time or another been used as mintmarks. In 1540, Francis I designated Paris, the principal mint of France, to have the mintmark "A" solely because it is the first letter of the alphabet. The other French mints are designated in an alphabetic sequence more or less corresponding to their importance.

Frequently the primary mint of a nation uses no mintmark. Coins struck at Philadelphia did not exhibit mintmarks until 1980 (with the exception of the 1942-45 silver *wartime* nickels).

It is also possible for one country to use the same mintmark more than once. The United States placed the mintmark "D' on its gold coins struck at the Dahlonega, Georgia, Mint (1838-

1861) and then recycled it for the Denver Mint which opened in 1906.

Mintmarks should not be confused with engravers' marks, designers' initials, mintmasters' marks, and all sorts of other symbols and letters which appear on coins.

mise (f.) [Fr.] (auction) bid.

mise ajoutée; mise de protection [Fr.] protective reserve bid.

mise suggérée (f.) [Fr.] suggested bid.

misgeslagen [Dut.] mis-struck.

mishkal מִשְׁקָל (m.) [Heb.] weight.

miso μισό (n.; adj.) [Grk.] half.

mispar siduri מִסְפָּר סִדּוּרִי (m.) [Heb.] serial number.

misslag (m.-c.) [Dut.] a mis-strike.

mit [Ger.] with.

mitad (f.) [Span.] half (the fraction).

mitali [Finn.] medal.

mitba'a מִטְבָּעָה (f.) [Heb.] mint.

mivkhar מִבְחָר (m.) [Heb.] variety.

m'khir מְחִיר (m.) [Heb.] price.

m'khiron מְחִירוֹן (m.) [Heb.] price list.

M.L. [abbr.] maple leaf.

modası geçmiş [Turk.] obsolete.

modèle (m.) [Fr.] pattern.

modelo (m.) [Span.] pattern.

modifica (v.) [Rom.] to modify; to alter.

modification (f.) [Fr.] modification; alteration.

modulo di offerta [Ital.] bid sheet.

modulo d'ordine [Ital.] order form.

moeda (f.) [Port.] coin; currency.

moeda cunhada à martelo [Port.] hammered coin.

moeda de emergência [Port.] emergency currency.

moeda de fábrica mecânica [Port.] milled coin.

moeda estrangeira (f.) [Port.] foreign currency.

moeda fiduciária (f.) [Port.] fiat money.

moeda provisória (f.) [Port.] scrip.

moitié (f.) [Fr.] half (the fraction).

monada chrimaton μονάδα χρημάτων [Grk.] denomination.

monadikos μαναδικός [Grk.] unique.

moneda [Tag.]; (f.) [Span.] coin; coinage; currency.

monedă (f.) [Rom.] coin; coinage; currency.

monedă accesorie privată [Rom.] scrip.

moneda acuñada a martillo [Span.] hammered coin.

moneda acuñada a molino [Span.] milled coin.

monedă bătută manual (f.) [Rom.] hammered coin.

monedă bătută mecanic (f.) [Rom.] milled coin.

moneda chapada (f.) [Span.] clad coinage.

moneda de necesidad (f.) [Span.] emergency currency; necessity money; scrip.

monedă de necesitate [Rom.] emergency currency; necessity money, scrip.

monedă din multiple straturi (f.) [Rom.] clad coinage.

moneda extranjera (f.) [Span.] foreign currency.

moneda falsa (f.) [Span.] counterfeit coin.

moneda fiduciaria (f.); **moneda fíat** (f.) [Span.] fiat money.

moneda forrada (f.) [Span.] clad coinage.

moneda tri-capa (f.) [Span.] clad coinage.

monedera [Tag.] mint.

moneta (f.) [Ital., Pol.] coin.

moneta a coniazione meccanica [Ital.] milled coin.

moneta battuta a mano [Ital.] hammered coin.

moneta bita maszynowo (f.) [Pol.] milled coin.

moneta bita młotem (f.) [Pol.] hammered coin.

moneta d'emergenza (f.) [Ital.] emergency currency.

moneta mal battuta (f.) [Ital.] mis-strike; badly struck coin.

monetair [Dut.] monetary.

monétaire [Fr.] monetary.

monetär [Ger.] monetary.

monetărie (f.) [Rom.] mint.

monetario [Span., Ital.] monetary.

monetário [Port.] (adj.) monetary; (m.) coin collection.

monetarny [Pol.] monetary.

monetnyy dvor монетный двор (m.) [Russ.] mint.

monety wielowarstwowe (f.pl.) [Pol.] clad coinage.

money Anything of accepted value which can readily be exchanged for goods or services or for settling debts.

Prior to the development of coins in the late seventh century B.C., livestock was a common

form of money. It was not only accepted in trade but was also the means by which men measured their wealth. Gold and silver were considered valuable then, but no one had yet figured out a way to forge precious metal into a form which would be automatically accepted as payment. In other words, everyone knew the value of a cow, but a gold ingot had to be weighed and checked for purity before it could be accepted in trade.

At various times and places, a great many items, both natural and man-made, have been used as a form of exchange. The list includes beads, shells, tusks, small forged items, chocolate, rice, gambling tokens, nails, woodpecker skulls, and even live rats intended to be eaten raw.

In some societies, the value of a money item was pegged on how many it took to buy a wife. The gizzi pennies[q.v.] of Africa, for example, were usually valued at 240 equal to one wife, although a larger number was needed if the pieces were rusted or if they were bent or broken. In the case of Siamese (Thai) wedding tokens (known as toks[q.v.]), a prospective husband needed two toks to buy a wife, and two more if he chose to divorce her.

The advent of coinage greatly simplified trade. The earliest staters[q.v.] of Asia Minor were little more than small ingots of electrum (a natural alloy of approximately three parts gold and one part silver) punched with just enough information to make them serviceable as a means of exchange. Within just a few centuries, coins became far more sophisticated, both in style and utility. The concept of coinage spread far beyond the Greek world and ultimately was accepted everywhere.

Paper money took a great deal longer to develop, because although paper notes represent something of value, they themselves do not contain value. A gold or silver disk has value whether it is stamped as a coin or not, but a note is only a paper guarantee. A note must either be exchangeable for precious metal or it must be issued by an agency with enough credibility or clout to convince people to accept it as a medium of exchange.

Fiat money (money not exchangeable for gold or silver) is now the norm. In the present world, practically no circulating money is backed by precious metal. Even most coins are made of "token" metals, the primary exceptions being high-priced commemoratives targeted to collectors and bullion coins which not only do not circulate but which often show unrealistic denominations representing only a fraction of their intrinsic value.

The end of the twentieth century has seen the definition of *money* become somewhat muddled. The concept of digital currency (a term coined by Bill Gates of Microsoft) brings into play a wide range of electronic methods for transacting business without the use of coins or notes. In theory, the so-called *smart cards* could someday make circulating money obsolete. In principle, it doesn't matter whether a person has in hand a group of coins with a total face value of ten dollars, or a note valued at ten dollars, or a plastic card with electronic coding that says it is worth ten dollars; all three will buy exactly ten dollars' worth of goods or services. All three media are subject to the same effects of inflation, they can all be taxed the same, and they are all worth the same in exchange for foreign currencies (assuming, of course, that a bank will even accept the coins). Electronic money has the advantage that it is harder to steal and easier for police authorities to trace. Hence, we have not yet seen the end of the evolution of money.

money of account Unit of currency or denomination of money that exists only for accounting purposes. There are usually no coins or paper money issued in those amounts.

One example is the *mill*, a sum equal to one-tenth of a U.S. cent or one-thousandth of a dollar. This unit of money is seen frequently in financial and legal documents but has never been used as the denomination of a U.S. coin.

Another example is the British *guinea*, equal to 21 shillings (the old pound Sterling equalled 20 shillings). Although coins were issued in that denomination at one time, the modern use of that unit was strictly as money of account. Until the adoption of the new pound in 1971,

prices of luxury items were quoted in guineas rather than pounds to give the seller a five percent bonus.

The Spanish *maravedí*[q.v.] is an example of a denomination which was used simultaneously as a circulating coin and as a money of account. By the sixteenth century, the maravedí had degenerated from a valued gold coin to a cheap copper coin. During the time when the copper pieces circulated, their value in trade steadily declined. Yet for many years the maravedí had a defined value against which the values of other coins could be calculated. In this sense, the maravedí was a money of account.

monnaie (*f.*) [*Fr.*] currency.

monnaie fiduciaire (*f.*) [*Fr.*] fiat money.

Monnaies Russes des Derniers Trois Siècles [*Fr.*] *Russian Coins of the Past Three Centuries.* Outstanding reference book published in 1857 by General Fedor Schubert. Included in the work are the actual weights of several thousand Russian coins struck during the sixteenth through nineteenth centuries.

monnayage (*m.*) [*Fr.*] coinage.

monogram Symbol of a king or queen, usually a crowned version of the monarch's initials. These are not only found on coins of Western Europe but are also seen on many imperial Russian coins with the initials written in the Cyrillic alphabet. For example, Catherine the Great's monogram resembles the letter "E" (Екатерина).

Swedish monograms: 1807 and 1965

The illustrated Swedish coins show the tradition of the royal monogram. The coin on the left is an 1807 1/4 skilling of Gustaf IV. The coin on the right, struck a century and a half later, shows virtually the same monogram. It is a 1965 50 öre coin of Gustaf VI.

monoplevro μονόπλευρο (*n.*) [*Grk.*] uniface.

mønster (*n.*) [*Nor., Dan.*] pattern.

mønt (*c.*) [*Dan.*] coin; mint.

møntenhed (*c.*) [*Dan.*] monetary unit; denomination.

month Very few dates on coins include the month of issue. Two of the few exceptions are the dates on the *gun money* issues of late-seventeenth century Ireland and on the Vatican's September 1978 *sede vacante* coins. In the later case, the month was needed because two popes died within the same calendar year. The coins dated simply 1978 (in roman numerals) were in honor of Pope Paul VI; the second issue dated September 1978 were for John Paul I.

møntmærke (*n.*) [*Dan.*] mintmark.

møntprægemaskine (*c.*) [*Dan.*] coinage press.

møntsamler (*c.*) [*Dan.*] coin collector; numismatist.

møntsystem (*n.*) [*Dan.*] monetary system.

møntværksted (*n.*) [*Dan.*] literally, *coin workshop.* Name given to Danish mints during the Middle Ages.

Franklin Mint moon medalet (enlarged)

moon medalet Small so-called *mini-coin* given to members of the Franklin Mint Collectors Society in 1971. The pieces were struck from silver taken aboard the Apollo XIV spacecraft by one of the astronauts in his personal belongings. Although the Franklin Mint was initially criticized for supposedly trying to capitalize on America's moon mission for its own financial gain, the company stated that it had never intended to sell the medalets but had only planned to give them free of charge to its subscribers as a momento of America's great space achievements.

The illustration has been enlarged to 400% to show detail. The obverse design consists of a "map" of the visible part of the moon. The reverse is taken up by an inscription telling where the silver came from.

These pieces are unique within the realm of numismatics because they are the only documented numismatic items whose roots go beyond the confines of the planet Earth.

Canadian coin with Morse Code inscription

Morse Code Just within the rim on the reverse of the Canadian wartime 5 cent pieces is an inscription in Morse Code: *We Win When We Work Willingly*. This appears on the coins showing the so-called "Victory" design of 1943 (tombac composition) and 1944-45 (chromium-plated steel).

Morgan Dollar U.S. silver dollar minted from 1878 to 1904 and again in 1921. It is named for its designer, Charles Morgan. The coin was authorized by the Act of February 28, 1878, known as the Bland-Allison Act, that brought back a denomination which had not been coined since 1873.

The obverse shows the capped head of Liberty. As per law, the reverse features an eagle, although this particular design was not well-received when the coin was first released. One writer of the time declared that it looked like a "scared hen."

For whatever reason, many millions of Morgan Dollars, particularly those struck in New Orleans and Carson City, were minted in the 1880s and 1890s but not released. They sat in bags in Treasury Department vaults until they were discovered in the early 1960s. Great numbers of uncirculated dollars from the

Philadelphia, New Orleans, and San Francisco mints were released at face value to banks. Most of the Carson City coins were kept until the 1970s when they were sold to collectors at a premium.

Morgan Dollar

Morgan Dollars became the center of attention in the 1980s when third-party grading services became popular. Many millions were graded and slabbed (i.e., encapsulated in plastic holders by the grading companies), and their prices skyrocketed. The market finally collapsed in late 1989 when the market saw far more sellers than buyers.

Although the term *cartwheel* applies to any U.S. silver dollar, it was most often used in reference to the Morgan Dollar.

Mormon issues Many of the so-called Forty-niners who participated in the California Gold Rush in the mid-19th century were Mormons, i.e., members of the Church of Latter Day Saints. A great deal of gold was brought back to what is now Salt Lake City, Utah, where the Church is headquartered.

The Church's leader, Brigham Young, conceived the idea of creating a mint for the territory and of producing a local coinage. Because the people of the Eastern United States would not accept the Mormon view on bigamy, the Mormons had gone west to establish a territory of their own and to create their own society. Young and his followers believed that producing local coinage fit this intent.

Mormon $5 gold coin (enlarged)

In all, six types of gold coins were struck. Their denominations include $2.50 (dated 1849), $10 (1849), $20 (1849), and three different types of $5 (1849, 1850, and 1860). The coins were actually struck from 1848 to 1861.

On all but the 1860-61 issue of $5 coins, the principal device is a three-pointed Phrygian crown above the All-Seeing Eye

The coins were determined to be non-current as of March 5, 1862.

[Walter Breen, *Complete Encyclopedia of U.S. and Colonial Coins*, pp. 655-56.]

Moses crown Series of World War II ghetto money showing Moses holding the Ten Commandments. These notes were issued by the Germans in 1943 in denominations of 1, 2, 5, 10, 20, 50, and 100 kronen and were produced for use in the ghetto at Theresienstadt, Czechoslovakia.

Moses crowns would have been offensive to the Jews under any circumstances, but the insult was made even greater because the portrait of Moses was modeled after one of the German guards, and the lettering on the tablets was in Modern Hebrew instead of the Paleo-Hebrew used in Biblical days.

"Moses" and the decalog on a Moses crown

See *ghetto money* and *World War II* for additional information and page 312 for a color illustration.

mosiądz (*m.*) [*Pol.*] brass (the alloy).

mostra (*f.*) [*Ital.*] exhibition.

motā sikkä मोटा सिक्का [*Hin.*] piéfort, piedfort.

motief (*n.*) [*Dut.*] pattern.

motif (*m.*) [*Fr.*] design.

motsa מוֹצָא (*m.*) [*Heb.*] pedigree (list of previous and present owners).

mountzoura μουντζούρα (*f.*) [*Grk.*] tarnish.

moyen pour contrer la contrefaçon [*Fr.*] anti-counterfeiting device.

mprountzos μπρούντζος (*m.*) [*Grk.*] bronze (the alloy).

m'til matekhet מְטִיל מַחֶכֶת (*m.*) [*Heb.*] ingot.

muchie (*f.*) [*Rom.*] edge.

muestra (*f.*) [*Span.*] specimen.

muinainen [*Finn.*] ancient.

muinaisaika [*Finn.*] antiquity.

muisto- (*adj.*) [*Finn.*] commemorative.

muka [*Indo.*] obverse.

mule A coin or medal made from mismatched dies. This error has rarely occurred in the twentieth century but was more common in earlier times.

One of the most recent mules is the Bahamas/New Zealand mule of 1967. The

color photos on page 317 show the coins as they were supposed to be and the mule which resulted from combining the obverse die of the Bahamas 5 cent piece with the reverse die of the New Zealand 2 cent piece. The mule itself shows no date because both of the mismatched dies came from the undated side of their respective coins. The mule was supposed to be the New Zealand 2 cent coin and has its correct bronze planchet.

mulinadong moneda [*Tag.*] milled coin.

mulya varg मूल्य वर्ग [*Hin.*] denomination.

munt (*m.-c.*) [*Dut.*] coin; mint.

munteenheid (*f.-c.*) [*Dut.*] monetary unit.

muntloon (*n.*) [*Dut.*] seigniorage.

muntpers (*m.-c.*) [*Dut.*] coinage press.

muntplaatje (*n.*) [*Dut.*] planchet.

muntplaats (*f.-c.*) [*Dut.*] mint.

muntslag [*Dut.*] coinage.

muntstelsel (*n.*) [*Dut.*] monetary system.

muntstempel (*m.-c.*) [*Dut.*] coinage die.

muntteken (*n.*) [*Dut.*] mintmark.

Münzamt (*n.*) [*Ger.*] mint.

Münze (*f.*) [*Ger.*] coin.

Münzfehler (*m.*) [*Ger.*] error (i.e., an error coin).

Münzprägeanstalt (*f.*) [*Ger.*] mint.

Münzprägemaschine (*f.*) [*Ger.*] coinage press.

Münzzeichen (*n.*) [*Ger.*] mintmark.

muotoilu [*Finn.*] design.

muotokuva [*Finn.*] effigy; portrait.

Murabit dinar Muslim gold coin which circulated extensively in Spain prior to the thirteenth century and was the predecessor of the Spanish gold *maravedí*[q.v.]. In Spanish, this coin is known as *marabotín*.

murni [*Indo.*] fineness; fine (purity of metal).

murto-osa [*Finn.*] fraction.

musta [*Finn.*] black.

musta pörssi [*Finn.*] black market.

Muster (*n.*) [*Ger.*] specimen.

mustuma [*Finn.*] tarnish.

mutsmad מֻצְמָד [*Heb.*] accolated[q.v.], conjoined, jugate.

muutettu vuosiluku [*Finn.*] altered date.

muutos [*Finn.*] alteration.

muuttaa (*v.*) [*Finn.*] to alter (a date, mint mark, or die).

muy buena conservación [*Span.*] Grade of banknote approximating Extremely Fine to About Uncirculated. The note may have one fold but no tears. Abbreviated "M.B.C."

muy escaso [*Span.*] very scarce. Strictly speaking, *escaso* ("scarce") indicates the known or assumed existence of 200 to 1000 specimens, while *muy escaso* refers to 20 to 200 existing examples.

müzayede ile satış [*Turk.*] auction sale.

Mylar Tradename of the Dupont Company for a class of clear polyester films currently used for packaging coins. It is stiffer than P.C.V.[q.v.] but does not need plasticisers.

mynt (*n.*) [*Swed.*]; (*m.*) [*Nor.*] coin.

mynt- [*Nor., Swed.*] monetary.

myntenhet (*m.*) [*Nor.*] monetary unit.

mynting (*m.*) [*Nor.*] coinage.

myntmerke (*n.*) [*Nor.*] mintmark.

myntning (*r.*) [*Swed.*] coinage.

myntortsmärke (*n.*) [*Swed.*] mintmark.

myntpress (*r.*) [*Swed.*] (coinage) press.

myntstempel (*n.*) [*Nor.*] (coinage) die.

myntsystem (*n.*) [*Nor.*] coinage.

myntverk (*n.*) [*Nor., Swed.*] mint.

myntvitenskap (*m.*) [*Nor.*] numismatics; coin collecting.

myydä (*v.*) [*Finn.*] to sell.

myyjä [*Finn.*] seller.

m'zuman מְזֻמָּן (*m.*) [*Heb.*] cash (ready money).

m'zuyaf מְזֻיָּף (*m.*) [*Heb.*] a counterfeit.

N n

naarmu [*Finn.*] scratch.

nabycie (*n.*) [*Pol.*] acquisition.

nabywca (*m.*) [*Pol.*] buyer.

nacionalidad (*f.*) [*Span.*] nationality.

naderwanie (*n.*) [*Pol.*] a tear (as in a banknote or bond).

naderwany [*Pol.*] torn.

nadir [*Turk.*] rare, scarce.

nadruk (*m.*) [*Pol.*] overprint.

nagy [*Hun.*] large.

Nagy-Britannia [*Hun.*] Great Britain.

nagyító [*Hun.*] magnifying glass.

nahezu [*Ger.*] almost.

naing ngyan cha nhwe နိုင်ငံခြား:ငွေ [*Bur.*] foreign currency.

najniższa cena (*f.*) [*Pol.*] minimum bid.

nakit [*Turk.*] cash (ready money).

na lewo [*Pol.*] left (direction or position).

nalyot налет (*m.*) [*Russ.*] tarnish.

namaak (*m.-c.*) [*Dut.*] imitation.

namaaksel (*n.*) [*Dut.*] a fake.

não [*Port.*] no; not.

não circulado [*Port.*] uncirculated.

não classificado [*Port.*] not classified; unattributed.

na odwrociu; na rewersie [*Pol.*] on the back.

não emitido [*Port.*] not issued.

não publicado [*Port.*] unpublished (not listed in any book or catalogue).

não se aceitam propostas sem limites [*Port.*] no unlimited bids accepted.

napis (*m.*) [*Pol.*] inscription.

Napoléon Name of two French rulers and one pretender.

1. Napoléon I [né *Napoleone*, translated in French to *Napoléon Bonaparte*; nicknamed *Le Petit Caporal*, the "Little Corporal."] Military leader and self-proclaimed emperor of France. Born August 15, 1769, in Ajaccio on the island of Corsica; died May 5, 1821, at Longwood on St. Helena.

The greatest military genius of his time, Napoléon distinguished himself early in his career by becoming an officer in the French Army at the age of sixteen and then by leading his revolutionary French army troops to a series of decisive victories. His leadership not only provided military successes but also contributed great sums of money to the revolutionary cause.

Napoléon ultimately created an empire (which for sixteen years covered most of Europe) and crowned himself Emperor of France. He established many reforms in France such as a strong centralized government, and he reorganized the French laws into codes, seven in number. They incorporated the freedoms gained by the people of France during the French Revolution, including religious tolerance and the abolition of serfdom.

Although his empire included most of Europe, only England stood in the way of his complete mastery of Western Europe. His plans to invade Great Britain in 1805 never materialized. The French fleet was destroyed at Trafalgar on October 21, 1805, by the English Navy. Napoléon realized then that whatever hopes he might have had of avenging himself on England were ended.

He then turned his attention to Russia. On September 12, 1812, he engaged the Russians in battle at Borodino. The results of the battle were indecisive and he was forced to retreat. His army of 500,000 was reduced to barely 20,000 ragged, freezing, starving men who staggered across the Russian frontier in the dead of winter.

This defeat gave his enemies— England, Austria, Prussia, and now Russia— their chance. Paris was captured on March 30, 1814, and Napoléon was forced to abdicate on April 11. Sent into exile, his "empire" consisted of a few square miles of Elba, a tiny island on the west coast of Italy.

Refusing to admit defeat, he escaped from Elba and returned to Paris. With the help of hundreds of his old officers and soldiers, he enjoyed a brief return to his old glory. The end came with the Battle of Waterloo on June 18, 1815.

Exiled to St. Helena, he died there, alone without family or friends, on May 5, 1821. His remains were returned to France in 1840 and buried under the dome of the Hôtel des Invalides.

Napoléon made a huge impact on numismatics, not so much in France as in virtually every other part of the Western World. His exploits disrupted established governments throughout Europe, triggering all sorts of political changes. For example, his conquest of Spain so weakened that nation that it gave Spanish colonies in the Western Hemisphere the opportunity to break away from the mother country. Hence, a tremendous number of coinage issues connected in some way to the colonies' fight for independence can trace their roots to Napoléon and his empire. Even in today's world, many current or recent coins and notes of Latin American countries bear the likenesses of heroes from their various wars of independence. Were it not for Napoléon, modern coins and notes of Mexico would probably not portray Father Hidalgo and Josefina, coins of Chile would not show Bernardo O'Higgins, and Venezuelan money would not honor Simón Bolívar.

2. Napoléon II [né *Napoléon Francis Joseph Charles* (1811-1832); nicknamed *l'Aiglon* ("Little Eagle")]. Son of Napoléon Bonaparte and his second wife Marie Louise, daughter of Francis I of Austria.

After Napoléon Bonaparte's fall at Waterloo, he intended for his son to succeed him as French emperor and proclaimed the boy

as such to the French Assembly in 1815. On June 23 of that year, the four-year-old child was in fact proclaimed emperor by the Chamber of Deputies, but this honor lasted exactly one day.

pretender coinage: 5 franc crown of Napoléon II

Because the child's mother was an Austrian princess, she wanted her son to be brought up an Austrian prince and not a French emperor, an idea Bonaparte vehemently opposed. But after his first exile, Bonaparte had little to say in the matter. Marie Louise took her son to live at Schönbrunn Palace in Vienna and then left him there in the care of servants while she and her advisor, Count Adam Adalbert Neipperg (with whom she had a love affair), went to rule the duchy of Parma which her father had given her. Francis I gave his grandson the title Duc de Reichstadt and prepared him to be part of the Austrian army.

The Little Eagle died just after his twenty-first birthday in 1832 of tuberculosis. By 1852 the Bonapartists gained power in France and placed his cousin, Charles Louis Napoléon, on the throne as Napoléon III.

Largely to bolster his position with old-line Bonapartists, Napoléon III issued a set of presentation coins with his late cousin's effigy. The coins, all dated 1816, were in denominations of 1, 3, 5, and 10 centimes as well as 1/4, 1/2, 1, 2, and 5 francs. The obverse inscription encircles the effigy and reads *NAPOLÉON II — EMPEREUR*. The reverse shows the date, denomination, and inscription *EMPIRE FRANÇAIS*. The coins, which fall

under the category of pretender coinage[q.v.], were struck for political purposes and probably never circulated.

[John W. Dunn, "Napoléon II: Emperor for a Day," *World Coins*, January 1973, pp. 34-48; David T. Alexander, "The Eaglet: Napolean's offspring adds to numismatic legacy," *Coin World*, February 12, 1996, p. 60.]

3. Napoléon III [né *Louis Napoléon Bonaparte*.] French emperor. Born April 20, 1808, in Paris; died in exile on January 9, 1873, at Chislehurst, England.

Napoléon III was the son of King Louis and Queen Hortense of Holland, and was thus a nephew of Napoléon Bonaparte. Because the Bonaparte family was banished from France, the young Louis Napoléon was educated in Switzerland and Bavaria.

He was sentenced to life for two unsuccessful attempts to overthrow the French government of King Louis Philippe but escaped in 1846. When Louis Philippe was ousted in 1848, Louis Napoléon ran for the presidency of the new French republic and won an astonishing victory. When the new French constitution forbade him to run for a second 4-year term, he assumed dictatorial powers and extended his term to ten years. By 1852 he had gained enough personal support to re-establish the French Empire and to name himself Emperor Napoléon III (Napoléon Bonaparte's son had been accorded the title *Napoléon II*; see #2 above).

Napoléon III's rule is generally regarded as having been a failure, both for his domestic policies and especially because he led France to a devastating loss in the Franco-Prussian War of 1870. His regime was overthrown on September 4, 1870, and he died in exile in England in 1873.

Although his face appears on the whole gamut of circulating coins from this period, his most significant numismatic legacy was probably the many satirical pieces carved from those coins. His effigy was often retooled to create outlandish images as a way of mocking him for his failed foreign and domestic policies. Retooled coins exist showing him

portrayed as everything from a clown to a jackass. Many of the pieces were enameled with bright colors to enhance the coins' garish appearance.

And like his namesake Napoléon Bonaparte, Louis Napoléon's actions affected numismatics long after his death. When he failed to defeat the Prussians in 1870, they imposed a huge war indemnification on France which nearly bankrupted the country. The French did not forget this. A half century later, France convinced its allies to impose enormous payments on Germany and Austria after World War I. This helped create the hyperinflation of the early 1920s from which the many thousands of different Notgeld[q.v.] notes, coins, and miscellaneous items emerged.

[Contributed by Ruth Ann Davis. *Compton's Encyclopedia and Fact Index*, Vol. 17, pp. 8-13 et al.]

naprawiony [*Pol.*] repaired.

na prawo [*Pol.*] right (direction or position).

narodowość (*f.*) [*Pol.*] nationality.

narodowy [*Pol.*] national.

naslag (*m.-c.*) [*Dut.*] restrike.

National Bank note Type of U.S. paper money issued from 1863 to 1935.

As in the case of postage currency, fractional currency, encased postage stamps[qq.v.], and a host of other monetary items, these notes resulted from the many economic problems stemming from the U.S. Civil War and its aftermath. The Lincoln administration, with the help of Congress, brought about the National Banking Act of February 25, 1863, an act intended to generate more money to fight the war. It was also intended to regulate and stabilize the nation's currency system. This act encouraged private banks to become "national banks" by applying for federal charters. In so doing, these banks could then issue their own federal bank notes. To do so, the national banks needed only to use their funds to buy Union bonds, money which would be used to fight the war. If they deposited these funds with the Treasurer of the United States, they could then issue their own paper money up to 90 percent of the value of the bonds which they had deposited.

National Bank note

In 1863 a total of 179 banks had gained federal charters, and by 1865 the number approached two thousand. In 1935 when the system finally ended, the number of participating banks was 14,348, most of which (but not all) had actually issued their own paper money. Every U.S. state and territory had banks which issued these notes, although some areas (e.g., Hawaii) produced very few.

From 1863 to 1875, the federal government allowed private printing companies to produce these notes. But in 1875, the government decided to begin printing all the notes at its own facilities. The notes were printed in sheets with only the signatures missing. The sheets were then sent to the various banks where local officials either hand-signed the notes or stamped them with a rubber stamp bearing their signature. The largest banks had the signatures applied at the time of printing, much the way signatures are applied to paper money today.

A strange bit of irony occurred in 1929 when U.S. paper money was reduced in size from a larger note (sometimes called a *horse blanket*) to the size used by Americans today. Shortly after the reduction in size, the Stock Market crashed, throwing the U.S. economy (as well as that of the rest of the world) into chaos. Many of the banks which were issuing these notes failed, and many others were found to be unsound. In March 1933 when President Franklin D. Roosevelt temporarily closed all the banks as a way of avoiding more bank failures, a nation-wide examination of the country's banking system showed the national bank note program to be incapable of managing the nation's money during a time of Depression. The Federal Reserve System was created, and in 1935 the national banks were no longer authorized to issue money.

[Richard G. Doty, *The Macmillan Encyclopedic Dictionary of Numismatics*, pp. 223-25.]

Nationalität (*f.*) [*Ger.*] nationality.

nationaliteit (*f.-c.*) [*Dut.*] nationality.

nationalitet (*r.*) [*Swed.*] nationality.

natural toning Discoloration which appears on the surfaces of coins or medals over a period of time. This oxidation usually results from the item's exposure to air or sunlight or from a chemical reaction caused by the substances that have touched those coins or medals during storage. Numismatic items are frequently stored in paper or cellophane envelopes, cardboard albums, velvet-lined cabinets, and a variety of other containers, and most of these are made of materials which can cause a chemical reaction in metal that results in toning.

The beauty of a coin may be enhanced by toning or be ruined by it. Toning may take the form of ugly black tarnish that eats into the surface of the coin, forever destroying its natural luster. But toning may also appear as a glint of glorious color as though the coin had been touched by the brush of an angelic artist.

These are the coins and medals whose beauty and value are magnified by their glimmering hues.

Coins can tone in any color or shade of the spectrum, and the specific color generally indicates what type of container was used to store the piece. The amount of sulfur present in the container is often the determining factor as to what color the coin will tone. Sulfur in the air can have the same effect.

Sometimes attempts are made to tone coins and medals through artificial means in order to increase their value and marketability. These efforts are seldom successful. See *artificial toning*.

nature printing on 18th century note

nature printing   Process used by Benjamin Franklin to reproduce the image of a leaf on eighteenth century Pennsylvania Continental Currency and in his *Poor Richard's Almanac* of 1737. The technique was ultimately copied by other money printers.

Because of the biological accuracy of the image, it is obvious that real leaves were used somehow in this process. Unfortunately, the method was never recorded, and it has been necessary for twentieth century experts to try to reconstruct the process.

Apparently a piece of wet fabric was laid on some smooth soft plaster. A leaf, either moistened or covered with some sort of adhesive, was placed on the cloth in such a way that it would adher to the cloth after drying. Something with a flat surface was then pressed against this so that the leaf and fabric would be flush with each other. After this unit dried, a plaster negative was made by applying an oil to the leaf and cloth and then by covering the whole unit with a mixture of plaster and some heat-resistant substance such as asbestos. Molten metal would be poured into the hardened plaster negative to make the printer's cut which would actually be used in the printing process.

[Eric P. Newman, "Nature Printing on Colonial and Continental Currency," *The Numismatist*, February and March, 1964, pp. 147-154 (February) and pp. 299-305 (March).]

naula [*Finn.*] pound (unit of weight). [Pound Sterling (£) is *punta.*]

näyte [*Finn.*] specimen.

näyttely [*Finn.*] exhibition.

nazionale [*Ital.*] national.

nazionalità (*f.*) [*Ital.*] nationality.

N.C.L.T. [*abbr.*] non-circulating legal tender[*q.v.*].

N.D. [*abbr.*] no date.

neatribuit; nedeterminat [*Rom.*] unattributed.

necesidad (*f.*) [*Span.*] necessity; *de necesidad* refers to *obsidional* money.

necirculat [*Rom.*] uncirculated.

necunoscut [*Rom.*] unknown.

Nederland [*Dut.*] The Netherlands. The complete official name in the Dutch language is *Koninkrijk der Nederlanden.*

Nederländerna [*Swed.*] Netherlands, Holland.

nedsænket præg [*Dan.*] incuse.

ne-emis [*Rom.*] not issued.

negen [*Dut.*] nine.

negentig [*Dut.*] ninety.

negro [*Span.*] black.

negru [*Rom.*] black.

négy [*Hun.*] four.

negyed [*Hun.*] fourth, quarter.

négyszögletes [*Hun.*] rectangular; square.

negyven [*Hun.*] forty.

nelikulmainen [*Finn.*] square.

neljä [*Finn.*] four.

neljäkymmentä [*Finn.*] forty.

neljäsosa [*Finn.*] fourth; quarter.

nemesfémrúd [*Hun.*] ingot.

Németország [*Hun.*] Germany.

nem hivatalos [*Hun.*] unofficial.

nemzeti [*Hun.*] national.

nemzetiség [*Hun.*] nationality.

nemzetközi [*Hun.*] international.

Nennwert (*m.*) [*Ger.*] denomination; face value.

neoficial [*Rom.*] unofficial.

nepublicat [*Rom.*] unpublished.

neregulat [*Rom.*] irregular.

nero [*Ital.*] black.

nesher נֶשֶׁר (*m.*) [*Heb.*] eagle.

netekh נֵתֶךְ (*m.*) [*Heb.*] alloy (of metals).

neu [*Ger.*] new.

neuf [*Fr.*] nine; new.

neun [*Ger.*] nine.

neunzig [*Ger.*] ninety.

Neuprägung (*f.*) [*Ger.*] a restrike.

Neuseeland [*Ger.*] New Zealand.

neutron activation analysis A non-destructive method for determining the chemical composition of samples. In numismatics, activation analysis can be used to determine the metallic composition of coins without damaging them. A less expensive method is X-ray fluorescent analysis, but fluorescent analysis can determine only the composition of the surface of an object and consequently tells the investigator nothing about the interior of the coin. The composition of the surface of a coin may have been altered by cleaning or corrosion (which may selectively remove metals like zinc or copper).

The coin to be analyzed using neutron activation is subjected to bombardment by neutrons, usually in a nuclear reactor. A small part of most of the metals in the coin will be with energy levels characteristic of the elements involved and intensities proportional to the amounts of the parent metals in the coin. The measurements of the gamma rays from a treated coin are made with a gamma ray spectrometer.

There are two principal uses of this sort of analysis: to determine whether a coin is counterfeit and to investigate the sources of the metals used by various mints and to assign coins to specific mints. The detection of counterfeits by activation analysis in not fool-proof; the fact that a given coin has the same composition as a genuine specimen may mean only that the counterfeiter melted inexpensive coins of the period to use in counterfeiting an expensive one. On the other hand, if a counterfeiter uses modern silver to manufacture an ancient coin, the fraud can be detected easily. Silver ores are rarely if ever found which do not contain at least a small amount of gold; the history of silver refining is a story of learning more efficient methods of removing the gold from the silver.

In a test case, a suspect Roman denarius (a silver coin) was alleged by a dealer to be an ancient counterfeit. For the analysis, six samples were used: a Roman denarius of the Republican period, one from the Imperial period, the suspect, a U.S. silver dime, a sample of pure silver, and a sample of pure gold. The conditions of the neutron bombardment and its duration were chosen to accentuate the difference between silver and gold. The results clearly demonstrated that the counterfeit coin was made using modern silver and that the Romans improved their method of purifying silver between Republican and Imperial times.

This analysis indicated that the republican denarius contained about 0.5% gold, the imperial denarius perhaps 0.1%. As expected, the imperial denarius contained a substantial amount of copper; beginning with Emperor Nero, Roman silver coins were alloyed,

containing about 10% copper. The counterfeit and the U.S. dime each contained about 0.025% gold.

[Contributed by David Block. Karl Schmitt-Korte and Michael Cowel, "Nabatæan coinage, Part 1," *Numismatic Chronicle*, 1989, pp. 33-58 (The authors discuss different analytical methods and techniques); D. De Soete, R. Gijbels, and J. Hoste, *Neutron Activation Analysis*.]

Neuvostoliitto [*Finn.*] Soviet Union.

névérték [*Hun.*] face value.

New Zealand, Royal Numismatic Society of see *Royal Numismatic Society of New Zealand*.

ngày tháng [*Viet.*] date.

ngoại tệ [*Viet.*] foreign currency.

người làm giả [*Viet.*] counterfeiter.

nguyên chất [*Viet.*] fineness; fine (purity of metal).

ngwe ၁ [*Bur.*] silver.

ni [*Nor., Dan.*] nine.

nichel (*m.*) [*Ital.*]; (*n.*) [*Rom.*] nickel (the metal).

Nicholas I Memorial crown (1859)

Nicholas Name of two Russian czars (or *tsars*).

1. Nicholas I. Born in 1796 at Tsarskoye Selo (Pushkin), Russia; died in 1855.

Nicholas I came to the throne in 1825 after the death of his brother Alexander I. His first action was to put down the *Decembrist* uprising led by liberal-minded noblemen who desired wide reforms. A harsh ruler, he created a powerful police, banned political organizations, introduced censorship, refused to abolish serfdom, and exiled liberal writers. Yet Nicholas is also known to have promoted the economic growth of his country by establishing a stable currency and putting in place protective tariffs. He also began construction of a national railroad, introduced a new law code, and established vocational schools.

Hoping to enlarge his empire, Nicholas I engaged in wars in Central and East Asia. In 1828 he began his war against Turkey and nearly realized his dream of taking the Dardanelles. The Hapsburgs, under the leadership of Francis Joseph, called upon Nicholas and his armies in 1849 to assist in putting an end to the Hungarian uprisings.

The Crimean War proved to be his downfall. Not only was Russia was defeated in its attempt to add more Turkish territory to its domain, but Nicholas himself died in 1855 during that war.

Nicholas I's reign left a very significant numismatic legacy, because it was from 1828 to 1845 that Russia issued platinum coins in the denominations of 3, 6, and 12 rubles. In the entire history of world coinage, these are the only circulating coins ever struck from platinum (although this metal has been used in patterns and is currently found in some bullion coins). However, many of the issues were restruck at later dates, using original dies in unrecorded quantities.

Another significant numismatic treasure from his reign are the Family rubles struck in 1836. These presentation pieces show the effigy of Nicholas on the obverse and individual effigies of his wife and children on the reverse. See *Family ruble* for additional information and illustrations.

2. Nicholas II [né *Nicholas Alexandrovich Romanov*] was the last czar. Born May 18, 1868, in St. Petersburg, Russia, to Czar Alexander III and Marie Fyodorovna; died by execution on July 16, 1918.

Nicholas II became czar in 1894 upon the death of his father. His wife was Princess Alix

of Hesse-Darmstadt who took the name of Alexandra Fyodorovna. The couple had one son and four daughters.

Though ill-prepared politically and militarily, Nicholas II ruled from 1894 to 1917. After his military defeat by Japan, he took little notice of the many warnings he received of future trouble such as the student riots of St. Petersburg in 1899, and the rebellions all over the country that began in 1905 due to the harsh conditions under which the peasants and city dwellers lived. As a result of the unrest, Nicholas issued a manifest on October 30, 1905, in which he promised to establish an elected legislative body— the State Duma— and guaranteed civil liberties to his subjects.

During the reign of Nicholas II, Russia became a major industrial power; science, music, and literature flourished; and the Trans-Siberian railroad was completed. In 1914 Russia entered World War I, largely to help defend its Slavic neighbor Serbia. Military losses, the threat of famine, and the disorganization of the economy led to the riots of 1917. The communist uprising was lead by Lenin and Trotsky and began on October 25, 1917. Nicholas and his family were held under house arrest, and were executed on July 16, 1918, thus ending the rule of the czars.

[Contributed by Ruth Ann Davis. Frank W. Weis, *Lifelines: Famous Contemporaries from 600 B.C. to 1975,* p. 373; Duncan M. White (editor), *Caesar to Churchill: The Years of Fulfillment*; Chester L. Krause and Clifford Mishler, *Standard Catalog of World Coins* (1985), p. 1804.]

nicht ausgegeben [*Ger.*] not issued.

nicht zugeschrieben [*Ger.*] unattributed.

1951 Canadian 5 cent "nickel" commemorative

nickel A very popular metal used for coinage purposes. [element: group VIII of the period table; atomic weight 58.70; atomic number 28; specific gravity 8.90; symbol Ni; magnetic.]

The first use of pure nickel for coinage came in 1881 in Switzerland, although copper-nickel alloys had long been in use worldwide. The metal is silvery white but wears to a dull gray. Its hardness makes it difficult to strike a deep design, but the coins do wear well. Canada's current circulating 5, 10, 25, and 50 cent coins are of pure nickel.

The element nickel was isolated and named by the Swedish chemist A. F. Cronstedt in 1751. Because Canada is the world's largest producer of nickel, that nation issued a circulating commemorative 5 cent piece in 1951. The reverse (shown in the illustration) features a nickel refinery.

[Contributed by Halbert Carmichael.]

niè 镍 [*Chin.-py./sc.*] nickel (the metal).

niebieski [*Pol.*] blue.

Niedrigstgebot (*f.*) [*Ger.*] minimum bid.

niekompletny [*Pol.*] incomplete.

Niemcy [*Pol.*] Germany.

Niemcy Wschodnie [*Pol.*] East Germany (D.D.R.).

Niemcy Zachodnie [*Pol.*] West Germany (B.R.D.).

nieobiegowy [*Pol.*] uncirculated.

nieoficjalny; nieurzędowy [*Pol.*] unofficial.

nieokreślony [*Pol.*] unattributed.

nie przyjmuje się zleceń bez limitu [*Pol.*] no unlimited bids accepted.

niepublikowany [*Pol.*] unpublished (not listed in any book or catalogue).

nieregularny; nietypowy [*Pol.*] irregular.

niet compleet [*Dut.*] incomplete.

niet gepubliceerd [*Dut.*] unpublished (not listed in any book or catalogue).

niet in omloop gebracht [*Dut.*] uncirculated.

niet langer in gebruik [*Dut.*] obsolete.

niet toegeschreven [*Dut.*] unattributed.

niet uitgegeven [*Dut.*] not issued.

nieuw [*Dut.*] new.

Nieuw-Zeeland [*Dut.*] New Zealand.

nie wprowadzony do obiegu [*Pol.*] not issued.

nieznany [*Pol.*] unknown.

nikel נִיקֶל (*m.*) [*Heb.*] nickel (the metal).

nikelio νικέλιο (*n.*) [*Grk.*] nickel.

nikiel (*m.*) [*Pol.*] nickel.

nikkel [*Hun.*]; (*n.*) [*Dan., Dut.*]; (*m.*) [*Nor.*] nickel.

nikkeli [*Finn.*] nickel.

nimellisarvo [*Finn.*] denomination; face value.

nimikirjoitus [*Finn.*] signature.

nio [*Swed.*] nine.

niquel (*m.*) [*Span.*] nickel.

níquel (*m.*) [*Port.*] nickel.

nitti [*Nor.*] ninety.

nittio [*Swed.*] ninety.

n'khoshet נְחֹשֶׁת (*f.*) [*Heb.*] copper.

N.M. [*abbr.*] no motto. This is used most often in reference to U.S. coins lacking the motto *In God We Trust.*

no atribuido [*Span.*] unattributed.

no circulado [*Span.*] uncirculated.

no debe circular [*Span.*] not for circulation.

nödmynt (*n.*) [*Swed.*] emergency currency.

nødspenger (*n.pl.*) [*Nor.*] emergency currency; obsidional money.

no emitido [*Span.*] not issued.

noir [*Fr.*] black.

noll [*Swed.*] zero.

nolla [*Finn.*] zero.

nominal номинал (*m.*) [*Russ.*] denomination.

nominał (*m.*) [*Pol.*] denomination.

nominale waarde (*f.-c.*) [*Dut.*] face value.

nominellt värde (*n.*) [*Swed.*] face value.

nomisma νόμισμα (*n.*) [*Grk.*] coin; currency.

nomismata νομίσματα [*Grk.*] coinage.

nomismata ektaktis anagkis νομίσματα ἐκτάκτης ἀνάγκης (*n.*) [*Grk.*] emergency currency.

nomismatiki monada νομισματική μονάδα (*f.*) [*Grk.*] monetary unit.

nomismatiko systima νομισματικό σύστημα [*Grk.*] monetary system.

nomismatokopion νομισματοκοπείον (*n.*) [*Grk.*] mint.

non attribué [*Fr.*] unattributed.

non attribuito [*Ital.*] unattributed.

non catalogato [*Ital.*] unpublished (not listed in any book or catalogue).

non circolato [*Ital.*] uncirculated.

non-circulating legal tender [abbreviated *N.C.L.T.*] Gold or silver commemorative coins technically possessing legal tender status even though they do not circulate. They are targeted to collectors and souvenir hunters and are sold at high prices. Although a few major countries like Canada have issued coins of this type, most N.C.L.T. coins are the products of small countries which were able to obtain a large portion of their revenue from the sale of these coins.

N.C.L.T. coins do not circulate anywhere. They usually cannot be converted into other currencies at foreign exchange offices and can only be exchanged in the country of issue.

N.C.L.T. coins were most popular in the 1960s and 1970s. Collectors and the general public soon realized that these coins had poor investment potential and quit buying them. Huge numbers of them were destroyed in the Great Silver Melt of 1979.

non emesso [*Ital.*] not issued.

non-émis [*Fr.*] not issued.

non publié [*Fr.*] unpublished (not listed in any book or catalogue).

Non Sine Diis Animosus Infans [*Lat.*] The courageous child was not without divine assistance. Inscription found on the *Libertas Americana* Medal[*q.v.*] of 1783.

[Louis C. Sass, "Medals of Friendship and Thanks", *The Numismatist*, July 1990, pp. 1080-1084.]

noodgeld (*n.*) [*Dut.*] emergency currency; necessity money, obsidional.

Noord-Ierland [*Dut.*] Northern Ireland.

Noorwegen [*Dut.*] Norway.

no publicado [*Span.*] unpublished (not listed in any book or catalogue).

Nordirland [*Ger., Swed., Dan.*] Northern Ireland.

Nord-Irland [*Nor.*] Northern Ireland.

Noreg [*Nor.*] Norway.

Norge [*Swed., Nor., Dan.*] Norway.

Norja [*Finn.*] Norway.

Norton I, Emperor of the United States [né *Joshuah Abraham Norton*]. Born in 1818 to a Jewish family in London, England. Norton was a businessman who was raised in South Africa but made and lost his fortune in San Francisco in the 1850s. It is believed that the shock of bankruptcy made him mentally unstable. He declared himself to be Norton I, Emperor of the United States, on Sept. 17, 1859. For his remaining twenty years he issued a variety of

scrip, usually denominated 50 cents, by which he sustained himself. He was a local celebrity, and the local citizenry, as well as some old business colleagues, supported his modest life style.

Most notes portray the Emperor's bust in his familiar military uniform with sundry other vignettes and the claim that they are convertible into interest-bearing bonds.

[Contributed by Simcha Kuritzky. Edward Schuman, "Emperor Norton I," *The Shekel*, November-December 1988, pp. 3-7.]

No-S Mint error in which U.S. proof coins produced at the San Francisco Mint are inadvertently struck without the "S" mintmark. The mistake is not the result of filled dies[q.v.], as has sometimes been the case. In this instance, it is caused by the failure of mint employees to punch the mintmark into the die when the die was being prepared for shipment to San Francisco from the Philadelphia Mint where it was made. The scarcest example of this error is probably the 1968 "No-S" proof dime, although similar errors have been discovered on 1990 cents, 1971 5 cent pieces, and 1970, 1975, and 1983 dimes. All are scarce.

The 1968 "No-S" proof dimes show a peculiarity on the reverse which makes authentication easier. The genuine specimens can be identified by a patch of small scratches resembling a wisp of smoke. This "smoke signal" rises from the top of the torch and extends to the lower left of the letter "o" in the word "of".

[J. Bruce Jackson, "The 1968 'No-S' Proof Set," *The Numismatist*, April 1987, pp. 740-1.]

no se aceptan licitaciones sin límite; **no se aceptan pujas sin límite** [*Span.*] no unlimited bids accepted.

notă propagandistică (*f.*) [*Rom.*] propaganda note.

Notgeld (*n.*) [*Ger.*] Literally, *emergency money*.

Although the simple meaning of this German term is *emergency money*, its usage is generally restricted to those non-imperial and non-federal notes and coins produced in Germany or Austria from the beginning of the First World War to the end of the inflation period in 1923. In a more limited sense it includes only the part of these issues called *series notes*, sets of several designs of the same denomination and/or the same design in several denominations. These *Serienscheine*, to use the German term, were issued primarily to raise money for the cities or other entities issuing them. Collecting these notes became the hobby of a great number of German people; societies were formed, dealerships became established, and several ephemeral periodicals came into existence to cater to the hobby and to dealers.

There exist many types of Notgeld money manufactured on substances other than paper. The list includes linen, silk, leather, wood, porcelain, and a variety of metals. Most of these pieces were manufactured as souvenirs or novelty items and were never intended to be circulating currency. Nevertheless, perhaps as much as 99% of all Notgeld pieces produced were paper notes of varying sizes, denominations, and quality of workmanship.

Many collectors unfamiliar with this money have great difficulty in distinguishing where the various notes were printed. The denomination provides the best clue for determining the country of origin. Notes denominated in Heller or Kronen are Austrian; those using the Pfennig or Mark are German.

The doyen of Notgeld was Dr. Arnold Keller, an orientalist by education whose hobby was collecting paper money. He began collecting the emergency issues of towns in his native Alsace in 1914 while still a university student. During and after the war his interest expanded to include not only all German issues of emergency money but also the war-time issues from other countries, from Portugal to Russia. In 1920 Keller became the editor of *Das Notgeld*, the earliest and longest lasting of the periodicals devoted to emergency money. In addition to the notices of new issues published in *Das Notgeld*, Keller produced or sponsored catalogs, periodically revised, to cover the field of German emergency money: 1. Emergency notes of 1914; 2. Fractional notes, 1916-1922; 2-A. Circulation issues; 2-

B. Series notes; 3. Emergency coins; 4. Large notes of 1918-19 and 1920-21; 5. Notes of prisoner-of-war camps; 6. Inflation notes of 1922; 7. Inflation notes of 1923; 8. Notes tied to the U.S. dollar. New editions of 2-A & B were published by Battenberg Verlag, Munich, edited by Albert Pick and Carl Siemsem, in 1976 and 1975. Battenberg has since reprinted the other catalogs of the series. More recently (1989) a new edition of 2-B has been edited by Kai Lindman and published by K. K. K. Verlag, Sassenburg, Germany.

Also see *emergency currency*. Additionally, page 319 of the color section illustrates a variety of Notgeld pieces made from materials other than paper.

[Contributed by David Block. Arnold Keller, the introductions to *Kleingeldscheine* ("Fractional Notes") in *N.I. Bulletin*, November 1979, and April 1978. Reprinted as *Notgeld Handbook No. 1*, Manor Press, 1981; Arnold Keller, "Recollections of a Notgeld Collector," *N.I. Bulletin*, September 1989, pp. 201-222; David Block, "The Life of a Journal: *Das Notgeld*," *The Asylum*, Winter 1988, pp. 103-114.]

Notgeldwährung (*f.*) [*Ger.*] emergency money; necessity money.

not issued 1. Numismatic item which is produced by a government or other issuing agency but is never released to the public, such as the gasoline rationing coupons that the United States printed by the millions in the early 1970s but never distributed and the British 1937 proof set of Edward VIII.

2. Anticipated items which the issuing agency fails to produce for whatever reason.

nou [*Rom.*] new.

nouă [*Rom.*] nine.

nouăzeci [*Rom.*] ninety.

Noua Zeelandă [*Rom.*] New Zealand.

no unlimited bids accepted Bidders at an auction or mail bid sale are not permitted to offer to pay a percentage above the actual highest bid from the floor rather than to submit a specific bid themselves.

In the 1940s and 1950s, unlimited bidding was popular with many multi-millionaire collectors who expected to purchase anything they bid on, especially King Farouk of Egypt.

The auctioneer would be told in advance that Farouk (or whomever) wanted a certain item on auction for his collection and that he would pay a specified percentage above the highest actual bid.

Unlimited bidding has two drawbacks. First, it creates tremendous animosity among the bidders on the floor when they realize they cannot purchase the item no matter how high they go. Secondly, what happens if two people place an unlimited bid on the same item? Obviously, one of the unlimited bids has to be rejected, but whose? Farouk's bid was virtually always accepted because of his tremendous wealth. He was such a "high roller" that no auction house dared to turn down his bid.

nouveau [*Fr.*] new.

Nouvelle-Zélande [*Fr.*] New Zealand.

Nova Zelândia [*Port.*] New Zealand.

nove [*Port., Ital.*] nine.

noventa [*Span., Port.*] ninety.

no verso [*Port.*] on the back.

novo [*Port.*] new.

novodel новодел [*Russ.*] Literally, *new made*. Numismatically, the term refers to restrikes of early coin issues made for collectors by the Russian mints from 1738-1890.

Nowa Zelandia [*Pol.*] New Zealand.

nowe bicie (*n.*) [*Pol.*] a restrike.

nowy [*Pol.*] new.

N.R. [*abbr.*] no record, no records.

nudity In ancient times, nudity appeared on coins and other works of art as a celebration of the human form. The Roman coin in the illustration is one such example. It is a follis of Maximian Herculius struck around A.D. 295 at Ticinum which features the nude allegorical figure of the Genio Populi Romani, the genius of the Roman people.

nudity: Roman follis of ca. A.D. 295

In the nineteenth and twentieth centuries, a number of countries issued coins featuring nudes, and most have been regarded in good taste. Among them are the Italian nickel 20 centesimo coins of 1908-35 showing a naked woman and the stainless steel 50 lira coins of 1954-82 revealing the rear view of a naked man.

nudity: naked woman and naked man on Italian coins

Probably the greatest controversy came in 1916 and 1917 when the United States issued its only coin ever to show nudity. The original design of the Standing Liberty Quarter Dollar portrayed Ms. Liberty with one bare breast exposed. The American people were so outraged that the coin was redesigned later in 1917 with Liberty encased in a suit of armor.

Most art critics agree that the controversy surrounding the Standing Liberty Quarter was unwarranted. However, some very recent coins and notes featuring nudity have been soundly criticized by artists as well as the general public, and probably with just cause. Two of the most blatant examples are the series of coins and notes issued by Cook Islands since the 1970s. Crown-size coins, introduced in 1972, show Tangaroa[q.v.], the Polynesian god of creation and fertility, in a very provocative profile. He also appears in full frontal nudity on $3 notes first issued in the early 1990s. The back of the notes shows a naked maiden riding a shark. Cook Islands has generated a sizable profit by "selling" many thousands of these coins and notes to the outside world. Yet many people question the ethics of producing what is generally regarded as numismatic pornography.

Nueva Zelanda; **Nueva Zelandia** [*Span.*] New Zealand.

nueve [*Span.*] nine.

nuevo [*Span.*] new.

nul [*Dan., Dut.*] zero.

null [*Nor.*] zero.

Null (*f.*) [*Ger.*] zero.

număr (*n.*) [*Rom.*] number.

număr de serie (*n.*) [*Rom.*] serial number.

numer (*m.*) [*Pol.*] number.

numéraire de nécessité; **numéraire d'urgence** [*Fr.*] emergency currency.

numerals, letters used as See *gematria*.

numerar (*n.*) [*Rom.*] cash (ready money).

numero (*m.*) [*Ital.*]; [*Finn.*] number.

número (*m.*) [*Span., Port.*] number.

numéro (*m.*) [*Fr.*] number.

número de serie [*Span.*] serial number.

número de série [*Port.*] serial number.

nudity on paper money: Tangaroa, the Polynesian god of creation and fertility

numéro de série [*Fr.*] serial number.

numero di serie (*m.*) [*Ital.*] serial number.

numismaat (*m.-c.*) [*Dut.*] numismatist.

numismaattinen [*Finn.*] numismatic.

numismata (*m.*) [*Port.*] numismatist.

numismate (*m.*) [*Fr.*] numismatist.

numismati נוּמִיסְמָטִי [*Heb.*] numismatic.

numismatica (*f.*) [*Ital.*] numismatics.

numismática (*f.*) [*Span., Port.*] numismatics.

numismatico [*Ital.*] (*adj.*) numismatic; (*m.*) numismatist.

numismático [*Span., Port.*] (*adj.*) numismatic; (*m.*) numismatist.

numismatics The examination and study of coins, banknotes, medals, tokens, and primitive forms of money. In the strictest sense, the word has no commercial connotation. An investor who does not study coins is not a true numismatist, but someone who researches coins, notes, and the like but without actually collecting them can claim the title.

This word was derived from *nomisma* (νόμισμα), the Greek word for *coin* or *currency*.

Numismatic Society of Ireland The Numismatic Society of Ireland was founded in Dublin in 1961, the object being to promote interest in the study of coins, medals, tokens, and currency, particularly those relating to Ireland. A branch of the Society was formed in Belfast in 1963.

In conjunction with the Northern Branch, the Society publishes its *Occasional Papers* and a members' *Bulletin*, both of which are distributed free to members.

For membership information, contact the Hon. Secretary, Numismatic Society of Ireland, St. Heliers, Stillorgan Park, Blackrock, Co. Dublin, Ireland.

numismatiek (*f.-c.*) [*Dut.*] numismatics.

numismatiikka [*Finn.*] numismatics.

numismatik (*c.*) [*Dan.*]; (*r.*) [*Swed.*] numismatics; (*adj.*) [*Turk.*] numismatic.

nümismatik [*Turk.*] numismatics.

Numismatik (*f.*) [*Ger.*] numismatics.

numismatikah נוּמִיסְמָטִיקָה (*f.*) [*Heb.*] numismatics.

numismatiker (*m./f.*) [*Swed.*]; (*c.*) [*Dan.*]; (*m.*) [*Nor.*] numismatist; coin collector.

Numismatiker (*m.*) [*Ger.*] numismatist.

numismatikk (*m.*) [*Nor.*] numismatics.

numismatique [*Fr.*] (*f.*) numismatics; (*adj.*) numismatic.

numismatisch (*adj.*) [*Ger., Dut.*] numismatic.

Numismatist, The Official journal of the American Numismatic Association. It first appeared in the fall of 1888 as a simple four-page leaflet, but has since grown to become a first-class professional journal.

Its creator was Dr. George F. Heath, a respected collector and part-time dealer from Monroe, Michigan, He devised the publication as an advertising medium to further his own professional numismatic activities.

The first issue, dated September-October of 1888, was titled *The American Numismatist* and was judiciously listed as Volume 1, Number 1. The November-December issue was shortened to *The Numismatist*, the title that has remained to this day.

Dr. Heath founded the American Numismatic Association in 1891, but wanted a publication known as *Plain Talk* to be its official organ rather than his beloved *Numismatist*. But Charles T. Tatman, *Plain Talk*'s publisher, failed to adequately pursue the endeavor, thereby causing *The Numismatist* to attach itself to the A.N.A. despite Dr. Heath's desires. Thus began a marriage which has lasted more than a century. Only during a few years in the 1890s has there been a separation.

Upon Dr. Heath's death in 1908, his heirs sold the publication to A.N.A. President Farran Zerbe. Three years later, the A.N.A. acquired ownership of the journal through the generosity of W. C. C. Wilson, a philanthropist from Montreal. *The Numismatist* has remained an A.N.A. property ever since.

The journal's format has been revised and expanded several times during its first century. The most recent change came in January 1988 when its dimensions were modified to give the work a more contemporary look.

[Q. David Bowers, "Plain Talk About *The Numismatist*," *The Numismatist*, October 1988, pp. 1732-38.]

numizmatika [*Hun.*] numismatics.

numizmatikai *(adj.)* [*Hun.*] numismatic.

numizmatyczny *(adj.)* [*Pol.*] numismatic.

numizmatyk *(m.)* [*Pol.*] numismatist; coin collector.

numizmatyka *(f.)* [*Pol.*] numismatics.

nummer *(n.)* [*Nor., Dan., Swed.*] number.

Nuova Zelanda [*Ital.*] New Zealand.

nuovo [*Ital.*] new.

nur einseitig geprägt [*Ger.*] uniface.

ny [*Nor., Dan., Swed.*] new.

Nya Zeeland [*Swed.*] New Zealand.

nyelv [*Hun.*] language.

nyomtatni *(v.)* [*Hun.*] to print.

nyprägling *(r.)* [*Swed.*] a restrike.

nypregning *(m.)* [*Nor.*] a restrike.

Nyugat-Németország [*Hun.*] West Germany (B.R.D.).

nyugta [*Hun.*] receipt.

O o

OB. [*abbr. from Lat.*] *obryza* or *obryziacum aurum*, referring to refined gold.

obca waluta (*f.*) [*Pol.*] foreign currency.

obieg (*m.*) [*Pol.*] circulation.

obiegowy [*Pol.*] circulated.

oblężniczy [*Pol.*] obsidional.

obligasjon (*m.*) [*Nor.*] (commercial) bond.

obligatie (*f.-c.*) [*Dut.*] (commercial) bond.

oblitération (*f.*) [*Fr.*] cancellation.

oblitération au poinçon [*Fr.*] punch cancellation.

oblitération par coupure [*Fr.*] cut cancellation.

obol One of the basic units of the silver coinage system of ancient Greece. Six obols equaled one drachm.

obryziacum aurum [*from Lat.*] refined gold. The abbreviation *OB* is sometimes found in the exergue of late Roman coins.

obrzeże (*n.*) [*Pol.*] edge (of a coin or medal).

obsidional (*adj.*) Money issued by towns or cities under attack. Most of these *siege pieces* were struck during the late Middle Ages, but some came as late as the nineteenth century. Their purpose was to enable commerce to continue even during the siege.

obverse Usually but not always the "heads" side of a coin. It is the primary side showing the ruler or some symbolic device, and it gives certain key information such as the country of issue.

In the United States, the obverse is defined by federal law. Most key information (denomination, name of the issuing country, etc.) is on the reverse. In some Latin American countries such as Mexico, the obverse is the side showing the nation's emblem. Therefore, in Mexico, effigies appear on the reverse.

In many European languages, the slang terms for "obverse" and "reverse" translate to "face" and "cross" (*cara* and *cruz* in Spanish, for example), because so many coins of the Middle Ages showed the reigning (or recent) monarch on the obverse and a cross on the reverse.

The equivalent term for paper money is *face*, and the reverse is called the *back*.

ocirkulerad [*Swed.*] uncirculated.

odcinek (*m.*) [*Pol.*] exergue.

odlewać (*v.*) [*Pol.*] to cast.

odmiana (*f.*) [*Pol.*] variety.

odznaczenie wojskowe (*n.*) [*Pol.*] military decoration.

oferta (*f.*) [*Span., Pol., Port.*] an offer, bid.

ofertă (*f.*) [*Rom.*] offer.

oferta cenowa (*f.*) [*Pol.*] (auction) bid.

ofertă de rezervă (pentru protecție) (*f.*) [*Rom.*] protective reserve bid.

oferta de salida (*f.*) [*Span.*] minimum bid.

oferta mínima (*f.*) [*Port.*] minimum bid.

oferta recomendada (*f.*) [*Span.*] suggested bid.

oferta sugerida (*f.*) [*Port.*] suggested bid.

off-center U.S. cent and nickel

off-center In the coinage process, if the collar fails to rise and retain the blank, and if the blank happens to fall on the center of the die, a broadstrike results. However, if the blank falls partially on the die, only part of the coin is struck. An off-center coin can be off by as little as one or two percent or as much as ninety-nine percent. Generally speaking, part

of the design or lettering is missing from one or both sides. This is different from misaligned dies which result in one side of the coin being almost perfectly centered and the other side appearing to be off-center.

[Contributed by Coleman Ezkovich.]

offerta (*f.*) [*Ital.*] an offer.

offerta (ad un'asta) (*f.*) [*Ital.*] (auction) bid.

offerta indicativa (*f.*) [*Ital.*] suggested bid.

offerta minima (*f.*) [*Ital.*] minimum bid.

offerta minima di riserva [*Ital.*] protective reserve bid.

offerta suggerita (*f.*) [*Ital.*] suggested bid.

offerte illimitate sono proibite [*Ital.*] no unlimited bids accepted.

official melt see *melt, official.*

offre (*f.*) [*Fr.*] an offer; (auction) bid.

offre minimum (*f.*) [*Fr.*] minimum bid.

offrire in vendita (*v.*) [*Ital.*] to offer.

ofullständig [*Swed.*] incomplete.

oikea [*Finn.*] right (direction or position).

okänd [*Swed.*] unknown.

okolicznościowy (*adj.*) [*Pol.*] commemorative.

ókori [*Hun.*] ancient.

okrągły [*Pol.*] round.

Olanda [*Ital., Rom.*] Holland, Netherlands.

Olaszország [*Hun.*] Italy.

Old Coppernose Nickname given to King Henry VIII of England because of the way his portrait degenerated on certain coins. In need of money, he concocted a method of inflicting a "hidden tax" on his subjects by debasing the silver testoons, which were major circulating coins of the time and which bore his effigy. He reduced the percentage of silver and increased the percentage of copper in these coins to such a degree that they contained less than 50% pure silver, an alloy known as *billon*[q.v.]. Because of the way billon coins are manufactured, they tend to have a shiny silver appearance when they are freshly minted, but the silvery surface soon begins to wear off after the coins have been in circulation for only a short time. The coins start to take on a copper tone, with the highest points on the coins' design being the first to turn a brassy color.

Henry VIII discovered, to his chagrin, that one of the highest points on the testoon was his nose! It turned coppery almost immediately after the coins entered circulation, thereby not only embarrassing the king in a personal way but also exposing conclusively the debasement of the coinage.

[Richard G. Doty, *The Macmillan Encyclopedic Dictionary of Numismatics*, p. 49.]

olimiterade bud accepteras ej [*Swed.*] no unlimited bids accepted.

omioma ομοίωμα (*n.*) [*Grk.*] effigy.

omløb (*n.*) [*Dan.*] circulation.

omloop (*m.-c.*) [*Dut.*] circulation.

omologia ομολογία (*f.*) [*Grk.*] (commercial) bond.

omote 表 [*Jpn.*] obverse.

on [*Turk.*] ten.

onbekend [*Dut.*] unknown.

onça (*f.*) [*Port.*] ounce.

once [*Span.*] eleven; (*f.*) [*Fr.*] ounce.

oncia (*f.*) [*Ital.*] ounce.

önerilen fiat [*Turk.*] suggested bid.

ongecirculeerd [*Dut.*] uncirculated.

ongedekt papiergeld (*n.*) [*Dut.*] fiat money.

ongepubliceerd [*Dut.*] unpublished.

ön ödeme [*Turk.*] prepayment.

onofficieel [*Dut.*] unofficial.

onomastiki aksia ονομαστική αξία (*f.*) [*Grk.*] face value.

ons [*Turk.*]; (*n.*) [*Dut.*] ounce.

ontwerp (*n.*) [*Dut.*] design.

onuitgegeven [*Dut.*] not issued.

ön yüz [*Turk.*] obverse.

onza (*f.*) [*Span.*] ounce.

Oost-Duitsland [*Dut.*] East Germany (D.D.R.).

Oostenrijk [*Dut.*] Austria.

opbevaringsslid (*n.*) [*Dan.*] cabinet friction.

op de achterkant; op de achterzijde [*Dut.*] on the back.

opdruk (*m.-c.*) [*Dut.*] overprint.

opgæld (*c.*) [*Dan.*] seigniorage.

opłata (*f.*) [*Pol.*] fee.

opschrift (*n.*) [*Dut.*] motto.

opsidiano οψιδιανό [*Grk.*] obsidional.

opublicerad [*Swed.*] unpublished (not listed in any book or catalogue).

op zicht [*Dut.*] on approval.

or (*m.*) [*Fr.*] gold.

Orden (*m.*) [*Ger.*] decoration; distinctive medal.

order see *fraternal order*.

ordreseddel (*m.*) [*Nor.*] order form.

orichalcum A light-colored copper alloy used in a number of Roman sestertii. In most cases it consists of copper alloyed with 10% or more of tin or lead.

Oriental Numismatic Society The aims of the Society are to promote the systematic study of the coins, medals, and currency, both ancient and modern, of India, the Far East, the Islamic countries, and their non-Western predecessors. The Society was founded in 1970, and its membership of some 600 people are spread over 46 countries.

Membership is individual. It is open to anyone with a genuine interest in the numismatic series of any of these areas, but it is not open to companies or organizations.

The activities of the Society are financed by an Initial Subscription and an Annual Subscription, the amounts being calculated to cover the expected costs of each year's operations. The Annual Subscription if due on each anniversary of the member's admission to the Society. Donations to a specific cause or publication are welcome.

For membership information, contact the Oriental Numismatic Society, 30 Warren Road, Woodley, Reading, Berks. RG5 3AR United Kingdom.

origami Japanese art of paper folding. Its numismatic application lies in folding pieces of paper money into intricate designs or in folding large numbers of notes in such a way that they can be assembled into a lovely mosaic. Ideally, of course, the notes are not cut in any way; they remain undamaged and could be unfolded and spent.

[Marion Muller, "Folding Money," *The Numismatist*, February 1988, pp. 254-260; Cyril Tessier, "How Do I Fold Thee? Let Me Count the Ways," *The Numismatist*, September 1988, p. 1523.]

Ormonde money Emergency coins issued in 1643 and 1644 by the Lords Justices at Dublin who sided with Charles I during the Great Rebellion. To show their allegiance to him, they stamped the coins with the crowned monogram "CR" (the "R" meaning *rex*, the Latin word for "king"). The coins were named after the Lord of Ormonde who was appointed Lieutenant of Ireland in 1643.

Ormonde crown

Ormonde money consisted of crude silver coins in the denominations of twopence, threepence, groat (4d), sixpence, shilling, halfcrown, and crown. The coin in the illustration is an Ormonde crown. The large "V" on the reverse is the roman numeral for five, indicating that the coin had the standard crown value of five shillings.

Also see *Blacksmith's halfcrown*, *Dublin money*, and *Inchiquin money*.

[Peter Seaby & P. Frank Purvey, *Coins of Scotland, Ireland & the Islands* (Seaby), pp. 143-47.]

örn (*r.*) [*Swed.*] eagle.

ørn (*c.*) [*Dan.*]; (*m.*) [*Nor.*] eagle.

oro (*m.*) [*Span., Ital.*] gold.

oroide An alloy of copper and tin with enough tin to yield a distinct golden color (hence the name, since the word *oro* means "gold" in Spanish). It was used in some United States pattern coins of 1854-55.

Oroszország [*Hun.*] Russia.

Ortiz de Domínguez, Josefa [a.k.a., *La Corregidora*.] see *Josefina*.

oryol орел (*m.*) [*Srb., Bul.*]; орёл (*m.*) [*Russ.*] eagle.

orzel (*m.*) [*Pol.*] eagle.

Osborne Coinage Company Oldest private mint in the United States. Established in 1835 in Cincinnati, Ohio, as the Z. Bisbee Company, it has been in continuous operation since its inception.

Osborne's first products were trade checks, but it ultimately expanded its production line to

include a wide range of transportation tokens, advertising pieces, coal mine scrip[q.v.] tokens, and even the 5 billion blue and red food ration tokens used in the United States during World War II. Some of the well-known Civil War tokens[q.v.] came from this facility. The firm also produced campaign medals for nine American presidential candidates, including the 1860 medals for Abraham Lincoln.

Two of the company's most popular current products are the Presidential Series medals, depicting all U.S. presidents and issued since the 1930s, and the Zodiac Series of 12 medals.

[Paul Gilkes, "Cincinnati's Osborne Oldest Private Mint," *Coin World*, January 31, 1990, pp. 115-9.]

oscuro [*Span.*] dark.

osef אֹסֶף (*m.*) [*Heb.*] collection.

ossidazione (*f.*) [*Ital.*] tarnish, oxidation.

ossidionale [*Ital.*] obsidional; reference to seige money.

összeg [*Hun.*] amount.

ostaa (*v.*) [*Finn.*] to buy.

ostaja [*Finn.*] buyer.

ostemplowanie (*n.*) [*Pol.*] cancellation.

Österreich [*Ger.*] Austria.

Østerrike [*Nor.*] Austria.

Österrike [*Swed.*] Austria.

Østrig [*Dan.*] Austria.

ostromlott városban forgalomba hozott pénz [*Hun.*] obsidional.

Östtyskland [*Swed.*] East Germany (D.D.R.).

Østtyskland [*Dan.*] East Germany.

Øst-Tyskland [*Nor.*] East Germany.

osztály [*Hun.*] grade, condition.

osztályozás [*Hun.*] classification.

osztályozni (*v.*) [*Hun.*] to classify; to grade.

öt [*Hun.*] five.

ottone (*m.*) [*Ital.*] brass.

ötven [*Hun.*] fifty.

ötvözet [*Hun.*] alloy (of metals).

otwór (*m.*) [*Pol.*] hole.

oud [*Dut.*] old; ancient.

ouggia ουγγιά [*Grk.*] ounce.

ouro (*m.*) [*Port.*] gold.

overstrike A previously-minted coin which is struck at a later time by a different set of dies in order to produce an entirely new coin. The original coin is called the *host* coin. The design

on the host coin prior to the overstriking is referred to as the *undertype*, and the new design which is overstruck is known as the *overtype*.

Overstrikes have been very uncommon in the twentieth century. Occasionally overstrikes are created when finished coins accidentally go through the stamping machine a second time. The resulting coins are called *errors* and are not made this way intentionally.

The term *overstrike* is usually reserved for those coins which have been stamped a second time on purpose. This practice was common from ancient times through the nineteenth century and was done for a variety of reasons. Coins issued by an overthrown ruler were sometimes overstruck as a simple and useful way of destroying them. Coins confiscated in war could be easily and quickly overstruck to provide new coins for the victors.

Some governments overstruck their own coins as a way of updating them. The Spanish copper *maravedí* shown in color on page 310 was overstruck as a means of devaluing it, a move necessary due to the maravedí's drop in value. One side of the illustrated coin shows its original date of 1622, and the other side gives the overstruck date of 1641.

For whatever the need, coins were generally overstruck because this method was faster, easier, and cheaper than melting the old coins and making new planchets. Probably the most famous incidence of this occurred in 1804 in England resulting from the financial crisis caused by the Napoleonic Wars. The Royal Mint overstruck many silver Spanish-American 8-real coins with new dies to create the Bank of England dollars. Although the mint made an effort to obliterate the original design prior to overstriking, some of the undertype usually can be seen on these pieces.

[Richard G. Doty, *The Macmillan Encyclopedic Dictionary of Numismatics*, pp. 242-243.]

övertryck (*n.*) [*Swed.*] overprint.

overtryk (*n.*) [*Dan.*] overprint.

overtrykk (*n.*) [*Nor.*] overprint.

ovpt. [*abbr.*] overprint.

oz. [*abbr.*] ounce.

P p

päällystetty raha [*Finn.*] clad coinage.

paavi [*Finn.*] pope.

på bagsiden [*Dan.*] on the back.

padrão (*f.*) [*Port.*] pattern.

pagamento antecipado (*m.*) [*Port.*] prepayment.

pagamento anticipato (*m.*) [*Ital.*] prepayment.

pagbaba ng halaga [*Tag.*] devaluation.

pagmomoneda [*Tag.*] coinage.

pago adelantado (*m.*) [*Span.*] prepayment.

paiement anticipé (*m.*) [*Fr.*] prepayment.

paiements par carte de crédit acceptés [*Fr.*] credit cards accepted.

paikallisseteli [*Finn.*] scrip.

pài mài 拍卖 [*Chin.-py./sc.*] auction.

painaa (*v.*) [*Finn.*] to print.

painter coin Popular name of the 1987 Portuguese commemorative 100-escudo coin honoring the centennial of the birth of Amadeo de Souza-Cardoso, regarded as a pioneer of modern European art. Despite the stated date, the coins were actually struck in 1989.

["Portuguese Commemorative Honors Painter's Birth," *Coin World*, January 24, 1990, p. 50.]

País de Gales [*Port.*] Wales.

Países Bajos [*Span.*] Netherlands, Holland.

paksu erikoislyönti [*Finn.*] piéfort, piedfort.

palaganapin [*Tag.*] circulated.

pale gold Common term for electrum[*q.v.*], a mix of approximately three parts gold and one part silver as found in Nature. The first coins were made of this alloy around 620-600 B.C. in Asia Minor. Also known as *white gold*.

palindrome A word or number which reads the same forward or backward, such as the number 85266258. Some collectors of paper money save banknotes with palindrome serial numbers. These notes are usually referred to as *radar notes*.

palios παλιός [*Grk.*] old.

pålydende (*n.*) [*Nor.*] denomination.

pålydende verdi [*Nor.*] face value.

pamiątkowy (*adj.*) [*Pol.*] commemorative.

pananalapi [*Tag.*] currency.

pananalapi ng ibang bansa [*Tag.*] foreign currency.

pankki [*Finn.*] bank.

papa [*Turk., Tag.*]; (*m.*) [*Ital., Span., Port.*] pope (of the Roman Catholic Church).

papă (*m.*) [*Rom.*] pope.

papas πάπας (*m.*) [*Grk.*] pope.

pape (*m.*) [*Fr.*] pope.

på prøve [*Nor., Dan.*] on approval.

papel (*m.*) [*Span., Port.*] paper.

papel-moeda (*m.*) [*Port.*] paper money.

papel moneda [*Span.*] paper money.

paperiraha [*Finn.*] paper money.

papier (*m.*) [*Fr., Pol.*] paper.

papiergeld (*n.*) [*Dut.*] paper money.

Papiergeld (*n.*) [*Ger.*] paper money.

papier-monnaie (*m.*) [*Fr.*] paper money.

papier wartościowy (*m.*) [*Pol.*] (commercial) bond; certificate.

papież (*m.*) [*Pol.*] pope.

papir (*n.*) [*Nor., Dan.*] paper.

papír [*Hun.*] paper.

papirpenger (*m.pl.*) [*Nor.*] paper money.

papírpénz [*Hun.*] paper money.

pappersvaluta (*r.*) [*Swed.*] fiat money.

Papst (*m.*) [*Ger.*] pope.

para [*Turk.*] coinage; money; currency; cash (ready money).

para birimi [*Turk.*] monetary unit.

paracharagmeno παραχαραγμένο [*Grk.*] misstruck.

paracharaksi παραχάραξη (*f.*) [*Grk.*] a misstrike.

paracharasso παραχαράσσω (*v.*) [*Grk.*] to counterfeit.

paralarla ilgili; paraya ait [*Turk.*] monetary.

paranın değerini düşürmek [*Turk.*] demonetization.

para sistemi [*Turk.*] monetary system.

páratlan [*Hun.*] unique.

på reversen [*Swed.*] on the back.

parfait [*Fr.*] perfect, flawless.

parit פְּרִיט (*m.*) [*Heb.*] (auction) lot.

parte inferior (*f.*) [*Span.*] bottom.

parte superior (*f.*) [*Span.*] top.

parti (*n.*) [*Nor.*] (auction) lot.

particulier geld (*n.*) [*Dut.*] scrip.

parvis sammenstilt [*Nor.*] accolated[q.v.], conjoined, jugate.

pase kä darär पासे का दरार [*Hin.*] die break.

Pass and Stow, Philada., MDCCLIII Pass and Stow is the name of the firm that recast the Liberty Bell after it cracked while being tested for tone. The roman numeral (1753) refers to the year it was recast.

This phrase can be seen immediately above the upper terminus of the crack on the Liberty Bell as it appears on the reverse of the Franklin Half Dollar[q.v.] (1948-63). The Philadelphia Assembly had ordered the inscription to be placed on the bell as a courtesy to Pass and Stow.

[Clifford Mishler, *Coins: Questions and Answers*, p. 76.]

passive Metallic object covered with a fine layer of tarnish which protects the metal from further oxidation. One example is the very thin layer of aluminum oxide which forms on the surface of aluminum coins.

Unprotected metal is known as *active*[q.v.].

pastilă monetară (*f.*) [*Rom.*] planchet.

pată (*f.*) [*Rom.*] stain.

patina Corrosion, usually green in color, often seen on ancient bronze coins as well as on other objects of art. It is an adhering film of oxidized material which cannot be removed without doing substantial damage to the coin. In particular, coins which have had patina removed tend to show surface pitting. Depending on the degree and nature of the corrosion, patina can either diminish or enhance the beauty of a bronze coin.

pătrat [*Rom.*] square.

pătrime (*f.*) [*Rom.*] a fourth, quarter.

patru [*Rom.*] four.

patruzeci [*Rom.*] forty.

pàtryk (*n.*) [*Dan.*] overprint.

Paul VI [né *Giovanni Battista Montini.*] Pope of the Roman Catholic Church (1963-78). Born September 26, 1897, in Concessio, Italy; died August 6, 1978, at Castel Gandolfo.

Pope Paul VI was the son of a well-to-do, middle-class newspaper editor, banker, and member of Parliament. After training at Milan and Georgian University in Rome, Montini was ordained to the priesthood in May 1920. His work from 1923 until 1932 was in the Secretariat of State working closely with Eugenio Pacelli, the future Pius XII. In 1937, Montini was promoted to the position of *sostituto* (Under-Secretary of State). Pope Pius confirmed him in this position as one of Pius's first acts as pope. This was the beginning of a close relationship between the two which lasted until 1954.

In 1954, Montini was appointed Archbishop of Milan which signified a break with Pius XII after twenty-five years of cooperation. The reason for the break is unknown. In Milan, he undertook visits to all of his 912 parishes, established some 100 new churches, and a Diocesan Office for Social and Pastoral action. His vital pastoral experience as Archbishop of Milan eventually resulted in his election to the Papacy.

Prior to the enclave of cardinals following the death of Pope John XXIII, Montini made his own position quite clear that the initiatives of Pope John XXIII must be followed up. On the morning of July 21, 1963, Montini was presented to Rome and to the world as Paul VI. His realistic, objective approach followed the deeply human sympathetic approach of Pope John XXIII. Pope Paul declared that the Roman Curia needed to be adapted to the modern age. To look critically at an institution with which one is so closely related requires much courage, honesty, and independence of thought— virtues which he possessed in great abundance.

Pope Paul VI appears on a wide range of Vatican type coins. Among the more unusual

coins of his papacy are the undated F.A.O. coins struck in 1968 for the United Nations Food and Agriculture Organization.

[Contributed by Ruth Ann Davis. Eric John (editor), *The Popes: A Concise Biographical History*.]

pa'und לִטְרָה (*f.*) [*Heb.*] pound (unit of weight).

paus (*m.-c.*) [*Dut.*] pope.

pave (*c.*) [*Dan.*]; (*m.*) [*Nor.*] pope.

påve (*m.*) [*Swed.*] pope.

paymenten [*Dut.*] small change, i.e., minor coins.

Pays Bas [*Fr.*] Holland, Netherlands.

Pays de Galles [*Fr.*] Wales.

P.C. [*Span. abbr.*] precaria conservación. Grade of banknotes approximating Good. The note has tears, folds, patches, etc., but the date, series, and serial number are legible.

Peace Dollar

Peace Dollar Type of United States silver dollar issued from 1921-1928 and 1934-1935.

The birth of the Peace Dollar resulted from two occurrences, both involving World War I. The first, the passage of the Pittman Act of 1918, was an attempt on the part of the United States to help Great Britain control war-induced inflation and the hoarding of silver in India, then a British possession. The Pittman Act enabled the U.S. to melt great numbers of dollar coins and to use that silver to flood the Indian silver market, thereby deflating the price of silver. Additional silver was to be purchased from U.S. mines and used in the minting of new dollars.

Silver dollars had been minted sporadically from 1794 to 1904, but the coins had never really been popular, especially in the eastern portion of the country. Cartwheels, as they were called, were discontinued in 1904 because so many millions of them were sitting in bank vaults collecting dust. If their importance had only been as a circulating medium of exchange, there would have been no need to replace the ones that were melted due to the provisions of the Pittman Act. However, these coins also provided the backing for the silver certificates which accounted for the bulk of the lower-denomination notes in circulation. For every silver dollar that was melted, a silver certificate had to be retired. Part of the problem was alleviated by issuing Federal Reserve Bank notes denominated at one and two dollars. Nevertheless, a sizable number of new silver dollars did have to be struck.

The Pittman Act made no mention of coin design, leaving the assumption that the Morgan Liberty Head used from 1878 to 1904 would be retained. When the first of these dollars rolled from the presses in 1921, the Morgan design was preserved. A total of more than 85 million silver dollars with this motif were produced at the three mints.

The second of the afore-mentioned occurrences was the declaration of peace between the United States and Germany at the conclusion of the war. There was strong popular support for a commemorative coin honoring this peace, which incidentally, did not formally transpire until 1921. The American Numismatic Association went one step further by passing a resolution at its 1920 convention urging that the new silver dollars be the vehicle for this commemoration.

The A.N.A. got its wish, although the finished coins were not at all what anyone expected. Instead of a stereotypical commemorative design, the new dollars exhibited the same devices as regular issue coins but with the addition of the single word "PEACE" at the bottom of the reverse. The coin was designed by Anthony de Francisci, who used his wife as the model for the stylized representation of Liberty on the obverse.

Slightly more than a million Peace Dollars were issued in 1921. These first pieces were struck in unusually high relief, a characteristic that caused the coins not to stack well. The relief was lowered in the 1922 and subsequent issues.

An attempt was made to revive the Peace Dollars in 1964. The Denver Mint produced 316,076 of the dollars before the plan was abandoned. Although official records indicate that all of these coins were melted, unsubstantiated rumors persist that a few escaped the melting pot. Anyone possessing such coins would be doing so illegally, and the pieces could be confiscated by the F.B.I. if they remained within U.S. territory.

[David W. Lange, "Examining the Peace Dollar Series," *The Numismatist*, October 1988, pp. 1767-70; R. S. Yeoman, *A Guide Book of United States Coins* (44th Ed.), pp. 158-9.]

Pearl Black Crown Coin with the denomination of one crown issued in 1990 by the Isle of Man to commemorate the 150th anniversary of the emission of the British *Penny Black* stamp, the world's first adhesive, prepaid postage stamp. The coins were struck by the Pobjoy Mint which developed a special black satin finish that it applied to the background areas of the coin to give the stamp design the appearance of black ink on paper as the original stamp had looked when it was issued in 1840. Never before had this Pearl Black coloration been used on a coin.

The Isle of Man authorized the mint to strike an unlimited number of uncirculated copper-nickel coins, plus 50,000 proof specimen pieces in copper-nickel, and 30,000 sterling silver proof crowns. All of these pieces exhibit the Pearl Black backgrounds. Additionally, a limited number of presentation pieces in gold and platinum were offered, but these are completely metallic in color and do not include the Pearl Black coloration.

See page 308 for color illustration.

["Isle of Man: Pearl Black Crown Bridges Numismatics and Philately," *The Numismatist*, October 1990, pp. 1554-6.]

pecete (*f.*) [*Rom.*] seal.

pedido (*m.*) [*Span.*] order form.

pedigree A complete list of all former and present owners of a numismatic item (including books or journals). When a piece is extremely rare but not unique, a pedigree or partial pedigree reference is often used to pinpoint which specific specimen is under discussion (e.g., "from the Col. Green collection" or "Farouk specimen").

Most collectors only care about the pedigrees of items which are exceedingly scarce or expensive, unless a more common piece was previously owned by a famous person.

Pegasus

Pegasus According to Greek mythology, Pegasus was a winged horse which sprang from the blood of Medusa, the Gorgon, when Perseus cut off her head with magic weapons given to him by the gods. Bellerophon rode Pegasus when he fought against the chimaera. The winged horse symbolizes the power of natural forces to convert evil into good.

Pegasus is featured on some ancient Greek coins, most notably staters of Corinth.

pęknięcie stempla (*n.*) [*Pol.*] die break.

pembuatan wang logam [*Indo.*] coinage.

pengar (*r.pl.*) [*Swed.*] money.

penge (*pl.*) [*Dan.*] money.

pengeanvisning (*m.*) [*Nor.*] money order.

pengeerstatning (*m.*) [*Nor.*] scrip.

penger (*m.pl.*) [*Nor.*] money.

pengeseddel (*c.*) [*Dan.*]; (*m.*) [*Nor.*] note, banknote.

pengesystem (*n.*) [*Nor.*] monetary system.

penge uden guldværdi (*pl.*) [*Dan.*] literally, "money without gold value"; known in English as *fiat money*.

pengumpul wang logam [*Indo.*] coin collector; numismatist.

peninta πενήντα [*Grk.*] fifty.

penning (*m.-c.*) [*Dut.*] medal. This word can also be attached to the end of other words to create specific types of tokens, such as *telefoonpenning* for *telephone token*.

penningkunde (*f.-c.*) [*Dut.*] numismatics; coin collecting.

penningstempel (*m.-c.*) [*Dut.*] coinage die.

English "Long Cross" silver penny of Henry III (1247-72)

penny [pl.: *pence* or *pennies*, depending on usage.] Primary coin of England from the late eighth century A.D. until the beginning of the fourteenth century. In today's world, it is a minor denomination used at one time or another in Australia, Bahamas, Barbados, Bermuda, British West Africa, Falkland Islands, Fiji, Gambia, Ghana, Great Britain, Guernsey, Ireland, Isle of Man, Jamaica, Jersey, Malawi, New Brunswick, New Guinea, New Zealand, Nigeria, Rhodesian & Nyasaland, St. Helena & Ascension, Sierra Leone, South Africa, Southern Rhodesia, Trinidad & Tobago, Tristan da Cunha, Zambia, and Zimbabwe.

The word *penny* is assumed to be derived from *denarius*, a popular silver coin of ancient Rome. Because of this derivation, the abbreviation for the traditional penny has been *d.* instead of *p.* (as in the Sterling designations £.*s.d.*).

The first English pennies were presumably struck by Offa, king of Mercia, around 755-780, although pennies are known to have been minted by Heaberht and Ecgberht, two kings of Kent, at around the same time. All of these coins were tiny pieces of silver, slightly smaller than the modern cent.

Coins of this type were an instant success, not only in England but throughout Europe. By the year 1000 much of Western Europe had developed its own silver coins similar in size and type to the penny, and most had names derived from the denarius (e.g., *denier* of France, *dinero* of Spain, *denaro* of Italy, etc.). The various coins were so popular and so interchangeable that by the mid-14th century, England was forced to redesign its entire coinage output to remove the foreign coins from circulation.

The penny became the standard unit of currency in Scotland and was the only denomination struck from around 1136 (under the rule of King David I) until the 1280s when Alexander III issued halfpennies and farthings. The penny continued to be the primary coin of Scotland until 1513. Part of the penny's popularity in Scotland was undoubtedly due to the existence of silver mines, which gave Scottish rulers an abundance of that metal for coinage purposes.

With some modifications, the penny continued to be struck in silver until the end of the eighteenth century. Its fractional components, the farthing[*q.v.*] (quarter penny) and halfpenny, had originally been minted in silver, but those coins had been switched over to copper by the seventeenth century. A gold penny was attempted by Henry III in 1257, but it was discontinued after only a few years.

Henry III was also responsible for a major design change. In 1247 he introduced what are now called the *Long Cross* coins, so named because the four arms of the cross on the reverse extend all the way to the edge to discourage clipping, a common practice of the time.

The penny underwent an amazing change in 1797. A whole new type, made from a full ounce of copper, was introduced. Even more amazing, a twopence coin containing two full ounces of copper was presented at the same

time (see *cartwheel* for additional information and page 308 of the color section for an illustration). Both coins were manufactured by Matthew Boulton and James Watt in Birmingham, using their state-of-the-art minting machinery. Interesting though the coins were, they were also very cumbersome and much too large and heavy for normal circulation. Hence the types were soon abandoned.

1951 bronze penny of George VI

The pennies were reduced in size and weight in 1806 and 1807, but they were still more troublesome than the public could handle, and the coins soon slipped out of circulation. As a side note, there exists one single known specimen of the 1808 penny, making it one of the world's great numismatic rarities.

Penny production did not resume until 1825 during the reign of George IV. Penny production was somewhat sporadic until 1853, when it finally exceeded one million pieces. From then on, it was produced with greater regularity.

Part of the problem facing the penny at this time was the matter of production costs. Copper prices were climbing, and the coin was becoming less and less economical to mint. In 1860 the composition was changed to bronze.

The manufacturing of some pennies struck from 1874 to 1919 was farmed out to two private firms, the Heaton Mint (today known simply as *The Mint*) and Kings Norton Metal Company, Ltd. Pennies produced at these facilities exhibit the mintmarks "H" and "KN" respectively.

Two very great rarities exist of twentieth century British pennies— the 1933 specimens, of which only six are presumed to have been struck (all intended for museum collections or building cornerstones), and the 1954 specimen, of which only one unique specimen is known to have survived.

Except for that one specimen, no pennies were issued from 1954 to 1960, because the Bank of England had an enormous surplus which it had to unload. Pennies dated 1953 would not have been minted, either, had it not been for Elizabeth II's coronation. Penny production resumed in 1961 and continued until 1967.

The following year the decision was made to adopt the decimal system. The final issuance of British pennies came in 1970 as part of the "Last Sterling" Proof Set.

The word *penny* is a common fixture in the United States and Canada, but it is only a slang term referring to the *cent* and is not an official denomination of either country.

[David Thompson, "Empire and penny linked— Britannia copper symbolized age," *Numismatic News*, January 2, 1996, pp. 64-66; Stephen Mitchell & Brian Reeds (editors), *Coins of England and the United Kingdom* (Seaby, 1991), p. 46; Peter Seaby & P. Frank Purvey, *Coins of Scotland, Ireland & the Islands* (Seaby), pp. 1-12.]

pennyweight Measure equal to 0.05 troy ounce or 24 grains. Abbreviated *dwt.* or *pwt.*

pente πέντε [*Grk.*] five.

pénz [*Hun.*] money.

pénzegység [*Hun.*] monetary unit.

pénzrendszer [*Hun.*] monetary system.

pénzügyi [*Hun.*] monetary.

pénzügyminiszter [*Hun.*] finance minister.

pénzverde [*Hun.*] mint.

pénzverés [*Hun.*] coinage.

pequeno [*Port.*] small, little.

pequeño [*Span.*] small, little.

pera [*Tag.*] money.

perak [*Indo.*] silver.

percetakan uang logam [*Indo.*] mint.

perełka (*f.*) [*Pol.*] bead (raised dot on the surface of a coin or medal).

perem [*Hun.*] edge; rim.

perfecto [*Span.*] perfect, flawless.

perfeito [*Port.*] perfect, flawless.

perikliomeno grammatosimo περικλειόμενο γραμματόσημο (*n.*) [*Grk.*] encased postage stamp (such as the type used in the United States in the 1860s as an emergency substitute for coins).

peringatan (*adj., noun*) [*Indo.*] commemorative.

perle (*f.*) [*Fr.*] pearl; bead (raised dot on the surface of a coin or medal).

Pérou [*Fr.*] Peru.

pers (*m.-c.*) [*Dut.*] (coinage) press.

perunggu [*Indo.*] copper.

peşin (*n.*) [*Rom.*] cash (ready money) [archaic term].

peso (*m.*) 1. [*Span., Ital., Port.*] weight.

2. Current or former unit of currency of Argentina, Cambodia, Chile, Colombia, Costa Rica, Cuba, Dominican Republic, Culion Island, Curaçao, El Salvador, Guatemala, Guinea-Bissau, Honduras, Mexico, Paraguay, Peru, Philippines, Puerto Rico, and Uruguay.

The silver Spanish-American *peso de a ocho* ("piece of eight") which circulated in the eighteenth century helped inspire the creation of the U.S. dollar in 1792.

Peter's pence 1. Prior to England's conversion to Protestantism, the head of every household was required to donate a penny to the papel see. This annual tribute became known as *Peter's pence.*

2. An annual cash contribution which Roman Catholics voluntarily make to the pope.

petit [*Fr.*] small.

pfennig 1. The German version of the French denier, English penny, or Spanish dinero. It was a small silver coin used from the tenth to the late thirteenth centuries. Later it was minted in copper and base metals.

2. Minor denomination introduced in 1948 in West Germany (B.D.R.) and now used in unified Germany. One hundred pfennig equal one Deutsche Mark.

Pfund (*n.*) [*Ger.*] pound (unit of weight).

Pfund Sterling (*n.*) [*Ger.*] pound Sterling (£).

phone card Popular name for a prepaid, opaque plastic card, about 54mm x 86mm, used to pay for a telephone call at any suitably equipped pay phone (British: coin box). While the conventional credit card, payable once a month after usage, continues to be the standard in the United States and Canada, around 100 other countries have already gone to the new prepaid phone cards, and further changeovers are expected. These colorful cards have become much sought after by collectors. In Japan alone, over a hundred thousand different phone cards have been produced, and the collecting fever there continues unabated.

[Contributed by Robert Doyle. S. E. R. Hiscocks, *The Stanley Gibbons Catalogue of Telephone Cards*, Stanley Gibbons Publications, England (1990); Note: the Hiscocks catalogue covers all countries except Japan.]

Phrygian cap Cloth head-piece originating in the ancient country of Phrygia, now part of Turkey. The cap was worn by freed slaves in Roman times to indicate their liberation.

During the French Revolution, the cap was adopted not only as a symbol of immolation (killing as a sacrifice) but also as a symbol of freedom. Americans continued this tradition by issuing a number of coins, revenue stamps, and various other official items portraying the personification of Liberty wearing a Phrygian cap and laurel wreath.

[J. E. Cirlot, *A Dictionary of Symbols* (2nd Ed.), 1983, Philosophical Library, New York, p. 254; *Funk & Wagnalls New Encyclopedia* (1984), Vol. 20, p. 407.]

piccolo [*Ital.*] small.

pidyon haben פִּדְיוֹן הַבֵּן [*Heb.*] literally, *Redemption of the son.*

A ceremony where a Jewish father symbolically redeems his first-born son from service in the Temple. The redemption is based on Biblical commandments (*Numbers 3:47-48 & 18:16*; *Exodus 13:13 & 34:20*), and takes place on the 31st day after birth, unless delayed by the Sabbath or festivals. The father gives a Cohen (descendant of the ancient priests) five shekalim (five "shekels") or 100 grams of pure silver, usually in the circulating coinage of the day.

The Israeli government issued special *pidyon haben* coins from 1970 to 1977. These were sold as individual coins and in sets of five with a scroll attesting to the coins' suitability for use in accordance with religious law. The 1970-74 coins were denominated 10 lirot, and

the 1975-77 coins were 25 lirot. In 1982, a pidyon haben medal was produced for the same purpose.

[Contributed by Simcha Kuritzky. "Israel Issues a New Pidyon Haben Medal," *The Shekel*, November-December 1982; Government of Israel, *Pidyon Haben Coin* (pamphlet); *Encyclopedia Judaica*, Vol. 6, p. 1306.]

1974 pidyon haben silver 10 lirot coin

pięć [*Pol.*] five.

pięćdziesiąt [*Pol.*] fifty.

pièce à métal emrobé [*Fr.*] clad coin.

pièce à motif concave [*Fr.*] brockage.

pièce au moulin [*Fr.*] milled coin.

pièce de monnaie (*f.*) [*Fr.*] coin.

pièce d'essai (*f.*) [*Fr.*] pattern.

pièce frappée au marteau; pièce martelée [*Fr.*] hammered coin.

piece of eight Popular name for the pillar dollar[*q.v.*], a Spanish-American coin struck from 1537 to 1772.

pieczęć (*f.*) [*Pol.*] seal (in the numismatic sense).

pied (*m.*) [*Fr.*] foot. The term *à pied*[*q.v.*] refers to the portrayed person on a coin or medal shown in a standing position.

piéfort; piedfort (*m.*) [*Fr.*] Literally, *strong foot*.

1. Specimen coin or medal struck on a planchet which is at least twice normal thickness. Although some are of copper or other base metals, the majority are struck in gold or silver.

The earliest piéforts are thought to have been minted in the late thirteenth century. Most came from Germany, Bohemia (now part of the Czech Republic), France, and England. They were produced sporadically throughout the late Middle Ages and well into Modern times.

Scholars are not certain as to why these pieces were minted, but there is great likelihood that they were not intended for general circulation. The piéforts may have been test pieces made by the master engravers to check the quality and style of their work. The pieces could then have been sent to other engravers and mint workers to demonstrate what the finished product was supposed to resemble. The very thickness of the piéforts would have precluded their being confused with other coins or trial pieces. Their unusual nature would have lessened their chances of being lost or stolen.

In more recent times, some pattern coins exhibiting new designs have been minted as piéforts. The 1907 U. S. $20 gold design struck on a planchet the diameter of a $10 gold piece but twice as thick is an oft-cited example. The U.S. Mint clearly wanted to introduce an extraordinary coin with the new St. Gaudens design and took great pains to produce numerous patterns and presentation pieces, such as the high relief specimens with the dates in Roman numerals. The piéforts were just one portion of this group.

2. Contemporary piéforts are usually nothing more than glorified commemorative coins targeted to the lucrative numismatic market. They are different only because they are struck on very thick planchets. The 1980s saw an upsurge in their popularity, as such numismatically-significant countries as Great Britain and France produced these pieces. On the one hand, the 1982 British 20p pieces were struck with the same designs as on the circulation coins of that denomination; on the other hand, the 1986 French silver crowns

commemorating the hundredth anniversary of the Statue of Liberty were coined with special dies not used for circulation strikes. In both cases, the coins were issued for marketing purposes rather than to deal with production necessities.

[L. A. Lawrence, "English Piedforts and Their Purposes," *British Numismatic Journal*, 16 (2nd Series, Vol. 6) 1924, pp. 113-117, as quoted in Doty, pp. 255-256.]

Piéfort-Münze (*f.*) [*Ger.*] piéfort, piedfort.

piega (*f.*) [*Ital.*] a crease, fold.

piękny [*Pol.*] fine (grade or condition).

pieni [*Finn.*] small.

pieniądz papierowy (*m.*) [*Pol.*] note, banknote; paper money.

pieniądz zastępczy (*m.*) [*Pol.*] emergency currency; scrip.

piiritykseen liittyvä (esim. hätäraha) [*Finn.*] obsidional.

pikilia ποικιλία (*f.*) [*Grk.*] variety.

pilak [*Tag.*] silver.

1763 Pillar Dollar (Mexico)

pillar dollar [Also known as the *Spanish milled dollar*; it is the so-called *piece of eight* of pirate lore.] Large silver Spanish-American coin

valued at 8 *reales* which circulated extensively throughout the New World. It was first minted at the newly-created Mexico City Mint in 1537 and was ultimately struck at various mints throughout Latin America until 1772. Its name is derived from its principal device, crowned hemispheres between the Pillars of Hercules. Coins of this type were issued in units of 1/2, 1, 2, 4, and 8 reales.

The pillar dollar is regarded as the precursor of the U.S. silver dollar. It was one of most popular of the many coins which circulated in the American colonies, and it influenced the direction the U.S. coinage system would take.

pinaka-larawan [*Tag.*] effigy.

pinakamababang tawad [*Tag.*] minimum bid.

pinanday na moneda [*Tag.*] hammered coin.

pinched penny Oval-shaped souvenir better known as an *elongated coin*[q.v.].

pig rupee Type of Indian rupee of 1911 showing an elephant with pig-like feet and a short tail. The elephant, part of the representation of the Order of the Indian Empire, was incorporated into King George V's robe on the coin's obverse. The rupees were rejected by the public because the elephant supposedly resembled a pig, an animal considered unclean by Indians. The Calcutta and Bombay mints had together minted 9.4 million pieces, but only 700,000 had been released when the public voiced its opposition. The coins were withdrawn from circulation and many were melted down, along with all the unreleased pieces. The coin was redesigned to show an elephant with an outlined ear, heavy feet, and a long tail.

[Chester L. Krause and Clifford Mishler, *Standard Catalog of World Coins* (1985), p. 1006.]

pirinç [*Turk.*] brass (the alloy).

piros [*Hun.*] red.

pistole Spanish gold coin (22 carat) introduced by Charles V in 1537 to replace the pure gold *excelente* of Isabella and Ferdinand first issued in 1497. The pistole was one of the coins authorized to be struck at the new mint in Mexico to make use of gold mined in the New World. It is the beginning of the series of

Spanish or Spanish American coins referred to as the *doblón* (or *doubloon* in English).

pistotiki karta πιστωτική κάρτα (*f.*) [*Grk.*] credit card.

Pistrucci, Benedetto Italian coin engraver (1784-1855). Protégé of British Mintmaster William Wellesley Pole. Pistrucci is best known for creating the *St. George Slaying the Dragon*[q.v.] design seen on British gold sovereigns (plus a few silver coins) since 1817. The motif is still used on some British coins today.

Scottish plack

plack Popular billon coin of Scotland begun by James II around 1470 and continued until 1590. Originally it was valued at fourpence but its value fluctuated considerably, sometimes being issued as low as one penny.

plads til omskrift [*Dan.*] exergue.

Plain Talk Journal originally adopted as the official organ of the American Numismatic Association when the organization was founded in 1891. The publication soon failed because its publisher, Charles T. Tatman, was lax in his duties. By the end of the 1890s, *The Numismatist* became the official journal of the A.N.A. and has remained so to the present day.

See *Numismatist, The.*

[Q. David Bowers, "Plain Talk about *The Numismatist*," *The Numismatist*, October 1988, pp. 1732-8.]

plama (*f.*) [*Pol.*] stain (on a banknote or bond).

planchet Metal disc struck by two dies to make a coin, medal, or token. Although the planchet can be a previously manufactured coin which is being overstruck, the vast majority are blank discs which are going through the minting process for the first time.

In modern times, planchets are produced in huge quantities by punching the discs out of sheets of metal that have been rolled to the appropriate thickness. The flans (another name for planchets) are fed into an upsetting machine where the edges are raised up to allow for better rims on the finished coins. As the final step, the planchets are placed in a collar and stamped by the two dies.

The rolling and punching processes are attributed to the Venetians who developed the methods in 1528. These techniques quickly became popular but did not gain universal acceptance until the nineteenth century.

Producing acceptable planchets had been a major headache for moneyers for two thousand years, and even those made from the Venetian system were not always consistent. The flans could not be of an arbitrary weight or fineness; they had to conform to a prescribed standard, although in ancient times such conformity was difficult if not impossible. If the planchets or finished coins were overweight, they could be adjusted by filing excess metal from the edge. If they were underweight, they were usually melted down because merchants would not accept them in trade.

Lincoln Cent: planchet and finished coin

The methods used to make early planchets varied greatly. Precious metal could be hammered into a sheet and the blanks could be cut or chiseled from it. Planchets were sometimes cast from sand molds. Spaniards converted gold and silver from the New World into flans by casting the metal into bars and then slicing coin-shaped discs from it, somewhat akin to the way a butcher slices a bologna. The coins produced this way are known as *cobs*[q.v.] and are very crude.

Special treatment of the planchets is required for the preparation of some presentation or trial pieces. Coins and medals known as *piéforts* are struck with regular dies but on extra thick flans. Proof specimens are produced on planchets which have been cleaned and polished and checked for flaws or scratches.

Most experts agree that the words *planchet, blank*, and *flan* are synonymous and can be used interchangeably. Walter Breen, however, insisted that the word *planchet* be reserved for a metal disc which has already been stamped as a coin, and that *blank* be used to refer to the disc prior to stamping. In his opinion, *flan* usually means *blank*.

[Richard G. Doty, *The Macmillan Encyclopedic Dictionary of Numismatics*, pp. 260-1; Walter Breen, *Complete Encyclopedia of U.S. and Colonial Coins*, p. 706.]

planşet [*Turk.*] planchet.

plants (*r.*) [*Swed.*] planchet.

plass til innskrift [*Nor.*] exergue.

plasto πλαστό (*n.*) [*Grk.*] a forgery, fake, counterfeit.

plata [*Tag.*]; (*f.*) [*Span.*] silver; common term for *money.*

platin [*Turk.*]; (*n.*) [*Dan.*] platinum.

Platin (*n.*) [*Ger.*] platinum.

platina [*Finn., Hun.*]; (*f.*) [*Port.*]; (*n.*) [*Dut.*]; (*r.*) [*Swed.*]; (*m.*) [*Nor.*] platinum.

platine (*m.*) [*Fr.*] platinum.

platino [*Tag.*]; (*m.*) [*Span., Ital.*] platinum.

1832 Russian 12 ruble platinum coin

platinum A very precious metal which has not seen considerable use in coinage. [element:

group VIII of the periodic table; atomic weight 195.09; atomic number 78; specific gravity 21.447; symbol Pt.]

Platinum is a dense dark silver-gray noble metal. Its most significant use in coinage was the series of Russian 3, 6, and 12 ruble coins issued from 1828 to 1845 under Nicholas I. Today its use is limited to bullion coins produced by Australia, the Isle of Man, etc.

[Contributed by Halbert Carmichael.]

1990 Australian platinum $50 bullion coin

playing card money Emergency issue of paper money introduced in 1685 by Jacques de Meulles, French commissariat office, in New France (now Québec). Because of a coin shortage, there was no way to pay the troops.

De Meulles solved the problem by producing "notes" on the back of playing cards. Unlike regular paper, playing cards were not only plentiful but durable enough to withstand circulation. For lack of printing presses, the notes were hand-written.

French-Canadian playing card money

The first series consisted of three denominations: four *livres* (equal to four English pounds) printed on a full playing card; two livres on a half-card; and 15 *sols* (the sol equaling an English shilling) on a quarter-card. Eventually even cut-off pieces circulated.

The idea was so successful that it was continued until 1760 with new series replacing old ones. Because stiff penalties were imposed on anyone holding old cards after new ones were issued, there are no known specimens of any card from the first eight series known to exist today. The later issues are also quite scarce, and many surviving examples are in museums. Canada is so anxious to keep the survivors at home, that the Heritage and Culture Act forbids playing card money specimens to be exported abroad.

[J. A. Haxby and R. C. Willey, *Coins of Canada* (9th Ed.), pp. 121-22.]

plet (*c.*) [*Dan.*] stain.

pli (*m.*) [*Fr.*] a crease, fold.

plistiriasmos πλειστηριασμός (*m.*) [*Grk.*] auction sale.

pliu (*n.*) [*Rom.*] a fold, crease.

p'liz פְּלִיז (*m.*) [*Heb.*] brass (the alloy).

plug 1. Base metal or precious metal used to fill a hole in a coin or medal after that piece was minted.

2. Core of precious metal attached to a coin to bring its weight up to a specified standard.

pney matbeya פְּנֵי מַטְבֵּעַ (*m.*) [*Heb.*] obverse.

pochodzenie (*n.*) [*Pol.*] pedigree (list of previous and present owners).

pocket piece [also known as a *touch piece*.] Coin, medal, token, or note which is carried in a person's pocket or purse for superstitious, religious, or nostalgic reasons. St. Christopher medals are very popular. Coins bearing the date of their owners' birth or of the owners' children are also commonly found.

poco común [*Span.*] somewhat common.

podatek (*m.*) [*Pol.*] tax.

poddelka подделка (*f.*) [*Russ.*] a counterfeit, fake.

poddelyvat подделывать (*v.*) [*Russ.*] to counterfeit.

podpis (*m.*) [*Pol.*] signature.

podrabiać (*v.*) [*Pol.*] to alter.

podrobienie (*n.*); **podróbka** (*f.*) [*Pol.*] alteration.

podrobiona data (*f.*) [*Pol.*] altered date.

pohja [*Finn.*] bottom.

pohjahinta [*Finn.*] minimum bid.

pohjatarjous [*Finn.*] protective reserve bid.

Pohjois-Irlanti [*Finn.*] Northern Ireland.

poids (*m.*) [*Fr.*] weight.

poikkeavuus [*Finn.*] anomaly.

poinçon (*m.*) [*Fr.*] mintmark.

poker chip from the 1930s

poker chip Type of gambling token used to facilitate the making of bets in card playing. Although most modern poker chips are made of plastic, they have also been made of wood, cardboard, and a variety of other substances. Some of the older specimens are quite beautiful and very collectable.

pokwitowanie (*n.*) [*Pol.*] receipt.

pół (*adj.*) [*Pol.*] half.

pola [*Indo.*] pattern.

Polar Bear Canadian bimetallic $2 coin introduced on February 19, 1996, as a permanent replacement for the $2 note.

The reverse feature of the $2 coin is a polar bear standing at the edge of an ice flow. It was designed by wildlife artist Brent Townsend. Dora dePedery-Hunt's rendition of Queen Elizabeth II graces the obverse.

This is the first bimetallic Canadian coin intended for general circulation. The outer ring, with a diameter of 28 mm, is made of nickel and includes all of the coin's inscriptions. One of its key features is an interrupted serrated edge to enable blind people to

recognize the coin more readily. The center core is made from an alloy of aluminum (aluminium) and bronze.

The Polar Bear coin is part of Canada's plan to eliminate small-denomination notes and replace them with coins. The first phase of this goal was put in place in 1987 with the introduction of the Loon[q.v.] $1 coin and subsequent withdrawal of the $1 note. The appearance of the Polar Bear coincides with Canada's elimination of the $2 note.

Almost immediately upon their release, some of the $2 coins were reported to have fallen apart, their core separating from the ring. Some Canadians attributed this problem to the timing of the coins' release in mid-winter. Because the coins were shipped in unheated vehicles in the middle of a very cold Canadian winter, a theory was proposed that the aluminum-bronze cores contracted in the cold at a faster rate than the nickel rings and simply fell out.

To test this theory, the chemistry department at North Carolina State University ran an experiment, similar to one performed by the Royal Canadian Mint. Three Polar Bears were immersed in liquid nitrogen to bring them to a temperature of -320° F (-196° C). After being chilled, they were dropped on the floor but failed to separate. Two of them were re-chilled and then hit with a rubber hammer. One separated cleanly and the other bent. In sum, chilling the coins did increase their propensity to separate, but probably not enough to cause them to do so in Canada's temperatures which at worst are not likely to go below -40° F.

An examination of the disassembled coin shows that the two pieces are held together with bevels. According to the Royal Canadian Mint, the coins are sufficiently bonded that they should not come apart in normal use. The R.C.M. claims that all the separated coins it has examined were tampered with, perhaps by being struck with a hammer. Yet this argument is disputed by some collectors who insist that their coins separated naturally and without undue force.

In addition to issuing business strikes, the Royal Canadian Mint also produced a limited quantity of presentation pieces using 22 carat gold in place of the aluminum-bronze alloy for the center core and white gold (17.2% gold, 77.6% silver, and 5.2% copper) for the ring. Five thousand pieces were struck, all of which sold out quickly. Additionally, a proof version of the base metal $2 was offered, as well as a special set containing the proof base metal coin and an uncirculated $2 replacement note with "X" as the third character in the serial number. Quantities were limited to 30,000.

Prior to issuing the actual coins, the Royal Canadian Mint sold test tokens identical in size, weight, and composition to the Polar Bear. The tokens were not only offered to vending machine companies to enable them to retool their equipment, but were also sold to the general public as souvenirs.

See page 317 for color illustrations of a separated Polar Bear.

[Experiment conducted by Dr. Halbert Carmichael. Richard Giedroyc, "Royal Canadian Mint confident $2 coin likely to remain intact," *Coin World*, April 1, 1996, p. 1 et al; "Gold $2 sells out," *World Coin News*, March 1996, p. 1; "R.M.C. unveils $2 test token to commons committee," *Canadian Coin News*, July 4-17, 1995, p. 1.]

polegada (*f.*) [*Port.*] inch.

polet (*c.*) [*Dan.*] token.

polett (*m.*) [*Nor.*] token; scrip.

poletti [*Finn.*] token.

Polierte Platte (*f.*) [*Ger.*] proof (*re*: coins or medals).

polisi mesou tachidromiou πώληση μέσω ταχυδρομείου [*Grk.*] mail bid sale.

political badge Political campaign button or inauguration souvenir.

Political badges have been popular in the United States since the nineteenth century, but they are much less common elsewhere. Their popularity in America developed primarily because the U.S. is one of the few major countries where the chief of state is elected directly by the people rather than being chosen by the ruling political party. Although thousands of different campaign buttons have

been issued to promote local, state, and congressional candidates in the U.S., many of the most desirable political badges are those heralding presidential candidates. Collectors especially like pre-World War II badges which feature the candidate's photo.

souvenir badge from L.B.J.'s inauguration (1965)

Political badges can also include inauguration souvenirs and related items. The illustrated badge with ribbon was given to participants in President Lyndon B. Johnson's Inaugural Parade in 1965.

pollett (*r.*) [*Swed.*] token; scrip.

polymethylmethacrilate A rigid thermoplastic often used in coin holders. It is chemically inert and may be either clear or colored.

polyvinyl chloride [Abbreviated *P.V.C.*] Type of plastic from which many coin holders were made in the 1960s and 1970s. Collectors discovered that the coins stored in these holders became discolored or pitted or suffered other damage. In some cases, the damage did not become evident until after the coins had been in those containers for a period of years. In other cases, the problem showed itself quickly, often within a few months.

The best coin holders manufactured since the late 1970s have not been made from this substance nor from any other substances known to harm coins. However, holders made from P.V.C. are still being sold. They are sometimes acceptable for short-term use, but the wise collector totally avoids them.

[Douglas G. Borden, "Storage Vital Numismatic Aspect," *Coin World*, February 4, 1981, pp. 81-98.]

pond (*n.*) 1. [*Dut.*] pound (16 ounces avdp., 12 oz. troy). 2. [*Rom.*] weight.

pond sterling (*n.*) [*Dut.*] pound Sterling (£).

ponto (*m.*) [*Port.*] bead (raised dot on the surface of a coin or medal).

portcullis on 1953 British threepence

portcullis An iron grating, also known as a drop-gate, hung over the entrance of a castle or other fortified building which is raised or lowered to allow or prevent passage. It is found on many British coins, either as a mint mark or as a primary device. Ironically, the two monarchs whose coinage best features this design are the two Elizabeths. The crowns, half-crowns, shillings, and sixpences struck for the East India Company in 1600 and 1601 under the reign of Elizabeth I feature this device. Three and a half centuries later, the brass threepence of her namesake, Elizabeth II, became the best known coin showing this design. A crowned portcullis dominates the reverse of the 12-sided threepences, issued from 1953 until 1967.

A small number of groats and farthings struck under the rule of Henry VIII exhibit a portcullis. Because of their unusual rarity and careful striking, Junge suggests that these pieces were patterns.

[Ewald Junge, *World Coin Encyclopedia*, p. 203.]

porthole note Nickname of United States $5 silver certificate of series 1923. Unlike most U.S. notes with portraits in the configuration of an oval, on this note the vignette of President Abraham Lincoln is surrounded by an unusual round design, resembling a porthole on a ship.

Portogallo [*Ital.*] Portugal.

portr. [*abbr.*] portrait.

portræt (*n.*) [*Dan.*] portrait.

portrætbillede (*n.*) [*Dan.*] effigy.

porträtt (*n.*) [*Swed.*] portrait.

portret (*n.*) [*Dut., Rom.*]; (*m.*) [*Pol.*] portrait; effigy.

portret podwójny ("gemmowy") [*Pol.*] conjoined, accolated, jugate.

portrett (*n.*) [*Nor.*] portrait; effigy.

pospolity [*Pol.*] common.

postać (*f.*) [*Pol.*] effigy.

postage currency The first general emission of United States fractional currency issued from August 21, 1862 to May 27, 1863. They were printed in denominations of 5, 10, 25, and 50 cents. These notes were called *postage currency* because they actually picture 5 and 10 cent postage stamps.

See *fractional currency*.

postage stamp currency; **postage currency** General term for any postal item which has circulated as money, usually during wartime when coins have been hoarded. Forty-three countries have used some form of postal currency, either issued with the official sanction of the government or done unofficially by private citizens as a way of overcoming coin shortages. The following are three of the best-known examples:

1. During the U.S. Civil War (1861-65), there was a great shortage of small circulating coins. In addition to the issuance of Civil War tokens[*q.v.*] by merchants and others, postage stamps were used to alleviate the shortage. Some were encased in mica containers (see *encased postage stamp*); others were affixed to advertising cards and circulated as if they were paper money. The piece illustrated in color on page 316 is one such example. Its ten cents' worth of uncancelled postage stamps made it legitimately worth ten cents in trade.

postage stamp money from Spanish Civil War

2. Postage stamps were affixed to round disks of thin cardboard and circulated as coins during the Spanish Civil War (1936-39). The royal crown printed on the disk indicates that these items were authorized by the government and were not simply concocted by private citizens.

Russian postage currency of Nicholas II

3. Czar Nicholas II faced a severe coin shortage during World War I. He authorized the production of small banknotes made from postage stamp dies to alleviate the shortage. The face of the notes are identical to the stamps, but the backs are not gummed and the notes are printed on thin cardboard instead of normal postage stamp paper. Also, the backs of the notes carry an inscription stating that the items are notes worth a certain amount of kopecks in trade. Similar mini-notes were issued for Ukraine.

These notes are erroneously listed in many world stamp catalogues as postage stamps. Although they are not stamps, they were sometimes glued onto envelopes and used as postage.

postage stamps on currency paper World War I left a severe shortage of paper throughout Europe. In some countries, paper could not be wasted under any circumstances.

Latvia was one of the places hit the hardest; its very limited supply of paper had to be distributed judiciously. Preference had to be given to paper currency in order to keep the economy intact, and practically none was left for the production of postage stamps. Thus, stamps were printed on any paper that the printers could find. During the post-war period, some stamps were printed on the back of old maps and some on leftover wallpaper.

The item in the illustration on the opposite page is a block of twelve stamps printed on discarded money paper. The stamps on the front are perfectly normal and are perforated in the usual way. The back of the block, however, shows a full banknote. The banknote side is gummed just as the back side of any group of stamps would be.

postanvisning (c.) [Dan.] postal money order.

postauksjon (m.) [Nor.] mail bid sale.

postautalvány [Hun.] postal money order.

Posten (m.) [Ger.] (auction) lot.

postihuutokauppa [Finn.] mail bid sale.

postväxel (r.) [Swed.] postal money order.

postwissel (m.-c.) [Dut.] postal money order.

potwierdzenie odbioru (n.) [Pol.] receipt.

pouce (m.) [Fr.] inch.

pound; pound sterling [£] Unit of currency of Great Britain. The term originated in eighth-century Anglo-Saxon Britain as a monetary unit known as the *sterling* which was worth 1/240 of a pound of silver. Two hundred forty sterlings were referred to as a *pound of sterling* and then simply a *pound sterling*.

The pound was redeemable in silver until 1717 when Britain temporarily went on the gold standard and redeemed the pound in gold. Britain abandoned the gold standard in 1797, re-established it in 1816, abandoned it again during World War I, restored it in 1925, and finally did away with it forever in 1931.

The symbol for the pound sterling [£] resembles the letter "L" because it comes from the Latin word *libra* meaning "pound."

pour approbation [Fr.] on approval.

povrch zkoušky [Cz.] proof surface (of a coin or medal).

P.Q. [abbr.] premium quality. Controversial description of some uncirculated coins which have been graded and encapsulated by third-party grading services. The *M.S.* ("mint state") system introduced in the United States theoretically has 70 different grades, including eleven (MS-60 through MS-70) in uncirculated. The presumption is that a coin in MS-64 P.Q. is nicer (for whatever *subjective* reasons) than an average MS-64 coin, but is not as nice (for whatever *objective* reasons) as an MS-65 coin. To avoid confusion, many dealers refuse to use the P.Q. designation.

[Robert R. Van Ryzin, "PQ?— Or Not PQ?" *Numismatic News*, January 2, 1990, pp. 30-32.]

prægestempel (n.) [Dan.] (coinage) die.

Prägestempel (m.) [Ger.] (coinage) die.

Prägestempelsprung (m.) [Ger.] die break.

Prägevorlage (f.) [Ger.] pattern.

Pragmatic Sanction of Medina del Campo Monetary reform established on June 3, 1497, by Isabella and Ferdinand of Spain. It authorized the issuance of a new gold coin, the *excelente de la granada*[q.v.], later known as the *ducado*.

[Manuel Moreno Fraginals and José A. Pulido Ledesma, *Cuba: A Country and Its Currency*, National Bank of Cuba, pp. 27-28.]

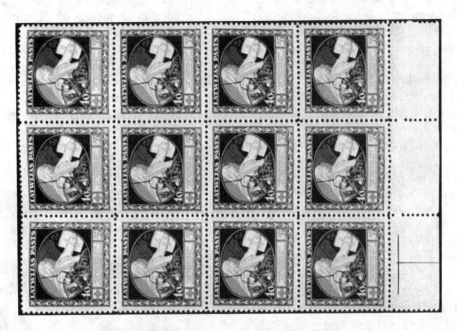

Latvian postage stamps printed on discarded banknote paper

Prägung (*f.*); **Prägungen** (*f.pl.*) [*Ger.*] coinage.

prangko [*Tag.*] franc (French unit of currency).

prasa mennicza (*f.*) [*Pol.*] coinage press.

prasasti [*Indo.*] inscription.

Präsident (*m.*) [*Ger.*] president.

prata (*f.*) [*Port.*] silver.

prawa strona (*f.*) [*Pol.*] right (direction or position).

prawdziwy [*Pol.*] genuine.

prawie [*Pol.*] almost.

precaria conservación [*Span.*] Grade of paper money roughly similar to Good. The note has tears, folds, patches, etc., but the date, series, and serial number are readable. Abbreviated *P.C.*

précieux [*Fr.*] valuable.

precinto (*m.*) [*Span.*] seal (in the numismatic sense).

precio (*m.*) [*Span.*] price.

precio de reserva [*Span.*] protective reserve bid.

preço (*m.*) [*Port.*] price.

preço mínimo de adjudicação [*Port.*] protective reserve bid.

preg (*n.*) [*Nor.*] incuse.

pregepresse (*m.*) [*Nor.*] (coinage) press.

Preis (*m.*) [*Ger.*] price.

Preisliste (*f.*) [*Ger.*] price list.

prensa (*f.*) [*Span., Port.*] (coinage) press.

presă de bani (*f.*) [*Rom.*] coinage press.

prescurtare (*f.*) [*Rom.*] abbreviation.

presque [*Fr.*] almost.

pressa (*f.*) [*Ital.*] (coinage) press.

presse (*m.*) [*Nor.*] (coinage) press.

presse monétaire (*f.*) [*Fr.*] coinage press.

preto [*Port.*] black.

prezzo (*m.*) [*Ital.*] price.

preţ (*n.*) [*Rom.*] price; (auction) bid.

prijs (*m.-c.*) [*Dut.*] price.

prijslijst (*m.-c.*) [*Dut.*] price list.

pris (*n.*) [*Swed.*]; (*c.*) [*Dan.*]; (*m.*) [*Nor.*] price.

prislista (*r.*) [*Swed.*] price list.

prisliste (*c.*) [*Dan.*]; (*m.*) [*Nor.*] price list.

[#1] South African P.O.W. token

prisoner-of-war token 1. Coin retooled by a prisoner interned in a P.O.W. camp as a way of passing time. Unlike hobo nickels and satire pieces, in which the carver has a specific purpose in choosing which coins he retools, prisoner-of-war tokens are carved on whatever coins the prisoner has in his possession.

It is likely that P.O.W. tokens are a thing of the past, because prisoners in modern internment camps are far less likely to be permitted to keep knives and other sharp tools needed for carving.

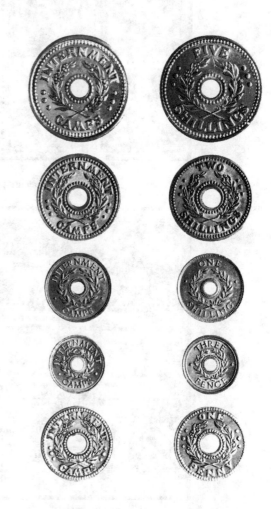

[#2] Australian P.O.W. tokens

2. Tokens issued to prisoners-of-war for use in internment camps. They are often referred to as internment tokens or internment money.

One of the most notable sets of P.O.W. tokens was issued by Australia during World

War II. The set consists of five tokens issued in denominations of a penny, threepence, shilling, 2 shillings, and 5 shillings.

Tennessee State Prison token

prison token A form of scrip[q.v.] used in prisons to permit some exchange to go on behind bars yet without the need to allow prisoners to keep actual cash money.

private scrip Tokens or other money substitute issued by an individual or firm for non-fraudulent purposes. Although the term *private scrip* is commonly used, it is actually a redundancy because all scrip is privately issued.

See *scrip* for additional information and page 316 for color illustrations.

Privatgeldschein (*m.*); **Privatschein** (*m.*) [*Ger.*] scrip.

privatpenge (*pl.*) [*Dan.*] scrip.

privy purse Historical name for the allowance given to British monarchs for their personal expenses.

prix (*m.*) [*Fr.*] price.

Polish pattern coin with the word *PRÓBA*

próba (*f.*) [*Pol.*] proof [re: coins]; pattern.

In Poland, coins with rejected designs have often been minted in quantities ranging from a few to many thousands for sale to collectors. The word *próba* is placed on them to indicate that they are patterns and not regular issues.

Probe (*f.*) [*Ger.*] pattern.
proiect (*n.*) [*Rom.*] pattern.
pronssi [*Finn.*] bronze (alloy).
proof 1. Specimen coin or medal exhibiting a mirror-like surface and very sharp detail in its designs. To achieve the reflective surface, each planchet is examined for flaws, and any with blemishes are discarded. The survivors are carefully washed and polished before the coins are produced. The die is also polished.

The coin or medal is carefully struck two or more times to assure virtually perfect sharpness. The multiple striking gives most proof coins a sharper and more defined rim and edge than those of identical regular-issue pieces.

If the entire die has been polished, including the lettering and all devices, the entire coin will have a reflective look and will be referred to as a *brilliant* proof. If only the die's surface has been polished, and particularly if some form of acid has been applied to the die prior to its polishing, the surfaces of the coin will be mirror-like, but the devices will not and in fact will stand out in sharp contrast. This process produces what is known as a *frosted* proof.

During the early twentieth century, the United States and a few other countries experimented with a process known as *matte* proofing. Proof coins were made through the usual process but were then sandblasted to give them a rough, matted finish. The coins proved to be unpopular, and the method is rarely used today.

The term *proof* refers to a specific type of manufacture and not a grade or condition. A proof coin which has been placed into circulation may show a tremendous amount of wear, but it is still and will forever be a proof coin. A proof coin or medal which is no longer in its original uncirculated state is called an impaired proof. Although the term *proof condition* is frequently seen in books and catalogues, it is not correct terminology and should be avoided.

The earliest known pieces of this type were struck in England in the 1660s, although some experts theorize that a few examples may have

been produced in the previous decade. From their inception until the mid-twentieth century, proof coins were almost always produced in small qualities and were often intended to be presented to some special person. An example is the magnificent group of United States proof coins known as the King of Siam[q.v.] set. Notable, too, are the presentation sets created by Great Britain at the beginning of the reign of each new monarch.

Britain is also responsible for having produced what is believed to be the longest running series of annual proof emissions, the *Maundy*[q.v.] coins. These four-piece sets consist of a tiny silver penny, twopence, threepence, and fourpence which are struck each year to be given on Maundy Thursday to poor people on behalf of the reigning monarch. The presentation is part of a religious ceremony dating back to medieval times.

The advent of high-powered machinery enabled mints to produce quality proof coins in large quantities which were targeted to collectors. Nowhere was this more evident than in the United States in the 1950s. The Philadelphia Mint produced outstanding proof sets (cent, nickel, dime, quarter, and half) in whatever quantity the market demanded. Since 1968 the San Francisco Assay Office has manufactured U.S. proof sets, as well as proof commemorative coins and some proof medals. Many other countries have jumped on the proof bandwagon and are now producing beautiful proof sets and individual proof coins, many on an annual basis.

[Richard G. Doty, *The Macmillan Encyclopedic Dictionary of Numismatics*, p. 270-2.]

2. An accepted design for a piece of paper money, certificate, bond, check, etc., which is impressed on India paper, card, or rice paper. Some isolated examples of proofs exist on other types of paper.

The softer paper provides a surface that will show the best example of the engraving. As the design is being engraved, partial progressive proofs are made from the original die; final die proofs are made at completion.

When the design is finished and transferred to the final printing plate, such an impression is called a *plate proof*. All proofs are uniface. Proofs can be in black and white or in color.

Book illustrations on counterfeit detection as well as remaining unsigned notes, intended for use and often in sheets, can be mistaken for proofs by an inexperienced collector.

Proofs lack serial numbers and signatures, unless the signatures were actually engraved in the plate. Unlike proof coins, "paper" proofs are made for technical reasons and not for general distribution. Consequently, these paper proofs are scarce and often very hard to obtain.

[Contributed by Gene Hessler. Gene Hessler, *U.S. Essay, Proof and Specimen Notes*, BNR Press, p. 32; Dr. Howard S. Friedman, "Essays, Proofs and Specimens," *The Essay-Proof Journal*, Vol. 31, No. 1, 1974, p. 17.]

plate proof with engraved signatures

propaganda note Any note which deliberately exhibits written or pictorial information or allegations intended to further the issuing agency's cause or to damage an opposing cause. The cause itself may be political, religious, economic, or military, or it may involve the aspirations of an individual.

Propagandanote (*f.*) [*Ger.*] propaganda note.

propuesta (*f.*) [*Span.*] an offer, proposal.

prosfora προσφορά (*f.*) [*Grk.*] (auction) bid.

prosfores anef oriou den apodechonte προσφορές άνευ ορίου δέν αποδέχονται [*Grk.*] no unlimited bids accepted.

prosthios πρόσθιος (*m.*) [*Grk.*] obverse.

prostokątny [*Pol.*] rectangular.

protective reserve bid An auction bid made by the auctioneer on behalf of the seller of the lot in order to bring the price up to a level acceptable to the seller. This is usually done only if the bids from the floor are very low and the auctioneer does not believe that the bids will rise significantly. If no one offers a bid higher than the reserve bid, then the lot goes unsold.

prøveeksemplar (*n.*) [*Dan.*] specimen.

prøvemønt (*c.*) [*Dan.*] pattern.

proveniens (*r.*) [*Swed.*] pedigree.

provmynt (*n.*) [*Swed.*] pattern.

proweniencja (*f.*) [*Pol.*] pedigree (list of previous and present owners).

prueba; prueba fondo espejo [*Span.*] proof (*re*: coins or medals).

Judean pruta of Alexander Yannai, ca. 100 B.C.E. (enlarged)

pruta פְּרוּטָה (*f.*) [*Heb.*] (also romanized as *prutah*). A coin of low value issued in both ancient and modern Israel. A few decades after the Jews regained autonomy and established the Second Jewish Commonwealth (165 B.C.E.), the Selukid kings permitted the Jews to issue their own copper coinage. These took the form of half, one, and one and a half pruta coins, which portrayed such designs as anchors, eight-pointed stars, palm branches, cornucopias, and long inscriptions. The coins' legends were in Greek and/or Paleo-Hebrew, an alphabet based on the Phoenician, which was already out of date. The original pruta were worth two lepta, and 192 pruta equalled a denarius (also called *drachma* or *zuz*). King Agrippa I (37-44 C.E.) increased the size of the pruta from 2 grams to 2.55 grams, and the value changed to 144 pruta per denarius.

Second Commonwealth coins are mentioned in the Talmud (since they are too recent to be mentioned in the Jewish Bible) and in the Christian Gospels. The *widow's mite*, the offering made by a poor widow which Jesus declared was worth more than gold given by the wealthy (*Mark 22:41-44*), was probably a lepta or half pruta coin, the smallest denomination then in circulation.

After winning her independence (1949 C.E.), the Third Jewish Commonwealth replaced the Palestine pound and mil with the Israeli lira[*q.v.*] and pruta. Due to inflation, the pruta was replaced with the agora in 1960, with ten prutot equal to one agora.

[Contributed by Simcha Kuritzky. *Encyclopedia Judaica*, Vol. 14, p. 1347 and Vol. 5, p. 697; James Hastings (ed.), *Dictionary of the Bible*.]

przedpłata (*f.*) [*Pol.*] prepayment.

przepołowiony (*adj.*) [*Pol.*] half.

przestarzały [*Pol.*] obsolete.

przyjmujemy karty kredytowe [*Pol.*] credit cards accepted.

przypisywać (*v.*) [*Pol.*] to attribute.

publikálatlan [*Hun.*] unpublished.

puheenjohtaja [*Finn.*] president.

puja (*f.*) [*Span.*] (auction) bid.

pulgada (*f.*) [*Span.*] inch.

punainen [*Finn.*] red.

punch cancellation Invalidation of a note, bond, or philatelic item by punching one or more holes through it. This method was most often used in the nineteenth century to prevent notes and other certificates from being re-circulated

once they had been redeemed. Its twentieth century application was limited mostly to post-World War I emergency currency.

pund (n.) [*Nor., Swed.*] pound (unit of weight).

pund sterling [*Dan., Swed.*] pound Sterling (£).

punta [*Finn.*] pound Sterling (£).

punzone (m.) [*Ital.*] (coinage) die.

puoli (adj.) [*Finn.*] half.

puolikas [*Finn.*] half (the fraction).

purana पुराण [*Hin.*] ancient.

puro [*Span., Port.*] pure; fine (purity of metal), fineness.

Purple Heart U.S. military decoration awarded to those killed or wounded in action against an enemy. On the back, the Purple Heart shows the recipient's name engraved under the inscription *For Military Merit*.

The Order of the Purple Heart is America's oldest military decoration, having been originally established by George Washington in 1782. Originally known as the Badge for Military Merit, it consisted of a purple heart-shaped piece of silk edged with a narrow binding of silver. The word *Merit* appeared stitched across the face, also in silver.

The Purple Heart was revived in the form of a military medal in 1932, the 200th anniversary of George Washington's birth. It is faced with purple enamel upon which is placed a gold relief bust of Washington in the uniform of a general of the Continental Army. The Washington coat of arms between two sprays of leaves in green enamel is incorporated in the ring which attaches it to a purple ribbon bordered with white.

See page 311 for a color illustration.

[Contributed by Robert A. Carpenter. Evans Kerrigan, *American Medals and Decorations*, pp. 4-5, 23; David L. Riley, *Uncommon Valor: Decorations, Badges, and Service Medals of the U.S. Navy and Marine Corps*.]

puur [*Dut.*] fine (purity of metal), fineness.

P.V.C. [*abbr.*] polyvinyl chloride[q.v.]. Plastic coin holders made from this substance can cause discoloration and pitting on the coins stored within them.

pwt. [*abbr.*] pennyweight[q.v.]; *dwt.* is also used.

pyke san ၃ၵၽ [*Bur.*] money.

pyke san pya ၃ၵၽ ၍ [*Bur.*] coinage.

pyöreä [*Finn.*] round.

Q q

qián 钱 [*Chin.-py./sc.*] money.

qīng tǒng 青铜 [*Chin.-py./sc.*] bronze (the alloy).

quadrado (*adj.*) [*Port.*] square.

quadratisch (*adj.*) [*Ger.*] square.

quadrato (*adj.*) [*Ital.*] square.

quadrigatus (pl.: *quadrigati.*) A silver coin of the Roman Republican era issued to replace the didrachm, and, in turn, supplanted by the denarius (which adopted its chariot motif). This issue came into being circa 222 B.C. and lasted until ca. 170 B.C. It was coined on the 6-scruple standard and was part of the first systematic attempt to unify the coinage. The intention was to supersede all coins then circulating on the Italian peninsula, whether produced domestically or at a foreign mint.

The quadrigatus was plentifully struck. It overtook and replaced other forms of coinage as it spread from Rome to other mints in Italy and Sicily. Even the Carthaginians mimicked it.

These pieces underwent a gradual but severe debasement and weight reduction occasioned by the financial strains of the Second Punic War. They fell to perhaps half of their original weight, and can be less than 3.2 grams or 50 grains.

Quadrigati are of a uniform type, but can display some differences in style which could be indicative of different mints and dates. Changes are most notable on the obverse. The characteristic obverse depicts a laureate head of Janus/Frontus/Dioscuri with side curls.

The reverse shows Jupiter hurling a thunderbolt and holding a sceptre. He may appear either in or in front of a fast quadriga (four-horse chariot from which the name of this coin has been derived) driven by Victory. This ordinarily faces to the observer's right, but a few are to the left. *ROMA* is written beneath in letters that can be either incuse or in relief. A corn (maize) ear sometimes can be noted under that, and could signify Sicilian vintage.

[Contributed by William F. Mross. Sydenham, *The Coinage of the Roman Republic*; Sutherland, *Roman Coins*; Mattingly, *Roman Coins*; G. F. Hill, *Historical Roman Coins*; David R. Sear, *Roman Coins and Their Values*.]

quahaug; quahog A type of clam the hard shell of which was used for making *wampum*, strings of beads utilized as a means of exchange by some North American Indians prior to the arrival of Europeans. The quahog shells produced blue-black beads. These dark beads had about twice the trading value of white wampum beads, which came from whelk shells.

[A. George Mallis, "A Numismatic Primer— Part 1," *The Numismatist*, July 1988, p. 1217.]

qualidade (*f.*) [*Port.*] grade; quality.

qualità (*f.*) [*Ital.*] grade; quality.

quaranta [*Ital.*] forty.

quarante [*Fr.*] forty.

quarenta [*Port.*] forty.

quart (*m.*) [*Fr.*] fourth (fraction), quarter.

quarto (*m.*) [*Ital., Port.*] fourth (fraction), quarter.

quase [*Port.*] almost.

quatre [*Fr.*] four.

quatre-vingt-dix [*Fr.*] ninety.

quatre-vingts [*Fr.*] eighty.

quatro [*Port.*] four.

quattro [*Ital.*] four.

quetzal Unit of currency of Guatemala introduced in 1925 and nominally equivalent to the United States dollar. Between 1925 and 1964 the quetzal and its fractions were of lower fineness than the equivalent U.S. coins but contained as much silver.

The resplendent quetzal (Pharomacrus mocinno) is the national bird of Guatemala and is a member of the trogon family. Its range is limited to Central America, and it is renowned for its long green tail feathers.

[Contributed by Halbert Carmichael.]

quinto (*m.*) [*Span., Port.*] fifth (the fraction).

Quittung (*f.*) [*Ger.*] 1. receipt.

2. Name given by the Germans to ghetto money[q.v.] which Jews were required to use while interned in the ghettos of Theresienstadt (Czechoslovakia) and Litzmannstadt (Poland) during World War II. These notes were also called Moses crowns[q.v.].

R r

r. [*abbr.*] right (direction or position).

R, RR *et al* [*abbr.*] Indications of various degrees of rarity. "R" means *rare*, usually indicating that 13 to 20 specimens are believed to exist (although the specific numbers attached to these abbreviations vary from country to country). "RR" means *very rare* (7 to 12 examples believed to exist); "RRR" is *extremely rare* (4 to 6 specimens); "RRRR" equals *exceedingly rare* (2 or 3 specimens); and "RRRRR" indicates that only one unique specimen is known.

The purpose of using these rarity indicators is to denote the number of specimens in existence and not necessarily to indicate a high price. Because of supply and demand considerations, high prices and rarity are not necessarily synonymous.

rachunek (*m.*) [*Pol.*] account (financial or transactional).

radar note Banknote with a palindrome serial number, i.e., a number which reads the same forward or backward such as 32988923. Notes with these numbers are popular collector's items. They are so named because the word *radar* is itself a palindrome.

raha [*Finn.*] money; coinage; currency.

raha- (*adj.*) [*Finn.*] monetary.

rahajärjestelmä [*Finn.*] monetary system.

rahake [*Finn.*] token.

rahaleimasin [*Finn.*] (coinage) die.

rahan poistaminen käytöstä [*Finn.*] demonetization.

rahapaja [*Finn.*] mint.

rahapajan tunnus [*Finn.*] mint mark.

rahapötkö [*Finn.*] roll (of coins).

rahasto [*Finn.*] treasure.

railroad rim In normal coin production, a collar rises above the anvil die (the stationary die) so that when the blank is struck, it does not spread (see *broadstrike*). If the collar fails to rise all the way, part of the blank is above the collar. When the hammer die (the movable die) strikes the blank, part of the metal spreads over the top of the collar. Thus the coin looks like the wheel of a railroad car. If the collar is slightly tilted, the resulting coin is said to have a partial railroad rim.

[Contributed by Coleman Ezkovich.]

rainha (*f.*) [*Port.*] queen.

raising the cross Symbolic act of taking possession of a territory. It is frequently seen in vignettes showing Christopher Columbus dedicating newly-discovered lands to Spain.

rajoittamattomia tarjouksia ei hyväksytä [*Finn.*] no unlimited bids accepted.

rame (*m.*) [*Ital.*] copper (the metal).

rand (*m.-c.*) [*Dut.*]; (*c.*) [*Dan.*]; (*m.*) [*Nor.*] edge; rim.

Rand (*m.*) [*Ger.*] edge; rim.

Rändelmünze (*f.*) [*Ger.*] milled coin.

Randschrift (*f.*) [*Ger.*] inscription; motto; legend.

Rangoon Ship that sank in 1871 while en route from London to Melbourne. Part of the lost cargo included the entire supply of coinage dies destined for the Melbourne Mint. In subsequent years, all shipments of dies from England to Australia were divided in two and sent separately.

[John Sharples, "Australian Coins 1919 to 1924," *Journal of the Numismatic Association of Australia*, July 1985, p. 5.]

Ranska [*Finn.*] France.

rant (*m.*) [*Pol.*] edge.

rar [*Ger., Rom.*] rare, scarce.

rareté (*f.*) [*Fr.*] rarity.

rareza (*f.*) [*Span.*] rarity.

rarità (*f.*) [*Ital.*] rarity.

raritate (*f.*) [*Rom.*] rarity.

raro [*Span., Ital.*] rare, scarce.

rasgado [*Span., Port.*] torn.

rasgadura (*f.*); **rasgón** (*m.*) [*Span.*] a tear (as in a banknote or bond).

rasguño (*m.*) [*Span.*] a scratch.

ratsa ράτσα (*f.*) [*Grk.*] pedigree (list of former and present owners).

rauta [*Finn.*] iron (metal).

R.C. [*Span. abbr.*] *regular conservación.* Spanish term for a grade of paper money similar to Fine. The note may show some folds and tears, but the date, series, and serial number must be legible.

rdza (*f.*) [*Pol.*] rust.

re (*m.*) [*Ital.*] king.

real (*m.*) [*Span., Port.*] literally, an adjective meaning *royal.*

The *real* was a silver coin introduced at virtually the same time in Spain and Portugal in the mid-1300s. It remained a silver coin in Spain (and later in Spanish America) for five hundred years. The 8 *real* coin (better known as the *Pillar Dollar* or *piece of eight*) was very popular throughout the New World in the eighteenth century and was in fact a precursor of the U.S. dollar. In Spain, coins denominated in *reales* [the plural form of *real* in Spanish] were struck until 1864 and were a part of Spain's first attempt at decimalizing its coinage.

The Portuguese version was not as popular as its Spanish counterpart and ultimately became a copper coin in the 1500s. The Portuguese *real* [plural: *reais*] underwent a name change and became the *rei*, literally meaning "king" [plural: *réis*]. Coins with denominations in *réis* were used in Portugal and Brazil even into the twentieth century.

rebro ребро (*n.*) [*Russ.*] edge.

rechteckig [*Ger.*] rectangular.

rechthoekig [*Dut.*] rectangular.

rechts [*Ger., Dut.*] right (direction or position).

recibo (*m.*) [*Span., Port.*] receipt.

recto (*m.*) [*Fr.*] front side; face (of a banknote).

reçu (*m.*) [*Fr.*] receipt.

Red Book See *Guide Book of United States Coins.*

redondo [*Span., Port.*] round.

reeded edge

reeded edge Continuous even cuts around the edge of a coin. Historically it has been called a *milled edge* because the development of milled coinage[*q.v.*] in the sixteenth century permitted this type of configuration to be used. The term *milled edge* is now considered archaic.

Reeded edges were introduced primarily to discourged clipping of slivers of precious metal from the edges of coins. The reeding also made counterfeit coins more readily noticeable, because it is nearly impossible for a counterfeiter to reproduce a good reeded edge on a phony coin.

In the late twentieth century, reeded edges found a new purpose. Italy, Canada, and various other countries began placing interrupted reeded edges on certain coins to make them easily identifiable by people with visual impairments. This type of edge has a short length of reeding followed by a non-reeded section, followed by more reeding, etc., all the way around the coin. A blind person is unlikely to mistaken a coin with this type of reeding for a token or a coin of a different denomination.

re-emisión (*f.*) [*Span.*] restrike; re-issuance.

re-emissão (*f.*) [*Port.*] restrike; re-issuance.

Regatul Unit [*Rom.*] United Kingdom (U.K.).

rege (*m.*) [*Rom.*] king.

regent (*c.*) [*Dan.*] sovereign.

regina (*f.*) [*Ital., Lat.*] queen.

regină (*f.*) [*Rom.*] queen.

Regno Unito [*Ital.*] United Kingdom (U.K.).

regula 1. [*Lat.*] rule.

2. [*Eng.*] The line separating the numerator from the denominator in a fraction. Also known as *fraction line.*

[Alan Herbert, "Coin Clinic," *Numismatic News,* December 19, 1989, p. 46.]

regular conservación (*f.*) [*Span.*] Grade of banknotes approximately equal to Fine. The

note may have some folds and small tears, but the date, series, and serial number must all be readable. Abbreviated *R.C.*

regular conservada [*Span.*] Approximate equivalent of Good as a grade or condition of coins.

rei (*m.*) [*Port.*] king.

reiällinen [*Finn.*] holed.

Reihe (*f.*) [*Ger.*] series.

Reihenbezeichnung (*f.*) [*Ger.*] serial number.

reikä [*Finn.*] hole.

reikämitätöinti [*Finn.*] punch cancellation.

réimpression (*f.*) [*Fr.*] restrike.

rein [*Ger.*] fineness; fine (purity of metal).

reina (*f.*) [*Span.*] queen.

reine (*f.*) [*Fr.*] queen.

Reino Unido [*Span., Port.*] United Kingdom.

reject tab Small square of adhesive paper attached to a note or sheet of notes during the manufacturing process to indicate that an inspector has found a defect and that the item should be rejected.

rekening (*f.-c.*) [*Dut.*] account (financial or transactional).

reklamepenge (*pl.*) [*Dan.*] scrip.

rekwerdong moneda [*Tag.*] token.

relief [also written as *bas-relief.*] Design or lettering on a coin or medal which is raised up above the field. This is in contrast to *incuse*, a design which sinks into the surface of the coin.

Except for the 1908-29 U.S. Indian Head $2.50 and $5 gold coins and for incuse inscriptions on the wide rims of some British coins (e.g., the 7-sided 20 pence pieces introduced in 1982), virtually all modern coins have been struck in relief.

Current coins are almost always designed with relatively high relief to enable them to withstand additional years of circulation. One major exception is the 1965 Churchill Crown of Great Britain. The side showing Churchill's effigy was struck in extremely low relief as a way of creating an artistic effect. The coins were expected to be kept as souvenirs and not to circulate, so there was no need to put any anti-wear protection into the design.

remainder Security paper of any type which remains at the printing facility or at the place of issue. These notes, certificates, bonds, etc., could be incomplete or could be complete with serial numbers and signatures but most often lack one or both, and on occasion bear a cancellation mark.

Remainders, since they were expected to be issued, are always found on the normal paper intended for that purpose. Remainders of early uniface notes and certificates are often offered as proofs[*q.v.*].

The term *remainder* was coined by Dr. Julian Blanchard, pioneer of paper money research.

[Contributed by Gene Hessler. Dr. Howard S. Friedman, "Essays, Proofs and Specimens," *The Essay-Proof Journal*, Vol. 31, No. 1, 1974, p. 17; Gene Hessler, *U.S. Essay, Proof and Specimen Notes*, BNR Press, p. 33.]

ren [*Swed.*] fine (purity of metal), fineness.

repa (*r.*) [*Swed.*] a scratch.

reparado [*Span., Port.*] repaired.

réparé [*Fr.*] repaired.

repariert [*Ger.*] repaired.

repeämä [*Finn.*] a tear (as in a note or bond).

repedés a verőtövön [*Hun.*] die break.

repeytynyt [*Finn.*] torn.

réplica (*f.*) [*Port.*] a duplicate; replica; reproduction.

Repubblica Democratica Tedesca [*Ital.*] East Germany (D.D.R.).

Repubblica Federale Tedesca [*Ital.*] West Germany (B.R.D.).

Repubblica Popolare Cinese [*Ital.*] People's Republic of China (P.R.C.).

república (*f.*) [*Span., Port.*] republic.

República de ... [*Span., Port.*] Republic of .... [Note: If the name of the country that follows always uses its gender designation, then the word *de* may be changed to incorporate some form of the word *the*. For example, "Republic of Brazil" is written in Portuguese as *República do Brasil*.]

República de China [*Span.*] Republic of China (Taiwan).

República Democrática de Alemania [*Span.*] East Germany (D.D.R.).

República Federal de Alemania [*Span.*] West Germany (B.R.D.).

Republica Populară Chineza [*Rom.*] People's Republic of China (P.R.C.).

Republik China [*Ger.*] Republic of China. The name *Taiwan* is more commonly used in German.

Republiken Kina [*Swed.*] Republic of China (Taiwan).

Republikken Kina [*Nor., Dan.*] Republic of China.

république (*f.*) [*Fr.*] republic.

République de Chine [*Fr.*] Republic of China.

République Populaire de Chine [*Fr.*] People's Republic of China (P.R.C.).

requer-se um depósito [*Port.*] deposit required.

reserve bid see *protective reserve bid.*

Reserveschutzgebot (*n.*) [*Ger.*] protective reserve bid.

részvény [*Hun.*] (commercial) bond.

retooled South African florin

retooled coin Satirical or artistic piece created by altering a genuine coin.

In the 1860s and '70s, the effigy of France's Napoleón III was often retooled to create outlandish images as a way of mocking him for his failed foreign and domestic policies. Many of the pieces were enameled with bright colors to enhance the coins' garish appearance.

Some prisoner-of-war tokens[*q.v.*] fall into this category. Prisoners sometimes re-carved coins in their possession as a way of passing time. This activity is probably a lost art, because prisoners in today's internment camps are not likely to be permitted to keep sharp tools necessary to do this type of carving.

As collector's items, some of the most popular retooled coins are hobo nickels[*q.v.*]

carved from U.S. Buffalo Nickels. Many were carved in the 1930s by victims of the Great Depression. (See *Hughes, "Bo".*)

Also popular is the love token[*q.v.*], a coin re-engraved on one side with a creative design or with the initials of the person for whom it was intended. The South African florin in the illustration was retooled in this style.

retouche (*f.*) [*Fr.*] alteration.

retoucher (*v.*) [*Fr.*] to alter.

retrato (*m.*) [*Span., Port.*] portrait.

rettangolare [*Ital.*] rectangular.

reuna [*Finn.*] rim.

Canadian large cent die reused on Chinese coin

reused die 1. A coinage die used from one year to the next without a change in date. For example, all U.S. silver dollars produced in 1804 were struck on old dies dated 1803. Dollars bearing the date 1804 were produced from 1834 to around 1858.

2. An old die which has had its date retooled to show the current year. This often produces visible overdates. Whether the date is changed or not, a die reused in this way sometimes rusts with age, leaving noticeable marks on coins produced from it.

3. In 1920 Canada switched from the large cent to the small cent. Some of the large cent dies were sold to China for reuse. The illustrations show the identical ring of maple leafs on both coins.

It is somewhat ironic that China would purchase those particular dies, because Canadian large cent dies had a design flaw which caused ghosting[*q.v.*]. As a result of this flaw, the two middle letters of the word *CANADA* on the illustrated coin were struck so weakly as to be barely visible.

revalidado [*Span.*] revalidated. This word is often seen stamped on notes which circulated during the Mexican Revolution of the 1910s. The stamping indicated that the note had passed through the hands of revolutionary authories and was thereby deemed "acceptable" for use by supporters of the revolutionary movement.

See *revolutionary piece*.

revers (*m.*) [*Fr.*]; (*c.*) [*Dan.*] reverse.

Revers (*m.*) [*Ger.*] reverse.

reverse Usually but not always the "tails" side of a coin. In theory, the reverse is the less important side of a coin. Yet in the United States, the obverse and reverse are defined by law. Similarly, in Mexico and some other Latin American countries, the obverse is the side showing the nation's emblem, and the reverse features the effigies of people.

In many European countries, the slang expression "tails" translates to "cross" (just as "heads" translates to "face"). Many coins of the Middle Ages, especially the silver penny-size coins most apt to be used by peasants, showed a cross on the reverse.

The equivalent term for paper money is *back*, and the obverse is called the *face*.

reverso (*m.*) [*Span., Port.*] reverse.

revet [*Nor.*] torn.

revolutionary piece Any standard circulating coin which has been marked in some way by revolutionary officials to show that the coin has passed through their hands and is therefore acceptable to be used in trade by anyone sympathetic to the revolutionary cause. Coins, by their nature, are made and distributed by the regime in power. Revolutionists do not normally have the means to issue their own money until and unless they actually gain control of the government. The marked coins serve as a symbolic coinage of the revolutionary movement. Having such coins in one's possession enables a person to prove his or her loyalty to the revolutionary cause, but possessing them can be considered evidence of treason.

The illustrated piece on page 310 of the color section is from Mexico. An "X" was scratched on each side as the official mark of the revolution.

rewers (*m.*) [*Pol.*] reverse.

rey (*m.*) [*Span.*] king.

réz [*Hun.*] brass (the alloy).

ricevuta (*f.*) [*Ital.*] receipt.

ridse (*c.*) [*Dan.*] a scratch.

riemissione (*f.*) [*Ital.*] restrike.

Ries Wiener, Gerta Gerta Ries was born in England in 1898. After being trained in Germany, Ms. Ries came to New York in 1921. However, it was not until a half century later (1971) that she created her first medal, honoring U.S. Supreme Court Justice Louis Brandeis. This was commissioned by the Jewish-American Hall of Fame, as were nearly a dozen notable medals since: patriot Gershom Seixas (1975), humanitarian Henrietta Szold (1976), Israeli Prime Minister Golda Meir (1978), philanthropist Rebecca Gratz (1981), violin virtuoso Isaac Stern (1982), poet Emma Lazarus (1983), publisher Adolph Ochs (1985), Justice Benjamin Cardozo (1987), and pediatrician Dr. Béla Schick (1990).

Gerta Ries Wiener's medals have been exhibited at the Smithsonian Institution, the San Francisco Mint, the Newark Museum, and they are on permanent display at the Magnes Museum.

[Contributed by Mel Wacks on behalf of the Magnes Museum.]

rift (*c.*) [*Dan.*]; (*m.*) [*Nor.*] a tear (as in a banknote or bond).

rim The raised portion around the circumference of a coin or medal where the face meets the edge. It tends to be sharp and distinct on proof coins and somewhat rounded and a little flatter on business strikes.

Although the words *rim* and *edge* are translated the same in many foreign languages, they should not be confused with each other in English. The *edge* is the outside portion which is often reeded or lettered and which touches the paper when coins are rolled. The *rim* can be thought of as a peripheral part of the obverse and reverse designs.

riparato [*Ital.*] repaired.

ripe (*m.*) [*Nor.*] a scratch.

riproduzione (*f.*) [*Ital.*] reproduction.

Riß (*m.*) [*Ger.*] a tear (in a banknote or bond).

ritka [*Hun.*] rare, scarce.

ritkaság [*Hun.*] rarity.

rito ρητό (*n.*) [*Grk.*] motto.

ritratto (*m.*) [*Ital.*] portrait.

rød [*Nor., Dan.*] red.

roedura (*f.*) [*Span.*] corrosion.

roenoke Strings of shell money used by some North American Indians. These beads were popular as a medium of exchange with white settlers during the seventeenth century. Many of the white traders even exchanged these beads among themselves. The term *roenoke* was used in the Virginia region, but the item is better known by its New England name, *wampum*. It was called *seawan* in New York.

[A. George Mallis, "A Numismatic Primer— Part 1," *The Numismatist*, July 1988, p. 1217.]

roi (*m.*) [*Fr.*] king.

rojo [*Span.*] red.

rok (*m.*) [*Pol.*] year.

rol (*m.-c.*) [*Dut.*] roll (of coins).

rolka (*f.*) [*Pol.*] roll.

Rolle (*f.*) [*Ger.*] roll.

rolo (*m.*) [*Port.*] roll.

rolos ρολός [*Grk.*] roll.

Roman coinage Roman coinage was developed in the third century B.C. primarily to facilitate trade with Greece. Prior to that time, Roman coins consisted mostly of large bronze pieces known as the *aes rude* and *aes grave*. But around 211 B.C., a silver coin based on the Greek weight system was introduced. The *denarius*[*q.v.*] quickly became popular and was struck in one form or another until the middle of the third century A.D.

Ancient Roman coins are generally grouped into two categories: those from the Republican period and those of the Roman Empire. The dividing point was 29 B.C., the year in which Octavian (better known today as Augustus) received the title of emperor.

Imperial coins were much improved over those from the Republic because their designs were more sophisticated and their denominations were issued with greatly regularity. Augustus was also responsible for making gold an integral part of the coinage system.

The quality of the Roman coins and the fate of the Empire itself seemed to rise and fall together. By the beginning of the fifth century, the state of Roman coins had greatly declined. The end came in A.D. 476 when the western portion of the Empire fell, bringing to a close one of the most important eras in numismatic history.

roman numerals on Spanish and Canadian coins

roman numerals [sometimes written as *Roman numerals* with the first word capitalized.] Numbering system used by ancient Romans. The "numbers" are composites of letters of the alphabet, usually (but not always) capitalized. Roman numerals and their arabic counterparts are as follows: I (1), II (2), III (3), IV (4), V (5), VI (6), VII (7), VIII (8), IX (9), X (10), XI (11), XII (12), XIII (13), XIV (14), XV (15), XVI (16), XVII (17), XVIII (18), XIX (19), XX (20), XXI (21), XXII (22), ..., XXX (30), XXXI (31), ..., XL (40), XLI (41), ..., L (50), LI (51), ..., LX (60), ..., LXX (70), ..., LXXX (80), ..., XC (90), ..., C (100), CI (101), CII (102), ..., CC (200), CCI (201), ..., CCC (300), ..., CD (400), ..., D (500), ..., DC (600), ..., DCC (700), ..., DCCC (800), ..., CM (900), ..., M (1000), MI (1001), ..., MM (2000), ..., MMM (3000), ..., $\bar{V}$ (5000), ..., $\bar{X}$ (10,000), ..., $\bar{C}$ (100,000), ..., $\bar{M}$ (1,000,000), etc. There is no roman numeral equivalent for zero.

In the modern world, a few countries have used roman instead of arabic numerals for dates to give a certain flair to their coins. United States gold bullion coins struck since 1986 are a well known example. The U.S. also used this technique in 1907 on some of the earliest specimen strikes of the St. Gaudens $20

gold pieces. One of the most beautiful of all British coins is the Victorian £5 gold piece (*Una and the Lion*[q.v.]) which shows the date 1839 in roman numerals.

Occasionally the insertion of roman numerals creates a different variety. Some of the 1887 British double-florins show the date as I887 with a roman one instead of the standard arabic 1887.

The most common use of roman numerals on coins is in the numbering of kings and queens. Most collectors are familiar with the designations *George VI* and *Elizabeth II* on the coins of U.K. and the Commonwealth. But the coins of George I and Elizabeth I did not include the roman numeral; those monarchs are simply stated as *George* and *Elizabeth*. This is not the case with Spanish coins issued since 1975. King Juan Carlos is designated *Juan Carlos I*, perhaps in anticipation that there will be a Juan Carlos II, Juan Carlos III, etc.

Roman numerals were used to indicate the values of crude emergency coins issued during the Irish Great Rebellion. See *Dublin money* and *Ormonde money* for illustrations.

The United States used the roman numeral "V" to designate the denomination of its Liberty Head Nickels[q.v.] (1883-1913). Canada got double use of this letter on its tombac and steel 5 cent pieces issued during World War II. The "V" represented both the denomination and the word "Victory."

rond [*Fr., Dut.*] round.

rondell (*m.*) [*Nor.*] planchet, coin blank.

róng yù de 荣誉的 [*Chin.-py./sc.*] laureate.

rood [*Dut.*] red.

Roosevelt Dime U.S. 10 cent piece struck since 1946. The Roosevelt Dime honors Franklin Delano Roosevelt[q.v.], the U.S. president who is generally credited with pulling the nation out of the Great Depression and who presided over the government during most of World War II. Roosevelt died in 1945 shortly after his unprecedented fourth inauguration.

The dime was designed by John R. Sinnock, whose initials JS appear on the truncation of the neck. It replaced the Winged Liberty ("Mercury") Dime which had been minted from 1916 to 1945. Sinnock's rendition is bold and simple and appears more modernistic than designs on previous U.S. coins. The obverse features the profile of F.D.R. facing left. The principal device on the reverse is a torch, representing purification through illumination. This seems an appropriate symbol on a coin dedicated to a man who had just been instrumental in achieving an Allied victory in World War II.

From 1946 to 1964 the Roosevelt Dime was struck from an alloy of .900 silver and .100 copper, the same as that used in U.S. quarter dollars, half dollars, and dollar coins. In 1965 the planchets of all U.S. dimes and quarters were changed to a clad composition with outer layers of .750 copper and .250 nickel bonded to an inner core of pure copper.

The greatest rarities in the Roosevelt Dime series are the 1968, '70, "75, and '83 proof specimens inadvertently struck with no S mintmark. See *smoke signal*.

Roosevelt Dime

Roosevelt, Franklin Delano President of the United States (1933-45). Born January 30, 1882, in Hyde Park, New York; died suddenly on April 12, 1945, in Warm Springs, Georgia.

F.D.R., as he was affectionately called, was elected to four terms as president of the United States. His nomination in 1932 turned solely on the Great Depression issue. On March 4, 1933, he was inaugurated president of a nation on the verge of panic. His inaugural address inspired new confidence with his famous statement that "the only thing we have to fear is fear itself." He followed by declaring a national bank holiday to stop disastrous runs, and on the same day began a program of sweeping legislation known as the "New Deal." A reorganization of

government functions and powers occurred which created many agencies known as the "alphabet agencies" such as the F.D.I.C. (Federal Deposit Insurance Corporation) and the S.S.A. (Social Security Administration).

By 1937 the New Deal was encouraging recovery and a cutback in government spending. But within two years foreign policy was engaging more attention than domestic problems. Roosevelt had maintained a policy of neutrality, but Japanese aggression in China, as well as the rise of Adolf Hitler in Germany and Benito Mussolini in Italy, brought about a deterioration of U.S. relations.

In 1940 Roosevelt won an unprecedented third term. But in 1941 the international situation worsened. Hitler had overrun most of Europe, and the Japanese were approaching a level of absolute strength in the Atlantic. Opposition to Roosevelt increased as he persisted in giving aid to the Allies but without committing U.S. troops.

Finally on December 7, 1941, Japanese aircraft attacked the U.S. Naval Base at Pearl Harbor in Hawaii. The next day, the president obtained a declaration of war from Congress. The course of the war was marked by a series of meetings with heads of state such as Winston Churchill and Joseph Stalin to plan the strategy of the war.

By this time, Roosevelt's health had become a serious problem. In 1921 he was stricken with polio myelitis. He had very little use of his legs and remained crippled throughout his life. He traveled to Warm Springs, Georgia, to rest for an upcoming meeting in San Francisco. Two weeks before the scheduled meeting, he suddenly died.

F.D.R. was both loved and hated, admired and feared. A consummate politician and a bold, courageous president, he left his mark on the nation and on the world. The year after his death, the United States honored him by placing his likeness on the dimes. The Roosevelt Dime[q.v.] is still being issued today.

[Contributed by Ruth Ann Davis. Charles van Doren (editor), *Webster's American Biographies*; Ted Morgan, *FDR: A Biography*.]

rose-ryal of James I

rose-ryal English gold coin issued by James I. It is distinguished by its elegant portrayal of the king sitting on an ornate throne. The reverse shows the coat of arms against a rose, from which the coin gets its name.

From its inception around 1604 until 1612, the rose-ryal was valued at 30 shillings. In 1612, all gold coins were raised in value by ten percent, thus bringing the rose-ryal to 33 shillings. It remained at this value until 1619 when it was brought back to 30 shillings where it remained until the end of its run in 1625 at the death of James I.

[Stephen Mitchell & Brian Reeds (editors), *Coins of England and the United Kingdom* (Seaby, 1991), pp. 177-79.]

Rosja [*Pol.*] Russia.

rosso (*m.*) [*Ital.*] red.

rosszul vert (pénz) [*Hun.*] badly struck; misstruck.

Rost (*m.*) [*Ger.*] rust.

roşu [*Rom.*] red.

rot [*Ger.*] red.

rotocalco (*m.*) [*Ital.*] intaglio.

rotolo (*m.*) [*Ital.*] roll (of coins).

rotondo [*Ital.*] round.

rotura de cuño; **rotura de matriz**; **rotura de troquel** [*Span.*] die break.

rouge [*Fr.*] red.

rouille (*f.*) [*Fr.*] rust.

rouleau (*m.*) [*Fr.*] roll (of coins).

silver round of Princess Grace

round (*noun*) 1. Circular disk, usually containing one ounce of pure silver, which resembles a medal or large coin. This item became popular in the 1980s and was intended to make investing in small quantities of silver easy and convenient. Many rounds portray famous people or illustrate popular cartoon characters.

2. Crown-size wooden disks commonly known as wooden nickels.

rovescio (*m.*) [*Ital.*] reverse; on the back.

rövidítés [*Hun.*] abbreviation.

Royal Numismatic Society The Royal Numismatic Society was founded in 1836 as the Numismatic Society of London and received the title of the Royal Numismatic Society by Royal Charter in 1904. The Society is an academic body of charitable status concerned with research into all branches of numismatics. Its lectures and publications deal with classical, oriental, medieval, and modern coins, paper money, tokens, and medals.

The Society does not undertake the classification, authentication, or valuation of coins. It has no institutional connection with the British Museum. Fellows are entitled to no special privileges at the Department of Coins and Medals.

Fellowship of the Society is by nomination and election. For additional information, contact the Royal Numismatic Society, c/o Department of Coins and Medals, British Museum, London, WCIB 3DG, U.K.

Royal Numismatic Society of New Zealand Founded in 1931, the Royal Numismatic Society of New Zealand was originally incorporated as the New Zealand Numismatic Society. The prefix "Royal" was granted in 1947. The Society was established to encourage and promote the study of numismatics and other related subjects.

The Society awards Fellowships to members in recognition of outstanding service to the Society. It is based in Wellington with a branch in Dunedin. An annual magazine, the New Zealand Numismatic Journal, is published and sent to all members. Articles cover a wide range of numismatic interest, especially those pertaining to New Zealand. Two or three times a year, newsletters on current and general topics are also produced.

Membership is open to any person interested in the objectives of the Society and willing to abide by the Society's rules. An application form can be obtained by contacting the Honorable Secretary at the Royal Numismatic Society of New Zealand, Inc., P.O. Box 2023, Wellington 6015, New Zealand.

Royaume Uni [*Fr.*] United Kingdom (U.K.).

rückseitig [*Ger.*] on the back.

rugină (*f.*) [*Rom.*] corrosion.

ruilen (*v.*) [*Dut.*] to trade.

rull (*m.*) [*Nor.*] roll (of coins).

rulle (*c.*) [*Dan.*]; (*r.*) [*Swed.*] roll.

rund [*Ger., Swed., Nor., Dan.*] round.

ruoste [*Finn.*] rust.

Ruotsi [*Finn.*] Sweden.

rupt [*Rom.*] torn.

ruptură (*f.*) [*Rom.*] a tear (in a banknote or bond).

Rusia [*Span.*] Russia.

ruskea [*Finn.*] brown.

Rusland [*Dan., Dut.*] Russia.

Russland [*Nor.*] Russia.

Rußland [*Ger.*] Russia.

rust An oxide of iron, the product of the corrosion of iron objects.

Rust is rarely seen on coins because few coins have been made from iron or non-stainless steel. A major exception was the 1943 zinc-coated steel cent struck by the United States as a way of conserving copper for war purposes. When it came time to dispose of the cents, the government simply dumped tons of them into San Francisco Bay and allowed them to rust into an unrecognizable blob in the harsh salt water.

A more widespread problem was the rusting of coinage dies, a fairly common occurrence in the eighteenth and nineteenth centuries if the same dies were re-used from year to year. This concerns collectors, because rusted dies leave telltale marks on the coins struck from them.

rysa (*f.*) [*Pol.*] a scratch.

Ryssland [*Swed.*] Russia.

rzadki [*Pol.*] rare, scarce.

rzadkość (*f.*) [*Pol.*] rarity.

S s

s. [*abbr.*] shilling[*q.v.*].

saanti [*Finn.*] acquisition.

saddle blanket Nickname for any large-size U.S. note issued prior to 1929. Also known as *horse blanket*.

sælge (*v.*) [*Dan.*] to sell.

sælger (*c.*) [*Dan.*] seller.

sælgers minimumpris [*Dan.*] protective reserve bid.

saf [*Turk.*] fineness; fine (purity of metal).

sağ [*Turk.*] right (direction or position).

sahte [*Turk.*] a fake, forgery.

säilytyskuluma [*Finn.*] cabinet friction.

St. Gaudens Double Eagle U.S. $20 gold piece struck from 1907 to 1933. The initial pieces in 1907 were extremely high relief patterns with the date in roman numerals. These, plus the circulation strikes in 1907 and early 1908 did not show the motto *In God We Trust* at the request of President Theodore Roosevelt, who opposed mentioning the Deity on coins. The motto was added later in 1908.

The St. Gaudens double eagle is universally hailed as one of America's most beautiful coins. The design was brought back in 1986 for the obverse of the $5, $10, $25, and $50 gold bullion coins.

St. George Slaying the Dragon Reverse design seen on British gold sovereigns and some large silver coins since 1817. It was the creation of Benedetto Pistrucci, who was criticized for not making the dragon formidable enough and for allowing the saint to appear naked. St. George, patron saint of England, is shown on horseback and is wearing only a cloak and a helmet, probably the last piece of armor he is likely to have wanted when fighting a dragon.

Whatever the St. George motif lacks in logic, it makes up for in beauty. It is truly one of the most attractive and enduring designs in the history of coinage and still appears on some British gold coins today.

[Graham P. Dyer, "Five Centuries of the British Gold Sovereign," *The Numismatist*, March 1989, p. 396.]

St. George Slaying the Dragon

St. Nicholas note Any of a group of obsolete United States notes picturing St. Nicholas (a.k.a. Santa Claus, Father Christmas, Kris Kringle, et al). All were printed in the mid-nineteenth century and included five different "Santa Claus" designs. Additionally, the St. Nick motif can be found on checks issued by some of the same banks that distributed the notes, and several Austrian and German communities printed Notgeld[*q.v.*] notes in the early 1920s showing the good saint.

[Gene Hessler, "St. Nick Notes," *The Numismatist*, December 1989, pp. 1934-42.]

säkerhets- [*Swed.*] anti-counterfeiting.

Saksa [*Finn.*] Germany.

salakauppa [*Finn.*] black market.

salapi [*Tag.*] money.

salaping pilak [*Tag.*] crown (large silver coin).

säljare (*m./f.*) [*Swed.*] seller.

sällsynt [*Swed.*] rare, scarce.

samlare (*m./f.*) [*Swed.*] collector.

samler (*m.*) [*Nor.*]; (*c.*) [*Dan.*] collector.

samling (*c.*) [*Dan.*]; (*r.*) [*Swed.*]; (*m.*) [*Nor.*] collection.

sammeln (*v.*) [*Ger.*] to collect.

sammensat [*Dan.*] accolated, conjoined, jugate.

Sammler (*m.*) [*Ger.*] collector.

Sammlung (*f.*) [*Ger.*] collection.

sampu [*Tag.*] ten.

sanat [*Turk.*] art.

"sandwitch"-mynt (*m.*) [*Nor.*] clad coinage.

Santa Margarita *Saint Margaret.* Spanish sailing vessel which sank in 1622 while carrying an estimated $20 million in gold coins and artifacts. The wreckage was located by Mel Fisher and his crew in 1980 as they were searching for the Santa Margarita and its treasure-laden sister ship, Nuestra Señora de Atocha.

Although the State of Florida attempted to claim 25% of the treasure and the U.S. federal government tried to claim 100%, the U.S. Supreme Court in 1982 ruled that Fisher was entitled to whatever he found.

See *Atocha, Nuestra Señora de.*

santimetre [*Turk.*] centimeter, centimetre.

sárga [*Hun.*] yellow.

sarja [*Finn.*] an issue, issuance; series.

sarjanumero [*Finn.*] serial number.

sas [*Hun.*] eagle.

Sassanian coinage Coins struck during the Persian dynasty of A.D. 226-641. The coins generally were thin silver *drachmai*, the earliest of which had fairly standard designs but which degenerated over the centuries until they featured ghoulish effigies suggestive of death. See *drachm* for illustrations.

sata [*Finn.*] hundred.

satavuotinen [*Finn.*] centennial, centenary.

satuan mata wang [*Indo.*] denomination.

S.C. [*Lat. abbr.*] Senatus Consulto ("By Decree of the Senate"). In imperial Rome, the emperor was responsible for precious metals and the coins minted from them, but the Senate determined the production of coins made from base metals. Because of this, the letters "SC" are prominently displayed on imperial bronze coins.

Roman Senatorial coin showing *SC*

scambiare (*v.*) [*Ital.*] to trade.

sceau (*m.*) [*Fr.*] seal (in the numismatic sense).

schaars [*Dut.*] scarce.

schat (*m.-c.*) [*Dut.*] treasure.

Schatz (*m.*) [*Ger.*] treasure.

Schauthaler [*Ger.*] (also spelled *Schautaler*). Silver piece, described as a medal by some experts and as a coin by others, struck in northern Germany during an 80-year period from the late 1500s to the mid-1600s. Most of these pieces presumably were produced by the Hamburg Mint and were intended to commemorate the birth, baptism, and crucifixion of Jesus Christ. Some also honor such religious events as marriage.

The lack of agreement as to whether these are coins or medals exists because of the unusual nature of the pieces. The weights and fineness of the planchets equalled those of partial or multiple thaler coins. Yet, they were struck as commemorative pieces and were not intended for circulation. In other words, they were not supposed to be a form of money, but they could have been used as money because they had the same intrinsic qualities as the circulating coins of the time.

No matter what their intended purpose, these pieces exhibit magnificent workmanship and are considered among the finest examples of numismatic art.

[Arthur R. Doumaux, Jr., "The Hamburg Connection," *The Numismatist*, February 1989, pp. 242-52 (This article includes a detailed compilation of the obverse and reverse dies used to produce the Hamburg Marriage Schauthalers, as well as a list of the Hamburg

and non-Hamburg mintmasters as compiled by O. C. Gædechens.); Richard G. Doty, *The Macmillan Encyclopedic Dictionary of Numismatics*, p. 289.]

Scheck (*m.*) [*Ger.*] check, cheque.

schedio σχέδιο (*n.*) [*Grk.*] pattern; design.

scheur (*m.-c.*) [*Dut.*] a tear (in a note or bond).

schismeno σχισμένο [*Grk.*] torn.

Schlagschatz (*m.*) [*Ger.*] seigniorage.

schlechte Prägung [*Ger.*] bad strike.

Schnittentwertung (*f.*) [*Ger.*] cut cancellation.

Schotland [*Dut.*] Scotland.

Schottland [*Ger.*] Scotland.

Schrötling (*m.*) [*Ger.*] planchet.

Schubert, General Fedor (1789-1865) Author of the monumental *Monnaies Russes des Derniers Trois Siècles* ("Russian Coins of the Past Three Centuries"), a major scholarly work published in 1857 which listed the actual weights of several thousand sixteenth-nineteenth century Russian coins. Schubert was regarded as one of the greatest numismatic scholars of his time.

[R. W. Julian, "The Russian Silver Coinage of 1796-1917," *The Numismatist*, December 1989, pp. 1952-59.]

schwach ausgeprägt [*Ger.*] badly struck.

schwarz [*Ger.*] black.

Schwarzmarkt (*m.*) [*Ger.*] black market.

Schweiz [*Dan., Ger.*] Switzerland.

sconosciuto [*Ital.*] unknown.

Scozia [*Ital.*] Scotland.

scrap 1. Broken jewelry, heavily damaged coins, etc., which no longer have value as collectors' items and are worth only their metallic value.

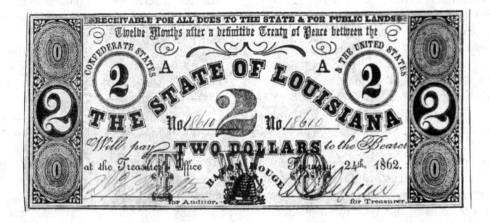

scrap [#4]: 1862 C.S.A. (Louisiana) note printed on discarded money paper

2. Mint scraps are the odd pieces of metal that remain after coin blanks are punched from sheets of rolled metal. Minting facilites normally collect the scraps and return them for re-melting, so it is somewhat unusual to see mint scraps in a coin collection. See page 317 for color illustrations.

3. Postage stamps printed on discarded money paper. This was done in 1919 in Latvia due to a severe paper shortage resulting from the effects of World War I. See *postage stamps on currency paper.*

4. Paper money printed on discarded money paper. The illustration shows an 1862 Confederate States of America note from Louisiana printed on paper originally processed for notes from Mississippi. The two sides are completely different in that they represent different states, different denominations, and even two different printing methods.

It is incorrect to call this note an error, because it was produced this way more or less intentionally. There were few printing houses in the South during the U.S. Civil War, and the few that did exist were often called upon to print notes from many different states. In some cases, state-issued notes of the Civil War era were uniface, so it did not matter if they were printed on the clean side of soiled paper. And since the South was suffering from a paper shortage, nothing could be wasted. Thus, it was not unusual for notes of this type to be printed on scrap.

scrip Tokens or paper notes issued by companies, private individuals, or governmental agencies as a temporary replacement for legitimate money. These items are not counterfeits and are not intended to deceive or defraud anyone. Rather, they are most often issued in times of economic stress to alleviate a shortage of circulating money. Users normally understand the scrip's purpose.

Some authorities insist that the term *scrip* be reserved strictly for emergency money. The *Notgeld* of post-World War I Germany and Austria and some of the inflation-riddled notes of post-World War II Hungary fall into this category, as do the store cards and various emergency notes emanating from the Union (the North) during the U.S. Civil War of 1861-65. Not all emergency money stemmed from the economic uncertainties or military defeat of war, however. The Depression of 1837 and the Great Depression of the 1930s gave rise to a considerable amount of scrip in the United States and Canada.

In its broadest sense, the word *scrip* can refer to any temporary substitute for money. Stores may give scrip in lieu of small coins to customers during times of coin shortages or to make change for purchases made with government-issued food stamps. While incarcerated, prisoners may be required to use special scrip instead of regular money. Coal miners and other employees working in isolated regions have sometimes received part of their salaries in scrip which could only be redeemed at the company's general store, although this practice is no longer in vogue. Many present-day pieces of scrip are tokens or note-like coupons issued by businesses for the convenience of customers or for purposes of advertising.

The term *scrip* does not cover tax receipts, theater tickets, bus tokens, or any other pieces purchased for a very specific purpose, nor does it include coins or notes produced by governmental agencies that are normally authorized to issue money.

Many people use the term *private scrip*, yet this is an unnecessary redundancy because all scrip is privately issued.

See *prison token, Notgeld, trade token,* and *coal company scrip.* Also see pages 316 and 319 for color illustrations.

[Richard G. Doty, *The Macmillan Encyclopedic Dictionary of Numismatics,* pp. 292-3.]

script Printed lettering resembling handwriting, a technique virtually never seen on coins. The recent French 1 and 5 centime pieces are among the rare exceptions. [Note: The word *script* should not be confused with *scrip.*]

scyphate Cup-shape coin, somewhat resembling an elephant-size contact lens. The coin gets this shape when the blank is struck by a convex reverse die into a concave obverse die.

Although coins of this type are thought to have existed as early as the second century B.C., the most pronounced use of this technique came from the Byzantine Empire. Doty states that Emperor Constantine IX, who ruled from A.D. 1042-1055, adopted this minting procedure in order to distinguish heavy gold coins from lighter ones.

Spanish brass stamp seal [photo courtesy Harlan J. Berk, Ltd.]

Byzantine scyphate

The Byzantine Empire, as well as some of the neighboring states, minted scyphate coins along with the usual flat coins until around 1400. Although gold remained the preferred metal for this kind of coinage, many of these pieces were also made of electrum[q.v.], copper, and silver.

The gold scyphate was called the *nomisma*, a name that had been given to the gold *solidus* as early as the fourth century A.D. in the Eastern Roman Empire. The immediate predecessor of the scyphate nomisma was the *stamenon nomisma*, a gold coin which was flat and not as broad.

[A. George Mallis, "A Numismatic Primer— Part 4," *The Numismatist*, October 1988, pp. 1760-61; Richard G. Doty, *The Macmillan Encyclopedic Dictionary of Numismatics*, p. 293.]

se aceptan tarjetas de crédito [*Span.*] credit cards accepted.

seal Device with a cut or raised emblem used to certify a signature or to authenticate a document, or an engraved medallion which can be pressed into wax to officially seal envelopes or authenticate documents.

The illustration shows the male and female sides of a Spanish brass stamp seal from the thirteenth century. The seal features the Tree of Life and is bordered with a Hebrew inscription that reads, "Moses, Son of Joseph of Merena."

Seated Liberty coins [a.k.a. *Liberty Seated* coins.] Popular design found on many series of silver U.S. coins issued during the nineteenth century. Specifically, this motif appeared on the half dimes (i.e., silver 5 cent pieces, 1837-1873), dimes (10 cent pieces, 1837-1891), 20 cent pieces (1875-1878), quarter dollars (1838-1891), half dollars (1839-1891), and dollars (1836-1873).

The design is attributed to Mint Engraver Christian Gobrecht, whose last name appears below or on the base upon which Liberty is sitting on some of the earliest dollars of this type. During the late 1830s, modifications were made on several denominations, but by 1840 the Liberty design was finalized and remained unchanged until it was abandoned in 1891.

Seated Liberty Quarter

Several changes not involving the actual Liberty design itself occurred on some of these coins. From 1853 to 1855 arrows were placed next to the date on the half dimes, dimes, quarters, and halves to indicate a small reduction of weight. In 1853 only, the quarters

and halves also displayed rays around the eagle on the reverse. The motto *In God We Trust* was added to the reverse side of the larger coins in 1866, just two years after it made its debut on two cent pieces. In 1873 and 1874, the arrows surfaced again next to the dates on the dimes, quarters, and halves, this time to signify a very slight increase in weight.

[R. S. Yeoman, *A Guide Book of United States Coins* (44th Ed.), pp. 171-174, et al; Karl L. Guntermann, "An Analysis of Liberty Seated Half Dimes," *The Numismatist,* March 1988, pp. 455-60.]

seawan Strings of shell money used by some North American Indians. These beads were popular as a medium of exchange with white settlers during the seventeenth century. Many of the white traders even exchanged these among themselves. The term *seawan* was used in the New York area, but the item is better known by its New England name, *wampum*[q.v.]. It was called *roenoke* in Virginia.

[A. George Mallis, "A Numismatic Primer— Part 1," *The Numismatist*, July 1988, p. 1217.]

sechs [*Ger.*] six.

sechzig [*Ger.*] sixty.

lettered edge (above); complex & decorative edges (below)

security edge Any special design or lettering placed on the edge of a coin to make counterfeiting more difficult or to prevent the shaving off of bits of precious metal from the edge of a gold or silver coin (known as *clipping*[q.v.]).

The first illustration shows part of a lettered edge in relief (i.e., with the letters raised up from the surface) from a U.S. Bust Type Half Dollar. The original purpose of this type of lettering was to thwart clipping. But today, lettered edges are added primarily to make commemorative coins more esthetically pleasing to add to their marketability.

The second illustration exhibits the complex security edge on a British West Africa threepence. Clipping was not a concern because the coins were made of non-precious metals (copper and nickel). The security edges were needed to discourage counterfeiting, a serious problem in the parts of the world where these coins circulated. The fact that the coins were of such small denomination did not diminish the need to encircle them with a complex security device.

The third illustration shows a security edge with a stylized design. It has little functional use and is primarily utilized as a decoration. The coin is a 1987 German 1 mark piece.

sedek b'matba'at סֶדֶק בְּמַטְבֵּעַ (*m.*) [*Heb.*] die break.

sedel (*r.*) [*Swed.*] note, banknote.

sede vacante (*f.*) [*Ital.*] vacant see. The period between the death of an ecclesiastical ruler and the appointment of his successor. Numismatically, the term refers to coins issued during this period. The tradition began in the Middle Ages in various cities in Europe which were controlled by religious leaders who also enjoyed temporal power.

In today's world, the term is used almost exclusively in reference to the death of the pope. Vatican City regularly issues special coins and stamps during interregnal periods, such as in 1963 at the death of Pope John XXIII and in 1978 at the deaths of Paul VI and John Paul I.

The issuance of *sede vacante* coins and stamps in 1978 was complicated by the death of John Paul I, who died within only a month of his ascension to the papacy. In keeping with tradition, the Vatican did in fact issue a 500 lire coin at the death of Paul VI and then produced a different 500 lire coin two months later upon the death of John Paul I. This latter coin is somewhat unique, because it was dated not only with the year of emission but also the month (September 1978) in order to clarify which interregnum it represented.

sedlar (*r.pl.*) [*Swed.*]; (*c.pl.*) [*Dan.*] paper money.

segno di rifilatura; segno di riporto [*Ital.*] adjustment mark.

segno di zecca [*Ital.*] mintmark.

segnoragium (*n.*) [*Pol.*] seigniorage.

sei [*Ital.*] six.

Seidenfaden (*m.*) [*Ger.*] silk thread.

seigneuriage (*m.*) [*Fr.*] seigniorage.

seigniorage (also spelled *seignorage* and *seigneurage*.)

1. The difference between the bullion value of a coin and the coin's denomination. As early as the thirteenth century, this "profit" was retained by the moneyer to defray the costs of refining, minting, etc. In the later Middle Ages in such places as England and France, the seigniorage might be kept by the king, who would sometimes debase the precious metal content of coins in order to make the seigniorage even greater. This only served to create a form of inflation by decreasing the buying power of those coins.

2. In the most contemporary sense as this term is understood by marketers, seigniorage is the difference between the "selling" price of a modern coin (when "sold" by the government which minted it) and the total cost of producing that coin. Total cost is determined by taking into account the cost of the metal, labor costs, wear and tear on the machinery, distribution costs, et al. In other words, seigniorage is the profit which a government earns by making and distributing coins, irrespective of whether those coins are general circulation coins, bullion coins for investors, or proof sets or non-circulating legal tender[*q.v.*] (N.C.L.T.) coins for collectors and souvenir hunters.

In the more traditional sense, if Canada must pay a total cost of ten cents to produce and distribute a quarter dollar coin, then its seigniorage (or "profit") is fifteen cents, because Canada is "selling" that coin for 25 cents by declaring it to be of that value and by placing it into general circulation for that amount. In a more modern economic sense, if the United States must pay a total cost of $3 to produce a five-coin proof set which it then (literally) sells for $7 to collectors, its seigniorage is $4; the fact that the five coins have a total face value of 91 cents is absolutely irrelevant (as long as the total face value is less than the selling price). Similarly, if the U.S. Mint produces a Presidential Medal, a non-money item having no face value, the difference between the total cost and selling price is still regarded as the item's seigniorage.

Although not universally accepted by all economists, this last definition of seigniorage is very important to numismatics, because it is the reason why N.C.L.T. coins proliferated during the 1960s and '70s and why such countries as Austria, Canada, the United States, and many others have flooded the market with recent commemorative issues. Governments produce these coins to make money, either for their general funds or for special projects such as the Canadian Olympics. In some cases, seigniorage has been a very large source of revenue.

seis [*Span., Port.*] six.

seitsemän [*Finn.*] seven.

seitsemänkymmentä [*Finn.*] seventy.

sekki; šekki [*Finn.*] check, cheque.

seks [*Nor., Dan.*] six.

seksti [*Nor.*] sixty.

selge (*v.*) [*Nor.*] to sell.

selger (*m.*) [*Nor.*] seller.

sello (*m.*) [*Span.*] 1. postage stamp. 2. seal (in the numismatic sense).

sello encapsulado (*m.*) [*Span.*]; **selo encapsulado** (*m.*) [*Port.*] encased postage stamp (such as the type used as an emergency substitute for small coins during the U.S. Civil War of 1861-65).

selo (*m.*) [*Port.*] seal (in the numismatic sense).

selten [*Ger.*] rare, scarce.

Seltenheit (*f.*) [*Ger.*] rarity.

selyemszál [*Hun.*] silk thread.

semé (or **semée**) **of hearts** Ornamental pattern of hearts which appears on some varieties of the 1787 British shillings of George III. They are (or are not) found within the shield on the left side of the reverse design.

[Stephen Mitchell & Brian Reeds (editors), *Coins of England and the United Kingdom* (Seaby, 1991), p. 261]

semi-commemorative [a.k.a. *circulating commemorative.*] Commemorative coin issued for general circulation and intended to take the place of the prevailing regular-issue coins for

one or two years. Some of the best-known examples are the 1967 Canadian coins (cent, 5 cents, 10 cents, 25 cents, 50 cents, and dollar) struck to honor the hundredth anniversary of the formation of the Dominion of Canada, and the 1976 U.S. Bicentennial coins (25 cents, 50 cents, and dollar). The Canadian designs replaced the regular issues for only the year 1967. The U.S. pieces replaced the regular coinage in 1975 and 1976.

semnătură (*f.*) [*Rom.*] signature.

semn de ajustare (*n.*) [*Rom.*] adjustment mark.

semnul monetăriei (*n.*) [*Rom.*] mintmark.

senhoriagem (*f.*) [*Port.*] seigniorage.

senioriaj (*n.*) [*Rom.*] seigniorage.

señoreaje (*m.*); **señoraje** (*m.*) [*Span.*] seigniorage.

senttimetri [*Finn.*] centimeter, centimetre.

senza rovescio [*Ital.*] uniface.

seppelöity (laakeriseppele) [*Finn.*] laureate.

sept [*Fr.*] seven.

sepuluh [*Indo.*] ten.

seratus [*Indo.*] hundred.

se requiere un depósito [*Span.*] deposit required.

serial number Sequential numbering on paper money. Serials numbers are also occasionally found on coins, tokens, and commemorative medals.

There are several areas of note collecting which focus on special serial numbers. One example is the collection of notes and sheets with Serial Number 1. Although this is a fairly popular area of notaphily (the study and collection of paper money), assembling a collection of these items can be difficult and expensive. Many Number 1 notes and sheets are not available at any price because they reside in museum collections. An alternative is the saving of the nine-digit serial number 100000000 (100 million), which is the highest number to be found on any U.S. paper money.

Two other widely collected types of serial numbers are the "solid" numbers (all of the digits are identical, such as 22222222) and "radar" notes (technically known as *palindromes*) in which the serial number reads the same from the front to the end or from the end to the front (e.g., 24688642). Both of these types can command significantly higher premiums than similar notes without the peculiar serial number arrangements.

Some note collectors look for serial numbers that have some personal meaning but may not be important to anyone else. These notes are often difficult to locate, because no one else is searching for them and no dealer is likely to carry them.

Serial numbers are sometimes placed on commemorative medals, usually on the edge. The numbers indicate that the medals are a limited edition, making them more marketable.

serie (*f.*) [*Ital., Span.*] series.

Serie (*f.*) [*Ger.*] series.

série (*f.*) [*Fr., Port.*] series.

serienummer (*n.*) [*Nor., Swed.*] serial number.

seri numarası [*Turk.*] serial number.

Roman denarius with serrated edge

serrated Continuous deep indentations cut into the edge of a coin. This characteristic is most often seen on silver Roman republican denarii of the first two centuries B.C., although the technique was also occasionally used in ancient Greece. No one knows for sure why this type of edge was used, but it is certain that the method was slow and difficult for the moneyers who produced it.

sertifikat (*n.*) [*Nor.*] certificate.

sérült [*Hun.*] damaged.

sesenta [*Span., Port.*] sixty.

sessanta [*Ital.*] sixty.

sessenta [*Port.*] sixty.

sestertius Originally a small Roman Republican silver coin valued at two and a half asses, the sestertius ultimately became the primary bronze coin of the Roman Empire. The bronze version was introduced around 23 B.C. by Augustus and was valued at a quarter-denarius. It not only circulated widely but it was an

esthetically pleasing coin upon which many interesting designs were placed. The coins were a forum for political slogans and are of key interest to historians. The last of the pieces were struck ca. A.D. 265.

Roman sestertius

seteli [*Finn.*] note, banknote.

set-up trial piece (a.k.a. *adjustment trial piece* or *set-up trial.*) Coin struck while the die is in the process of being aligned. See *adjustment.*

strung coins of Persia

sewn money Coins sewn together or onto clothing as a way of preventing them from getting lost. During the Middle Ages, holes were often punched into small coins to enable the coins to be strung together. The strung coins could either be kept in that manner or attached to a garment. In some parts of the world, coins have been sewn onto clothing as a decoration.

sewn token Fourteenth century farthing token of England, usually round, which contained a large, square, two-holed appendage that was used to sew the token to an alms purse.

[Saul B. Needleman, "The Farthing as an Economic Necessity," *The Numismatist*, April 1987, p. 764.]

sfragida σφραγίδα (*f.*) [*Grk.*] seal (as defined in numismatics.).

sfragismeno nomisma σφραγισμένο νόμισμα (*n.*) [*Grk.*] milled coin.

sheared coin Coin cut into two or more pieces to provide small change or to make the coin acceptable for circulation in a country other than the one where it was minted. See *cut coin.*

shekel [from Hebrew שֶׁקֶל or ∠שׁ] (also romanized as *sheqel*; plural forms are *sheqalim* or *shekalim.*)

1. Babylonian and Canaanite weight mentioned in the Jewish Bible. It was equal to 20 gerahs, and there were sixty shekels to a minah and 3600 shekels to a talent.

2. Silver coin introduced by the Phoenicians in the fourth century B.C.E, weighing 26.4 grams.

3. Weight and coin used by the Jews for religious purposes (see *temple tax* and *pidyon haben*). A shekel was equal to 20 gerah (גֵּרָה), 4 zuz (זוּז), or 2 beka (בֶּקַע). In turn, 50 shekels made a maneh (מָנֶה) and 3000 shekels a kikkar (כִּכָּר). Coined silver shekels from Ptolemy II (285-246 B.C.E.) through the Bar Kokhba Revolt (132-135 C.E.) weighed between 13.5 and 14.5 grams. The first Jewish shekel coins were issued in the War Against Rome (65-70 C.E.) and portray a wine cup on one side and a pomegranate branch on the other. The second series was issued during the Bar Kokhba Revolt and portray the Temple façade on the obverse and a *lulav* and *etrog* (tree branches and fruit used in the harvest holiday services) on the reverse.

false shekel (souvenir) [#4]

4. Souvenirs (called *false shekels*) issued for pilgrims to the Holy Land. These were originally issued by Georg Emerich (1422-1507), burgomaster of Gerlitz, Germany, himself a pilgrim to the Holy Land. The coins are usually large brass or bronze reproductions based on a description of the Bar Kokhba shekels in a commentary by Nakhmanides. They are easily identified since they use the modern, Aramaic-based Hebrew alphabet (שקל ישראל), whereas the Bar Kokhba coins used the old, Paleo-Hebrew alphabet (⌐Ⴎ⥀Wℵ ⌐ႮꟼW).

5. The cost of one year's membership in the World Zionist Organization, starting in 1897. It was officially valued at 1 French franc, 1 German mark, 1 Austrian crown, 2 British shillings, 50 U.S. cents, or 40 Russian kopeks. Membership cards were issued, often portraying shekel coins of the War Against Rome. The number of cards sold was 164,333 in 1907, which grew to 2.16 million in 1946.

6. A modern Israeli coin and monetary unit. The Knesset (parliament) voted to replace the lira (pound) with the shekel in 1970, but it was not carried out until 1980 (when the shekel was valued at 10 lirot). In 1985, due to inflation, a *new shekel* (שֶׁקֶל חָדָשׁ) equal to 1000 shekalim was introduced. All Israeli silver commemorative shekalim but the first one are produced according to the ancient Phoenician standard of 14.4 grams of .850 fine silver (1980-1990) or .925 fine silver (1991 on).

[Contributed by Simcha Kuritzky. *Encyclopedia Judaica*, Vol. 14, p. 1347; James Hastings (ed.), *Dictionary of the Bible*; Peter S. Horvitz, "Pilgrim Medals: Old Tradition and New," *The Shekel*, July-August 1988, pp. 4-6.]

shelo bamakhazor שֶׁלֹּא בַּמַּחְזוֹר [*Heb.*] uncirculated.

shelo nitba kahalakha שֶׁלֹּא נִטְבַּע כַּהֲלָכָה [*Heb.*] mis-struck.

shelo pursam שֶׁלֹּא פּוּרְסַם [*Heb.*] unpublished (not listed in any book or catalogue).

shelo ya'tsa l'hanpakah שֶׁלֹּא יָצָא לְהַנְפָּקָה [*Heb.*] not issued.

shenitba b'ofen lakuy שֶׁנִּטְבַּע בְּאֹפֶן לָקוּי [*Heb.*] badly struck.

sheqalim plural of *shekel*[*q.v.*] (or *sheqel*).

sheqel See *shekel*.

shekel [#5]: World Zionist Organization membership card

shihei 紙幣 [*Jpn.*] paper currency. The general term for currency, referring both to coins and paper money, is *tsûka* 通貨 .

shill Phony bidder at an auction who bids against the real bidders in order to prop up the price. He does this on behalf of either the seller or auction house.

shilling [abbreviated *s.*] Minor denomination used at one time or another by Australia, British Honduras (Belize), Biafra, British Virgin Islands, British West Africa, Cyprus, Dominica, East Africa, El Salvador, Fiji, Gambia, Ghana, Great Britain, Guernsey, Ireland, Isle of Man, Jamaica, Jersey, Kenya, Malawi, Mozambique, New Guinea, New Zealand, Nigeria, Rhodesia, Rhodesia & Nyasaland, St. Vincent, Somalia, South Africa, Southern Rhodesia, Trinidad, Uganda, and Zambia.

Originally known as a *testoon*, the silver shilling was introduced in England by Henry VII around 1504 to compete with the Italian *testone*. The name *shilling* was applied to the testoon in 1549 during the brief reign of Edward VI. The exact origin of the word shilling is uncertain, but the word was used as early as the ninth century as a unit of account.

During most of its history, the shilling was valued at twelve pence or 1/20 of a pound. After the decimal conversion of 1970, the equivalent value became five new pence.

Canadian "shinplaster"

shinplaster Common term for any of the U.S. notes issued from 1862-1876 bearing a denomination of less than one dollar. The term also applies to the Canadian 25 cent notes first issued in 1870 as a way of preventing U.S. quarter dollar coins from entering Canada. The notes proved so popular that additional printings of the Canadian notes were made in 1900 and 1923.

See *fractional currency*.

shinui ta'arikh שִׁנּוּי תַאֲרִיךְ (*m.*) [*Heb.*] altered date.

shit'ray kesef שְׁטָרֵי כֶּסֶף [*Heb.*] paper money.

shiyô sareta 使用された [*Jpn.*] circulated.

Swiss Shooting Festival Taler

Shooting Festival Medals and Talers Collection of medals and crown-size silver coins issued at various times from 1822 to 1913 to commemorate the Shooting Festivals. These festivals were competitions among skilled riflemen and were held to strengthen the sense of unity among the various Swiss cantons after the Napoleonic wars. Approximately 100 types and varieties of these medals were issued, and they were struck in silver, bronze, aluminum, tin, and lead. There were 22 talers issued,

mostly in the denomination of 5 francs, although some authorities feel that as many as five of these were really medals, not coins.

Some additional silver (5 franc) and gold (100 franc) pieces were struck in 1934 and 1939 on behalf of the cities of Fribourg and Lucerne.

[Delbert Kay Krause, "Swiss Shooting Festival Medals and Talers," *The Numismatist*, May 1964, pp. 579-585.]

sh'tar שְׁטָר (*m.*) [*Heb.*] note.

sh'tar kesef שְׁטָר כֶּסֶף (*m.*) [*Heb.*] banknote.

sh'tar ta'amulah שְׁטָר תַּעֲמוּלָה (*m.*) [*Heb.*] propaganda note.

shuleyim שׁוּלַיִם [*Heb.*] rim.

shwe ၁ [*Bur.*] gold.

sidiros σίδηρος (*m.*) [*Grk.*] iron (the metal).

sieben [*Ger.*] seven.

siebzig [*Ger.*] seventy.

Siegel (*n.*) [*Ger.*] seal (in the numismatic sense).

siete [*Span.*] seven.

sigiliu (*n.*) [*Rom.*] seal.

sigill (*n.*) [*Swed.*] seal.

sigillo (*m.*) [*Ital.*] seal.

sign. [*abbr.*] signature, signatures.

signoraggio (*m.*) [*Ital.*] seigniorage.

sikkerhetsfibre [*Nor.*] silk thread.

Silber (*n.*) [*Ger.*] silver.

silked paper Small pieces of brightly colored silk thread are sometimes embedded in the paper upon which stamps and paper money are printed as a device for making counterfeiting more difficult.

The silk threads may be evenly distributed throughout the paper (as with U.S. notes) or may be concentrated in one specific area.

The Paraguayan note in the color illustration on page 318 is a somewhat of an anomaly, because it represents a banknote with "fake" silked paper. The silk threads were actually glued on, giving the illusion of having been embedded in the paper. This qualifies as the "poor man's" anti-counterfeiting device.

silketråd (*c.*) [*Dan.*] silk thread.

silkkilanka [*Finn.*] silk thread.

silver One of the most popular metals from which coins have been minted. [element: group Ib of the periodic table; atomic weight 107.868; atomic number 47; specific gravity 10.50; symbol Ag.]

A white, easily worked metal that resists corrosion but takes on a patina that often enhances the struck design. Silver coins have a satisfying ring when struck against a hard object. Silver has been used since ancient times. It is almost always alloyed, usually with copper. A number of different finenesses have been used in the twentieth century: .925 (Great Britain), .900 (United States), .835 (France), .800 (Canada), .720 (Mexico), .625 (West Germany, 1951-74), et al.

Specific alloys often have names: sterling silver, coin silver, billon, etc. Alloys with less than 50% silver (known as *billon*) frequently have nickel and zinc added to hide the yellow color of the copper.

[Contributed by Halbert Carmichael.]

United Netherlands "Silver Rider"

Silver Rider Popular name of the silver ducaton issued by United Netherlands from 1759 to 1792. The coin was of .941 silver, an unusually high level of purity for coinage purposes.

Silver Star Small silver star worn on the ribbon of a campaign medal. It was authorized on July 9, 1918, as the *Citation Star* of the U.S. Army. However, the use of these caused some confusion, as they were worn in the same manner by those who had been wounded in action.

After the authorization of the Purple Heart to persons wounded in action in 1932, the Silver Star was redesigned as a medal on August 8 of

that year. It became a small silver star 4.5 mm in diameter encircled by a laurel wreath. The wreath was placed in the center of a 32 mm bronze star, and a ribbon of red, white, and blue was added.

The Silver Star, awarded for combat action only, takes precedence over the Legion of Merit and under special circumstances may be awarded to civilians. It can be given to any member of the U.S. armed forces who, while serving in any capacity (including with friendly forces), distinguishes himself or herself by gallantry in action against an armed enemy of the United States, but not warranting the Medal of Honor or Distinguished Service Cross.

The award was made retroactive as far back as the Spanish American War (1898), and subsequently the Phillipine insurrection, Boxer Rebellion, and World War I.

In the case of the U.S. Army, the Silver Star was given on or after December 7, 1941, but could be awarded retroactively prior to that date on the orders of a general officer. The Silver Star joined the naval "Pyramid of Honor" in 1942, citing conspicuous gallantry but not at the level of the Medal of Honor or Navy Cross.

Designed by the Philadelphia jewelry firm of Bailey, Banks, and Biddle, the first Navy medals struck were in general thicker than their Army counterparts, thus being helpful in authenticating a particular medal's age.

[Contributed by Robert A. Carpenter. Evans Kerrigan, *American Medals and Decorations*, pp. 18-19; Capt. H. Taprell Dorling, *Ribbons and Medals*, pp. 207-8.]

siman hamitba'a סִימָן הַמַּטְבֵּעָה (*m.*) [*Heb.*] mint-mark.

siman hat'ama סִימָן הַתְאָמָה (*m.*) [*Heb.*] adjust-ment mark.

siman mayim סִימָן מֵימִי (*m.*) [*Heb.*] watermark.

símbolo (*m.*) [*Span., Port.*] symbol.

sin atribución [*Span.*] unattributed (not listed in any book or catalogue).

sin circular [*Span.*] uncirculated.

sininen [*Finn.*] blue.

sinistra (*f.*) [*Ital.*] left (direction or position).

sinsilyo [*Tag.*] coin.

sirküle etmiş [*Turk.*] circulated.

sirkulert [*Nor.*] circulated.

sisma סִיסְמָה (*f.*) [*Heb.*] motto.

sistema monetario (*m.*) [*Span., Ital.*] monetary system.

sistema monetário (*m.*) [*Port.*] monetary system.

situado (*m.*) [*Span.*] An allowance received from New Spain (Mexico) or the Mainland (Colombia and Venezuela) to cover the costs of building and maintaining forts and garrisons throughout the Spanish Caribbean territories in the sixteenth century. In essense, Carlos V (Charles V) of Spain decided that the gold-producing areas in the New World would be responsible for financing the protection of the entire territory conquered by Spain. The *situado* was simply an accounting method used to enable the expenses to be assigned to the proper viceroyalties.

[Manuel Moreno Fraginals and José A. Pulido Ledesma, *Cuba: A Country and Its Currency*, National Bank of Cuba, pp. 33-37.]

sjælden [*Dan.*] rare, scarce.

sjældenhed (*c.*) [*Dan.*] rarity.

sjekk (*m.*) [*Nor.*] check, cheque.

sjelden [*Nor.*] rare, scarce.

sjeldenhet (*m.*) [*Nor.*] rarity.

skat (*c.*) [*Dan.*] tax; treasure.

skatt (*r.*) [*Swed.*]; (*m.*) [*Nor.*] tax; treasure.

ślad justowania (*m.*) [*Pol.*] adjustment mark.

slagskatt (*r.*) [*Swed.*] seigniorage.

slave token

slave token Identification tags for African slaves brought to the New World were often made from coins. Copper coins were the right size and shape. They were also plentiful and were far less expensive to use than specially-prepared tags would have been.

slicewood Thin sheets of wood used for printing various cards and novelties, including some flat wooden tokens, referred to simply as *flats*[q.v.].

slider A virtually uncirculated coin. The fact that it is attractive and blends well in an uncirculated set does not change its grade; it is still About Uncirculated.

slijschat (*m.-c.*) [*Dut.*] seigniorage.

slijtage (*m.-c.*) [*Dut.*] wear.

slitage (*n.*) [*Swed.*] wear.

slitasje (*m.*) [*Nor.*] wear.

small cent 1. U.S. one cent piece introduced as a pattern in 1856 and established as a circulating coin the following year. With modifications, the small cent has been issued every year from 1857 to the present.

Large cents[q.v.] had been struck in the U.S. since 1793. By the mid-1850s they had become too expensive to produce, and an alternative was sought. In 1857 the large cent (29 mm in diameter; 10.89 grams) was replaced with a smaller coin, and the half cent was abandoned altogether. The Coinage Act of February 21, 1857, not only provided for the minting of small cents but also officially invalidated the use of foreign coins in the United States.

The first small cents were of the Flying Eagle type, designed by James B. Longacre. They were only 19 mm in diameter and with a weight of 4.67 grams. The cents were thick and rather white in color due to their composition of 88% copper and 12% nickel.

Neither the composition nor the design survived. The design was changed in 1859 to the Indian Head type (also designed by Longacre), and the metallic composition was switched in 1864 to a bronze planchet. This remained its basic type until its discontinuance in 1909 when the Lincoln Cent was introduced.

The Lincoln Cent was struck in honor of the hundredth anniversary of Abraham Lincoln's birth. The reverse was changed in 1959 by replacing the wheat stalks with the Lincoln Memorial. All 1943 cents were minted from zinc-coated steel because copper was needed for the war effort, and many cents of 1944 to 1946 were made from retrieved shell cases. In the 1970s, clad blanks with bronze as the outside layers and aluminum as the center core were adopted.

More coins have been struck with the Lincoln obverse than any other type in history. Since 1909, more than 250,000,000,000 cents with Lincoln's likeness have been produced.

2. Canada switched to the small cent in 1920 after having minted large cents intermittently since 1858. In the early 1920s Canada decided to sell some of its old large cent dies to China for "recycling." Hence, the familiar ring of Canadian maple leaves adorns a number of Chinese bronze coins (see *reused die* for illustration).

A few George V 1936 cents were issued with a dot under the date signifying that they were struck in 1937 under the reign of George VI. Edward VIII's unexpected abdication in December 1936 disrupted the schedule for preparing new dies, and the Royal Canadian Mint wanted to be ready for any further delays.

The independence of India in 1947 required new obverse dies with *ET IND. IMP.* ("and Emperor of India") deleted from the king's title. A small maple leaf was placed near the date 1947 to show that the coins had actually been struck in 1948. This procedure was done to all denominations, not just the cent.

The small cent has undergone many changes during the reign of Elizabeth II. Her portrait has been updated as she has aged, and some changes have been made in the size and metallic composition of the cents due to an increase in the price of copper as well as other considerations. For example, the cents were made 12-sided in 1982 as a way of assisting the blind.

smoke signal Small group of die scratches resembling a wisp of smoke appearing on the reverse of genuine 1968 "No-S" proof U.S. dimes. See *No-S*.

soberano (*m.*) [*Span., Port.*] sovereign.

sobre el reverso [*Span.*] on the back, on the reverse.

sobreestampa (*f.*); **sobreimpressão** (*f.*) [*Port.*] overprint.

sobreimpresión (*f.*) [*Span.*] overprint.

Sociedad Numismática de México The Numismatic Society of Mexico is a cultural organization founded in 1952, which throughout its years of existence has promoted Mexican numismatics and has attracted many people to it.

Mexico was the first country in America to have a print shop on the continent, and it was also the first to found a mint in the New World (1536). Since then the coins minted in Mexico have circulated throughout most of the world. The study of Mexican coins is a subject of deep interest, since it allows us to acquire an extensive knowledge of the historical, economic, political, and cultural development of the country. Numismatics is a science which also leads us to a world where art and esthetics join with the benefits derived from economic investment.

The Numismatic Society of Mexico has members throughout the Republic as well as abroad. Its activities are varied and multiple; all are oriented towards numismatics in general and Mexican numismatics in particular.

Among its membership benefits are monthly meetings, a quarterly *Boletín* (Journal) which offers articles of high cultural and informative quality, use of its extensive library facilities, auctions, and an annual international numismatic convention.

For membership information, contact the Sociedad Numismática de México, A.C., Eugenia 13-301, México, D.F. 03100.

Société des Bains de Mer de Monaco Corporation which runs the Casino of Monte Carlo. This name appears on many of the Casino's gambling tokens. See *casino token.*

Société d'Études Numismatiques et Archéologiques *Society of Numismatics and Archeologic Studies.*

The S.E.N.A. was founded in 1963 by three eminent French numismatists, Dr. J. B. Colbert de Beaulieu, Paul Lafolie, and Max Le Roy. It has been a member of the International Commission of Numismatics which 1989.

Its principal activity consists of the publication of the quarterly magazine *Cahiers*

Numismatiques ("Numismatic Notebooks") of which the first issue appeared in March 1964. The founders and successive presidents of the Society have wished to devote the *Cahiers* to the publication of innovative monetary and archeological studies without consideration of date or country, but with a priority for those matters involving France. This provides ample opportunity for the exploitation of unpublished documents from the archives.

The articles published emanate essentially from researchers (in particular, members of the National Center of Scientific Research), from librarians or museum curators (principally of the Bibliothèque Nationale [the National Library]), and from collectors of known competence. The most significant studies published since 1964 concern the knowledge of the coinages of ancient Gaul, and the description of medieval Roman treasures. Key subject areas on modern issuances have included the discovery of some previously unknown cameos and medals, a re-examination of French monies from the Renaissance to the Revolution, the monetary history of the Principality of Monaco, and certain coinages of the Far East, previously unpublished or little known.

The S.E.N.A. holds a monthly meeting with diverse conferences or communications at the Musée de la Monnaie (Museum of Money) in Paris. Its audience, in addition to amateurs and collectors, extends to numerous museums, libraries, collections or medals, and universities, both French and foreign.

For membership information, contact Société d'Études Numismatiques et Archéologiques, Secrétariat Administratif, 3, Rue des Arts, 92100 Boulogne, C.C.P. Paris 20 780 21 Z.

soeverein (*m.-c.*) [*Dut.*] sovereign.

soixante [*Fr.*] sixty.

soixante-dix [*Fr.*] seventy.

sokszorosítani (*v.*) [*Hun.*] to duplicate.

sol 1. [*Turk.*] left (direction or position). 2. (*m.*) [*Span.*] sun.

sølv (*n.*) [*Nor., Dan.*] silver.

soma (*f.*) [*Port.*] amount.

sönderriven [*Swed.*] torn.

sono accettate le carte di credito [*Ital.*] credit cards accepted.

soon-do 순도 [*Kor.*] fineness; fine (purity of metal).

sorozat [*Hun.*] series.

sorszám [*Hun.*] serial number.

sort [*Dan.*] black.

sortbørsmarked (*n.*) [*Dan.*] black market.

sötét [*Hun.*] dark.

sotilaskunniamerkki [*Finn.*] military decoration.

soumission minimum (*f.*) [*Fr.*] minimum bid.

sous condition [*Fr.*] on approval.

souverain (*m.*) [*Fr.*] sovereign.

Souverän (*m.*) [*Ger.*] sovereign.

sovereign British gold coin introduced on October 18, 1489, by Henry VII. At one-half troy ounce and with a diameter of more than 40 mm, it was the largest gold coin issued by England up to that time. Its value was placed at one pound (20 shillings).

The earliest strikings show the king holding an orb and scepter while seated on a high-backed, ornamental throne. This design concept had not appeared on an English gold coin since the short-lived florin of 1344. The reverse features a crowned shield quartered with the arms of England and France. The shield is superimposed on an open double rose, symbolizing the union of the White Rose of York and the Red Rose of Lancaster.

The creation of the sovereign may have been prompted by the appearance in 1487 of the large gold *réal d'or*, struck by Emperor Maximilian in The Netherlands. For commercial reasons (as well as reasons of pride), the introduction of a well-received coin by one nation or ruler has often led to the sudden appearance of similar coins from neighboring or competing nations. The réal d'or had been copied by other rulers on the Continent, and Henry VII apparently saw the need to present a similar coin of his own.

Yet the argument has been made that this coin was more ceremonial than commercial, because Henry decreed that only a small number would be minted. It has been suggested that Henry struck this coin so that it would be seen by certain key rulers of Europe who would then perceive him to be at their level, i.e., the king of a united empire.

When Henry VIII ascended to the throne, the sovereign began a roller-coaster ride. First, as part of the coinage reforms initiated by Cardinal Wolsey, the value of the sovereign was increased to 22 shillings and later to the unlikely value of 22 shillings 6 pence. Then, in the 1540s when Henry VIII was well into his coinage debasement, the value was reduced back to 20 shillings. Of course, the purity of the gold had dropped from *fine* gold (.989 pure or about 23 3/4 carat, the purest gold obtainable with the technology of the day) to 23 carat gold (.958 pure).

In her attempt to restore integrity to the nation's coinage (which her father had seriously damaged through his debasement), Elizabeth I brought the sovereign back to fine gold, but gave the coin a value of 30 shillings. Curiously, she also introduced another coin called a sovereign which was somewhat smaller, contained only 22 carat gold, and was valued at 20 shillings. Despite the common name, the two sovereigns were so different in appearance that they apparently circulated side by side without confusion. So as to avoid confusion today, numismatists regularly refer to the 20 shilling coin as simply a *pound*.

Under James I the name *sovereign* lapsed, not to be revived until 1663 when Charles II issued 20 shilling coins, even though the pieces were more regularly referred to as *guineas*. The guinea took on a life of its own in 1717 when it was established at the fixed value of 21 shillings. It then became the principal British gold coin of the eighteenth century.

The sovereign did not re-establish itself until 1817 when the now-famous *St. George and the Dragon* reverse of Benedetto Pistrucci was introduced. The guinea, relegated to the status of money of account, was never again coined.

Since the reign of George III, every British monarch has issued sovereigns, even including Edward VIII whose sovereigns were never officially released and are virtually unique today.

Some sovereigns have been struck at the branch mints in Australia (Perth, Melbourne, and Sydney), Canada (Ottawa), and South Africa (Pretoria). Sovereigns have been accepted in trade in many places, even well beyond the confines of the British Empire in such unlikely places as Brazil.

The sovereign no longer circulates anywhere, but it is amazing to note that these gold coins struck by Henry VII in 1489 are still legal tender for the sum of £1, more than five hundred years after he made them.

[Graham P. Dyer, "Five Centuries of the British Gold Sovereign," *The Numismatist*, March 1989, pp. 392-400; Stephen Mitchell & Brian Reeds (editors), *Coins of England and the United Kingdom* (Seaby, 1991), pp. 141-42 et al.]

Sovjetsamveldet [*Nor.*] Soviet Union (U.S.S.R.).

Sovjet-Unie [*Dut.*] Soviet Union.

Sovjetunionen [*Dan.*] Soviet Union.

sovrano (*m.*) [*Ital.*] sovereign (i.e., a king or queen). The gold coin known as a *sovereign* is *sterlina oro* in Italian.

sovrastampa (*f.*) [*Ital.*] overprint.

Sowjetunion [*Ger.*] Soviet Union.

English "spade" guinea

spade guinea Series of British gold guineas[q.v.] (1787-1799) and half-guineas (1787-1800) issued by George III. They are named for the spade-shaped shield on the reverse. This design was noticeably different because most shields on British coins are more square-shaped in appearance.

Spagna [*Ital.*] Spain.

Spania [*Nor.*] Spain.

Spanien [*Ger., Dan.*] Spain.

spanio σπάνιο [*Grk.*] rare, scarce.

Spanje [*Dut.*] Spain.

Spanyolország [*Hun.*] Spain.

specie Precious metal in the form of minted coins as opposed to ingots or other uncoined metal. The term can also refer to paper money which is readily redeemable in coin or to certain coins which replaced paper notes.

The word is seen most frequently in numismatics when paper money backed by gold or silver is described. Although the backing for notes can be in the form of coins, it is more likely to be in large bars, such as those stored at the U.S. federal gold depository in Fort Knox, Kentucky.

specie strikes See *currency strikes*.

specimen 1. Generic term for any numismatic item; i.e., "Mary Smith's collection included many outstanding specimens."

2. The complete face and back design of any banknote, certificate, bond, check, etc., which is stamped or perforated with the word "SPECIMEN" (in English or in any other language). On occasion, the identifying word is "CANCELLED". Although these items are most often printed on the same kind of paper which would be used if the notes were intended for general circulation, face and back designs are at times printed separately on heavier paper.

Specimens can have a conventional serial number but usually show multiple zeros or a sequential set of numerals, e.g., "12345678". Specimen notes are most often prepared by a government or central bank for use by other governments and central banks around the world or by its own domestic banks and law enforcement agencies as an example of authentic notes. Specimen notes are non-negotiable.

Some proofs and essais have incorrectly been stamped or perforated with the word "SPECIMEN".

3. A standard coin with the word "SPECIMEN" (again, in whatever language) added to the normal legends. These coins are made for such purposes as introducing new designs or denominations to banks or for providing rejected designs to collectors. Far fewer coins of this nature have been produced than the above-described notes, mostly because

there has not been as great a need for specimen coins.

[Contributed by Gene Hessler. Dr. Howard S. Friedman, "Essays, Proofs and Specimens," *The Essay-Proof Journal*, Vol. 31, No. 1, 1974, p. 17; Gene Hessler, *U.S. Essay, Proof and Specimen Notes*, BNR Press, p. 33.]

Spem Reducis, Mentibus Anxiis [*Lat.*] Hope of return to anxious minds.

spider press Nineteenth century printing press so named because its five rotating handles have the appearance of legs protruding from a spider.

spigolo (*m.*) [*Ital.*] edge.

spit spots Small spots of tarnish on coins or medals resulting from tiny droplets of saliva which land on the pieces while someone is talking over them. These marks reduce the attractiveness and value of the pieces.

splav сплав (*m.*) [*Russ.*] alloy (of metals).

splendido [*Ital.*] fine (grade or condition).

Sprache (*f.*) [*Ger.*] language.

språk (*n.*) [*Swed., Nor.*] language.

spre aprobare [*Rom.*] on approval.

springbok on South African crown

springbok Small antelope (*Antidorcas marsupialis*) native to the southern African plains. It is featured on the reverse of the South African 5 shilling crown minted from 1947 to 1959.

sprog (*n.*) [*Dan.*] language.

sprzedający (*m.*) [*Pol.*] seller.

sprzedawać (*v.*) [*Pol.*] to sell.

sprzedaż aukcyjna [*Pol.*] auction sale.

srebro (*n.*) [*Pol.*] silver.

średnica (*f.*) [*Pol.*] diameter.

S.S.C. Initials of the South Sea Company, the supplier of the bullion used to strike some of the silver coins of George I of Great Britain from 1723 to 1726. The initials W.C.C. (Welsh Copper Company, another supplier of silver) are also found on some of the coins.

S.S. Central America See *Central America, S.S.*

staaf (*m.-c.*) [*Dut.*] ingot.

staal (*n.*) [*Dut.*] steel.

staalgravure [*Dut.*] steel engraving.

stagno (*m.*) [*Ital.*] tin.

Stahl (*m.*) [*Ger.*] steel.

Stahlstich (*m.*) [*Ger.*] steel engraving.

stal (*f.*) [*Pol.*] steel.

stål (*n.*) [*Nor., Dan.*]; (*r.*) [*Swed.*] steel.

stålgravering (*c.*) [*Dan.*]; (*m.*) [*Nor.*] steel engraving.

stålgravyr (*r.*) [*Swed.*] steel engraving.

ställa ut (*v.*) [*Swed.*] to exhibit.

staloryt (*m.*) [*Pol.*] steel engraving.

Stammbaum (*m.*) [*Ger.*] pedigree.

stamp (*r.*) [*Swed.*] (coinage) die.

stampare (*v.*) [*Ital.*] to print.

stampée (above); Cayenne Colony 2 sous (below)

stampée Colloquial English term for a *tempé* (also written *tampé* or *étampé*) or *Creole tempé*. The stampée is a coin made from base metal which was first issued by the French in 1763 for use in the French West Indies (also known as the French Antilles). The first of these were made by merely counterstamping a crowned "C" over a large number of billon (base metal)

coins valued a 2 sols (24 deniers) which had been accumulating in the French treasury.

Even prior to being counterstamped, the old 2 sol coins had been very popular in the West Indies. French traders called this coin *la marque noire* ("the black mark"), probably because base metal coins tend to tarnish a black color due to the nature of their metallic content. English traders and colonists also found favor with this coin by allowing it to substitute for their *black dogg* (coin of 1 1/2 pence) which had been in very short supply.

The counterstamped stampée quickly became as popular as the old 2 sol piece had been, and a shortage soon resulted. Two million additonal stampées were authorized in 1774, but there was not a sufficient number of host coins available for counterstamping. The 1774 issue was struck on original flans made of brass, bronze, copper, and an alloy with a low silver content.

A major drawback of this coin was its popularity among counterfeiters. By the end of the eighteenth century, a great many phony pieces were being produced, the majority coming from Birmingham, England.

Although the stampées continued to circulate until the middle of the nineteenth century, their official end came on June 8, 1844, when they were demonetized in French Guiana, the last place in which their use was recognized.

Another popular coin which circulated along with the stampée in the French colonies in the Americas was the Cayenne Colony 2 sous coin. It was issued from 1780 to 1790 and was variously minted in billon, copper, or bronze.

[Jan M. Dyroff, "The Quaint and Curious Stampée," *The Numismatist*, April 1987, pp. 756-760.]

stampskada (*r.*) [*Swed.*] die break.

stamtræ (*n.*) [*Dan.*] pedigree.

stan (**zachowania**) (*m.*) [*Pol.*] a grade, condition.

standard 1. Legally or officially designated weight or fineness for a coin.

2. A counterweight (also known as a *coin weight*) used for checking the accuracy of the weight of newly-minted coins. The example in the illustration is from the late eighteenth century. It was used to check the weight of the silver Spanish 8 *real* pieces. The standard itself is made from base silver and was stamped with the royal crown to give it authenticity.

"standard" for Spanish silver 8 *real* coin

Standing Liberty Quarter United States quarter dollar coin struck from 1916 to 1930. The designer was Herman A. MacNeil, whose initial "M" appears in the lower right-hand corner of the obverse design. The advent of this coin coincided with the arrival of the Winged Liberty ("Mercury") Dime and the Walking Liberty Half Dollar[q.v.], all of which were intended to replace the Barber design which had graced the three silver coins since 1892.

The Standing Liberty Quarter caused an immediate controversy, as Ms. Liberty was shown "topless" with her right breast exposed. Very few pieces were produced in 1916, so her naked condition was not noticed until early in 1917. A great uproar ensued when the American public realized exactly how their new coins looked. Later in 1917 the design was changed, placing Ms. Liberty in an appropriately modest suit of armor. At the same time, the eagle on the reverse was raised slightly and three stars were placed under it.

Stanton, Edwin McMasters United States Attorney General and Secretary of War. Born December 19, 1814, in Steubenville, Ohio; died of pneumonia in Washington, D.C., on December 24, 1869.

Edwin M. Stanton performed as U.S. Attorney General under President James Buchanon in the late 1850s. In 1862 he became Secretary of War in Abraham Lincoln's cabinet.

Stanton distinguished himself through efficiency and hard work and contributed significantly to the ultimate military success of the Union (the North) in the U.S. Civil War (1861-65). He quickly became regarded as a Civil War hero.

Edwin M. Stanton

Upon the assassination of Lincoln in 1865, Vice President Andrew Johnson ascended to the presidency. Johnson greatly disliked Stanton and removed him from his cabinet without the approval of Congress. The Congress reinstated Stanton, but Johnson dismissed him again, prompting the House of Representatives to impeach Johnson. Although the Senate failed to ratify the impeachment by only one vote, saving Johnson's presidency, Johnson's political career was damaged beyond repair and General Ulysses S. Grant was elected president in 1868.

At Grant's first opportunity, he appointed Stanton to the U.S. Supreme Court, a goal Stanton had cherished all his professional life. The coveted seat was still to elude Stanton, however, because he died just a few days before he was to be sworn in as Associate Justice.

Stanton's portrait appears on two different 50 cent fractional currency[q.v.] notes issued in the 1870s and a $1 note from 1890.

[R. Scott Carlton, "A Numismatic Journey Through Steubenville," *The Numismatist,* July 1991, pp. 1054-55; *Funk & Wagnalls New Encyclopedia* (1984), Vol. 24, p. 317.]

starcie (*n.*) [*Pol.*] wear.
stare de conservare (*f.*) [*Rom.*] grade, condition.
starinnyy старинный [*Russ.*] ancient.
starożytny (*m.*) [*Pol.*] ancient.

Aegina stater (404-430 B.C.): land turtle (obv.), mill-sail (rev.)

stater The generic term for many different ancient Greek coins. The world's earliest coins (those struck in Asia Minor ca. 620-600 B.C. and made from electrum[q.v.]) were referred to as staters. Most of the later coins called by this name were silver, but some parts of the ancient world used the term for their gold coinage. Staters were issued for approximately six hundred years and as far away as Britain where the earliest gold Gallo-Belgic coins struck around 125-100 B.C. were known by this name.

The word *stater* comes from the Greek word meaning *weigher*, a reference to a custom practiced in the eastern Mediterranean of minting coins of a basic unit and of its subunits. Hence, the staters had to be fairly large coins, often the equivalents of didrachmæ or tetradrachmæ, to allow for the practicality of minting fractional coins, sometimes as small as 1/96 of a basic unit. (By contrast, in the western regions it was more common to produce coins of a basic unit and its multiples.)

Many scholars regard the stater not so much as a denomination but as a reference to any given city-state's unit of currency. This would account for the very diverse range of coins issued under this name. The value of a stater could also reflect the power and influence of the city which produced it. For example, a wealthier city-state might produce a stater of gold while a less affluent region might strike staters of silver.

Heraldic designs on staters often reflected legends or the historical background of the city-state that issued them. Thus, the staters of

Corinth show Pegasus, the mythical flying horse; those of Poseidonia in Southern Italy display the image of Poseidon; and the coins of Tarentum show their mythical founder Taras being carried to the site of the city astride a dolphin.

Some of the designs seem bizarre to those of us in the modern world. We can only guess why some cities in Thrace chose for their coinage design a scene of a satyr raping a nymph.

The reverses of some staters show a geometric design somewhat resembling a swastika known technically as a *mill-sail* [q.v.] pattern. It appears in the form of an incuse punch. A panther peers out from one of the incuse squares on early Athenian coins.

Only one thing can be said for certain about the stater: no two experts define this term exactly the same. Some regard it as a weight, a few call it a denomination, and others refer to it as a non-specific unit of currency. But all experts agree that the stater played a very important role in the development of coins as we in today's world understand the term.

[David Van Meter, *Collecting Greek Coins*, p. 18.]

Stellas: coiled hair & flowing hair with common reverse

stella 1. (*f.*) [*Ital.*] star.

2. Gold $4 pattern coins struck in the United States in 1879 and 1880. Their name comes from the large five-pointed star on the reverse. Two obverse types exist: the *flowing hair* type designed by Charles E. Barber, and the *coiled hair* created by George T. Morgan. Contrary to what many collectors believe, these were only patterns and were not adopted as regular-issue coins.

stemma στέμμα (*n.*) [*Grk.*] crown (royal headpiece).

stempel (*m.-c.*) [*Dut.*] (coinage) die.

Stempel (*m.*) [*Ger.*] (coinage) die.

stempelbreuk (*f.-c.*) [*Dut.*] die break.

stempelbrud (*n.*) [*Dan.*] die break.

stempelbrudd (*n.*) [*Nor.*] die break.

stempelglanz [*Ger.*] uncirculated.

stempel menniczy (*m.*) [*Pol.*] (coinage) die.

Stempelriß (*m.*) [*Ger.*] die break.

Stempelsprung (*m.*) [*Ger.*] die break.

stentryk (*n.*) [*Dan.*] lithography.

ster (*m.-c.*) [*Dut.*] star.

sterlina (*f.*) [*Ital.*] pound (£).

sterlina oro [*Ital.*] gold coin referred to in English as a *sovereign*.

sterling Monetary unit of eighth-century Anglo-Saxon Britain from which the current *pound sterling* was derived. Because the sterling was worth 1/240 of a pound of silver, 240 sterlings became known as a *pound of sterling* and later simply as a *pound sterling*.

sterling silver [or simply *sterling*.] Alloy of .925 silver and .075 copper. This was the recognized standard alloy for British coinage from before the Norman Conquest until 1919.

Stern (*m.*) [*Ger.*] star.

Steuer (*f.*) [*Ger.*] tax.

stille ut (*v.*) [*Nor.*] to exhibit.

stjärna (*r.*) [*Swed.*] star.

stjerne (*m.*) [*Nor.*]; (*c.*) [*Dan.*] star.

sto [*Pol.*] hundred.

støbe (*v.*) [*Dan.*] to cast.

stop (*m.*) [*Pol.*] alloy (of metals).

støpe (*v.*) [*Nor.*] to cast.

stor [*Nor., Swed.*] large.

Storbritannia [*Nor.*] Great Britain; United Kingdom (U.K.).

Storbritannien [*Dan., Swed.*] Great Britain; United Kingdom.

store card Token showing a merchant's name and address and bearing some advertising message. The token's value may be stated as a

certain amount of money or may be exchangeable for a specific item such as a glass of beer.

Despite the word *card*, these pieces are almost always made of metal. Until the twentieth century, the vast majority of store cards resembled whatever small copper coins circulated in that time and place. For example, the English store cards of the seventeenth century were of the same basic sizes and metallic content as the farthings, halfpennies, and pennies which they imitated. This practice extended into the nineteenth century. The many *Hard Times* tokens[q.v.] issued by American merchants in the 1830s and 1840s resulting from the Panic of 1837 and subsequent depression, resembled the U.S. large cents. United States Civil War tokens[q.v.] of the 1860s were similar to the small cents which had been introduced only a few years earlier.

Although these tokens had no legal status as circulating money and were usually frowned upon by the government, they frequently appeared during those times when the legitimate coins had been driven out of circulation, either due to the uncertainties of war or because of other economic instability. Because small change was so badly needed to allow for the steady flow of commerce, merchants were usually glad to accept store cards in payment, even if they themselves had not issued those particular tokens. Various governments attempted to put a halt to this practice but with varying degrees of success. In 1864 an Act of Congress was passed prohibiting the further issuance of Civil War tokens in the United States, but the existing pieces continued to circulate until economic order was restored after the war.

[Richard G. Doty, *The Macmillan Encyclopedic Dictionary of Numismatics*, p. 317.]

straniero [*Ital.*] foreign.

strappato [*Ital.*] torn.

strappo (*m.*) [*Ital.*] a tear.

stratiotikon parasimon στρατιωτικόν παράσημον (*n.*) [*Grk.*] military decoration.

stretched coin Oval-shaped souvenir better known as an *elongated coin*[q.v.].

stroggilos στρογγυλός [*Grk.*] round.

stuletni (*m.*) [*Pol.*] centennial, centenary.

subasta (*f.*) [*Span.*] auction.

subasta por correo [*Span.*] mail bid sale.

Subducendis Rationibus [*Lat.*] Calculations must be made.

subsidiary 1. Fractionary or minor coin, i.e., a coin denominated at less than one principal unit of currency (such as a quarter dollar in the U.S. or Canada).

2. Silver coins valued at less than 25 kopecks in Czarist Russia. Silver coins of 25 kopecks or more were referred to as *banco*.

[R. W. Julian, "The Russian Silver Coinage of 1796-1917," *The Numismatist*, December 1989, p. 1956.]

Sudáfrica; Suráfrica [*Span.*] South Africa. Also written as *África del Sur* (although the accent over the "A" is usually omitted).

Sud Africa [*Ital.*] South Africa.

Südafrika [*Ger.*] South Africa.

sự dúc tiền [*Viet.*] coinage.

Suecia [*Span.*] Sweden.

Suède [*Fr.*] Sweden.

Suedia [*Rom.*] Sweden.

Suíça [*Port.*] Switzerland.

Suisse [*Fr.*] Switzerland.

Suiza [*Span.*] Switzerland.

sujeito aprovação [*Port.*] on approval.

sukupuu [*Finn.*] pedigree (list of former and present owners).

suma (*f.*) [*Span., Pol.*] amount.

sumă (*f.*) [*Rom.*] amount.

summa [*Finn.*] amount.

Suomi [*Finn.*] Finland.

suorakulmainen [*Finn.*] rectangular.

supratipar (*n.*) [*Rom.*] overprint.

surface The outermost layer of molecules of metal in a coin or medal which comes in contact with the atmosphere. Simply put, it is any portion of the metal which the human eye actually sees. In the case of a tarnished or corroded coin, the surface is the portion which the human eye would see if oxidation were not present.

surimpression (*f.*) [*Fr.*] overprint.

sürüm [*Turk.*] circulation.

sus [*Rom.*] top.

sută [*Rom.*] hundred.

sutime (*f.*) [*Rom.*] hundredth.

sutler token A sutler was a vendor of provisions during the United States Civil War of 1861-65 who was allowed to follow the army and sell his goods to the soldiers.

The word *sutler* is not new. It was mentioned as early as 1599 in a quotation from the play Henry V by William Shakerspeare: "I shall Sutler be onto the Campe and profits will acrue."

The sutler of the Civil War era was equivalent to the post exchange or commissary of today. His purpose was to provide the military with a convenient place to purchase necessities and luxury items.

Sutlers, who were civilians, issued tokens primarily to simplify the process of extending credit. The soldier, facing long periods without pay, bought from the sutler on credit. The sutler would give him the amount desired in tokens and have him sign a paymaster's order. Finally, on payday, the sutler sat at the paymaster's table and collected his amount due.

Several manufacturers struck sutler tokens and some can be identified by the style of die cutting or by a signature on the token. Most sutler tokens were issued in small face amounts from five cents to a dollar. The denomination usually appeared on one side and the name of the military post or unit on the other.

The metal most often used for the striking of sutler tokens was brass. However, copper, lead, white metal, German silver, nickel, and bronze were also used.

All sutler tokens are scarce and hard to find in nice condition. Most were lost on the battlefields. The sutler continued to serve the military until the late 1870s. Then, as more permanent military posts were established, the sutler faded into history and the post exchange was born.

[Contributed by Gerald L. Kochel. James J. Curto, "Sutlers and Their Tokens," reprint from *The Numismatist*, 1960, pp. 109-121; David E. Schenkman, *Civil War Sutler Tokens and Cardboard Scrip*, 1983, Jade House Publications; Jim Hancock, "Army Commissary System, A Historical Review," *Troop Support Digest*, Summer 1984, pp. 8-12.]

suurennuslasi [*Finn.*] magnifying glass.

suuri [*Finn.*] large.

suveran (*m.*) [*Rom.*] sovereign.

suverän (*m./f.*) [*Swed.*] sovereign.

suweren (*m.*) [*Pol.*] sovereign.

Svájc [*Hun.*] Switzerland.

svalutazione (*f.*) [*Ital.*] devaluation.

svart [*Nor., Swed.*] black.

svarta börsen (*r.*) [*Swed.*] black market.

svartebørs (*m.*) [*Nor.*] black market.

Svédország [*Hun.*] Sweden.

Sveits [*Nor.*] Switzerland.

Sveitsi [*Finn.*] Switzerland.

Sverige [*Swed., Nor., Dan.*] Sweden.

Svezia [*Ital.*] Sweden.

Svizzera [*Ital.*] Switzerland.

Swiss Shooting Festival Medals and Talers See *Shooting Festival Medals and Talers*.

sword dollar Silver *ryal* of 30 shillings issued by James VI of Scotland from 1567 to 1571. It is so named because the reverse features a crowned sword dividing the first two and last two digits of the date. Next to the sword is the roman numeral XXX indicating 30 shillings. Similar two-thirds ryal (with roman numeral XX) and one-third ryal (X) coins were also issued of the same dates.

Sword in Hand Note issued by Paul Revere on December 7, 1775, during the American Revolution. The note is so named because it shows a Minute-Man (soldier in the American militia) holding a sword in one hand and the Magna Charta in the other. The face value of the note is 3 shillings 4 pence.

Sydafrika [*Dan., Swed.*] South Africa.

Syd-Afrika [*Nor.*] South Africa.

syngraphics The study and collecting of paper money and related items.

The Reverend Richard Doyle, Chairman of the Department of Classical Languages at Fordham University in New York, coined this long-needed word. It was introduced in the first edition of *The Comprehensive Catalog of U.S. Paper Money* by Gene Hessler.

The word comes from the Greek *syn*, meaning "with" or "together" (as a *synagogue* is a place where people come together), and *graphikos*, which means "to write". Addition-

ally, the first paper money in the Western world was a handwritten goldsmith receipt. In Latin, *syngrapha* refers to a written agreement to pay, a promissory note, a bond. *The Oxford Dictionary* defines *paper money* as "a written promise to pay". In the same source, *syngraph* is defined as "a written contract or bond signed by both or all parties, an obligation or bond between two or more."

The art of engraving, etching and other methods by which copies of an original design are printed from a plate, block or the like is referred to as *graphic art*. Modern bank notes are no longer handwritten but are made from engraved plates. Therefore, *syngraphics* is interpreted as the collecting of paper money. A researcher or collector is a syngraphist.

[Contributed by Gene Hessler with assistance from Rev. Richard Doyle. Gene Hessler, *The Comprehensive Catalog of U.S. Paper Money*, BNR Press, 1983, p. ix.]

syngraphist A person who studies or collects paper money or related items. See *syngraphics*.

syöpyminen [*Finn.*] corrosion.

syrjä [*Finn.*] edge (of a coin or medal).

système monétaire (*m.*) [*Fr.*] monetary system.

system monetarny (*m.*) [*Pol.*] monetary system.

szabálytalan [*Hun.*] irregular.

szakadás [*Hun.*] a tear (in a banknote or bond).

szakadt [*Hun.*] torn.

szám [*Hun.*] number.

számla [*Hun.*] account (financial or transactional).

száz [*Hun.*] hundred.

század [*Hun.*] hundredth (the fraction).

szelvény [*Hun.*] exergue.

szép [*Hun.*] fine (grade or condition).

szerzemény [*Hun.*] acquisition.

szín [*Hun.*] color, colour.

szín- [*Hun.*] fine (purity of metal), fineness.

Szkocja [*Pol.*] Scotland.

Szovjetúnió [*Hun.*] Soviet Union (U.S.S.R.).

sztaba (*f.*); **sztabka** (*f.*) [*Pol.*] ingot.

sztuka (*f.*) [*Pol.*] art.

szükségpénz [*Hun.*] emergency currency.

T t

taal (*f.-c.*) [*Dut.*] language.

tache (*f.*) [*Fr.*] stain (on a banknote or bond).

tacka (*r.*) [*Swed.*] ingot.

tæring (*c.*) [*Dan.*] corrosion.

taglio (*m.*) [*Ital.*] edge.

tahor טָהוֹר [*Heb.*] fineness; fine (purity of metal).

tahra [*Finn.*] stain; tarnish.

tähti [*Finn.*] star.

tahvil seneti [*Turk.*] (commercial) bond.

taide [*Finn.*] art.

taitos [*Finn.*] a crease or fold (as in a piece of paper money).

takasivu [*Finn.*] reverse.

takasivulla [*Finn.*] on the back.

tampé [*Fr.*] Also known as *tempé*, *Creole tempé*, *étampé*, or *stampée*. Base metal coin first struck in 1763 by the French for use in the French West Indies. See *stampée*.

tam tanımlanmamış [*Turk.*] unattributed.

Tangaroa on Cook Islands crown

Tangaroa Polynesian god of creation and fertility who appears on two types (round and scalloped) of Cook Islands regular-issue crowns first issued in 1972 and on the back of that nation's $3 note.

The coins and notes bearing Tangaroa's image have generated a great deal of controversy. Many people were offended when the coins first came out because he is shown blatantly naked. It also seemed inappropriate to show such an "obscene" design on a British Commonwealth coin with Queen Elizabeth II's effigy on the flip side.

The appearance of the $3 notes in the 1990s incensed critics even more. The grotesque portrayal of Tangaroa shows full frontal nudity. On the other side of the note, a young naked maiden is seen riding a shark.

Whether or not these coins and notes are in poor taste is up to one's own judgment, but beyond a doubt the pieces have been a marketing success for Cook Islands. Due to their unusual (and controversial) nature, the items have sold very well and have generated large profits.

tanımlama [*Turk.*] attribution (the complete identification of a coin, medal, or banknote).

tan pho ∞ई ई: [*Bur.*] face value.

Tanska [*Finn.*] Denmark.

tanso [*Tag.*] copper.

tantusz [*Hun.*] token.

tantuz тантуз (*m.*) [*Serb.-Cr.*] token.

Țara Galilor [*Rom.*] Wales.

tarih [*Turk.*] date.

tarihi sahte olarak değiştirilmiş [*Turk.*] altered date.

tarikh ditukar [*Indo.*] altered date.

tarjeta de crédito [*Span.*] credit card.

tarjota (*v.*) [*Finn.*] to offer; to bid (at an auction).

tarjous [*Finn.*] an offer; a bid.

tarjouslista [*Finn.*] bid sheet.

tarnish A coating caused by oxidation which dulls the luster of metals. Unlike patina,

tarnish is often considered a detraction to the coin or medal's beauty.

Tarraco Mint Tarraco was the capital of a Spanish province called Hispania Tarraconensis and is located at the mouth of a river. It is now known as Tarragona and is situated on the Catalonian coast. Its foundations are ascribed to Scipio Africanus. The Romans there had assisted Caesar against Pompey and displayed a great devotion to Augustus, having shown kindness to the latter when he became ill there. They raised an altar (from which a palm tree grew) to him subsequent to his recovery.

The mint at Tarraco (also perhaps a mint under Augustus) was created by Galba to fill his immediate need for coinage in A.D. 69 when he became emperor and had to have specie to pay his troops as he left Spain for Rome. The coinage consisted of gold and silver, with the addition of a few copper asses. Vitellius also utilized the facility to produce gold, silver, and a large selection of asses. Vespasian's issue was of gold, silver, and rare sestertii and asses. The mint closed in either A.D. 71 or 73-74 (depending on the authority consulted), the reason for its existence having terminated. It is likely that certain of its personnel were transferred to Rome, for the portraiture of that main plant seemed to begin to betray traces of Terraconian style at about that time.

Although all Terraco issues are rare, they are not up to the style of the Rome Mint. Its chief characteristics are a fine neat lettering that is usually rather small. Unnaturally thin and lanky but not unpleasing figures mark its reverses. They may show little consistency or be true to life because of an absence of reliable models.

It has been argued that the mintmark "T" stood for Terraco. Later scholarship has rebutted this. It may have marked certain of its issues with a globe, as did Lugdunum. Coins may have the letters CVT (Colonia Victrix Tarraco) or CVTT (Colonia Victrix Togata Tarraco). The former would denote a reward as a place founded or re-established by Julius Caesar, and the latter would mean both this and also give attention to the practice of toga-wearing by its inhabitants as if they were Romans.

Reverses of Tarraco products show similar themes such as LIBERTAS RESTITVTA, ROMA RENASCENS, and VESTA P(OPULI) R(OMANI) QVIRITIVM.

[Contributed by William F. Mross. Harold Mattingly, *Roman Coins*; Percy H. Webb, *Third Century Roman Mints and Marks*; C.H.V. Sutherland, *Roman Coins*; Stevenson & Smith, *Dictionary of Roman Coins*; Mattingly & Sydenham, *Roman Imperial Coinage*.]

ta sait ဆ ၆ၐ [*Bur.*] medal.

tassa (*f.*) [*Ital.*] tax.

tasso di scambio (*m.*) [*Ital.*] exchange rate.

tauschen (*v.*) [*Ger.*] to trade.

tausend [*Ger.*] thousand.

ta'ut טָעוּת (*f.*) [*Heb.*] error.

taux de change [*Fr.*] exchange rate.

taxa (*f.*) [*Port.*] fee.

taxă (*f.*) [*Rom.*] tax.

taxa de câmbio [*Port.*] exchange rate.

taxe (*f.*) [*Fr.*] tax.

techmirio τεκμήριο (*n.*) [*Grk.*] token.

tedavülden kaldırmak [*Turk.*] demonetization.

tedavüle çıkarılmamış [*Turk.*] not issued.

tegnforklaring (*m.*) [*Nor.*] legend.

teklif [*Turk.*] (auction) bid.

tek yüzlü [*Turk.*] uniface.

telephone card See *phone card*.

Hungarian telephone token

telephone token A token intended to operate a pay phone (British: *coin box*) or to otherwise pay for one or more phone calls. These tokens should not be confused with other types of telephone memorabilia not intended to be used in payment for a phone call nor those which carry a telephone number merely as part of an

advertising message. The category of telephone tokens does not include various miscellaneous tokens which coincidentally are the same size as regular coins and which can be illegally used to operate pay telephones.

[Contributed by Robert Doyle.]

tempé [*Fr.*] Also known as *Creole tempé, tampé, étampé,* or *stampée.* Base metal coin first struck in 1763 by the French for use in the French West Indies. See *stampée.*

Tempo koban kin see *koban.*

Tempo tsuho [*Jpn.*] Circulating currency of the *Tempo* period. A large oval copper coin, it was issued from 1835 to around 1865. Its nominal value is 100 mon.

Tempo tsuho

Tsuho has no meaning today as an individual word; it has been variously translated from either Chinese or Japanese as "circulating currency," "circulating treasure," "current treasure," and other similar phrases. Most contemporary dictionaries state its meaning as "coins circulated in earlier times."

Virtually every cash-style coin minted in east Asia after 1700 uses *tsuho* as the final two characters, as do hundreds of types from earlier periods.

Also see *cash* and *amulet.*

[Contributed by Joseph E. Boling.]

tentoonstelling (*f.-c.*) [*Dut.*] exhibition.

tepian [*Indo.*] edge.

teräskaiverrus [*Finn.*] steel engraving.

terbitan [*Indo.*] an issue, issuance.

tercio (*m.*) [*Span.*] third (the fraction).

tercer (*m.adj.*); **tercera** (*f.adj.*) [*Span.*] third.

têrço (*m.*) [*Port.*] third (the fraction).

ternissure (*f.*) [*Fr.*] tarnish.

tersi [*Turk.*] reverse.

terzo (*m.*) [*Ital.*] third (the fraction).

tesorería general (*f.*) [*Span.*] general treasury.

tesoro (*m.*) [*Ital., Span.*] treasure; treasury.

tesouro (*m.*) [*Port.*] treasure.

tessera τέσσερα [*Grk.*] four.

teston (*m.*) [*Fr.*] French version of the Italian silver coin known as a *testone.* It was introduced in France by Louis XII in 1513 after he had produced some Italian-style testoni for his Italian possessions.

testone (*m.*) [*Ital.*] Italian silver coin introduced in 1474 by Galeazzo Maria Sforza, Duke of Milan. Its name is derived from the Italian word *testa* meaning "head," a reference to the coin's obverse which features a bust of the ruler.

The testone quickly became a popular coin and was copied by other Italian rulers. By 1504 it was being produced in England by Henry VII and was called a *testoon*[*q.v.*], the anglicanized version of its name. Its next incarnation came from France's Louis XII who first produced testoni for his Italian possessions and then ultimately introduced a French version, the *teston*, for his own subjects in 1513. Scottish testoons were struck from 1553-1562.

testoon of Mary Queen of Scots

testoon Silver coin of England's Henry VII and Henry VIII and Scotland's Mary Queen of Scots. It was first issued as a shilling by Henry VII in 1504 to compete with the Italian testone.

Under Henry VIII, the testoon was part of the infamous debased Third coinage of 1544-47. These were among the coins from which Henry VIII got the name *Old Coppernose*[q.v.], because as soon as a freshly-minted coin started to circulate, the highest points on the coin (such as his nose) immediately started tarnishing a coppery brown.

The first Scottish testoon (1553) was valued at four shillings, but was replaced in 1555 with a five shilling version. This value remained until 1562. Although the word *testoon* is derived from *testa*, the Italian word for "head" (and thus refers to a portrait piece), some Scottish testoons feature a crowned monogram on the obverse.

tête-bêche design on Brazilian note

tête-bêche (*f.*) [*Fr.*] literally, *head-spade.*

Anti-counterfeiting device on paper money which consists of a design that appears twice, each occurrence being upside-down relative to the other. Its purpose is to make counterfeiting of that note more detectable, even to the average citizen not well-versed in determining the authenticity of paper money.

The illustrated note is from Brazil. The tête-bêche technique was used on both sides. To the viewer, the note appears exactly the same whether right-side up or upside-down.

The technique itself goes back to the coins of Istros, located in what is now Romania. This town was apparently quite wealthy and produced a sizable coinage. The distinguishing feature on its coins was an obverse design consisting of two male faces, one of them inverted. The reason why the moneyers of Istros used this design is unknown, but its purpose was surely not to deter counterfeiting.

tetradrachm Very popular silver coin of ancient Greece. *Tetra* means four, so its value was equal to four drachmai.

Athenian tetradrachm

The city-state of Athens produced the earliest of these around the middle of the sixth century B.C. and gave them a weight of slightly more than 17 grams. Other Greek city-states adopted this coin (with some variations in weight and size), but the Athenian version set the standard even though its weight did fluctuate somewhat.

By the beginning of the fifth century B.C., the tetradrachm was no longer a crude coin with only a punchmark on the reverse. The redesigned piece with the head of Athena on the obverse and an owl on the back in essence became the world's first trade coin, a concept that has endured even into the twentieth century via the Maria Theresa Thaler[q.v.] and the British trade dollar. Athenian moneyers allowed the tetradrachm's weight and design to remain sufficiently consistent to make it recognizable and acceptable to traders throughout the Greek world.

Alexander the Great's conquests into Asia in the fourth century B.C. allowed the tetradrachm to gain acceptance well beyond its original borders. The coin added a stabilizing effect to the money of the region. It was not only copied by other Greek city-states but also

became the medium for some magnificent Greek art.

By the second century B.C., the Roman Empire was on the rise and the tetradrachm began to decline in importance. The last of the tetradrachmai were debased pieces struck in Egypt around A.D. 300.

[David Van Meter, *Collecting Greek Coins*, p. 29; Richard G. Doty, *The Macmillan Encyclopedic Dictionary of Numismatics*, pp. 325-26.]

1486 Tirolean Guldengroschen

Thaler [*Ger.*] [Often spelled *taler* in English texts.] Large silver coin first struck in 1486 in Hall in the Austrian Tirol. Its initial German appearance came around 1500 in Saxony.

The discovery of huge silver deposits in the German city of Joachimsthal in 1519 led to the building of new mint facilities and to the production of great quantities of silver coins which became known as *Joachimsthalers*. Eventually the name was shortened to *Thaler*, although its official name *Guldengroschen* (or *Guldiner*) continued to be used in government documents for many years.

The Thaler quickly became popular and spread to other parts of Europe. The name became generic for many large silver coins of this type. The word *Thaler* underwent slight changes as it was adopted by one country after another. Centuries later it reached the New World as the *dollar*, probably by way of the Dutch version, *daaler*.

The Thalers' popularity was based both on their practical use as trade coins and on the beautiful artistic designs which could be placed on such large heavy planchets. Rulers of small principalities often used Thalers to honor themselves and to promote their own cause.

As trade coins, Thalers were universally accepted in all areas where they circulated. The most popular trade coin of all time, the 1780 Maria Theresa Thaler[q.v.], circulated freely in many parts of the world and were still issued as restrikes (with the 1780 date) even into the 1960s.

The last original circulating Thalers were issued in 1867 in Austria and 1871 in Germany. The final issues were the magnificent "Victory" Thalers of Prussia commemorating the German victory over France in the Franco-Prussian War. Immediately thereafter, the various German States banded together into a unified Germany. The Empire adopted the mark as its unit of currency, thus bringing the German Thaler to a glorious end.

Austrian 1620 Joachimsthal half-taler

thẻ tín dụng [*Viet.*] credit card.

Thistle Crown Common name for two types of English gold coins struck by James I. The first was valued at four shillings and was struck

from 1604-12. As the result of a decision in 1612 to increase the gold content of all gold coins by ten percent, a new issue was created that was denominated at four shillings fivepence. These coins were produced from 1612-19.

[Stephen Mitchell & Brian Reeds (editors), *Coins of England and the United Kingdom* (Seaby, 1991), pp. 177-79, et al.]

thỏi [*Viet.*] ingot.

thuộc về tiền tệ [*Viet.*] monetary.

ti [*Nor., Dan.*] ten.

tidak beredar [*Indo.*] uncirculated.

tien [*Dut.*] ten.

tiers (*m.*) [*Fr.*] third (the fraction).

tilapäisseteli [*Finn.*] scrip.

tilauslomake [*Finn.*] order form.

tilbud (*n.*) [*Nor., Dan.*] an offer.

tilbudsskjema (*n.*) [*Nor.*] bid sheet.

til gennemsyn [*Dan.*] on approval.

tili [*Finn.*] account (financial or transactional).

tillagt egenskap (*m.*) [*Nor.*] attribution.

till påseende [*Swed.*] on approval.

timbre-poste enchassé [*Fr.*] encased postage stamp.

timi τιμή (*f.*) [*Grk.*] price.

timi katalogou τιμή καταλόγου [*Grk.*] catalogue value.

timi sinalagmatos τιμή συναλλάγματος [*Grk.*] exchange rate.

tinta [*Hun.*]; (*f.*) [*Span., Port.*] ink.

Tinte (*f.*) [*Ger.*] ink.

tio [*Swed.*] ten.

tipo de cambio (*m.*) [*Span.*] exchange rate.

titolo (*m.*) [*Ital.*] (commercial) bond; title; certificate.

título (*m.*) [*Port.*] (commercial) bond.

tíz [*Hun.*] ten.

tjockmynt (*n.*) [*Swed.*] piéfort, piedfort.

tjue [*Nor.*] twenty.

tjugo [*Swed.*] twenty.

tłok menniczy (*m.*) [*Pol.*] (coinage) die.

to [*Nor., Dan.*] two.

todistus [*Finn.*] certificate.

toeschrijven (*v.*) [*Dut.*] to attribute.

toeschrijving (*f.-c.*) [*Dut.*] attribution.

tok Thai wedding token. The tok is a crude heavy disk of low-grade silver used to buy a wife. Two hundred years ago, it cost two toks to buy a wife and two more to divorce her.

In addition to being a form of money, it was also a type of good luck charm. As the color illustration on page 305 shows, a hole was placed near one edge so that the tok could be worn on a string. The red and yellow stains are said to be chicken blood and egg yolk, symbols of fertility (although some authorities claim the discoloration is nothing but impurities in the metal). The bride would wear the tok around her neck on her wedding night but then had to give it up the next morning.

[Charles J. Opitz, *Odd and Curious Money: Descriptions and Values*, p. 80.]

tökéletes [*Hun.*] perfect.

token A coin-like object used in lieu of legal tender coins to compensate for goods or services, to make change where no suitable legal tender coins exist, or to operate various vending or amusement devices. They are usually of metal but may also be of pressed fiberboard, ceramic materials, paper, plastics, cardboard, etc. (with certain limitations regarding usage when a non-metal is used).

Metal tokens are most frequently made of brass, bronze, copper, copper-nickel, white metal, or aluminum, but these are often replaced by zinc or steel during periods of wartime shortages. Plated tokens are common. Most tokens are round but they may also be triangular, square, scalloped, hexagonal, octagonal, etc., or may take the shape of such objects as a four-leaf clover.

In addition to those pieces which may be strictly defined as tokens, many other coin-like pieces, never intended to be used in payment, are collected along with tokens. These include advertising pieces, commemorative and political medals or medalets (small medals), communion tokens, good luck pieces, key tags, Masonic "pennies" and issues of many fraternal organizations, apothecary weights, magician's "coins", "personal" tokens, watch fobs, wooden "nickels", and a diverse range of other items which are of about coin size.

Also see *sutler token*, *Civil War token*, *coal company store scrip*, *encased coin*, *trans-*

portation token, exonumia, Hard Times token, machine token, maverick, military token, store card, phone card, telephone token, Van Buren token, and *vecture.*

[Contributed by Robert Doyle.]

token coinage Coins whose face value is considerably greater than the intrinsic value of the metal from which they were made. The term usually refers to nickel alloy coins previously issued in silver or to recently-created coins of cheaper metals which would have been made of silver had they been issued in an earlier era. This is the coinage equivalent of fiat money[q.v.], paper money which is not redeemable for specie nor for gold or silver coins. Both fiat money and token coinage are good in trade only because the people using them have faith in the issuing agency or because the issuing agency has the clout to enforce that the money be accepted.

A hundred years ago, the concept of token coinage was unthinkable. Today it is the norm. As recently as the 1950s, coins were supposed to be "worth their weight in gold (or silver)." But by the 1960s, the price of gold and silver had escalated to the point where the intrinsic value of these metals exceeded the face value of coins made from them. World governments had no choice but to replace precious metals with cheap metals. In other words, if a 50 cent coin has 75 cents worth of silver in it, the coin is going to be pulled from circulation and melted so that a profit can be made. Although it was a federal crime in the United States to melt U.S. coins, the government finally decriminalized such melting, realizing that it was trying to impose an unenforceable law which violated all rules of economics.

tombac A brass alloy of 88% copper and 12% zinc. It is best known for having been the substitute for nickel in the 1942 and 1943 Canadian "wartime" 5 cent pieces.

tomme (c.) [Dan.]; (m.) [Nor.] inch.

tóng 铜 [Chin.-py./sc.] copper.

tong-hwa 통화 [Kor.] currency.

törtszám [Hun.] fraction.

tospråklig [Nor.] bilingual.

tosproget [Dan.] bilingual.

trade coin A coin intended to circulate outside the political region where it is issued.

The ancient Greek tetradrachm[q.v.] is regarded by many as the world's first trade coin. Originally it was intended for use primarily by the citizens of the city-state where it was struck, but its popularity soon spread as far and wide as Greek traders could take it. One of the reasons the moneyers of Athens kept the familiar Athena/owl motifs for hundreds of years was because they realized that coins needed to be consistent to be accepted as trade coins.

The Maria Theresa Thaler[q.v.] is by far the most famous trade coin in history. As in the case of the tetradrachm, the design, weight, and purity of the Thaler were left unchanged because many foreign traders would not accept coins with variations. Maria Theresa's effigy was retained on restrikes for 180 years after her death.

Britain (1895-1935) and the United States (1873-1885) issued trade dollars specifically for use in the Orient. Many existing specimens are covered with chop marks[q.v.] placed there by Far East traders and bankers who examined each piece for purity and authenticity.

two aluminum trade tokens (*good fors*)

trade token (Pieces of this type are also called *merchant tokens* and *good fors.*) Token issued by an individual merchant to be an incentive

for sales, to make change, or to pay for goods (like eggs) brought to the merchant's store to be sold.

To promote sales, a merchant might give away a certain amount in tokens with each purchase over some minimum. The tokens then become, in effect, a discount on the purchase price. He might also sell thirteen loaves of bread for the price of twelve but then give the buyer tokens "Good for 1 loaf of Bread" so that the buyer would not need to accept all the bread at one time. This inscription also explains why these pieces are sometimes called *good fors*. Equivalent specimens exist in other languages, such as the German *gut für* beer token illustrated in color on page 316.

[Contributed by Robert Doyle.]

tranche (*f.*) [*Fr.*] edge (of a coin or medal).

bus token from the 1950s

transportation token (abbreviated *t.t.*) Token used in payment for the fare or toll or as a pass on bridges, buses, ferries, street cars (trolleys), taxis, toll roads, amusement rides, etc.

tre [*Ital., Swed., Dan., Nor.*] three.

Treasury Seal of the United States Official seal of the Department of the Treasury. The date 1789 represents the year in which the Department was created. Within the shield are the balance scales of justice and the key of official authority, separated by a chevron containing one star for each of the thirteen original colonies which banded together to form a new government.

trediedel (*c.*) [*Dan.*] third (the fraction).

tredive [*Dan.*] thirty.

tredjedel (*m.*) [*Nor.*]; (*r.*) [*Swed.*] third.

trei [*Rom.*] three.

treinta [*Span.*] thirty.

treizeci [*Rom.*] thirty.

trenta [*Ital.*] thirty.

trente [*Fr.*] thirty.

tres [*Span.*] three; [*Dan.*] sixty.

três [*Port.*] three.

trésor (*m.*) [*Fr.*] treasure.

tressure Hexagon-shaped figure but with concave sides. If a fleur-de-lis appears at each point, it is called a *fleured tressure*.

tretti [*Nor.*] thirty.

trettio [*Swed.*] thirty.

tria τρία [*Grk.*] three.

tribute penny: denarius of Tiberius (A.D. 14-37)

tribute penny Common name for the silver denarius issued by the Roman Emperor Tiberius (A.D. 14-37). The coin was in circulation in Judæa during the time of Christ and is known for having been the annual amount each citizen was taxed by the Romans. As a point of reference, one denarius was equal to a day's wages for a Roman soldier. Although the tax could be paid with old coins struck by previous emperors, the term *tribute penny* generally applies specifically to the denarius of Tiberius which portrays him on the obverse and the seated figure of his wife Livia on the reverse.

trime United States silver 3 cent pieces issued from 1851 to 1873. The term is not normally used in reference to the U.S. 3 cent coins of 75% copper and 25% nickel issued from 1865 to 1889.

Both the silver and copper-nickel coins owe their existence to the U.S. Post Office, which lowered the rate of sending a one ounce, first-class letter from 5 cents down to 3 cents in 1851. The coin's primary purpose was to enable post office customers to use a single coin when purchasing a stamp. Similarly, the $3 gold pieces of 1854-1889 were issued for the purpose of expediting the purchase of a full pane of 100 stamps.

Silver trimes were so small (14mm) that they often fell out of pockets or purses. Those that were not lost were snatched out of circulation during the economic instability of the U.S. Civil War (1861-1865). At the end of the war, larger non-precious versions were introduced (the copper-nickel coins) and the silver trimes were phased out.

The word is derived from the prefix *tri*, meaning "three", and the word *dime*, the official and legal name of the U.S. 10 cent pieces struck since 1796.

[Tom LaMarre, "The Trouble with Trimes," *Coins*, February 1996, pp. 48-50; R. W. Julian, "In the Grips of a Gold Rush," *Coins*, August 1988, pp. 62-64.]

trinta [*Port.*] thirty.

triskeles

triskeles Configuration of three legs extending outward from the center. It is emblematic of the Isle of Man and has appeared on many of its coins.

trivi kermatos apo tin thiki τριβή κέρματος απο την θήκη [*Grk.*] cabinet friction.

trocar (*v.*) [*Port.*] to trade.

trois [*Fr.*] three.

troquel (*m.*) [*Span.*] (coinage) die.

trou (*m.*) [*Fr.*] hole.

troy Common measurement of weight of precious metals. One troy pound equals 12 troy ounces, and one troy ounce equals 20 pennyweights, 480 grains, 31.103 grams, or 1.097 avoirdupois ounces.

trzy [*Pol.*] three.

tseke [*Tag.*] check, cheque.

tsûka 通貨 [*Jpn.*] currency (referring collectively to coins and paper money. Paper currency is *shihei* 紙幣).

tsura mutba'at צוּרָה מֻטְבַּעַת [*Heb.*] incuse.

tughra; toughra Monogram configured from the sultan's name and title in the Arabic language. It was introduced on Ottoman coinage in the fifteenth century and has appeared on coins of Turkey, Egypt, Pakistan, and elsewhere as late as 1974. This calligraphic design substituted for the ruler's effigy which, according to Islamic law, may not appear on coins.

tükörfényes [*Hun.*] proof (*re:* coins or medals).

tulajdonítás; tulajdonság [*Hun.*] attribution.

tum (*r.*) [*Swed.*] inch.

tumma [*Finn.*] dark.

tunnuskuva [*Finn.*] symbol.

tuntematon [*Finn.*] unknown.

tusen [*Nor., Swed.*] thousand.

tusind [*Dan.*] thousand.

tuuma [*Finn.*] inch.

två [*Swed.*] two.

tvåspråkig [*Swed.*] bilingual.

tvi'a meykhadash טְבִיעָה מְחֻדָּשׁ (*f.*) [*Heb.*] a restrike.

tvi'a m'yukhedet טְבִיעָה מְיוּחֶדֶת (*f.*) [*Heb.*] piéfort, piedfort.

tvi'a shelo kahalakha טְבִיעָה שֶׁלֹא כַּהֲלָכָה [*Heb.*] a mis-strike.

tvi'at matb'ot טְבִיעַת מַטְבְּעוֹת (*f.*) [*Heb.*] coinage.

twee [*Dut.*] two.

tweetalig [*Dut.*] bilingual.

twintig [*Dut.*] twenty.

type 1. A classification of coins by their metal, denomination, nationality, and principal devices. Major symbolic devices such as a coat of arms, the effigy, and the presence or absence of key mottoes are all determining factors. A *variety* is a minor die variation within a given type.

2. As an investment term, *type coin* refers to the least expensive dates and mintmarks within a type.

type metal An alloy of lead, tin, and antimony. It has occasionally been used in die trials or counterfeits.

tysiąc [*Pol.*] thousand.

Tyskland [*Nor., Dan., Swed.*] Germany.

tysk mark (*m.*) [*Nor.*] mark (German unit of currency).

tyve [*Dan.*] twenty.

U u

Überdruck (*m.*) [*Ger.*] overprint.
ubrugt [*Dan.*] uncirculated.
üç [*Turk.*] three.
uchikomimoyô 打ち込み模様 [*Jpn.*] incuse.
udenlandsk [*Dan.*] foreign.
udenlandsk valuta (*c.*) [*Dan.*] foreign currency.
udgive (*v.*) [*Dan.*] to issue.
udgivelse (*c.*) [*Dan.*] an issue, issuance.
udmøntning (*c.*) [*Dan.*] coinage.
udstede (*v.*) [*Dan.*] to issue.
ufficiale [*Ital.*] official.
ufficioso [*Ital.*] unofficial.
ufuldstændig [*Dan.*] incomplete.
ufullstendig [*Nor.*] incomplete.
ufullstendig identifisert [*Nor.*] unattributed.
ugyldiggørelse (*c.*) [*Dan.*] demonetization.
uim bog [*Ire.*] Literally, *soft copper*. Term given by the Irish to some of the *Gun money*[q.v.] coins of King James II of England. These were base metal token coins issued by James when he was forced into exile and was preparing to attempt to re-take his throne. The tokens had the appearance of standard coins but were made of whatever scrap metal was available, including the metal from melted-down cannons (from which the coins get their name). This metal was quite soft, inducing the populace to nickname the pieces *uim bog*. James intended to redeem the tokens for genuine silver coins when he regained the throne, but he was unable to recapture it.
[Leon Lindheim, "Coins" Column, *The Plain Dealer* (Cleveland, Ohio), September 15, 1985, p. 16P.]
uitgeven (*v.*) [*Dut.*] to issue.
uitstekend [*Dut.*] excellent.
új [*Hun.*] new.
Új-Zéland [*Hun.*] New Zealand.
ukendt [*Dan.*] unknown.
ukjent [*Nor.*] unknown.

ulkomaan raha [*Finn.*] foreign currency.
ulkomainen [*Finn.*] foreign.
um (*m.adj.*); **uma** (*f.adj.*) [*Port.*] one.
umändern (*v.*) [*Ger.*] to alter.
Umänderung (*f.*) [*Ger.*] alteration.
Umlauf (*m.*) [*Ger.*] circulation.
Umschrift (*f.*) [*Ger.*] legend.
un (*m.adj.*) [*Fr., Span.*] one.
una (*f.adj.*) [*Ital., Span.*] one.

Una and the Lion

Una and the Lion Magnificent reverse design of the 1839 £5 gold piece showing the young Queen Victoria in the role of William Spencer's character from *The Fairie Queene*. This issue has been called the high point of the English

engraver's art and is one of the most beautiful coins ever created. A presentation piece, it was issued only in proof and with the date in roman numerals (MDCCCXXXIX). The *Young Head* design of Queen Victoria graces the obverse.

Also see page 308 for color photos.

unattributed A numismatic item which has not been fully identified. A complete identification of the piece, including such elements as the issuing agency, date of issue, exact substance from which the item was made, condition, pedigree, etc., is known as its *attribution.*

unbekannt [*Ger.*] unknown.

uncia [*Hun.*] ounce.

uncirculated Grade of a coin or note in mint state which shows no signs of having been placed in circulation. For coins, this means absolutely no surface wear. For notes, it means no creases or folds.

It is permissible for an uncirculated coin to show some signs of cabinet friction or for a note to have pin holes if thin stacks of notes of that type were commonly pinned together at the bank for easy handling. Some uncirculated coins and notes show signs of having been cleaned. In each of the above cases, the grade of uncirculated can be assigned but then must be followed by an explanation of the coin or note's impairment.

Since the advent of third-party grading services, uncirculated coins can theoretically be placed into any of eleven levels of excellence, ranging from a low of MS-60, which might have a weak strike and many bag marks but still shows no signs of having circulated, up to MS-70, a coin in a perfect state of preservation. Some experts doubt if such a coin exists.

uncja (*f.*) [*Pol.*] ounce.

underprint [abbreviated *unpt.*] Network of background printing on a banknote.

underskrift (*m.*) [*Nor.*]; (*c.*) [*Dan.*] signature.

une (*f.adj.*) [*Fr.*] one.

ungedecktes Papiergeld (*n.*) [*Ger.*] fiat money.

União Soviética [*Port.*] Soviet Union (U.S.S.R.).

unico [*Ital.*] unique.

único [*Span., Port.*] unique.

unidade monetária [*Port.*] monetary unit.

unidad monetaria (*f.*) [*Span.*] monetary unit.

uniek [*Dut.*] unique.

unifaţă [*Rom.*] uniface.

unifaz [*Span.*] uniface.

Unione delle Repubbliche Socialiste Sovietiche [*Ital.*] Soviet Union (U.S.S.R.).

Unión de Repúblicas Socialistas Soviéticas; Unión Soviética [*Span.*] Soviet Union.

unique Only one specimen known to exist, either because only one single piece was originally produced (such as the 1787 Brasher Half Doubloon) or because multiple examples were produced but all were later destroyed except one (as was presumably the case with the 1954 British penny).

If no specimens are known to survive, the piece is referred to in catalogues as *unknown*, even if it is certain that at least one was made. This was the case with the Templeton Reid $25 California gold piece. Only one piece was struck, but it was ultimately stolen from the Cabinet of the U.S. Mint in 1858. It was never recovered.

unità monetaria (*f.*) [*Ital.*] monetary unit.

unitate monetară (*f.*) [*Rom.*] monetary unit.

unite Large gold coin of England and Scotland first struck in 1604 by James I (known as James VI in Scotland) to honor the merging of the two countries. The first issues had a value of 20 shillings (1604-12). This was increased to 22 shillings in 1612 and maintained until 1619. The unites of Charles I (begun in 1625 and discontinued just after his death in 1649 at the beginning of the Commonwealth) went back to 20 shillings. At the restoration of the monarchy, Charles II issued the unite as one of his first coins (1662).

See page 308 for color photos.

unité monétaire (*f.*) [*Fr.*] monetary unit.

unkiya אוּנְקְיָה (*f.*) [*Heb.*] ounce.

unknown Not known to exist in any collection. In some cases there is a question as to whether the piece was ever actually produced. In other cases, it is certain that at least one was made but none can be accounted for. An example is the 1873-S U.S. silver dollar of which 700 were struck. Apparently none has survived.

uno (*m.adj.*) [*Ital., Span.*] one.

unpt. [*abbr.*] underprint. A network of background printing on a banknote.

unpublished A coin, note, medal, or any other numismatic item which is unlisted in any book or catalogue. Unpublished pieces are not necessarily rare if they are from a series which has not been well researched, such as German or Austrian Notgeld, or if they are part of an area where reliable information is difficult to obtain, such as U.S. trade tokens.

unregelmäßig [*Ger.*] irregular.

uns (*n.*) [*Swed.*] ounce.

unse (*m.*) [*Nor.*] ounce.

unssi [*Finn.*] ounce.

unten [*Ger.*] bottom; below, beneath.

Unterschrift (*f.*) [*Ger.*] signature.

unu [*Rom.*] one.

unveröffentlicht [*Ger.*] unpublished.

unvollständig [*Ger.*] incomplete.

Unze (*f.*) [*Ger.*] ounce.

unzirkuliert [*Ger.*] uncirculated.

uofficiel [*Dan.*] unofficial.

Upper Mint Popular name of the minting facility built in England in 1560 to accommodate Elizabeth I's "recoinage" program intended to bring integrity back to the nation's money. This was in response to the gross debasement of coins done some years earlier by Henry VIII.

After the recoinage program was completed, the facility was used to make coins for Ireland which was suffering from a severe coin shortage. Thus the facility became known as the *Irish Mint*.

upubliceret [*Dan.*] unpublished.

uralkodó [*Hun.*] sovereign.

uregelmæssig [*Dan.*] irregular.

urzędowy [*Pol.*] official.

usado [*Span., Port.*] used.

usagé [*Fr.*] used.

usato [*Ital.*] used.

usirkulert [*Nor.*] uncirculated.

uso (*m.*) [*Span., Port.*] use; wear.

üstüste ve aynı yöne bakan [*Turk.*] accolated, conjoined, jugate.

usura (*f.*) [*Ital.*] wear.

usura da contenitore (*f.*) [*Ital.*] cabinet friction.

usure (*f.*) [*Fr.*] wear.

uszkodzenie (*n.*) [*Pol.*] defect; damage.

uszkodzenie kolekcjonerskie (*n.*) [*Pol.*] cabinet friction.

uszkodzony [*Pol.*] damaged; defective.

utánzat [*Hun.*] imitation.

utenlandsk [*Nor.*] foreign.

utenlandsk mynt (*m.*) [*Nor.*] foreign currency.

utforming (*m.*) [*Nor.*] design.

utgåva (*r.*) [*Swed.*] an issue, issuance.

utge; ge ut (*v.*) [*Swed.*] to issue.

utländsk [*Swed.*] foreign.

utländsk valuta [*Swed.*] foreign currency.

utmärkt [*Swed.*] excellent.

utmerket [*Nor.*] excellent.

utropspris (*n.*) [*Swed.*]; (*m.*) [*Nor.*] suggested bid.

utställning (*r.*) [*Swed.*] exhibition.

utstede (*v.*) [*Nor.*] to issue.

utstedelse (*m.*) [*Nor.*] an issue, issuance.

utstilling (*m.*) [*Nor.*] exhibition.

uusintalyönti [*Finn.*] a restrike.

Uusi-Seelanti [*Finn.*] New Zealand.

uwieńczony [*Pol.*] laureate.

uzură (*f.*) [*Rom.*] wear.

uzură de cabinet (*f.*) [*Rom.*] cabinet friction.

V v

väärennös [*Finn.*] a counterfeit; fake; forgery.

väärentäjä [*Finn.*] counterfeiter.

väärentämisen ehkäisykeino [*Finn.*] anti-counterfeiting device.

vægt (*c.*) [*Dan.*] weight.

vaglia (*m.*) [*Ital.*] postal money order.

værdi (*c.*) [*Dan.*] value.

værdifuld [*Dan.*] valuable.

vahingoittunut [*Finn.*] damaged.

vaihtokurssi [*Finn.*] exchange rate.

valaminek az alja [*Hun.*] bottom.

választék [*Hun.*] variety.

vale (*m.*) [*Port.*] (commercial) bond.

vale de propaganda [*Span.*] propaganda note.

vale por ... [*Span.*] good for ....

vale postal (*m.*) [*Port.*] postal money order.

valeur (*f.*) [*Fr.*] value.

valeur de catalogue [*Fr.*] catalogue value.

valeur faciale (*f.*) [*Fr.*] face value.

valeurs (*f.pl.*) [*Fr.*] (commercial) bond.

valgspråk (*n.*) [*Nor.*] motto.

valioso [*Span., Port.*] valuable.

valkoinen [*Finn.*] white.

valoare (*f.*) [*Rom.*] value.

valoare de catalog (*f.*) [*Rom.*] catalogue value.

valoare nominală (*f.*) [*Rom.*] denomination; face value.

valódi [*Hun.*] genuine.

valor (*m.*) [*Span., Port.*] value; denomination.

valör (*r.*) [*Swed.*] denomination.

valor de cambio (*m.*) [*Span.*] exchange rate.

valor de catálogo (*m.*) [*Span., Port.*] catalogue value.

valore (*m.*) [*Ital.*] value; denomination.

valore di catalogo (*m.*) [*Ital.*] catalogue value.

valore facciale (*m.*); **valore nominale** (*m.*) [*Ital.*] face value.

valor facial (*m.*); **valor nominal** (*m.*) [*Span., Port.*] face value.

valsverkspräglat mynt (*n.*) [*Swed.*] milled coin.

valtiovarainministeri [*Finn.*] finance minister.

valuta [*Hun.*]; (*f.*) [*Ital.*]; (*m.-c.*) [*Dut*]; (*c.*) [*Swed., Dan.*]; (*m.*) [*Nor.*] currency.

valută (*f.*) [*Rom.*] currency.

valuta- [*Swed.*] monetary.

valuta di propaganda [*Ital.*] propaganda note.

valutaenhet (*r.*) [*Swed.*] monetary unit.

valută străină (*f.*) [*Rom.*] foreign currency.

valuta straniera (*f.*) [*Ital.*] foreign currency.

valutasystem (*n.*) [*Swed.*] monetary system.

valuutta [*Finn.*] foreign currency.

Van Buren token

Van Buren token In 1837 when Martin van Buren succeeded Andrew Jackson as president of the United States, the U.S. was in the middle of a great financial crisis. Among the consequences of this economic depression was the hoarding of hard money, even copper cents and half cents.

To facilitate commerce, many manufacturers, innkeepers, goldsmiths, boot makers, and all sorts of other tradesmen issued their own copper tokens. Most did not resemble the U.S. large cents of the time and were not intended as counterfeit coins. These Hard Times tokens[q.v.], as they are known, were not only used to help pay employees' salaries and to provide small change for making trans-

actions, but they also provided a "public forum" for expressing critical opinions of the president and his policies.

Although Jackson was the target of the most satirical tokens (some portrayed him as a mule because of his well-known stubbornness), the later tokens attacked Van Buren (also sometimes portrayed as a mule). One token quotes him as saying, "I take responsibility for the measures that I propose..." The sentence should have stopped there. But the token maker added, "...to take the money of the state."

The token in the illustration reflects the frustration of the American people and the feelings of the token maker that Daniel Webster, not Van Buren, should have been elected president.. On one side is seen the Ship of State in great disrepair, at risk of shipwreck in 1837 as the consequence of some measures introduced by Van Buren. On the other side is a grand sailing vessel, suggesting what the Ship of State would have looked like had Webster been elected.

vandmærke (n.) [*Dan.*] watermark.

vanha [*Finn.*] old.

vannmerke (n.) [*Nor.*] watermark.

vänster [*Swed.*] left (direction or position).

vânzător (m.) [*Rom.*] seller.

varausmaksu [*Finn.*] deposit.

varausmaksu vaaditaan [*Finn.*] deposit required.

värde (n.) [*Swed.*] value.

väri [*Finn.*] color, colour.

variant (m.-c.) [*Dut.*] variety.

variedad (f.) [*Span.*] variety.

varietà (f.) [*Ital.*] variety.

variété (f.) [*Fr.*] variety.

variëteit (m.-c.) [*Dut.*] variety.

variety A minor die variation, specifically something noticeably different in two coins of the same type, date, and mint. The *large motto* and *small motto* varieties of the 1864 U.S. 2 cent pieces are one such example, as are the date varieties (*near 6* and *far 6*) of the 1926 Canadian 5 cent pieces.

varmuustekijä [*Finn.*] anti-counterfeiting device.

vas [*Hun.*] iron (the metal).

vásárló [*Hun.*] buyer.

vasen [*Finn.*] left (direction or position).

vastagveret [*Hun.*] piéfort, piedfort.

Västtyskland [*Swed.*] West Germany (B.R.D.).

vattenmärke (n.) [*Swed.*] watermark.

växelkurs (r.) [*Swed.*] exchange rate.

vecchio [*Ital.*] old.

veck (n.) [*Swed.*] a fold (in a banknote).

vecturist A collector of transportation tokens. See *vecture.*

viejo [*Span.*] old.

vekt (m.) [*Nor.*] weight.

veiling (f.-c.) [*Dut.*] auction, auction sale.

veilingkatalogus (m.-c.) [*Dut.*] auction catalogue.

veinte [*Span.*] twenty.

vekselkurs (c.) [*Dan.*] exchange rate.

velho [*Port.*] old.

velkakirja [*Finn.*] bond.

Venäjä [*Finn.*] Russia.

venda em leilão [*Port.*] auction sale.

vender (v.) [*Span., Port.*] to sell.

vendedor (m.) [*Span., Port.*] seller.

vendere (v.) [*Ital.*] to sell.

vendeur (m.) [*Fr.*] seller.

vendita all'asta (f.) [*Ital.*] auction sale.

vendita all'asta per posta [*Ital.*] mail bid sale.

venditore (m.) [*Ital.*] seller.

vendre (v.) [*Fr.*] to sell.

venstre [*Nor., Dan.*] left (direction or position).

venta en subasta (f.) [*Span.*] auction sale.

vente aux enchères [*Fr.*] auction; auction sale.

vente aux enchéres par correspondance [*Fr.*] mail bid sale.

venti [*Ital.*] twenty.

veraltet [*Ger.*] obsolete.

verbonden [*Dut.*] accolated, conjoined, jugate.

Verbriefte Schuldverpflichtung (f.) [*Ger.*] scrip.

verde [*Span., Ital., Port., Rom.*] green.

verdejegy [*Hun.*] mintmark.

verdi [*Nor.*] value.

verdifull [*Nor.*] valuable.

Vereinigtes Königreich [*Ger.*] United Kingdom.

Vereinigte Staaten von Amerika [*Ger.*] United States of America.

vereint [*Ger.*] accolated[q.v.], conjoined, jugate.

Verenigde Staten van Amerika [*Dut.*] United States of America.

Verenigd Koninkrijk [*Dut.*] United Kingdom.

vergrootglas (*n.*) [*Dut.*] magnifying glass.

Vergrößerungsglas (*n.*) [*Ger.*] magnifying glass.

verhandelen (*v.*) [*Dut.*] to trade.

veritabil [*Rom.*] authentic, genuine.

véritable [*Fr.*] authentic, genuine.

verkaufen (*v.*) [*Ger.*] to sell.

Verkäufer (*m.*) [*Ger.*] seller.

verkopen (*v.*) [*Dut.*] to sell.

verkoper (*m.-c.*) [*Dut.*] seller.

vermelho [*Port.*] red.

vero [*Finn.*] tax.

verőgép [*Hun.*] (coinage) press.

verőtő [*Hun.*] (coinage) die.

verouderd [*Dut.*] obsolete.

verso (*m.*) [*Ital.*] obverse.

Versteigerung (*f.*) [*Ger.*] auction.

vert [*Fr.*] green.

vertieft [*Ger.*] incuse.

vervalsen (*v.*) [*Dut.*] to counterfeit.

vervalser (*m.-c.*) [*Dut.*] counterfeiter.

vervalsing (*f.-c.*) [*Dut.*] a counterfeit, fake, forgery.

verzamelaar (*m.-c.*) [*Dut.*] collector.

verzameling (*f.-c.*) [*Dut.*] collection.

vésett [*Hun.*] engraved.

vesileima [*Finn.*] watermark.

Vest-Tyskland [*Nor.*] West Germany (B.R.D.).

viallinen [*Finn.*] defective.

Victoria Queen of the United Kingdom of Great Britian and Ireland from 1837 to 1901 and Empress of India, 1876-1901. Born May 24, 1819, in Kensington Palace, London; died January 22, 1901 in London.

Victoria became queen at the age of eighteen upon the death of her uncle, King William IV, who had no legitimate heirs. Her reign of 63 years made hers the longest of any monarch in British history and one of the longest anywhere in Europe. Many thousands of British subjects were born and died having only known her as their monarch.

Victoria was neither brilliant nor witty, but she was very conservative, stable, and patriotic, making her the personification of the English ideal of her time. Her personality and demeanor were a perfect match for what British citizens of the nineteenth century wanted, so it is no surprise that this period became known as the Victorian Era. The Victorian Age, as it was also known, was marked by prosperity and the rise of the middle class. In many respects, Victoria truly was the "Fairie Queene" as she was portrayed on the 1839 gold £5 coin known as *Una and the Lion*[q.v.]. [See page 308 for color illustration.]

Queen Victoria

Victoria's popularity was enhanced by the success of the British military. During her long reign, many diverse parts of the world became part of the British Empire on which, as it was said, "the sun never sets." The vastness of this empire contributed greatly to Victoria's importance in numismatic history. Not only did she appear on the vast number of British coins expected from someone who would reign for sixty-three years, but she also was portrayed on many coins produced in an attempt to match local denominations found in the far-off corners of the Empire. This is the sole reason why her image appears on coins valued at a quarter-farthing (for use in Ceylon), a third-farthing (for Malta), and three-halfpence (for use in various colonial territories). And, of course, the coinages of Canada and India, both struck in local denominations, feature Victoria's portrait.

Queen Victoria's presence was everywhere. In addition to her effigy found on so very many

coins, she also was the first person ever to be portrayed on a postage stamp (the *Penny Black* of 1840; see page 308 for a color photo of a 1990 Isle of Man crown commemorating this event and struck with a special proof surface).

Because of her very long reign, mint officials changed her effigy twice so that she and her portrait would both "age" (although not at the same rate), a situation not unlike that of her great-great-granddaughter, Elizabeth II. The first design, known as the *Young Head* coinage, shows Victoria as she appeared as a child of eighteen. This youthful effigy was used on various coins from 1838 until 1887 when Victoria was 66 years old. A slightly modified version known as *Bun Head*[q.v.] was introduced on bronze coins in 1860 and not discontinued until 1895 when the queen was 74.

The Young Head was not the only design used during this period. From 1847 to 1887 the silver florins (2 shilling pieces) and crowns (5 shillings) showed an alternative design known as the *Gothic*[q.v.] type. These pieces show a youthful crowned head of Victoria.

To honor her first fifty years on the throne, the effigy was changed in 1887 to what is known as the *Jubilee* coinage exhibiting the portrait of a more mature Victoria wearing a small crown.

From 1893 (or 1895 on bronze pieces) until her death in 1901, coins bearing her likeness showed a much older queen wearing a draped crown. The drape represented her state of mourning which had begun in 1861 on the death of her beloved husband, Prince Albert, who was also her first cousin. Five years before his death, Albert and Victoria created the Victoria Cross, the highest British award for wartime valor. This decoration was first given to military heroes who distinguished themselves in the Crimean War.

Victoria's descendants included forty grandchildren, some of whom ultimately married into nearly every royal family in Europe. In a sense this could be called Victoria's curse, because she carried the gene responsible for hemophilia. The best-known recipient to suffer this affliction transmitted by Victoria was Alexis, son of the Russian Czar Nicholas II, who was killed along with his entire family in 1918 by the Bolsheviks.

Queen Victoria was a classic. She will live forever in numismatics.

Victoria, Museum of Institution possessing the largest and finest numismatic collection in Australia. The numismatic holdings include the former collections of the National Gallery of Victoria and of the Melbourne Branch of the Royal Mint.

Perhaps the best-known pieces of this group are those from the A. M. LeSouef Collection[q.v.]. LeSouef was the Deputy Master of the Melbourne Mint from 1919 to 1926 and acquired many of the new coins as they were being minted. His pieces have great historical significance.

[John Sharples, "The Numismatic Collection of the Museum of Victoria," *Journal of the Numismatic Association of Australia*, Vol. 2, (July 1986), pp. 37-52.]

Vielfalt (*f.*) [*Ger.*] variety.

vier [*Ger., Dut.*] four.

vierde [*Dut.*] fourth, quarter.

vierkant (*adj.*) [*Dut.*] square.

Viertel (*n.*) [*Ger.*] fourth, quarter.

vierzig [*Ger.*] forty.

vieux [*Fr.*] old.

vignette Portrait or other pictorial design on a banknote or bond that shades off gradually into the surrounding ground or unprinted paper. The U.S. note in the illustration is a good example of how extensive a vignette can be on a piece of paper money.

Extensive vignette on U.S. note.   [Photo courtesy Stanley Morycz.]

Although many vignettes are beautiful works of art, their primary purpose has been as an anti-counterfeiting device. The work is very intricate and detailed and historically has been difficult for counterfeiters to reproduce.

The advent of high-quality photography and computerized photocopy equipment has made the fraudulent reproduction of vignettes easier, but some governments have redesigned their notes to make falsifying more difficult. For example, in 1996 the United States introduced a new series of notes in which the portrait on the face and the vignette on the back blend into backgrounds of concentric fine lines. This configuration is nearly impossible to duplicate with any degree of efficiency, even with sophisticated equipment.

VIGO on Queen Anne crown of 1702

Vigo In 1702 a combined English and Dutch fleet captured a group of Spanish treasure ships just arriving from the New World. The attack took place in Vigo Bay off the coast of northwestern Spain. Some of the Spanish ships were sunk and their cargoes were never recovered, but a large quantity of gold and silver bullion was seized before the ships went down. Much of this metal was sent to England where it was used to mint gold 5 guineas, guineas, and half-guineas, as well as silver crowns, halfcrowns, and shillings. The word VIGO was placed under Queen Anne's bust on the coins produced from the seized bullion. All of the coins were dated 1702 or 1703.

viidesosa [*Finn.*] fifth (the fraction).

viisi [*Finn.*] five.

viisikymmentä [*Finn.*] fifty.

vijf [*Dut.*] five.

vika [*Finn.*] defect.

Vikariatsthaler [*Ger.*] Large silver ornate coin issued in Germany during the seventeenth and eighteenth centuries to mark an interregnum (the period between the death of an ecclesiastical leader and the appointment of his successor). They are regarded as among the most grandiose coins ever made.

These pieces served much the same purpose as the modern sede vacante[q.v.] coins issued by the Vatican upon the death of the pope.

vikt (*r.*) [*Swed.*] weight.

Vilda Hiya Name of the so-called "wildman" who appears with an unrooted fir tree on a variety of coins struck by Brunswick-Lüneburg, Brunswick-Wolfenbuttel, Prussia and several other German states from the mid-1500s until the early nineteenth century. The figure is based on a mythological character originating in the Harz Mountains during the Middle Ages.

vínculo (*m.*) [*Span.*] (commercial) bond.

vingt [*Fr.*] twenty.

vinte [*Port.*] twenty.

virallinen [*Finn.*] official.

virhe [*Finn.*] error.

virheetön [*Finn.*] perfect.

virhelyönti [*Finn.*] a mis-strike.

virhelyöty [*Finn.*] mis-struck.

vis-à-vis portraits on 1518 Austrian Thaler

vis-à-vis [*Fr.*] literally, *opposite*. Two separate portraits which face each other on the same side of a coin or medal. The French term *tête-à-tête* is also used.

This style is rarely seen, in part because it tends to be esthetically displeasing. The placement of two independent portraits is not well suited for a round coin, creating a lot of wasted space. And since the portraits must be very small to fit them into the allotted area, detail and artistic quality have usually suffered, especially on hammered coins of ancient and medieval times.

A better reason why this technique is seen infrequently is because its usage has seldom been appropriate. Vis-à-vis effigies signify two co-rulers or two rulers of equal status, or a ruler who is indicating his choice of successor.

Coins of Isabella and Ferdinand of Spain show the vis-à-vis configuration, because the king and queen had inherited separate kingdoms and, in essence, sat on separate thrones. Spain was not united under one ruler until the death of Ferdinand in 1516 when their grandson Charles (Charles I of Spain, later Charles V of the Holy Roman Empire) inherited the second of the two kingdoms. Because Ferdinand and Isabella were of equal status, neither could be portrayed in a superior position to the other. [See *excelente de la granada.*]

The Austrian Thaler of 1518 shows Holy Roman Emperor Maximilian I facing his grandson, the above-mentioned Charles. Maximilian, Charles' paternal grandfather, used the coin in his campaign to have his grandson succeed him as Holy Roman emperor. The tactic worked, and Charles was elected emperor on the death of Maximilian in 1519.

When two people of unequal status are featured on the same coin, they are generally placed in an accolated[q.v.] fashion (i.e., overlapped) and with the person of higher status in the forefront.

vízjegy [*Hun.*] watermark.

volgnummer (*n.*) [*Dut.*] serial number.

Volksrepublik China [*Ger.*] People's Republic of China (P.R.C.).

voorgesteld bod (*n.*) [*Dut.*] suggested bid.

voorkant (*m.-c.*) [*Dut.*] front.

vooruitbetaling (*m.-c.*) [*Dut.*] prepayment.

voorzijde (*f.-c.*) [*Dut.*] obverse.

Vorauszahlung (*f.*) [*Ger.*] prepayment.

Vorderseite (*f.*) [*Ger.*] front.

vörösréz [*Hun.*] copper.

Roman votive coin

votive coin Any Roman coin which reaffirms the emperor's vows or records his public prayers. In some cases they were intended to give thanks for major achievements.

The position of emperor did not accord that person the status of deity, but he was regarded as being above other human beings. As such, it became customary for him to make and periodically reaffirm certain vows. The votive coins were simply public documentation of those vows.

Votive coins began with Augustus, the first Roman emperor (31 B.C.), and continued sporadically until the late Constantine period when they became most popular.

Votive coins can be identified by their inscriptions on the reverse side which always include *votis, vota,* or some other form of the Latin word *votum,* a reference to the vows. They are usually in combination with words such as *publica* ("public") or *soluta* ("thanks") and include indications of how many years these vows are good for, either in roman numerals (V, X, or XX) or in words (e.g., *decennalia,* ten years).

vuosiluku [*Finn.*] date.

W w

w/ [*abbr.*] with.

waarborgsom vereist [*Dut.*] deposit required.

waarde (*m.-c.*) [*Dut.*] value.

waardebon (*m.-c.*) [*Dut.*] certificate.

waardevol [*Dut.*] valuable.

wadium (*n.*) [*Pol.*] deposit (of funds).

wadium wymagane [*Pol.*] deposit required.

wadliwie wybity [*Pol.*] mis-struck.

waga (*f.*) [*Pol.*] weight.

Wahlspruch (*m.*) [*Ger.*] motto, slogan.

Währung (*f.*) [*Ger.*] currency.

Währungssystem (*n.*) [*Ger.*] monetary system.

wài bì 外币 [*Chin.-py./sc.*] foreign currency.

New Zealand Waitangi crown

Waitangi crown Silver 5 shilling crown of New Zealand issued in 1935 to commemorate the 1840 Treaty of Waitangi. The obverse shows the traditional crowned bust of George V, and the reverse features the British governor and Maori chief shaking hands. A total of 1128 pieces (764 business strikes, 364 proofs) were struck in .500 silver.

Walia [*Pol.*] Wales.

Walking Liberty Half Dollar [a.k.a. *Liberty Walking Half Dollar.*] Magnificent design of U.S. half dollars issued from 1916-1947. This type was created by Adolph A. Weinman, the designer of the Winged Liberty ("Mercury") Dime. The Walking Liberty Half Dollar is considered one of America's most beautiful coins. The design is so popular that it was brought back in 1986 as the obverse design on the silver 1 ounce bullion coins.

Walking Liberty design on U.S. silver bullion coin

waluta (*f.*) [*Pol.*] currency.

wampum Cylindrical beads made from conch shells and used as a form of exchange by New England-area natives from an undetermined time prior to the seventeenth century up through the nineteenth century. Some were purple in color (although they were called *black* wampum) and others were white. In 1648 Connecticut decreed that four white wampum beads were equal to one English penny.

Throughout the Virginia area, wampum was known as *roenoke*; in New York the beads were called *seawan*.

[Charles J. Opitz, *Odd and Curious Money: Descriptions and Values*, p. 83.]

wang [*Indo.*] money.

wang kertas [*Indo.*] banknote; paper money.

wang logam [*Indo.*] coin.

wariant (*m.*) [*Pol.*] variety.

wartime nickel [nicknamed *warnick.*]

    1. U.S. 5 cent piece struck from 1942 to 1945 using an alloy of 56% copper, 35% silver, and 9% manganese. This alloy was substituted because nickel was a critical metal for the war effort.

    2. Canadian 5 cent piece, struck in 1942 (with traditional reverse design) and 1943 ("Victory" reverse) in tombac, a brass alloy of 88% copper and 12% zinc. The 1944 and 1945 5 cent pieces were made from chromium-plated steel and carried the "Victory" reverse. All Canadian war nickels are 12-sided instead of round, and the one with the Victory design includes a Morse Code inscription around the reverse rim: *We Win When We Work Willingly.*

1806 "wart on nose" farthing (enlarged 3x)

wart on nose Unusual die break on some 1806 British farthings. Its unfortunate location gives George III the appearance of having a wart on his nose and a runny nose. Numismatic catalogers of the time were hesitant to make public mention of this die break for fear of retribution.

wartość (*f.*) [*Pol.*] value.

wartościowy [*Pol.*] valuable.

wartość nominalna (*f.*) [*Pol.*] face value.

washer Coins are often punched with holes and used as washers, especially in Third World countries. In British West Africa, the tenth-penny coins were perfect as struck, because they were of very low value and the hole was already there. A very large number of these coins were used for that purpose.

B.W.A. tenth-penny commonly used as washer

Washington, George [nicknamed *The Father of His Country*]. General of the American forces in the American Revolutionary War and first president of the United States. Born February 22, 1732, in Westmoreland County, Virginia (then a part of the British colonies in America); died December 14, 1799, at Mount Vernon, Virginia, reportedly from over-exposure to the elements.

    Washington was not a particularly brilliant student and he received little in the way of formal education, yet he was a hard worker and an avid reader. He became self-taught by reading extensively on such diverse subjects as agriculture, military history, and geography. At the age of seventeen Washington was asked to join a team of surveyors. He showed great aptitude for this profession and spent the next several years surveying for the local Virginia landowners.

    His knowledge of surveying helped him enter the Virginia militia where he quickly rose to the rank of lieutenant colonel. He was ultimately given command of that militia and was instrumental in keeping the Virginia frontier safe during the war between France and England in the mid-1750s. After the war, he was elected to the House of Burgesses where he served for more than ten years.

    Because of his tough stand against unpopular British policies, Washington was elected as a Virginia delegate to the First Continental Congress in 1774 and to the Second Congress in 1775. When fighting broke out

between the Massachusetts colonists and English troops in 1775, the Congress appointed Washington to command its newly-formed army, in part to promote unity between Virginia and the New England colonies. From 1775 until the Americans finally achieved victory at the Battle of Yorktown in 1781, Washington led his troops through a long string of successes and failures. He is best remembered today for his famous crossing of the Delaware River with his poorly-clad soldiers on Christmas night, 1776. The next morning they pulled a successful surprise attack on the British at Trenton, a battle which became one of the turning points of the war.

Because of his proven leadership abilities and his wide-spread popularity and because he was an outspoken advocate for developing a strong central federal government, Washington became elected as the first U.S. president in 1788 and was re-elected in 1792. He declined a third term. He is the only U.S. president not to belong to any political party.

To a large degree, the nature of the presidency was designed around his own personal talents and beliefs. For example, he created the concept of the presidential cabinet, something which had not been provided by the Constitution.

George Washington is one of the most significant people in numismatic history. As the result of his immense popularity after the Revolutionary War, tokens known as Washington pieces were issued by private individuals, both in America and in England. These pieces were dated from 1783 to 1795, although some were produced later than their dates indicate. In a few cases, the tokens were intended to be patterns for which their creators expected to receive manufacturing contracts if their designs were adopted for general use as U.S. coins. The likenesses of Washington are generally true-to-life and the inscriptions and devices are highly patriotic in nature.

Washington was the first U.S. citizen ever to appear on any legitimate coin. His effigy conjoined with that of General Lafayette appear on the obverse of the 1900 Lafayette

Dollar[q.v.], one of America's earliest commemorative coins.

To honor the 200th anniversary of his birth, a semi-commemorative quarter dollar was issued in 1932. The Washington Quarter became so popular that it was retained and is still being issued today. Washington's 250th birthday in 1982 was noted by the issuance of a commemorative half dollar showing him on horseback. The reverse depicts his beloved home, Mount Vernon.

Martha and George Washington

As every American knows, Washington's greatest numismatic claim to fame is his portrait on the dollar bill. Although his face appeared on a variety of notes in the late nineteenth and early twentieth century, including on some fractional currency[q.v.], the dollar note bearing his likeness is special because more of these have been printed than any other banknote in the history of the world. This is due not only to Washington's popularity but also to America's reluctance to redesign its coins and paper money.

Even if Washington's face had never appeared on a coin or note, his place in numismatic history would be secured because of his involvement with the creation of the United States Mint in 1792. After he secured authorization to build the facility in Philadelphia, he rejected the proposal to place

his own image on the coins in favor of an allegorical Liberty. Before the building was even completed, he and his wife Martha donated a silver tea service to be melted down as part of the silver for use in the first silver coins, an issue of 1500 half-dismes (5 cent pieces). There is speculation that Martha was the model for those coins.

Without the efforts of George Washington, the United States might never have been created. It is only fitting that Washington has played such a huge role in American numismatics.

Washington Pieces Collective name for the private copper tokens struck in the late eighteenth century and bearing the likeness of George Washington. Although these pieces were dated from 1783-1795, many of them were manufactured later than their dates indicate. Some of the coppers were minted in the United States, others in England.

The pieces were struck for a variety of unrelated reasons. Some manufacturing companies produced these as samples of their work in an attempt to influence the U.S. Congress to award those companies coinage contracts. Others were made to satisfy a collector demand in England. Still others were stamped from the same dies used to make buttons, and a few were nothing more than advertising promotions. In some cases, the tokens were intended to alleviate a severe shortage of minor coins in the young country; in all cases, the pieces paid tribute to Washington, the man univerally recognized as the hero of the American Revolution.

These tokens may have contributed to Congress's decision not to portray the incumbent president's effigy on the nation's coins. Doing so would have been more symbolic of European monarchy than of New World republicanism, as Washington himself insisted. The decision was therefore made to place an allegorical figure on the coins rather than the effigy of a living person.

Although the Washington motif did not take hold, these pieces did greatly influence future designs of U.S. coins. The American eagle, the shield, and stars were among the devices advocated by these early coppers.

[William Justin DeLeonardis, "The Liberty Motif on Early American Coinage," *The Numismatist*, October 1988, pp. 1741-2; R. S. Yeoman, *A Guide Book of United States Coins* (44th Ed.), pp. 51-55.]

Washington Quarter U.S. twenty-five cent piece first struck in 1932. It was originally intended to be a semi-commemorative issue to honor the two hundredth anniversary of the birth of George Washington, but the coin became so popular that it was brought back in 1934 as a regular issue (there were no U.S. quarters struck in 1933). It is still being minted today. This was only the second U.S. series to portray an actual person, the first being the Lincoln Cent in 1909. All previous U.S. series in all denominations either featured the allegorical figure of Liberty or showed a patriotic device such as a shield or eagle.

The coin was designed by John Flannagan, a sculptor from New York. His initials are located on the truncation of the neck. The reverse shows an eagle perched on a bundle of arrows.

From 1932 to 1964 Washington Quarters were made of an alloy of .900 silver and .100 copper with a weight of 6.25 grams. By the mid-1960s the price of silver had risen to the point where it was no longer feasible to make circulating coins from that metal. Starting in 1965 the U.S. mints began striking Washington Quarters and Roosevelt Dimes on clad planchets, i.e., blanks made of three separate layers of metal. The outer layers are of .250 nickel and .750 copper (the same alloy used in U.S. five cent pieces since 1866), and the middle layer is pure copper. This type of blank was chosen because it is far cheaper than silver and yet has the metallurgical properties to fool vending machines which were geared only to accept legitimate silver coins.

As part of the U.S. Bicentennial celebration in 1976, the reverse of the Washington Quarters was changed to a patriotic design showing a colonial drummer. This design, as well as those of the Bicentennial half dollar and dollar, resulted from a nation-wide

competition. The winning entry for the quarter dollar came from Jack L. Ahr. Proof specimens were struck on special clad planchets with outer layers of .800 silver and .200 copper and a core of .209 silver and .791 copper.

Washington Quarters have been struck at the Philadelphia, Denver, and San Francisco mints. From 1932 to 1964, the "D" and "S" mintmarks appeared on the reverse under the wreath below the eagle. Quarters struck from 1965 to 1967 had no mintmarks, regardless of their mint of origin. Since 1968 mintmarks from all three mints have appeared on the obverse immediately to the right of the ribbon next to Washington's neck.

[R. S. Yeoman, *A Guide Book of United States Coins* (44th Ed.), pp. 140-44.]

Wasserzeichen (*n.*) [*Ger.*] watermark.

watermark A pattern pressed into paper during its manufacture and visible when the paper is held up to the light. The image results from differences in thickness in the paper created by using a mold or processing roll to press a likeness of the pattern into the paper while the paper is still in a semi-soft pulp state.

Watermarks are frequently used as an anti-counterfeiting device in paper money, bonds, and other securities. The Bank of England issued the first banknotes of this type in 1697, and the concept has remained popular ever since.

In the past, the watermark often encompassed the entire surface of the note with the design printed over the watermark. Most modern notes leave the watermarked area unprinted. As an added security measure, the watermark and printed portrait often show the same person.

watermerk (*n.*) [*Dut.*] watermark.

Wechselkurs (*m.*) [*Ger.*] exchange rate.

wedding token see *tok*.

weiß [*Ger.*] white.

Wells Fargo Bank Museum One of the finest museums of Western Americana in the United States. Located in San Francisco, its displays include coins (mostly gold) and paper money from the California gold rush days of the mid-nineteenth century, gold samplings ranging from dust to nuggets, tools of the era, guns, stagecoaches, old plate photos, art of various types, and an unusual display cabinet full of letters, stamps, checks, and the like.

[V. M. Hanks, Jr., "Valuable gold up close," *Coins*, August 1988, pp. 52-56. The article includes extensive photos of the interior and exterior of the museum.]

Wenezuela [*Pol.*] Venezuela.

Werbenote (*f.*) [*Ger.*] propaganda note.

Wert (*m.*) [*Ger.*] value.

Wertpapier (*n.*) [*Ger.*] bond.

wertvoll [*Ger.*] valuable.

West-Duitsland [*Dut.*] West Germany (B.R.D.).

We Win When We Work Willingly Inscription in Morse Code[q.v.] found just within the rim on the reverse of the Canadian wartime 5 cent pieces. It appears on those coins showing the so-called "Victory" design of 1943 (tombac composition) and 1944-45 (chromium-plated steel).

wewnętrzny [*Pol.*] intrinsic.

whelk Large marine snail. Its shell was used for making *wampum*[q.v.], strings of beads utilized as a means of exchange by some North American Indians. Whelk shells produced white beads which were only worth about half as much as the dark colored beads made from *quahog* shells.

[A. George Mallis, "A Numismatic Primer— Part 1," *The Numismatist*, July 1988, p. 1217.]

white gold Common term for electrum[q.v.], a mix of approximately three parts silver and one part gold as found in Nature. The first coins were made of this alloy around 620-600 B.C. in Asia Minor. Also known as *pale gold*.

white josefa Popular name of the 1950 Mexican 5 centavo coin struck in copper-nickel. It portrays Josefa Ortiz de Domínguez (a.k.a. *Josefina*[q.v.] and *La Corregidora*), a key figure in Mexico's struggle for independence from Spain. Although Josefina appeared on several types of Mexican 5 centavo coins from 1942 to 1976, all the others were of brass or bronze. This one-year type was the only one white in color, which gave rise to its nickname.

widow's mite See *prutah*.

Wielka Brytania [*Pol.*] Great Britain.

Wiener, Gerta Ries see *Ries Wiener, Gerta*.

Elie Wiesel on Jewish-American Hall of Fame Medal

Wiesel, Elie Elie Wiesel was born on September 30, 1928, in Sighet, a small town in Romania. His grandfather told the young Elie Hasidic tales which later inspired Wiesel's writings. In 1944, the Nazis deported all of Sighet's 15,000 Jews to the Auschwitz concentration camp. Wiesel's mother and younger sister died in the gas chambers, and his father died later on a forced march to Buchenwald.

Wiesel miraculously survived, settling in France where he studied literature and philosophy at the Sorbonne University. Afterwards, he became a journalist for various Jewish, French, and American periodicals. In 1957 he joined the staff of the Jewish Daily Forward, and he became a United States citizen in 1963.

Not until ten years after his release from Buchenwald did Elie Wiesel begin writing about the Holocaust. His first biographical book *And the World Remained Silent* appeared in Yiddish; it was published four years later in English as the novel *Night*. This was followed by over two dozen semi-autobiographical novels, plays, and essays, all bearing witness to the Holocaust.

Wiesel served as chairman of the United States Holocaust Memorial Council from 1978 to 1987, and later founded the Elie Wiesel Gold Medal of Achievement in 1984. He was made a Grand Officer in the French Legion of Honor in 1990.

When presenting Wiesel with the Nobel Peace Prize, Egil Aavik said, "Wiesel is a messenger to mankind. His message is one of peace, atonement, and human dignity. Wiesel's commitment, which originated in the suffering of the Jewish people, had been widened to embrace all oppressed peoples and races."

Wiesel's words, "Never shall I forget," are engraved on the reverse of the Jewish-American Hall of Fame Medal dedicated to him in 1995. The obverse was designed by Alex Shagin, and the reverse by Mel Wacks. Proceeds from the medal go to support the Magnes Museum, a non-profit organization.

[Contributed by Mel Wacks on behalf of the Magnes Museum.]

wijzigen (*v.*) [*Dut.*] to alter.

wijziging (*f.-c.*) [*Dut.*] alteration.

Wildman coinage Series of coins issued in Brunswick and other German states from the sixteenth to the ninettenth centuries. See *Vilda Hiya.*

window-type holder Coin holder with cellophane on each side to allow the coin to be easily and clearly seen. Because they are so inexpensive and easy to use, they are very popular and are available in a variety of styles and sizes.

Winged Liberty Dime U.S. 10 cent piece struck from 1916 to 1945. It is almost universally known as the *Mercury Dime.*

The coins were designed by Adolph A. Weinman, who also created the Walking Liberty Half Dollars of 1916-1947. His monogram "AW" appears at the right of

Liberty's neck on the obverse side of the dime. Elsie Kachel Stevens, wife of poet Wallace Stevens, sat as the model for this lovely design as well as for the half dollar.

U.S. Winged Liberty ("Mercury") Dime

The wings (or wing, as only one is visible) on Liberty's cap are responsible for the misconception that the effigy is of Mercury, the wing-footed Roman messenger. The winged cap is intended to symbolize "liberty of thought." Misnomer or not, the name has stuck and the coin will probably forever be known as the *Mercury* Dime.

The primary feature on the reverse of this coin is the fasces, a bundle of rods bound by a leather strap and topped by an ax blade. The fasces was an ancient Roman symbol of strength and authority. A laurel branch, symbolizing peace, is draped around the fasces.

Also see *dog on a bridge*.

[David W. Lange, "Mercury Dimes— Challenging Yet Affordable," *The Numismatist*, February 1988, pp. 289-293; R. S. Yeoman, *A Guide Book of United States Coins* (44th Ed.), p. 110; Jay Pastor, "Don't Call It *Mercury*," *Coins*, February 1996, pp. 52-54.]

wire money 1. Thin silver bar in the shape of a fish hook used in parts of the Persian Gulf region from the sixteenth to the early twentieth centuries. It was called a *larin* (pl.: *lari*).

2. Small crude coins of Imperial Russia. When they were introduced in the fourteenth century, their denomination was referred to as the *denga* (деньга, spelled деига prior to the nineteenth century). From the 1534 Monetary Reform came a newly designed coin showing a horseman with a spear (копье) from which the coin got its new name *kopeck*.

Wire money coins similar to the denga were produced in other parts of Europe, most notably in Denmark. Christian IV introduced

the *denning* in 1619, the first of which were virtually identical to the Russian denga pieces.

Coins of this type were made by rolling silver into a wire, cutting it into sections of correct weight, and then hammering it until it was flat and somewhat oval. The silver flan was heated and struck with a pair of coinage dies.

[#2] Russian wire money (enlarged)

Peter the Great decided to abandon wire money in favor of more modern coinage in 1700, but it took nearly twenty years for the changeover to take place. The Russian people were so accustomed to the small crude silver pieces that they did not immediately accept larger copper substitutes.

[Randolph Zander, *Russian-English Numismatic Dictionary*, p. 25.]

3. The 1792 British Maundy coins, so named because of their thin and fancy numerals.

wisselkoers (*f.-c.*) [*Dut.*] exchange rate.

wit [*Dut.*] white.

withdrawn type British sixpence of 1887 which was withdrawn and redesigned after only one year because it so closely resembled the gold half-sovereign. Both the sixpence and half-sovereign feature Victoria's *Jubilee Head* on the obverse and a shield on the reverse, although the sixpence's shield is within a garter. The redesign shows the words *SIX PENCE* surrounded by a wreath and topped with a crown.

wizerunek (*m.*) [*Pol.*] effigy.

wklęsły (stempel) [*Pol.*] incuse.

Włochy [*Pol.*] Italy.

wmk. [*abbr.*] watermark.

w/o [*abbr.*] without.

wolność (*f.*) [*Pol.*] liberty.

WWI commemorative Peace Medal

World War I The Great War of 1914-18 was responsible for many changes which affected numismatics. The most obvious effect was the dissolution of some countries and the creation of others. Another effect was Czar Nicholas II's need to print postage stamp currency[q.v.] to alleviate a severe shortage of small coins in Russia.

World War I left a severe paper shortage throughout Europe. Latvia was forced to print postage stamps on discarded banknote paper. [See *postage stamps on banknote paper*.] And, of course, the rampant inflation which took place in Germany and Austria in the early 1920s was a direct result of the war. This inflation led to the issuance of thousands of unusual Notgeld items, some of which are shown on page 319 of the color section.

In the years immediately following World War I, many medals and other commemorative items were struck to honor veterans of the war or to raise money for building monuments. The medal in the illustration was given to many U.S. veterans. Thousands of similar items were issued throughout the world.

World War II The Second World War was the most devastating war in history, yet it left a huge numismatic legacy.

Many coins had to be modified because their metals were needed for the war effort. The 1943 U.S. cents were made of zinc-plated steel, and the 1944 Belgian 2 franc coins were made from the same blanks. Nickel was temporarily removed from U.S. 5 cent pieces in 1942 and replaced with an alloy of 56% copper, 35% silver, and 9% manganese. The regular copper-nickel alloy was restored in 1946. Canadian 5 cent coins underwent a similar change. In 1942, nickel was replaced with tombac, a brass alloy of 88% copper and 12% zinc, and the coins were made 12-sided instead of round. In 1944 chromium-plated steel was used.

In France, the Nazi-backed Vichy government issued its own coins. In Germany and in German-controlled regions, the notorious ghetto money[q.v.] was printed for use by Jews interned in the ghettos. And back in the United States, special paper money overprinted with the word HAWAII was issued for use in the Pacific with the idea that the money could be quickly invalidated if large quantities of it were captured by enemy forces.

The end of the war saw the unification of Yugoslavia, the breakup of Germany into two countries, and the takeover by the Soviet Union of many of its Eastern European neighbors. Thus, the ramifications of World War II affected the world throughout the twentieth century.

See pages 312-313 for color illustrations.

wrijfschade (door lade of album veroorzaakt) [*Dut.*] cabinet friction.

wydanie (*n.*) [*Pol.*] an issue, issuance.

wydawać (*v.*) [*Pol.*] to issue.

wyobrażenie (*n.*) [*Pol.*] pattern.

wystawa (*f.*) [*Pol.*] exhibition.

wystawiać (*v.*) [*Pol.*] to exhibit.

wzór (*m.*) [*Pol.*] pattern; design.

X x   Y y

xelin (*m.*) [*Port.*] (British) shilling.

xeraphim (*m.*) [*Mid. Port.*] literally, *seraphim.* Silver coin issued by Portugal for its Indian colonies from 1570 to 1871. Officially it was valued at 360 *réis* (later reduced to 300 réis), but it was really intended to match up with the local half-rupee.

The early issues portrayed various saints instead of the Portuguese monarch. In 1570 the Inquisition was still very active in the Iberian Peninsula, and it is likely that the king was being pressured to convert the people of India to Christianity. The presence of saints on coins was to reinforce the missionaries' efforts.

xiāo xiàng 肖像 [*Chin.-py./sc.*] effigy; portrait.

xī chéng yìn bì 铣成硬币 [*Chin.-py./sc.*] milled coin.

xī hǎn 稀罕 [*Chin.-py./sc.*] rarity.

xìn yòng kǎ 信用卡 [*Chin.-py./sc.*] credit card.

xī shǎo 稀少 [*Chin.-py./sc.*] scarce.

yabancı para [*Turk.*] foreign currency.

yakhid b'mino יָחִיד בְּמִינוֹ [*Heb.*] unique.

yayınlanmamış [*Turk.*] unpublished (not listed in any book or catalogue).

yazı [*Turk.*] inscription; legend.

yazı yeri [*Turk.*] exergue.

year set All of the coins issued by a government or other issuing agency in a given year. The set may have no particular numismatic significance except that it represents one's birthyear, wedding anniversary, or other special event.

Yeni Zelanda [*Turk.*] New Zealand.

yerro (*m.*) [*Span.*] error.

yhdeksän [*Finn.*] nine.

yhdeksänkymmentä [*Finn.*] ninety.

yhdistetty [*Finn.*] accolated[*q.v.*], conjoined, jugate.

Yhdistynyt Kuningaskunta [*Finn.*] United Kingdom (U.K.).

yıl [*Turk.*] year.

yín 银 [*Chin.-py./sc.*] silver.

yìn bǎn jī 印版机 [*Chin.-py./sc.*] (coinage) press.

yīng 鹰 [*Chin.-py./sc.*] eagle.

yīng bàng 英磅 [*Chin.-py./sc.*] pound Sterling.

yìng bì 硬币 [*Chin.-py./sc.*] coin.

yirmi [*Turk.*] twenty.

Yisra'el יִשְׂרָאֵל [*Heb.*] Israel.

yitur dafnah עֲטוּר דַּפְנָה (*m.*) [*Heb.*] laureate.

yitur ts'va'i עֲטוּר צְבָאִי (*m.*) [*Heb.*] military decoration.

y'khidah kaspit יְחִידָה כַּסְפִּית (*f.*) [*Heb.*] monetary unit.

yksi [*Finn.*] one.

yksipuolinen [*Finn.*] uniface.

yläosa [*Finn.*] top.

yleinen [*Finn.*] common.

yuán 元 [*Chin.-py./sc.*] dollar.

yuán jīn shǔ piàn 园金属片 [*Chin.-py./sc.*] planchet.

Yunanistan [*Turk.*] Greece.

yu-tong-doen 유통된 [*Kor.*] circulated.

yuvarlak [*Turk.*] round.

yüz [*Turk.*] hundred.

yüzüncü yıl dönümü [*Turk.*] centennial, centenary.

Z z

zabezpieczenie przed fałszerstwem (*n.*) [*Pol.*] anti-counterfeiting device.

zadrapanie (*n.*) [*Pol.*] a scratch.

zahav זָהָב (*m.*) [*Heb.*] gold.

Zahl (*f.*) [*Ger.*] number.

Zahlungsanweisung (*f.*) [*Ger.*] money order.

zào bì 造币 [*Chin.-py./sc.*] coinage.

zào bì chǎng 造币厂 [*Chin.-py./sc.*] mint.

za zgodą [*Pol.*] on approval.

zbieracz (*m.*) [*Pol.*] collector.

zbiór (*m.*) [*Pol.*] collection.

zecca (*f.*) [*Ital.*] mint.

zece [*Rom.*] ten.

zegel (*m.-c.*) [*Dut.*] seal.

zehn [*Ger.*] ten.

Zeichen (*n.*) [*Ger.*] token.

Zeichnung (*f.*) [*Ger.*] design; model.

żelazo (*n.*) [*Pol.*] iron (the metal).

zeldzaam [*Dut.*] rare.

Zentimeter (*m.*) [*Ger.*] centimeter, centimetre.

zerrissen [*Ger.*] torn.

Zertifikat (*n.*) [*Ger.*] certificate.

zes [*Dut.*] six.

zestaw (*m.*) [*Pol.*] (auction) lot.

żeton (*m.*) [*Pol.*] token.

zgârietură (*f.*) [*Rom.*] a scratch.

zhèng miàn 正面 [*Chin.-py./sc.*] obverse.

zhēn huò 真货 [*Chin.-py./sc.*] authentic, genuine.

zheton жетон (*m.*) [*Russ.*] token.

zhǐ bì 纸币 [*Chin.-py./sc.*] paper money, note.

Zhōng Guó 中国 [*Chin.-py./sc.*] China.

zilver (*n.*) [*Dut.*] silver.

zinc Metal infrequently used in coinage. [element: group IIb of the periodic table; atomic weight 65.38; atomic number 30; specific gravity 7.138; symbol Zn.]

Zinc is a soft metal that corrodes very rapidly from silvery gray to dark dull gray. It was used largely for minor coins during the two World Wars in such places as Denmark, Netherlands, and Germany.

Zink (*n.*) [*Ger.*] zinc.

Zinn (*n.*) [*Ger.*] tin.

zirkuliert [*Ger.*] circulated.

Zjednoczone Królestwo [*Pol.*] United Kingdom.

zlato злато (*n.*) [*Serb.-Cr.*] gold (the metal).

źle wybity [*Pol.*] badly struck.

złoto (*n.*) [*Pol.*] gold (the metal).

złoty [*Pol.*] Polish unit of currency.

zmatowienie (*n.*) [*Pol.*] tarnish.

znaczek kapslowy [*Pol.*] encased postage stamp.

znak menniczy (*m.*) [*Pol.*] mintmark.

znak wodny (*m.*) [*Pol.*] watermark.

zôheigoku-in 造幣極印 [*Jpn.*] mintmark.

Zoll (*m.*) [*Ger.*] inch.

zoloto золото (*n.*) [*Russ.*] gold (the metal).

zseton [*Hun.*] token.

Zuid-Afrika [*Dut.*] South Africa.

zur Ansicht [*Ger.*] on approval.

Zuschreibung (*f.*) [*Ger.*] attribution.

Zuytdorp Dutch sailing ship that crashed off the coast of Western Australia in June 1812 while en route from the Cape of Good Hope to Batavia. The ship is believed to have been carrying approximately two million coins, only about nine thousand of which were recovered.

[Stan Wilson, "Coins from the *Zuytdorp*," *Journal of the Numismatic Association of Australia*, July 1985, pp. 24-30. (This article contains a detailed listing of the coins which have thus far been recovered.)]

zwanzig [*Ger.*] twenty.

zwart [*Dut.*] black.

zwarte markt (*f.-c.*) [*Dut.*] black market.

zwei [*Ger.*] two.

zweisprachig [*Ger.*] bilingual.

Związek Radziecki (Z.S.R.R.) [*Pol.*] Soviet Union.

zysk menniczy (*m.*) [*Pol.*] seigniorage; mint profit.

key money, above; *pants* or *saddle* money, below.

Siamese wedding token *(tok)*

primitive money Since the dawn of civilization, many unusual objects have been used as a means of exchange. These *odd and curious* items have included such diverse things as live rats intended to be eaten raw (not pictured here) to the Siamese wedding token (above, right).

The objects at the upper left are examples of cast Chinese "key" money (A.D. 9-23) and "pants" money (1122-225 B.C.; a.k.a. "saddle" or "shirt" money). Many old counterfeits exist of both. The red and yellow splotches on the wedding token (or *tok*) are said to be chicken blood and egg yolk, symbols of fertility. It cost two toks to buy a wife and two more to divorce her.

The low-grade silver pieces below are also from Siam (Thailand). The shorter item is called "canoe" money. The longer piece is referred to as a "tiger tongue" and is another type of canoe money. The yellowish-green seashells are money cowry shells. Although most cowries come from the Maldive Islands, these shells have been used as a form of exchange in nearly every part of the world. Their use started in ancient times and continued in some places until the middle of the twentieth century. Cowries enjoyed such popularity in part because they are probably the only form of money ever concocted which cannot be counterfeited.

canoe money, above; *tiger tongue*, below; cowry shells, at right.

Lydia, Croesus (561-546 B.C.); stater.   Athens; tetradrachm, ca. 440-415 B.C.

Metapontum; tetrobol (1/3 stater), ca. 302 B.C.   Ptolemy II (285-246 B.C.); octadrachm.

Rhoontopates; tetradrachm, 334-333 B.C.   Demetrios Poliorcetes (294-288 B.C.); tetradrachm.

Ancient Greece The world's first coins came from Lydia in Asia Minor around 620-600 B.C. Although the earliest were crude (e.g., the *stater* pictured above), coins soon became a medium for the great artists of Greek society. More importantly, the social, political, and economic impact caused by the creation and evolution of coins soon extended far beyond the boundaries of Greece and is still felt in all parts of the world even to the present day.

One of the most popular designs of ancient Greek coins is that of the silver tetradrachm (top row, right). The obverse portrays the helmeted head of the goddess Athena; the reverse features an owl.

Another common motif was the human form, as seen on another tetradrachm above (bottom row, right). In ancient Greek times, nudity in art was not suppressed, it was glorified.

[Photos courtesy Harlan J. Berk, Ltd., Chicago.]

Vespasian (A.D. 69-79); aureus.

Maximianus Herculius (A.D. 286-305); aureus.

Augustus; denarius showing Haley's Comet (ca. 18-17 B.C.).

Hadrian (A.D. 117-138); sestertius.

Theodosius II; solidus, A.D. 408-419.

Xusro II; dinar, A.D. 616.

Ancient Rome The coins of the Roman Empire include some of great majesty, and others which are inferior in design and workmanship to many coins minted hundreds of years earlier in Greece. To a degree, the state of the coins reflected the state of the Empire.

A feature of Roman imperial coins (as opposed to the republican coinage) is the presence of the letters "SC" which stand for *Senatus Consulto* ("By decree of the Senate"). The sestertius (second row, right) bears those letters. This coin is particularly significant because it makes reference to the end of the Jewish wars (*Bar Kochba*).

The dinar (bottom row, right) is actually a post-Roman Byzantine coin. It shows the stylistic direction coins took after the fall of the Roman Empire. The designs of many coins of this era were affected by the influence of Christianity.

[Photos courtesy Harlan J. Berk, Ltd., Chicago.]

Victoria 1839 £.5 pattern ("Una and the Lion")

Isle of Man 1990 Penny Black crown

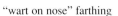

"wart on nose" farthing

earrings from hand-enameled 1850s 4d coins

1816 shillings: genuine (left) and fake (right)

Great Britain The wonderful world of British numismatics ranges from the magnificent gold coins of Victoria and James I to the clumsy 1797 2d "cartwheel" of George III to the 1990 Isle of Man "Pearl Black" proof surface crown commemorating Victoria's appearance on the world's first postage stamp (the Penny Black) in 1840. The realm of British coins also includes such oddities as the 1806 farthing with a die break that gives George III a wart on his nose and a runny nose. George III also appears on the counterfeit 1816 shilling which was produced about the same time as its genuine counterpart. The lovely earrings pictured above were made by hand-enameling the reverses of a pair of silver 4d coins from the 1850s.

The coins shown on this page are just a small sample of Britain's rich contribution to numismatics over the past two thousand years.

George III 1797 2d "cartwheel"

James I (known as James VI in Scotland) gold unite, ca. 1608

[Photo courtesy Stack's, New York]

King of Siam Set In 1834 the Philadelphia Mint prepared a special eleven-piece proof set of U.S. coins to be given to the King of Siam as a diplomatic gift. All of the coins were dated 1834 except the silver dollar and gold eagle ($10 gold piece). Because no coins of those two denominations had been issued for thirty years, dies bearing the date 1804 were used. This was highly unusual, as the dollars issued in 1804 were actually struck from reused dies dated 1803. Eight specimens of the 1804 dollar (today known as *originals*) were made in 1834-35 for presentation sets, and seven more (called *restrikes*) were produced in 1858 by mint employees to satisfy collectors' demands for this coin. Of all the 1804 dollars known to exist, the King of Siam specimen is among the finest. The 1804-dated $10 gold piece is also extraordinary, being one of only four specimens struck in proof.

After its presentation to the king, the set disappeared from numismatic annals. It resurfaced briefly at the 1962 American Numismatic Association convention but with two pieces missing. One of the missing coins was almost definitely a half-dime. The other missing piece is probably not a coin but a gold medal struck for President Andrew Jackson's second inaugural.

The set did not come into public view again until 1987. It was placed on auction as a single lot but failed to sell. Two years later the set was purchased for a reported price of more than two million dollars.

bit cut from 4 R. coin   *bit* cut from 8 R. coin   bisected English penny   Nepal clipped coin (3 petals)

Hejaz c/m on Turkish 20 para   Costa Rica c/m on English 6d   *maravedi:* host date (1622) and overstruck date (1641)

multiple countermarks for Malta   British trade dollar w/ 8 *chop* marks   Mexican revolutionary piece

counterstamped, overstruck, and cut coins Every coin on this page is a genuine mint issue that has been doctored in some way to make it acceptable for trade. The top row begins with two sheared pieces known as *bits*, the first cut in the 1700s from a Spanish 4 *real* coin and the second from a crown-size 8 *real* piece. This was done to provide fractional currency, i.e., small change. The next coin, half of an English silver penny from ca. 1200, was bisected for the same reason. The last piece is a Nepal coin clipped for use in Tibet. The "denomination" was determined in part by how many petals are visible.

The first coin in the second row is a Turkish 20 para countermarked *Hejaz* to authorize it for use in Saudi Arabia, a practice done from 1916-23. Similarly, Costa Rica counterstamped English sixpences and shillings in 1857 as substitutes for 1 and 2 *real* coins. The Spanish copper *maravedí* was overstruck to devalue it. One side shows the host date 1622, the other side the overstruck date 1641.

The third row starts with a copper coin counterstamped six times over a period of 150 years to continually re-authorize it for use in Malta. The center coin is a British trade dollar made to circulate in the Orient. The obverse shows 8 *chop marks*, each applied by a Chinese trader to guarantee the coin's weight and purity. The final coin is a Mexican revolutionary piece. The scratches were added by revolutionary authorities to show that the coin had passed through their hands and was "acceptable" for trade.

military and civil orders and decorations Decorations are different from medals because they are intended to be worn, not just stored in an album or box. Although some decorations are given as prizes or to indicate membership in a fraternal organization, military decorations and civil orders are special because they are presented for merit, valor, good conduct, or service in defense of one's country.

The piece on the left is the German Iron Cross, Second Class, bestowed during World War I on behalf of Kaiser Wilhelm II. The campaign service award in the center is Britain's Africa Star given for service in the Allied North African theater of World War II. It bears the crowned monogram of King George VI. The item on the right is America's Purple Heart, presented to those killed or wounded in action against an enemy. Traditionally the Purple Heart had the recipient's name engraved on the back under the inscription *For Military Merit*, but the most recent ones are unnamed.

QUITTUNG ÜBER ZWANZIG KRONEN

20

WER DIESE QUITTUNG VERFÄLSCHT ODER NACHMACHT ODER GEFÄLSCHTE QUITTUNGEN IN VERKEHR BRINGT, WIRD STRENGSTENS BESTRAFT.

20

World War II Every major war creates monetary problems, but World War II was so devastating that it left an indelible mark on numismatic history. From the accursed Moses crowns (above) of the Theresienstadt ghetto to the metallic varieties of U.S., Belgian, and Canadian coins (shown below) necessitated by shortages of copper and nickel, World War II affected nearly every aspect of numismatics.

The U.S. and Belgian steel coins were struck in the United States from the same group of zinc-plated steel blanks. Some 1944 and 1945 U.S. cents were made from melted rifle shell cases. The U.S. silver-alloy wartime nickel (the *warnick*) shows its distinguishing large mintmark above Monticello's dome. The Canadian "V" 5 cent pieces of tombac (1943) and steel (1944-45) have an inscription in Morse Code around the rim: *We Win When We Work Willingly.*

U.S. 1943 Steel cent   Belgian 1944 2 Fr on same steel planchet   1944 U.S. "shell case" cent   U.S. 1943-D "warnick"

Can. 1942 nickel 5c   Can. 1942 tombac five cents (12-sided)   Can. 1943 "V" tombac 5c   Can. 1944 "V" steel 5c

Vichy 2 Fr (top); U.S. ration tokens (bottom)

U.S. military payment certificate

The aluminum coin shown above was issued by the collaborationist (pro-German) French government headquartered in Vichy. The small red and blue pieces beneath it are ration tokens which U.S. citizens were required to use when purchasing a wide variety of scarce goods during the war. The colorful note above is a military payment certificate, first issued shortly after World War II to U.S. soldiers stationed in occupied territories as a way of preventing military personnel from profiting on the black market. The note below is a specimen issued as a type of souvenir by Czechoslovakia, sold to raise money for the war effort. The official stamp was affixed to give value to an otherwise unredeemable note.

The items illustrated on these two pages are just a small sample of the many notes and coins resulting from the terrible demands of a terrible war.

American Numismatic Association Since its inception in 1891, the A.N.A. has played a major role in the numismatic world. The organization maintains a world-class museum and research library, sponsors two major national conventions each year, and publishes *The Numismatist,* an outstanding monthly journal.

The photo above shows former A.N.A. president John Jay Pittman and his wife Gehring, two very dedicated exhibitors, placing their display at the 1994 A.N.A. convention in Detroit. Mr. Pittman is holding in his hand a U.S. Assay Commission Medal.

When the A.N.A. celebrated its hundredth anniversary in 1991, it received accolades from throughout the world. The Isle of Man issued a commemorative crown, shown below. The U.S. Postal Service put out a commemorative postage stamp which it released at the A.N.A.'s national convention in Chicago. The stamp with its first-day cancellation also appears below.

Throughout the years the American Numismatic Association has issued many beautiful medals and related items, some of which are shown above. The medal in the lower left-hand corner is given to 25-year members. The other items have been issued at various A.N.A. conventions.

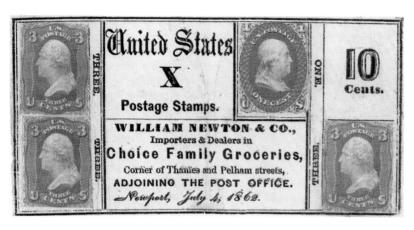

advertising scrip from the U.S. Civil War

U.S. and German *good fors*

Alaskan trade dollar

exonumia Contrary to what many numismatists believe, exonumia deals with more than just bus tokens. It encompasses the entire range of scrip, trade tokens, flats, sales tax receipts, coin-like advertising pieces, philatelic items used as currency, hobo nickels, love tokens, and many objects which resemble money but are not.

The paper item above is advertising scrip affixed with 10c in postage. Such pieces helped alleviate a coin shortage during the U.S. Civil War. Next to it are a U.S. fish store token (a *good for*) and a German beer token (a *gut für*). At the left is a 1959 Alaskan dollar, among the most beautiful trade tokens ever made.

The bottom row starts with a Siamese porcelain gambling token. They were first issued by gambling houses around 1760 and eventually became lawful money. The next piece is a greeting token given by the Israel Government Coins and Medals Corporation. Next is coal mine company scrip from West Virginia. The final piece is a telephone token issued through the Hungarian post office.

gambling token (Siam)

greeting token (Israel)

coal company scrip (U.S.)

telephone token (Hungary)

Bahamas obverse   +   New Zealand reverse (and bronze planchet)   =   Bahamas/New Zealand mule

good hole   bad hole   no hole   unwanted hole: a separated Polar Bear

1955 double die cent   double strike cent   partial plated cent (both sides)   off-center nickel

mint errors The coins shown on this page were all struck between 1942 and 1996 and represent just a few of the error types that have occurred in recent years.

The top row shows the Bahamas 5 cent and New Zealand 2 cent coins whose dies were inadvertently matched together to create a *mule* in 1967. The mule itself shows no date because both of the mismatched dies came from the undated side of their respective coins. The mule was supposed to be the New Zealand 2 cent coin and has its correct bronze planchet.

The second row starts with a pair of Hungarian 2 filler coins, one correctly holed and the other with the hole off-center. The Thai coin with its hole missing is not a mint error in the strictest sense because all the pieces of that type lack holes, even though they were designed to have them. The final coin is a bimetallic Canadian $2 Polar Bear whose center core popped out.

The third row shows a group of recent U.S. errors. The first is the famous 1955 double die Lincoln Cent. The coin next to it is a double strike, a common error. The partial plated cent is one of several error types resulting from America's switch to clad coinage. The last coin is an off-center nickel, another common error.

The items on the right are mint scraps. The "error" was on the part of mint officials who allowed these pieces to leave the mint. Because scraps are usually gathered up and re-melted, they seldom fall into the hands of collectors.

mint scraps

Paraguayan note with "fake" silked paper

Canadian 25c "shinplaster"

Colombian half peso "bisect"

Pakistani "haj" note

paper money Each of the notes pictured above represents a specific numismatic term or concept. The Paraguayan note at the top was printed on red and blue silked paper, a commonly used device to prevent counterfeiting. However, these threads are fake. Instead of being embedded in the paper, as they are in the U.S. and elsewhere, they were glued on (and can be pulled off). The second item is a 25c fractional currency note of Canada. Despite its popularity, it was known as a *shinplaster* because it was a paper note of low value. Next to it is a Colombian provisional *bisect*, a 1 peso note cut in half and overprinted to give it a circulating value of one-half peso. It is also known as a *cut note*. The final piece is the multi-lingual *haj* note of Pakistan, used by Muslims while doing their required pilgrimage (the "haj") to Mecca.

Notgeld   Although most German and Austrian Notgeld of the post-World War I era was produced on paper, many interesting pieces were made from other materials. The Sachsen "coin" shown above is a German piece made of ceramic. The colorful note next to it was produced in Bielefeld, Germany, on high quality linen.

The rectangular Notgeld piece below is an Austrian wooden flat highlighted by a portrait of two rabbits. Both of the coins next to the flat are German and were struck in iron. The piece on the top was minted in Bonn in 1920 and features its most famous son, Ludwig van Beethoven. The larger coin was made in 1919 in Bingen and includes the word *Notgeld* ("emergency money") on the reverse.

Above, what sighted people see. Below, what blind people feel. [Actual size 7.5 cm x 13.6 cm.]

blind assistance Since World War II, many countries have begun producing money that can be identified by blind people. The Dutch note above is one such example. An exaggerated intaglio process produces inking so thick that key features can actually be felt by the blind. The drawing shows what blind people feel when they run their finger over the note.

The Paraguayan coin on the left is easy for blind people to identify because of its scalloped shape and because its bold number 10 can be "read" by touching it. The Italian coin beneath it includes an inscription in braille. To further assist the blind, the edge of the Italian coin has an interrupted reeded edge, a characteristic also found on other recent coins such as the Canadian $2 Polar Bear.

Greek Alphabet

All words in Modern Greek

Α α

Αγγλία England.
άγνωστος unknown (no specimens are known to exist in any collection).
αγοράζω (v.) to buy.
αγοραστής buyer.
αετός (m.) eagle.
αιχμή (f.) rim.
άκρον (n.) edge.
ακυκλοφόρητα uncirculated.
ακύρωση κοπής (f.) cut cancellation.
αλλοδαπός foreign.
αλλοίωση (f.) alteration.
αμοιβή (f.) fee.
αναγνωρισμένο accolated[q.v.], conjoined, jugate.
αναξιόχρεον κέρμα (n.) hammered coin.
αναπαραγωγή (f.) copy; reproduction.
Ανατολική Γερμανία East Germany (D.D.R.).
ανεπίσημον unofficial.
ανεστραμμένο inverted.
ανταλλάσσω (v.) to trade.
αντίγραφο (n.) copy.
αντιγράφω (v.) to copy.
ανωμαλία (f.) anomaly.
ανώμαλος irregular.
αξία (f.) value.
απαρχαιομένο obsolete.
απόδειξη (f.) receipt.
απόδειξη προσφορών (f.) bid sheet.
αποδίδω (v.) to attribute.
απόκτηση (f.) acquisition.
απόσυρσης νομίσματος απο την κυκλοφορία demonetization.
αποτύπωμα (n.) fingerprint.

αριθμός (m.) number.
αρχαίον ancient.
αρχαιότης (f.) antiquity.
Αργεντινή Argentina.
αργυρός silver.
αριστερός left (direction or position).
άσπρο white.
άστρο (n.) star.
ατελές incomplete.
Αυστραλία Australia.
Αυστρία Austria.
αυτοκράτορας (m.) emperor.
αχαρακτηριστικός unattributed (not fully identified or classified).
άψογος perfect.

Β β

βαθμολογώ (v.) to grade.
βαθμός (m.) grade, condition (of a coin or note).
βάρος (n.) weight.
βασιλιάς (m.) king.
βασίλισσα (f.) queen.
Βέλγιο Belgium.
Βενεζουέλα Venezuela.
Βόρεια Ιρλανδία Northern Ireland.
Βουλγαρία Bulgaria.
Βραζιλία Brazil.

Γ γ

γαλβανισμένα electrotype.
Γαλλία France.
Γερμανία Germany.
Γιουγκοσλαβία Yugoslavia, Jugoslavia.
γλώσσα (f.) language.
γνήσιον genuine, authentic.
γραμμάτιο (m.) note, banknote.
γρατσουνιά (f.) scratch.

Δ δ

Δανία Denmark.
δαφνοστεφής laureate.
δείγμα (*n.*) specimen.
δέκα ten.
δέκατον tenth (the fraction).
δελτίον παραγγελιών (*n.*) order form.
δέμα (*n.*) package.
δεξιός right (direction or position).
δεχόμαστε πιστωτικές κάρτες credit cards accepted.
δημοκρατία (*f.*) republic.
Δημοκρατία τής Κίνας Republic of China.
δημοπρασία (*f.*) auction; auction sale.
διάβρωση (*f.*) corrosion.
διαδοχικός αριθμός (*m.*) serial number.
διακανονισμένο σημείο αναγνώρισης adjustment mark.
διακοπτόμενη σφραγίδα νομίσματος die break.
διάμετρος (*f.*) diameter.
διαφυλασσόμενη προσφορά protective reserve bid.
δίγλωσσος bilingual.
διεθνής international.
διπλασιάζω (*v.*) to duplicate.
διπλοτυπωμένο (*adj.*) duplicate.
διπλότυπον a duplicate.
διπλώνω (*v.*) to fold.
διχοτομισμένο bisected.
δοκίμιον proof [re: coins].
δολλάριο (*n.*) dollar.
δύο two.
Δυτική Γερμανία West Germany (B.R.D.).

Ε ε

εβδομήντα seventy.
έγγλυφο (*n.*) incuse.
εγχάραξη (*f.*) intaglio.
εθνικός national.

εθνικότητα (*f.*) nationality.
εικονογραφία (*f.*) portrait.
είκοσι twenty.
ειρήνη (*f.*) peace.
εισηγούμενη προσφορά (*f.*) suggested bid.
εκατό hundred.
εκατομμύριο (n.) million.
εκατονταετηρίδα (*f.*) centennial, centenary.
εκατοστό (*n.*) centimeter.
εκατοστόν hundredth.
εκδίδω (*v.*) to issue.
έκδοση (*f.*) an issue, issuance.
έκθεση (*f.*) exhibition.
έκθεση (*n.*) essay.
εκθέτω (*v.*) to exhibit.
ελαττωματικό defective.
ελάχιστη προσφορά (*f.*) minimum bid.
Ελβετία Switzerland.
ελευθερία (*f.*) liberty.
Ελλάς Greece.
ελλιπώς κομμένο κέρμα (*n.*) brockage.
ένα one.
ένδειξη νομισματοκοπείου mintmark.
εννέα nine.
εξαίρετος fine; excellent (condition of coins).
έξεργον (*n.*) exergue.
έξι six.
επιγραφή (*f.*) legend; inscription.
επιδιορθωμένο repaired.
επικεκομμένο (*n.*) a restrike.
επί πιστώσει on approval.
επίσημος official.
επισφράγισης (*f.*) overprint.
επιταγή (*f.*) check, cheque.
επιφάνεια (*f.*) surface.
εσφαλμένη χάραξη badly struck.
εσωτερική αξία (*f.*) intrinsic.
έτος year.

Η η

ηγεμόνας sovereign.
ήλεκτρον (*n.*) electrum.
ημερομηνία (*f.*) date.

Ηνωμένον Βασίλειον United Kingdom (U.K.).
Ηνωμένες Πολιτείες τής Αμερικής United States of America (U.S.A.).

Θ θ

Θεός (*m.*) God (in the Judaic-Christian sense).
θησαυρός (*m.*) treasure.

Ι ι

Ιαπωνία Japan.
ιδιωτικό προσωρινό νόμισμα scrip.
ίντσα (*f.*) inch.
Ιρλανδία Ireland.
Ισπανία Spain.
Ισραήλ Israel.
Ιταλία Italy.

Κ κ

καθαρός fineness; fine (purity of metal).
καινούργιο new; crisp (in reference to paper money).
καλό good.
καλός fair.
καλουπώνω (*v.*) to cast.
Καναδάς Canada.
κασσίτερος (*n.*) tin; pewter.
κατάλογος (*m.*) catalog, catalogue.
κατάλογος πλειστηριασμού (*m.*) auction catalogue.
κατάσταση (*f.*) grade, condition (of a coin or note).

κατάταξη (*f.*) classification.
κατατάσσω (*v.*) to classify.
κάτω bottom.
κίβδηλον (*n.*) a fake, forgery.
κινούμενον πινακίδιον με γραφίδα planchet.
Κίνα China.
κλάσμα (*n.*) (mathematical) fraction.
κοινός common.
κόκκινο red.
Κολομβία Colombia.
κορνίζα (*f.*) frame (part of a banknote or bond's outer design that encloses or surrounds the vignette).
κορυφή (*f.*) top.
κορώνα (*f.*) crown (generic name for any large silver coin).
κρατικό κέρδος απο έκδοση νομισμάτων seigniorage.
κυκλοφορία (*f.*) circulation (of a coin or note).
κυκλοφορημένο circulated.

Λ λ

Λαϊκή Δημοκρατία τής Κίνας People's Republic of China.
λάθος (*n.*) error.
λαχνός (*m.*) (auction) lot.
λεύκωμα (*n.*) album.
λίβρα (*f.*) pound (16 ounces avdp., 12 oz. troy).
λιθογραφία (*f.*) lithography.
λίρα (*f.*) lira; pound Sterling.
λογαριασμός (*m.*) account (financial or transactional).

Μ μ

μάρκο (*n.*) mark (German unit of currency).
μαύρη αγορά (*f.*) black market.
μαύρο black.

324

Μεγάλη Βρεττανία Great Britain.
μεγάλο large.
μεγενθυτικός φακός (m.) magnifying glass.
μελάνι (n.) ink.
Μεξικό Mexico.
μεταβάλλω (v.) to alter.
μεταλλικό κράμα (n.) (metal) alloy.
μετάλλιον (n.) medal.
μέταλλο (n.) metal.
μεταξωτή κλωστή (f.) silk thread.
μεταποιημένη ημερομηνία altered date.
μεταχειρισμένο used.
μηδέν (n.) zero.
μή εκδοθέντα not issued.
μή εκδοθέν unpublished (not listed in any book or catalogue).
μήνας (m.) month.
μήτρα (f.) (coinage) die.
μηχανισμός αναγνώρισης πλαστογραφίας anti-counterfeiting device.
μικρό small.
μίμηση (f.) imitation.
μισό (n.; adj.) half.
μονάδα χρημάτων denomination.
μοναδικός unique.
μονόπλευρο (n.) uniface.
μουντζούρα (f.) tarnish.
μπλέ blue.
μπρούντζος (m.) bronze (the alloy).

N ν

Νέα Ζηλανδία New Zealand.
νικέλιο (n.) nickel (the metal).
νόμισμα (n.) coin; currency.
νομίσματα; νομισματοκοπία coinage.
νομίσματα έκτακτης ανάγκης (n.) emergency currency.
νομισματική μονάδα (f.) monetary unit.
νομισματικό σύστημα monetary system.
νομισματοκοπείον (n.) mint.
νομισματικός monetary.
Νορβηγία Norway.
Νότιος Αφρική South Africa.

Ξ ξ

ξένος foreign.
ξένο νόμισμα (n.) foreign currency.

O o

ογδόντα eighty.
οικιακός domestic.
οκτώ eight.
Ολλανδία The Netherlands, Holland.
ομοίωμα (n.) effigy.
ομολογία (f.) (commercial) bond.
ονομαστική αξία (f.) face value.
οπή (f.) hole.
όπισθεν on the back.
οπισθότυπος (m.) reverse.
ορθογώνιο rectangular.
Ουαλία Wales.
ουγγιά ounce.
οψιδιανό obsidional.

Π π

παλινδρομική επιγραφή (f.) palindrome (serial number of a banknote which reads the same forwards or backwards; a banknote with this type of number is known as a *radar note*).
παλιός old.
πάπας (m.) pope (of the Roman Catholic Church).
παράσημο (n.) decoration.
παραχάραξη (f.) mis-strike.
παραχαραγμένο mis-struck.
παραχαράσσω (v.) to counterfeit.
πάχος (n.) thickness.

πέμπτον fifth (the fraction).
πενήντα fifty.
πέντε five.
περικλειόμενο γραμματόσημο (n.) encased postage stamp (such as the type used in the United States in the 1860s as an emergency form of circulating money).
Περού Perú.
πεσέτα (f.) peseta (Spanish unit of currency).
πέσο (n.) peso (unit of currency used by many countries in Latin America).
πιεφόρτ piedfort, piéfort.
πίστωση (f.) credit.
πιστωτική κάρτα (f.) credit card.
πλαστικός plastic.
πλαστό (n.) a forgery, fake, counterfeit.
πλαστογράφος (m.) counterfeiter.
πλατίνα (f.) platinum.
πλειστηριασμός (m.) auction sale.
πλήρες complete.
ποικιλία (f.) variety.
πολύτιμος valuable.
πολύχρωμο multicolored, multicoloured.
Πορτογαλία Portugal.
πορτοκαλί orange.
πορτραίτο (n.) portrait.
πορφυρές purple.
ποσόν (n.) amount.
πουλώ (v.) to sell.
πράσινο green.
πρέσσα τυπώσεως νομισμάτων (f.) (coinage) press.
πρόεδρος president.
προκαταβολή (f.) (bank or financial) deposit.
προπαγανδιστικό σημείωμα (n.) propaganda note.
προπληρωμή (f.) prepayment.
πρόσθιος (m.) obverse.
πρόσοψη (f.) front.
προσφέρω (v.) to bid; to offer.
προσφορά (f.) an offer; a bid (at an auction or mail bid sale).
προσφορές άνευ ορίου δέν αποδέχονται no unlimited bids accepted.
προσωρινά χαρτονομίσματα (n.pl.) scrip.
προσωρινόν (n.) provisional.
πρωτότυπος original.
πτυχή (f.) a fold, crease.

πυθμένας bottom.
πώληση μέσω ταχυδρομείου mail bid sale.
πωλητής seller.

Ρ ϱ

ράτσα (f.) pedigree (list of former and present owners).
ρητό (n.) motto.
ρολός roll (of coins).
ρυθμίζω (v.) to adjust.
Ρωσσία Russia.

Σ σ ς

Σαουδική Αραβία Saudi Arabia.
σαράντα forty.
σειρά (f.) series.
σίδηρος (m.) iron (the metal).
σκωρία (f.) rust.
Σκωτία Scotland.
Σοβιετική Ένωση Soviet Union.
Σουηδία Sweden.
σπάνιο rare, scarce.
σπανιότητα (f.) rarity.
στέμμα (n.) crown (royal headpiece).
στίγμα (n.) stain.
στρατιωτικόν παράσημον (n.) military decoration.
στρογγυλός round.
συλλέγω (v.) to collect.
συλλέκτης collector.
συλλογή (f.) collection.
σύμβολο (n.) symbol.
σύντμηση (f.) abbreviation.
σφαιροειδής round.
σφραγίδα (f.) seal (as defined in numismatics).
σφραγισμένο νόμισμα (n.) milled coin.
σχέδιο (n.) pattern; design.

σχεδόν almost.
σχίζω (v.) to tear.
σχίσιμο (n.) a tear (as in a banknote, bond, or certificate).
σχισμένο torn.

T τ

ταξινομία classification.
ταξινομώ (v.) to classify.
τεκμήριο (n.) token.
τέσσερα four.
τέταρτον fourth.
τετραγωνικό (adj.) square.
τέχνη (f.) art.
τιμή (f.) price.
τιμή καταλόγου catalogue value.
τιμή συναλλάγματος exchange rate.
τιμοκατάλογος (m.) price list.
τράπεζα (f.) bank (savings institution).
τρία three.
τριάντα thirty.
τριβή κέρματος απο την θήκη cabinet friction.
τρίτον (n.) third (the fraction).
τροποποίηση (f.) alteration.
τρύπα hole.
τσακίζω (v.) to crease.
τσάκισμα (n.) a crease, a fold (as in a note or bond).
τυπογραφία (f.) typography.
τυπώνω (v.) to print.

Y υ

υδατόσημο (n.) watermark.
υπογραφή (f.) signature.
υποτίμηση (f.) devaluation.
υπουργός οικονομικών (m.) finance minister.

Φ φ

φαιό grey.
φθορά (f.) wear.
Φιλανδία Finland.
φόρος (m.) tax.
φράγκο (n.) franc (French unit of currency).
φωτογραβούρα (f.) photogravure.
φωτογραφία (f.) photo.

X χ

χαλασμένο damaged.
χαλκός (m.) copper (the metal).
χάλυβας (m.) steel.
χάνδρα (f.) bead (raised dot on the surface of a coin or medal).
χαρακτηριστικόν (n.) attribution.
χαρακτικόν engraved.
χάραξη επί χάλυβδος steel engraving.
χαρτί (n.) paper.
χαρτονόμισμα (n.) paper money; banknote; certificate.
χίλια (n.pl.) thousand.
χιλιοστό (n.) millimeter, millimetre.
χιλιοστόν thousandth.
Χόνγκ Κόνγκ Hong Kong.
χρήματα (n.pl.) money; cash.
χρόνος (m.) year.
χρυσός (m.) gold (the metal).
χρώμα (n.) color, colour.
χρώμιο (n.) chromium.
χυτός ογκος μετάλλου ingot.

Ψ ψ

ψευδάργυρος (m.) [literally "fake silver."] zinc.

Cyrillic Alphabet

Words in Russian, Serbian, and Bulgarian

А а

абдрук (*m.*) [*Russ.*] trial impression; essay strike.

аванс (*m.*) [*Russ.*] prepayment.

аверс (*m.*) [*Russ.*] obverse.

Австралия [*Russ.*] Australia.

Австрия [*Russ.*] Austria.

автентичен [*Bul.*] authentic, genuine.

албум (*m.*) [*Serb.*] album.

альбом (*m.*) [*Russ.*] album.

Александр [*Russ.*] Alexander.

Англия [*Russ.*] England.

аномалија (*f.*) [*Serb.*] anomaly.

аномалия (*f.*) [*Russ.*] anomaly.

Аргентина [*Russ., Serb.*] Argentina.

атрибуција (*f.*) [*Russ.*] attribution (complete identification of a coin, medal, or note).

аукцион (*m.*) [*Russ.*] auction.

аукционная продажа (*f.*) [*Russ.*] auction sale.

Аустралија [*Serb.*] Australia.

Аустрија [*Serb.*] Austria.

аутентичан [*Serb.*] authentic, genuine.

Б б

бакар (*m.*) [*Serb.*] copper.

банк (*m.*) [*Russ.*] bank (financial institution).

банка (*f.*) [*Bul., Serb.*] bank.

банкнота (*f.*) [*Bul., Russ., Serb.*] note, banknote.

Белгија [*Serb.*] Belgium.

Бельгия [*Russ.*] Belgium.

белый [*Russ.*] white.

бео [*Serb.*] white.

битни [*Serb.*] intrinsic.

благо (*n.*) [*Serb.*] treasure.

бланк (*m.*) [*Russ.*] order form.

Бог (*m.*) [*Bul., Serb., Russ.*] God (in the Judaic-Christian sense).

бонови (*m.pl.*) [*Serb.*] scrip.

боја (*f.*) [*Serb.*] color, colour.

большой [*Russ.*] large.

Бразилија [*Serb.*] Brazil.

Бразилия [*Russ.*] Brazil.

бракованный [*Russ.*] mis-struck.

браун [*Serb.*] brown.

брид кованог новца (*m.*) [*Serb.*] edge (of a coin or medal).

број (*m.*) [*Serb.*] number.

бронза (*f.*) [*Russ.*] bronze (the alloy).

бронца (*f.*) [*Serb.*] bronze (the alloy).

бумага (*f.*) [*Russ.*] paper.

бумажные деньги (*pl.*) [*Russ.*] paper money.

бусина (*f.*) [*Russ.*] bead (raised dot on the surface of a coin or medal).

бывший в обращении [*Russ.*] circulated.

В в

валута (*f.*) [*Bul., Serb.*] currency.

валюта (*f.*) [*Russ.*] currency.

ваљан [*Serb.*] good (grade or condition).

ван оптицаја [*Serb.*] not issued.

вар (*m.*) [*Serb.*] stain (on a banknote or bond).

Велика Британја [*Serb.*] Great Britain; United Kingdom (U.K.).

велик; велики [*Serb.*] large.

Великобритания [*Russ.*] Great Britain; United Kingdom.

Велс [*Serb.*] Wales.

верх (*m.*) [*Russ.*] top.

вес (*f.*) [*Russ.*] weight.

видоизменять (*v.*) [*Russ.*] to alter.

водени жиг (*m.*) [*Serb.*] watermark.

водяной знак (*m.*) [*Russ.*] watermark.

воинская награда (*f.*) [*Russ.*] military decoration.

војно одликовање [*Serb.*] military decoration.

восемь [*Russ.*] eight.

восемьдесят [*Russ.*] eighty.

Восточная Германия [*Russ.*] East Germany (D.D.R.).

вредност (*f.*) [*Serb.*] value.

вредност означена у каталогу [*Serb.*] catalogue value.

врх (*m.*) [*Serb.*] top.

выпуск (*m.*) [*Russ.*] an issue, issuance.

выпускать (*v.*) [*Russ.*] to issue.

выставка (*f.*) [*Russ.*] exhibition.

выставлять (*v.*) [*Russ.*] to exhibit.

вычеканенный [*Russ.*] incuse.

възпоменателен (*adj.*) [*Bul.*] commemorative.

Г г

гарантована понуда (*f.*) [*Serb.*] protective reserve bid.

гашение компостером (*n.*) [*Russ.*] punch cancellation.

гашение надрезом (*n.*) [*Russ.*] cut cancellation.

гвожђе (*n.*) [*Serb.*] iron (the metal).

Германия [*Russ.*] Germany.

глубокая печать (*f.*) [*Russ.*] intaglio.

год (*m.*) [*Russ.*] year.

година (*f.*) [*Serb.*] year.

Голландия [*Russ.*] Holland, Netherlands.

Гонконг [*Russ.*] Hong Kong.

готовина (*f.*) [*Serb.*] cash (ready money).

гравирование по стали (*m.*) [*Russ.*] steel engraving.

гравированный [*Russ.*] engraved.

Греция [*Russ.*] Greece.

грешка (*f.*) [*Serb.*] error.

гривенник (*m.*) [*Russ.*] grivennik.

гривна (*f.*) [*Russ.*] grivna.

Грчка [*Serb.*] Greece.

Д д

давни [*Serb.*] old; ancient.

Дания [*Russ.*] Denmark.

дата (*f.*) [*Russ.*] date.

датум (*m.*) [*Serb.*] date.

два [*Russ., Serb.*] two.

двадесет [*Serb.*] twenty.

двадцать [*Russ.*] twenty.

две [*Bul.*] two.

двојезичан [*Serb.*] bilingual.

двуязычный [*Russ.*] bilingual.

девалвација (*f.*) [*Serb.*] devaluation.

девальвация (*f.*) [*Russ.*] devaluation.

деведесет [*Serb.*] ninety.

девет [*Serb.*] nine.

девиз (*m.*) [*Russ.*] motto.

девиза (*f.*) [*Serb.*] foreign currency.

девяносто [*Russ.*] ninety.

девять [*Russ.*] nine.

действительный [*Russ.*] intrinsic.

демонетизация (*f.*) [*Russ.*] demonetization.

денежная единица (*f.*) [*Russ.*] monetary unit.

денежная система (*f.*) [*Russ.*] monetary system.

денежный [*Russ.*] monetary.

денежный перевод (*m.*) [*Russ.*] money order.

деньги (*pl.*) [*Russ.*] money.

десет [*Bul., Serb.*] ten.

десетина (*f.*) [*Serb.*] tenth (the fraction).

десно [*Serb.*] right (direction or position).

десятая часть (*f.*) [*Russ.*] tenth (the fraction).

десять [*Russ.*] ten.

дефект (*m.*) [*Serb., Russ.*] defect.

дефектный [*Russ.*] defective.

дефицитный [*Russ.*] rare, scarce.

диаметр (*m.*) [*Russ.*] diameter.

дизајн (*m.*) [*Serb.*] design; pattern.

добар [*Serb.*] good (grade or condition).

долар (*m.*) [*Serb.*] dollar ($).

доллар (*m.*) [*Russ.*] dollar ($).
доплата (*f.*) [*Russ.*] surcharge.
древан [*Serb.*] ancient.
древност (*f.*) [*Serb.*] antiquity.
древность (*f.*) [*Russ.*] antiquity.
дубликат (*m.*) [*Russ.*] a duplicate.
дубликатный (*adj.*) [*Russ.*] duplicate.
дублировать (*v.*) [*Russ.*] to duplicate.
дюйм (*m.*) [*Russ.*] inch.

Е е

едно [*Bul.*] one.
електротип (*m.*) [*Serb.*] electrotype.
Екатерина [*Russ.*] Catherine.
Елизавета [*Russ.*] Elizabeth.
Енглеска [*Serb.*] England.

Ж ж

железо (*n.*) [*Russ.*] iron (the metal).
жёлтый [*Russ.*] yellow.
жетон (*m.*) [*Russ.*] token.
жут [*Serb.*] yellow.

З з

задаток (*m.*) [*Russ.*] deposit (of funds).
зазубрина (*f.*) [*Russ.*] adjustment mark.
за одобрение [*Bul.*] on approval.
Западни Немачка [*Serb.*] West Germany (B.R.D.).
запис (*m.*) [*Serb.*] inscription.
застарео [*Serb.*] obsolete.

зачёхленная марка (*f.*) [*Russ.*] encased postage stamp (such as the type used as an emergency substitute for small coins during the U.S. Civil War of 1861-65).
заштитни знак ковнице [*Serb.*] mintmark.
заявка на торгах (*f.*) [*Russ.*] bid sheet.
збирка (*f.*) [*Serb.*] collection.
званичан [*Serb.*] official.
звезда (*f.*) [*Russ., Serb.*] star.
зелен [*Serb.*] green.
зелёный [*Russ.*] green.
злато (*n.*) [*Bul., Serb.*] gold (the metal).
золото (*n.*) [*Russ.*] gold (the metal).
Западная Германия [*Russ.*] West Germany.

И и

ивица (*f.*) [*Serb.*] edge; rim.
идеальный [*Russ.*] perfect, flawless.
изврстан [*Serb.*] excellent.
издавати; издати (*v.*) [*Serb.*] to issue.
издање (*n.*); изливање (*n.*) [*Serb.*] an issue, issuance.
изложба (*f.*) [*Serb.*] exhibition.
изложити (*v.*) [*Serb.*] to exhibit.
измененная дата (*f.*) [*Russ.*] altered date.
Израел [*Serb.*] Israel.
Израиль [*Russ.*] Israel.
имитация (*f.*) [*Russ.*] imitation.
император (*m.*) [*Russ., Serb.*] emperor.
ингот (*m.*) [*Serb.*] ingot.
иностранная валюта (*f.*) [*Russ.*] foreign currency.
иностранный [*Russ.*] foreign.
интаглио (*m.*) [*Serb.*] intaglio.
интернациональный [*Russ.*] international.
инч (*m.*) [*Serb.*] inch.
Ирландия [*Russ.*] Ireland.
Ирска [*Serb.*] Ireland.
искусство (*n.*) [*Russ.*] art.
Испания [*Russ.*] Spain.
истёртый [*Russ.*] badly worn.
Источна Немачка [*Serb.*] East Germany.

исходная монета (*f.*) [*Russ.*] host coin (i.e., a coin upon which a countermark or overstrike is applied).

итоговый список [*Russ.*] list of prices realized.

J j

Јапан [*Serb.*] Japan.
један [*Serb.*] one.
јединствен [*Serb.*] unique.
једноглав; једнолик [*Serb.*] uniface.
језик (*m.*) [*Serb.*] language.
јемствена обавезница (*f.*) [*Serb.*] (commercial) bond.
Југославија [*Serb.*] Yugoslavia, Jugoslavia.
Јужна Африка [*Serb.*] South Africa.

K к

кабинет; минцкабинет [*Russ.*] coin cabinet, as a reference to a coin collection.
казна (*f.*) [*Russ.*] treasure; treasury.
казначейский билет [*Russ.*] treasury note. The term usually applies to Soviet notes of 1, 3, or 5 rubles.
калај (*m.*) [*Serb.*] tin.
калуп преса [*Serb.*] coinage die.
Канада [*Russ., Serb.*] Canada.
каталог (*m.*) [*Bul., Russ., Serb.*] catalog, catalogue.
каталог аукциона (*m.*) [*Russ.*] auction catalogue.
каталогизация [*Russ.*] cataloguing.
каталог лицитације (*m.*) [*Serb.*] auction catalogue.
кауција (*f.*) [*Serb.*] deposit (of funds).
кауција обавезна [*Serb.*] deposit required.
квадратный (*adj.*) [*Russ.*] square.

квитанция (*f.*) [*Russ.*] receipt.
Кина [*Serb.*] China.
Китай [*Russ.*] China.
класификација (*f.*) [*Serb.*] classification.
класифицирати (*v.*) [*Serb.*] to classify.
классификация (*f.*) [*Russ.*] classification.
классифицировать (*v.*) [*Russ.*] to classify.
ковани новац; ковница новца [*Serb.*] mint.
кованица (*f.*) [*Serb.*] coin.
ковање новца [*Serb.*] coinage.
колајна (*f.*) [*Serb.*] medal.
колекција (*f.*) [*Serb.*] collection.
колекционар (*m.*) [*Serb.*] collector.
колекционарски примерак (*m.*) [*Serb.*] proof (*re*: coins).
коллекционер (*m.*) [*Russ.*] collector.
коллекционировать (*v.*) [*Russ.*] to collect.
коллекция (*f.*) [*Russ.*] collection.
комеморативан (*adj.*) [*Serb.*] commemorative.
копейка (*f.*) [*pl.:* копейки] [*Russ.*] kopek.
копија (*f.*) [*Serb.*] a copy.
копировать (*v.*) [*Russ.*] to copy.
копирати (*v.*) [*Serb.*] to copy.
копия (*f.*) [*Russ.*] a copy.
коричневый [*Russ.*] brown.
королева (*f.*) [*Russ.*] queen.
король (*m.*) [*Russ.*] king.
корона (*f.*) [*Bul., Russ.*] crown (royal headpiece).
коррозия (*f.*) [*Russ.*] corrosion.
краљ (*m.*) [*Serb.*] king.
краљица (*f.*) [*Serb.*] queen.
красный [*Russ.*] red.
кредит (*m.*) [*Russ., Serb.*] credit.
кредитна карта (*f.*) [*Serb.*] credit card.
кредитне карте важе [*Serb.*] credit cards accepted.
кредитная карточка (*f.*) [*Russ.*] credit card.
кредитные карточки принимаются [*Russ.*] credit cards accepted.
кризисные деньги (*pl.*) [*Russ.*] emergency currency.
крона (*f.*) [*Russ.*] crown (numismatic term for a large silver coin).
круглый [*Russ.*] round.
крузейро (*n.*) [*Russ.*] cruzeiro (Brazilian unit of currency).
крузеро (*m.*) [*Serb.*] cruzeiro.

круна (*f.*) [*Serb.*] crown (royal headpiece; large silver coin).

крупан [*Serb.*] large.

купац (*m.*) [*Serb.*] buyer.

купити; **куповати** (*v.*) [*Serb.*] to buy.

купон (*m.*) [*Bul., Russ., Serb.*] coupon; scrip.

Л л

латунь (*f.*) [*Russ.*] brass (the alloy).

лауреат [*Serb.*] laureate.

лево [*Serb.*] left (direction or position).

левый [*Russ.*] left (direction or position).

легенда (*f.*) [*Serb.*] legend.

легура (*f.*) [*Serb.*] alloy (of metals).

лик (*m.*) [*Serb.*] effigy.

литография (*f.*) [*Russ.*] lithography.

лице (*n.*) [*Serb.*] front; obverse.

лицевая сторона (*f.*) [*Russ.*] front; obverse.

лицитација (*f.*) [*Serb.*] auction; auction sale.

лицитација путем поште [*Serb.*] mail bid sale.

лупа (*f.*) [*Bul., Russ., Serb.*] magnifying glass.

М м

мален [*Serb.*] small.

маленький [*Russ.*] small.

марка (*f.*) [*Bul., Serb., Russ.*] postage stamp; mark (German unit of currency).

мастило (*n.*) [*Serb.*] ink.

мед (*m.*) [*Bul.*] copper.

медаль (*f.*) [*Russ.*] medal.

медаља (*f.*) [*Serb.*] medal.

медь (*f.*) [*Russ.*] copper.

међународни [*Serb.*] international.

Мексика [*Russ.*] Mexico.

Мексико [*Serb.*] Mexico.

месинг (*m.*) [*Serb.*] brass (the alloy).

метал (*m.*) [*Serb.*] metal.

металл (*m.*) [*Russ.*] metal.

метални новац веће дебљине [*Serb.*] piéfort, piedfort.

метални новчић (*m.*) [*Serb.*] coin.

милиметар (*m.*) [*Serb.*] millimeter, millimetre.

миллиметр (*m.*) [*Russ.*] millimeter, millimetre.

милион [*Serb.*] million.

миллион (*m.*) [*Russ.*] million.

минимальное предложение цены (*n.*) [*Russ.*] minimum bid.

министар финансија [*Serb.*] finance minister.

министр финансов (*m.*) [*Russ.*] finance minister.

многоцветный [*Russ.*] multicolored, multicoloured.

монета (*f.*) [*Bul., Russ.*] coin; [*Serb.*] currency.

монета машинного изготовления (*f.*) [*Russ.*] milled coin.

монета ручного изготовления (*f.*) [*Russ.*] hammered coin.

монетен двор (*m.*) [*Bul.*] mint.

монетный двор (*m.*) [*Russ.*] mint.

монетный диск (*m.*) [*Russ.*] planchet.

Москва [*Russ.*] Moscow.

мото (*m.*) [*Serb.*] motto.

мрачан [*Serb.*] dark.

мрља (*f.*) [*Serb.*] tarnish (on a coin or medal); stain (on a banknote or bond).

Н н

надпечатка (*f.*) [*Russ.*] overprint.

надпись (*f.*) [*Russ.*] inscription; legend.

назнака (*f.*) [*Serb.*] attribution (the complete identification of a coin, medal, or banknote).

назначити порекло (*v.*) [*Serb.*] to attribute.

најнижа понуда (*f.*) [*Serb.*] minimum bid.

најнижи [*Serb.*] bottom.

налет (*m.*) [*Russ.*] tarnish.

наличје (*n.*) [*Serb.*] reverse.

наличные деньги (*pl.*) [*Russ.*] cash (i.e., ready money).

налог (*m.*) [*Russ.*] tax.

наложенный [*Russ.*] accolated[q.v.], conjoined, jugate.

на полеђини [*Serb.*] on the back.

нарицательная стоимость [*Russ.*] face value.

Народна Република Кина [*Serb.*] People's Republic of China (P.R.C.).

наруџбеница (*f.*) [*Serb.*] order form.

на увид [*Serb.*] on approval.

национальный [*Russ.*] national.

националност [*Serb.*] nationality.

национальная принадлежность (*f.*) [*Russ.*] nationality.

нацрт (*m.*) [*Serb.*] design.

не бывший в обращении [*Russ.*] uncirculated.

незваничан; неслужбени [*Serb.*] unofficial.

неидентифицированный [*Russ.*] unattributed (not fully identified).

неисправан [*Serb.*] defective.

неисправност (*f.*) [*Serb.*] defect.

неизвестный [*Russ.*] unknown.

неизданный [*Russ.*] not issued.

неиздат [*Serb.*] not issued.

нејасан отисак пресе [*Serb.*] badly struck.

Немачка [*Serb.*] Germany.

немецкая марка (*f.*) [*Russ.*] mark (German unit of currency).

необјављен [*Serb.*] unpublished (not listed in any book or catalogue).

необращавшийся [*Russ.*] uncirculated.

необычный [*Russ.*] irregular.

неопредељен [*Serb.*] unattributed (not fully identified).

неопубликованный [*Russ.*] unpublished (not listed in any book or catalogue).

непознат [*Serb.*] unknown.

непотпун [*Serb.*] incomplete.

неофициальный [*Russ.*] unofficial.

неполный [*Russ.*] incomplete.

неразменные деньги [*Russ.*] fiat money.

изван оптицаја [*Serb.*] uncirculated.

Нидерланды [*Russ.*] Netherlands, Holland.

никель (*m.*) [*Russ.*] nickel (the metal).

никл (*m.*) [*Serb.*] nickel (the metal).

Николай [*Russ.*] Nicholas.

низ (*m.*) [*Russ.*] bottom.

новац (*m.*) [*Serb.*] money.

новац без подлоге [*Serb.*] fiat money.

новац излизан трењем [*Serb.*] cabinet friction.

новац искован у три слоја [*Serb.*] clad coinage.

новац произведен са дефектом [*Serb.*] a mis-strike.

новац у оптицају [*Serb.*] circulated.

Новая Зеландия [*Russ.*] New Zealand.

нови [*Serb.*] new.

Нови Зеланд [*Serb.*] New Zealand.

новодел (*m.*) [*Russ.*] a restrike; *novodel.*

ново издање (*n.*) [*Serb.*] a restrike.

новчана јединица (*f.*) [*Serb.*] denomination; monetary unit.

новчана уплатница (*f.*) [*Serb.*] money order.

новчан; новчани [*Serb.*] monetary.

новчани систем [*Serb.*] monetary system.

новчаница (*f.*) [*Serb.*] banknote.

новый [*Russ.*] new.

номер (*m.*) [*Russ.*] number.

номинал (*m.*) [*Russ.*] denomination.

номинална вредност (*f.*) [*Serb.*] face value.

Норвегия [*Russ.*] Norway.

Норвешка [*Serb.*] Norway.

нула [*Serb.*] zero.

нуль (*m.*) [*Russ.*] zero.

нумизмат (*m.*) [*Bul., Russ.*] numismatist; coin collector.

нумизматика (*f.*) [*Bul., Russ., Serb.*] numismatics.

нумизматичар (*m.*) [*Serb.*] numismatist; coin collector.

нумизматичен (*adj.*) [*Bul.*] numismatic.

нумизматический (*adj.*) [*Russ.*] numismatic.

нумизматички (*adj.*) [*Serb.*] numismatic.

O o

обичан [*Serb.*] common.

облигация (*f.*) [*Russ.*] (commercial) bond.

обмениваться (*v.*) [*Russ.*] to trade.

обменный курс (*m.*) [*Russ.*] exchange rate.

образец (*m.*) [*Russ.*] pattern.
обратная сторона (*f.*) [*Russ.*] reverse.
обращение (*n.*) [*Russ.*] circulation.
обрез (*m.*) [*Russ.*] exergue.
обыкновенный [*Russ.*] common.
овенчан [*Serb.*] laureate.
ограничене понуде [*Serb.*] no unlimited bids accepted.
огреботина (*f.*) [*Serb.*] a scratch.
один [*Russ.*] one.
односторонка (*f.*) [*Russ.*] brockage.
односторонний [*Russ.*] uniface.
одличан [*Serb.*] excellent (grade or condition).
одузимање вредности новчићу [*Serb.*] demonetization.
округао [*Serb.*] round.
окупациони новац (*m.*) [*Serb.*] obsidional money.
олово (*n.*) [*Russ.*] tin.
определять (*v.*) [*Russ.*] to attribute.
оптицај (*m.*) [*Serb.*] circulation.
орао (*m.*) [*Serb.*] eagle.
орел (*m.*) [*Bul.*] eagle.
орёл (*m.*) [*Russ.*] eagle.
оригинал [*Russ.*] original.
оригиналан [*Serb.*] original; genuine.
осадный [*Russ.*] obsidional.
осам [*Serb.*] eight.
осамдесет [*Serb.*] eighty.
отверстие (*n.*) [*Russ.*] hole.
отечественный [*Russ.*] domestic.
отливать (*v.*) [*Russ.*] to cast.
отличный [*Russ.*] excellent.
отреставрированный [*Russ.*] repaired.
официальный [*Russ.*] official.
ошибка (*f.*) [*Russ.*] error.
оштећен [*Serb.*] damaged.
оштећен при ковању [*Serb.*] mis-struck.

П п

набавка (*f.*) [*Serb.*] acquisition.
палиндром (*m.*) [*Russ., Serb.*] palindrome ("radar" serial number on banknotes).

памятный (*adj.*) [*Russ.*] commemorative.
папа (*m.*) [*Bul., Serb., Russ.*] pope (of the Roman Catholic Church).
папир (*m.*) [*Serb.*] paper.
папирна новчаница (*f.*) [*Serb.*] paper money.
пари (*f.pl.*) [*Bul.*] money.
паричен [*Bul.*] monetary.
партија (*f.*) [*Serb.*] (auction) lot.
партия (*f.*) [*Russ.*] (auction) lot.
педесет [*Serb.*] fifty.
Перу [*Russ., Serb.*] Peru.
пезо (*m.*) [*Serb.*] peso (Spanish-American unit of currency).
песета (*f.*) [*Russ., Serb.*] peseta (Spanish unit of currency).
песо (*n.*) [*Russ.*] peso (Spanish-American unit of currency).
пет [*Bul., Serb.*] five.
петдесет [*Bul.*] fifty.
петина (*f.*) [*Serb.*] fifth (the fraction).
Петр [*Russ.*] Peter.
печат (*m.*) [*Serb.*] seal (in the numismatic sense).
печатать (*v.*) [*Russ.*] to print.
печать (*f.*) [*Russ.*] seal (in the numismatic sense).
плав; плаветан [*Serb.*] blue.
плакированная монета (*f.*) [*Russ.*] clad coinage.
платина (*f.*) [*Bul., Russ., Serb.*] platinum.
плохо отштампованный [*Russ.*] badly struck.
пљосница (*f.*) [*Serb.*] planchet.
повреждённый [*Russ.*] damaged.
подделка (*f.*) [*Russ.*] a counterfeit; a fake, forgery.
подделывать (*v.*) [*Russ.*] to counterfeit.
подлинный [*Russ.*] authentic, genuine.
подпись (*f.*) [*Russ.*] signature.
покидан [*Serb.*] torn.
покупатель (*m.*) [*Russ.*] buyer.
покупать (*v.*) [*Russ.*] to buy.
полный [*Russ.*] complete.
половина (*f.*) [*Russ.*] half (the fraction).
половинный (*adj.*) [*Russ.*] half.
половица (*f.*) [*Serb.*] half (the fraction).
половичан (*adj.*) [*Serb.*] half.
полтина (*f.*) [*Russ.*] poltina.
полтинник (*m.*) [*Russ.*] poltinnik.

полушка (*f.*) [*pl.*: полушки] [*Russ.*] polushka.

поништавање рупицама или урезом [*Serb.*] cut cancellation.

понуда (*f.*) [*Serb.*] an offer; a bid (at an auction or mail bid sale).

понудити (*v.*) [*Serb.*] to offer; to bid.

порванный [*Russ.*] torn.

порез (*m.*) [*Serb.*] tax.

порекло (*n.*) [*Serb.*] pedigree (list of previous and present owners).

портрет (*m.*) [*Russ., Serb.*] portrait; effigy.

портретная медаль (*f.*) [*Russ.*] portrait medal.

Португалија [*Serb.*] Portugal.

Португалия [*Russ.*] Portugal.

порча монет [*Russ.*] debasement.

потврда (*f.*) [*Serb.*] certificate.

потертость от хранения (*f.*) [*Russ.*] cabinet friction.

потпис (*m.*) [*Serb.*] signature.

потпун [*Serb.*] complete.

похабаност (*f.*) [*Serb.*] wear (on a coin).

поцепотина (*f.*) [*Serb.*] a tear (in a banknote or bond).

почетна понуда (*f.*) [*Serb.*] suggested bid.

почка (*f.*) [*Russ.*] pochka (1/25 zolotnik).

почти [*Russ.*] almost.

пошлина за право чеканки монет [*Russ.*] seigniorage.

прави [*Serb.*] genuine.

правоугаони [*Serb.*] rectangular.

правый [*Russ.*] right (direction or position).

прегиб (*m.*) [*Serb.*] a crease, a fold (as in a banknote or bond).

предлагаемая цена (*f.*) [*Russ.*] suggested bid.

предлагать (*v.*) [*Russ.*] to offer.

предлагать цену (*v.*) [*Russ.*] to bid (at an auction or mail bid sale).

предложение (*n.*) [*Russ.*] an offer.

предложение цены (*n.*) [*Russ.*] (auction) bid.

предложения цен ограниченны [*Russ.*] no unlimited bids accepted.

предња страна (*f.*) [*Serb.*] obverse.

председник (*m.*) [*Serb.*] president.

президент (*m.*) [*Bul., Russ.*] president.

прейскурант (*m.*) [*Russ.*] price list.

преса (*f.*) [*Serb.*] (coinage) press.

пресс (*m.*) [*Russ.*] (coinage) press.

претплата (*f.*) [*Serb.*] prepayment.

пречник (*m.*) [*Serb.*] diameter.

признаница (*f.*) [*Serb.*] certificate; receipt.

пријава за учествовање на лицитацији [*Serb.*] bid sheet.

примерак (*m.*) [*Serb.*] specimen.

примитивно искован новац (*m.*) [*Serb.*] milled coin.

приобретение (*n.*) [*Russ.*] acquisition.

пробный образец (*m.*) [*Russ.*] specimen.

продавати (*v.*) [*Serb.*] to sell.

продавать (*v.*) [*Russ.*] to sell.

продавац (*m.*) [*Serb.*] seller.

продавец (*m.*) [*Russ.*] seller.

продати (*v.*) [*Serb.*] to sell; to trade.

происхождение (*n.*) [*Russ.*] pedigree (list of previous and present owners).

промена (*f.*) [*Serb.*] alteration.

промењен датум (*m.*) [*Serb.*] altered date.

пропагандистская банкнота (*f.*) [*Russ.*] propaganda note.

процена (*f.*) [*Serb.*] grade, condition.

проценити (*v.*) [*Serb.*] to grade.

пруф [*Russ.*] proof (re: coins).

прямоугольный [*Russ.*] rectangular.

пятая часть (*f.*) [*Russ.*] fifth (the fraction).

пятно (*n.*) [*Russ.*] stain (on a banknote or bond).

пять [*Russ.*] five.

пятьдесят [*Russ.*] fifty.

Р р

разновидность (*f.*) [*Russ.*] variety.

разноликост (*f.*) [*Serb.*] variety.

разрыв (*m.*) [*Russ.*] a tear (in a banknote or bond).

разрывать (*v.*) [*Russ.*] to tear.

раритет (*m.*) [*Russ., Serb.*] rarity.

распродажа по почте (*f.*) [*Russ.*] mail bid sale.

рачун (*m.*) [*Serb.*] account (financial or transactional).

рђа (*f.*) [*Serb.*] rust.

ребро (*n.*) [*Russ.*] rim; edge.

редак [*Serb.*] rare, scarce.

редкий [*Russ.*] rare.

резервная цена (*f.*) [*Russ.*] protective reserve bid.

реклама (*f.*) [*Serb.*] propaganda note.

репродукция (*f.*) [*Russ.*] reproduction.

република (*f.*) [*Serb.*] republic.

Република Кина [*Serb.*] Republic of China (Taiwan).

республика (*f.*) [*Russ.*] republic.

Республика Китай [*Russ.*] Republic of China (Taiwan).

ржавчина (*f.*) [*Russ.*] rust.

рисунок (*m.*) [*Russ.*] design.

рола (*f.*) [*Serb.*] roll (of coins).

Россия [*Russ.*] Russia.

руб (*m.*) [*Serb.*] rim.

рубль (*m.*) [*pl.*: рубли] [*Russ.*] rouble, ruble.

руком ковани новац [*Serb.*] hammered coin.

румен [*Serb.*] red.

рупица (*f.*) [*Serb.*] hole.

Русија [*Serb.*] Russia.

рядък [*Bul.*] rare, scarce.

С с

савршен [*Serb.*] perfect, flawless.

Санкт-Петербург [*Russ.*] St. Petersburg (Russia).

сантиметр (*m.*) [*Russ.*] centimeter, centimetre.

састављен [*Serb.*] accolated[q.v.], conjoined, jugate.

свилена нит (*f.*) [*Serb.*] silk thread.

свота (*f.*) [*Serb.*] amount.

Северна Ирска [*Serb.*] Northern Ireland.

Северная Ирландия [*Russ.*] Northern Ireland.

седам [*Serb.*] seven.

седамдесет [*Serb.*] seventy.

семь [*Russ.*] seven.

семьдесят [*Russ.*] seventy.

сентиметар (*m.*) [*Serb.*] centimeter, centimetre.

серебро (*n.*) [*Russ.*] silver.

серийный номер (*m.*) [*Russ.*] serial number.

серија (*f.*) [*Serb.*] series.

серијски број на новчаници [*Serb.*] serial number.

серия (*f.*) [*Russ.*] series.

сертификат (*m.*) [*Russ.*] certificate.

сечене на пари (*n.*) [*Bul.*] coinage.

символ (*m.*) [*Serb.*] symbol.

символ (*m.*) [*Bul., Russ.*] symbol.

синий [*Russ.*] blue.

ситан [*Serb.*] small.

Сједињене Америчке Државе [*Serb.*] United States of America (U.S.A.).

складка (*f.*) [*Russ.*] a fold, crease.

складывать (*v.*) [*Russ.*] to fold, to crease.

скраћеница (*f.*) [*Serb.*] abbreviation.

скупљати (*v.*) [*Serb.*] to collect.

скупоцен [*Serb.*] valuable.

слепая сторона (*f.*) [*Russ.*] blank side (of a uniface coin or medal).

слика (*f.*) [*Serb.*] effigy.

слиток (*m.*) [*Russ.*] ingot.

службен; службени [*Serb.*] official.

Советский Союз [*Russ.*] Soviet Union (U.S.S.R.).

Совјетски Савез [*Serb.*] Soviet Union.

Соединенные Штаты Америки [*Russ.*] United States of America (U.S.A.).

соединённый [*Russ.*] accolated[q.v.], conjoined, jugate.

сокращение (*n.*) [*Russ.*] abbreviation.

сорок [*Russ.*] forty.

сортировать (*v.*) [*Russ.*] to grade; to sort.

состояние (*n.*) [*Russ.*] grade; condition.

сотая часть (*f.*) [*Russ.*] hundredth (the fraction).

Союз Советских Социалистических Республик [*Russ.*] Union of Soviet Socialist Republics (U.S.S.R.).

список (*m.*) [*Serb.*] catalog, catalogue.

сплав (*m.*) [*Bul., Russ.*] alloy (of metals).

спојен [*Serb.*] accolated[q.v.], conjoined, jugate.

сребрни новац (*m.*) [*Serb.*] crown (numismatic term for a large silver coin).

сребро (*n.*) [*Bul., Serb.*] silver.

средство против подделки [*Russ.*] anti-counterfeiting device.

средство спречавања кривотворби [*Serb.*] anti-counterfeiting device.

ставка (*f.*) [*Serb.*] (auction) lot.

сталь (*f.*) [*Russ.*] steel.
стар; старн [*Serb.*] old; ancient.
старина (*f.*) [*Serb.*] antiquity.
старинный [*Russ.*] ancient.
старый [*Russ.*] old.
статер [*Bul., Russ.*] stater[q.v.].
стварни [*Serb.*] intrinsic.
степен (*m.*) [*Serb.*] grade, condition.
стилизованный [*Russ.*] stylized.
сто [*Bul., Russ., Serb.*] hundred.
стогодишњица (*f.*) [*Serb.*] centennial, centenary.
столетие (*n.*) [*Russ.*] centennial, centenary.
стопа размене (*f.*) [*Serb.*] exchange rate.
стопка монет (*f.*) [*Russ.*] roll (of coins).
стоти [*Serb.*] hundredth (the fraction).
стран; страни [*Serb.*] foreign.
страни новац (*m.*) [*Serb.*] foreign currency.
суверен (*m.*) [*Russ., Serb.*] sovereign.
сумма (*f.*) [*Russ.*] amount.
счёт (*m.*) [*Russ.*] account (financial or transactional).

Т т

Тайвань [*Russ.*] Taiwan (Republic of China).
Тајван Taiwan (Republic of China).
тантуз (*m.*) [*Serb.*] token.
тежина (*f.*) [*Serb.*] weight.
таман [*Serb.*] dark.
тёмный [*Russ.*] dark; deep (*re:* color).
тетрадрахма [*Bul., Russ.*] tetradrachm[q.v.].
траг турпије [*Serb.*] adjustment mark.
трговати (*v.*) [*Serb.*] to trade.
требуется задаток (*m.*) [*Russ.*] deposit required.
третья часть (*f.*) [*Russ.*] third (the fraction).
трећина (*f.*) [*Serb.*] third (the fraction).
трещина в штампе (*f.*) [*Russ.*] die break.
три [*Bul., Russ., Serb.*] three.
тридесет [*Serb.*] thirty.
тридцать [*Russ.*] thirty.
туђи [*Serb.*] foreign.
туч (*m.*) [*Serb.*] bronze (the alloy).

тысяча (*f.*) [*Russ.*] thousand.
търг (*m.*) [*Bul.*] auction.
тяжёлая монета (*f.*) [*Russ.*] piéfort, piedfort.

У у

увенчанный [*Russ.*] laureate.
угравиран [*Serb.*] engraved.
узорак (*m.*) [*Serb.*] specimen.
Уједињено Краљевство [*Serb.*] United Kingdom (U.K.).
уметност (*f.*) [*Serb.*] art.
уникальный [*Russ.*] unique.
унца (*f.*) [*Serb.*] ounce.
унция (*f.*) [*Russ.*] ounce.
уоквирена, оклопљена марка [*Serb.*] encased postage stamp (such as the type used as an emergency substitute for small coins during the U.S. Civil War of 1861-65).
устаревший [*Russ.*] obsolete.
Уэльс [*Russ.*] Wales.

Ф ф

фабричное клеймо (*n.*) [*Russ.*] mintmark.
фактура (*f.*) [*Serb.*] order form; account (financial or transactional).
фалсификат (*m.*) [*Serb.*] a counterfeit; a fake, forgery.
фалсификатор (*m.*) [*Serb.*] counterfeiter.
фалсификовати (*v.*) [*Serb.*] to counterfeit.
фальшивомонетчик (*m.*) [*Russ.*] counterfeiter.
фарба (*f.*) [*Serb.*] color, colour.
фин [*Serb.*] fine (grade or condition).
Финляндия [*Russ.*] Finland.
финоћа (*f.*) [*Serb.*] fineness; fine (purity of metal).
франк (*m.*) [*Russ., Serb.*] franc (French unit of currency).

Франция [*Russ.*] France.

Француска [*Serb.*] France.

фригийский колпак [*Russ.*] Phrygian cap[q.v.].

фунт (*m.*) [*Russ.*] pound (unit of weight; pound Sterling - £).

фунта (*f.*) [*Serb.*] pound (unit of weight; pound Sterling - £).

фунт стерлингов (*m.*) [*Russ.*] pound Sterling.

X   x

хартија (*f.*) [*Serb.*] paper.

хиљада [*Serb.*] thousand.

ходячая монета (*f.*) [*Russ.*] circulating currency.

Холандија [*Serb.*] Holland, Netherlands.

Хонг Конг [*Serb.*] Hong Kong.

хороший [*Russ.*] fine (grade or condition).

хрђа (*f.*) [*Serb.*] corrosion; rust.

хром (*m.*) [*Bul., Russ., Serb.*] chromium (the metal).

Ц   ц

цар (*m.*) [*Serb.*] emperor; czar, tsar.

царь (*m.*) [*Russ.*] emperor; czar, tsar.

царица (*f.*) [*Russ.*] empress; czarina, tsarina.

царапина (*f.*) [*Russ.*] a scratch.

цвет (*m.*) [*Russ.*] color, colour.

цена (*f.*) [*Bul., Russ., Serb.*] price.

цена по каталогу (*f.*) [*Russ.*] catalogue value.

ценность (*f.*) [*Russ.*] value.

ценный [*Russ.*] valuable.

ценовник (*m.*) [*Serb.*] price list.

ценоразпис (*m.*) [*Bul.*] price list.

центровка (*f.*) [*Russ.*] zinc.

церковная марка (*f.*) [*Russ.*] church token; communion token[q.v.].

цинк (*m.*) [*Serb.*] zinc.

црвен [*Serb.*] red.

црн [*Serb.*] black.

црна берза (*f.*) [*Serb.*] black market.

цянь [*Russ.*] cash (Chinese coin).

Ч   ч

частный сертификат (*m.*) [*Russ.*] scrip.

часть (*f.*) [*Russ.*] fraction.

червонец (*m.*) [*Russ.*] chervonetz.

чест [*Serb.*] common.

чек (*m.*) [*Bul., Serb., Russ.*] check, cheque.

чеканка (*f.*) [*Russ.*] coinage.

чеканить (*v.*) [*Russ.*] to coin, to strike.

челик (*m.*) [*Serb.*] steel.

чёрный [*Russ.*] black.

чёрный рынок (*m.*) [*Russ.*] black market.

четверть (*f.*) [*Russ.*] fourth (the fraction), quarter.

четвртаст (*adj.*) [*Serb.*] square.

четвртина (*f.*) [*Serb.*] fourth (the fraction), quarter.

четири [*Bul., Serb.*] four.

четрдесет [*Serb.*] forty.

четыре [*Russ.*] four.

чистоћа метала (*f.*) [*Serb.*] fineness; fine (purity of metal).

чистый [*Russ.*] fineness; fine (purity of metal).

чужда валута (*f.*) [*Bul.*] foreign currency.

Ш   ш

Швајцарска [*Serb.*] Switzerland.

Шведска [*Serb.*] Sweden.

Швейцария [*Russ.*] Switzerland.

Швеция [*Russ.*] Sweden.

шездесет [*Serb.*] sixty.

шёлковая нить [*Russ.*] silk thread.

шест [*Serb.*] six.

шесть [*Russ.*] six.
штамп (*m.*) [*Russ.*] (coinage) die.
штампање поврх текста [*Serb.*] overprint.
штампати (*v.*) [*Serb.*] to print.
штамповочный брак (*m.*) [*Russ.*] a mis-strike.
штемпельный блеск [*Russ.*] mint luster; *fleur de coin*.

Э э

экземпляр [*Russ.*] specimen.
электр (*m.*); **электрум** (*m.*) [*Russ.*] electrum, a naturally-found alloy containing approximately three parts gold to one part silver from which the world's earliest coins were struck (staters of Asia Minor, ca. 620-600 B.C.).
электротипия (*f.*) [*Russ.*] electrotype.

Ю ю

Югославия [*Russ.*] Yugoslavia, Jugoslavia.
Южная Африка [*Russ.*] South Africa.
юстировка (*f.*) [*Russ.*] adjustment (the filing away of excessive metal on an overweight planchet or coin); adjustment mark.

Я я

язык (*m.*) [*Russ.*] language.
Япония [*Russ.*] Japan.

Hebrew Alphabet

Unlike European languages, Hebrew reads from right to left. In order to accommodate the natural flow of the Hebrew language, columns are snaked from right to left and pages turn in reverse order from that of English. But to satisfy the requirements of a book intended for English speakers, pages are numbered in accordance with English usage. Hence, this section begins on page 345 and ends on page 340.

The letters of the Hebrew alphabet are consonants while the vowels appear in the form of diacritical marks. In everyday usage, Hebrew words do not normally show vowel points. Inscriptions on coins, banknotes, and medals are almost always written exclusively in consonants. For reference purposes, Hebrew words in this glossary are shown in their complete form, including vowels.

Although English verbs are given in their infinitive form (as they are throughout this dictionary), Hebrew verbs are in the plene form, i.e., third person male singular past tense which corresponds to the three-letter root of the word.

Hebrew grammar often requires that letters be added to the beginnings of words, such as to infinitives which always start with the letter ל. If a particular word in Hebrew cannot be found under its first letter, it may be found under its second letter, although usually with some slight modification in spelling.

ר

top (m.) רֹאשׁ
square (adj.) רָבוּעַ
fourth (the fraction), quarter (m.) רֶבַע
Russia (f.) רוּסְיָה
acquisition (f.) רְכִישָׁה
republic (f.) רֶפּוּבְּלִיקָה
People's Republic of China (P.R.C.) (f.) רֶפּוּבְּלִיקָה הָעֲמָמִית שֶׁל סִין
Republic of China (Taiwan) (f.) רֶפּוּבְּלִיקָה שֶׁל סִין
official רִשְׁמִי

ש

(mathematical) fraction (m.) שֶׁבֶר
seven שִׁבְעָה
seventy שִׁבְעִים
Sweden (f.) שְׁוֶדְיָה
Switzerland (f.) שְׁוַיְץ
rim שׁוּלַיִם
black market (m.) שׁוּק שָׁחוֹר
black שָׁחוֹר
certificate (m.) שְׁטָר
banknote (m.) שְׁטַר כֶּסֶף
(commercial) bond (m.) שְׁטַר עֵרֶךְ
propaganda note (m.) שְׁטַר תַּעֲמוּלָה
paper money שִׁטְרֵי כֶּסֶף
common שָׁכִיחַ
to duplicate (v.) שִׁכְפֵּל
uncirculated שֶׁלֹּא בַּמַּחֲזוֹר
not issued שֶׁלֹּא יָצָא לְהַנְפָּקָה
mis-struck שֶׁלֹּא נִטְבַּע כַּהֲלָכָה
unpublished (a coin or banknote not listed in any book or catalogue). שֶׁלֹּא פּוּרְסַם
peace (m.) שָׁלוֹם
sovereign (m.) שַׁלִּיט
third (the fraction) (m.) שְׁלִישׁ
complete שָׁלֵם
three שְׁלֹשָׁה
thirty שְׁלֹשִׁים
left (direction or position) שְׂמֹאל
eight שְׁמוֹנָה
eighty שְׁמוֹנִים
"Hear, O Israel..." (the first line of the essential Jewish creed, *Deut. 6:4*). שְׁמַע יִשְׂרָאֵל
year (f.) שָׁנָה
to alter (a date, mintmark, or coinage die, either for legal or fraudulent reasons). (v.) שִׁנָּה
alteration (of a date, mintmark, coinage die, etc.). (m.) שִׁנּוּי
altered date (m.) שִׁנּוּי תַּאֲרִיךְ
badly struck שֶׁנִּטְבַּע בְּאֹפֶן לָקוּי
two שְׁנַיִם
exchange rate (m.) שַׁעַר הַחֲלִיפִין
reproduction (m.) שַׁעְתּוּק
language (f.) שָׂפָה
shekel, sheqel (ancient Judaic coin; also a coin of modern Israel). שֶׁקֶל
finance minister (m.) שַׂר הָאוֹצָר
a scratch (f.) שְׂרִיטָה
six שִׁשָּׁה
sixty שִׁשִּׁים

ת

date (m.) תַּאֲרִיךְ
Torah תּוֹרָה
bottom (f.) תַּחְתִּית
design (m.) תֶּכֶן
exhibition (f.) תַּעֲרוּכָה
monetary reform תִּקּוּן כַּסְפִּי
fee (m.) תַּשְׁלוּם
prepayment (m.) תַּשְׁלוּם מֵרֹאשׁ
nine תִּשְׁעָה
ninety תִּשְׁעִים

[ס *continued from page 342*]

domestic פְּנִים

peso (Spanish-American currency) (m.) פֶּסוֹ

peseta (monetary unit of Spain) (f.) פֶּסֵטָה

deposit (of funds) (m.) פִּקְדוֹן

deposit required פִּקְדוֹן דָרוּשׁ

pruta, prutah (unit of Israeli money) פְּרוּטָה

(auction) lot (m.) פָּרִיט

franc (French unit of currency) (m.) פְרַנְק

steel engraving (m.) פִּתּוּחַ פְּלָדָה

to trade (v.) סָחַר

mintmark (m.) סִימָן הַמַּטְבֵּעָה

adjustment mark (m.) סִימָן הַתְאָמָה

watermark (m.) סִימָן מֵימִי

motto (f.) סִיסְמָה

amount (m.) סְכוּם

symbol (m.) סֵמֶל

centimeter, centimetre (m.) סֶנְטִימֶטֶר

Spain (f.) סְפָרַד

צ

color, colour (m.) צֶבַע

front (m.) צַד הַקִּדְמִי

reverse (m.) צַד הַשֵּׁנִי

yellow צָהֹב

incuse צוּרָה מָטְבַּעַת

to cast (e.g., a coin or medal) (v.) צָקַת

France (f.) צָרְפַת

ע

Hebrew (language) עִבְרִית

round עָגֹל

laureate עָטוּר דַפְנָה

military decoration (m.) עִטּוּר צְבָאִי

on the back עַל הַגַּב

Saudi Arabia (f.) עֲרָב הַסַּעוּדִית

value (m.) עֵרֶךְ

intrinsic value (m.) עֵרֶךְ בְּשׁוּק

denomination; face value (m.) עֵרֶךְ נָקוּב

catalogue value (m.) עֵרֶךְ קָטָלוֹגִי

tenth (the fraction) (f.) עֲשִׂירִית

ten עֲשָׂרָה

twenty עֶשְׂרִים

ancient עַתִּיק

antiquity (f.) עַתִּיקוּת

a copy, reproduction (m.) עֹתֶק

ק

receipt (f.) קַבָּלָה

Colombia (f.) קוֹלוֹמְבִּיָה

buyer (m.) קוֹנֶה

catalog, catalogue (m.) קָטָלוֹג

auction catalogue (m.) קָטָלוֹג מְכִירָה פֻּמְבִּית

small קָטָן

diameter (m.) קֹטֶר

emperor (m.) קֵיסָר

a crease, fold (as in a banknote) (m.) קֶמֶט; קֶפֶל (m.)

Canada (f.) קַנַדָה

to buy (v.) קָנָה

to fold (v.) קָפַל

edge (of a coin or medal) (m.) קָצֶה

abbreviation (m.) קִצוּר

cruzeiro (Brazilian currency) (m.) קְרוּזֵרוֹ

torn קָרוּעַ

a tear (in a banknote or bond) (m.) קֶרַע

to tear (v.) קָרַע

פ

damaged פָּגוּם

Portugal (f.) פּורטוּגַל

devaluation (m.) פְּחוּת

Finland (f.) פִינְלַנְד

steel (f.) פְּלָדָה

platinum (f.) פְּלָטִינָה

brass (the alloy) (m.) פְּלִיז

obverse (m.) פְּנֵי מַטְבֵּעַ

king (m.) מֶלֶךְ
queen (f.) מַלְכָּה
United Kingdom (U.K.) (f.) מַמְלָכָה הַמְאֻחֶדֶת
menorah מְנוֹרָה
tax (m.) מַס
number (m.) מִסְפָּר
serial number (m.) מִסְפָּר סִדּוּרִי
monetary system (f.) מַעֲרֶכֶת הַכְּסָפִים
excellent מְצֻיָּן
accolated, conjoined, jugate (two or more מְצֻמָּד effigies overlapped and facing in the same direction on a coin, medal, or banknote).
original מְקוֹרִי
Mexico (f.) מֶקְסִיקוֹ
mark (German unit of currency) (m.) מַרְק
perfect, flawless מֻשְׁלָם
weight (m.) מִשְׁקָל
metal (f.) מַתֶּכֶת
repaired מְתֻקָּן

נ

fine (grade or condition) נָאֶה
rare, scarce נָדִיר
rarity (f.) נְדִירוּת
numismatic (adj.) נוּמִיסְמָטִי
numismatics (f.) נוּמִיסְמָטִיקָה
Norway (f.) נוֹרְבֶגְיָה
copper (f.) נְחֹשֶׁת
New Zealand (f.) נְיוּ זִילַנְד
nickel (the metal) (m.) נִיקֶל
paper (m.) נְיָר
president (m.) נָשִׂיא
eagle (m.) נֶשֶׁר
alloy (of metals) (m.) נֶתֶךְ

ס

die break (m.) סֶדֶק בְּמַטְבֵּעַ
series (f.) סִדְרָה

---

lithography (f.) לִיתוֹגְרַפְיָה
on approval לְנִסָּיוֹן
defective לָקוּי
a defect (m.) לִקּוּי

מ

hundred מֵאָה
Golda Meir מֵאִיר, גּוֹלְדָה
hundredth (the fraction) (f.) מֵאִית
variety (m.) מִבְחָר
Shield of David (m.) מָגֵן דָּוִד
Red Shield of David (insignia of (m.) מָגֵן דָּוִד אָדֹם the Israeli Chapter of International Red Cross).
medal (f.) מֶדַלְיָה
grade, condition (f.) מַדְרֵגָה
seller (m.) מוֹכֵר
pedigree (list of all previous and (m.) מוֹצָא present owners of a collectible item).
a counterfeit (m.) מְזֻיָּף
cash (ready money) (m.) מְזֻמָּן
obsolete מָחוּץ לְמַחֲזוֹר
circulation (m.) מַחֲזוֹר
price (m.) מְחִיר
price list (m.) מְחִירוֹן
coin; currency (m.) מַטְבֵּעַ
foreign currency (m.) מַטְבֵּעַ זָר
milled coin (m.) מַטְבֵּעַ מְכֻרְסָם
hammered coin (m.) מַטְבֵּעַ מְעֻצָּב בַּפַּטִּישׁ
clad coinage (m.) מַטְבֵּעַ תְּלַת שִׁכְבָתִי
mint (f.) מִטְבָּעָה
obsidional מַטְבְּעוֹת חֵרוּם
(coinage) die (f.) מַטְבַּעַת
ingot (m.) מְטִיל מַתֶּכֶת
classification (m.) מִיּוּן
mil (unit of Israeli currency) מִיל
millimeter, millimetre (m.) מִילִימֶטֶר
to classify (v.) מִיֵּן
(coinage) press (m.) מַכְבֵּשׁ מַטְבְּעוֹת
mail bid sale מְכִירָה פּוּמְבִּית דֶּרֶךְ הַצָּעוֹת נִשְׁלָחוֹת בְּדוֹאַר
auction; auction sale (f.) מְכִירָה פֻּמְבִּית
to sell (v.) מָכַר
million מִילְיוֹן
rectangular מַלְבֵּנִי

unique   יָחִיד בְּמִינוֹ
monetary unit (*f.*)   יְחִידָה כַּסְפִּית
to attribute (*v.*)   יִחֵס
right (direction or position)   יָמִין
Japan (*f.*)   יַפָּן
green   יָרֹק
old   יָשָׁן
Israel (*f.*)   יִשְׂרָאֵל

כ

dark   כֵּהֶה
star (*m.*)   כּוֹכָב
Western Wall (usually referred by   כּוֹתֶל הַמַּעֲרָבִי
gentiles as the *Wailing Wall*).
blue   כָּחֹל
almost   כִּמְעַט
money; silver (*m.*)   כֶּסֶף
emergency currency (*m.*)   כֶּסֶף חֵרוּם
fiat money (paper money or   (*m.*) כֶּסֶף מֻכְרָז
token coinage not redeemable in gold or silver).
monetary   כַּסְפִּי
duplicate (*adj.*)   כָּפוּל
a duplicate (*m.*)   כֶּפֶל
chromium (*m.*)   כְּרוֹם
credit card (*m.*)   כַּרְטִיס אַשְׁרַאי
credit cards accepted   כַּרְטִיסֵי אַשְׁרַאי מִתְקַבְּלִים
tarnish; stain (*m.*)   כֶּתֶם
crown (headpiece or large silver coin) (*m.*)   כֶּתֶר

ל

no unlimited bids   לֹא מִתְקַבְּלוֹת הַצָּעוֹת בִּלְתִּי מֻגְבָּלוֹת
accepted (at an auction or mail bid sale).
unofficial   לֹא-רִשְׁמִי
nationality (*m.*)   לְאוֹם
national   לְאֻמִּי
white   לָבָן
planchet (*f.*)   לוּחִית
pound (unit of weight) (*f.*)   לִטְרָה
pound Sterling (£) (*f.*)   לִירָה שְׁטֶרְלִינְג

[ח *continued from page 344*]

hole (*m.*)   חוֹר
seal (device with a cut or raised (*m.*)   חוֹתָם
emblem used to certify a signature or
authenticate a document, or a medallion of this
type that can be pressed into wax to give
official validity to envelopes or documents).
palindrome ("radar" serial (*f.*)   חִידַת רָצוֹא וָשׁוֹב
number on banknotes, i.e., a number that reads
the same forwards or backwards).
five   חֲמִשָּׁה
fifty   חֲמִשִּׁים
Hanukkah   חֲנוּכָּה
half (*adj.*)   חֲצִי
half (the fraction) (*m.*)   חֲצִי
imitation (*m.*)   חִקּוּי
engraved   חָרוּת
irregular   חָרִיג
account (financial or transactional) (*m.*)   חֶשְׁבּוֹן
signature (*f.*)   חֲתִימָה

ט

restrike (a modern re-issuance (*f.*)   טְבִיעָה מְחֻדָּשׁ
of a coin or medal).
piéfort, piedfort (*f.*)   טְבִיעָה מְיֻחֶדֶת
a mis-strike (*f.*)   טְבִיעָה שֶׁלֹּא כַּהֲלָכָה
fingerprint (*f.*)   טְבִיעַת אֶצְבַּע
coinage (*f.*)   טְבִיעַת מַטְבְּעוֹת
fineness, fine (re: purity of metal)   טָהוֹר
good (generic grade or condition of a coin   טוֹב
or banknote).
order form (*m.*)   טוֹפֶס הַזְמָנָה
bid sheet (*m.*)   טוֹפֶס הַצָּעָה
error (*f.*)   טָעוּת

י

Yugoslavia, Jugoslavia (*f.*)   יוּגוֹסְלַבְיָה
Greece (*f.*)   יָוָן
attribution (the complete identi- (*m.*)   יִחוּס
fication of a coin or banknote).

ג

large גָּדוֹל
roll (of coins) (m.) גָּלִיל
Germany (f.) גֶּרְמַנְיָה
East Germany (D.D.R.) (f.) גֶּרְמַנְיָה הַמִּזְרָחִית
West Germany (B.R.D.) (f.) גֶּרְמַנְיָה הַמַּעֲרָבִית

ד

pattern (m.) דֶּגֶם
bilingual דּוּ-לְשׁוֹנִי
specimen (f.) דּוּגְמָא
dollar ($) (m.) דּוֹלָר
ink (m./f.) דְּיוֹ
portrait (m.) דְּיוֹקָן
effigy (f.) דְּמוּת
Denmark (f.) דַּנְמַרְק
intaglio; photogravure (m.) דְּפוּס שֶׁקַע
to grade (v.) דֵּרַג
South Africa (f.) דְּרוֹם אַפְרִיקָה
liberty (m.) דְּרוֹר

ה

to print (v.) הִדְפִּיס
overprint (m.) הֶדְפֵּס מֵעַל
Holland, The Netherlands (f.) הוֹלַנְד
Hong Kong (f.) הוֹנְג-קוֹנְג
demonetization (f.) הוֹצָאָה מִתּוֹקֶף
commemorative issue הוֹצָאַת זִכָּרוֹן
scrip (privately-issued tokens הוֹצָאַת כֶּסֶף פְּרָטִית
or other substitute for circulating currency; the
term sometimes refers to emergency money).
check, cheque (f.) הַמְחָאָה
money order (f.) הַמְחָאַת כֶּסֶף
to issue (v.) הַנְפִּיק
an issue, issuance הַנְפָּקָה
to copy (v.) הַעְתֵּק

---

electrotype (m.) הֶעְתֵּק אֶלֶקְטְרוֹטִיפִּי
seigniorage הֶפְרֵשׁ הָעֵרֶךְ (שֶׁל מַטְבֵּעַ)
to exhibit (v.) הִצִּיג
to offer (v.) הִצִּיעַ
to bid (at an auction or at a mail (v.) הִצִּיעַ מְחִיר
bid sale).
an offer (f.) הַצָּעָה
suggested bid (f.) הַצָּעָה מֻצַעַת
protective reserve bid (f.) הַצָּעָה שְׁמוּרָה מוּגֶנֶת
(auction) bid (f.) הַצָּעַת מְחִיר
minimum bid (f.) הַצָּעַת מְחִיר מִינִימוּם
Benjamin (Theodor) Zeev Herzl הֶרְצֵל, בִּנְיָמִין זְאֵב
cabinet friction (f.) הִתְחַכְּכוּת בַּתֵּיבָה
anti-counterfeiting device (m.) הֶתְקֵן כְּנֶגֶד זִיּוּף

ו

Wales (f.) וֵיילְס
Chaim Weizmann וַיצְמַן, חַיִּים
Venezuela (f.) וֶנֶצוּאֶלָה

ז

gold (m.) זָהָב
a fake, forgery (m.) זִיּוּף
to counterfeit (v.) זִיֵּף
counterfeiter (m.) זַיְפָן
magnifying glass (f.) זְכוּכִית מַגְדֶּלֶת
foreign זָר

ח

centennial, centenary (f.) חֲגִיגַת שְׁנַת הַמֵּאָה
uniface חַד-פָּנִים
new חָדָשׁ
silk thread חוּט מֶשִׁי
brown חוּם

Hebrew Alphabet

All words in Modern Hebrew

This section is formatted in accordance with accepted Hebrew usage. Pages and columns flow from right to left and all Hebrew entries are right-justified exactly as they are found in standard Israeli dictionaries.

See page 339 for additional information and explanations.

art (f.) אָמָנוּת
authentic, genuine; real אֲמִתִּי
England (f.) אַנְגְלִיָה
token (m.) אַסִימוֹן
collection (m.) אֹסֶף
to collect (v.) אָסַף
collector (m.) אַסְפָן
numismatist; coin collector (m.) אַסְפָן מַטְבְּעוֹת
pope (of the Roman Catholic Church) (m.) אַפִּיפְיוֹר
zero אֶפֶס
exergue אֶקְסֶרְג
four אַרְבָּעָה
forty אַרְבָּעִים
Argentina (f.) אַרְגֶנְטִינָה
bronze (the alloy) (m.) אָרָד
United States of America (U.S.A.) (f.) אַרְצוֹת הַבְּרִית
credit (m.) אַשְׁרַאי

א

zinc (m.) אָבָץ
agora, agorah (Israeli unit of currency) אֲגוֹרָה
bead (a raised dot on the surface of a (m.) אֶגֶל
coin, medal, or token).
red אָדֹם
ounce (of weight) (f.) אוּנְקִיָה
Austria (f.) אוֹסְטְרִיָה
Australia (f.) אוֹסְטְרַלִיָה
treasure (m.) אוֹצָר
one (f.adj.) אַחַת; (m.adj.) אֶחָד
Italy (f.) אִיטַלְיָה
inch (unit of measure equal to 2.54 cm.) (m.) אִינְץ'
Albert Einstein אַינְשְׁטַיִן, אַלְבֶּרְט
(Republic of) Ireland (f.) אִירְלַנְד
Northern Ireland (f.) אִירְלַנְד הַצְפוֹנִית
corrosion (m.) אִכּוּל
God (in the Judaic-Christian sense) (m.) אֵל
album (m.) אַלְבּוֹם
thousand (m.) אֶלֶף
electrum, a naturally-found alloy (m.) אֶלֶקְטְרוּם
containing approximately three parts gold to
one part silver from which the world's earliest
coins were struck (staters of Asia Minor, ca.
620-600 B.C.E.).

ב

tin (the metal) (m.) בְּדִיל
encased postage stamp (type (m.) בּוּל בְּצוּרַת נַרְתִּיק
of token used in the United States in the 1860s
as a form of circulating currency).
cut cancellation (m.) בִּטוּל בְּחִתּוּךְ
punch cancellation (m.) בִּטוּל בְּנִקּוּב
international בֵּין-לְאֻמִי
wear (degree of visible cir- (f.) בְּלִיָה ;(m.) בְּלַאי
culation on a coin).
Belgium (f.) בֶּלְגִיָה
unknown (not listed in any book or בִּלְתִּי יָדוּעַ
catalogue).
unattributed בִּלְתִּי מְזֹוהֶה
incomplete בִּלְתִּי מֻשְׁלָם
circulated בַּמַחֲזוֹר
David Ben-Gurion בֶּן גוּרְיוֹן, דָוִד
bank (m.) בַּנְק
holed בַּעַל-חוֹר
valuable בַּעַל-עֶרֶךְ
brockage בְּרוֹקֵיגִ'
Brazil (f.) בְּרָזִיל
iron (the metal) (m.) בַּרְזֶל
Great Britain (f.) בְּרִיטַנְיָה הַגְּדוֹלָה
Soviet Union (U.S.S.R.) (f.) בְּרִית הַמוֹעָצוֹת

Symbols

↑↑ Indicator of *medal struck*, i.e., the obverse and reverse sides are aligned with the top of both sides being on the same end of the coin. To turn the coin over so that the reverse is right side up, the coin must be rotated on an axis running north and south. Britain and British Commonwealth countries currently use this alignment.

↑↓ Indicator of *coin struck*, i.e., the obverse and reverse sides are aligned with the top of one side corresponding to the bottom of the other. To turn the coin over so that the reverse is right side up, the coin must be rotated on an axis running east and west. Current U.S. coins are struck with this alignment.

←→ When placed between two photos or line drawings, these arrows (or one continuous two-headed arrow) indicate that the illustrations are the obverse and reverse of the same coin or medal. This symbol is occasionally seen in current sales and auction catalogues, but it was quite common in books published in the nineteenth and early twentieth centuries.

$ 1. *dollar*, unit of currency of the U.S.A., Canada, Australia, New Zealand, and many other countries (see *dollar* for the entire list).
   2. *peso*, monetary unit of Mexico and elsewhere, although not all countries with the peso as its unit of currency use this symbol. Historically, there have been slight differences between the symbols for the dollar and for the peso, but the advent of the typewriter and now the word processor have ultimately rendered the symbols identical.

¢ *cent*, the minor monetary unit of the United States and Canada equal to the hundredth part of a dollar.

£ *pound Sterling*, the British unit of currency.

Ø *Diameter* of a coin or medal, usually given in millimeters.

number (catalogue or serial).

R$_x$ Symbol seen in numismatic books and catalogues indicating what is to be found on the reverse side of the described piece. Sometimes abbreviated *rev*.

☧ *Christogram*[q.v.], an ancient symbol of Christianity formed by the superimposition of the Greek letters χ (*chi*) and P (*rho*), the first two letters in the Greek word for *Christ*.

⊞ *mill-sail*[q.v.] pattern. Swastika-like design found in the form of an incuse punch on the reverse of many early Greek stater coins.

⚜ *fleur-de-lis*. A type of heraldic flower which does not exist in nature even though it looks somewhat like an iris. It has been a symbol of royalty since ancient times. During the Middle Ages the *lis* was emblematic of illumination and of religious faith. It was popular among Christian monarchs because its central flower rises straight up from a horizontal connector creating something that resembles a cross.

⌇ *fasces*. Bundle of rods, usually bound by a leather cord or strap, and topped with an ax blade. It was an ancient Roman symbol of strength and authority. Among the coins exhibiting the fasces are the U.S. Mercury (Winged Liberty) Dimes of 1916-1945 and some of the 2 lira Italian coins issued by Benito Mussolini in the 1920s.

♔ *monogram*. Stylized initials of the monarch, usually crowned. Designer's initials and mintmarks can be stylized as a monogram.

Multi-Language Matrix

The Multi-Language Matrix provides translations of 360 numismatically-useful terms into twenty modern languages. Included are many business and general words likely to be found in coin catalogues and price lists, as well as the technical terminology unique to the field.

Languages are not absolute. Regional differences within the same language do exist, and not every possible translation of an English word can be incorporated into a matrix. For that reason, the translators have made every effort to include only the most universal choices when several possible translations could be given. If a translation is omitted, either the term does not exist in that language or there was no consensus among the experts.

Specifics:

—Verbs are given in their infinitive form in all languages except Hebrew. Hebrew verbs are in the *plene* form, third person singular past tense which corresponds to the three-letter root of the word.

—For gender languages (French, Russian, Spanish, etc.), adjectives are normally given in their masculine singular form.

—Words on this list are only capitalized if they are *always* capitalized, such as the names of countries and all German nouns.

—The form of Chinese used here is Simplified Character, the preferred version in the P.R.C.

—*Cash* as it appears in this matrix means "ready money" and is not a reference to the small Oriental coin of the same name.

—The term *clad coinage* has many strange translations because it is a new concept used only in the United States and few other places. Many of the foreign terms translate literally to *sandwich coin*, *layer cake coin*, or the like.

—The English word *proof* on this list refers to the special striking of coins. The foreign translations may or may not be applicable to the term as it is used for paper money.

ENGLISH	GERMAN	FRENCH
abbreviation	Abkürzung (f.)	abréviation (f.)
accolated	vereint	accolé
account (financial or transactional)	Konto (n.)	compte (m.)
acquisition	Erwerbung (f.)	acquisition (f.)
adjustment mark	Eichmarkierung (f.); Justierspur (f.)	marque d'ajustage
album	Album (n.)	album (m.)
alloy (of metals)	Legierung (f.)	alliage (m.)
alter (verb)	umändern	retoucher; altérer; modifier
alteration	Umänderung (f.)	modification (f.); retouche (f.)
altered date	abgeändertes Datum (n.)	date changée (f.)
amount	Betrag (m.)	montant (m.)
ancient	antik	ancien
anti-counterfeiting device	Fälschungsschutz (m.)	moyen pour contrer la contrefaçon
antiquity	Antiquität (f.)	antiquité (f.)
Argentina	Argentinien	Argentine
art	Kunst (f.)	art (m.)
attribute (verb)	zuschreiben; kennzeichnen	attribuer; imputer
attribution	Zuschreibung (f.); Kennzeichnung (f.)	attribution (f.); imputation (f.)
auction	Auktion (f.); Versteigerung (f.)	vente aux enchères; á l'encan
auction catalogue	Auktionskatalog (m.)	catalogue de vente aux enchères
auction sale	Auktionsverkauf (m.)	vente aux enchères
Australia	Australien	Australie
Austria	Österreich	Autriche
authentic	authentisch; echt	authentique
badly struck	schwach ausgeprägt; schlechte Prägung	mal frappé
bank (financial institution)	Bank (f.)	banque (f.)
banknote	Banknote (f.)	billet de banque (m.)
Belgium	Belgien	Belgique
bid (noun: auction bid)	Gebot (n.)	enchère (f.); offre (f.); mise (f.)
bid (verb)	bieten	faire une offre; faire une mise
bid sheet	Gebot (n.)	feuille se soumission des offres
bilingual	zweisprachig	bilingue
black	schwarz	noir
black market	Schwarzmarkt (m.)	marché noir (m.)
blue	blau	bleu
bond (commercial)	Wertpapier (n.)	valeurs (f.pl.)

PORTUGUESE	ITALIAN	SPANISH
abreviatura (*f.*)	abbreviazione (*f.*)	abreviatura (*f.*)
conjugado; acolado	accollato	acolado
conta (*f.*)	conto (*m.*)	cuenta (*f.*)
aquisição (*f.*)	acquisto (*m.*)	adquisición (*f.*)
marca de ajuste	segno di rifilatura (*m.*); segno di riporto (*m.*)	marca de ajuste
álbum (*m.*)	album (*m.*)	álbum (*m.*)
liga (*f.*)	lega (*f.*)	aleación (*f.*)
alterar	alterare	alterar
alteração (*f.*)	alterazione (*f.*)	alteración (*f.*)
data falsificada (*f.*)	data alterata (*f.*)	fecha alterada (*f.*); fecha retocada (*f.*)
soma (*f.*)	somma (*f.*)	cantidad (*f.*); suma (*f.*)
antigo	antico	antiguo
invento contra falsificação	dispositivo antifalsificazione (*m.*)	dispositivo de antifalsificación
antiguidade (*f.*)	antichità (*f.*)	antigüedad (*f.*)
Argentina	Argentina	Argentina
arte (*f.*)	arte (*f.*)	arte (*m./f.*)
atribuir	attribuire	atribuir
atribuição (*f.*)	attribuzione (*f.*)	atribución (*f.*)
hasta pública (*f.*); leilão (*f.*)	asta (*f.*)	subasta (*f.*)
catálogo de leilão	catalogo d'asta (*m.*)	catálogo de subasta
venda em leilão	vendita all'asta (*f.*)	venta en subasta (*f.*)
Austrália	Australia	Australia
Austria	Austria	Austria
autêntico	autentico	auténtico
mal cunhado	mal battuto; mal stampato	mal acuñado
banco (*m.*)	banca (*f.*)	banco (*m.*)
cédula (*f.*); nota (*f.*)	banconota (*f.*)	billete de banco
Bélgica	Belgio	Bélgica
lanço (*m.*); oferta (*f.*)	offerta (ad un'asta) (*f.*)	oferta (*f.*); licitación (*f.*); puja (*f.*)
fazer uma oferta; lançar	fare un'offerta	ofrecer; licitar
impresso de oferta	foglio d'offerta; modulo di offerta	hoja de licitación (*f.*); hoja de oferta (*f.*)
bilíngüe	bilingue	bilingüe
preto	nero	negro
mercado negro (*m.*)	mercato nero (*m.*)	mercado negro (*m.*)
azul	blu	azul
título (*m.*); vale (*m.*)	titolo (*m.*)	bono (*m.*); obligación (*f.*); vínculo (*m.*)

ENGLISH	GERMAN	FRENCH
bottom	unten	bas (*m.*)
brass (the alloy)	Messing (*n.*)	laiton (*m.*)
Brazil	Brasilien	Brésil
brockage	Brockageprägung	pièce à motif concave
bronze (the alloy)	Bronze (*f.*)	bronze (*m.*)
brown	braun	brun
buy (*verb*)	kaufen	acheter
buyer	Käufer (*m.*)	acheteur (*m.*)
cabinet friction	Isolierreibung (*f.*)	marques de frottement
Canada	Kanada	Canada
cash (ready money)	Bargeld (*n.*)	espèces (*f.pl.*)
cast (*verb*)	gießen	couler
catalog; catalogue	Katalog (*m.*)	catalogue (*m.*)
catalogue value	Katalogwert (*m.*)	valeur de catalogue
centennial; centenary	Hundertjahrfeier (*f.*)	centenaire (*m.*)
centimeter; centimetre	Zentimeter (*m.*)	centimètre (*m.*)
certificate	Zertifikat (*n.*)	certificat (*m.*)
check; cheque	Scheck (*m.*)	chèque (*m.*)
China	China	Chine
chromium	Chrom (*n.*)	chrome
circulated	zirkuliert	circulé
circulation	Umlauf (*m.*)	circulation (*f.*)
clad coinage	Mehrschichtgepräge (*n.pl.*)	pièce à métal emrobé
classification	Klassifikation (*f.*)	classement (*m.*)
classify (*verb*)	klassifizieren	classer
coin	Münze (*f.*)	pièce de monnaie (*f.*)
coinage	Prägung (*f.*); Prägungen (*f.pl.*)	monnayage (*m.*)
collect (*verb*)	sammeln	collectionner
collection	Sammlung (*f.*)	collection (*f.*)
collector	Sammler (*m.*)	collectionneur (*m.*)
Colombia	Kolumbien	Colombie
color; colour	Farbe (*f.*)	couleur (*f.*)
commemorative (*adjective*)	Gedenk-	commémoratif
common	gewöhnlich	courant
complete	vollständig	complet
conjoined	vereint	conjugué; accolé

PORTUGUESE	ITALIAN	SPANISH
fundo (*m.*); base (*f.*)	basso (*m.*)	parte inferior (*f.*); fondo (*m.*)
latão (*m.*)	ottone	latón (*m.*); bronce amarillo (*m.*)
Brasil	Brasile	Brasil
brockage	inclusione (*f.*)	incusa (*f.*)
bronze (*m.*)	bronzo (*m.*)	bronce (*m.*)
castanho; marrom	marrone	marrón; moreno; pardo
comprar	comprare	comprar
comprador (*m.*)	compratore (*m.*)	comprador (*m.*)
fricção de arrumação	usura da contenitore (*f.*)	deterioro por contacto (*m.*)
Canadá	Canada	Canadá
cash; dinheiro disponível (*m.*)	contante (*m.*)	dinero contante y sonante (*m.*)
fundir; amoedar por fundição	coniare a fusione	fundir
catálogo (*m.*)	catalogo (*m.*)	catálogo (*m.*)
valor de catálogo	valore di catalogo (*m.*)	valor de catálogo (*m.*)
centenário (*m.*)	centenario (*m.*)	centenario (*m.*)
centímetro (*m.*)	centimetro (*m.*)	centímetro (*m.*)
certificado (*m.*)	titolo (*m.*); certificato (*m.*)	certificado (*m.*)
cheque (*m.*)	assegno (*m.*)	cheque (*m.*); talón (*m.*)
China	Cina	China
crómio (*m.*)	cromo (*m.*)	cromo (*m.*)
circulado	circolato	circulado
circulação (*f.*)	circolazione (*f.*)	circulación (*f.*)
amoedação «sanduíche» (*f.*)	multistrato	moneda forrada (*f.*); moneda chapada (*f.*)
classificação (*f.*)	classificazione (*f.*)	clasificación (*f.*)
classificar	classificare	clasificar
moeda (*f.*)	moneta (*f.*)	moneda (*f.*)
cunhagem (*f.*)	coniatura (*f.*)	acuñación (*f.*)
colecionar	collezionare	coleccionar
monetário (*m.*); coleção (*f.*)	collezione (*f.*)	colección (*f.*)
colecionador (*m.*)	collezionista (*m./f.*)	coleccionista (*m./f.*)
Colômbia	Colombia	Colombia
cor (*f.*)	colore (*m.*)	color (*m.*)
comemorativo	commemorativo	conmemorativo
comum; ordinário	comune	común
completo	completo	completo
conjugado; acolado	accollato	acolado

ENGLISH	GERMAN	FRENCH
copper (the metal)	Kupfer (n.)	cuivre (m.)
copy (noun)	Kopie (f.); Reproduktion (f.)	exemplaire (m.)
copy (verb)	kopieren; reproduzieren	copier
corrosion	Korrosion (f.)	corrosion (f.)
counterfeit (noun)	Fälschung (f.)	contrefaçon (f.)
counterfeit (verb)	fälschen	contrefaire
counterfeiter	Fälscher (m.)	contrefacteur (m.)
crease (noun)	Falte (f.)	pli (m.)
credit	Kredit (m.)	crédit (m.)
credit card	Kreditkarte (f.)	carte de crédit
credit cards accepted	Kreditkarten akzeptiert	paiements par carte de crédit acceptés
crown (royal headpiece)	Krone (f.)	couronne (f.)
crown (large silver coin)	Krone (f.); Halbtaler (m.)	couronne (f.)
cruzeiro	Cruzeiro (m.)	cruzeiro (m.)
currency	Währung (f.)	monnaie (f.)
damaged	beschädigt	endommagé
dark	dunkel	foncé
date	Datum (n.)	date (f.)
defect	Fehler (m.); Defekt (m.)	défaut (m.)
defective	mangelhaft	défectueux
demonetization	Demonetisierung (f.)	démonétisation (f.)
Denmark	Dänemark	Danemark
denomination	Nennwert (m.)	dénomination (f.)
deposit (of funds)	Anzahlung (f.)	dépôt (m.)
deposit required	anzahlungspflichtig	un dépôt est requis; un accompte est requis
design (noun)	Entwurf (m.); Zeichnung (f.)	motif (m.)
devaluation	Abwertung (f.)	dévaluation (f.)
diameter	Durchmesser (m.)	diamètre (m.)
die (i.e., coinage die)	Prägestempel (m.); Stempel (m.)	coin (m.)
die break	Stempelriß (m.); Prägestempelsprung (m.)	cassure de coin; bris de coin
dollar	Dollar (m.)	dollar (m.)
duplicate (adjective)	dupliziert	double
duplicate (noun)	Duplikat (n.)	double (m.)
duplicate (verb)	duplizieren	faire un double
eagle	Adler (m.)	aigle (f.)
East Germany (D.D.R.)	Deutsche Demokratische Republik	Allemagne de l'Est

PORTUGUESE	ITALIAN	SPANISH
cobre (*m.*)	rame (*m.*)	cobre (*m.*)
cópia (*f.*)	copia (*f.*)	copia (*f.*); reproducción (*f.*)
copiar	copiare	copiar
corrosão (*f.*)	corrosione (*f.*)	corrosión (*f.*); roedura (*f.*)
contrafação (*f.*); falsificação (*f.*)	contraffazione (*f.*)	falsificación (*f.*); moneda falsa (*f.*)
contrafazer; falsificar	contraffare; falsificare	falsificar; contrahacer
falsificador (*m.*)	falsario (*m.*)	falsificador (*m.*)
ruga (*f.*); prega (*f.*); dobra (*f.*)	piega (*f.*)	agujeta (*f.*); pliegue (*m.*); arruga (*f.*)
crédito (*m.*)	credito (*m.*)	crédito (*m.*)
cartão de crédito	carta di credito	tarjeta de crédito
aceitam-se cartões de crédito	sono accettate le carte di credito	se aceptan tarjetas de crédito
coroa (*f.*)	corona (*f.*)	corona (*f.*)
coroa (*f.*)	corona (*f.*)	corona (*f.*); duro (*m.*)
cruzeiro (*m.*)	cruzeiro (*m.*)	cruzeiro (*m.*)
moeda (*f.*)	valuta (*f.*)	circulación monetaria (*f.*); circulante (*m.*)
danificado; estragado	danneggiato (*m.*)	dañado
escuro	scuro	oscuro
data (*f.*)	data (*f.*)	fecha (*f.*)
defeito (*m.*)	difetto (*m.*)	defecto (*m.*)
defectivo; defeituoso	difettoso	defectuoso
desmonetização (*f.*)	fuoricorso (*m.*)	desmonetización (*f.*)
Dinamarca	Danimarca	Dinamarca
denominação (*f.*)	valore (*m.*)	denominación (*f.*); valor (*m.*)
depósito (*m.*)	caparra (*f.*); anticipo (*m.*)	depósito (*m.*)
requer-se um depósito	deposito obbligatorio (*m.*)	se requiere un depósito
desenho (*m.*)	disegno (*m.*)	diseño (*m.*)
desvalorização (*f.*)	svalutazione (*f.*)	devaluación (*f.*)
diâmetro (*m.*)	diametro (*m.*)	diámetro (*m.*)
cunho (*m.*)	punzone (*m.*)	cuño (*m.*); troquel (*m.*)
fissura de cunho	incrinatura del punzone	rotura de cuño; rotura de troquel
dólar (*m.*)	dollaro (*m.*)	dólar (*m.*)
duplo	doppio	duplicado
duplicado (*m.*); cópia (*f.*); réplica (*f.*)	doppio (*m.*)	duplicado (*m.*)
duplicar	duplicare	duplicar
águia (*f.*)	aquila (*f.*)	águila (*f.*)
Alemanha Oriental	Repubblica Democratica Tedesca	República Democrática de Alemania

ENGLISH	GERMAN	FRENCH
edge	Rand (*m.*)	tranche (*f.*); bord (*m.*)
effigy	Bildnis (*n.*)	effigie (*f.*)
eight	acht	huit
eighty	achtzig	quatre-vingts
electrotype	Galvanotypie (*f.*)	électrotypie (*f.*); galvanoplastie (*f.*)
electrum	Elektrum (*n.*)	électrum (*m.*); or vert (*m.*)
emergency currency	Notgeldwährung (*f.*); Notgeld (*n.*)	numéraire de nécessité
emperor	Kaiser (*m.*)	empereur (*m.*)
England	England	Angleterre
engraved	eingraviert; graviert	gravé
error	Fehler (*m.*); Münzfehler (*m.*)	erreur (*f.*)
excellent	ausgezeichnet	excellent
exchange rate	Wechselkurs (*m.*)	taux de change
exergue	Abschnitt (*n.*)	exergue (*m.*)
exhibit (*verb*)	ausstellen	exposer
exhibition	Ausstellung (*f.*)	exposition (*f.*)
face value	Nennwert (*m.*)	valeur faciale (*f.*)
fake (*noun*)	Fälschung (*f.*)	faux (*m.*)
fee	Gebühr (*f.*)	cotisation (*f.*)
fiat money	ungedecktes Papiergeld (*n.*)	monnaie fiduciaire (*f.*)
fifty	fünfzig	cinquante
finance minister	Finanzminister (*m.*)	ministre des finances
fine (grade or condition)	schön	beau
fine (purity of metal)	rein	fin
Finland	Finnland	Finlande
five	fünf	cinq
fold (*noun*)	Falte (*f.*); Knick (*m.*)	pli (*m.*)
foreign	ausländisch; fremd	étranger
foreign currency	Auslandswährung (*f.*); Fremdwährung (*f.*)	devise étrangère (*f.*)
forgery	Fälschung (*f.*)	contrefaçon (*f.*)
forty	vierzig	quarante
four	vier	quatre
fourth (*noun*)	Viertel (*n.*)	quart (*m.*)
fraction	Bruchteil (*f.*)	fraction (*f.*)
franc	Franc (*m.*)	franc (*m.*)
France	Frankreich	France

PORTUGUESE	ITALIAN	SPANISH
bordo (*m.*)	taglio (*m.*); spigolo (*m.*)	canto (*m.*)
efígie (*f.*)	effige (*f.*)	efigie (*f.*)
oito	otto	ocho
oitenta	ottanta	ochenta
eletrótipo (*m.*)	galvanoplastica (*f.*)	electrotipia (*f.*)
electro (*m.*)	elettro (*m.*)	electro (*m.*)
moeda de emergência	moneta d'emergenza (*f.*)	moneda de necesidad (*f.*)
imperador (*m.*)	imperatore (*m.*)	emperador (*m.*)
Inglaterra	Inghilterra	Inglaterra
gravado	inciso	grabado
erro (*m.*)	errore (*m.*)	error (*m.*); yerro (*m.*)
excelente; esplêndido	eccellente	excelente
taxa de câmbio	tasso di scambio (*m.*)	cambio (*m.*); valor de cambio (*m.*)
exergo (*m.*)	esergo (*m.*)	exergo (*m.*)
exibir	mettere in mostra; esporre	exponer; exhibir; presentar
exibição (*f.*)	mostra (*f.*); esposizione (*f.*)	exposition (*f.*); exhibición (*f.*)
valor facial (*m.*)	valore nominale (*m.*); valore facciale (*m.*)	valor facial (*m.*); valor nominal (*m.*)
falsificação (*f.*)	falso (*m.*)	falso (*m.*); falsificación (*f.*)
taxa (*f.*)	onorario (*m.*)	honorario (*m.*)
moeda fiduciária (*f.*)	carta moneta inconvertibile	moneda fiduciaria (*f.*); moneda fíat (*f.*)
cinqüenta	cinquanta	cincuenta
ministro das finanças	ministro delle finanze	ministro de finanzas
belo	splendido	bien conservada
puro	fino	puro; fino
Finlândia	Finlandia	Finlandia
cinco	cinque	cinco
dobra (*f.*)	piega (*f.*)	pliegue (*m.*); doblez (*m.*)
estrangeiro	straniero	extranjero
moeda estrangeira (*f.*)	valuta straniera (*f.*)	moneda extranjera (*f.*); divisa (*f.*)
contrafração (*f.*); falsificação (*f.*)	falso (*m.*)	falsificación (*f.*)
quarenta	quaranta	cuarenta
quatro	quattro	cuatro
quarto (*m.*)	quarto (*m.*)	cuarto (*m.*)
fração (*f.*)	frazione (*f.*)	fracción (*f.*)
franco (*m.*)	franco (*m.*)	franco (*m.*)
França	Francia	Francia

ENGLISH	GERMAN	FRENCH
front	Vorderseite (f.)	recto (m.)
genuine	echt	véritable
Germany	Deutschland	Allemagne
gold (the metal)	Gold (n.)	or (m.)
good	gut	bon
grade (noun)	Erhaltungsgrad (m.)	état de conservation
grade (verb)	einstufen	classer; évaluer l'état de conservation
Great Britain	Großbritannien	Grande Bretagne
Greece	Griechenland	Grèce
green	grün	vert
half (adjective)	halb	demi
half (noun)	Hälfte (f.)	moitié (f.)
hammered coin	Hammerprägung (f.); gehämmerte Münze	pièce martelée (f.); pièce frappée au marteau
hole	Loch (n.)	trou (m.)
holed	gelocht	troué
Hong Kong	Hongkong	Hong-kong
hundred	hundert	cent
hundredth (noun)	Hundertstel (n.)	centième (m.)
imitation	Imitation (f.)	imitation (f.)
inch	Zoll (m.); Inch (m.)	pouce (m.)
incomplete	unvollständig	incomplet
incuse	vertieft; incus	incuse (f.); en creux
ingot	Barren (m.)	lingot (m.)
ink	Tinte (f.)	encre (f.)
inscription	Beschriftung (f.); Randschrift (f.)	inscription (f.)
intaglio	Heliogravüre (f.)	gravure en creux
international	international	international
intrinsic	intrinsisch	intrinsèque
Ireland	Irland	Irlande
iron (the metal)	Eisen (n.)	fer (m.)
irregular	unregelmäßig	irrégulier
Israel	Israel	Israël
issue (noun)	Ausgabe (f.)	émission (f.)
issue (verb)	herausgeben	émettre
Italy	Italien	Italie
Japan	Japan	Japon

PORTUGUESE	ITALIAN	SPANISH
frente (f.)	fronte (f.); coperta (f.)	frente (m.); faz (f.); cara (f.)
genuíno; autêntico	autentico	genuino; auténtico; legítimo
Alemanha	Germania	Alemania
ouro (m.)	oro (m.)	oro (m.)
bom (m.adj.); boa (f.adj.)	bello	bueno; regular conservada
grau (m.); qualidade (f.)	qualità (f.)	graduación (f.); grado de conservación
classificar; determinar	esaminare qualitativamente	graduar; clasificar
Grã-Bretanha	Gran Bretagna	Gran Bretaña
Grécia	Grecia	Grecia
verde	verde	verde
meio	mezzo	medio
metade (f.)	metà (f.)	mitad (f.)
moeda cunhada à martelo	moneta battuta a mano	moneda acuñada a martillo
furo (m.)	foro (m.)	agujero (m.)
furado	forato	agujereado
Hong Kong	Hong Kong	Hong Kong
cem	cento	cien; ciento
centésimo (m.)	centesimo (m.)	centésimo (m.)
imitação (f.)	imitazione (f.)	imitación (f.)
polegada (f.)	pollice (m.)	pulgada (f.)
incompleto	incompleto	incompleto
incuso	incuso	incuso; hueco
lingote (m.)	lingotto (m.)	lingote (m.)
tinta (f.)	inchiostro (m.)	tinta (f.)
inscrição (f.)	iscrizione (f.)	inscripción (f.)
entalhe (m.)	rotocalco (m.)	impresión intaglio (f.)
internacional	internazionale	internacional
intrínseco	intrinseco	intrínseco
Irlanda	Irlanda	Irlanda
ferro (m.)	ferro (m.)	hierro (m.)
irregular	irregolare	irregular
Israel	Israele	Israel
emissão (f.)	emissione (f.)	emisión (f.)
emitir	emettere	emitir
Itália	Italia	Italia
Japão	Giappone	Japón

ENGLISH	GERMAN	FRENCH
king	König (*m.*)	roi (*m.*)
language	Sprache (*f.*)	langue (*f.*)
large	groß	grand; gros
laureate	lorbeerbekranzt	lauré; lauréate
left (direction or position)	links	gauche (*f.*)
legend	Inschrift (*f.*)	légende (*f.*)
lithography	Lithographie (*f.*)	lithographie (*f.*)
lot (*i.e.,* auction lot)	Los (*n.*); Posten (*m.*)	lot (*m.*)
magnifying glass	Vergrößerungsglas (*n.*)	loupe (*f.*)
mail bid sale	Auktion per Postweg; Briefauktion (*f.*)	vente aux enchéres par correspondance
mark (German currency)	Mark (*f.*)	mark (*m.*)
medal	Medaille (*f.*)	médaille (*f.*)
metal	Metall (*n.*)	métal (*m.*)
Mexico	Mexiko	Mexique
military decoration	Militärorden (*m.*)	médaille militaire (*f.*)
milled coin	Rändelmünze (*f.*)	pièce au moulin
millimeter; millimetre	Millimeter (*m.*)	millimètre (*m.*)
million	Million (*f.*)	million
minimum bid	Niedrigstgebot (*f.*)	soumission minimum; offre minimum
mint	Münzprägeanstalt (*f.*); Münzamt (*n.*)	Hôtel de la Monnaie; atelier monétaire (*m.*)
mintmark; mint mark	Münzzeichen (*n.*)	marque monétaire (*f.*); poinçon (*m.*)
mis-strike (*noun*)	Fehlprägung (*f.*); Verprägung (*f.*)	défaut de frappe (*m.*)
mis-struck	fehlgeprägt	ayant un défaut de frappe
monetary	monetär	monétaire
monetary system	Währungssystem (*n.*)	système monétaire (*m.*)
monetary unit	Geldeinheit (*f.*)	unité monétaire (*f.*)
money	Geld (*n.*)	argent (*m.*)
money order	Geldanweisung (*f.*); Zahlungsanweisung (*f.*)	mandat (*m.*)
motto	Wahlspruch (*m.*); Motto (*n.*)	devise (*f.*)
national	national	national
nationality	Nationalität (*f.*)	nationalité (*f.*)
Netherlands; Holland	Holland	Pays Bas; Hollande
new	neu	nouveau
New Zealand	Neuseeland	Nouvelle-Zélande
nickel (the metal)	Nickel (*n.*)	nickel (*m.*)
nine	neun	neuf

PORTUGUESE	ITALIAN	SPANISH
rei (*m.*)	re (*m.*)	rey (*m.*)
língua (*f.*)	lingua (*f.*)	lengua (*f.*); idioma (*m.*)
grande	grande	grande
laureado	laureato; coronato di lauro	laureado
esquerdo	sinistra (*f.*)	izquierda (*f.*)
legenda (*f.*)	leggenda (*f.*)	leyenda (*f.*); inscripción (*f.*)
litografia (*f.*)	litografia (*f.*)	litografía (*f.*)
lote (*m.*)	lotto (*m.*)	lote (*m.*)
lupa (*f.*)	lente d'ingrandimento (*f.*)	lupa (*f.*); lente de aumento
leilão por correspondência	vendita all'asta per posta	subasta por correo
marco (*m.*)	marco (*m.*)	marco (*m.*)
medalha (*f.*)	medaglia (*f.*)	medalla (*f.*)
metal (*m.*)	metallo (*m.*)	metal (*m.*)
México	Messico	México; Méjico
condecoração militar	decorazione militare (*f.*)	condecoración militar (*f.*)
moeda de fábrica mecânica	moneta a coniazione meccanica	moneda acuñada a molino
milímetro (*m.*)	millimetro (*m.*)	milímetro (*m.*)
milhão	milione	millón
oferta mínima (*f.*)	offerta minima (*f.*)	licitación mínima (*f.*); oferta de salida (*f.*)
casa da moeda (*f.*)	zecca (*f.*)	casa de moneda (*f.*); ceca (*f.*)
marca de cunhagem	segno di zecca (*m.*)	marca de ceca (*f.*)
cunhagem defeituosa	moneta mal battuta (*f.*)	acuñación defectuosa (*f.*)
mal cunhado	mal battuto	mal acuñado
monetário	monetario	monetario
sistema monetário (*m.*)	sistema monetario (*m.*)	sistema monetario (*m.*)
unidade monetária	unità monetaria (*f.*)	unidad monetaria (*f.*)
dinheiro (*m.*)	denaro (*m.*)	dinero (*m.*)
vale postal (*m.*)	vaglia (*m.*)	giro (*m.*); libranza (*f.*)
lema (*m.*)	motto (*m.*)	divisa (*f.*); lema (*f.*)
nacional	nazionale	nacional
nacionalidade (*f.*)	nazionalità (*f.*)	nacionalidad (*f.*)
Holanda; Países Baixos	Olanda	Holanda; Países Bajos
novo	nuovo	nuevo
Nova Zelândia	Nuova Zelanda	Nueva Zelandia; Nueva Zelanda
níquel (*m.*)	nichel (*m.*)	niquel (*m.*)
nove	nove	nueve

ENGLISH	GERMAN	FRENCH
ninety	neunzig	quatre-vingt-dix
Northern Ireland	Nordirland	Irlande du Nord
Norway	Norwegen	Norvège
note (*i.e.*, banknote)	Geldschein (*m.*)	billet de banque
not issued	nicht ausgegeben	non-émis
no unlimited bids accepted	-----	les offres sans limite ne sont pas acceptées
number	Zahl (*f.*)	numéro (*m.*)
numismatic (*adjective*)	numismatisch	numismatique
numismatics (*noun*)	Numismatik (*f.*)	numismatique (*f.*)
numismatist	Numismatiker (*m.*)	numismate (*m.*)
obsidional	Belagerungsmünze (*f.*)	obsidional
obsolete	veraltet	hors d'usage
obverse	Avers (*m.*)	avers (*m.*)
offer (*noun*)	Angebot (*n.*)	offre (*f.*)
offer (*verb*)	anbieten	offrir
official	amtlich	officiel
old	alt	vieux
on approval	zur Ansicht	pour approbation; à condition
one	eins	un (*m.adj.*); une (*f.adj.*)
on the back	rückseitig	au verso
order form	Bestellformular (*n.*)	bon de commande; bulletin de commande
original	original	original
ounce	Unze (*f.*)	once (*f.*)
overprint	Überdruck (*m.*)	surimpression (*f.*)
palindrome	Palindrom (*n.*)	palindrome (*m.*)
paper	Papier (*n.*)	papier (*m.*)
paper money	Papiergeld (*n.*); Geldscheine (*m.pl.*)	papier-monnaie (*m.*)
pattern	Prägevorlage (*f.*); Probe (*f.*)	modèle (*m.*); pièce d'essai (*f.*)
pedigree	Stammbaum (*m.*)	lignée (*f.*)
People's Republic of China (P.R.C.)	Volksrepublik China	République Populaire de Chine
perfect	makellos; perfekt	parfait
Peru	Peru	Pérou
peseta	Peseta (*f.*)	péséta (*f.*)
peso	Peso (*m.*)	péso (*m.*)
photogravure	Photogravüre (*f.*)	photogravure (*f.*)
piéfort; piedfort	Piéfort-Münze (*f.*)	piéfort (*m.*)

PORTUGUESE	ITALIAN	SPANISH
noventa	novanta	noventa
Irlanda do Norte	Irlanda del Nord	Irlanda del Norte
Noruega	Norvegia	Noruega
nota (*f.*); cédula (*f.*)	bancanota (*f.*)	billete (*m.*)
não emitido	non emesso	no emitido
não se aceitam propostas sem limites	offerte illimitate sono proibite	no se aceptan licitaciones sin límite
número (*m.*)	numero (*m.*)	número (*m.*)
numismático	numismatico	numismático
numismática (*f.*)	numismatica (*f.*)	numismática (*f.*)
numismata (*m.*)	numismatico (*m.*)	numismático (*m.*)
obsidional	ossidionale	obsidional; de necesidad
obsoleto	obsoleto; fuoricorso	anticuado; obsoleto; en desuso
anverso (*m.*)	verso (*m.*); diritto (*m.*)	anverso (*m.*)
oferta (*f.*)	offerta (*f.*)	oferta (*f.*); propuesta (*f.*)
oferecer	offrire in vendita	ofrecer
oficial	ufficiale	oficial
velho	vecchio	viejo
sujeito aprovação	invio a scelta	en espera de aprobación
um (*m.adj.*); uma (*f.adj.*)	uno (*m.adj.*); una (*f.adj.*)	un (*m.adj.*); uno (*m.adj.*); una (*f.adj.*)
no verso	rovescio (*m.*)	en el reverso; sobre el reverso
formulário de pedido	modulo d'ordine	pedido (*m.*); formulario de pedido (*m.*)
original	originale	original
onça (*f.*)	oncia (*f.*)	onza (*f.*)
sobreimpressão (*f.*); sobreestampa (*f.*)	sovrastampa (*f.*)	sobreimpresión (*f.*)
capicua (*f.*)	palindromo (*m.*)	capicúa (*f.*)
papel (*m.*)	carta (*f.*)	papel (*m.*)
papel-moeda (*m.*)	carta moneta (*f.*)	papel moneda
desenho (*m.*); padrão (*f.*)	disegno (*m.*)	modelo (*m.*)
pedigree (*m.*)	pedigree	pedigrí (*m.*)
República Popular da China	Repubblica Popolare Cinese	República Popular China
perfeito	perfetto	perfecto
Peru	Perù	Perú
peseta (*f.*)	peseta (*f.*)	peseta (*f.*)
peso (*m.*)	peso (*m.*)	peso (*m.*)
fotogravura (*f.*)	fotoincisione (*f.*)	fotograbado (*m.*)
piéfort	piéfort (*m.*)	piéfort (*m.*)

ENGLISH	GERMAN	FRENCH
planchet	Schrötling (*m.*)	flan (*m.*); planchet (*m.*)
platinum (the metal)	Platin (*n.*)	platine (*m.*)
pope	Papst (*m.*)	pape (*m.*)
portrait	Bildnis (*n.*); Porträt (*n.*)	portrait (*m.*)
Portugal	Portugal	Portugal
pound (unit of weight)	Pfund (*n.*)	livre (*f.*)
pound (£)	Pfund Sterling (*n.*)	livre (*f.*)
prepayment	Vorauszahlung (*f.*)	paiement anticipé (*m.*)
president	Präsident (*m.*)	président (*m.*)
press (*i.e.*, coinage press)	Münzprägemaschine (*f.*)	presse monétaire (*f.*)
price	Preis (*m.*)	prix (*m.*)
price list	Preisliste (*f.*)	liste de prix
print (*verb*)	drucken	imprimer
proof (*re*: coins or medals)	Polierte Platte (*f.*)	épreuve numismatique (*f.*)
propaganda note	Werbenote (*f.*); Propagandanote (*f.*)	billet de propagande
protective reserve bid	Reserveschutzgebot (*n.*)	mise ajoutée; mise de protection
queen	Königin (*f.*)	reine (*f.*)
rare	selten	rare
rarity	Seltenheit (*f.*)	rareté (*f.*)
receipt	Quittung (*f.*)	reçu (*m.*)
rectangular	rechteckig	rectangulaire
red	rot	rouge
repaired	repariert	réparé
reproduction	Nachprägung (*f.*); Reproduktion (*f.*)	reproduction (*f.*)
republic	Republik (*f.*)	république (*f.*)
Republic of China (Taiwan)	Taiwan (i.e, Republik China)	République de Chine
restrike (*noun*)	Neuprägung (*f.*)	réimpression (*f.*)
reverse	Revers (*m.*)	revers (*m.*)
right (direction or position)	rechts	droite (*f.*)
rim	Rand (*m.*)	listel (*m.*)
roll (of coins)	Rolle (*f.*)	rouleau (*m.*)
round	rund	rond
Russia	Rußland	Russie
Saudi Arabia	Saudi-Arabien	Arabie Séoudite
scarce	rar; selten	rare
Scotland	Schottland	Ecosse

PORTUGUESE	ITALIAN	SPANISH
flan (m.)	tondino (m.)	cospel (m.)
platina (f.)	platino (m.)	platino (m.)
papa (m.)	papa (m.)	papa (m.)
retrato (m.)	ritratto (m.)	retrato (m.)
Portugal	Portogallo	Portugal
libra (f.)	libbra (f.)	libra (f.)
libra esterlina (f.)	sterlina (f.)	libra esterlina (f.)
pagamento antecipado (m.)	pagamento anticipato (m.)	pago adelantado (m.)
presidente (m.)	presidente (m.)	presidente (m.)
prensa (f.)	pressa (f.)	prensa (f.)
preço (m.)	prezzo (m.)	precio (m.)
lista de preços (f.)	listino prezzi (m.)	lista de precios
imprimir	stampare	imprimir
proof	fondo a specchio (m.)	prueba; prueba fondo espejo
folheto de propaganda	valuta di propaganda	vale de propaganda; billete de propaganda
preço mínimo de adjudicação	offerta minima di riserva	precio de reserva
rainha (f.)	regina (f.)	reina (f.)
raro	raro	raro
raridade (f.)	rarità (f.)	rareza (f.)
recibo (m.)	ricevuta (f.)	recibo (m.)
retangular	rettangolare	rectangular
vermelho	rosso	rojo
reparado	riparato	reparado
reprodução (f.); réplica (f.)	riproduzione (f.)	reproducción (f.); copia (f.)
república (f.)	repubblica (f.)	república (f.)
República da China; Formosa	Formosa	República de China
re-emissão (f.)	riemissione (f.)	re-emisión (f.)
reverso (m.)	rovescio (m.)	reverso (m.)
direito	destra (f.)	derecha (f.)
bordo (m.)	orlo	borde (m.)
rolo (de moeda) (m.)	rotolo (m.); bobina (f.)	cartucho (m.)
redondo	rotondo	redondo
Rússia	Russia	Rusia
Arábia Saudita	Arabia Saudita	Arabia Saudita; Arabia Saudí
escasso	raro	raro; escaso
Escócia	Scozia	Escocia

ENGLISH	GERMAN	FRENCH
scratch (*noun*)	Kratzer (*m.*)	égratignure (*f.*)
scrip	Verbriefte Schuldverpflichtung (*f.*)	billet privé (*m.*)
seal (*noun*)	Siegel (*n.*)	sceau (*m.*)
seigniorage	Schlagschatz (*m.*)	seigneuriage (*m.*)
sell (*verb*)	verkaufen	vendre
seller	Verkäufer (*m.*)	vendeur (*m.*)
series	Serie (*f.*); Reihe (*f.*)	série (*f.*)
serial number	Reihenbezeichnung (*f.*)	numéro de série
seven	sieben	sept
seventy	siebzig	soixante-dix
signature	Unterschrift (*f.*)	signature (*f.*)
silk thread	Seidenfaden (*m.*)	filament de soie
silver (the metal)	Silber (*n.*)	argent (*m.*)
six	sechs	six
sixty	sechzig	soixante
small	klein	petit
South Africa	Südafrika	Afrique du Sud
sovereign	Souverän (*m.*)	souverain (*m.*)
Soviet Union (U.S.S.R.)	Sowjetunion	Union Soviétique
Spain	Spanien	Espagne
specimen	Muster (*n.*)	spécimen (*m.*)
square (*adjective*)	quadratisch	carré
stain	Makel (*m.*); Fleck (*m.*)	tache (*f.*)
star	Stern (*m.*)	étoile (*f.*)
steel	Stahl (*m.*)	acier (*m.*)
steel engraving	Stahlstich (*m.*)	gravure sur acier
suggested bid	Bietempfehlung (*f.*)	mise suggérée (*f.*)
Sweden	Schweden	Suède
Switzerland	Schweiz, die	Suisse
symbol	Symbol (*n.*)	symbole (*m.*)
tarnish	Belag (*m.*)	ternissure (*f.*)
tax (*noun*)	Steuer (*f.*)	taxe (*f.*)
tear (*noun*)	Riß (*m.*)	déchirure (*f.*)
ten	zehn	dix
tenth (*noun*)	Zehntel (*n.*)	dixième (*m.*)
third (*noun*)	Drittel (*n.*)	tiers (*m.*)

PORTUGUESE	ITALIAN	SPANISH
arranhão (*m.*); arranhadura (*f.*)	graffio (*m.*)	rasguño (*m.*)
moeda provisória (*f.*)	assegno (*m.*)	vale de necesidad; moneda de necesidad
selo (*m.*)	sigillo (*m.*)	sello (*m.*); precinto (*m.*)
senhoriagem (*f.*)	signoraggio (*m.*); diritto di conio (*m.*)	señoraje (*m.*); señoreaje (*m.*)
vender	vendere	vender
vendedor (*m.*)	venditore (*m.*)	vendedor (*m.*)
série (*f.*)	serie (*f.*)	serie (*f.*)
número de série	numero di serie (*m.*)	número de serie
sete	sette	siete
sesenta	settanta	setenta
assinatura (*f.*)	firma (*f.*)	firma (*f.*)
fio de seda	filo di seta	hilo de seda
prata (*f.*)	argento (*m.*)	plata (*f.*)
seis	sei	seis
sessenta	sessanta	sesenta
pequeno	piccolo	pequeño
África do Sul	Sud Africa	África del Sur; Suráfrica; Sudáfrica
soberano (*m.*)	sovrano (*m.*); sterlina oro [coin]	soberano (*m.*)
União Soviética	Unione delle Repubbliche Socialiste Sovietiche	Unión Soviética
Espanha	Spagna	España
espécime (*m.*)	esemplare (*m.*)	muestra (*f.*); ejemplar (*m.*)
quadrado	quadrato	cuadrado
mancha (*f.*)	macchia (*f.*)	mancha (*f.*)
estrela (*f.*)	stella (*f.*)	estrella (*f.*)
aço (*m.*)	acciaio (*m.*)	acero (*m.*)
gravura em aço	incisione su acciaio	grabado en acero (*m.*)
oferta sugerida (*f.*)	offerta suggerita (*f.*); offerta indicativa (*f.*)	licitación sugerida (*f.*)
Suécia	Svezia	Suecia
Suíça	Svizzera	Suiza
símbolo (*m.*)	simbolo (*m.*)	símbolo (*m.*)
deslustre (*m.*)	ossidazione (*f.*)	deslustre (*m.*)
imposto (*m.*)	tassa (*f.*)	impuesto (*m.*)
rasgadela (*f.*)	strappo (*m.*)	rasgón (*m.*); rasgadura (*f.*)
dez	dieci	diez
décimo (*m.*)	decimo (*m.*)	décimo (*m.*)
têrço (*m.*)	terzo (*m.*)	tercio (*m.*)

ENGLISH	GERMAN	FRENCH
thirty	dreißig	trente
thousand	tausend	mille
three	drei	trois
tin	Zinn (n.)	étain (m.)
token	Zeichen (n.); Marke (f.)	jeton (m.)
top	oben	haut (m.)
torn	zerrissen	déchiré
trade (verb)	tauschen	échanger
treasure	Schatz (m.)	trésor (m.)
twenty	zwanzig	vingt
two	zwei	deux
unattributed	nicht zugeschrieben	non attribué
uncirculated	unzirkuliert; stempelglanz	hors circulation; F.D.C.
uniface	nur einseitig geprägt	uniface
unique	einzigartig	unique
United Kingdom (U.K.)	Vereinigtes Königreich	Royaume Uni
United States of America (U.S.A.)	Vereinigte Staaten von Amerika	États-Unis d'Amérique
unknown	unbekannt	inconnu
unofficial	nicht amtlich	non officiel
unpublished	unveröffentlicht	non publié
used	gebraucht	usagé
valuable	wertvoll	précieux
value	Wert (m.)	valeur (f.)
variety	Vielfalt (f.)	variété (f.)
Venezuela	Venezuela	Vénézuéla
Wales	Wales	Pays de Galles
watermark	Wasserzeichen (n.)	filigrane (m.)
wear (noun)	Abnutzung (f.)	usure (f.)
weight	Gewicht (n.)	poids (m.)
West Germany (B.R.D.)	Bundesrepublik Deutschland	Allemagne de l'Ouest
white	weiß	blanc
year	Jahr (n.)	année (f.)
yellow	gelb	jaune
Yugoslavia; Jugoslavia	Jugoslawien	Yougoslavie
zero	Null (f.)	zéro
zinc	Zink (n.)	zinc (m.)

PORTUGUESE	ITALIAN	SPANISH
trinta	trenta	treinta
mil	mille	mil
três	tre	tres
estanho (*m.*)	stagno (*m.*)	estaño (*m.*)
ficha (*f.*)	gettone (*m.*)	ficha (*f.*)
topo (*m.*); cimo (*m.*)	alto (*m.*)	parte superior (*f.*); parte de arriba (*f.*)
rasgado	strappato	rasgado
trocar	scambiare	comerciar
tesouro (*m.*)	tesoro (*m.*)	tesoro (*m.*)
vinte	venti	veinte
dois (*m.adj.*); duas (*f.adj.*)	due	dos
inatribuído; não classificado	non attribuito	no atribuido; sin atribución
não circulado	non circolato	sin circular; no circulado
uniface	senza rovescio	unifaz
único	unico	único
Reino Unido	Regno Unito	Reino Unido
Estados Unidos da América	Stati Uniti d'America	Estados Unidos de América (EE.UU.)
desconhecido	sconosciuto	desconocido
não oficial	ufficioso	no oficial; oficioso
não publicado	non catalogato	no publicado
usado	usato	usado
valioso	di gran valore	valioso; de valor
valor (*m.*)	valore (*m.*)	valor (*m.*)
variedade (*f.*)	varietà (*f.*)	variedad (*f.*)
Venezuela	Venezuela	Venezuela
País de Gales	Galles	Gales
filigrana (*f.*)	filigrana (*f.*)	filigrana (*f.*); marca de agua (*f.*)
uso (*m.*)	usura (*f.*)	desgaste por el uso (*m.*)
peso (*m.*)	peso (*m.*)	peso (*m.*)
Alemanha Ocidental	Repubblica Federale Tedesca	República Federal de Alemania
branco	bianco	blanco
ano (*m.*)	anno (*m.*)	año (*m.*)
amarelo	giallo	amarillo
Iugoslávia	Jugoslavia	Yugoslavia
zero	zero	cero
zinco (*m.*)	zinco (*m.*)	zinc (*m.*); cinc (*m.*)

368

ENGLISH	DUTCH	FINNISH
abbreviation	afkorting (f./c.)	lyhenne
accolated	verbonden	yhdistetty
account (financial or transactional)	rekening (f./c.)	tili
acquisition	aanwinst (f./c.)	hankinta; saanti
adjustment mark	aanpassingsteken (n.)	jälki metallin poistamisesta
album	album (n.)	albumi; kansio
alloy (of metals)	legering (f./c.)	metalliseos
alter (verb)	wijzigen	muuttaa
alteration	wijziging (f./c.)	muutos
altered date	gewijzidge datum (m./c.)	muutettu vuosiluku
amount	bedrag (n.)	summa
ancient	oud	muinainen; antiikinaikainen
anti-counterfeiting device	anti-vervalsingkenmerk (n.)	väärentämisen ehkäisykeino
antiquity	antiquiteit (f./c.)	antiikki; muinaisaika
Argentina	Argentinië	Argentiina
art	kunst (f./c.)	taide
attribute (verb)	toeschrijven	määrittää
attribution	toeschrijving (f./c.)	määritys
auction	veiling (f./c.)	huutokauppa
auction catalogue	veilingkatalogus (m./c.)	huutokauppaluettelo
auction sale	veiling (f./c.)	huutokauppa
Australia	Australië	Australia
Austria	Oostenrijk	Itävalta
authentic	authentiek	aito
badly struck	slecht geslagen	huonosti lyöty
bank (financial institution)	bank (f./c.)	pankki
banknote	bankbiljet (n.)	seteli
Belgium	België	Belgia
bid (noun: auction bid)	bod (n.)	tarjous
bid (verb)	bieden	tarjota
bid sheet	biedformulier (n.)	tarjouslista
bilingual	tweetalig	kaksikielinen
black	zwart	musta
black market	zwarte markt (f./c.)	salakauppa; musta pörssi
blue	blauw	sininen
bond (commercial)	obligatie (f./c.)	arvopaperi; velkakirja

SWEDISH	DANISH	NORWEGIAN
förkortning (r.)	forkortelse (c.)	forkortelse (m.)
bredvid varandra	sammensat	forbundet; parvis sammenstilt
konto (n.)	konto (c.)	konto (m.)
förvärv (n.)	erhvervelse (c.)	akkvisisjon (m.)
filspår (n.)	justeringsmærke (n.)	justeringsmerke (n.)
album (n.)	album (n.)	album (n.)
legering (r.)	legering (c.)	legering (m.)
förändra	ændre	forandre
förändring (r.)	forandring (c.)	forandring (m.)
ändrat datum (n.)	forandret årstal (n.)	forandret dato (m.)
belopp (n.)	beløb (n.)	beløp (n.)
antik	antikke	eldgammel
säkerhets-	antiforfalskningskarakteristika (n.)	sikkerhetselement mot forfalskning
antiken	antikvitet (c.)	antikvitet (m.)
Argentina	Argentina	Argentina
konst (r.)	kunst (c.)	kunst (m.)
attribuera	henføre til	tilskrive; tillegge
bestämning (r.)	attribut (c.); kendetegn (n.)	tillagt egenskap (m.)
auktion (r.)	auktion (c.)	auksjon (m.)
auktionskatalog (r.)	auktionskatalog (n.)	auksjonskatalog (m.)
auktionsförsäljning (r.)	auktionssalg (n.)	auksjon (m.)
Australien	Australien	Australia
Österrike	Østrig	Østerrike
autentisk	ægte; autentisk	ekte; autentisk
dåligd präglad	dårligt præget	dårlig preget
bank (r.)	bank (c.)	bank (m.)
sedel (r.)	pengeseddel (c.)	pengeseddel (m.)
Belgien	Belgien	Belgia
anbud (n.)	bud (n.)	bud (n.)
bjuda	byde	by
anbudslapp (r.)	budliste (c.)	tilbudsskjema (n.)
tvåspråkig	tosproget	tospråklig
svart	sort	svart
svarta börsen (r.)	sortbørsmarked (n.)	svartebørs (m.)
blå	blå	blå
obligation (r.)	obligation (c.)	obligasjon (m.)

ENGLISH	DUTCH	FINNISH
bottom	onderkant (m./c.)	alaosa; pohja
brass (the alloy)	messing (n.); geelkoper (n.)	messinki
Brazil	Brazilië	Brasilia
brockage	incusum (n.)	jälki leimasimien lyömisestä yhteen
bronze (the alloy)	brons (n.)	pronssi
brown	bruin	ruskea
buy (verb)	kopen	ostaa
buyer	koper (m./c.)	ostaja
cabinet friction	wrijfschade (door lade of album veroorzaakt)	säilytyskuluma
Canada	Canada	Kanada
cash (ready money)	contant geld (n.)	käteinen raha
cast (verb)	gieten	valaa
catalog; catalogue	katalogus (m./c.)	luettelo
catalogue value	kataloguswaarde (m./c.)	luetteloarvo
centennial; centenary	honderdjarig	satavuotinen
centimeter; centimetre	centimeter (m./c.)	senttimetri
certificate	waardebon (m./c.)	todistus
check; cheque	cheque (m./c.)	sekki; šekki
China	China	Kiina
chromium	chroom (n.)	kromi
circulated	in omloop geweest; gecirculeerd	kierrossa ollut
circulation	omloop (m./c.); circulatie (m./c.)	kierto
clad coinage	gelaagde munten; gelaagd muntmetaal	päällystetty raha
classification	classificatie (f./c.)	luokitus
classify (verb)	indelen; klasseren	luokitella
coin	munt (m./c.); geldstuk (n.)	metalliraha
coinage	muntslag	raha
collect (verb)	verzamelen	kerätä
collection	verzameling (f./c.)	kokoelma
collector	verzamelaar (m./c.)	keräilijä
Colombia	Colombia	Kolumbia
color; colour	kleur (f./c.); tint (f./c.)	väri
commemorative (adjective)	herdenkings-	muisto-
common	gewoon	yleinen
complete	volledig	täydellinen
conjoined	geaccoladeerd	yhdistetty

SWEDISH	DANISH	NORWEGIAN
botten (r.)	bund (c.)	bunn (m.)
mässing (r.)	messing (n.)	messing (m.)
Brasilien	Brasilien	Brasil
brockage (r.)	dobbeltstansning	-----
brons (r.)	bronze (c.)	bronse (m.)
brun	brun	brun
köpa	købe	kjøpe
köpare (m.)	køber (c.)	kjøper (m.)
-----	opbevaringsslid (n.)	kabinettslitasje (m.)
Kanada	Canada	Canada
kontanter (r.pl.)	kontant	kontant (m.; adj.)
gjuta	støbe	støpe
katalog (r.)	katalog (n.)	katalog (m.)
katalogvärde (n.)	katalogværdi (c.)	katalogverdi (m.)
hundraårsjubileum (n.)	hundredårsdag (c.)	hundreårsjubileum (n.)
centimeter (r.)	centimeter (c.)	centimeter (m.)
certifikat (n.)	certifikat (n.)	garantibevis (n.); sertifikat (n.)
check (r.)	check (c.)	sjekk (m.)
Kina	Kina	Kina
krom (n.)	krom (n.)	krom (n.)
cirkulerad	cirkuleret	sirkulert
cirkulation (r.)	omløb (n.)	sirkulasjon (m.)
treskiktsmynt	lagkagelegering (c.)	lagdelt mynt (m.); "sandwitch"-mynt (m.)
klassificering (r.)	klassifikation (c.)	klassifikasjon (m.)
klassificera	klassificere	klassifisere
mynt (n.)	mønt (c.)	mynt (m.)
myntning (r.)	udmøntning (c.)	mynting (m.); myntsystem (n.)
samla	samle	samle
samling (r.)	samling (c.)	samling (m.)
samlare (m./f.)	samler (c.)	samler (m.)
Colombia	Colombia	Colombia
färg (r.)	farve (c.)	farge (m.)
minnes-	erindrings-	minne-
vanlig	almindelig	alminnelig
fullständig	komplet	fullstendig
bredvid varandra	sammensat	forbundet; dobbelportrettert

ENGLISH	DUTCH	FINNISH
copper (the metal)	koper (n.)	kupari
copy (noun)	kopie (f./c.)	kopio
copy (verb)	kopiëren	kopioida; jäljentää
corrosion	corrosie (f./c.)	syöpyminen
counterfeit (noun)	vervalsing (f./c.)	väärennös
counterfeit (verb)	vervalsen	väärentää
counterfeiter	vervalser (m./c.)	väärentäjä
crease (noun)	vouw (f./c.)	taitos
credit	krediet (n.)	luotto
credit card	credit card	luottokortti
credit cards accepted	kredietkaarten aanvaard	luottokortit hyväksytään
crown (royal headpiece)	kroon (m./c.)	kruunu
crown (large silver coin)	groot zilverstuk (n.)	kruunu; crown
cruzeiro	cruzeiro (m./c.)	cruzeiro
currency	valuta (m./c.)	raha
damaged	beschadigd	vahingoittunut
dark	donker	tumma
date	jaartal (n.); datum (m./c.)	vuosiluku
defect	fout (f./c.)	vika
defective	foutief	viallinen
demonetization	buiten koers stelling	rahan poistaminen käytöstä
Denmark	Denemarken	Tanska
denomination	denominatie (f./c.)	nimellisarvo
deposit (of funds)	aanbetaling (m./c.)	käsiraha; varausmaksu
deposit required	waarborgsom vereist	varausmaksu vaaditaan
design (noun)	ontwerp (n.)	muotoilu
devaluation	devaluatie (f./c.)	arvonalennus; devalvaatio
diameter	diameter (m./c.)	halkaisija; läpimitta
die (i.e., coinage die)	muntstempel (m./c.); penningstempel (m./c.)	meisti; rahaleimasin
die break	stempelbreuk (f./c.)	meistivirhe
dollar	dollar (m./c.)	dollari
duplicate (adjective)	dubbel	kaksois-
duplicate (noun)	dubbel (n.); duplicaat (n.)	kaksoiskappale
duplicate (verb)	verdubbelen; in duplo maken	jäljentää
eagle	adelaar (m./c.)	kotka
East Germany (D.D.R.)	Oost-Duitsland	Itä-Saksa

SWEDISH	DANISH	NORWEGIAN
koppar (r.)	kobber (n.)	kobber (n.)
kopia (r.)	kopi (c.)	kopi (m.)
kopiera	kopiere	kopiere
korrosion (r.)	tæring (c.)	korrosjon (m.)
förfalskning (r.)	forfalskning (c.)	forfalskning (m.)
förfalska	forfalske	forfalske
förfalskare (m./f.)	falskner (c.)	forfalsker (m.)
veck (n.)	fold (c.)	brett (m.)
kredit (r.)	kredit (c.)	kreditt (m.)
kreditkort (n.)	kreditkort (n.)	kredittkort (n.)
kreditkort gäller	kreditkort accepteres	kredittkort akseptert
krona (r.)	krone (c.)	krone (m.)
krona (r.)	krone (c.); crown (c.)	crown (n.)
cruzeiro (r.)	cruzeiro (c.)	cruzeiro (m.)
valuta (r.)	valuta (c.)	gangbar mynt (m.); valuta (m.)
skadad	beskadiget	skadet
mörk	mørk	mørk
datum (n.)	årstal (n.)	dato (m.)
defekt (r.)	defekt (c.)	mangel (m.)
felaktig	defekt	mangelfull
indragning (r.)	ugyldiggørelse (c.)	inndraging (m.)
Danmark	Danmark	Danmark
valör (r.)	møntenhed (c.)	pålydende (n.)
handpenning (r.)	depositum (n.)	depositum (n.)
handpenning erfordras	depositum nødvendigt	depositum nødvendig
design (r.)	design (n.)	utforming (m.); design (m.)
devalvering (r.)	devaluering (c.)	devaluering (m.)
diameter (r.)	diameter (c.)	diameter (m.)
stamp (r.)	prægestempel (n.)	myntstempel (n.)
stampskada (r.)	stempelbrud (n.)	stempelbrudd (n.)
dollar (r.)	dollar (c.)	dollar (m.)
dubblett-	ens	duplisert
dubblett (r.)	dublet (c.)	duplikat (n.)
duplicera	duplikere; efterligne	duplisere
örn (r.)	ørn (c.)	ørn (m.)
Östtyskland	Østtyskland	Øst-Tyskland

ENGLISH	DUTCH	FINNISH
edge	rand (*m./c.*); kant (*m./c.*)	syrjä
effigy	portret (*n.*)	muotokuva
eight	acht	kahdeksan
eighty	tachtig	kahdeksankymmentä
electrotype	galvano	elektrotyyppi
electrum	electrum (*n.*)	elektron
emergency currency	noodgeld (*n.*)	hätäraha
emperor	keizer (*m./c.*)	keisari
England	Engeland	Englanti
engraved	gegraveerd	kaiverrettu
error	fout (*f./c.*)	virhe
excellent	uitstekend	erinomainen
exchange rate	wisselkoers (*f./c.*)	vaihtokurssi
exergue	afsnede (*f./c.*)	eksergi; leike
exhibit (*verb*)	tentoonstellen	asettaa näytteille
exhibition	tentoonstelling (*f./c.*)	näyttely
face value	nominale waarde (*f./c.*)	nimellisarvo
fake (*noun*)	vervalsing (*f./c.*); namaaksel (*n.*)	väärennös
fee	honorarium (*n.*)	maksu; palkkio
fiat money	ongedekt papiergeld (*n.*); fudiciair geld (*n.*)	katteeton raha
fifty	vijftig	viisikymmentä
finance minister	minister van financiën (*m./c.*)	valtiovarainministeri
fine (grade or condition)	fraai	kohtalainen
fine (purity of metal)	fijn; zuiver; puur	puhdas; hieno
Finland	Finland	Suomi
five	vijf	viisi
fold (*noun*)	vouw (*f./c.*)	taitos; laskos
foreign	buitenlands	ulkomainen
foreign currency	buitenlandse valuta (*f./c.*)	ulkomaan raha; valuutta
forgery	vervalsing (*f./c.*)	väärennös
forty	veertig	neljäkymmentä
four	vier	neljä
fourth (*noun*)	vierde	neljäsosa
fraction	fractie (*f./c.*)	murto-osa
franc	franc (*m./c.*); frank (*m./c.*)	frangi
France	Frankrijk	Ranska

SWEDISH	DANISH	NORWEGIAN
kant (r.)	kant (c.)	kant (m.); rand (m.)
avbildning (r.)	portrætbillede (n.)	bilde (n.); portrett (n.)
åtta	otte	åtte
åttio	firs	åtti
galvanokopia (r.)	elektrotypi (c.)	elektrotypi (m.)
elektron (r.)	elektrum (n.)	elektrum (n.)
nödmynt (n.)	nødpenge (pl.)	nødspenger (n.pl.)
kejsare (m.)	kejser (c.)	keiser (m.)
England	England	England
graverad	graveret	gravert
fel (n.)	fejl (c.)	feil (m.)
utmärkt	fremragende	utmerket
växelkurs (r.)	vekselkurs (c.)	kurs (m.)
avskärning (r.)	plads til omskrift; exergue; udenværk	plass til innskrift
ställa ut	udstille	utstille; stille ut
utställning (r.)	udstilling (c.)	utstilling (m.)
nominellt värde (n.)	pålydende værdi (c.)	pålydende verdi
förfalskning (r.)	forfalskning (c.)	forfalskning (n.)
avgift (r.)	gebyr (n.)	gebyr (n.)
pappersvaluta (r.)	penge uden guldværdi (pl.)	penger uten motverdi i edelt metall
femtio	halvtreds	femti
finansminister (m./f.)	finansminister (c.)	finansminister (m.)
fin	fin	kvalitet (m.)
ren	finhed (c.)	finhet (m.)
Finland	Finland	Finnland
fem	fem	fem
veck (n.)	fold (c.)	brett (m.)
utländsk	udenlandsk	utenlandsk
utländsk valuta	udenlandsk valuta (c.)	utenlandsk mynt (m.)
förfalskning (r.)	forfalskning (c.)	forfalskning (m.)
fyrtio	fyrre	førti
fyra	fire	fire
fjärdedel (r.)	fjerdedel (c.)	fjerdedel (m.)
del (r.)	brøkdel (c.)	brøkdel (m.)
franc (r.)	franc (c.)	franc (m.)
Frankrike	Frankrig	Frankrike

ENGLISH	DUTCH	FINNISH
front	voorkant (*m./c.*)	etusivu
genuine	echt	aito
Germany	Duitsland	Saksa
gold (the metal)	goud (*n.*)	kulta
good	goed	heikko; hyvä
grade (*noun*)	kwaliteitsaanduiding (*f./c.*)	kuntoluokka
grade (*verb*)	klasseren; kwalificeren	luokitella
Great Britain	Groot-Brittannië	Iso-Britannia
Greece	Griekenland	Kreikka
green	groen	vihreä
half (*adjective*)	half	puoli
half (*noun*)	helft (*f./c.*)	puolikas
hammered coin	handmatig geslagen munt (*m./c.*)	käsinlyöty
hole	gat (*n.*)	reikä
holed	doorboord; met gat	reiällinen
Hong Kong	Hong-Kong	Hongkong
hundred	honderd	sata
hundredth (*noun*)	honderdste	sadasosa
imitation	namaak (*m./c.*); imitatie (*f./c.*)	jäljitelmä
inch	inch (*m./c.*)	tuuma
incomplete	onvolledig; niet compleet	epätäydellinen
incuse	inwaarts; incuus; incusum	kuvio tai kirjoitus syvennöksenä
ingot	baar (*f./c.*); staaf (*m./c.*)	metalliharkko
ink	inkt (*m./c.*)	muste
inscription	inscriptie (*f./c.*)	inskriptio; kirjoitus
intaglio	diepdruk (*n.*)	intaglio-painanta
international	internationaal	kansainvälinen
intrinsic	intrinsiek	itseis-
Ireland	Ierland	Irlanti
iron (the metal)	ijzer (*n.*)	rauta
irregular	onregelmatig	epäsäännöllinen
Israel	Israël	Israel
issue (*noun*)	emissie	sarja
issue (*verb*)	uitgeven; emitteren	laskea liikkeeseen
Italy	Italië	Italia
Japan	Japan	Japani

SWEDISH	DANISH	NORWEGIAN
framsida (r.)	forside (c.)	forside (m.)
äkta	ægte	ekte
Tyskland	Tyskland	Tyskland
guld (n.)	guld (n.)	gull (n.)
god	god	fin
grad (r.); klass (r.)	kvalitet (c.); konserveringsgrad (c.)	klasse (m.)
gradera	kvalitetsbedømme	klassifisere
Storbritannien	Storbritannien	Storbritannia
Grekland	Grækenland	Hellas
grön	grøn	grønn
halv	halv	halv
halva (r.)	halvdel (c.)	halvpart (m.)
hammarpräglat mynt (n.)	håndslået mønt (c.)	hammerpreget mynt (m.)
hål (n.)	hul (n.)	hull (n.)
med hål	gennemhullet	hullet
Hong Kong	Hong Kong	Hong Kong
hundra	hundrede	hundre
hundradel (r.)	hundrededel (c.)	hundrededel (m.)
imitation (r.)	efterligning (c.); imitation (c.)	etterligning (m.)
tum (r.)	tomme (c.)	tomme (m.)
ofullständig	ufuldstændig	ufullstendig
inkus prägling (r.)	indslået; nedsænket præg	preg (n.)
tacka (r.)	barre (c.)	barre (m.)
bläck (n.)	blæk (n.)	blekk (n.)
inskription (r.)	inskription (c.)	inskripsjon (m.)
intaglio (r.)	indskåret	intaglio gravering (m.)
internationell	international	internasjonal
inneboende	egenværdi (c.)	egenverdi; markedsverdi
Irland	Irland	Irland
järn (n.)	jern (n.)	jern (n.)
oregelbunden	uregelmæssig	irregulær
Israel	Israel	Israel
utgåva (r.)	udgivelse (c.)	utstedelse (m.)
utge; ge ut	udstede; udgive	utstede
Italien	Italien	Italia
Japan	Japan	Japan

ENGLISH	DUTCH	FINNISH
king	koning (*m./c.*)	kuningas
language	taal (*f./c.*)	kieli
large	groot	suuri
laureate	gelauwerd; met lauwerkrans	seppelöity (laakeriseppele)
left (direction or position)	links	vasen
legend	omschrift (*n.*)	kehäkirjoitus; legenda
lithography	lithografie (*f./c.*)	litografia
lot (*i.e.,* auction lot)	lot (*n.*)	huutokauppakohde
magnifying glass	vergrootglas (*n.*)	suurennuslasi
mail bid sale	post-veiling verkoop (*m./c.*); mail bid sale	postihuutokauppa
mark (German currency)	mark (*m./c.*)	markka
medal	penning (*m./c.*); medaille (*f./c.*)	mitali
metal	metaal (*n.*)	metalli
Mexico	Mexico	Meksiko
military decoration	militaire onderscheiding (*f./c.*)	sotilaskunniamerkki
milled coin	machinaal geslagen munt (*m./c.*)	koneella lyöty raha
millimeter; millimetre	millimeter (*m./c.*)	millimetri
million	miljoen	miljoona
minimum bid	laagste bod (*n.*)	pohjahinta
mint	munt (*m./c.*); muntplaats (*f./c.*)	rahapaja
mintmark; mint mark	muntteken (*n.*)	rahapajan tunnus
mis-strike (*noun*)	misslag (*m./c.*)	virhelyönti
mis-struck	misgeslagen	virhelyöty
monetary	monetair	raha-
monetary system	muntstelsel (*n.*)	rahajärjestelmä
monetary unit	munteenheid (*f./c.*)	rahayksikkö
money	geld (*n.*)	raha
money order	postwissel (*m./c.*)	maksumääräys
motto	opschrift (*n.*); motto (*n.*)	motto
national	nationaal	kansallinen
nationality	nationaliteit (*f./c.*)	kansallisuus
Netherlands; Holland	Koninkrijk der Nederlanden; Nederland	Alankomaat
new	nieuw	uusi
New Zealand	Nieuw-Zeeland	Uusi-Seelanti
nickel (the metal)	nikkel (*n.*)	nikkeli
nine	negen	yhdeksän

SWEDISH	DANISH	NORWEGIAN
kung (*m.*)	konge (*c.*)	konge (*m.*)
språk (*n.*)	sprog (*n.*)	språk (*n.*)
stor	stor	stor
lagerkransad	laurbærkranset	laurbærkronet
vänster	venstre	venstre
inskrift (*r.*)	inskription (*c.*); indskrift (*c.*)	innskrift (*m.*); tegnforklaring (*m.*)
litografi (*r.*)	litografi (*c.*); stentryk (*n.*)	litografi (*n.*)
lot (*r.*)	auktionsnummer (*n.*)	parti (*n.*)
förstoringsglas (*n.*)	forstørrelsesglas (*n.*)	forstørrelsesglass (*n.*)
anbudsauktion (*r.*)	brevbudsauktion (*c.*)	postauksjon (*m.*)
mark (*r.*)	mark (*c.*)	tysk mark (*m.*)
medalj (*r.*)	medalje (*c.*)	medalje (*m.*)
metall (*r.*)	metal (*n.*)	metall (*n.*)
Mexiko	Mexico	Mexico
militär dekoration	orden (*c.*)	militær orden (*m.*)
valsverkspräglat mynt (*n.*)	præget mønt (*c.*)	maskinfremstilt mynt
millimeter (*r.*)	millimeter (*c.*)	millimeter (*m.*)
miljon (*r.*)	million	million (*m.*)
minimibud (*n.*)	minimumsbud (*n.*)	minstebud (*n.*)
myntverk (*n.*)	mønt (*c.*)	myntverk (*n.*)
myntortsmärke (*n.*)	møntmærke (*n.*)	myntmerke (*n.*)
felprägling (*r.*)	fejlprægning (*c.*)	feilpregening (*m.*)
felpräglad	fejlpræget	feilpreget
valuta-; mynt-	monetær	mynt-
valutasystem (*n.*)	møntsystem (*n.*)	pengesystem (*n.*)
valutaenhet (*r.*)	møntenhed (*c.*)	myntenhet (*m.*)
pengar (*r.pl.*)	penge (*pl.*)	penger (*m.pl.*)
postväxel (*r.*)	postanvisning (*c.*)	pengeanvisning (*m.*)
motto (*n.*)	motto (*n.*)	motto (*n.*); valgspråk (*n.*)
nationell	national	nasjonal
nationalitet (*r.*)	nationalitet (*c.*)	nasjonalitet (*m.*)
Nederländerna; Holland	Nederlandene	Nederland; Holland
ny	ny	ny
Nya Zeeland	New Zealand	New Zealand
nickel (*r.*)	nikkel (*n.*)	nikkel (*m.*)
nio	ni	ni

ENGLISH	DUTCH	FINNISH
ninety	negentig	yhdeksänkymmentä
Northern Ireland	Noord-Ierland	Pohjois-Irlanti
Norway	Noorwegen	Norja
note (*i.e.,* banknote)	biljet (*n.*)	seteli
not issued	niet uitgegeven; onuitgegeven	liikkeeseen laskematon
no unlimited bids accepted	geen ongelimiteerde biedingen geaccepteerd	rajoittamattomia tarjouksia ei hyväksytä
number	nummer (*n.*); getal (*n.*)	numero
numismatic (*adjective*)	numismatisch	numismaattinen
numismatics (*noun*)	numismatiek (*f./c.*); penningkunde (*f./c.*)	numismatiikka
numismatist	numismaat (*m./c.*)	numismaatikko
obsidional	belegerings-; noodgeld (*n.*)	piiritykseen liittyvä (esim. hätäraha)
obsolete	verouderd; niet langer in gebruik	käytöstä poistettu
obverse	voorzijde (*f./c.*)	etusivu
offer (*noun*)	aanbieding (*m./c.*)	tarjous
offer (*verb*)	aanbieden	tarjota
official	officieel	virallinen
old	oud	vanha
on approval	op zicht	hyväksyttäväksi
one	één	yksi
on the back	op de achterkant; op de achterzijde	takasivulla
order form	bestelformulier (*n.*)	tilauslomake
original	origineel	alkuperäinen
ounce	ons (*n.*)	unssi
overprint	opdruk (*m./c.*)	lisäpainama
palindrome	palindroom (*n.*)	palindromi
paper	papier (*n.*)	paperi
paper money	papiergeld (*n.*)	paperiraha
pattern	motief (*n.*)	kuvio
pedigree	herkomst (*m./c.*)	sukupuu
People's Republic of China (P.R.C.)	Chinese Volksrepubliek	Kiinan kansantasavalta
perfect	volmaakt; perfect	virheetön
Peru	Peru	Peru
peseta	peseta (*m./c.*)	peseta
peso	peso (*m./c.*)	peso
photogravure	fotogravure (*m./c.*)	fotogravyyri
piéfort; piedfort	piedfort	paksu erikoislyönti

SWEDISH	DANISH	NORWEGIAN
nittio	halvfems	nitti
Nordirland	Nordirland	Nord-Irland
Norge	Norge	Norge; Noreg
sedel (r.)	seddel (c.)	pengeseddel (m.)
ej utgiven	ikke udgivet	ikke utgitt
olimiterade bud accepteras ej	bud uden øvre grænse accepteres ikke	kun faste bud akseptert
nummer (n.)	nummer (n.)	nummer (n.)
numismatisk	numismatisk	numismatisk
numismatik (r.)	numismatik (c.)	myntvitenskap (m.); numismatikk (m.)
numismatiker (m./f.)	numismatiker (c.); møntsamler (c.)	numismatiker (m.)
belägrings-	belejringspenge	nødspenger
föråldrad	forældet	foreldet
åtsida (r.)	avers (c.)	forside; advers
anbud (n.)	tilbud (n.)	tilbud (n.)
offerera	tilbyde	tilby
officiell	officiel	offisiell
gammal	gammel	gammel
till påseende	på prøve; til gennemsyn	på prøve
en	en (c.); et (n.)	en
på reversen; på frånsidan	på bagsiden	på baksiden
beställningssedel (r.)	bestillingsformular (c.)	ordreseddel (m.)
original	original	original
uns (n.)	ounce (c.)	unse (m.)
övertryck (n.)	overtryk (n.); påtryk (n.)	overtrykk (n.)
palindrom (n.)	palindrom (n.)	palindrom (n.)
papper (n.)	papir (n.)	papir (n.)
sedlar (r.pl.)	sedler (c.pl.)	papirpenger (m.pl.)
provmynt (n.)	mønster (n.); prøvemønt (c.)	mønster (n.)
proveniens (r.)	stamtræ (n.)	liste over tidligere eiere
Folkrepubliken Kina	Folkerepublikken Kina	Folkerepublikken Kina
perfekt	perfekt	perfekt
Peru	Peru	Peru
peseta (r.)	peseta (c.)	peseta (m.)
peso (r.)	peso (c.)	peso (m.)
fotogravyr (r.)	fotogravure (c.)	fotogravyre (m.)
tjockmynt (n.)	piéfort	piéfort; piedfort

ENGLISH	DUTCH	FINNISH
planchet	muntplaatje (n.)	aihio
platinum (the metal)	platina (n.)	platina
pope	paus (m./c.)	paavi
portrait	portret (n.)	muotokuva
Portugal	Portugal	Portugali
pound (unit of weight)	pond (n.)	naula
pound (£)	pond sterling (n.)	punta
prepayment	vooruitbetaling (m./c.)	ennakkomaksu
president	president (m./c.)	presidentti; puheenjohtaja
press (i.e., coinage press)	muntpers (m./c.); pers (m./c.)	leimauspuristin
price	prijs (m./c.)	hinta
price list	prijslijst (m./c.)	hintaluettelo; hinnasto
print (verb)	drukken	painaa
proof (re: coins or medals)	proof; kwaliteit (f./c.)	kiiltolyönti
propaganda note	propagandabiljet (n.)	propagandaseteli
protective reserve bid	beschermend bod (n.)	pohjatarjous
queen	koningin (f./c.)	kuningatar
rare	zeldzaam	harvinainen
rarity	zeldzaamheid (m./c.)	harvinaisuus
receipt	ontvangstbewijs (n.)	kuitti
rectangular	rechthoekig	suorakulmainen
red	rood	punainen
repaired	gerepareerd	korjattu
reproduction	reproduktie (m./c.)	jäljennös
republic	republiek (m./c.)	tasavalta
Republic of China (Taiwan)	Chinese Republiek	Kiinan tasavalta
restrike (noun)	naslag (m./c.)	uusintalyönti
reverse	keerzijde	takasivu
right (direction or position)	rechts	oikea
rim	kant (m./c.); rand (m./c.)	reuna
roll (of coins)	rol (m./c.)	rahapötkö
round	rond	pyöreä
Russia	Rusland	Venäjä
Saudi Arabia	Saoudi-Arabië	Saudi-Arabia
scarce	schaars	melko harvinainen
Scotland	Schotland	Skotlanti

SWEDISH	DANISH	NORWEGIAN
plants (r.)	blanket (c.)	blankett (m.); rondell (m.)
platina (r.)	platin (n.)	platina (m.)
påve (m.)	pave (c.)	pave (m.)
porträtt (n.)	portræt (n.)	portrett (n.)
Portugal	Portugal	Portugal
pund (n.)	engelsk pund (c.)	pund (n.)
pund sterling (n.)	pund sterling	pund (n.)
förskottsbetalning (r.)	forudbetaling (c.)	forhåndsbetaling (m.)
president (m./f.)	præsident (c.)	president (m.)
myntpress (r.)	møntprægemaskine (c.)	presse (m.); pregepresse (m.)
pris (n.)	pris (c.)	pris (m.)
prislista (r.)	prisliste (c.)	prisliste (m.)
trycka	trykke	trykke
spegelblank	medaljepræg	proof
propagandasedel (n.)	propaganda seddel (c.)	propagandabrev (n.)
bevakningspris (n.)	sælgers minimumpris	minstepris (m.)
drottning (f.)	dronning (c.)	dronning (m./f.)
sällsynt	sjælden	sjelden
raritet (r.)	sjældenhed (c.)	sjeldenhet (m.)
kvitto (n.)	kvittering (c.)	kvittering (m.)
rektangulär	rektangulær	rektangulær
röd	rød	rød
lagad	repareret	reparert
reproduktion (r.)	reproduktion (c.)	reproduksjon (m.)
republik (r.)	republik (c.)	republikk (m.)
Republiken Kina	Republikken Kina	Republikken Kina
nyprägling (r.)	nypræg (n.)	nypregning (m.)
frånsida (r.)	bagside (c.); revers (c.)	bakside; revers
höger	højre	høyre
kant (r.)	rand (c.)	kant (m.); rand (m.)
rulle (r.)	rulle (c.)	rull (m.)
rund	rund	rund
Ryssland	Rusland	Russland
Saudiarabien	Saudi Arabien	Saudi-Arabia
sällsynt	sjælden	sjelden
Skottland	Skotland	Skottland

ENGLISH	DUTCH	FINNISH
scratch (noun)	kras (m./c.)	naarmu
scrip	particulier geld (n.)	tilapäisseteli; paikallisseteli
seal (noun)	zegel (m./c.)	sinetti
seigniorage	slijschat (m./c.); muntloon (n.)	lyöntivero
sell (verb)	verkopen	myydä
seller	verkoper (m./c.)	myyjä
series	serie (m./c.)	sarja
serial number	volgnummer (n.)	sarjanumero
seven	zeven	seitsemän
seventy	zeventig	seitsemänkymmentä
signature	handtekening (m./c.)	nimikirjoitus; allekirjoitus
silk thread	draadje (n.)	silkkilanka
silver (the metal)	zilver (n.)	hopea
six	zes	kuusi
sixty	zestig	kuusikymmentä
small	klein	pieni
South Africa	Zuid-Afrika	Etelä-Afrikka
sovereign	soeverein	hallitsija
Soviet Union (U.S.S.R.)	Sovjet-Unie	Neuvostoliitto
Spain	Spanje	Espanja
specimen	specimen (n.); exemplaar (n.)	näyte; mallikappale
square (adjective)	vierkant	nelikulmainen
stain	vlek (m./c.)	tahra
star	ster (m./c.)	tähti
steel	staal (n.)	teräs
steel engraving	staalgravure	teräskaiverrus
suggested bid	voorgesteld bod (n.); adviesprijs (m./c.)	ehdotettu tarjous
Sweden	Zweden	Ruotsi
Switzerland	Zwitserland	Sveitsi
symbol	symbool (n.)	tunnuskuva; symboli
tarnish	ontlvistering	tahra; mustuma
tax (noun)	belasting (m./c.)	vero
tear (noun)	scheur (m./c.)	repeämä
ten	tien	kymmenen
tenth (noun)	tiende	kymmenesosa
third (noun)	derde	kolmasosa

SWEDISH	DANISH	NORWEGIAN
repa (r.)	ridse (c.)	ripe (m.)
pollett (r.)	reklamepenge (pl.); privatpenge (pl.)	pengeerstatning (m.); polett (m.)
sigill (n.)	segl (n.)	segl (n.)
slagskatt (r.)	opgæld (c.); fortjeneste (c.)	seigniorage
sälja	sælge	selge
säljare (m./f.)	sælger (c.)	selger (m.)
serie (r.)	serie (c.)	serie (m.)
serienummer (n.)	løbenummer (n.)	serienummer (n.)
sju	syv	sju
sjuttio	halvfjerds	sytti
signatur (r.)	underskrift (c.)	underskrift (m.)
säkerhetstråd (r.)	silketråd (c.)	sikkerhetsfibre
silver (r.)	sølv (n.)	sølv (n.)
sex	seks	seks
sextio	tres	seksti
liten	lille	liten
Sydafrika	Sydafrika	Syd-Afrika
suverän (m./f.)	regent (c.)	hersker (m.); sovereign (m.) [the coin]
Sovjetunionen	Sovjetunionen	Sovjetsamveldet
Spanien	Spanien	Spania
specimen (n.)	prøveeksemplar (n.)	eksemplar (n.)
kvadratiskt	firkantet; kvadratisk	kvadratisk
fläck (r.)	plet (c.)	flekk (m.)
stjärna (r.)	stjerne (c.)	stjerne (m.)
stål (r.)	stål (n.)	stål (n.)
stålgravyr (r.)	stålgravering (c.)	stålgravering (m.)
utropspris (n.)	foreslået bud (n.)	utropspris (m.)
Sverige	Sverige	Sverige
Schweiz	Schweiz	Sveits
symbol (r.)	symbol (n.)	symbol (n.)
glanslöshet (r.)	anløbe	flekk (m.)
skatt (r.)	skat (c.)	skatt (n.)
reva (r.)	rift (c.)	rift (m.)
tio	ti	ti
tiondel (r.)	tiendedel (c.)	tiendedel (m.)
tredjedel (r.)	trediedel (c.)	tredjedel (m.)

ENGLISH	DUTCH	FINNISH
thirty	dertig	kolmekymmentä
thousand	duizend	tuhat
three	drie	kolme
tin	tin (*n.*)	tina
token	token; -penning (*m./c.*)	rahake; poletti
top	bovenkant (*m./c.*)	yläosa; huippu
torn	gescheurd	repeytynyt
trade (*verb*)	verhandelen; ruilen	vaihtaa; käydä kauppaa
treasure	schat (*m./c.*)	rahasto
twenty	twintig	kaksikymmentä
two	twee	kaksi
unattributed	niet toegeschreven	määrittelemätön
uncirculated	ongecirculeerd; niet in omloop gebracht	käyttämätön
uniface	eenzijdig	yksipuolinen
unique	uniek	uniikki
United Kingdom (U.K.)	Verenigd Koninkrijk	Yhdistynyt kuningaskunta
United States of America (U.S.A.)	Verenigde Staten van Amerika	Amerikan Yhdysvallat
unknown	onbekend	tuntematon
unofficial	onofficieel	epävirallinen
unpublished	ongepubliceerd; niet gepubliceerd	julkaisematon
used	gebruikt	käytetty
valuable	waardevol	arvokas
value	waarde (*m./c.*)	arvo
variety	variant (*m./c.*); variëteit (*m./c.*)	variantti
Venezuela	Venezuela	Venezuela
Wales	Wales	Wales
watermark	watermerk (*n.*)	vesileima
wear (*noun*)	slijtage (*m./c.*)	kuluma
weight	gewicht (*n.*)	paino
West Germany (B.R.D.)	West-Duitsland	Länsi-Saksa
white	wit	valkoinen
year	jaar (*n.*)	vuosi
yellow	geel	keltainen
Yugoslavia; Jugoslavia	Joegoslavië	Jugoslavia
zero	nul	nolla
zinc	zink (*n.*)	sinkki

SWEDISH	DANISH	NORWEGIAN
trettio	tredive	tretti
tusen	tusind	tusen
tre	tre	tre
tenn (*n.*)	tin (*n.*)	tinn (*n.*)
pollett (*r.*)	polet (*c.*)	polett (*m.*); betalingsmerke (*n.*)
topp	top (*c.*)	øverst
sönderriven	iturevet	revet
handla med	bytte	handle; bytte
skatt (*r.*)	skat (*c.*)	skatt (*m.*)
tjugo	tyve	tjue
två	to	to
obestämt	ikke identificeret	ufullstendig identifisert
ej cirkulerad; ocirkulerad	ubrugt; ikke været i cirkulation	usirkulert
ensidig	ensidig	ensidig
unik	enestående; unik	unik
Storbritannien	Storbritannien	Storbritannia
Amerikas Förenta Stater	Forenede Stater	Forente Stater
okänd	ukendt	ukjent
inofficiell	uofficiel	uoffisiell
opublicerad	upubliceret	ikke katalogført
använd	brugt	brukt
värdefull	værdifuld	verdifull
värde (*n.*)	værdi (*c.*)	verdi
mångfald (*r.*)	variant (*c.*)	mangfoldighet (*m.*)
Venezuela	Venezuela	Venezuela
Wales	Wales	Wales
vattenmärke (*n.*)	vandmærke (*n.*)	vannmerke (*n.*)
slitage (*n.*)	slid (*n.*)	slitasje (*m.*)
vikt (*r.*)	vægt (*c.*)	vekt (*m.*)
Västtyskland	Vesttyskland	Vest-Tyskland
vit	hvid	hvit
år (*n.*)	år (*n.*)	år (*n.*)
gul	gul	gul
Jugoslavien	Jugoslavien	Jugoslavia
noll	nul	null
zink (*n.*)	zink (*c.*)	sink (*m.*)

ENGLISH	POLISH	HUNGARIAN
abbreviation	skrót (*m.*)	rövidítés
accolated	portret podwójny ("gemmowy")	egyirányba néző kettős portré
account (financial or transactional)	rachunek (*m.*); konto (*n.*)	számla
acquisition	nabycie (*n.*); zakup (*m.*)	szerzemény
adjustment mark	ślad justowania (*m.*)	kiegyenlítési jegy
album	album (*m.*)	album
alloy (of metals)	stop (*m.*)	ötvözet
alter (*verb*)	podrabiać	megváltoztatni
alteration	podrobienie (*n.*); podróbka (*f.*)	változtatás
altered date	podrobiona data (*f.*)	dátumváltozás
amount	suma (*f.*); kwota (*f.*)	összeg
ancient	starożytny (*m.*)	ókori
anti-counterfeiting device	zabezpieczenie przed fałszerstwem (*n.*)	hamisítás elleni eszköz
antiquity	starożytność (*f.*)	ókor
Argentina	Argentyna	Argentína
art	sztuka (*f.*)	művészet
attribute (*verb*)	przypisywać; atrybuować	tulajdonítani
attribution	atrybucja (*f.*)	tulajdonítás; tulajdonság
auction	aukcja (*f.*)	árverés
auction catalogue	katalog aukcyjny (*m.*)	árverési katalógus
auction sale	sprzedaż aukcyjna	árverés
Australia	Australia	Ausztrália
Austria	Austria	Ausztria
authentic	autentyczny	hiteles
badly struck	źle wybity	rosszul vert (pénz)
bank (financial institution)	bank (*m.*)	bank
banknote	banknot (*m.*)	bankjegy
Belgium	Belgia	Belgium
bid (*noun:* auction bid)	cena licytowana (*f.*); oferta cenowa (*f.*)	árajánlatot tesz
bid (*verb*)	licytować	árajánlat
bid sheet	zlecenie zakupu (*n.*)	árverési lap
bilingual	dwujęzyczny	kétnyelvű
black	czarny	fekete
black market	czarny rynek (*m.*)	fekete piac
blue	niebieski	kék
bond (commercial)	papier wartościowy (*m.*)	részvény

ROMANIAN	GREEK	HEBREW
abreviere (f.); prescurtare (f.)	σύντμηση (f.)	קִצּוּר (m.)
acolat; alăturat; acostat	αναγνωρισμένο	מְצֹמָד
cont (n.)	λογαριασμός (m.)	חֶשְׁבּוֹן (m.)
achiziție (f.)	απόκτηση (f.)	רְכִישָׁה (f.)
semn de ajustare (n.)	διακανονισμένο σημείο αναγνώρσης	סִימָן הַתְאָמָה (m.)
album (n.)	λεύκωμα (n.)	אַלְבּוֹם (m.)
aliaj (n.)	μεταλλικό κράμα (n.)	נֶתֶךְ (m.)
altera; modifica	μεταβάλλω	שִׁנָּה
alterare (f.); modificare (f.)	αλλοίωση; τροποποίηση	שִׁנּוּי (m.)
dată shimbată (f.)	μεταποιημένη ημερομηνία	שִׁנּוּי תַּאֲרִיךְ (m.)
sumă (f.)	ποσόν (n.)	סְכוּם (m.)
antic	αρχαίον	עַתִּיק
procedeu contra falsificării (n.)	μηχανισμός αναγνώρσης πλαστογραφίας	הֶתְקֵן כְּנֶגֶד זִיּוּף (m.)
antichitate (f.)	αρχαιότης (f.)	עַתִּיקוּת (f.)
Argentina	Αργεντινή	אַרְגֶּנְטִינָה
artă (f.)	τέχνη	אָמָּנוּת (f.)
atribui	αποδίδω	יִחֵס
atribuire (f.); identificare (f.)	χαρακτηριστικόν (n.)	יִחוּס (m.)
licitație (f.)	δημοπρασία (f.)	מְכִירָה פֻּמְבִּית (f.)
catalog de licitație (n.)	κατάλογος πλειστηριασμού (m.)	קָטָלוֹג מְכִירָה פֻּמְבִּית (m.)
licitație (f.)	πλειστηριασμός (m.)	מְכִירָה פֻּמְבִּית (f.)
Australia	Αυστραλία	אוֹסְטְרַלְיָה
Austria	Αυστρία	אוֹסְטְרְיָה
autentic; veritabil	γνήσιον	אֲמִתִּי
bătut defectuos	εσφαλμένη χάραξη (f.)	שֶׁנִּטְבַּע בְּאֹפֶן לָקוּי
bancă (f.)	τράπεζα (f.)	בַּנְק (m.)
bancnotă (f.)	χαρτονόμισμα (n.)	שְׁטַר כֶּסֶף (m.)
Belgia	Βέλγιο	בֶּלְגִּיָה
licitare (f.); pret (n.)	προσφορά (f.)	הַצַּעַת מְחִיר
licita	προσφέρω	הִצִּיעַ מְחִיר
ofertă de licitație (f.)	απόδειξη προσφορών (f.)	טוֹפֶס הַצָּעָה (m.)
bilingv	δίγλωσσος	דּוּ-לְשׁוֹנִי
negru	μαύρο	שָׁחוֹר (m.)
bursă neagră (f.)	μαύρη αγορά (f.)	שׁוּק שָׁחוֹר (m.)
albastru	μπλέ	כָּחֹל (m.)
actiune (f.)	ομολογία (f.)	שְׁטַר עֵרֶךְ (m.)

ENGLISH	POLISH	HUNGARIAN
bottom	dół (*m.*)	fenék; valaminek az alja
brass (the alloy)	mosiądz (*m.*)	réz
Brazil	Brazylia	Brazília
brockage	-----	-----
bronze (the alloy)	brąz (*m.*)	bronz
brown	brązowy	barna
buy (*verb*)	kupować	vásárolni
buyer	nabywca (*m.*)	vásárló
cabinet friction	uszkodzenie kolekcjonerskie (*n.*)	lekopott
Canada	Kanada	Kanada
cash (ready money)	gotówka (*f.*)	készpénz
cast (*verb*)	odlewać	önteni (fémet)
catalog; catalogue	katalog (*m.*)	katalógus
catalogue value	cena katalogowa	katalógus érték
centennial; centenary	stuletni (*m.*)	százéves évforduló
centimeter; centimetre	centymetr (*m.*)	centiméter
certificate	certyfikat (*m.*); papier wartościowy (*m.*)	tanúsítvány
check; cheque	czek (*m.*)	csekk
China	Chiny	Kína
chromium	chrom (*m.*)	króm
circulated	obiegowy	forgalomban lévő
circulation	obieg (*m.*)	forgalom
clad coinage	monety wielowarstwowe (*f.pl.*)	plattírozott érme
classification	klasyfikacja (*f.*)	osztályozás
classify (*verb*)	klasyfikować	osztályozni
coin	moneta (*f.*)	érme
coinage	mennictwo (*n.*)	pénzverés
collect (*verb*)	kolekcjonować; zbierać	gyűjteni
collection	kolekcja (*f.*); zbiór (*m.*)	gyűjtemény
collector	kolekcjoner (*m.*); zbieracz (*m.*)	gyűjtő
Colombia	Kolumbia	Kolumbia
color; colour	kolor (*m.*)	szín
commemorative (*adjective*)	okolicznościowy; pamiątkowy	emlék-
common	pospolity	mindennapos; általános
complete	kompletny	teljes; egész
conjoined	portret podwójny ("gemmowy")	egyirányba néző kettős portré

ROMANIAN	GREEK	HEBREW
jos; dedesubt	κάτω; πυθμένας	תַּחְתִּית (f.)
alamă (f.)	ορείχαλκος (n.)	פְּלִיז (m.)
Brazilia	Βραζιλία	בְּרָזִיל
monedă incusă (f.)	ελλιπώς κομμένο κέρμα (n.)	בְּרוֹקֵיג'
bronz (n.)	μπρούντζος (m.)	אָרָד (m.)
cafeniu	καφέ	חוּם
cumpăra	αγοράζω	קָנָה
cumpărător (m.)	αγοραστής (m.)	קוֹנֶה (m.)
uzură de cabinet (f.)	τριβή κέρματος απο την θήκη	הִתְחַכְּכוּת בַּתֵּיבָה (f.)
Canada	Καναδάς	קַנָדָה
numerar (n.)	χρήματα (n.pl.)	מְזֻמָּן (m.)
turna	καλουπώνω	לָצֶקֶת
catalog (n.)	κατάλογος (m.)	קַטָלוֹג (m.)
valoare de catalog (f.)	τιμή καταλόγου	עֵרֶךְ קַטָלוֹגִי (m.)
centenar (n.)	εκατονταετηρίδα (f.)	חֲגִיגַת שְׁנַת הַמֵּאָה (f.)
centimetru (m.)	εκατοστό (n.)	סֶנְטִימֶטֶר (m.)
certificat (n.)	χαρτονόμισμα (m.)	שְׁטָר (m.)
cec (n.)	επιταγή (f.)	הַמְחָאָה (f.)
China	Κίνα	סִין
crom (n.)	χρώμιο (n.)	כְּרוֹם (m.)
circulat	κυκλοφορημένο	בַּמַחֲזוֹר
circulație	κυκλοφορία (f.)	מַחֲזוֹר (m.)
monedă din multiple straturi (f.)	ενδεδυμένη νομισματοκοπία (f.)	מַטְבֵּעַ תְּלָת שִׁכְבָתִי (m.)
clasificare (f.)	ταξινόμηση (f.); κατάταξη (f.)	מִיּוּן (m.)
clasifica	ταξινομώ; κατατάσσω	מִיֵּן
monedă (f.)	νόμισμα (n.)	מַטְבֵּעַ (m.)
monedă (f.)	νομισματοκοπία; νομίσματα (n.pl.)	טְבִיעַת מַטְבְּעוֹת (f.)
colecționa	συλλέγω	אָסַף
colecție (f.)	συλλογή (f.)	אֹסֶף (m.)
colecționar (m.)	συλλέκτης	אַסְפָן (m.)
Columbia	Κολομβία	קוֹלוּמְבִּיָה
culoare (f.)	χρώμα (n.)	צֶבַע (m.)
comemorativ	αναμνηστικόν	הוֹצָאַת זִכָּרוֹן
comun	κοινός	שָׁכִיחַ
complet	πλήρες	שָׁלֵם
acolat; alăturat; acostat	αναγνωρισμένο	מְצֻמָּד

ENGLISH	POLISH	HUNGARIAN
copper (the metal)	miedź (f.)	vörösréz
copy (*noun*)	kopia (f.)	másolat
copy (*verb*)	kopiować	másolni
corrosion	korozja (f.)	korrózió
counterfeit (*noun*)	fałszerstwo (n.)	hamisítvány
counterfeit (*verb*)	fałszować	hamisítani
counterfeiter	fałszerz (m.)	hamisító
crease (*noun*)	załamanie (n.); zagięcie (n.)	hajtás; gyűrődés
credit	kredyt (m.)	hitel
credit card	karta kredytowa (f.)	hitelkártya
credit cards accepted	przyjmujemy karty kredytowe	hitelkártya-elfogadás
crown (royal headpiece)	korona (f.)	korona
crown (large silver coin)	korona (f.)	korona
cruzeiro	cruseiro (n.)	cruzeiro
currency	waluta (f.)	valuta
damaged	uszkodzony	sérült; megrongált
dark	ciemny	sötét
date	data (f.)	dátum
defect	uszkodzenie (n.); defekt (m.)	hiba
defective	uszkodzony	hibás; hiányos
demonetization	demonetyzacja (f.)	forgalomból kivont
Denmark	Dania	Dánia
denomination	nominał (m.)	címlet
deposit (of funds)	wadium (n.); kaucja (f.)	letét; betét; foglaló
deposit required	wadium wymagane	foglaló kötelező
design (*noun*)	wzór (m.)	minta; terv
devaluation	dewaluacja (f.)	leértékelés
diameter	średnica (f.)	átmérő
die (*i.e.*, coinage die)	tłok menniczy (m.); stempel menniczy (m.)	verőtő
die break	pęknięcie stempla (n.)	repedés a verőtövön
dollar	dolar (m.)	dollár
duplicate (*adjective*)	skopiowany	kettős; kétszeres
duplicate (*noun*)	duplikat (m.)	másolat
duplicate (*verb*)	kopiować; duplikować	sokszorosítani; másolni
eagle	orzeł (m.)	sas
East Germany (D.D.R.)	Niemcy Wschodnie	Kelet-Németország

ROMANIAN	GREEK	HEBREW
cupru (n.); aramă (f.)	χαλκός (m.)	נְחֹשֶׁת (f.)
copie (f.)	αντίγραφο (n.)	עֹתֶק (m.)
copia	αντιγράφω	הֶעְתֵּק
coroziune (f.); rugină (f.)	διάβρωση (f.)	אִכּוּל (m.)
fals (n.); falsificare (f.)	πλαστό (n.)	מְזֻיָּף (m.)
falsifica	παραχαράσσω	זִיֵּף
falsificator (m.)	πλαστογράφος	זַיְּפָן
cută (f.)	τσάκισμα (n.)	קֶמֶט (m.)
credit (n.)	πίστωση (f.)	אַשְׁרַאי (m.)
carte de credit (f.)	πιστωτική κάρτα (f.)	כַּרְטִיס אַשְׁרַאי (m.)
carți de credit acceptate	δεχόμαστε πιστωτικές κάρτες	כַּרְטִיסֵי אַשְׁרַאי מִתְקַבְּלִים
coroană (f.)	στέμμα (n.)	כֶּתֶר (m.)
coroană (f.)	κορώνα (f.)	כֶּתֶר (m.)
cruzeiro (m.)	κρουζιέρο (m.)	קְרוּזֵרוֹ (m.)
valută (f.); monedă (f.)	νόμισμα (n.)	מַטְבֵּעַ (m.)
deteriorat	χαλασμένο	פָּגוּם
închis	σκοτεινός	כֵּהֶה (m.)
dată (f.)	ημερομηνία (f.)	תַּאֲרִיךְ (m.)
defect (n.); imperfecțiune (f.)	ελάττωμα (n.)	לִקּוּי (m.)
cu defect	ελαττωματικό	לָקוּי
demonetizare (f.)	απόσυρσης νομίσματος απο την κυκλοφορία	הוֹצָאָה מִתּוֹקֶף (f.)
Danemarca	Δανία	דַּנְמַרְק
valoare nominală (f.)	μονάδα χρημάτων	עֵרֶךְ נָקוּב (m.)
acont (n.)	προκαταβολή (f.)	פִּקָּדוֹן (m.)
depozit obligatoriu	προκαταβολή απαιτείται	פִּקָּדוֹן דָּרוּשׁ
motiv (n.)	σχέδιο (n.)	תֶּכֶן (m.)
devalorizare (f.)	υποτίμηση (f.)	פִּחוּת (m.)
diametru (n.)	διάμετρος (f.)	קֹטֶר (m.)
matriță (f.); ștanță (f.); tipar (n.)	μήτρα (f.)	מַטְבַּעַת (f.)
fisură în matriță (f.); fisură în ștanță (f.)	διακοπτόμενη σφραγίδα νομίσματος	סֶדֶק בְּמַטְבַּעַת (m.)
dolar (n.)	δολλάριο (n.)	דּוֹלָר (m.)
duplicat	διπλοτυπωμένο	כָּפוּל
duplicat (n.)	διπλότυπον	כֶּפֶל (m.)
duplica	διπλασιάζω	שִׁכְפֵּל
vultur (m.)	αετός (m.)	נֶשֶׁר (m.)
Germania de Est	Ανατολική Γερμανία	גֶּרְמַנְיָה הַמִּזְרָחִית

ENGLISH	POLISH	HUNGARIAN
edge	rant (*m.*); obrzeże (*n.*)	perem
effigy	wizerunek (*m.*); postać (*f.*)	képmás
eight	osiem	nyolc
eighty	osiemdziesiąt	nyolcvan
electrotype	elektrotyp (*m.*); galwanotyp (*m.*)	galvánklisé
electrum	elektrum (*m.*)	elektron
emergency currency	pieniądz zastępczy (*m.*)	szükségpénz
emperor	cesarz (*m.*)	császár
England	Anglia	Anglia
engraved	-----	vésett
error	błąd (*m.*)	hiba
excellent	znakomity	kitűnő
exchange rate	kurs wymiany (*m.*)	árfolyam
exergue	egzerga (*f.*); odcinek (*m.*)	szelvény
exhibit (*verb*)	wystawiać; eksponować	kiállítani
exhibition	wystawa (*f.*); ekspozycja (*f.*)	kiállítás
face value	wartość nominalna (*f.*)	névérték
fake (*noun*)	falsyfikat (*m.*)	hamisítvány
fee	opłata (*f.*)	illeték
fiat money	-----	beválthatatlan papírpénz
fifty	pięćdziesiąt	ötven
finance minister	minister finansów (*m.*)	pénzügyminiszter
fine (grade or condition)	piękny; dobry	szép
fine (purity of metal)	czysty	finom; szín-
Finland	Finlandia	Finnország
five	pięć	öt
fold (*noun*)	zagięcie (*n.*); zgięcie (*n.*)	hajtás
foreign	zagraniczny; obcy	idegen
foreign currency	obca waluta (*f.*); dewizy (*f.pl.*)	idegen valuta
forgery	fałszerstwo (*n.*)	hamisítvány
forty	czterdzieści	negyven
four	cztery	négy
fourth (*noun*)	jedna czwarta (*f.*)	negyed
fraction	frakcja (*f.*)	törtszám
franc	frank (*m.*)	frank
France	Francja	Franciaország

ROMANIAN	GREEK	HEBREW
margine (f.); muchie (f.)	άκρον (n.)	קָצֶה (m.)
efigie (f.)	ομοίωμα (n.)	דְּמוּת (f.)
opt	οκτώ	שְׁמוֹנֶה
optzeci	ογδόντα	שְׁמוֹנִים
copie prin electroplastie (f.)	γαλβανισμένα	הֶעְתֵּק אֶלֶקְטְרוֹטִיפִּי (m.)
electrum (n.)	ήλεκτρον (n.)	אֶלֶקְטְרוּם (m.)
monedă de necesitate	νομίσματα έκτακτης ανάγκης (n.)	כֶּסֶף חֵרוּם (m.)
împărat (m.)	αυτοκράτορας (m.)	קֵיסָר (m.)
Anglia	Αγγλία	אַנְגְלִיָּה
gravat	χαρακτικόν	חָרוּת
eroare (f.); greşeală (f.)	λάθος (n.)	טָעוּת (f.)
excelent	εξαίρετος	מְצֻיָּן
curs de schimb (n.)	τιμή συναλλάγματος	שַׁעַר הַחֲלִיפִין (m.)
exergă (f.)	έξεργον (n.)	שׁוּל תַּחְתּוֹנִי מְסוּיָּם בַּמַּטְבֵּעַ ; אֶקְסֶרְג
expune	εκθέτω	הַצִּיג
expoziţie (f.)	έκθεση (f.)	תַּעֲרוּכָה (f.)
valoare nominală (f.)	ονομαστική αξία (f.)	עֵרֶךְ נָקוּב (m.)
fals (n.); imitaţie (f.)	πλαστό (n.)	מְזֻוָּף
taxă (f.)	αμοιβή (f.)	תַּשְׁלוּם (m.)
bani fără acoperire în aur sau argint	-----	כֶּסֶף מוּכְרָז (m.)
cincizeci	πενήντα	חֲמִשִּׁים
ministru de finanţe (m.)	υπουργός οικονομικών (m.)	שַׂר הָאוֹצָר (m.)
foarte bun	εξαίρετος	נָאֶה
fin; pur	καθαρός	טָהוֹר
Finlanda	Φιλανδία	פִינְלַנְד
cinci	πέντε	חֲמִשָּׁה
îndoitură (f.); pliu (n.)	πτυχή (f.)	קֶפֶל (m.)
străin	αλλοδαπός; ξένος	זָר
valută străină (f.)	ξένο νόμισμα (n.)	מַטְבֵּעַ זָר
fals (n.); falsificare (f.)	πλαστό (n.); κίβδηλον (n.)	זִיּוּף (m.)
patruzeci	σαράντα	אַרְבָּעִים
patru	τέσσερα	אַרְבָּעָה
pătrime (f.)	τέταρτον	רֶבַע (m.)
fracţiune (f.)	κλάσμα (n.)	שֶׁבֶר (m.)
franc (m.)	φράγκο (n.)	פְרַנְק (m.)
Franţa	Γαλλία	צָרְפַת

ENGLISH	POLISH	HUNGARIAN
front	front (*m.*)	előoldal; előlap
genuine	prawdziwy	valódi
Germany	Niemcy	Németország
gold (the metal)	złoto (*n.*)	arany
good	dobry	jó
grade (*noun*)	stan (zachowania) (*m.*)	fokozat; osztály
grade (*verb*)	oceniać (stan zachowania); klasyfikować	osztályozni
Great Britain	Wielka Brytania	Nagy-Britannia
Greece	Grecja	Görögország
green	zielony	zöld
half (*adjective*)	pół; przepołowiony	fél
half (*noun*)	połowa (*f.*); połówka (*f.*)	fele valaminek
hammered coin	moneta bita młotem (*f.*)	kézi veréssel készült pénz
hole	otwór (*m.*); dziura (*f.*)	lyuk
holed	z otworem	lyukas
Hong Kong	Hong Kong	Hongkong
hundred	sto	száz
hundredth (*noun*)	jedna setna (*f.*)	század
imitation	imitacja (*f.*)	utánzat
inch	cal (*m.*)	hüvelyk
incomplete	niekompletny	befejezetlen
incuse	wklęsły (stempel)	mélyített veret
ingot	sztaba (*f.*); sztabka (*f.*)	nemesfémrúd
ink	atrament (*m.*)	tinta
inscription	inskrypcja (*f.*); napis (*m.*)	felírás; felirat
intaglio	intaglio (*n.*)	intaglió
international	międzynarodowy	nemzetközi
intrinsic	wewnętrzny	belső
Ireland	Irlandia	Írország
iron (the metal)	żelazo (*n.*)	vas
irregular	nieregularny; nietypowy	szabálytalan
Israel	Izrael	Izrael
issue (*noun*)	emisja (*f.*); wydanie (*n.*)	kiadás; kibocsátás
issue (*verb*)	wydawać; emitować	kiadni; kibocsátani
Italy	Włochy	Olaszország
Japan	Japonia	Japán

ROMANIAN	GREEK	HEBREW
față (f.)	πρόσοψη (f.)	צַד הַקִּדְמִי (m.)
autentic; veritabil	γνήσιον	אֲמִתִּי
Germania	Γερμανία	גֶּרְמַנְיָה
aur (n.)	χρυσός (m.)	זָהָב (m.)
bun	καλό	טוֹב
stare de conservare (f.)	βαθμός (m.)	מַדְרֵגָה (f.)
califica; aprecia	βαθμολογώ	דֵּרַג
Marea Britanie	Μεγάλη Βρεττανία	בְּרִיטַנְיָה הַגְּדוֹלָה
Grecia	Ελλάς	יָוָן
verde	πράσινο	יָרֹק
jumătate	μισό	חֲצִי
jumătate (f.)	μισό (n.)	חֲצִי (m.)
monedă bătută manual (f.)	αναξιόχρεον κέρμα (n.)	מַטְבֵּעַ מְעוּצָב בַּפַּטִּישׁ (m.)
gaură (f.)	τρύπα (f.); οπή (f.)	חוֹר (m.)
găurit	τρυπημένο	בַּעַל-חוֹר
Hong Kong	Χόνγκ Κόνγκ	הוֹנְג-קוֹנְג
sută	εκατό	מֵאָה (f.)
sutime (f.)	εκατοστόν	מֵאִית (f.)
imitație (f.)	μίμηση (f.)	חִקּוּי (m.)
inci (m.)	ίντσα (f.)	אִינְץ' (m.)
incomplet	ατελές	בִּלְתִּי מָשְׁלָם
incus	έγγλυφο (n.)	צוּרָה מֻטְבַּעַת
lingou (n.)	χυτός όγκος μετάλλου	מְטִיל מַתֶּכֶת (m.)
cerneală (f.)	μελάνι (n.)	דְּיוֹ (m./f.)
inscripție (f.)	επιγραφή (f.)	כְּתוֹבִית
intaglio (n.)	εγχάραξη (f.)	דְּפוּס שֶׁקַע (m.)
internațional	διεθνής	בֵּין-לְאֻמִּי
intrinsec	εσωτερική αξία (f.)	עֵרֶךְ בְּשׁוּק (m.)
Irlanda	Ιρλανδία	אִירְלַנְד
fier (n.)	σίδηρος (m.)	בַּרְזֶל (m.)
neregulat	ανώμαλος	חָרִיג (m.)
Israel	Ισραήλ	יִשְׂרָאֵל
emisiune (f.)	έκδοση (f.)	הַנְפָּקָה
emite	εκδίδω	הַנְפֵּק
Italia	Ιταλία	אִיטַלְיָה (f.)
Japonia	Ιαπωνία	יָפָן

ENGLISH	POLISH	HUNGARIAN
king	król (*m.*)	király
language	język (*m.*)	nyelv
large	wielki; duży	nagy
laureate	uwieńczony	babérkoszorús
left (direction or position)	na lewo; lewa strona (*f.*)	bal
legend	legenda (*f.*)	legenda; felirat
lithography	litografia (*f.*)	litográfia
lot (*i.e.*, auction lot)	lot (*m.*); zestaw (*m.*)	lot
magnifying glass	lupa (*f.*); szkło powiększające (*n.*)	nagyító
mail bid sale	aukcja na oferty pocztowe (*f.*)	-----
mark (German currency)	marka (*f.*)	márka
medal	medal (*m.*)	érem
metal	metal (*m.*)	fém
Mexico	Meksyk	Mexikó
military decoration	odznaczenie wojskowe (*n.*)	katonai kitüntetés
milled coin	moneta bita maszynowo (*f.*)	hornyolt érem
millimeter; millimetre	milimetr (*m.*)	milliméter
million	milion	millió
minimum bid	najniższa cena (*f.*)	legalacsonyabb ár
mint	mennica (*f.*)	pénzverde
mintmark; mint mark	znak menniczy (*m.*)	verdejegy
mis-strike (*noun*)	destrukt menniczy (*m.*)	hibás veret
mis-struck	wadliwie wybity	rosszul vert (pénz)
monetary	monetarny	pénzügyi
monetary system	system monetarny (*m.*)	pénzrendszer
monetary unit	jednostka monetarna (*f.*)	pénzegység
money	pieniądze (*m.pl.*)	pénz
money order	przekaz pieniężny (*m.*)	postautalvány
motto	motto (*n.*)	jelmondat
national	narodowy	nemzeti
nationality	narodowość (*f.*)	nemzetiség
Netherlands; Holland	Holandia	Hollandia
new	nowy	új
New Zealand	Nowa Zelandia	Új-Zéland
nickel (the metal)	nikiel (*m.*)	nikkel
nine	dziewięć	kilenc

ROMANIAN	GREEK	HEBREW
rege (m.)	βασιλιάς (m.)	מֶלֶךְ (m.)
limbă (f.)	γλώσσα (f.)	שָׂפָה (f.)
mare	μεγάλο	גָּדוֹל
laureat	δαφνοστεφής	עֲטוּר דַּפְנָה (m.)
stânga	αριστερός	שְׂמֹאל
legendă (f.)	επιγραφή (f.)	כְּתוֹבִית
litografie (f.)	λιθογραφία (f.)	לִיתוֹגְרַפְיָה (f.)
lot (n.)	λαχνός (m.)	פְּרִיט (m.)
lupă (f.)	μεγενθυτικός φακός (m.)	זְכוּכִית מַגְדֶּלֶת (f.)
licitaţie prin poştă (f.)	πώληση μέσω ταχυδρομείου	מְכִירָה פּוּמְבִּית דֶּרֶךְ הַצָעוֹת נִשְׁלָחוֹת בַּדּוֹ אַר
marcă (f.)	μάρκο (n.)	מַרְק (m.)
medalie (f.)	μετάλλιον (n.)	מֶדַלְיָה (f.)
metal (n.)	μέταλλο (n.)	מַתֶּכֶת (f.)
Mexic	Μεξικό	מֶקְסִיקוֹ
decoraţie militară (f.)	στρατιωτικόν παράσημον (n.)	עֲטוּר צְבָאִי (m.)
monedă bătută mecanic (f.)	σφραγισμένο νόμισμα (n.)	מַטְבֵּעַ מְכוּרְסָם (m.)
milimetru (m.)	χιλιοστό (n.)	מִילִימֶטֶר (m.)
milion	εκατομμύριο (n.)	מִילְיוֹן (m.)
ofertă minimă de licitaţie (f.)	ελάχιστη προσφορά (f.)	הַצָּעַת מְחִיר מִינִימוּם (f.)
monetărie (f.)	νομισματοκοπείον (n.)	מִטְבָּעָה (f.)
semnul monetăriei (n.)	ένδειξη νομισματοκοπείου	סִימָן הַמִּטְבָּעָה (m.)
batere defectuoasă (f.)	παραχάραξη (f.)	טְבִיעָה שֶׁלֹּא כַּהֲלָכָה (f.)
bătut defectuos	παραχαραγμένο	שֶׁלֹּא נִטְבַּע כַּהֲלָכָה
monetar	νομισματικός	כַּסְפִּי
sistem monetar (n.)	νομισματικό σύστημα	מַעֲרֶכֶת הַכְּסָפִים (f.)
unitate monetară (f.)	νομισματική μονάδα (f.)	יְחִידָה כַּסְפִּית (f.)
bani (m.pl.)	χρήματα (n.pl.)	כֶּסֶף (m.)
mandat poştal (n.)	επιταγή (f.)	הַמְחָאַת כֶּסֶף (f.)
moto (n.); deviză (f.)	ρητό (n.)	סִיסְמָה (f.)
naţional	εθνικός	לְאֻמִּי
naţionalitate (f.)	εθνικότητα (f.)	לְאוֹם (m.)
Olanda	Ολλανδία	הוֹלַנְד
nou	καινούργιο	חָדָשׁ
Noua Zeelandă	Νέα Ζηλανδία	נִיוּ זִילַנְד
nichel (n.)	νικέλιο (n.)	נִיקֶל (m.)
nouă	εννέα	תִּשְׁעָה

ENGLISH	POLISH	HUNGARIAN
ninety	dziewięćdziesiąt	kilencven
Northern Ireland	Irlandia Północna	Észak-Írország
Norway	Norwegia	Norvégia
note (*i.e.*, banknote)	banknot (*m.*); pieniądz papierowy (*m.*)	bankjegy
not issued	nie wprowadzony do obiegu	kibocsátásra nem került
no unlimited bids accepted	nie przyjmuje się zleceń bez limitu	-----
number	numer (*m.*)	szám
numismatic (*adjective*)	numizmatyczny	numizmatikai
numismatics (*noun*)	numizmatyka (*f.*)	numizmatika
numismatist	numizmatyk (*m.*)	gyűjtő (pénz, érem, stb.)
obsidional	oblężniczy	ostromlott városban forgalomba hozott pénz
obsolete	przestarzały	forgalomból kivont
obverse	awers (*m.*)	előlap
offer (*noun*)	oferta (*f.*)	ajánlat
offer (*verb*)	oferować	ajánlani
official	oficjalny; urzędowy	hivatalos
old	stary	régi
on approval	za zgodą	jóváhagyással
one	jeden	egy
on the back	na odwrociu; na rewersie	hátoldalon
order form	formularz zamówienia (*m.*)	megrendelőlap
original	oryginalny	eredeti
ounce	uncja (*f.*)	uncia
overprint	nadruk (*m.*)	felülbélyegzés
palindrome	palindrom (*m.*)	-----
paper	papier (*m.*)	papír
paper money	pieniądz papierowy (*m.*)	papírpénz
pattern	wzór (*m.*); wyobrażenie (*n.*)	minta
pedigree	proweniencja (*f.*); pochodzenie (*n.*)	tulajdonosok listája
People's Republic of China (P.R.C.)	Chińska Republika Ludowa	Kínai Népköztársaság
perfect	doskonały	tökéletes
Peru	Peru	Peru
peseta	peseta (*f.*)	pezeta
peso	peso (*n.*)	pezó
photogravure	fotograwiura (*f.*)	fénynyomás
piéfort; piedfort	piedfort (*m.*)	vastagveret; piefort

ROMANIAN	GREEK	HEBREW
nouăzeci	ενενήντα	תִּשְׁעִים
Irlanda de Nord	Βόρεια Ιρλανδία	אִירְלַנְד הַצְּפוֹנִית
Norvegia	Νορβηγία	נוֹרְבֶּגְיָה
bancnotă (f.)	γραμμάτιο (m.)	שְׁטָר (m.)
ne-emis	μή εκδοθέντα	שֶׁלֹּא יָצָא לְהַנְפָּקָה
oferte nelimitate de licitaţie neacceptate	προσφορές άνευ ορίου δέν αποδέχονται	לֹא מִתְקַבְּלוֹת הַצָּעוֹת בִּלְתִּי מוּגְבָּלוֹת
număr (n.)	αριθμός (m.)	מִסְפָּר
numismatic	νομισματικόν	נוּמִיסְמָטִי
numismatică (f.)	νομισματικός	נוּמִיסְמָטִיקָה (f.)
numismat (m.)	νομισματικός	אַסְפָן מַטְבֵּעוֹת (m.)
obsidional	οψιδιανό	מַטְבְּעוֹת חֵרוּם
învechit	απαρχαιομένο	מִחוּץ לְמַחְזוֹר
avers (n.)	εμπροσθότυπος (m.)	פְּנֵי מַטְבֵּעַ (m.)
ofertă (f.)	προσφορά (f.)	הַצָּעָה (f.)
oferi	προσφέρω	הִצִּיעַ
oficial	επίσημος	רִשְׁמִי
vechi	παλιός	יָשָׁן
spre aprobare	επί πιστώσει	לְנִסָּיוֹן
unu	ένα	אֶחָד (m.adj.) ; אַחַת (f.adj.)
pe verso	όπισθεν	עַל הַגַּב
formular de comandă (n.)	δελτίον παραγγελιών (n.)	טוֹפֶס הַזְמָנָה (m.)
original	πρωτότυπος	מְקוֹרִי
uncie (f.)	ουγγιά	אוּנְקִיָּה (f.)
supratipar (n.)	επισφράγισης (f.)	הֶדְפֵּס מֵעַל (m.)
palindrom (n.)	παλινδρομική επιγραφή (f.)	חִידַת רָצוֹא וָשׁוֹב (f.)
hârtie (f.)	χαρτί (n.)	נְיָר (m.)
bancnotă (f.)	χαρτονόμισμα (n.)	שְׁטְרֵי כֶּסֶף
proiect (n.); model (n.); probă (f.)	σχέδιο (n.)	דֶּגֶם (m.)
listă de proprietari (f.)	ράτσα (f.)	מוֹצָא (m.)
Republica Populară Chineza	Λαϊκή Δημοκρατία τής Κίνας	הָרֶפּוּבְּלִיקָה הָעֲמָמִית שֶׁל סִין
perfect	άψογος	מְשֻׁלָּם
Peru	Περού	פֶּרוּ
peseta (f.)	πεσέτα (f.)	פֶּסֶטָה (f.)
peso (m.)	πέσο (n.)	פֶּסוֹ (m.)
fotogravură (f.)	φωτογραβούρα (f.)	דְּפוּס שֶׁקַע
piéfort (n.)	πιεφόρτ	טְבִיעָה מְיוּחֶדֶת (f.)

ENGLISH	POLISH	HUNGARIAN
planchet	blankiet (*m.*); krążek monetarny (*m.*)	fémlapka
platinum (the metal)	platyna (*f.*)	platina
pope	papież (*m.*)	pápa
portrait	portret (*m.*)	arckép; portré
Portugal	Portugalia	Portugália
pound (unit of weight)	funt (*m.*)	font
pound (£)	funt szterling (*m.*)	font
prepayment	przedpłata (*f.*)	előfizetés
president	prezydent (*m.*)	elnök
press (*i.e.,* coinage press)	prasa mennicza (*f.*)	verőgép
price	cena (*f.*)	ár
price list	cennik (*m.*)	árjegyzék
print (*verb*)	drukować	nyomtatni
proof (*re:* coins or medals)	próba (*f.*)	proof; tükörfényes
propaganda note	bon propagandowy (*m.*)	propaganda pénz
protective reserve bid	cena zabezpieczenia (*f.*)	-----
queen	królowa (*f.*)	királynő
rare	rzadki	ritka
rarity	rzadkość (*f.*)	ritkaság
receipt	pokwitowanie (*n.*)	nyugta
rectangular	prostokątny	derékszögű; négyszögletes
red	czerwony	piros
repaired	naprawiony	kijavított
reproduction	reprodukcja (*f.*)	másolat
republic	republika (*f.*)	köztársaság
Republic of China (Taiwan)	Tajwan	Kínai Köztársaság
restrike (*noun*)	nowe bicie (*n.*)	utánveret
reverse	rewers (*m.*)	hátlap; hátoldal
right (direction or position)	na prawo; prawa strona (*f.*)	jobb
rim	krawędź (*f.*)	perem
roll (of coins)	rolka (*f.*)	tekercs
round	okrągły	kerek
Russia	Rosja	Oroszország
Saudi Arabia	Arabia Saudyjska	Szaúd-Arábia
scarce	rzadki	ritka
Scotland	Szkocja	Skócia

ROMANIAN	GREEK	HEBREW
pastilă monetară (f.)	κινούμενον πινακίδιον με γραφίδα	לוּחִית (f.)
platină (f.)	πλατίνα (f.)	פְּלָטִינָה (f.)
papă (m.)	πάπας (m.)	אַפִּיפְיוֹר (m.)
portret (n.)	πορτραίτο (n.)	דִּיוֹקָן (m.)
Portugalia	Πορτογαλία	פּוֹרטוּגַל
livră (f.)	λίβρα (f.)	לִטְרָה (f.)
livră (f.)	λίρα (f.)	לִירָה שְׁטֶרְלִינְג (f.)
francare (f.)	προπληρωμή (f.)	תַּשְׁלוּם מֵרֹאשׁ (m.)
președinte (m.)	πρόεδρος	נָשִׂיא (m.)
presă de bani (f.)	πρέσσα τυπώσεως νομισμάτων (f.)	מַכְבֵּשׁ מַטְבְּעוֹת (m.)
preț (n.)	τιμή (f.)	מְחִיר (m.)
listă de prețuri (f.)	τιμοκατάλογος (m.)	מְחִירוֹן (m.)
tipări	τυπώνω	הַדְפֵּס
proof	δοκίμιον	מְיָחָד ; מַטְבֵּעַ קִשּׁוּט
notă propagandistică (f.)	προπαγανδιστικό σημείωμα (n.)	שְׁטַר תַּעֲמוּלָה (m.)
ofertă de rezervă (pentru protecție) (f.)	διαφυλασσόμενη προσφορά	הַצָּעָה שְׁמוּרָה מוּגֶנֶּת (f.)
regină (f.)	βασίλισσα (f.)	מַלְכָּה (f.)
rar	σπάνιο	נָדִיר
raritate (f.)	σπανιότητα (f.)	נְדִירוּת (f.)
chitanță (f.); recipisă (f.)	απόδειξη (f.)	קַבָּלָה (f.)
dreptunghiular	ορθογώνιο	מַלְבֵּנִי
roșu	κόκκινο	אָדֹם
reparat	επιδιορθωμένο	מְתֻקָּן
reproducere (f.)	αναπαραγωγή (f.)	שַׁעֲתוּק (m.)
republică (f.)	δημοκρατία (f.)	רֶפּוּבְּלִיקָה (f.)
Republica Chineză	Δημοκρατία τής Κίνας	הָרֶפּוּבְּלִיקָה שֶׁל סִין (f.)
re-emitere (f.)	επικεκομμένο (n.)	טְבִיעָה מֵחָדָשׁ (f.)
revers (n.)	οπισθότυπος (m.)	צַד הַשֵּׁנִי (m.)
dreapta	δεξιός	יָמִין
margine (f.)	αιχμή (f.)	שׁוּלַיִם
fișic (n.)	ρολός	גָּלִיל (m.)
rotund	στρογγυλός; σφαιροειδής	עָגֹל
Rusia	Ρωσσία	רוּסְיָה
Arabia Saudită	Σαουδική Αραβία	עֲרָב הַסַּעוּדִית
rar	σπάνιον	נָדִיר
Scoția	Σκωτία	סְקוֹטְלַנְד

ENGLISH	POLISH	HUNGARIAN
scratch (*noun*)	rysa (*f.*); zadrapanie (*n.*)	karcolás
scrip	pieniądz zastępczy (*m.*)	magán szükségpénz
seal (*noun*)	pieczęć (*f.*)	pecsét
seigniorage	segnoragium (*n.*); zysk menniczy (*m.*)	-----
sell (*verb*)	sprzedawać	eladni
seller	sprzedający (*m.*)	eladó
series	seria (*f.*)	sorozat
serial number	numer serii (*m.*)	sorszám
seven	siedem	hét
seventy	siedemdziesiąt	hetven
signature	podpis (*m.*)	aláírás
silk thread	jedwabna nitka (*f.*)	selyemszál
silver (the metal)	srebro (*n.*)	ezüst
six	sześć	hat
sixty	sześćdziesiąt	hatvan
small	mały	kicsi
South Africa	Afryka Południowa	Dél-Afrika
sovereign	suweren (*m.*)	uralkodó
Soviet Union (U.S.S.R.)	Związek Radziecki (Z.S.R.R.)	Szovjetúnió
Spain	Hiszpania	Spanyolország
specimen	specimen (*m.*)	minta
square (*adjective*)	kwadratowy	négyszögletes
stain	plama (*f.*)	folt; pecsét
star	gwiazda (*f.*)	csillag
steel	stal (*f.*)	acél
steel engraving	staloryt (*m.*)	acélba vésés
suggested bid	cena szacunkowa (*f.*)	ajánlott ár
Sweden	Szwecja	Svédország
Switzerland	Szwajcaria	Svájc
symbol	symbol (*m.*)	jelkép
tarnish	zmatowienie (*n.*)	elhomályosodás; bevonat; patina
tax (*noun*)	podatek (*m.*)	adó
tear (*noun*)	naderwanie (*n.*)	szakadás
ten	dziesięć	tíz
tenth (*noun*)	jedna dziesiąta (*f.*)	tized
third (*noun*)	jedna trzecia (*f.*)	harmad

ROMANIAN	GREEK	HEBREW
zgârietură (f.)	γρατσουνιά (f.)	שְׂרִיטָה (f.)
monedă accesorie privată	προσωρινά χαρτονομίσματα (n.pl.)	שְׁטַר כֶּסֶף זְמַנִּי ; הוֹצָאַת כֶּסֶף פְּרָטִית
sigiliu (n.); pecete (f.)	σφραγίδα (f.)	חוֹתָם (m.)
senioriaj (n.)	κρατικό κέρδος απο έκδοση νομισμάτων	הֶפְרֵשׁ הָעֵרֶךְ (שֶׁל מַטְבֵּעַ)
vinde	πουλώ	מָכַר
vânzător (m.)	πωλητής	מוֹכֵר (m.)
serie (f.)	σειρά (f.)	סִדְרָה (f.)
număr de serie (n.)	διαδοχικός αριθμός (m.)	מִסְפָּר סִדּוּרִי (m.)
şapte	επτά	שִׁבְעָה
şaptezeci	εβδομήντα	שִׁבְעִים
semnătură (f.)	υπογραφή (f.)	חֲתִימָה (f.)
fir de mătase (n.)	μεταξωτή κλωστή (f.)	חוּט מֶשִׁי
argint (n.)	αργυρός	כֶּסֶף (m.)
şase	έξι	שִׁשָּׁה
şaizeci	εξήντα	שִׁשִּׁים
mic	μικρό	קָטָן
Africa de Sud	Νότιος Αφρική	דְּרוֹם אַפְרִיקָה
suveran (m.)	ηγεμόνας	שַׁלִּיט (m.)
Uniunea Sovietică	Σοβιετική Ένωση	בְּרִית הַמּוֹעָצוֹת
Spania	Ισπανία	סְפָרַד
mostră (f.); specimen (n.)	δείγμα (n.)	דּוּגְמָא (f.)
pătrat	τετραγωνικό	רָבוּעַ
pată (f.)	στίγμα (n.)	כֶּתֶם (m.)
stea (f.)	άστρο (n.)	כּוֹכָב (m.)
oţel (n.)	χάλυβας (m.)	פְּלָדָה (f.)
gravură în oţel (f.)	χάραξη επί χάλυβδος	פִּתּוּחַ פְּלָדָה (m.)
ofertă sugerată (f.)	εισηγούμενη προσφορά (f.)	הַצָּעָה מֻצַּעַת (f.)
Suedia	Σουηδία	שְׁוֶדְיָה
Elveţia	Ελβετία	שְׁוַיִץ
simbol (n.)	σύμβολο (n.)	סֵמֶל (m.)
mat (adj.)	μουντζούρα (f.)	כֶּתֶם (m.)
taxă (f.)	φόρος (m.)	מַס (m.)
ruptură (f.)	σχίσιμο	קֶרַע (m.)
zece	δέκα	עֲשָׂרָה
zecime (f.)	δέκατον	עֲשִׂירִית
treime (f.)	τρίτον (n.)	שְׁלִישׁ (m.)

ENGLISH	POLISH	HUNGARIAN
thirty	trzydzieści	harminc
thousand	tysiąc	ezer
three	trzy	három
tin	cyna (*f.*)	ón; cin
token	żeton (*m.*)	zseton; tantusz
top	góra (*f.*)	csúcs
torn	naderwany	szakadt
trade (*verb*)	handlować	elcserélni; kereskedni
treasure	skarb (*m.*)	kincs
twenty	dwadzieścia	húsz
two	dwa	kettő
unattributed	nieokreślony	bizonytalan származású
uncirculated	nieobiegowy	forgalomba nem bocsátott
uniface	jednostronny	egyoldalú (pénz, érem)
unique	unikatowy	páratlan
United Kingdom (U.K.)	Zjednoczone Królestwo	Egyesült Királyság
United States of America (U.S.A.)	Stany Zjednoczone Ameryki Północnej	Amerikai Egyesült Államok
unknown	nieznany	ismeretlen
unofficial	nieoficjalny; nieurzędowy	nem hivatalos
unpublished	niepublikowany	publikálatlan; kiadatlan
used	używany	használt
valuable	wartościowy	értékes
value	wartość (*f.*)	érték
variety	odmiana (*f.*); wariant (*m.*)	választék
Venezuela	Wenezuela	Venezuela
Wales	Walia	Wales
watermark	znak wodny (*m.*)	vízjegy
wear (*noun*)	starcie (*n.*); zużycie (*n.*)	kopás
weight	waga (*f.*)	súly
West Germany (B.R.D.)	Niemcy Zachodnie	Nyugat-Németország
white	biały	fehér
year	rok (*m.*)	év
yellow	żółty	sárga
Yugoslavia; Jugoslavia	Jugosławia	Jugoszlávia
zero	zero	zéró
zinc	cynk (*m.*)	cink

ROMANIAN	GREEK	HEBREW
treizeci	τριάντα	שְׁלֹשִׁים
mie	χίλια (n.pl.)	אֶלֶף (m.)
trei	τρία	שְׁלֹשָׁה
cositor (n.)	κασσίτερος (n.)	בְּדִיל (m.)
fisă (f.); jeton (n.)	τεκμήριο (n.)	אֲסִימוֹן (m.)
sus; deasupra	κορυφή (f.)	רֹאשׁ (m.)
rupt	σχισμένο	קָרוּעַ
face comerţ	ανταλλάσσω	סָחַר
comoară (f.); tezaur (n.)	θησαυρός (m.)	אוֹצָר (m.)
douăzeci	είκοσι	עֶשְׂרִים
doi	δύο	שְׁנַיִם
neatribuit; nedeterminat; ne-identificat	αταύτιστος	בִּלְתִּי מְזוֹהֶה
necirculat	ακυκλοφόρητα	שֶׁלֹּא בַּמַּחֲזוֹר
unifaţă	μονόπλευρο (n.)	חַד-פָּנִים
unic	μαναδικός	יָחִיד בְּמִינוֹ
Regatul Unit	Ηνωμένον Βασίλειον	מַמְלָכָה הַמְאֻחֶדֶת
Statele Unite al Americii	Ηνωμένες Πολιτείες τής Αμερικής	אַרְצוֹת הַבְּרִית
necunoscut	άγνωστος	בִּלְתִּי יָדוּעַ
neoficial	ανεπίσημον	לֹא-רִשְׁמִי
nepublicat	μή εκδοθέν	שֶׁלֹּא פוּרְסַם
folosit; uzat	μεταχειρισμένο	מְשֻׁמָּשׁ
valoros	πολύτιμος	בַּעַל-עֵרֶךְ
valoare (f.)	αξία (f.)	עֵרֶךְ (m.)
varietate (f.)	ποικιλία (f.)	מִבְחָר (m.)
Venezuela	Βενεζουέλα	וֶנֶצוּאֵלָה
Ţara Galilor	Ουαλία	וֵילְס
filigran (n.)	υδατόσημο (n.)	סִימָן מֵימִי (m.)
uzură (f.)	φθορά (f.)	בְּלַאי (m.) ; בְּלָיָה (f.)
greutate (f.); pond (n.)	βάρος (n.)	מִשְׁקָל (m.)
Germania de Vest	Δυτική Γερμανία	גֶּרְמַנְיָה הַמַּעֲרָבִית
alb	άσπρο	לָבָן
an (m.)	έτος (n.)	שָׁנָה (f.)
galben	κίτρινο	צָהֹב
Iugoslavia	Γιουγκοσλαβία	יוּגוֹסְלַבְיָה
zero	μηδέν (n.)	אֶפֶס
zinc (n.)	ψευδάργυρος (m.)	אָבָץ (m.)

ENGLISH	RUSSIAN	TURKISH
abbreviation	сокращение (*n.*)	kisaltma
accolated	соединённый; наложенный	üstüste ve aynı yöne bakan
account (financial or transactional)	счёт (*m.*)	hesap
acquisition	приобретение (*n.*)	elde etme; kazanç
adjustment mark	зазубрина (*f.*)	ayar işareti
album	альбом (*m.*)	albüm
alloy (of metals)	сплав (*m.*)	alaşım
alter (*verb*)	видоизменять (*v.*)	değiştirmek
alteration	подделка (*f.*)	değiştirme
altered date	измененная дата (*f.*)	tarihi sahte olarak değiştirilmiş
amount	сумма (*f.*)	miktar
ancient	старинный	eski
anti-counterfeiting device	средство против подделки (*n.*)	kalpazanlığı önleme cihazı
antiquity	древность (*f.*)	eskilik
Argentina	Аргентина	Arjantin
art	искусство (*n.*)	sanat
attribute (*verb*)	определять (*v.*)	tanımlamak
attribution	атрибуция (*f.*)	tanımlama
auction	аукцион (*m.*)	mezat
auction catalogue	каталог аукциона (*m.*)	mezat kataloğu
auction sale	аукционная продажа (*f.*)	müzayede ile satış
Australia	Австралия	Avustralya
Austria	Австрия	Avusturya
authentic	подлинный	gerçek; hakiki; otantik
badly struck	плохо отштампованный	kötü vurulmuş
bank (financial institution)	банк (*m.*)	banka
banknote	банкнота (*f.*)	kağıt para; banknot
Belgium	Бельгия	Belçika
bid (*noun*: auction bid)	предложение цены (*n.*)	teklif
bid (*verb*)	предлагать цену	fiyat arttırmak; teklif vermek
bid sheet	заявка на торгах (*f.*)	teklif formu
bilingual	двуязычный	iki dil bilen
black	чёрный	siyah; kara
black market	чёрный рынок	karaborsa
blue	синий	mavi
bond (commercial)	облигация (*f.*)	tahvil seneti

KOREAN	JAPANESE	CHINESE
약자	省略	缩写
이중타의	結合	重童的
구좌	口座	帐目
취득	取得	获得
조절표지	調節の刈り	调整记号
앨범	アルバム	相簿
합금	合金	合金
개조하다	改変する	更改
개조	改変	改造
개조된 날짜	改竄された日付	日期被更改的钱币
금액	金額	金额
고대의	古い；昔の	古代
위조 방지 장치	偽造防止策	防伪造机关
고물	古代	文物
아르헨티나	アルゼンチン	阿根廷
예술	美術	美術
출처를 밝히다	分類する	鉴定
발행출처	分類	鉴定
경매	競売	拍卖
경매목록	競売目録	拍卖目录
경쟁입찰판매	競売	拍卖
호주	オーストラリア	澳大利亚
오스트리아	オーストリア	奥地利
진짜의	本物の	真货
덜찍힌	-----	铸造不佳的
음금	銀行	银行
지폐	銀行券	钞票
벨기에	ベルギー	比利时
입찰	入札	出价
입찰하다	入札する	投标
입찰용지	入札用紙	标价单
이개국어 병용의	二ケ国語併用（の）	双语的
흑색	黒い	黑
암시장	闇市場	黑市
청색	青い	蓝
채권	債券	证卷

ENGLISH	RUSSIAN	TURKISH
bottom	низ (*m.*)	alt
brass (the alloy)	латунь (*f.*)	pirinç
Brazil	Бразилия	Brezilya
brockage	односторонка (*f.*)	yanlışlıkla tek yüzü iki tarafa basılmış
bronze (the alloy)	бронза (*f.*)	bronz
brown	коричневый	kahverengi
buy (*verb*)	покупать	satın almak
buyer	покупатель (*m.*)	alıcı; satın alan
cabinet friction	потертость от хранения (*f.*)	depolanma esnasında aşınmış
Canada	Канада	Kanada
cash (ready money)	наличные деньги (*pl.*)	nakit; para
cast (*verb*)	отливать (*v.*)	dökmek; döküm yapmak
catalog; catalogue	каталог (*m.*)	katalog
catalogue value	цена по каталогу (*f.*)	katalog değeri
centennial; centenary	столетие (*n.*)	yüzüncü yıl dönümü
centimeter; centimetre	сантиметр (*m.*)	santimetre
certificate	сертификат (*m.*)	vesika; belge
check; cheque	чек (*m.*)	çek
China	Китай	Çin
chromium	хром (*m.*)	krom
circulated	бывший в обращении	sirküle etmiş; kullanılmış
circulation	обращение (*n.*)	sürüm; sirkülasyon
clad coinage	плакированная монета (*f.*)	üç katlı olarak metalden yapılmış para
classification	классификация (*f.*)	sınıflama
classify (*verb*)	классифицировать	sınıflamak
coin	монета (*f.*)	madeni para
coinage	чеканка (*f.*)	para
collect (*verb*)	коллекционировать	koleksiyon yapmak
collection	коллекция (*f.*)	koleksiyon
collector	коллекционер (*m.*)	koleksiyoncu
Colombia	Колумбия	Kolombiya
color; colour	цвет (*m.*)	renk
commemorative (*adjective*)	памятный	hatıra; anma
common	обыкновенный	alelade
complete	полный	tamam
conjoined	соединённый; наложенный	üstüste ve aynı yöne bakan

KOREAN	JAPANESE	CHINESE
밑바닥	下	下面
황동	真鍮 ; 真鍮色	黄铜
브라질	ブラジル	巴西
합면	陰打	双面相同的硬币
청동	ブロンズ	青铜
다갈색	茶色	棕色
사다	買う	买
구매자	買い手	买主
보관시마모	こすり傷	集邮册中的磨损
캐나다	カナダ	加拿大
현금	現金	现金
주조하다	鋳造する	铸造
목록	カタログ	目录
목록가격	カタログ価格	目录价格
백년제	百年祭	百年的
센티미터	センチメートル	公分
증권	券	证卷
수표	小切手	支票
중국	中国	中国
크롬	クローム	铬
유통된	使用された	流通的
유통	流通	流通
샌드위치 주화	-----	夹层硬币
분류	種別	类别
분류하다	分離する	分类
동전	コイン ; 貨幣	硬币
주조화폐	貨幣の鋳造	造币
수집하다	集める	收集
수집품	収集	收集物
수집가	収集家	收集者
콜롬비아	コロンビア	哥伦比亚
색	色	颜色
기념의	記念の	纪念邮票的
흔한	一般的	普通
완전한	完全	完整
이중타의	結合	重叠的

ENGLISH	RUSSIAN	TURKISH
copper (the metal)	медь (f.)	bakır
copy (noun)	копия (f.)	kopya
copy (verb)	копировать	kopya etmek
corrosion	коррозия (f.)	korozyon
counterfeit (noun)	подделка (f.)	kalp
counterfeit (verb)	подделывать	kalpazanlık yapmak
counterfeiter	фальшивомонетчик (m.)	kalpazan
crease (noun)	складка (f.)	kat
credit	кредит (m.)	kredi
credit card	кредитная карточка (f.)	kredi kartı
credit cards accepted	кредитные карточки принимаются	kredi kartı kabul edilir
crown (royal headpiece)	корона (f.)	taç
crown (large silver coin)	крона (f.)	kron
cruzeiro	крузейро (n.)	kruzero
currency	валюта (f.)	para
damaged	повреждённый	bozuk
dark	тёмный	koyu
date	дата (f.)	tarih
defect	дефект (m.)	kusur; defo
defective	дефектный	kusurlu
demonetization	демонетизация (f.)	tedavülden kaldırmak
Denmark	Дания	Danimarka
denomination	номинал (m.)	-----
deposit (of funds)	задаток (m.)	kaparo; depozito
deposit required	требуется задаток (m.)	depozito gereklidir
design (noun)	рисунок (m.)	desen; motif
devaluation	девальвация (f.)	devalüasyon; değer düşürme
diameter	диаметр (m.)	çap
die (i.e., coinage die)	штамп (m.)	kalıp
die break	трещина в штампе (f.)	kalıp kırığı; kalıp çatlağı
dollar	доллар (m.)	dolar
duplicate (adjective)	дубликатный	çift
duplicate (noun)	дубликат (m.)	suret
duplicate (verb)	дублировать	aynısından çoğaltmak
eagle	орёл (m.)	kartal
East Germany (D.D.R.)	Восточная Германия	Doğu Almanya

KOREAN	JAPANESE	CHINESE
동	銅	铜
사본	複製	复本
복사하다	複製する；コピーする	复制
부식	腐食	侵蚀
위조품	偽造；贋物	伪品
위조하다	偽造する	伪造
위조자	偽造者	货币伪造者
구김살	折り目	折痕
신용	融資	信用
신용카드	クレジットカード	信用卡
신용카드 사용가능	クレジットカードを受付ける	接受信用卡支付
왕관	王冠	皇冠
크라운화	大型銀貨；クラウン	五先令银币
크루제이로	クルゼイロ	巴西币
통화	通貨；紙幣	货币
손상된	傷んだ	受损的
짙은	濃い	深色
날짜	日付	日期
흠	欠点	缺陷
흠이 있는	欠点のある	有缺陷的
통화정지	廃貨	使货币废止通用
덴마크	デンマーク	丹麦
액면단위	単位	面额
예치금	頭金	定金
보증금 필요	頭金を要する	要求付押金
도안	デザイン	图样
평가절하	平価切り下げ	贬值
직경	直径	直径
극인	極印	铸模
손상된 극인	-----	铸模裂痕
달러	ドル	元
복사한	二重の	复制的
복사품	二重にする	复制品
복사하다	複製する	复制
독수리	鷲	鹰
동독	東ドイツ	东德

ENGLISH	RUSSIAN	TURKISH
edge	ребро (*n.*)	kenar
effigy	портрет (*m.*)	madeni paradaki portre
eight	восемь	sekiz
eighty	восемьдесят	seksen
electrotype	электротипия (*f.*)	elektrolizle sahtecilik
electrum	электр (*m.*); электрум (*m.*)	elektrum
emergency currency	кризисные деньги (*pl.*)	geçici para
emperor	император (*m.*)	imparator
England	Англия	İngiltere
engraved	гравированный	hakkedilmiş
error	ошибка (*f.*)	hata
excellent	отличный	çok iyi; mükemmel
exchange rate	обменный курс (*m.*)	kambiyo kuru
exergue	обрез (*m.*)	yazı yeri
exhibit (*verb*)	выставлять	sergilemek
exhibition	выставка (*f.*)	sergi
face value	нарицательная стоимость	itibari değer
fake (*noun*)	подделка (*f.*)	taklit
fee	взнос	harç
fiat money	неразменные деньги	yalnız hükümet kararına dayanan kağıt para
fifty	пятьдесят	elli
finance minister	министр финансов (*m.*)	maliye bakanı
fine (grade or condition)	хороший	iyi durumda
fine (purity of metal)	чистый	saf
Finland	Финляндия	Finlandiya
five	пять	beş
fold (*noun*)	складка (*f.*)	kat
foreign	иностранный	yabancı
foreign currency	иностранная валюта (*f.*)	döviz; yabancı para
forgery	подделка (*f.*)	sahte
forty	сорок	kırk
four	четыре	dört
fourth (*noun*)	четверть (*f.*)	dörtte
fraction	часть (*f.*)	parça; kesir
franc	франк (*m.*)	frank
France	Франция	Fransa

KOREAN	JAPANESE	CHINESE
테두리	へり	边
초상	肖像	肖像
팔	八	八
팔십	八十	八十
전기도금 복사품	電気板	电铸
호박금	エレクトルマ	琥珀金
비상통화	緊急紙幣	应急货币
황제	皇帝	皇帝
잉글랜드	英国；イングランド	英格兰
조판의	凹版の	嵌版印刷的
에러	間違い；エラー	错误
우수한	優秀な	优良
환율	両替相場；為替相場	兑换率
주화의 중앙 아랫부분	-----	凹下部分
전시하다	出品する	展出
전시회	展示；博覧会	展览
액면	額面価格	面额
위조품	贋物；模造品	伪物
수수료	料金	费用
불환지폐	不換紙幣	证券
오십	五十	五十
재무장관	大蔵大臣	财政部长
훌륭한	並	好的
순도	純粋	纯的
핀란드	フィンランド	芬兰
오	五	五
접은자국	折り目	折痕
외국의	外国の	外国的
외화	外国通貨	外币
위조품	模造品	伪造票
사십	四十	四十
사	四	四
사분의 일	四分の一	四分之一
분수	断片	零头
프랑	フランク	法郎
프랑스	フランス	法国

ENGLISH	RUSSIAN	TURKISH
front	лицевая сторона (f.)	ön yüz
genuine	подлинный	hakiki
Germany	Германия	Almanya
gold (the metal)	золото (n.)	altın
good	хорошо	iyi
grade (noun)	состояние (n.)	durum
grade (verb)	сортировать (v.)	derecelemek
Great Britain	Великобритания	Büyük Britanya
Greece	Греция	Yunanistan
green	зелёный	yeşil
half (adjective)	половинный	yarım
half (noun)	половина (f.)	yarı
hammered coin	монета ручного изготовления	elle dövülerek yapılmış para
hole	отверстие (n.)	delik
holed	с отверстием	delikli
Hong Kong	Гонконг	Hong Kong
hundred	сто	yüz
hundredth (noun)	сотая часть (f.)	yüzde
imitation	имитация (f.)	taklit
inch	дюйм (m.)	inç
incomplete	неполный	eksik
incuse	вычеканенный	hakkedilmiş
ingot	слиток (m.)	külçe
ink	чернила (n.pl.)	mürekkep
inscription	надпись (f.)	yazı
intaglio	глубокая печать (f.)	intaglio metodu ile basılmış
international	интернациональный	uluslar arası
intrinsic	действительный	maden değeri
Ireland	Ирландия	İrlanda
iron (the metal)	железо (n.)	demir
irregular	необычный	gayrı muntazam
Israel	Израиль	İsrail
issue (noun)	выпуск (m.)	emisyon
issue (verb)	выпускать	tedavüle çıkarmak
Italy	Италия	İtalya
Japan	Япония	Japonya

KOREAN	JAPANESE	CHINESE
앞면	表	正面
진짜의	本物の	真品
독일	ドイツ	德国
황금	金	金
좋은	よい	好
등급	状態	等级
등급을 매기다	格付けする	评审
영국	イギリス；英国	大英帝国
그리이스	ギリシャ	希腊
녹색	緑	绿色
절반의	半	一半的
반	半分	一半
타제화	-----	手工锻造硬币
구멍	穴	孔
구멍이난	穴のあいた；穴あき銭	有孔的
홍콩	香港	香港
백	百	百
백분의 일	百分の一	百分之一
모조품	模造品	仿造
인치	インチ	吋
불완전한	不完全	不完整
음각의	打ち込み模様	凹下的花纹
주괴	インゴット	铸块
잉크	インク	墨水
명각	銘	铭刻
요판	凹版印刷	凹版印刷
국제적인	国際	国际的
본질적	固有の；本来の	固有的
아일랜드	アイルランド	爱尔兰
철	鉄	铁
불규칙한	不規則な	不规则的
이스라엘	イスラエル	以色列
발행	発行	出版物
발행하다	発行する	发行
이탈리아	イタリア	意大利
일본	日本	日本

ENGLISH	RUSSIAN	TURKISH
king	король (*m.*)	kral
language	язык (*m.*)	dil
large	большой	büyük
laureate	увенчанный	defne yaprağı taçlı baş
left (direction or position)	левый	sol
legend	надпись (*f.*)	yazı
lithography	литография (*f.*)	taş basması
lot (*i.e.*, auction lot)	партия (*f.*)	lot
magnifying glass	лупа (*f.*)	büyüteç
mail bid sale	распродажа по почте (*f.*)	mektupla müzayede
mark (German currency)	немецкая марка (*f.*)	mark
medal	медаль (*f.*)	madalya
metal	металл (*m.*)	maden
Mexico	Мексика	Meksika
military decoration	воинская награда (*f.*)	askeri madalya; askeri nişan
milled coin	монета машинного изготовления (*f.*)	makinede basılmış para
millimeter; millimetre	миллиметр (*m.*)	milimetre
million	миллион (*m.*)	milyon
minimum bid	минимальное предложение цены (*n.*)	asgarî teklif
mint	монетный двор (*m.*)	darphane
mintmark; mint mark	фабричное клеймо (*n.*)	darphane işareti
mis-strike (*noun*)	штамповочный брак (*m.*)	bozuk basılmış madeni para
mis-struck	бракованный	bozuk basılmış
monetary	денежный	paralarla ilgili; paraya ait
monetary system	денежная система (*f.*)	para sistemi
monetary unit	денежная единица (*f.*)	para birimi
money	деньги (*pl.*)	para
money order	денежный перевод (*m.*)	posta havalesi
motto	девиз (*m.*)	işaret
national	национальный	ulusal
nationality	национальная принадлежность (*f.*)	milliyet
Netherlands; Holland	Нидерланды; Голландия	Hollanda
new	новый	yeni
New Zealand	Новая Зеландия	Yeni Zelanda
nickel (the metal)	никель (*m.*)	nikel
nine	девять	dokuz

KOREAN	JAPANESE	CHINESE
왕	王	国王
언어	言語	语言
큰	大きい	大
월계관을 쓴	月桂冠を戴いた	荣誉的
왼쪽	左	左
명각	銘	铭
평판	リトグラフ	石版印刷术
품목	ロット	堆
확대경	虫めがね	放大镜
우편경매판매	郵便入札競売	邮政投标拍卖
마르크	マルク	马克
메달	メダル	奖章
금속	金属	金属
멕시코	メキシコ	墨西哥
군훈장	征軍徽章	军功嘉奖
압인화	-----	铳成硬币
밀리미터	ミリメートル	公厘
백만	百万	百万
최소 입찰가	最低入札値	最低标价
조폐국	造幣局；鋳造所	造币厂
주조청 표지	造幣極印	造币厂记
잘못찍힌 주화	エラー	错误铸造币
잘못찍힌	エラーの	错误铸造的
화폐의	貨幣の	货币的
봉화제도	貨幣制度	货币制度
화폐단위	貨幣の単位	货币单位
돈	金	钱
소 액환	為替	汇票
제명	モットー；題銘	铭辞
전국적인	国家的	国有的
국적	国籍	国籍
네덜란드	オランダ	荷兰
새토운	新しい	新的
뉴질랜드	ニュージーランド	纽西兰
니켈	ニッケル	镍
구	九	九

ENGLISH	RUSSIAN	TURKISH
ninety	девяносто	doksan
Northern Ireland	Северная Ирландия	Kuzey İrlanda
Norway	Норвегия	Norveç
note (*i.e.,* banknote)	банкнота (*f.*)	kağıt para; banknot
not issued	неизданный	tedavüle çıkarılmamış
no unlimited bids accepted	предложения цен ограниченны	-----
number	номер (*m.*)	numara
numismatic (*adjective*)	нумизматический	numismatik
numismatics (*noun*)	нумизматика (*f.*)	nümismatik
numismatist	нумизмат (*m.*)	numismat
obsidional	осадный	kuşatılmış bölge parası
obsolete	устаревший	modası geçmiş
obverse	лицевая сторона (*f.*)	ön yüz
offer (*noun*)	предложение (*n.*)	teklif
offer (*verb*)	предлагать	teklif vermek
official	официальный	resmi
old	старый	eski
on approval	на оценку	beğenilme şartiyle
one	один	bir
on the back	на обороте	arka yüzde
order form	бланк (*m.*)	ısmarlama formu
original	оригинал	orijinal
ounce	унция (*f.*)	ons
overprint	надпечатка (*f.*)	sürşarj
palindrome	палиндром (*m.*)	iki yönden de aynı okuma
paper	бумага (*f.*)	kağıt
paper money	бумажные деньги (*pl.*)	kağıt para
pattern	образец (*m.*)	desen
pedigree	происхождение (*n.*)	şeceresi
People's Republic of China (P.R.C.)	Китайская Народная Республика	Çin Halk Cumhuriyeti
perfect	идеальный	kusursuz
Peru	Перу	Peru
peseta	песета (*f.*)	peseta
peso	песо (*n.*)	peso
photogravure	фотогравюра (*f.*)	fotogravür
piéfort; piedfort	тяжёлая монета (*f.*)	kalın para

KOREAN	JAPANESE	CHINESE
구십	九十	九十
북아일랜드	北アイルランド	北愛尔兰
노르웨이	ノルウェイ	挪威
지폐	紙幣	纸币
미발행의	不発行	未公开发行的
무제한 입찰 불가	制限なしの入札は受付けられぬ	要求自行投标
번호	番号	数目
고화폐의	古銭学の	古币的
화폐수집	古銭学	货币学
화폐수집가	貨幣（古銭）学者	古币收藏家
임시화폐의	-----	-----
사용되지 않는	昔の	陈旧的
앞면	表面；表	正面
매매제의	提出	出价
팔려고 내놓다	提出する	出价
공식의	公務；公式の	官方的
오래된	古い	古老的
현물점검후 지급조건	点検売買	试用后再购货
일	一	一
뒷면에	裏側	反面
주문용지	注文用紙	定购单
원래의	最初の	原版
온스	オンス	盎司
가쇄	加刷	加盖
회문	どちらから読んでも同じ語句	双向同字词
종이	紙	纸
지폐	紙幣	纸币
도안	試鋳	模型
계도	-----	持有人家谱
중화인민공화국	中華人民共和国	中华人民共和国
완전한	完全	完整
페루	ペルー	秘鲁
페세타	ペセタ	西班牙币
페소	ペソ	披索
그라비야	フォトグラビア	凹版印刷
피에포트	-----	-----

ENGLISH	RUSSIAN	TURKISH
planchet	монетный диск (*m.*)	planşet
platinum (the metal)	платина (*f.*)	platin
pope	папа (*m.*)	papa
portrait	портрет (*m.*)	portre
Portugal	Португалия	Portekiz
pound (unit of weight)	фунт (*m.*)	libre
pound (£)	фунт стерлингов (*m.*)	İngiliz lirası
prepayment	аванс (*m.*)	ön ödeme
president	прездент (*m.*)	başkan
press (*i.e.*, coinage press)	пресс (*m.*)	baskı makinesi
price	цена (*f.*)	fiyat
price list	прейскурант (*m.*)	fiyat listesi
print (*verb*)	печатать	basmak
proof (*re*: coins or medals)	пруф	proof; ispat
propaganda note	пропагандистская банкнота (*f.*)	propaganda broşürü
protective reserve bid	резервная цена (*f.*)	minimum müzayede değeri
queen	королева (*f.*)	kraliçe
rare	редкий	nadir; ender
rarity	раритет (*m.*)	nadirlik
receipt	квитанция (*f.*)	makbuz
rectangular	прямоугольный	dik dörtgen şeklinde
red	красный	kırmızı
repaired	отреставрированный	tamir edilmiş
reproduction	репродукция (*f.*)	kopya
republic	республика (*f.*)	cumhuriyet
Republic of China (Taiwan)	Республика Китай; Тайвань	Çin Cumhuriyeti
restrike (*noun*)	новодел (*m.*)	-----
reverse	обратная сторона (*f.*)	tersi; arka yüzü
right (direction or position)	правый	sağ
rim	ребро (*n.*)	kenar
roll (of coins)	стопка монет (*f.*)	tomar
round	круглый	yuvarlak
Russia	Россия	Rusya
Saudi Arabia	Саудовская Аравия	Suudi Arabistan
scarce	дефицитный	az bulunur; nadir
Scotland	Шотландия	İskoçya

KOREAN	JAPANESE	CHINESE
화폐판금	円形	园金属片
백금	プラチナ	白金
고황	ローマ法王	权威者
초상	肖像	肖像
포르투칼	ポルトガル	葡萄牙
파운드	ポンド	磅
파운드	ポンド	英磅
선불	前払い	预支
대통령	大統領	总统
압인기	鋳造機	印版机
가격	価格	价格
가격표	価格表	价目表
인쇄하다	印刷する	印刷
-----	プルーフ	精制
선전삐라	宣伝札	宣传币
최저 응찰가	安全のための最低値	保留投标值
여왕	女王	皇后
진기한	珍しい	少有的
진품	珍品	稀罕
영수증	領収書	收据
직사각형의	長方形の	长方形
적색	赤い	红色
수선된	直した	修好的
복제품	複製	复制; 仿造
공화국	共和国	共和的
중화민국	台湾; 中華民国	中华民国
재주조	改鋳	加印
후면	裏	反面
오른쪽	右	右
가장자리	緣	边
롤	ロール	一卷
둥근	丸い	园形
러시아	ロシア	俄國
사우디아라비아	サウジアラビア	沙特阿拉伯
드문	珍しい; 稀な	锈
스코틀랜드	スコットランド	苏格兰

ENGLISH	RUSSIAN	TURKISH
scratch (*noun*)	царапина (*f.*)	kazıntı; çizik
scrip	частный сертификат (*m.*)	geçici özel para
seal (*noun*)	печать (*f.*)	damga
seigniorage	пошлина за право чеканки монет	devlet kâr payı
sell (*verb*)	продавать	satmak
seller	продавец (*m.*)	satıcı
series	серия (*f.*)	seri
serial number	серийный номер (*m.*)	seri numarası
seven	семь	yedi
seventy	семьдесят	yetmiş
signature	подпись (*f.*)	imza
silk thread	шёлковая нить	ipek çizgi; ipek iplik
silver (the metal)	серебро (*n.*)	gümüş
six	шесть	altı
sixty	шестьдесят	altmış
small	маленький	küçük
South Africa	Южная Африка	Güney Afrika
sovereign	суверен (*m.*)	hükümdar
Soviet Union (U.S.S.R.)	Советский Союз (С.С.С.Р.)	Sovyetler Birliği
Spain	Испания	İspanya
specimen	пробный образец (*m.*)	spesimen
square (*adjective*)	квадратный	kare
stain	пятно (*n.*)	leke
star	звезда (*f.*)	yıldız
steel	сталь (*f.*)	çelik
steel engraving	гравирование по стали (*m.*)	çelik gravür
suggested bid	предлагаемая цена (*f.*)	önerilen fiat
Sweden	Швеция	İsveç
Switzerland	Швейцария	İsviçre
symbol	символ (*m.*)	simge
tarnish	налет (*m.*)	leke; kararma
tax (*noun*)	налог (*m.*)	vergi
tear (*noun*)	разрыв (*m.*)	yırtık
ten	десять	on
tenth (*noun*)	десятая часть (*f.*)	onda
third (*noun*)	третья часть (*f.*)	üçte

KOREAN	JAPANESE	CHINESE
긁힌자국	瑕	痕迹
가증권	仮の証券	-----
봉인	封；封印用ラベル	印
화폐주조차익	-----	制币盈利
팔다	売る	卖
매도인	売り手	卖主
시리이즈	シリーズ	成套
일련번호	発行番号	编号
칠	七	七
칠십	七十	七十
서명	署名	签名
명주실	絹糸	丝线
은	銀	银
육	六	六
육십	六十	六十
적은	小さい	小
남아프리카	南アフリカ	南非
군주	主権者	至高的
소련	ソビエト社会主義共和国連邦	苏联
스페인	スペイン	西班牙
견본	見本	样张
네모난	正方形の	方形的
얼룩	汚れ；シミ	污点
별	星	星
강철	鋼鉄	钢
강판조 각	-----	钢蚀制版
제안 입찰가	参考値	建议投标值
스웨덴	スエーデン	瑞典
스위스	スイス	瑞士
상징	象徴；シンボル	标记
변색	錆	变色
세금	税金	税
찢어진 틈	裂け目	撕破处
십	十	十
십분의 일	十分の一	十分之一
삼분의 일	三分の一	三分之一

ENGLISH	RUSSIAN	TURKISH
thirty	тридцать	otuz
thousand	тысяча (*f.*)	bin
three	три	üç
tin	олово (*n.*)	teneke
token	жетон (*m.*)	jeton
top	верх (*m.*)	üst
torn	порванный	yırtık
trade (*verb*)	обмениваться (*v.*)	değiş tokuş etmek
treasure	казна (*f.*)	hazine
twenty	двадцать	yirmi
two	два	iki
unattributed	неидентифицированный	tam tanımlanmamış
uncirculated	не бывший в обращении	sirküle etmemiş
uniface	односторонний	tek yüzlü
unique	уникальный	emsalsiz
United Kingdom (U.K.)	Великобритания	Birleşik Kırallık
United States of America (U.S.A.)	Соединенные Штаты Америки	Amerika Birleşik Devletleri
unknown	неизвестный	bilinmeyen
unofficial	неофициальный	gayrı resmi; resmi olmayan
unpublished	неопубликованный	yayınlanmamış
used	бывший в употреблении	kullanılmış
valuable	ценный	değerli
value	ценность (*f.*)	değer
variety	разновидность (*f.*)	tür; çeşit
Venezuela	Венесуэла	Venezüela
Wales	Уэльс	Galler
watermark	водяной знак (*m.*)	filigran
wear (*noun*)	износ	aşınma
weight	вес (*f.*)	ağırlık
West Germany (B.R.D.)	Западная Германия	Batı Almanya
white	белый	beyaz
year	год (*m.*)	yıl
yellow	жёлтый	sarı
Yugoslavia; Jugoslavia	Югославия	Yugoslavya
zero	нуль (*m.*)	sıfır
zinc	цинк (*m.*)	çinko

KOREAN	JAPANESE	CHINESE
삼십	三十	三十
천	千	千
삼	三	三
주석	すず	锡
토큰	代用貨幣	代用币
정상	上	上面
찢어진	裂けている	撕破的
서로교환하다	交換する	交易
보물	貴重品	宝物
이십	二十	二十
이	二	二
출처불명의	分類しない	未经确定的
유통되지않은	未使用の	不可流通的
일면각인의	片面の	单面的
유일한	唯一の	唯一的
영국	英国	英国
미국	米国；アメリカ合衆国	美利坚合众国
미지의	知られていない	不知的
비공식의	非公式の	非官方的
미발행의	未発行の	未公开发行的
사용제의	使用済みの	使用过的
값진	価値のある	有价值的
가치	価値	价值
변종	バラエティー	多种
베네수엘라	ベネズエラ	委内瑞拉
웨일즈	ウェールズ	威尔斯
무문	すかし	透明花纹
낡음	摩損	磨损度
중량	重量	重量
서독	西ドイツ	西德
백색	白い	白色
년	年	年
황색	黄色	黄色
유고슬라비아	ユーゴスラビア	南斯拉夫
영	ゼロ	零
아연	亜鉛	锌

Pictorial

Numismatic concepts illustrated and named.

issuing agency: **Great Britain**
denomination: **50 new pence**
purpose: **regular issue**
edge: **plain**
side pictured below: **reverse**

principal device: **Britannia**
date: **1969** [not shown]
metal: **copper-nickel; cupro-nickel**
rim: **plain**
relief: **average**

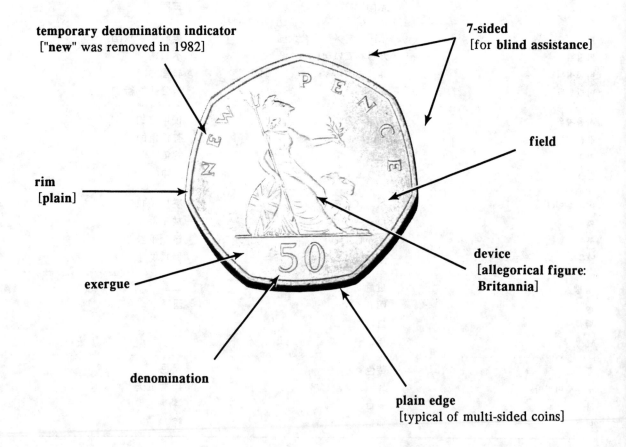

temporary denomination indicator
["**new**" was removed in 1982]

7-sided
[for **blind assistance**]

field

rim
[**plain**]

device
[**allegorical figure:**
Britannia]

exergue

denomination

plain edge
[typical of multi-sided coins]

issuing agency: **United States**
denomination: **50 cents; half dollar**
purpose: **regular issue**
edge: **security [reeded]**
side pictured below: **obverse**

effigy: **John F. Kennedy [head]**
date: **1995 [date of issue]**
metal: **clad [copper-nickel w/ copper core]**
rim: **plain**
relief: **relatively high**

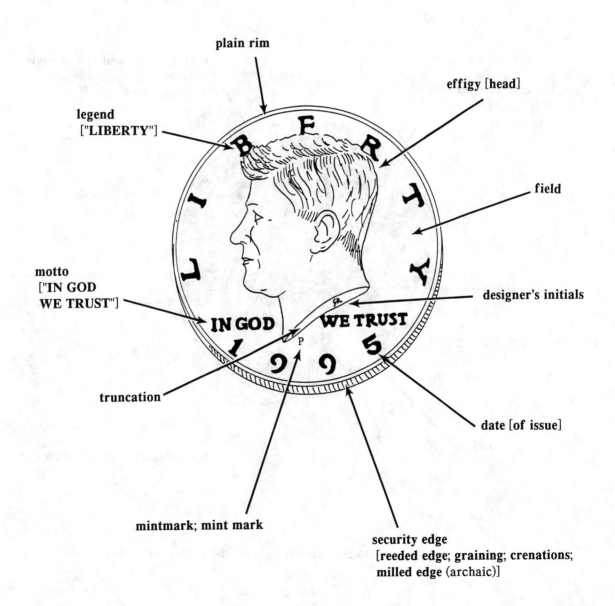

plain rim

effigy [head]

legend
["LIBERTY"]

field

motto
["IN GOD
WE TRUST"]

designer's initials

truncation

date [of issue]

mintmark; mint mark

security edge
[reeded edge; graining; crenations;
milled edge (archaic)]

issuing agency: **Austria**
denomination: **thaler; taler**
purpose: **trade coin**
edge: **security [lettered (in relief)]**
side pictured below: **reverse**

principal device: **crowned double eagle**
date: **1780** [restrike date]
metal: **silver**
rim: **minimally denticulated**
relief: **relatively low**

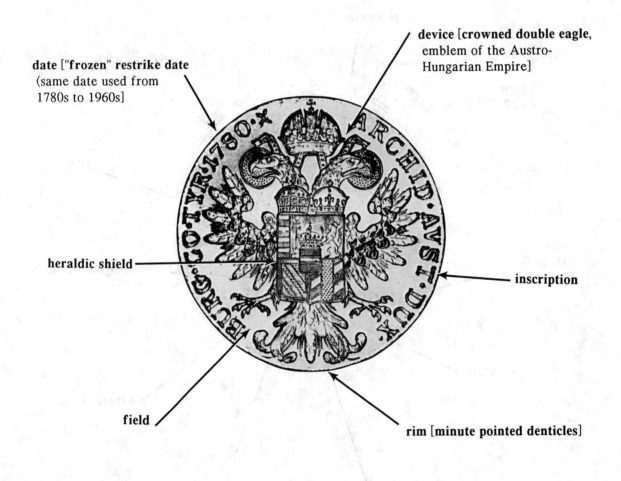

date ["frozen" restrike date]
(same date used from
1780s to 1960s]

device [**crowned double eagle**,
emblem of the Austro-
Hungarian Empire]

heraldic shield

inscription

field

rim [minute pointed denticles]

Maria Theresa Thaler [**Mariatheresientaler** in German]

issuing agency: **México**
value: **1 onza** [**1 ounce**]
purpose: **bullion coin**
edge: **security** [**lettered (incuse)**]
side pictured below: **reverse**

principal device: **Winged Liberty**
date: **1985** [**date of issue**]
metal: **silver**
rim: **denticulated**
relief: **average**

device [**Winged Liberty** (from which the coin's name **Libertad** is derived)]

metallic content [**plata pura**, "**pure silver**"]

rim [**partially denticulated**]

weight [**1 onza**, "**1 ounce**"]

mintmark; mint mark

date [**of issue**]

fineness [**Ley .999**, "**.999 fine**"]

legend [**issuing country**]

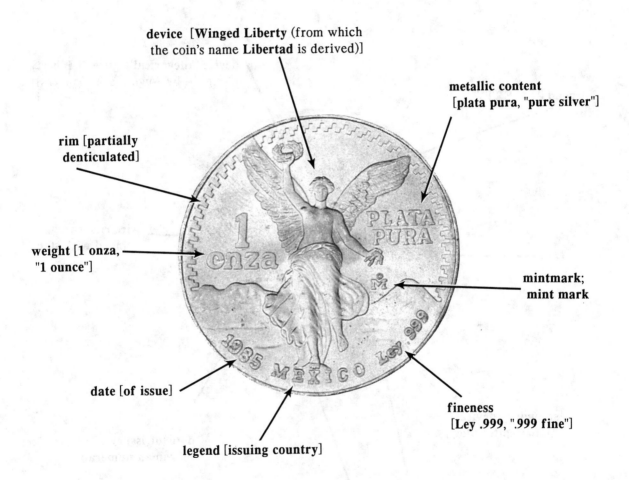

reverse [note: the "eagle" side is officially the obverse on Mexican coins]

issuing agency: **United States**
denomination: **double eagle; $20**
purpose: **regular issue**
edge: **security [lettered (in relief)]**
side pictured below: **obverse**

principal device: **St. Gaudens' Liberty**
date: **MCMVII [1907]**
metal: **gold**
rim: **wire**
relief: **very high**

device [**allegorical figure** of **Liberty**
designed by Augustus St. Gaudens]

legend ["**LIBERTY**"]

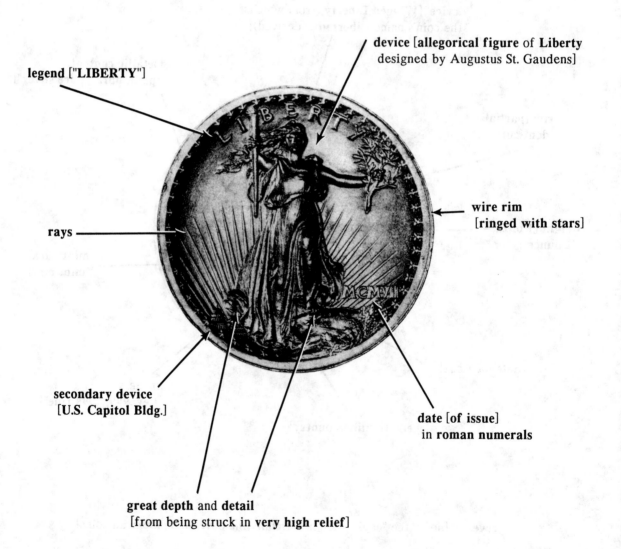

wire rim
[**ringed with stars**]

rays

secondary device
[**U.S. Capitol Bldg.**]

date [of issue]
in **roman numerals**

great depth and **detail**
[from being struck in **very high relief**]

issuing agency: **Isle of Man**
denomination: **£1**
purpose: **regular issue**
side pictured below: **face**

portrait: **Elizabeth II**
series: **none shown**
paper: **plasticized**
watermarked: **no**

promissory guarantee

issuing agency

portrait [in **vignette** style]

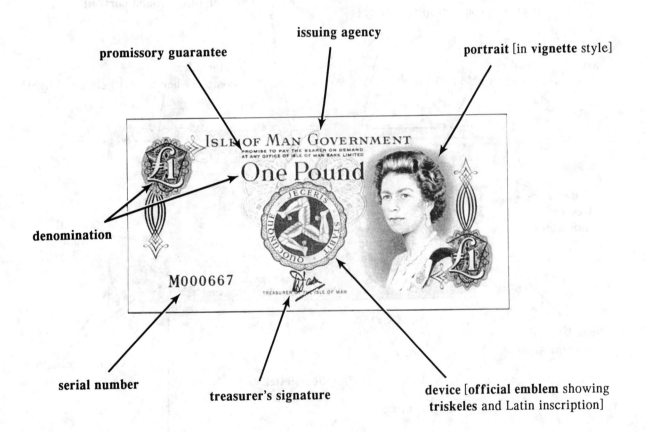

denomination

serial number

treasurer's signature

device [**official emblem** showing **triskeles** and Latin inscription]

plasticized [**polymerized**] **paper** to prevent tearing

issuing agency: **United States**
denomination: **$100**
purpose: **regular issue**
side pictured below: **face**

portrait: **Benjamin Franklin**
series: **1996**
paper: **high rag content**
watermarked: **yes**

portrait [larger than on previous series as an anti-counterfeiting device]

concentric fine lines around **portrait**

security thread [most visible when held up to light]

watermark [visible when note is held up to light]

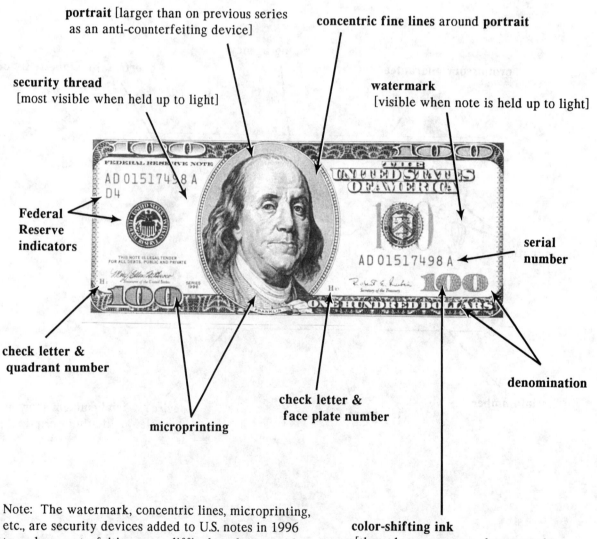

Federal Reserve indicators

serial number

check letter & quadrant number

denomination

check letter & face plate number

microprinting

color-shifting ink [the color appears to change as the number is viewed from different angles]

Note: The watermark, concentric lines, microprinting, etc., are security devices added to U.S. notes in 1996 to make counterfeiting more difficult and to provide easier detection.

Bibliography

Acar, Ozgen and Melik Kaylan. "Hoard of the Century." *Coin World*, July 6, 1988, p. 1 et al.

Alexander, David T. "Brass Tokens Recall Israel Birth Pangs." *The Shekel*, July-August 1986, pp. 28-31.

"Altered Coin Mimics Error." *Coin World*, August 30, 1989, pp. 1 & 13.

Banning, E. B. *Exploring Canadian Colonial Tokens*. Toronto: Charlton International Inc., 1988.

Barkay, Rachel. "The Numismatic Collection of the Bank of Israel." *The Shekel*, January-February 1989, p. 26.

Beals, Gary. *Numismatic Terms of Spain and Spanish America*. 1966.

Beresiner, Yasha. *A Collector's Guide to Paper Money*. New York: Stein & Day, 1977.

Block, David. "The Life of a Journal: *Das Notgeld*." *The Asylum*, Winter, 1988.

Breen, Walter. *Complete Encyclopedia of U.S. and Colonial Coins*. New York: F.C.I. Press Inc. (Doubleday), 1988.

—"The *S.S. Central America*: Tragedy and Treasure." *The Numismatist*, July 1990, pp. 1064-72 et al.

British Museum Catalogue of Greek Coins. London, 1873-1927.

Bryan, Florence Horn. *Susan B. Anthony: Champion of Women's Rights*. New York: Julian Messner, Inc., 1947.

Burnett, Andrew. *Coinage in the Roman World*. London, England: Seaby, 1987.

"Canada's Coin Dollar." *The Numismatist*, September 1993, p. 1196.

Carlton, R. Scott. "The Art and Science of Numismatic Exhibiting." *The Numismatist*, April 1990, pp. 550-54.

Carrigan, Pat. "Clydesdale Bank Plans New Note Trio." *World Coins*, April 1973, p. 532.

Charlton, J. E. *Standard Catalogue of Canadian Coins* (27th Ed.). Toronto: Charlton International Publishing Company, 1978.

Cervin, David R. "Legends of the Middle Ages." *The Numismatist*, March 1989, pp. 418-19 et al.

Cirlot, J. E. *A Dictionary of Symbols* (2nd Ed.). New York: Philosophical Library, 1983.

Clow, L. E. "Heraldic Lion Popular on Coins." *World Coins*, May 1973, pp. 678-80 et al.

Coin World Almanac (6th Ed.). Sidney, OH: Amos Press, 1990.

Compton's Encyclopedia and Fact Index, 1992.

Connell, "Christian Icons on Byzantine Coins." *The Numismatist*, October 1989, pp. 1610-14.

Cox, Arthur J. and Thomas Malim. *Ferracute: The History of an American Enterprise*. Bridgeton, New Jersey: Cowan Printing, Inc., 1985.

Craig, William D. *Coins of the World: 1750-1850* (3rd Ed.). Racine, WI: Western Publishing Company, 1976.

Day, Thomas C. "Casino Tokens of Monte Carlo." *The Numismatist*, June and July 1986, pp. 1124-42 (June) and 1372-79 (July).

DeLorey, Tom. "Longacre: Unsung Engraver of the U.S. Mint." *The Numismatist*, October 1985, pp. 1970-78.

De Soete, D., R. Gijbels, and J. Hoste. *Neutron Activation Analysis*. New York: John Wiley & Sons, 1972.

Doty, Richard G. *The Macmillan Encyclopedic Dictionary of Numismatics*. New York: Macmillan Publishing Company, 1982.

—"Boulton, Watt and the Canadian Adventure." *Canada's Money* (John M. Kleeberg, ed.). New York: American Numismatic Society, 1994.

Dunn, John W. "Napoléon II: Emperor for a Day." *World Coins*, January 1973, pp. 34-48.

Dyer, Graham P. "Five Centuries of the British Gold Sovereign." *The Numismatist*, March 1989, pp. 392-400.

Dyroff, Jan M. "The Quaint and Curious Stampée." *The Numismatist*, April 1987, pp. 756-60.

Encyclopedia Britannica; S.v. "Oliver Cromwell," 5:291-295; "Francisco Franco," 4:277; "Alexander Hamilton," 4:872. 1981.

Encyclopedia Judaica; S.v. "Coins," 5:697; "Firstborn," 6:1306; "Gemetria," 7:370; "Judenpfennige," 10:406; "Templers," 10:995; "Shekel," 14:1347. Jerusalem: Keter Publishing, 1973.

Entenmann, Lloyd L. "A Token Love Affair." *The Numismatist*, February 1992, pp. 187-90.

—"Love Token Pricing." *The Numismatist*, February 1988, pp. 271-3.

Feller, Steven A. and Barbara. "Ghetto Money of the Nazi Holocaust." *The Shekel*, September-October 1982, pp. 43-44.

Fisher, Jack H. "Lincoln and Kennedy: History Repeats Itself." *The Numismatist*, June 1989, pp. 908-10.

Frey, Albert R. *A Dictionary of Numismatic Names* (1973 reprint of 1916 monograph from the American Journal of Numismatics). London.

Friedenber, Daniel M. "Anti-Semitic Medals of Late Medieval Europe." *The Shekel*, July-August 1984, pp. 4-14.

Friedman, Dr. Howard S. "Essays, Proofs and Specimens." *The Essay-Proof Journal*, Vol. 31, No. 1, 1974, p. 17.

Fuld, George J. "New Franklin Medal by St. Gaudens," *TAMS Journal*, Token and Medal Society, March-April 1966.

Funk & Wagnalls New Encyclopedia, 1984.

Ganz, David L. "A Milestone for a Monumental Coin." *The Numismatist*, January 1994, pp. 42-46 et al.

Goglin, Dustin. "Charles Barber's Liberty Head Nickel." *The Numismatist*, June 1994, pp. 846-49.

Goldberg, Ira. "Abe Lincoln and Denver's First Federal Mint." *The Numismatist*, August 1991, pp. 1200-3.

Grant, Michael. *The Roman Emperors*. New York: Charles Scribner's Sons, 1985.

Greenspan, Michael. "Rebuilding a Coin Club." *The Numismatist*, June 1988, pp. 1025-29.

Gregory, Barbara J. "Marking the Campaign Trail." *The Numismatist*, November 1988, pp. 1906-10.

Guntermann, Karl L. "An Analysis of Liberty Seated Half Dimes." *The Numismatist*, March 1988, pp. 455-60.

Halperin, James L. *N.C.I. Grading Guide*. Dallas, TX: Ivy Press, 1986.

Hasting, James, ed. *Dictionary of the Bible*, 1963.

Haxby, J. A. and R. C. Willey. *Coins of Canada* (9th Ed.). Toronto: Unitrade Press, 1988.

Hébert, Raymond J. "Abjad and the Basmala—786." *NI Bulletin*, July 1986, pp. 162-65.

Hessler, Gene. *U.S. Essay, Proof, and Specimen Notes*, BNR Press.

—"St. Nick Notes." *The Numismatist*, December 1989, pp. 1934-42.

Hodder, Michael. "Ephraim Brasher's 1786 Lima Style Doubloon." *Money of Pre-Federal America*. New York: American Numismatic Society.

Hoenig, D. Bernard. "The Weeping Women of Judea." *The Shekel*, September-October 1983, pp. 19-23.

Holsen, Paul J., II. "Honduras Notes Interest Young Collector." *World Coins*, February 1970, pp. 206-10.

Horvitz, Peter S. "Pilgrim Medals: Old Tradition and New." *The Shekel*, July-August 1988, pp. 4-6.

Israel Government Coins and Medals Corporation. *Pidyon Haben Coin* (pamphlet). Jerusalem, 1970.

"Israel Issues a New Pidyon Haben Medal." *The Shekel*, November-December 1982, pp. 16-17.

Jourdan, Helen and Clarence. *Benjamin Franklin's Unfinished Business*. Philadelphia, PA: The Franklin Institute, 1956.

Julian, R. W. "The Russian Silver Coinage of 1796-1979." *The Numismatist*, December 1989, pp. 1952-59 et al.

Junge, Ewald. *World Coin Encyclopedia*. New York: William Morrow & Company, 1984.

Krause, Chester L., and Clifford Mishler, ed. *Standard Catalog of World Coins*. Iola, WI: Krause Publications, 1985 and 1995.

Keller, Arnold. The introduction to *Kleingeldscheine* ("Fractional notes") in *NI Bulletin*, November 1979 and April 1978. Reprinted as *Notgeld Handbook No. 1*. Ridge Manor: Manor Press, 1981.

Kuritzky, Simcha. "Give Credit Where Credit Is Due." *NI Bulletin*, October 1990, pp. 240-41.

LaMarre, Thomas. "The Lafayette Dollar: The Commemorative That Broke All the Rules." *The Numismatist*, July 1986, pp. 1359-61.

Lane, Peter. "The Love Tokens of Thomas Alsop." *Journal of the Numismatic Association of Australia*, July 1985, pp. 58-60.

Lange, David W. "Mercury Dimes— Challenging Yet Affordable." *The Numismatist*, February 1988, pp. 289-93.

Lapa, Frank A. *Russian Wire Money*. 1967.

Lee, Hans. "The Changing Face of Canada's Dollar." *The Numismatist*, July 1987, pp. 1441-45.

LeSouef, A.M. "Catalogue of Coins, Medals, and Checks in the A.M. LeSouef Collection." *Journal of the Numismatic Association of Australia*, July 1986, pp. 25-36.

Loperfido, John C. "Airborne Particulates: The Silent Nemesis." *The Numismatist*, Aptil 1983, pp. 706-9.

Mack, Walter R. "Collectors Are Indebted to Credit Cards." *The Numismatist*, January 1990, pp. 38-41 & 149-50.

Mackay, James. *Key Definitions in Numismatics*. London: Frederick Muller Limited, 1982.

Magnus, Sylvia Haffner, ed. *Israel's Money and Medals*. Bellevue, WA: Small Fry Press, 1979.

—"Palestine Numismatics: Part III." *The Shekel*, May-June 1986, pp. 17-18.

Mallis, A. George. "A Numismatic Primer— Part 1." *The Numismatist*, July 1988, p. 1217.

Marr, Dennis F. "Crusaders Against a Misunderstood Disease." *The Numismatist*, April 1988, pp. 657-62.

Mattingly, Harold. *Roman Coins from the Earliest Times to the Fall of the Western Empire*. New York: S. J. Durst, 1987.

McBride, David P. "Linked Rings: Early American Unity Illustrated." *The Numismatist*, November 1979, pp. 2373-93.

McKenzie, Lee F. "Longacre's Influence on Numismatic Art." *The Numismatist*, December 1991, pp. 1922-24.

Mendelssohn, Dr. Edwin. "Fiscus Judaicus." *The Shekel*, May-June 1986, pp. 3-8.

Menzel, Sewall H. "Tracking Down the Rare Gold *Star of Lima*." *The Numismatist*, June 1994, pp. 811-15 et al.

Migliavacca, Giorgio. "Mint Marks need further research." *Moneta International*, Vol. 1, No. 1, July 1989, pp. 10-12.

Mishler, Clifford. *Coins: Questions and Answers*. Iola, WI: Krause Publications, 1985.

Mitchell, Stephen and Brian Reeds (editors). *Coins of England and the United Kingdom,* 26th Ed. London: Seaby, 1991.

Moreno Fraginals, Manuel and José A. Pulido Ledesma. *Cuba: A Country and Its Currency*. Havana: National Bank of Cuba.

Morgan, Ted. *FDR: A Biography*. New York: Simon & Schuster, 1985.

Murray, Glenn S. "Exploring the Historic Lima Mint." *The Numismatist*, July 1988, pp. 1200-12.

Narbeth, Colin. *Collecting Paper Money*. London: Seaby, 1986.

Needelman, Chet. "The House of Rothschild." *Coin Illustrated*, July 1978, pp. 40-42.

Needleman, Saul B. "The Farthing as an Economic Necessity." *The Numismatist*, April 1987, pp. 764.

Newlon, Clarke. *The Men Who Made Mexico*. Dodd, Mead & Company.

Nuessel, Frank. "Currency Designations in Spanish-Speaking Nations." *The Numismatist*, November 1986, pp. 2260-65.

Obojski, Robert. "World's Fair Medal Weighs 365 Pounds." *Coin World*, October 15, 1986, p. 82.

Opitz, Charles J. *Odd and Curious Money: Descriptions and Values*. Ocala, FL: First Impressions Printing, 1986.

Pastor, Jay. "Don't Call It *Mercury*." *Coins*, February 1996, pp. 52-54.

Pick, Albert. *Standard Catalog of World Paper Money* (7th Ed.). Iola, WI: Krause Publications, 1994.

Plant, Richard. *Arabic Coins and How to Read Them.* London, England: Seaby's Numismatic Publications, 1973.

Potter, Clifton. "Images of Majesty." *The Numismatist,* June 1991, pp. 858-62 et al.

Read, Phyllis J. and Bernard L. Witlieb. *The Book of Women's Firsts.* New York: Randon House, 1992.

Reed, Mort. *Odd and Curious.* New York: Sanford J. Durst Numismatic Publications, 1979.

Reinfeld, Fred. *The Story of Paper Money.* New York: Sterling Publishing Company, 1960.

Reiter, Ed. "Minting the Impossible Dream: This American Lady Persuaded the Poles to Change Their Coinage." *Coinage,* October 1983, pp. 90-92.

Ricard, Charles J. "John C. Lighthouse: Numismatic Giant." *The Numismatist,* January 1988, pp. 47-54.

Romines, Delma K. *Hobo Nickels.* Lonesome John Publishing, 1982.

Room, Adrian. *Dictionary of Coin Names.* London: Routledge & Kegan Paul Ltd., 1987.

Ruehrmund, Jim. "Lucky Bucks." *The Numismatist,* November 1990, pp. 1814-15.

Sass, Louis C. "Medals of Friendship and Thanks." *The Numismatist,* July 1990, pp. 1080-84.

Schenkman, David E. *Civil War Sutler Tokens and Cardboard Scrip.* Jade House Publications, 1983.

Schmitt-Korte, Karl and Michael Cowell. "Nabatæan Coinage, Part 1." *Numismatic Chronicle.* 1989.

Schonwalter, Jean. "*Lost Wax* Cast Medals." *The Numismatist,* July 1994, pp. 1014-15.

Schwarz, Ted. "Ups and Downs of the U.S. Nickel." *Coins,* July 1983, pp. 56-61.

Schuman, Edward. "Emperor Norton I." *The Shekel,* November-December 1988, pp. 3-7.

Seaby, Peter and P. Frank Purvey. *Coins of Scotland, Ireland & the Islands.* London: Seaby, 1984.

Sear, R. David. *Greek Coins and Their Values,* Vol. I & II. London, England: Seaby, 1978.

Sebring, Thomas H. "Commodore Anson and the Lima Coinage." *The Numismatist,* November 1985, pp. 2164-71.

Sédillot, René. *Historia de las principales monedas.* Madrid, Spain: Ediciones Guadarrama, 1975.

Sharples, John. "Australian Coins 1919 to 1924." *Journal of the Numismatic Association of Australia,* July 1985, pp. 8-9.

—"The Numismatic Collection of the Museum of Victoria." *Journal of the Numismatic Association of Australia,* July 1986, pp. 37-52.

Sknouril, Evzen. "Thersienstadt's Bleak Bank Note Story." *The Shekel,* September-October 1982, pp. 27-33.

Slabaugh, Arlie R. *United States Commemorative Coinage.* Racine, WI: Whitman Publishng Company, 1962.

Smithsonian World: Voices of Latin America (script of television program), WETA (Washington, DC) & Smithsonian Institution, 1987.

State of Ohio Food Stamp Certification Handbook; *Encyclopedia of Social Work* (1973), Vols. 1 & 2.

Stevenson, William Seth. *A Dictionary of Roman Coins*. London, England: Seaby, 1982.

Tise, Larry E. *The Benjamin Franklin National Memorial Awards*. Philadelphia, PA: The Franklin Institute, 1990.

"Turkey Files Lawsuit to Regain Coin Hoard." *Coin World*, January 17, 1990, p. 1 et al.

Turner, Martha L. "Commemorative Medals of the American Revolution and the War of 1812." *The Numismatist*, January 1975, pp. 5-18.

Valbuena Briones, Angel. *Historia de la literatura española*, Vol. V: "Literatura hispanoamericana." Barcelona, Spain: Editorial Gustava Gili, S.A., 1969.

Van Meter, David. *Collecting Greek Coins*. Nashua, NH: Laurion Numismatics, 1990.

Van Valen, Frank. "Fishscales: My Favorite Canadian Import." *The Numismatist*, May 1987, pp. 991-994.

Webster's New World Dictionary. 2nd Collegiate ed. Cleveland, Ohio: The World Publishing Company, 1976.

Weis, Frank W. *Lifelines: Famous Contemporaries from 600 B.C. to 1975*. New York: Facts on File, Inc., 1982.

Welter, Gerhard. *Cleaning and Preservation of Coins and Medals*. New York: Sanford J. Durst Numismatic Publications, 1976-80.

White, Duncan M. (ed.). *Caesar to Churchill: The Years of Fulfillment (1783-1965)*. New York: Roy Publishers, 1969.

Whitney, David C. (ed.). *Founders of Freedom in America*. J. G. Ferguson Publishing Company.

Wilson, John and Nancy. "United States Postage and Fractional Currency." *The Centinel*, Vol. 28, No. 3, Fall 1980, pp. 15-28.

Yeoman, R. S. *A Guide Book of United States Coins* (44th Ed.), Racine, WI: Western Publishing Company, 1990.

York, Alan. "The Paper Money Used in the Thersienstadt Ghetto: The Inside Story." *The Shekel*, March-April 1983, pp. 27-33.

Zander, Randolph. *Russian-English Numismatic Dictionary*. Akron, OH: Russian Numismatic Society, 1990.

Contributing Scholars

The author wishes to express his appreciation to the following distinguished scholars for their outstanding technical assistance. Without their efforts, this encyclopædic dictionary would not have been possible.

Anca Arenas
[Berlitz Translation Service]
Chicago, Illinois
Romanian language

P. Arnold, Ph.D.
Staatliche Kunstsammlungen
Dresden, Germany
German language

Stewart and Marie Bailey
[American Philatelic Society]
Cincinnati, Ohio
Philatelic/numismatic expertise

Faith H. Barnett
Ohio Dept. of Human Services
Cuyahoga Falls, Ohio
Public assistance certificates

Autence A. Bason
Greensboro, North Carolina
Communion tokens

Harlan J. Berk
Harlan J. Berk, Ltd.
Chicago, Illinois
Ancient coins

Steve Bleeg
San Jose, California
German language

David Block
Gainesville, Florida
Physics; emergency money

Joseph E. Boling
[Chief Judge, A.N.A.]
Federal Way, Washington
Japanese numismatics and language

Hoang Bui
[Berlitz Translation Service]
San Francisco, California
Vietnamese language

Dmytro Bykovetz, Jr.
[Chairman, A.P.S. Translation Committee]
Melrose Park, Pennsylvania
Translation assistance

Halbert Carmichael, Ph.D.
North Carolina State University
Raleigh, North Carolina
Chemistry and metallurgy

Robert A. Carpenter
New Orleans, Louisiana
Military decorations

Mário de Castro Hipólito, Ph.D.
Fundação Calouste Gulbenkian
Lisbon, Portugal
Portuguese language

Lynn Chen
American Numismatic Association
Colorado Springs, Colorado
Library services; Chinese language

James J. Cleary, Jr.
Jersey City, New Jersey
German language

Charles G. Colver
Covina, California
Numismatic research

Richard Crum, Ph.D.
Berlitz Translation Service
Woodland Hills, California
General translation services

Ruth Ann Davis
Weirton, West Virginia
Latin language; biographies

Hüseyin Doğan & Yonca Poyraz-Doğan
[Texas Tech University (Lubbock, Texas)]
Istanbul, Turkey
Turkish language

Thomas "Chuck" Diezi
Harris County Engineering Department
Houston, Texas
Drawings and sketches

Robert Doyle
Clearwater, Florida
Exonumia

Sanae Eda
[Ohio State University (Columbus, Ohio)]
Okayama, Japan
Japanese language

Coleman Ezkovich
New Orleans, Louisiana
Mint errors

Diana C. Fabiano
Buffalo, New York
Serbo-Croatian language

Albert A. Feldmann
[American Translation Association]
Seattle, Washington
Hebrew language

M. Rafael Feria
Fábrica Nacional de Moneda y Timbre
Madrid, Spain
Spanish language

Horace P. Flatt
[American Numismatic Society]
Terrell, Texas
Spanish language

Barbara J. Fraize
Reston, Virginia
German language

James Galownia
Steubenville, Ohio
European coinages

Erika Garami, Ph.D.
National Bank of Hungary
Budapest, Hungary
Hungarian language

Jean Baptiste Giard
Bibliothèque Nationale
Paris, France
French language

Nick Gluschenko
Krasnodar, Russia
Russian language

Phil W. Greenslet
Reisterstown, Maryland
Commemorative medals

John Groot
Grand Rapids, Michigan
Dutch language

Flemming L. Hansen
Gentofte, Denmark
Danish language

Gene Hessler
St. Louis, Missouri
United States paper money

Karl Hnilicka, Ph.D.
German American Communications
Chicago, Illinois
German language

Amiteshwar Jha
Indian Institute of Research of
   Numismatic Studies
Maharashtra, India
Hindi language

Stanley S. Kim
Oakland, California
Korean language

Gerald L. Kochel
Lititz, Pennsylvania
Tokens

Ole-Robert Kolberg
Central Bank of Norway
Oslo, Norway
Norwegian language

Robert F. Kriz
Cocoa Beach, Florida
Research assistance

Simcha Kuritzky
Silver Spring, Maryland
Judaic Studies; Hebrew language

Hans E. Lee
Ottawa, Ontario
Indonesian language

Jacopo M. Madaro Moro, Ph.D.
[American Translation Association]
East Boston, Massachusetts
Italian language

Pam Makricosta
Weirton, West Virginia
Biographies

Yvon Marquis
[Canadian Numismatic Association]
Bic, Québec
French language

Very Rev. Dr. Mateja Matejič
Hilander Room, Ohio State University
Columbus, Ohio
Serbo-Croatian language

Marta Męclewska
Zamek Królewski w Warszawie
Warsaw, Poland
Polish language

Giorgio Migliavacca
[Editor, *Moneta International*]
Tortola, British Virgin Islands
Ancient coins; Italian language

Miriam S. Mirasol
[Berlitz Translation Service]
Fairfax, Virginia
Tagalog language

William F. Mross
Racine, Wisconsin
Ancient coins

Eugen Nicolae
Institutul de Arheologie
Bucharest, Romania
Romanian language

Michael S. Niddam
[American Translation Association]
Washington, D.C.
French and Spanish languages

Harold Nilsson
Kungl Myntkabinettet
Stockholm, Sweden
Swedish language

Pinar T. Ozand, M.D., Ph.D.
King Faisal Research Center
Riyadh, Saudi Arabia
Middle Eastern languages

Arent Pol
Rijksmuseum Het Koninklijk
  Penningkabinet
Leiden, The Netherlands
Dutch language

Very Rev. Slobodan Prodanovich
St. George "Lazarica" Church
Midland, Pennsylvania
Serbo-Croatian language

Bilha Ron
Canton, Ohio
Hebrew language

Salih Sari, Ph.D.
Yarmouk University
Irbid, Jordan
Arabic language

Rabbi John Spitzer, D.D.
Temple Israel
Canton, Ohio
Coins of Israel

Robert L. Starliper
Steubenville, Ohio
Research assistance

Tuukka Talvio
National Museum of Finland
Helsinki, Finland
Finnish language

Jian Tang
Chicago, Illinois
Chinese language

Jörg Tautenhahn
Feldberg, Germany
German language

George V. Tomashevich, Ph.D.
State University College at Buffalo
Buffalo, New York
Serbo-Croatian language

James A. Tyler, Ph.D.
Kent State University
Kent, Ohio
Spanish language

Emil Voigt
Nassau Point, Cutchogue, New York
Medallic art

Mel Wacks
PandaAmerica
Torrance, California
Judaic Studies

James R. Wilson
Computer Services Associates
North Ridgeville, Ohio
Computer and word processing expertise

John and Nancy Wilson
[American Numismatic Association]
Milwaukee, Wisconsin
United States paper money

Tin Win
[Berlitz Translation Service]
Houston, Texas
Burmese language

These Quality Numismatic Titles
Are Also Available From Krause Publications

NOTES

NOTES